Measuring Human Problems

A Practical Guide

Edited by
DAVID F. PECK
Highland Health Board, Scotland

and

COLIN M. SHAPIRO
Royal Edinburgh Hospital, Scotland

JOHN WILEY & SONS
Chichester · New York · Brisbane · Toronto · Singapore

Other Wiley Editorial Offices

John Wiley & Sons, Inc., 605 Third Avenue,
New York, NY 10158-0012, USA

Jacaranda Wiley Ltd, G.P.O. Box 859, Brisbane,
Queensland 4001, Australia

John Wiley & Sons (Canada) Ltd, 22 Worcester Road,
Rexdale, Ontario M9W 1L1, Canada

John Wiley & Sons (SAE) Pte Ltd, 37 Jalan Pemimpin #05-04,
Block B, Union Industrial Building, Singapore 2057

Library of Congress Cataloging-in-Publication Data:
Measuring human problems : a practical guide / edited by
David F. Peck and Colin M. Shapiro.
p. cm. — (The Wiley series in clinical psychology)
Includes bibliographical references.
Includes index.
ISBN 0 471 91206 9 (cloth)
1. Mental illness—Diagnosis. I. Peck, David F. II. Shapiro,
Colin M. III. Series.
[DNLM: 1. Adaptation, Psychological. 2. Eating Disorders—
— diagnosis. 3. Mental Disorders—diagnosis. 4. Sex Behavior.
5. Sleep Disorders—diagnosis. WM 141 M484]
RC469.M39 1990
616.89'075—dc20
DNLM/DLC
for Library of Congress

90-12398
CIP

British Library Cataloguing in Publication Data:
Measuring human problems.
1. Man. Mental disorders. Diagnosis
I. Peck, D. F. (David Francis), *1944–* II. Shapiro, Colin M.
616.89075

ISBN 0 471 91206 9

Typeset by Inforum Typesetting, Portsmouth
Printed and bound in Great Britain by Biddles Ltd, Guildford, Surrey

Contents

List of Contributors

JOHN BANCROFT	Assistant Director, MRC Reproductive Biology Unit, 37 Chalmers Street, Edinburgh
FIONA BARRY	Research Psychologist, Eating Disorders Research Group, Tipperlinn Cottage, Royal Edinburgh Hospital, Edinburgh, EH10 5HF
G.E. BERRIOS	Lecturer and Consultant Psychiatrist, Department of Psychiatry, University of Cambridge, Level 4, Addenbrooke's Hospital, Cambridge, CB2 2QQ
PATRICIA CASEY	Consultant Psychiatrist, Professorial Psychiatric Unit, Cork Regional Hospital, Wilton, Cork, Eire
JANICE CHRISTIE	Hon. Consultant Psychiatrist, MRC Brain Metabolism Unit, Ward 1A, Royal Edinburgh Hospital, Edinburgh, EH10 5HF
CHRIS CULLEN	Professor of Learning Difficuties, Department of Psychology, University of St Andrews, Fife, KY16 9JU
PAUL DICKENS	Area Psychologist, Department of Psychology, Royal Scottish National Hospital, Larbet, FK5 4SF
E.H.M. EURELINGS-BONTEKOE	Psychologist and Psychophysiologist, Department of Clinical and Health Psychology, Leiden University, Hooigracht 15, 2312 KM Leiden, The Netherlands
C.P. FREEMAN	Consultant Psychotherapist, Royal Edinburgh Hospital, Edinburgh, EH10 5HF
CHRIS GILLEARD	Department of Clinical Psychology, Springfield Hospital, London, SW17 7DJ

M. GOSSOP	Head of Research, Drug Dependence Clinical Research and Treatment Unit, Bethlem Royal Hospital, Beckenham, Kent, BR3 3BX
SUE GREY	Clinical Psychologist, Whitchurch Hospital, Cardiff
MAX HAMILTON (deceased)	Professor, Department of Psychiatry, University of Leeds
GEOFFREY LLOYD	Consultant Psychiatrist, Royal Free Hospital, Pond Street, Hampstead, London, NW3 2QG
JENNY MUNRO	Research Psychologist, Eating Disorders Research Group, Tipperlinn Cottage, Royal Edinburgh Hospital, Edinburgh, EH10 5HF
DAVID F. PECK	Area Clinical Psychologist, Craig Dunain Hospital, Inverness, IV3 6PJ
KATHERINE RATHOUSE	Department of Psychology, Oxford University
PAUL SALKOVSKIS	Research Psychologist, Department of Psychiatry, University of Oxford, Warneford Hospital, Oxford, OX3 7JX
COLIN M. SHAPIRO	Senior Lecturer, Department of Psychiatry, Royal Edinburgh Hospital, Morningside Park, Edinburgh
PHILIP SNAITH	Consultant Psychiatrist, St James University Hospital, Leeds, LS9 7TF
GRAHAM TURPIN	Lecturer, Department of Psychology, Polytechnic Southwest, Plymouth, PL4 8AA
PETER TYRER	Consultant Psychiatrist, St Charles Hospital, Exmoor Road, London W10 6TZ
ERIK VAN DE LOO	Department of Clinical and Health Psychology, Leiden University, Hooigracht 15, 2312 KM Leiden, The Netherlands

Series Preface

The Wiley Series in Clinical Psychology presents authoritative treatments of both new and established topics in clinical psychology. There are few more enduring tasks for practising clinical psychologists than the assessment and measurement of the human problems that are presented to them. I believe the present volume will prove a very valuable aid to busy clinicians in this aspect of their work, and that it will establish itself as a standard reference text.

Various other guides to clinical assessment are, of course, already available. However, the present volume has a breadth of coverage which I believe will make it particularly attractive. Not only is the range of human problems covered broader than in most comparable books, but there is also a more comprehensive coverage of the full range of assessment methods open to the clinicians. Clinical work too often suffers from an exclusive concentration on self-report measures. Valuable as these are, clinicians who want reliable, objective measures of the extent of clinical problems will often want to supplement them with biological measures and with the direct observation of behaviour. A particularly valuable feature of the present handbook is that, for each problem considered, it describes such measures in convenient, accessible form, alongside the more widely used self-report measures.

Though this book is published as part of a series on Clinical Psychology, it includes relevant measures which have been developed and employed in other disciplines, particularly in psychiatry. The editors are themselves a clinical psychologist (Peck) and a psychiatrist (Shapiro). This further underlines the commitment to comprehensiveness of approach which is the major feature of this book. We hope that it will appeal to a wide range of professions which are engaged in the assessment and measurement of human problems.

FRASER WATTS
Series Editor

Series Preface

Preface

This book is intended to act as a practical guide for all members of caring professions who wish to assess the problems of their patients and clients in a systematic and up-to-date way. The editors would argue that without such measurement we would not be able to convince ourselves nor our clients, patients and colleagues that change has taken place and we may therefore continue to apply ineffective and wasteful treatments. In addition to a simple listing of the relevant questionnaires and consideration of the merits and demerits of rating scales as used for particular problems and other methods of measurement, there is also an attempt to clarify diagnostic, definitional and other conceptual issues in relation to the problem area covered. It is intended that each chapter can be read alone, but some acquaintance with the material in Chapter 1 (on general measurement issues) is recommended.

All the authors are firmly of the view that problems are multi-faceted and therefore that as wide a range of measures as possible from subjective to biological should be employed. Various levels of measurement may cover different facets or components of a problem, and to use only one level would lead to false conclusions of little improvement, or to unsupportable claims of general effectiveness. For some problems (e.g. depression) the full range of measures may be applicable, whereas for others (e.g. mental handicap) the useful range may be narrower. Authors have placed different emphases in their chapters, both with regard to content and their particular approach and philosophy regarding the issue of measurement. These differences are reflected in the various chapters, and the editors hope that this will provide a broader view of measurement to the reader. An attempt at being comprehensive in covering the major areas in which most clinicians and researchers will wish to have ready access to measuring instruments has been made. Inevitably, readers will identify favoured measures which have been omitted. It may be that a particular topic might have been usefully included (for example, there is no chapter on the assessment of pain). We are aware that for many of the problems covered in this book there are no comprehensive reviews of the various approaches to measurement. If there are either topics that the readers feel merit such treatment or if there are particular measures that you believe should have been included, then the editors would be pleased if you would let them know.

Measurements of problems have several functions, mainly to help in diagnosis, to predict response to treatment and to monitor change. For research, measurement is essential. A familiarity with instruments of measurement in a particular area invariably leads to an enhanced understanding of the clinical nuances of the disorder, and therefore we encourage training professionals to read chapters relevant to their work and to consult references cited with regard to particular instruments. The emphasis in this book is on the one which is perhaps the most important, monitoring change. However, as will be apparent in several of the chapters, many of the measurement devices are used for more than one function and distinctions between diagnostic and change-monitoring functions of the measure are often arbitrary. Chapter 2 specifically focuses on diagnistic issues.

During the compiling of this book, one of the authors, Professor Max Hamilton, died. His contributions to measurement in psychiatry were immense and his thorough, clinically based, well-informed approach to the measurement of depression has been an inspiration to many. With gratitude and respect, this book is dedicated to him.

David F. Peck
Colin M. Shapiro

Chapter 1

Guidelines for the Construction, Selection and Interpretation of Measurement Devices

DAVID F. PECK and COLIN M. SHAPIRO

'When you can measure what you are speaking about, and express it in numbers, you know something about it; but when you cannot measure it, when you cannot express it in numbers, your knowledge is of a meagre and unsatisfactory kind' (cited in *Measurement in Medicine*, by Oldham, 1968)*

THE NATURE OF MEASUREMENT

Measurement is concerned with assigning numbers to objects or observations such that the numbers are amenable to manipulation and to the establishment of qualitative empirical relations. Typically, measurement involves the ordering or spacing of observations or objects along a dimension. These analyses and manipulations are conducted according to mathematical rules, which has the advantage that mathematics encompasses numerous well-validated and universally accepted arguments and theorems which may be applied to empirical propositions using a common language. The overall aim of this endeavour is to facilitate the drawing of conclusions, or the 'lubrication of deductive processes' (Michel, 1986), so that we can learn new things about the original objects or observations.

Measurement in all branches of science is an essential but difficult goal. Even in the natural sciences measurement problems abound, but when measuring human behaviour they occur in a more troublesome form, since the subject matter of human behaviour is more variable, both within and across individuals, than is the case within or across atoms or molecules.

* We have been unable to trace the original copyright holder for this quotation. However, full acknowledgement will be included, if available, in any subsequent editions of this book.

Measuring Human Problems. Edited by D.F. Peck and C.M. Shapiro

Furthermore, much of interest in human problems is not amenable to direct observation, adding to the complexity.

LEVELS OF MEASUREMENT

No form of measurement is perfect; all forms contain some degree of error, in both a statistical sense (i.e. variability) and in a more traditional sense (i.e. lack of accuracy). However, different forms of measurement will contain different levels of error. A multi-level approach to measurement (whereby a phenomenon is measured in several different forms simultaneously) will help to reduce the proportion of error, since each form will, to some extent, counterbalance the errors of the others. To use an analogy: each form of measurement acts like a layer of roofing thatch; each layer alone is not watertight but the different layers have different porous parts, so the stacking of layers will eventually produce a watertight structure. Similarly, by simultaneous use of several forms of measurement, error can be attenuated.

Applying this notion to human behaviour, it is possible to measure several modalities or at several different levels from subjective report to biochemical assays. At the level of subjective report, there are such problems as response set and individual interpretation of items; for observer-completed ratings, there are the problems of inter-observer agreement and halo effect; for naturalistic observations, of reactivity and observer drift; for psychophysiology, of low reliability over time and individual response specificity; and for biochemical assays, of sluggish response and wide individual variation. Although some sources of error are common across more than one level, generally the types of error differ. Using measures at more than one level will, therefore, serve to provide a secure basis for assessment.

Clearly, not all strategies are useful in the measurement of all problems. In the measurement of stereotyped behaviour in the severely mentally handicapped, subjective reports are, and biochemical assays may be, of little value but observer ratings and naturalistic observations are particularly appropriate. In measuring stress, however, measurement at all levels from subjective report to hormonal analysis is used. Which approaches to adopt will depend partly on the specific question to be answered and on the resources available. Also, individuals could differ as to which is the most appropriate level of measurement even when they have similar problems.

A further reason for the multi-level measurement strategy advocated here is that it would appear that these various response modalities do not necessarily change in synchrony. That is, subjective ratings, biological changes and overt behaviour do not necessarily change at the same rate or at the same time. A successful treatment intervention may produce its effects first, in the behavioural domain, second, in the biological domain, and only third, in the subjective domain. This 'response desynchronization' or 'response fractionation' is clearly important, since one may come to quite different conclusions about the effectiveness of a therapeutic intervention, according to the level at which measurement is pitched. Pitching measurement at several levels should encapsulate any changes which have occurred. An excellent discussion of this phenomenon can be found in Himadi *et al.* (1985). Furthermore, measures may be differentially sensitive to intervention methods. Subjective measures are appropriate for cognitive treatment approaches, whereas physiological measures are the key dependent variables in biofeedback studies. Finally, it has been noted that patient-completed scales and observer-completed checklists can tap different aspects of a problem, for example in depression (Fava *et al.*, 1986), and both should therefore be used. Even within a series of interview schedules purportedly assessing similar information, there may be a preponderance of items concerned with one facet in one instrument (e.g. the biological features of depression) and a different emphasis in the components making up another instrument (e.g. cognitive aspects of depression) (see Chapter 3).

EVALUATING AND DEVISING MEASURES

Traditionally, two main criteria have been used to evaluate psychological measurement devices; these are reliability and validity. Most often they have been applied to the traditional psychometric measures such as rating scales and questionnaires, but these criteria are applicable irrespective of level of measurement. The remainder of this chapter will describe the concepts of reliability and validity in some detail, paying particular attention to recent theoretical and practical developments.

RELIABILITY

Reliability addresses the question of consistency; that is, does the measure as a whole, and do the items comprising the measure, give roughly the same kind of results when used under the same circumstances? There are many kinds of reliability, and the results of reliability estimates are normally given in the form of a correlation coefficient.

Test–retest reliability

In this form of reliability the same measure is applied to the same group of subjects, under similar conditions and at two different times. If the measure is assessing the characteristic consistently, those who score high (or low) on the first occasion should score high (or low) on the second. Normally, the degree of relationship between the two sets of scores is expressed in the form of a product–moment correlation. There is no standard interval between the administrations of the measure, but a three-week interval is commonly used. This is long enough to reduce the risk of inflating consistency due to recall of previous responses, but short enough so that reliability is not reduced by major fluctuations in the characteristic being measured. For those problems which are naturally characterized by marked fluctuations (e.g. cyclothymic disorder), test–retest reliability will not be an appropriate measure of consistency. Furthermore test–retest reliability may vary according to the current stage of a problem, in that a measure may be reliable in acute stages but less reliable in the more chronic ones. Finally, as always the case with correlations, the test–retest reliability may be spuriously reduced if the range of scores is unduly narrow.

Alternative form reliability

With this, two alternative forms of the measure are devised, and administered to the same group of subjects under the same circumstances. If each is measuring the same characteristic, the correlation between them should be high. This form of reliability is not commonly used, partly because it is difficult to devise an equivalent measure without item overlap.

Split-half reliability

This form of reliability is different, in that instead of assessing consistency over time it assesses how far each item within a measure reflects the same characteristic. The classical way of assessing split-half reliability is literally to divide a measure into two halves (for example, first half versus second half, or odd- versus even-numbered items), to administer each half to the same group under similar circumstances, and to correlate the two halves together. Clearly, if the items are measuring the same characteristic, a high correlation would be expected, but because a measure can be split into two halves in many different ways, different split-half reliabilities may be obtained. Cronbach's coefficient alpha reduces this problem by providing an estimate of the average correlation between all possible ways of splitting the items. Briggs and Cheek (1986) have observed, however, that coefficient alpha may overestimate the mean inter-item correlation if the characteristic being measured is too broadly defined.

Inter-rater reliability

With this, two or more observers examine the same material or events and the degree of agreement between them is assessed. Although often reported, percentage agreement may be a misleading statistic. For example, suppose two observers view 100 events, of which five are critical. If one observer detects five of the critical events but the other only detects three, then widely differing percentage agreements will be obtained, depending on whether you include agreement on all 100 events (in which case, agreement will be 98 per cent) or whether one looks only at the critical events (in which case, agreement will be 60 per cent). An improvement which obviates this problem is the 'kappa' statistic and the similar 'weighted kappa' for use with scales based on ranks. Suen and Lee (1985) found that using kappa rather than percentage agreement resulted in considerably fewer judgements of good reliability. There is, however, a problem with kappa, since its value depends on the marginal totals or the overall frequencies of the various observations. A solution has been proposed by Kjaersgaard-Andersen *et al.* (1988). They describe a method which controls for chance agreement, and is independent of the marginal totals. Their method involves the use of generalized linear modelling, a form of chi-square test with multiple dimensions. Such relatively sophisticated methods of assessing inter-observer agreement have major advantages over previous methods and should receive greater attention in the psychological and psychiatric literature.

Intra-rater reliability

This is similar to inter-rater reliability, except that judgements are made by the same observers of the same material presented at two different times. Typically, this would include the use of video or tape recordings.

The size of reliability coefficients

Users should attempt to select only those measures which have high reliability coefficients, and authors of new measures should aim to maximize the reliability. An unreliable measure will include a great deal of random variability, which will make it considerably more difficult to produce statistically significant effects in research. Furthermore, it is undesirable in clinical work to use a measure which gives different results when used at different times. There is no absolute cut-off point above which reliability is acceptable and below which it is not. However, one should aim for a reliability of at least +0.8 when devising a measure, and treat with considerable caution any measure which has a reliability of less than +0.7.

In devising a new measure, authors should normally report a measure of temporal consistency (test–retest reliability) and a measure of internal reliability (kappa or similar method).

Alternatives and extensions to the assessment of reliability

Traditional methods of assessing reliability have served well in the measurement of human problems. Despite their widespread and continued use (e.g. Paykel, 1985) and a general consensus as to their utility, reservations have been expressed. In particular, one might query the assumption that reliability assessed in one study with one group of subjects and in one set of circumstances has established a level of reliability which applies equally to other studies, other subjects and other circumstances. There may be different reliabilities according to the sex of subjects, precise diagnosis, whether they are assessed at home or in hospital, singly or in a group, and according to which person does the assessment. Some measures may be particularly susceptible to influence by these variables whereas others may be relatively robust. Traditional forms of reliability assume a general robustness of measures which may be unwarranted.

Generalizability theory was put forward as an alternative to traditional reliability assessment in the late 1960s, and despite several pleas for its more common use (e.g. Owens, 1984), such pleas have gone unheeded and only rarely has generalizability theory been applied to the measurement of human problems. In essence, the theory makes use of the statistical technique of analysis of variance, instead of the usual correlation. The investigator sets up a study whereby variables which are considered to be possible influences on the measure are formally incorporated. For example, if a new scale was being devised to assess subjective anxiety levels, then one variable might be sex of subject; a second might be the particular type of anxiety; a third might be duration of the anxiety; a fourth might be whether the anxiety is assessed in the laboratory or in naturalistic settings; and a fifth may be later occasions of assessment. All these influences can be assessed using multivariate analysis of variance with repeated measures. An advantage of this approach is that the relative influence of all the variables can be directly compared; an even greater advantage is that interactions between them can be explored. For example, it may be found that temporal consistency is high for females with high levels of anxiety but poor for males with relatively low levels of anxiety. A good example of this approach has been described by Llabre *et al.* (1988). They investigated a number of possible sources of variability in blood pressure recordings; variation on the same day in the laboratory, home and work; variation across days in the laboratory; and variation across three measuring devices. Not only were the authors able to assess reliability under these conditions but they also calculated how many pressure readings may be required across the different conditions to achieve an acceptable level of reliability (that is, +0.8).

A further advance over traditional reliability assessment is 'item response theory', which investigates how far subjects at different levels of the measured characteristic vary in their response to each item. Gibbons *et al.* (1985), for example, take issue with the assumption that in measures which produce a total score by adding the individual items, the items have the same properties for all subjects throughout the range of scores. They re-examined the items of the Beck Depression Inventory (see Chapter 3) and obtained two subscales which they claimed to be particularly sensitive to different levels of depression.

Because of wide acceptability and easy interpretation, it is likely that in the measurement of human problems, traditional methods of reliability assessment will continue to be used. However, we would make a strong plea for investigators devising a new measure to consider applying the newer methods in the development and refinement of their scales.

VALIDITY

Validity addresses the question of whether a device is a true measure of the characteristic being assessed. Unlike reliability, where there is general agreement about its utility, how to assess it, and the appropriate terminology, there is considerable confusion about the concept of validity. Whereas some kinds of validity are reported in the form of a correlation, others are purely descriptive, and are not reported statistically. New kinds of validity are often suggested, some of which are taken up and used in the investigation of new measures whereas others are ignored. Some authors have applied different names to the same kind of validity, adding to the confusion.

These issues have led to a growing disenchantment with the concept of validity, a theme which will be explored later. Nevertheless, most authors of existing measures of human problems report validity data and will probably continue to do so. It is therefore important to outline some of the main kinds.

Face validity

This refers simply to whether the items in a measure appear on the surface to be measuring the characteristic of interest. There are no standard criteria to assess face validity, nor is it quantified, and therefore face validity is not reported by any summary statistic. It is mainly of interest because authors have to rely on face validity when drawing up the original list of items for a measure. Furthermore, it may be important if the author wishes to disguise the purpose of the measure, devising a measure with low face validity.

Sampling validity

Sampling validity is concerned with the content of measures; that is, whether the items tap all aspects of the characteristic in question. As with face validity, there are no standard guidelines for assessing sampling validity, nor is it quantified or reported statistically. As an example, suppose one wishes to devise a measure of anorexia nervosa. If all the items were purely concerned with eating, the measure would have low sampling validity because it omitted other aspects of anorexia such as hyperactivity and amenorrhea. The concept of sampling validity is important, but the lack of standard guidelines limits its usefulness.

Concurrent validity

The establishment of concurrent validity involves comparing a measure with a pre-existing external criterion, or an already existing measure of the same characteristic. For example, in order to establish the concurrent validity of a new measure of anxiety the scores could be compared with those obtained by the same subjects on the State–Trait Anxiety Inventory; or one may compare the mean scores of normals with those of patients with an anxiety state; or if it were a measure of laboratory-induced anxiety, concurrent validity could be established by looking at how far changes occurred in parallel with changes in heart rate in anticipation of electric shock. This is probably the most commonly used form of validity reported for new measures. It seems to be logical and systematic and can be reported statistically, for example in the form of a correlation or in terms of mean differences between groups.

There are, however, some problems. There are few definitive external criteria of psychological phenomena; concurrent validity can therefore only be assessed indirectly. Furthermore, if a new measure is compared with a pre-existing one, this assumes that this measure also has high validity; yet it will have faced the same problems in establishing its own validity. Furthermore, if there is a pre-existing measure, there may be little point in establishing the new one, unless it is easier or cheaper to administer and interpret. A final problem is that concurrent validity typically utilizes extreme samples in order to demonstrate that the measure can differentiate between different levels of the characteristic of interest. As mentioned, an anxiety measure may be validated by comparing normals with patients with diagnosed anxiety states. This procedure would not necessarily demonstrate that the measure can equally validly discriminate between less extreme values of the characteristic, or in borderline cases.

Predictive validity

Predictive validity is mainly of importance if one wishes to predict future clinical state. That is, it establishes the correlation between a measure and some future criterion. Although predictive validity can be very important if one wishes, for example, to predict which form of treatment will produce the best outcome for particular patients, it is not normally used in establishing the validity of measures to monitor changes in clinical state, which is the main topic of this book. The concept of predictive validity will not therefore be explored further.

However, it is worth noting in passing that predictive validity is seldom assessed because a large number of subjects is required and they need to be followed up for several years. This can make the process a prohibitively expensive (albeit an important) aspect of clinical endeavour.

Incremental validity

Irrespective of how a measure is to be used, incremental validity should be established but seldom is. Incremental validity assesses not just whether a measure 'works' in some way but whether it 'works' better than already existing or simpler measures. In other words, it examines whether it is worth devising a sophisticated, time-consuming measure of a characteristic if this new measure does not add anything substantial in terms of predictive ability or sensitivity. Mischel (1972) was a leading proponent of this form of validity. In a review of the literature on personality assessment, he concluded 'Predictions possible from a subject's own simple direct self-ratings and self-reports, generally have not been exceeded by those obtained from more indirect costly and sophisticated personality tests, from combined batteries and from expert clinical judgements'. Studies have shown that these conclusions apply to a wide range of problems: rehospitalization for discharged psychiatric patients, parole violations for delinquent children, academic achievement in college, professional success, treatment outcome in psychotherapy, drug treatment for depression, and vocational guidance. Often results are quite unexpected. For example, Farina *et al.* (1977) found that a simple rating of overall physical attractiveness of female patients was more predictive of a variety of clinical criteria than were diagnosis or clinical history.

It is incumbent therefore on the authors of new measures to establish not just that the measure has concurrent or predictive validity but that it actually improves upon simpler or already existing measures.

What is wrong with validity?

We have already noted that there is disenchantment with the concept of validity. As Bausell (1986) comments, physical measurements in physics or biology do not seem to have an equivalent concept. One does not, for example, see attempts to establish the validity of leukocyte counts or kilohms. No-one would doubt, however, that leukocyte counts and kilohm measurements are useful. Bausell goes so far as to say that we should de-emphasize validity and concentrate instead on utility. This could not be decided by one definitive study but would be a gradual build-up of information from many studies. If a measure proves useful, its continued use would be justified; if it does not prove useful, its use will decline. (However, the history of the use of projective techniques suggests that such optimism regarding the impact of research findings on clinical practice may be misguided.)

Bausell (1986) further suggests that utility is best seen as the end of a series of steps, including various forms of reliability and validity, with the final step being construct validity, encompassing all the previous kinds. That is, construct validity will be demonstrated when a measure has been shown to have high sampling validity, good internal test–retest and inter-rater reliability, and predictive validity. If these can be demonstrated with replications over different areas, construct validity would have been achieved. (We would strongly suggest adding incremental validity as a further step.)

How high should validity coefficients be? This does, of course, depend on the type of validity, but Guilford (1965) has devised an index of forecasting efficiency which specifies the improvement in predictive efficiency of various validity coefficients, compared to the predictive efficiency of making predictions based only on knowledge of the mean of the criterion. For example, validity coefficients need to be as high as +0.86 before errors in prediction are reduced by 50 per cent. Such high levels of coefficient are seldom, if ever, found for psychological measures.

If a measure is being used to monitor change over time and concurrent validity has been established, then the coefficient should be around +0.7 or higher. Measures with a validity coefficient of less than +0.7 must be viewed with some suspicion, since they share less than half of their variance with the criterion measure.

THE RELATIONSHIP BETWEEN RELIABILITY AND VALIDITY

The concepts of reliability and validity are more similar than may at first appear. As Mischel (1968) noted, the reliability of a measure is revealed by the size of correlation coefficients produced under maximally similar circumstances (e.g. a test correlated with itself), whereas validity coefficients are revealed by correlations obtained under maximal dissimilar circumstances (e.g. correlations between a psychological measure and a physiological measure).

Reliability and validity are closely related in other ways. For a test to be valid, it must be reliable. It is, however, possible to have a reliable test that is not valid. That is, for a measure to be accurate, it must be consistent; but a consistent measure could in practice be measuring something entirely different from that which is intended. Finally, if we increase reliability, it is likely that validity will also increase, but often not substantially. The better strategy may be to develop several imperfect measures rather than investing much time and effort in developing one measure very well.

SUMMARY AND CONCLUSIONS

Traditionally, concepts of reliability and validity have been of crucial importance in the development of psychological measures. They are applicable to all forms of measurement but are less frequently applied to the more biological approaches. For both reliability and validity, coefficients should be at least +0.7. There are, however, some major limitations with traditional notions of reliability and validity, and a range of more sophisticated psychometric concepts are becoming more widely used, although their impact on the measurement of human problems is small as yet.

REFERENCES AND FURTHER READING

Bausell, R.B. (1986) *A Practical Guide to Conducting Empirical Research*, Harper and Row, New York.

Briggs, S.R. and Cheek, J.M. (1985) The role of factor analysis in the development and evaluation of personality scales. *Journal of Personality*, **54**, 106–48.

Crocker, L. and Algina, J. (1986) *Introduction to Classical and Modern Test Theory*, Holt Rinehart and Winston, New York.

Farina, A., Fischer, E.H., Sherman, S., Smith, W.T., Groh, T. and Mermin, P. (1977) Physical attractiveness and mental illness. *Journal of Abnormal Psychology*, **86**, 510–17.

Fava, E.A., Kellner, R., Lisansky, J., Park, J., Perini, G.I. and Zielezny, M. (1986) Rating depression in normals and depressives: observer vs self-rating scales. *Journal of Affective Disorders*, **11**, 29–33.

Gibbons, R.D., Clark, D.C., Cavenaugh, S.V.A. and Davis, J.M. (1985) Application of modern psychometric theory in psychiatric research. *Journal of Psychiatric Research*, **19**, 43–55.

Goldstein, G. and Hersen, M. (1984) *Handbook of Psychological Assessment*, Pergamon Press, New York.

Guilford, J.P. (1965) *Fundamental Statistics in Psychology and Education*, 4th edn, McGraw-Hill, New York.

Himadi, W.G., Boice, R. and Barlow, D.H. (1985) Assessment of agoraphobia: triple response measurement. *Behaviour Research and Therapy*, **23**, 311–23.

Kjaersgaard-Andersen, P., Christensen, F., Schmidt, S.A., Pedersen, N.W. and Jorgensen, B. (1988) A new method of estimation of interobserver variation and its application to the radiological assessment of osteoarthrosis in hip joints. *Statistics in Medicine*, **7**, 639–47.

Llabre, M.M., Ironson, G.H., Spitzer, S.B., Gellman, M.D., Weidler, D.J. and Schneiderman, N. (1988) How many blood pressure measurements are enough? An application of generalisability theory to the study of blood pressure reliability. *Psychophysiology*, **25**, 97–106.

Martin, P. and Bateson, P. (1986) *Measuring Behaviour: An Introductory Guide*, Cambridge University Press, Cambridge.

Michel, J. (1986) Measurement methods and statistics: a clash of paradigms. *Psychological Bulletin*, **100**, 398–407.

Mischel, W. (1968) *Personality and Assessment*, John Wiley, New York.

Mischel, W. (1972) Direct versus indirect personality assessment: evidence and implications. *Journal of Consulting and Clinical Psychology*, **38**, 319–24.

Nelson, R.O. and Hayes, R.C. (1986) *Conceptual Foundations of Behavioral Assessment*, Guilford Press, New York.

Oldham, P.D. (1968) *Measurement in Medicine*, English Universities Press, London.

Owens, R.G. (1984) Psychological assessment. In P. McGuffin, M.F. Shanks and R.J. Hodgson (eds), *The Scientific Principles of Psychopathology*, Grune and Stratton, London.

Paykel, E.S. (1985) The clinical interview for depression: development, reliability and validity. *Journal of Affective Disorders*, **9**, 85–96.

Suen, H.K. and Lee, P.S. (1985) The effects of the use of percentage agreement in behavioral observation reliabilities: a reassessment. *Journal of Psychopathology and Behavioral Assessment*, **7**, 221–34.

Chapter 2

Screening and Detection of Psychiatric Illness

PATRICIA CASEY

The screening and detection of psychiatric illness have many purposes. These include not just estimating prevalence and incidence but also examining the course and prognosis of psychiatric illness, identifying aetiological factors and assisting in the planning of psychiatric services, although the latter is less important than is often initially assumed.

Since the first survey of psychiatric illness in the community by Edward Jarvis in 1855 there has been a considerable growth of such studies along with an increase in their sophistication. Studies of this type are not confined to the general population but occur in a variety of arenas, including prisons, general hospitals and general practices. Irrespective of the setting, there are a number of methodological issues which require consideration before embarking on such a study.

CASE DEFINITION

In psychiatry, where there are few biological markers for specific syndromes, the decision as to what constitutes a psychiatric 'case' is rather less of a philosophical and more of a clinical problem than might at first be thought. The notion of caseness being a fixed entity is dismissed by Copeland (1981) as a 'chimera existing in the mind of the investigator'. The debate is further compounded by the fact that psychiatric disturbance is not an entity separate from normality—rather, there is continuity between them (Schneider, 1950) and systems of establishing caseness suggesting qualitative differences are based on false premises. The view that caseness is defined by those who seek treatment from psychiatrists is fraught with pitfalls, as is the opinion that it should be defined in terms of social impairment (Ingham, 1981).

A further difficulty relating to psychiatric diagnosis and therefore to caseness is the notorious unreliability of these diagnoses. Several sources of

Measuring Human Problems. Edited by D.F. Peck and C.M. Shapiro

unreliability have been identified by Spitzer *et al.* (1975), and include the differing sources of information for clinicians, different stages of illness, differences in observation between clinicians and differing interpretations of the importance of individual symptoms. To reduce these sources of disagreement and to overcome the problem of defining caseness, diagnostic criteria have been developed and incorporated into operational definitions and structured interviews. This method is not without its critics when applied to non-hospital populations. Goldberg (1982) believes this technique is nothing more than projecting the concept of a case thought useful in one particular setting onto a quite different setting. Thus psychiatric patients in treatment may not be an appropriate criterion group from which to decide on caseness in general. In the absence of alternatives, however, psychiatric patients are likely to remain the standard population from which these decisions are made. It is important to understand that caseness is not an immutable entity and that it should be defined for the purpose of the individual study. The view of Wing *et al.* (1978) is apposite in this context: 'The term "case" can be used in any way that the purposes of the clinician require; no single set of definitions is likely to be of universal value.'

SCREENING VERSUS DIAGNOSTIC SCHEDULES

The choice between summation of symptoms or between combinations of symptoms to define caseness is reflected in the different schedules available. Those that rely on numbers of symptoms use an arbitrary cut-off score above which the person is said to be a case. Each symptom is equivalent to every other and there is no weighting for specific symptoms. Such scales are commonly called impairment or symptom scales. This type of schedule has the advantages of giving a measure of impairment on a continuous scale, and of being easy to administer and to score.

Their disadvantages are that those with physical illness frequently score highly and those with chronic psychiatric illness tend to obtain low scores. They fail to distinguish between the different diagnostic categories of illness and they do not take into account the amount of distress engendered by symptoms, with high scorers sometimes being less distressed than low scorers with just one or two symptoms (e.g. obsessional symptoms). Some researchers have begun to examine the problems associated with physical illness by isolating subscales measuring psychological symptoms, physiological symptoms or those that measure both.

Response bias, although a problem with all schedules, is a particular problem with screening schedules since there is no mechanism for scrutiny of the responses. The commonest cause of response bias is the tendency to give socially desirable answers and acquiescence (i.e. yea- or nay-saying). There is some evidence that social desirability is related to ethnic origin (Dohrenwend and Dohrenwend, 1969) and gender (Philips and Segal, 1969) while acquiescence set is not. Response bias has been found to affect both the *Langer Scale* and the *Health Opinion Survey* (Seiler, 1973) although not the *GHQ* (Goldberg, 1972).

A further problem with self-report schedules is non-response, and this may take the form of failure to co-operate at all or inability to answer one or more crucial questions relating to the disorder under study. The researcher has to decide how to handle these missing data—whether to exclude this group totally or to use the incomplete information. Missing data in themselves may not be a source of bias if the non-responders do not differ significantly from responders. Failure to respond commonly occurs in up to 30 per cent of those contacted, and investigators reporting such results have the onus of proving similarity between responders and non-responders.

Despite these drawbacks, they are useful as measures of reaction to stress (social, physical or psychological). They also identify those with probable psychiatric illness and in need of more detailed assessment. In this latter context they are used for initial screening in two-stage screening studies provided their sensitivity is acceptable. Although there is a prerequisite of adequate sensitivity it is also common practice to conduct second-stage assessments in a sample of those initially identified as non-cases to assess the magnitude of the percentage of false negatives.

Diagnostic instruments such as the *Present State Examination (PSE)* (Wing *et al.*, 1974) and the *Schedule for Affective Disorders and Schizophrenia (SADS)* (Endicott and Spitzer, 1978) have attempted to overcome some of the deficits inherent in screening schedules. They also solve many of the problems of reliability related to clinical diagnosis. Their main value is their ability to distinguish different categories of psychiatric illness. These are structured interviews, and each symptom is clearly defined and information is gathered in a systematic manner. Some, such as the PSE, concentrate on current mental state, others, such as SADS and the *Diagnostic Interview Schedule (DIS)* (Robins *et al.*, 1979, 1981), provide a lifetime diagnosis as well.

These instruments are time-consuming to administer and require special training. Also there are special problems relating to patients in remission and to interviewee recall which will be described in the next section. Nevertheless, diagnostic schedules do represent a major advance in psychiatric epidemiology.

TIME FRAME

The primary function of interview and screening schedules is to separate those who are psychiatrically ill from those who are not, and implicit in this is the identification of those who have undergone change from those with durable attributes. Conventionally, traits are thought of as belonging to the latter, while symptoms have a discrete onset and represent change from the individual's normal state. This distinction between personality and illness may seem obvious, but unfortunately it is not always made explicit in schedules that assess illness or in those purporting to examine personality.

The PSE is one commonly used schedule which clearly specifies a time frame (one month) in which the symptom must have been present. Although it has not been validated for use with longer periods, it has been used to assess symptoms over one year (Brown and Harris, 1978). The GHQ is more vague and inquires about change from 'usual'. This suggests that symptoms rather than traits are being identified but there is uncertainty about its ability to identify those with chronic disorders (Surtees, 1987). Other schedules such as the *Middlesex Hospital Questionnaire* (Crown and Crisp, 1966) do not specify a time frame and may thus be identifying personality disorder rather than illness.

While it is acknowledged that the specification of a time frame is highly desirable, the limitation of this is that patients in recent remission (e.g. schizophrenics) will not be identified as cases, although they may be heavy utilizers of the psychiatric services and may even be in-patients (Wing, 1976).

Schedules such as *SADS-L* and the *Structured Clinical Interview for DSM-III (SCID)* (Spitzer *et al.*, 1986), purporting to measure lifetime disorder, do so by inquiring about past symptoms and then identifying other symptoms present contemporaneously. Clearly, such measures will be influenced by interviewee recall and may in some circumstances not be valid. Little work has been carried out on the validity of lifetime diagnoses generated by these instruments. However, these schedules do utilize all sources of information, including case notes, and this may serve to make their validity less suspect.

ONSET OF DISORDER

Onset is of particular importance in disorders such as schizophrenia, where the type of onset is of prognostic significance. It is also a consideration in studies of incidence and in natural history studies. What constitutes an acute, subacute and insidious onset has rarely been made explicit. Traditionally, the onset of symptoms defines the onset of illness. However, many patients have changes in behaviour and in functioning or describe isolated symptoms long before the full-blown syndrome becomes apparent. Some define the type of onset by the time span between the first appearance of malfunctioning and the complete disorder. Others define it only in terms of the speed of onset of symptoms.

A further problem lies in deciding the number and severity of symptoms required before defining the full-blown condition. Can an episode of depression be regarded as present when only sleep and concentration are impaired or does it also require diurnal mood swing or any of the other commonly occurring symptoms? While consideration of the issues of 'caseness' may be helpful, the arguments are not defined exclusively in these terms. As already pointed out (see Case Definition), caseness is not an entity in nature. Rather, it is an arbitrary but useful concept developed to facilitate research. Thus defining the full disorder in terms of the appearance of 'caseness' may be procrustean. There are no definitive rules in this regard and researchers have to develop their own definition of, and requirements for, onset.

The difficulty of defining remission and relapse also requires consideration and is of special importance in incidence studies. Does the patient who has been free from depression for six months have a new episode or a continuing single episode if symptoms recur? Finally, the confounding effect of new symptoms developing in the course of a disorder, where hierarchical rules are applied, has only recently been addressed (Surtees *et al.*, 1986). The likelihood of the secondary disorder inflating the rate is a realistic concern, but one which can be overcome in longitudinal studies by careful attention to change points. As with the other issues raised in relation to onset, there are no definitive rules, and each researcher must define these *a priori*.

Reliability and Validity

The concepts of reliability and validity were discussed in Chapter 1 in this volume. Additional features of validity, sensitivity and specificity need to be noted here. The extent to which patients manifesting the disorder are so classified by the test is pertinent. The higher this value, the lower the percentage of false negatives. In two-stage screening studies high levels of sensitivity are imperative in the first-wave schedules if cases are not to be missed. Specificity is the extent to which those who do not manifest the disorder are so classified. It is therefore a measure of the percentage of false positives. These aspects of validity are demonstrated in a study by Myers and Weissman (1980), who found that the *CES-D* had a sensitivity of 66 per cent and a specificity of 94 per cent when validated concurrently against RDC criteria and clinical diagnosis. Changing the cut-off score for defining caseness from 16 to 5 resulted in an increase in sensitivity to 100 per cent but a drop in specificity to 70 per cent. Thus for screening for research this would be acceptable, but for other purposes such as prescriptive screening this would result in an excessively large number of non-depressed people being 'treated'.

Although sensitivity and specificity are commonly reported, a more appropriate but seldom-used measure for screening purposes is predictive value, defined as the proportion of true cases among those with a positive test. The value of this depends not only on sensitivity and specificity but also on the prevalence of the disorder. If this is low then the predictive value of a test of given sensitivity and specificity is low, and conversely, as the prevalence increases, so does the predictive value. Even tests with adequate sensitivity and specificity may have a predictive value worse than guessing (see Chapter 3, this volume). The CES-D was found to have a sensitivity of 64 per cent, a specificity of 94 per cent and a predictive value of 33 per cent when a cut-off score of 16 was used (Boyd *et al.*, 1982). Changing the cut-off as described in the previous paragraph resulted in a drop in predictive value to 14 per cent, although the sensitivity increased to 100 per cent. Consideration of predictive value is especially pertinent where tests with a high predictive value designed for use with hospital populations are unsuited for the general population. The issue of predictive value is succinctly discussed by Williams *et al.* (1982).

It is thus apparent that validity is not fixed but should be reassessed when a schedule is being used on a new population, especially when that population possesses different characteristics such as varying age or culture or is located in a different setting. Benjamin *et al.* (1982) found that in a community population the validity of the GHQ was unproven with a sensitivity of only 54.5 per cent. The specificity was 91.5 per cent. The validity of the GHQ had originally been assessed in a primary care setting and the finding of Benjamin and colleagues attests to the necessity for re-establishing validity.

SCHEDULES IN COMMON USE

The General Health Questionnaire (GHQ) was developed by Goldberg (1972) to detect probable cases of affective disorder that present to general practitioners. It is therefore a screening schedule and is most appropriately used as a measure of distress or as part of a two-stage screening programme. Those with threshold (or higher) scores should then have a full psychiatric interview to determine diagnosis. The GHQ is a 60-, 30-, 28- or 20-item self-administered questionnaire covering the 'past few weeks', rated on a four-point scale ranging from 'much more than usual' to 'not at all'. It was originally validated on a clinical population in a general practice setting and in an out-patient department. There is some evidence that the threshold score needs to be set independently for each population under study in order to improve sensitivity (Tarnopolsky *et al.*, 1979), and that in community samples the GHQ is unsuitable as a screening instrument due to its tendency to miss chronic cases (Benjamin *et al.*, 1982). Attempts to overcome this deficit have been only partially successful (Surtees, 1987). It has been widely used in a variety of settings that include general practitioner surgeries (Goldberg *et al.*, 1976; Skuse and Williams, 1984; Brodman, 1987), out-patient clinics (Sims and Salmons, 1975), hypertension clinics (Mann, 1977) and students enrolling at university (Szulecka *et al.*, 1986).

The Centre for Epidemiologic Studies Depression Scale (CES-D) was designed to measure depressive symptoms in the community (Radloff, 1977) by means of a self-rating questionnaire. It is composed of 20 symptoms of depression measured on a four-point scale and concerns the previous week. These symptoms are derived from other well-known and validated depression scales (e.g. Beck and Zung) and from the *Minnesota Multiphasic Personality Inventory (MMPI)*. A cut-off score of either 16 or 17 has been used in several studies (Weissman *et al.*, 1977; Roberts and Vernon, 1983) with little change in sensitivity and specificity. For use in the initial stage of two-stage screening projects, lowering the cut-off should be considered to maximize sensitivity (Boyd *et al.*, 1982). Predictive value is unacceptably low at between 14 per cent and 33 per cent. Problems with this scale include nay-saying and only a modest correlation with clinical depression in the community (Myers and Weissman, 1980). Ways of overcoming these problems are discussed by Boyd *et al.* (1982). This schedule has been little used in British studies but has found extensive use in North America (Comstock and Helsing, 1976; Radloff, 1977; Weissman *et al.*, 1977).

The Schedule for Affective Disorder and Schizophrenia (SADS) was developed by Endicott and Spitzer (1978) to reduce the variance in information elicited during clinical interviews for making RDC diagnoses. It covers symptoms, their duration and level of social functioning. Information from all three areas must be present before the criteria for a diagnosis can be met. SADS is best administered by those familiar with psychopathology and the issues involved in making clinical diagnoses. Training is necessary for achieving adequate reliability. The interview takes about one hour if the interviewee is largely free of symptoms, such as in community studies, but much longer if many symptoms are elicited.

There are three versions of SADS: the current SADS, a lifetime SADS (SADS-L) and a shorter version to measure change (SADS-C). SADS-L gives limited consideration to personality disorder identifying only antisocial, labile and cyclothymic types. Information is gathered from all available sources (for example, case notes and informants) as well as from the patient.

This schedule has been used most notably by Weissman *et al.* (1978) when they undertook a community study to estimate the prevalence of specific psychiatric disorders in the general population.

The Present State Examination (PSE) is a structured interview of excellent validity and reliability. Two versions are commonly used—a screening schedule assesses neurotic disorder and a full schedule which measures both neurotic and psychotic disorder. Both require training and are best used by personnel familiar with psychiatric symptomatology. Administration takes roughly 30 and 50 minutes respectively, depending on the amount of symptomatology. A ten-question version has been developed for predicting low scores (Cooper and Mackenzie, 1981) but has not been widely used.

The PSE allocates symptom clusters to diagnostic classes by means of a computer program (CATEGO) and these resemble the commonly used diagnostic classes, although organic states and personality disorder are not covered. In the presence of organic states the PSE is invalid and it is unsuitable for use with children. In addition to providing a research diagnosis it gives a measure of severity known as the Total Score, and provides a measure of the certainty with which a particular set of symptoms can be recognized as a psychiatric disorder. This is expressed as the Index of Definition and has eight levels. Those in levels 1 to 4 are described as 'non-cases', those in level 5 as 'borderline' and the remainder as 'definite' cases. It is to the latter group that CATEGO classes are assigned.

This covers symptoms which have been present in the previous month and only those of moderate or greater severity are rated. Diagnoses are thus cross-sectional rather than longitudinal, and there is no provision for lifetime diagnosis, although this may change in later versions. Each symptom is operationally defined and the questions are prescribed, although there is room for extra questions and clarification. The PSE has been used in numerous hospital (Wing, 1976; Tyrer *et al.*, 1983), community (Surtees *et al.*, 1983) and general practice studies (Casey *et al.*, 1984) but most notably in the US/UK diagnostic study (Cooper *et al.*, 1972) and the WHO schizophrenia study.

The tenth edition of the PSE is currently being tested in field trials and this will be included in a much larger constellation of schedules collectively to be called SCAN (Schedules for Clinical Assessment in Neuropsychiatry). In addition to PSE 10, which itself will have expanded to measure present state as well as previous episodes, the SCAN system will assess personality, social disablement and possible organic influences on symptomatology. It will generate diagnoses for ICD 10. A similar system—The Composite International Diagnostic Interview (CIDI) will generate diagnoses according to DSM III-R criteria and both will be able to generate diagnoses in the other system. These have not yet been used in epidemiological surveys.

The Diagnostic Interview Schedule (DIS) (Robins *et al.*, 1979, 1981) was developed to facilitate large-scale epidemiological studies and thus for use by lay interviewers. It provides diagnoses according to three systems—DSM III, RDC and Feighner—using rigidly prescribed questions and allowing little scope for improvisation. It is this aspect which makes it suitable, after training, for use by non-psychiatrists. Diagnosis is made on the basis of symptom severity and symptom cluster. Also for some diagnoses a maximum age of onset is specified. The schedule is complete in itself and, unlike SADS, does not require information from any other source such as case notes or relatives. Cut-offs are not used, thus minimizing the likelihood of false negatives. One can shorten the interview by omitting questions when enough positive or negative answers have been provided, although this is not advised. Diagnosis is given for lifetime initially and then for current illness defined by four time frames—two weeks, 1 month, 6 months and 1 year. This schedule will make possible comparison between various diagnostic systems and their application to outcome, response to treatments and those aspects of definitions relating to validity. It has not been used in Britain but has been widely publicized in the extensive ECA study (Robins *et al.*, 1984).

There are a host of other schedules available to the researcher but it is beyond the scope of this chapter to deal with all of these in detail. Well-known screening schedules include the *Langer 22-item Screening Score* (Langer, 1962), the *Health Opinion Survey* (Macmillan, 1957), the *Hopkins Symptom Checklist* (Derogatis, 1974), the *Psychiatric Epidemiology Research Interview (PERI)* (Dohrenwend *et al.*, 1980) and the *Psychiatric Status Schedule (PSS)* (Spitzer *et al.*, 1970). Diagnostic schedules include the *PSS/Diagno* system—a combination of a general psychopathology measure and a diagnostic computer program (Spitzer and Endicott, 1968), the *Current and Past Psychopathology Scales (CAPPS)* (Endicott and Spitzer, 1972) and the *Structured Clinical Interview for DSM III-R (SCID)* (Spitzer *et al.*, 1986). Some of these have proved to be less satisfactory than at first believed while others have not been widely used although of proven reliability and validity.

In summary, the specific circumstances of a particular screening exercise have to be considered in selecting the instruments for use in the detection of psychiatric illness. In general, a two-staged approach is likely to be both most effective and economical.

REFERENCES

Benjamin, S., Decalmer, P. and Haran, D. (1982) Community screening for mental illness: A validity study of the General Health Questionnaire. *British Journal of Psychiatry*, **140**, 174–80.

Boyd, J.H., Weissman, M.M., Thompson, D. and Myers, J.K. (1982) Screening for depression in a community sample: Understanding the discrepancies between symptom and diagnostic scales. *Archives of General Psychiatry*, **32**, 1195–1200.

Brodman, A.P. (1987) The General Health Questionnaire and the detection of emotional disorder by general practitioners. *British Journal of Psychiatry,* **151**, 373–81.

Brown, G. and Harris, T. (1978) *Social Origins of Depression,* Tavistock Publications, London.

Casey, P.R., Dillon, S. and Tyrer, P.J. (1984) The diagnostic status of patients with conspicuous psychiatric morbidity in primary care. *Psychological Medicine,* **14**, 673–83.

Comstock, G.W. and Helsing, K.J. (1976) Symptoms of depression in two communities. *Psychological Medicine,* **6**, 551–64.

Cooper, J.E., Kendell, R.E., Gurland, B.J., Sharpe, L., Copeland, J.R.M. and Simon, R. (1972) *Psychiatric Diagnosis in New York and London,* Maudsley Monograph, Oxford University Press, Oxford.

Cooper, J.E. and Mackenzie, S. (1981) The rapid prediction of low scores on a standardized psychiatric interview (Present State Examination). In J.K. Wing, P. Babbington and L.N. Robins (eds) *What is a Case? The problem of definition in community surveys,* Grant-McIntyre, London.

Copeland, J. (1981) What is a 'case'? A case for what? In J.K. Wing, P. Babbington and L.N. Robins (eds) *What is a Case? The problem of definition in community surveys,* Grant-McIntyre, London.

Crown, S. and Crisp, A.H. (1966) A short clinical diagnostic self-rating scale for psychoneurotic patients: the Middlesex Hospital Questionnaire (MHQ). *British Journal of Psychiatry,* **112**, 917–23.

Derogatis, L.R. (1974) The Hopkins symptom checklist. In P. Pichot (ed.), *Psychological Measures in Psychopharmacology,* Karger, Basel.

Dohrenwend, B.P. and Dohrenwend, B.S. (1969) *Social Status and Psychological Disorder: A Causal Inquiry,* John Wiley, New York.

Dohrenwend, B.P., Shrout, P.E., Egri, G. and Mendelsohn, F.S. (1980) Measures of nonspecific psychological distress and other dimensions of psychopathology in the general population. *Archives of General Psychiatry,* **37**, 1229–36.

Endicott, J. and Spitzer, R.L. (1972) Current and Past Psychopathology Scales (CAPPS): Rationale, reliability and validity. *Archives of General Psychiatry,* **27**, 678–87.

Endicott, J. and Spitzer, R.L. (1978) A diagnostic interview: the Schedule for Affective Disorders and Schizophrenia. *Archives of General Psychiatry,* **35**, 837–44.

Goldberg, D. (1972) *The Detection of Psychiatric Illness by Questionnaire,* Maudsley Monograph, No. 21, Oxford Unversity Press, Oxford.

Goldberg, D. (1982) The concept of a 'case' in general practice. *Social Psychiatry,* **17**, 61–5.

Goldberg, D., Kay, C. and Thompson, L. (1976) Psychiatric morbidity in general practice and the community. *Psychological Medicine,* **6**, 565–9.

Ingham, J. (1981) Neurosis: Disease or distress? In J.K. Wing, P. Babbington and L.N. Robins (eds), *What is a Case? The problem of definition in community surveys,* Grant-McIntyre, London.

Langer, T.S. (1962) A twenty-two item screening score of psychiatric symptoms indicating impairment. *Journal of Health and Social Behavior,* **3**, 269–76.

Macmillan, A.M. (1957) The Health Opinion Survey: Technique for estimating prevalence of psychoneurotic and related types of disorder in communities. *Psychological Reprints,* **3**, 325–9.

Mann, A.H. (1977) Psychiatric morbidity and hostility in hypertension. *Psychological Medicine,* **7**, 653–9.

Myers, J.K. and Weissman, M.M. (1980) Use of a self-report symptom scale to detect depression in a community sample. *American Journal of Psychiatry*, **137**, 1081–4.

Philips, D.L. and Segal, B.F. (1969) Sexual status and psychiatric symptoms. *American Sociological Review*, **34**, 58–72.

Radloff, L.S. (1977). The CES-D scale: A self-report depression scale for research in the general population. *Applied Psychological Measurement*, **1**, 385–401.

Roberts, R.E. and Venon, S.W. (1983) The Centre for Epidemiologic Studies Depression Scale: Its use in a community sample. *American Journal of Psychiatry*, **140**, 41–6.

Robins, L.N., Helzer, J.E., Croughan, J. and Ratcliff, K.S. (1981) National Institute of Mental Health Diagnostic Interview Schedule: its history, characteristics and validity. *Archives of General Psychiatry*, **38**, 381–9.

Robins, L.N., Helzer, J., Croughan, J., Williams, J.B.W. and Spitzer, R.L. (1979) *National Institute of Mental Health Diagnostic Interview Schedule*, Government Printing Office, Washington, DC.

Robins, L.N., Helzer, J.E., Weissman, M.M., Orvaschel, H., Gruenberg, E., Burke, J.D. and Regier, D.A. (1984) Lifetime prevalence of specific psychiatric disorders in three sites. *Archives of General Psychiatry*, **41**, 949–58.

Schneider, K. (1950) Systematic psychiatry. *American Journal of Psychiatry*, **107**, 334–5.

Seiler, L.H. (1973) The 12-item scale used in field studies of mental illness. A question of method, a question of substance, and a question of theory. *Journal of Health and Social Behavior*, **14**, 252–64.

Sims, A.C. and Salmons, P.H. (1975) Severity of symptoms of psychiatric outpatients. *Psychological Medicine*, **5**, 62–6.

Skuse, D. and Williams, P. (1984) Screening for psychiatric disorder in general practice. *Psychological Medicine*, **14**, 365–77.

Spitzer, R.L. and Endicott, J. (1968) DIAGNO: A computer program for psychiatric diagnosis utilizing the differential diagnosis procedure. *Archives of General Psychiatry*, **18**, 746–56.

Spitzer, R.L., Endicott, J., Fleiss, J.L. and Cohen, J. (1970) The Psychiatric Status Schedule: A technique for evaluating psychopathology and impairment in role functioning. *Archives of General Psychiatry*, **23**, 41–55.

Spitzer, R.L., Endicott, J. and Robins, E. (1975) Clinical criteria for psychiatric diagnosis and the DSM III. *American Journal of Psychiatry*, **132**, 1187–92.

Spitzer, R.L., Williams, J.B. and Gibbon, M. (1986) *Structured Clinical Interview for DSM III-R*, Biometrics Research Department, New York State Psychiatric Institute, New York.

Surtees, P.G. (1987) Psychiatric disorder in the community and the General Health Questionnaire. *British Journal of Psychiatry*, **150**, 828–35.

Surtees, P., Dean, C., Ingham, J.G., Kreitman, N.B., Miller, P. McC. and Sashidharan, S.P (1983) Psychiatric disorders in women from an Edinburgh community: associations with demographic factors. *British Journal of Psychiatry*, **142**, 238–46.

Surtees, P., Sashidharan, S.P. and Dean, C. (1986). Affective disorder amongst women in the general population: A longitudinal study. *British Journal of Psychiatry*, **148**, 176–86.

Szulecka, T.K., Springett, N.R., and DePauw, K.W. (1986) Psychiatric morbidity in first-year undergraduates and the effect of brief psychotherapeutic intervention—a pilot study. *British Journal of Psychiatry*, **149**, 75–81.

Tarnopolsky, A., Hand, D.J., McLean, E.K., Roberts, H. and Wiggins, R.D. (1979) Validity and uses of a screening questionnaire (GHQ) in the community. *British Journal of Psychiatry*, **134**, 508–15.

Tyrer, P.J., Casey, P.R. and Gall, J. (1983) The relationship between neurosis and personality disorder. *British Journal of Psychiatry*, **142**, 404–8.

Weissman, M.M., Myers, J.K. and Harding, P.S. (1978) Psychiatric disorders in a U.S. urban community. 1975–1976. *American Journal of Psychiatry*, **134**, 459–62.

Weissman, M.M., Scholomskas, D., Pottenger, M., Prusoff, B. and Locke, B. (1977) Assessing depressive symptoms in five psychiatric populations: A validation study. *American Journal of Epidemiology*, **106**, 203–14.

Williams, P, Hand, D. and Tarnopolsky, A. (1982) The problem of screening for uncommon disorders—a comment on the Eating Attitudes test. *Psychological Medicine*, **12**, 431–4.

Wing, J.K. (1976) A technique for studying psychiatric morbidity in in-patient and out-patient series and in general population samples. *Psychological Medicine*, **6**, 665–71.

Wing, J.K., Cooper, J.E. and Sartorius, N. (1974) *The Measurement and Classification of Psychiatric Symptoms*, Cambridge University Press, Cambridge.

Wing, J.K., Mann, S.A., Leff, J.P. and Nixon, J.M. (1978) The concept of a 'case' in psychiatric population surveys. *Psychological Medicine*, **8**, 203–17.

Chapter 3

Depression

MAX HAMILTON and COLIN M. SHAPIRO

INTRODUCTION

It is convenient to distinguish between detection and measurement of depression because, in practice, different methods will be used. Obviously, there is so much overlap that the difference could be regarded as merely quantitative, but it raises fundamental problems.

In sociology, human behaviour in all its variety forms a continuum, but in medicine the difference between health and sickness, between normal and abnormal, is fundamental. The reason is that this (qualitative) difference is the justification for therapeutic intervention. It is therefore necessary to be clear about the meaning of 'depression'. In psychiatry it has three different meanings. The first, as in common speech, defines depression as a normal human reaction to a loss. The loss may be real, such as the death of a relative, or potential, such as failing to obtain a job or promotion. The second and third meanings imply an abnormal state. Depression can be a symptom which appears in many different disorders (depressed mood) or a disorder which has not only symptoms, constituting a recognizable pattern, but also a definite course and incidence, a genetic basis and response to treatment (depressive illness). It can be very difficult to distingush between a depressive illness and reactions to stresses, but this does not mean that they are not essentially different. The main concern here will be with the measurement of depressive illness, even though most methods overlap with the measurement of depressive mood, whatever its nature.

Although the name emphasizes the subjective state, the condition involves changes in every aspect of the person's life. The obvious changes in affect and cognition are accompanied by alterations in facial expression, bodily posture and movements and also the response to environmental and social situations. In addition, there are physiological and biochemical changes. The last of these has become a very large field of research interest since the introduction and development of antidepressant drugs. With all these facets to the measurement of depressive illness it is a relatively easy matter to write a book on the measurement of depression and for the final

Measuring Human Problems. Edited by D.F. Peck and C.M. Shapiro

product not to be comprehensive (for example, Marsella *et al.*, 1987). This problem is more acute in a single chapter, and we have therefore opted to emphasize those forms of measurement that are currently used, especially rating scales. We also give attention to some of the other forms of measurement that have the potential of complementing rating scale assessment, that are currently much written about or that are likely to be accessible to most investigators and clinicians.

MEASUREMENT OF DEPRESSION

Detection

The detection of depression in the community is usually carried out by means of questionnaires, though interviewing is possible on a limited sample. In this situation the distinction between being dejected and suffering from a depressive illness becomes blurred. When the aim of the enquiry is to determine the presence of depressive illness in hospital in-patients the distinction is crucial. In this situation questionnaires are not likely to be useful; skilled interviewing may be necessary. Detection is then part of the process of making a diagnosis and measurement comes after. A good example of this two-step process is provided in the studies by Cox on post-natal depression in which some of the standard aspects of depressive symptomatology (e.g. sleeplessness) are not usefully included in the detection or measurement of depression (see Cox *et al.*, 1987).

At present there is no 'gold standard' by which to decide if a person is or is not depressed. It has become commonplace to use diagnostic criteria and rating scales, but the emergence of putative biological measures and measures of, for example, communication pattern which may change in relation to mental state should provide a broader perspective to the assessment of depression.

Scales

There are many scales in current use. The theoretical underpinnings and clinical orientation of a researcher when developing a new scale will greatly influence the composition of the items included in a scale. If the intention of a scale is the consideration of the cognitive aspects of depression, then the scale will emphasize these features. If the purpose in developing a scale is detection of changes in biological features following psychopharmacological treatments then a different cluster of factors will be incorporated. The use of different scales will highlight these differences.

Table 3.1. Facets of depression in commonly used scales

	BDI	CES-D	MMPI-D	SDS	HAMD	SADS
Style	Self-report	Self-report	Self-report	Self-rating	Clinical assessment	Interview
Items	21	20	60	20	17 + 4	
Scale	0–3	0–3	–	4 point	0–2 or 0–4	Yes/no or 3–9
Time frame	–	Past week	–	Past week	–	Present episode
Cut-offs	13 screening 21 research 9 normal	–	–	–	30 in-pt, 24 neurotic	
Affect	2	8	8	3	2	5a, 1b
Behaviour	2	4	1	4	5	7b 16c
Cognition	11	4	17	6	2	4b
Interpersonal symptoms	1	2	6	1	0	–
Somatic symptoms	5		18	6	8	1b, 1c
Behavioural signs	–	2	5		Yes	
Other	–		5			4d
Key reference	Beck *et al.* (1961)	Radloff (1977)	Hathaway and McKinlay (1951)	Zung (1965)	Hamilton (1967)	
Positive features	Easy to administer, sensitive to clinical change, wide usage, good discrimination, covalidated with clinical rating scales and behavioural observation scales	Assesses fluctuations in mood, differentiates acutely depressed sub-groups, and between clinical and normal populations	Sensitive to mood change, identifies research populations, correlates well with other scales	Good concurrent validity with other scales, sensitive to changes in clinical status. Short	Extensive usage, all information is applicable to interviews, inter-rater reliability 0.90, distinguishes depressed from non-depressed and level of depression. Sensitive to uni- versus bipolar	Use of operational criteria
Negative features	High correlation with anxiety	Not diagnostic, does not measure severity	Heterogeneous, lacks discriminant validity from anxiety	Discriminant validity is weak	Weighted to somatic, limited normative information for comparison	78 pages long, moderate concurrent validity

a = mood; b = endogenous; c = neuro-vegetative; d = suicidality

It is common for more than one scale to be used in studies of depression. It is unfortunate that often the scales chosen are similar in their emphasis, so that while one scale often supplements another, it often happens that the opportunity to select scales which are complementary in the sense of assessing a much wider range of facets of depression is lost. A limited comparison of the different facets measured by a few common scales is given in Table 3.1.

Scales can be classified in various ways:

(1) *Method of use:* (a) self-ratings or (b) ratings by observers, the latter being skilled (e.g. psychiatrist or psychologist), semi-skilled (e.g. nursing-aid) or unskilled (e.g. a relative). Information can be obtained through a structured, semi-structured or free interview. Paykel and Norton (1986) have tabulated the distinction between clinical interview and self-report assessments and these are shown in Table 3.2.
(2) *Content:* Behaviour in the Hospital Ward, Social Adjustment, Family Relationships, Working Capacity in occupational therapy or industrial

Table 3.2 Comparison of clinical interview and self-report assessments in depression (from Paykel and Norton, 1985, with permission).

Areas assessed	Self-report	Clinical interview
Subjective feelings/ moods	Yes	Less well
Verbal reports of symptoms	Yes	Yes
Observable behaviours	No	Yes
Judgements depending on insight	No	Yes
Specificity	More global	More specific
Range of severity	Less useful with severe depression, major retardation or psychotic features	Can be used over whole range. May be less sensitive in mild depression
Circumstances	Requires patient co-operation, motivation and ability to concentrate and read	Can be completed with minimal patient co-operation
Costs	Brief, easy, cheap in professional time	Longer. Requires professional rater
Potential biases	Pencil and paper response sets Complaining (sick) sets	Rater sets and bias

therapy. These features are not specific to depression and will therefore not be considered further here. They are covered in detail in other chapters in this book. One major aspect of content (symptoms) is considered in Table 3.1.

(3) *Form of items:* (a) with several grades of severity, (b) merely absent–present, (c) forced choice (in which the rater has to choose between alternative statements).

(4) *Function:* (a) scales for measuring severity of illness and, by implication, response to treatment, (b) prognostic scales, (c) scales for selection of treatment, (d) scales for diagnosis and classification.

Scales for prognosis and for selection of treatments are very similar, since prognosis in psychiatry has become essentially a prognosis after treatment. Such scales, together with diagnostic and classificatory ones, are not scales in the usual sense. They contain items which could be described as 'fixed', i.e. whatever the patient's condition, these items remain the same. Examples are: age, sex, a family history of manic-depressive disorder, length of illness or number of previous attacks.

The method of use and the form of the items will be given for each scale. The overwhelming majority of scales are designed for the measurement of symptoms and the severity of illness, and obviously they will be the major concern here. Prognostic scales and those for the selection of treatment have not been successful so far, except those that are implicit in classification scales. Of these, only the Newcastle scale will be considered (see below). There is an increasing number of scales designed for specific purposes or to assess depression in particular circumstances. Examples would be the Perinatal Grief Scale (Toedter *et al.*, 1988) and the Edinburgh Postnatal Depression Scale (Cox *et al.*, 1987). These specific scales, not surprisingly, prove to have greater sensitivity and specificity than more general scales when used in similar populations (Harris *et al.*, 1989). These specific scales will not be discussed in detail in this chapter.

Information for observer scales can be obtained through a structured, semi-structured or free interview.

Observer rating scales

A scale is simply a method of recording the judgement or opinion concerning a patient's condition. Those scales which are completed by a skilled and trained observer will usually yield the best information. This is shown by the high validity and reliability of such scales. What is recorded in a scale is either direct observations or inferences from them, though the distinction is not absolute. Raters who neglect to use their experience and powers of judgement are throwing away the most powerful instrument for measurement that they possess. A total score which may be derived from summing scores on items becomes a measure of severity by a clearly defined process, unlike the vague and unknown method of synthesis used by the clinician. A scale designed for use by unskilled raters should, as far as possible, be confined to observed behaviour and require the minimum of interpretation. A disadvantage of observer scales is that they require the time of skilled staff. This is a particular problem when patients do not attend a clinic for follow-up interviews and have then to be assessed in their homes.

SPECIFIC SCALES FOR DEPRESSIVE ILLNESS (MELANCHOLIA)

Observer rating scales

Hamilton Rating Scale for Depression (HAMD)

This is one of the oldest of observer rating scales and the most popular, so much so that it has become almost the standard by which other scales are judged. The first publication (Hamilton, 1960) was subsequently slightly revised and provided with better definitions and guides to the grades of severity (Hamilton, 1967). Since then, further details concerning its use have been published (Hamilton, 1980). Although designed for a skilled rater, very little training is required. It is easy to use in the course of a clinical interview but, as with all methods of assessment, the rater should utilize all sources of information. A guide to the use of the HAMD has been published (Loudon and Tiplady, 1981) and recently a further guide, apparently oblivious to the first and with unnecessary crudeness in the arrangement of questions, has slipped through the peer review process (Williams, 1988).

The scale contains 17 items for the assessment of severity of illness. Of these, five are concerned with somatic symptoms and with insomnia in its three phases (early, middle and delayed). The item 'Loss of Interest and Working Capacity' combines the two on the grounds that patients have difficulty in distinguishing between these two features. 'Loss of Interest' includes the symptoms currently termed 'anhedonia'.

Four other items were described in the original publication because, although of no value in assessing *severity*, it was considered that they would be of use in special circumstances (e.g. response to treatment). One symptom, Diurnal Variation, describes merely the form of the illness, not its severity. The other three (Derealization and Depersonalization, Paranoid symptoms and Obsessional symptoms) were omitted on the grounds that they occurred with insufficient frequency to merit inclusion.

The scale has high validity against global judgement and high reliability, both showing correlations round about +0.90. It has often been reported to be the most sensitive scale for measuring response to treatment. The scale was thoroughly reviewed by Hedlund and Vieweg (1979a).

One criticism is that too many items are concerned with 'somatic' symptoms, e.g. in comparison with the Beck, Bech–Rafaelsen and Montgomery–Asberg scales. However, with increasing interest in biological aspects of depression, this may be an advantage.

Some users preferred to include the supplementary four items. Others have added three psychological symptoms. In consequence, as the scale became increasingly used for the evaluation of antidepressant drugs, three versions emerged, containing 17, 21 and 24 items. The full scale is shown in Table 3.3. In the USA, the National Institute of Mental Health (NIMH) now recommends the original 17-item version. Unfortunately, the NIMH scale converted the grades of the items into a checklist, in an effort to improve the definitions of the items. A further deficiency was that it regarded the spontaneous mention of a symptom as indicating greater severity than if it had to be elicited by questioning. There are many reasons why patients may not mention a symptom at an interview. For example, they may not think it is relevant (e.g. feelings of guilt), they may be embarrassed (e.g. loss of libido) or they may be too polite to mention to the interviewer that they believe they are suffering from a physical illness.

The original recommendation for the scale was that it should not be used as a checklist but with the full clinical judgement of a skilled rater using all sources of information. Its most important limitation is that the rating should cover the condition of the patient for the last week or so, and therefore it cannot be used for frequent assessments. It has other deficiencies. There is no mention of the distinct quality of pathological depressed mood, though this is implicit in the diagnosis. Hypersomnia and increased appetite are not included and panic attacks are subsumed under Anxiety. Headaches have been included in two items, Anxiety Somatic and General Somatic, but should not be rated in the latter.

Bech–Rafaelsen Melancholia Scale

Bech *et al.* (1975) examined the Hamilton scale and concluded that it was unsatisfactory in a number of ways. For example, they disagreed, as did many others, with Baumann (1967), who had found it to be unifactorial. They then selected six items which they claimed to be of higher validity and more sensitive to the effects of treatment. Knesevitch *et al.* (1977) disagreed because they found that whereas the full scale and global judgement correlated (rho coefficient) 0.89, the same as the Bech subscale, for the remaining items the correlation was 0.81, and the Bech subscale and the remaining

Table 3.3 Hamilton Rating Scale.

1.	Depression	0–4	Occasional weeping 2 Frequent weeping 3 Severe 4	
2.	Guilt	0–4	Self-reproach 1 Ideas of guilt 2 Illness as punishment 3 Delusions, hallucinations 4	
3.	Suicidal ideas	0–4	Life not worth living 1 Wishing to be dead 2 Suicidal ideas + half-hearted attempts 3 Serious attempts 4	
4.	Insomnia initial	0–2	Account of severity—frequency	
5.	Insomnia middle	0–2		
6.	Insomnia delayed	0–2		
7.	Work + interest	0–4	Admission *due* to inability to carry on 4	
8.	Retardation	0–4	Flattened affect/fixed expression 1 Monotonous voice/delay in reply/tends to sit motionless 2 Prolonged difficult interview 3 Interview impossible 4	
9.	Agitation	0–4	Fidgetiness 1 Restlessness, clothes picking 2 Pacing 3 Interview 'on the run' 4	
10.	Anxiety (psychic)	0–4	Tension Difficulty in relaxing Irritability Worry over trivia Apprehension/panic/fear/'jumpy'	(discount if possible previous anxious disposition)
11.	Anxiety (somatic)	0–4	Autonomic overactivity RS, CUS, GI, Urinary	
12.	Gastrointestinal symptoms	0–2	Loss of appetite Constipation (indigestion rated under anxiety)	
13.	General somatic symptoms	0–2	Fatigue Muscular aching	
14.	Loss of libido	0–2	Assessed on *change* Rate 0 if no information	
15.	Hypochondriasis	0–4	Excessive preoccupation 1 Thoughts of organic disease 2 Strong conviction of organic disease 3 Hallucinations/delusions, e.g. rotting 4	
16.	Loss of insight	0–2		
17.	Loss of weight	0–2		

Score: Max. 52
Score 30 = severe illness

(Hamilton, 1967)

items correlated 0.94. Kearns *et al.* (1982) confirmed the sensitivity of the shorter scale but still considered the full Hamilton scale as appropriate for its purpose.

Other items and modifications were then added to the chosen six to produce a new scale (Bech and Rafaelson, 1980). It contains 11 items, five of which are identical to the Hamilton scale (Depressed mood, Guilt, Suicide, Work and interests, and Anxiety (Psychic) and a sixth, 'Tiredness and Pains', which is the equivalent of Somatic (General). The three items for insomnia have been compressed into one; Retardation has been expanded into four; Motor, Verbal, Intellectual and Emotional. This scale therefore concentrates chiefly on psychological symptoms.

The correlations of items with the total score of the other items range from 0.52 to 0.88. The inter-rater reliability ranges from 0.82 to 0.93, comparable to the Hamilton scale's figures of 0.79 to 0.93. The two scales correlate (rho) 0.97 (Rafaelsen *et al.*, 1980) and may be considered interchangeable.

The Montgomery–Asberg Depression Rating Scale (MADRS)

The Scandinavian Comprehensive Psychopathological Rating Scale (CPRS) is a general-purpose scale for psychiatric symptoms. It was so designed that specific scales could be made by extracting suitable items. The MADRS (Montgomery and Asberg, 1979) was constructed in this way. It consists of 10 out of the 17 items in the CPRS related to depression, selected because they had been found to be the most sensitive to changes produced by treatment. The items have seven grades of severity (including absent). Three of these grades are specified, the intermediate ones being left blank. Depressed Mood is split into three items: Apparent Sadness, Reported Sadness and Pessimistic Thoughts. Anxiety has two items: Inner Tension and Concentration Difficulties. Disturbances of sleep have only one item: Reduced Sleep. The item Inability to Feel covers anhedonia. Only two items are concerned with the somatic symptoms of depressive illness: Reduced Appetite and Lassitude.

The authors found that, using response category and change scores, the point biserial correlations were 0.70 compared with the Hamilton scale, which was 0.59. However, in the review of Kearns *et al.* (1982) the HAMD and MADRS came out equally well, in particular in discrimination of levels of severity.

The scale has high inter-rater reliability (up to 0.92), correlates 0.87 with a nurses' rating scale but only 0.63 with the Beck self-rating scale (Asberg *et al.*, 1973). This scale, and the Bech–Rafaelsen scale, have claimed an advantage over the Hamilton scale in that they are shorter, but as they require a full interview for completion, this makes little difference in practice. In a clinical trial of antidepressant drugs (Montgomery *et al.*, 1981) it was found that

MADRS was more sensitive to the improvement after treatment with Maprotiline than HAMD, but less so for Zimelidine. This example emphasizes the advantage of using more than one scale in the assessment of change.

Cronholm–Ottosson Scale

This is one of the earliest of specific scales (Cronholm and Ottosson, 1960), having been published in the same year as the Hamilton scale. Its publication in the middle of a monograph on electroconvulsive therapy may be one of the reasons why it has been comparatively neglected. The first version was a simple and short scale of eight items, later increased to 12. It is somewhat deficient in items on physical symptoms and perhaps gives too much emphasis to symptoms of anxiety (four items of 12).

In subsequent publications the scale was modified by better descriptions of the items, facilitating the use of half-steps (Asberg *et al.*, 1973). It has high reliability (ranging between 0.72 and 0.86) and validity, e.g. the rank correlation with the Beck Depression Inventory is about 0.63. The scale has been shown to have adequate sensitivity to effects of treatment. A comprehensive review of the scale was published by Cronholm *et al.* (1974).

Kellner Brief Depression Rating Scale (BDRS)

This scale (Simpson *et al.*, 1976; Kellner, 1986) was designed to be sensitive to changes produced by treatment. It contains eight items, scored 1–9. Five of the grades of severity are defined, the others left as intermediate values. There are four items on depressed mood, beliefs, appearance and suicidal thoughts; three items deal with anxiety, sleep and loss of interest; and one item with somatic symptoms. Symptoms are rated over the previous week, emphasis being placed on severity rather than frequency of occurrence.

The scale has high reliability: between raters ranging from 0.89 to 0.94 and between test and retest 0.85. Validity, tested by differentiation between groups and response to treatment, has been found to be very high. For 26 out-patients in various stages of treatment the correlation with the HAMD was 0.83. In a controlled trial of two levels of dosage of imipramine the total score discriminated significantly between the dosages.

Salpetriere Retardation Rating Scale

This scale (Widlocher, 1983) is based on a theory which regards retardation as a central feature of depressive illness; it therefore includes much more on the symptom of psycho-motor retardation. It contains 15 items, rated 0 to 4, the grades of which are described in detail. The scale correlates 0.46 with clinical evaluation and 0.69 with the HAMD scale.

Beck Depression Inventory

The Beck Depression Inventory (BDI) (Beck *et al.*, 1961) lies between self- and observer-rating scales. It was originally designed to be used by an interviewer who called out the items and the patients chose the appropriate response. This avoided some of the difficulties associated with self-rating scales. It is now generally used as a self-rating scale. It gives a 'here-and-now' assessment and is easy to use for frequent repetition.

The inventory contains 15 items on psychological symptoms and six on somatic ones, all scored 0–3. Some symptoms typical of depressive states are omitted (e.g. loss of appetite and libido), and it is somewhat deficient in anxiety items.

Bailey and Coppen (1976) compared it with the HAMD and found that there was good correspondence between the two scales for about two-thirds of the patients, but it was inexplicably poor for the others. This lack of concordance between scales is occasionally exploited in, for example, claims concerning new treatments. This emphasizes the advantage of having something other than rating scales as the assessment criterion of depression. The correlation between the two scales in the study by Bailey and Coppen (1976) was 0.68. Schwab *et al.* (1967) made a similar comparison on 153 medical in-patients, obviously with mild symptoms, and found a correlation (rho) of 0.75 between the two.

Metcalfe and Goldman (1965) found the BDI insensitive to the biases of physicians and nurses. It correlated 0.62 with global judgements. The inventory is sensitive to the effects of treatment but according to Edwards *et al.* (1984) it is inferior to the HAMD. Johnson and Heather (1974) found that as improvement occurred, decreases in scores paralleled those of ratings and sometimes even preceded them. The scale has been critically examined by Kearns *et al.* (1982), who concluded that the shorter version proposed by Bech *et al.* (1975) was an improvement.

Self-rating Scales

Self-assessment questionnaires have great attractions for those carrying out clinical trials. They can be repeated as often as required, they are reasonably valid and they do not take up the time of skilled clinicians. They (and analogue scales) are particularly useful when it is important to know the time of onset of therapeutic effect, because repeated assessments have to be made at about the time when the change would be expected. They should have clear and simple instructions for use and the vocabulary should be clearly understandable by the user. It may be necessary here to take local usage of words into account.

These scales suffer from certain disadvantages. The subjects must be cooperative and literate and must have sufficient insight. The responses are liable to exaggeration, to understatement and to attempts to 'save face'. Older patients tend to minimize their mental symptoms and emphasize their somatic complaints (Zung, 1967). Paykel and Prusoff (1973) found that older patients and 'psychotics' tended to under-rate themselves (see Leeds Scale, below), whereas younger patients and 'neurotics' over-rated, as did patients with neurotic, hysterical and obsessional personalities.

Arfwidsson *et al.* (1974) considered that they compared badly with observer scales. It would appear that if there are more than 20 items, reliability and sensitivity begin to decrease. Despite this and other criticisms, the scales are still frequently used in evaluating treatments. Observer scales and self-rating have high correlations among themselves but may have low correlations between them (Morrison and Peck, 1990), which indicates that the two types of scales are really measuring something different. Self-rating scales should therefore not be regarded as substitutes for observer scales, but as complementary. A common symptom in depression is an inability to concentrate. Therefore, if a self-rating questionnaire is used, patients should be kept under observation to see that they are completing it correctly.

Visual Analogue Scale (VAS)

Analogue scales now have a long history (Hayes and Patterson, 1921), but were rarely used in the clinic until Aitken (1969) drew attention to their value in research and encouraged their use. They cross the usual boundaries of classification, as they can be used by observers as well as by subjects. They can also be employed for global assessments as well as specific variables. They are best used for a 'here-and-now' assessment and can therefore be utilized as often as required. Their deficiency is that they are prone to contrast effects, i.e. rapid changes in state are given greater emphasis than slow ones. Serial use of analogue scales provides the best use of this technique. A valuable recent review on the subject of analogue scales (McCormack *et al.*, 1988) will prevent many (both experienced and uninitiated) researchers from making methodological errors in the use of this technique which, perhaps because of its apparent straightforwardness, has been used simplistically. The scores usually need some appropriate transformation for statistical analysis. A good example of the latter is described in the study by Adam and Oswald (1989).

In practice, patients are quite capable of producing meaningful assessments, despite the vagueness of the instructions and the apparent lack of a good basis for making a judgement. Folstein and Luria (1973) found a test–retest reliability over 24 hours of 0.61 and 0.73 in two groups of patients. Within-patient reliability is much less, doubtless reflecting the short-term changes which occur in symptoms. For depression, Little and McPhail (1973) found it compared favourably with the BDI.

Zealley and Aitken (1969) examined the correlations between VAS scores and clinical judgement and found that when patients were admitted for treatment, the correlation was as high as 0.78, but this fell to 0.36 during treatment and 0.13 on discharge. The corresponding correlations with the HAMD scores were 0.79, –0.06 and –0.06. In contrast, the respective figures between the HAMD score and clinical judgement were 0.90, 0.76 and 0.55.

Zung Self-Rating Depression Scale (Zung SDS)

This scale (Zung, 1965) was once very popular. It had high reliability but, as is the case with many self-assessment scales, its correlation with observer scales and with clinical judgement was moderate (at best, 0.69; Biggs *et al.*, 1978). Its use has declined since it was found to be insensitive to improvement following treatment (e.g. Rickels *et al.*, 1968; Feighner *et al.*, 1984). A comprehensive review is found in Hedlund and Vieweg (1979b).

Tiplady Self-Rating Scale

Tiplady (1980) used the same method as Montgomery and Asberg for constructing a self-rating scale. The data are based on 58 patients in a general practice who were involved in a clinical trial of two antidepressants compared with a placebo. The result is a 14-item scale which, at first, appears somewhat anomalous: it omits lack of energy, feelings of hopelessness and unworthiness, feeling scared, poor appetite and insomnia (initial and delayed). Obviously, it is not possible to say whether these omissions come from the type of patient or from the method.

Zerssen Adjective Checklist

In adjective checklists the subjects are asked to choose which of a pair of adjectives most corresponds to their feelings (e.g. joyful–tearful). The individual items are less informative than symptoms, but the scale is very sensitive to changes of mood, even short ones.

The checklist of von Zerssen *et al.* (1970, 1974) is now available in English and other European languages. There are two versions each containing 28 items. In a review of many scales, Heimann *et al.* (1975) found that the correlation between the two forms (split-half reliability) was 0.89 in a control group, 0.79 in newly admitted depressives and 0.93–0.96 in an antidepressant trial. Heimann and Schmocker (1974), assessing a mixed group of both depressive and schizophrenic patients, found that the scores correlated with a structured clinical interview 0.83 before treatment and 0.71 after, but with the HAMD the corresponding figures were 0.28 and 0.71.

General-purpose observer rating scales

Brief Psychiatric Rating Scale (BPRS)

This is one of the oldest of general-purpose scales (Overall and Gorham, 1962) and continues to be popular. It is used chiefly for the assessment of schizophrenia by a skilled observer but includes items on depression. Differential weighting of items produces scores on four syndromes or subtypes of depression: anxious, agitated, retarded and hostile. The relevant literature has been comprehensively reviewed by Hedlund and Vieweg (1980). As with all the general scales considered here, it has been used as a diagnostic scale.

Comprehensive Psychopathological Rating Scale (CPRS)

The English translation of this scale was published by Asberg *et al.* (1978). It was designed to be easy to use even by a semi-skilled rater. Although it is practicable to use the whole scale, it was recommended that items should be selected to make subscales for specific purposes. The MADRS is such a scale (see above).

Association for Methodology and Documentation in Psychiatry (AMDP)

This West German scale (AMDP, 1979) has now been translated into 11 languages. An English translation was published by Guy and Ban (1982). It contains five parts concerned with demographic data, life events, previous history of the patient, psychopathological symptoms and somatic signs. Reliability is high (Woggon *et al.*, 1978). Assessment of items is based on the events of the last 24 hours.

The Depression subscale contains 15 depressive items and has high inter-rater and test–retest reliabilities. The items for manic-depressive syndrome have been shown to correlate (rho) 0.62 with the HAMD.

Schedule for Affective Disorders and Schizophrenia (SADS)

This scale (Endicott and Spitzer, 1978) is based on a semi-structured interview and was developed to measure a number of dimensions of psychopathology. It could also be used as a diagnostic schedule. The items are clearly defined and are rated on six- or seven-point scales with defined levels of severity.

Endicott *et al.* (1981) extracted a subscale from the SADS which could be regarded as equivalent to the HAMD. The correlation between the two, based on 48 patients, was 0.92. The extracted scale was designed to have the same mean and standard deviation as the Hamilton scale.

Present State Examination

Although this scale (Wing *et al.*, 1974) is used chiefly for diagnostic purposes it can also be used for assessment. Items are scored 0–2 and assessment covers the previous month. It is therefore of no value for short-term changes.

Its chief advantage is that it has now been translated into many languages, including non-European ones. There is a shortened form of 140 items (Wing *et al.*, 1977). The computer program CATEGO classifies scores into diagnostic 'syndromes'. It requires training for its use, has high reliability and is particularly valuable for cross-national comparisons. Wing (1983) has produced a very useful review on the PSE which is broadly educational for trainees in psychology and psychiatry.

General-purpose questionnaires

Goldberg General Health Questionnaire (GHQ)

There have been severe criticisms of self-rating scales. Blumenthal (1975) demonstrated severe deficiencies in them when used for measuring symptomatology in a general population. Nevertheless, they are of real value and are still much used.

A popular questionnaire for detecting psychiatric symptoms is the General Hospital Questionnaire (GHQ) (Goldberg, 1972). A 28-item reduced version (Goldberg and Hillier, 1979) gives scores on four subscales, including one on depression. Its value has been demonstrated by Tarnopolsky *et al.* (1979). The original description by Goldberg is informative regarding the development of scales in general and the GHQ in particular.

Hopkins Symptom Check List (SCL-90)

This self-rating scale covers a wide range of symptoms. Factor-analytic methods have been used to split it into nine subscales (including one for depression) (Derogatis *et al.*, 1974). Test–retest correlations range from 0.75 to 0.84 over one week and internal consistency coefficients are about 0.86. It has been found to be sensitive to changes produced by antidepressants (Raskin *et al.*, 1970), though it would appear that the sensitivity resides chiefly in the anxiety and somatization clusters (Lipman *et al.*, 1969). In the 90-item version, Derogatis *et al.* (1976) found that the symptom clusters showed a high correlation with various scales of the MMPI.

Hospital Anxiety and Depression Scale (HAD)

This scale (Zigmund and Snaith, 1983) was designed to measure anxiety and depression in patients suffering from physical illness. It replaces the Wakefield (Snaith *et al.*, 1971) and Leeds (Snaith *et al.*, 1976) scales. It does not include such items as would be directly related to the patients' illness and provides ranges of scores indicating different levels of morbidity. Its validity has been confirmed by Bramley *et al.* (1988). The HAD has been used as an observer scale for the assessment of elderly patients with handicaps which would prevent them using the scale themselves (Kenn *et al.*, 1987).

'Paired' self and observer scales

A few scales have been designed to provide comparable self and observer versions. The Zung Depression Status Inventory (Zung, 1972) is designed to parallel Zung's self-assessment scale. It contains 20 items scored 1–4 and is based on a semi-structured interview. It has high internal consistency, the correlation between odd- and even-numbered items coming to 0.81 and its correlation with the self-assessment scale reaching 0.87.

The Carroll Self-Rating Scale (Carroll *et al.*, 1981a; Feinberg *et al.*, 1981) is designed to match the HAMD scale. The scale contains 52 statements, in random order, to which the subject responds yes or no. Each item scores one point. The split-half reliability is 0.87, correlation with the HAMD 0.80 and with the BDI 0.86. As a self-rating scale, it provides information of the same kind as other self-rating scales, especially the BDI, with the additional advantage of close correspondence with HAMD scores. When HAMD scale scores are not available, it would appear to provide a convenient and very useful substitute.

A Visual Analogue scale can, of course, be carried out by either an observer or by the patient.

Computer assessment

Patients have found 'computer interviews' quite acceptable, perhaps because the computer does not become impatient if a long time is required to respond. The computer can be programmed to analyse responses and report the results.

Carr *et al.* (1981) designed a computerized self-assessment questionnaire based on the HAMD. The correlation with a 10-point global rating was 0.78 for 75 out-patients and 0.72 for 24 in-patients. The program INTERACT is now available commercially (Ruby Computers, Watchmoor Trade Centre, Watchmoor Road, Camberley, Surrey, England).

Diagnostic scales

Newcastle Index

The Newcastle Index (Carney *et al.*, 1965) is a 'scale' designed to differentiate between 'neurotic' and 'endogenous' depression. It contains 10 items consisting of seven symptoms and three covering adequate personality, absence of psychological precipitation and previous episode. The items are given weights or scores ranging from −1 to +2, and a score of 6 or more indicates 'endogenous' depression and 5 or less, 'neurotic' depression.

The scale for predicting response to electroconvulsive therapy is closely associated with the index. It contains two items in common with the index, anxiety and weight loss over 7 pounds, six symptoms and two more items covering pyknic body type and 'hysterical'. Weights range from +3 to −3. A score of 1 or over predicts good response to the treatment; 0 or less predicts a poor response. A wider review of measurements covering outcome to specific treatment strategies is beyond the scope of this chapter. A comprehensive review on markers in ECT studies has been published (Scott, 1989) and serves as a model for the use of a multifaceted approach to outcome in depression.

BEHAVIOURAL MEASURES OF DEPRESSION

It is unfortunate that one can find complete books on the assessment of depression which make no mention of behavioural measures (Sartorius and Bann, 1986; Racagni and Smeraldi, 1987). A wider perspective is provided by Marsella *et al.* (1987) but they do not attempt to integrate the various forms of measurement of depression.

In the field of behavioural assessment of depression there are a number of theoretical orientations that have been applied. As in the case of items incorporated into rating scales, the specific theoretical orientation of the researcher has influenced facets of behaviour selected for measurement. Beck's emphasis on cognitive aspects of depression has been mentioned above. Other theoretical constructs are those of Seligman (1975), who emphasizes learned helplessness. Ferster (1973) has stressed the overt behaviour of depressed patients, particularly reduced activity as a key feature, and has therefore paid specific attention to activity measures in the assessment of depression. Wolpe's emphasis on anxiety within depression has led to a variety of treatment modalities (e.g. assertion training, desensitization and measures to assess these features) and would be better indexed by different measures of depression. Rehm (1977) emphasizes self-control as the core deficit in depression and highlights measures of control as crucial in a behavioural assessment. Finally, several authors have emphasized interpersonal aspects of depression and have developed assessments of social skill, interpersonal anger and the negative effect of depression on others (Coyne, 1976).

In several of these areas, both the form of behaviour (e.g. agitation or retardation) are assessed as well as the degree of the behaviours present (e.g. severity of motor retardation). It is not possible to give a detailed account of all aspects of behaviour in depression.

Greden and Carroll (1981) have commented on the poor level of psychomotor assessment in depressed patients and suggest that 'objective psychomotor assessment may improve classification, longitudinal monitoring, treatment selection, and prediction of outcome for patients with depression and mania'. Clinical assessment of depressed behaviour usually relies on subjective observations during other aspects of a clinical interview or global questions directed to relatives. It is a common clinical observation that when patients present with a range of features of depression, including behavioural, interpersonal, somatic and even cognitive aspects of depression, but are lacking in verbal descriptions of being depressed (i.e. affect) the patient is referred to as having 'masked depression'. This is in many senses a clinical error based on the absence of sufficiently broad assessment measures of depression.

There are four facets of behaviour which have been measured in relation to depression: gross motor behaviour; somatic measures; verbal utterances; and cognitive aspects.

Gross body activity

It has long been recognized that motor activity is altered in depression. In the current era of research, one of us (Hamilton, 1960) has pointed out that psychomotor retardation and agitation, which are often perceived as opposites, may coexist. In a series of studies using telemetric techniques,

Kupfer and colleagues (see Foster and Kupfer, 1975) observed that there are motility differences between unipolar and bipolar patients, that motility changes with treatment and that motility patterns can distinguish between groups of psychiatrically ill patients. Blackburn (1975) in a study of mental and psychomotor speed in patients with affective disorders concluded that 'unipolar depression does not seem to affect speed functions very significantly, but bipolar depression does decrease mental and psychomotor speeds significantly'. The measure of psychomotor speed used in this study was the Gibson Spiral Maze (Gibson, 1965) on the basis of its 'simplicity, shortness and ease of administration and the important fact that it is not contaminated by IQ'. A variety of physical behaviours including those of gesture (Ekman and Friesen, 1974), posture (Waxer, 1974) and head nods or head aversions (Ranelli, 1978) have been described in depressed patients.

The range of techniques applied to behaviour analysis in depression range from simple observational measures (Bunney and Hamburg, 1963) to more complex systems (Fisch *et al.*, 1983). There is (limited) evidence that behavioural change provides a better indicator of post-hospitalization improvement (Hersen *et al.*, 1973) than clinical assessment or rating scales. It is therefore surprising that more systematic study of this area has not been carried out.

A wider description of activity that has implications for depression has been attempted. A 'pleasant events schedule' (MacPhillamy and Lewinsohn, 1971) and subsequently an 'unpleasant events schedule' (Lewinsohn and Talkington, 1979) have been developed. These instruments have been used in tailoring treatment (Lewinsohn, 1976) but remain of questionable reliability as a more global assessment of depression. There are almost no measures of other behavioural aspects of depression, including sexual behaviour and appetite. Changes in sleep and polysomnographic changes of sleep in depression have been more intensively studied (see below).

Somatic manifestations

A range of psychophysiological techniques has been used to assess somatic facets of depression. A series of EMG studies has shown alterations in muscle tone of the corrugator supercilii muscle (Schwartz, 1975; Schwartz *et al.*, 1976; Teasdale and Bancroft, 1977; Teasdale and Rezin, 1978; Blackburn and Bonham, 1980).

In a general (but now slightly dated) review of peripheral indices of depression, Christie *et al.* (1980) emphasized the limitations of the techniques that have been used to date. Storrie *et al.* (1981) found skin conductance responses (SCR) in depressed subjects to be lower than those of controls and that these responses did not change with treatment. They implied that SCR may be useful as a trait marker in depression, but in the same year, far more negative results were obtained by Toone *et al.* (1981). Iacono *et al.* (1982) established that eye tracking in patients with either unipolar or bipolar affective disorder is not different from that of normal controls. Similarly, cardiovascular measures have not provided a useful tool for the somatic behavioural assessments of depression (Blackburn, 1988).

In a recent review of psychophysiological measures of depression Henriques and Davidson (1989) have assimilated the information, suggesting that there are relatively consistent EEG changes in depression and that there is a pattern of change with recovery.

Verbal behaviour

Studies in this area have measured speed and form of speech (including pauses), content of speech and interaction by verbal communication. Simply measuring the number of words used in a short period was demonstrated to be a useful measure of depression (Robinson and Lewinsohn, 1973). Szabadi *et al.* (1976) established that pause time was longer in depressed patients and that these intervals decreased with treatment. In an admirably clear synthesis of some of her earlier work, Rehm (1987) concluded that of a series of 11 different verbal measures taken during interviews, only 'loudness and latency discriminate depressed from non-depressed subjects'. She goes on to point out that 'while the measures have face validity in assessing depression, correlations with traditional measures are not supportive of consensual validity'. Stringent attention to the circumstances in which verbal measures of depression are obtained is necessary.

With regard to content, Hinchliffe *et al.* (1971) have described differences between depressed patients and controls concerning expressions of feeling and direct, non-personal and personal references. Andreasen and Pfohl (1976) describe differences in the use of overstatement and achievement-related words.

A variety of techniques has been used to attempt to classify the interaction of speech in depressed and non-depressed individuals. These include studies in couples in which an asymmetric verbal relationship is described (Hautzinger *et al.*, 1982); the use of assessment in small groups (Jacobson, 1981) and structured interviews. In all these circumstances, successful characterization of depressed and non-depressed individuals has been achieved, but as yet there is little work indicating the utility of these measures (e.g. treatment outcome measures).

Cognitive assessment

This comprises mood, affect, cognitive distortions, thought process and learning. Some of these can be measured behaviourally, but for others a rating scale is necessary.

It is useful to distinguish between subjective mood and affect, which is the therapist's perception of that mood. Rehm (1987) has drawn attention to the variability of depression scales with regard to the number of mood-related items. In the Hamilton scale there is only one affect item (5 per cent of the scale) whereas in the Centre for Epidemiological Studies Depression Scale (CES-D) there are seven affect items (one-third of the scale) (see Table 3.1).

A second facet of cognitive symptoms in depression is that of cognitive distortions. These are specifically assessed in certain scales, e.g. Hopelessness Scale (Beck *et al.*, 1974), Cognitive Bias Questionnaire (Krantz and Hammen, 1979), the Automatic Thoughts Questionnaire which emphasizes negative thoughts (Hollon and Kendall, 1980) and the Dysfunctional Attitudes Scale (Weissman and Beck, 1978). Changes in measures with these scales have been recorded with a variety of treatment modalities (Blackburn *et al.*, 1986).

A third aspect of cognitive measure in depression is that of thought process. In tasks involving varying combinations of chance and skill, depressed subjects have been shown to have different expectations compared to normal controls (Klein and Seligman, 1976). Similar results are recorded in the subjective perception of the performance of a task (Werner and Rehm, 1975). Questionnaire instruments assessing this behaviour have been developed, e.g. Cognitive Error Questionnaire (Lefebvre, 1981), Attribution Style Questionnaire (Peterson *et al.*, 1982), Cognitive Response Tests (Watkins and Rush, 1983) and the Cognitions Questionnaire (Fennell and Campbell, 1984).

The final area in which cognitive measurements have been made and shown to be different in depression is that of learning and memory. Using a simple technique of time to recall pleasant and unpleasant experiences in response to specific stimulus words, Lloyd and Lishman (1975) found that the ratio of these two retrieval processes increased with depression. Weingartner *et al.* (1977) described a state-dependent process of recall in relation to affective state. In a later study, Weingartner *et al.* (1981) were able to show that depressed patients are unable to use complex strategies to enhance recall, leading, for example, to poorer recall for words requiring more complex cognitive processing. This research, and many other studies (see Blackburn, 1988), indicates that learning deficits in depression are specifically related to 'the transfer of material to long-term memory and that short-term memory is not affected'. This specific observation as a measure of depression has not as yet been fully utilized.

PHYSIOLOGICAL MEASURES

There is much misunderstanding about the nature of measurement in physiology and biochemistry. Many measurements have the appearance of being quite straightforward; technically they are 'ratio' measurements, but functionally they are not. A pulse rate of 80/min is four times greater than one of 20/min, but functionally there is a world of difference. A blood glucose of 70 mg/100 ml is seven times greater than one of 10 mg/100 ml, but in the latter case the patient is dead.

Physiological and biochemical changes are integral to psychopathology. In practice, the fundamental problem is the establishment of their validity. They can have no significance until they have been shown to correlate adequately with psychopathological manifestations (though one day the reverse may be true). A particular problem here is that most of the physiological and biochemical changes associated with depression (regarded either as a symptom or as a syndrome) are unduly subject to other influences, i.e. they are insufficiently specific. It is therefore not surprising that Loo (1987), in his extensive review, came to the conclusion that there were no genuine biological diagnostic markers of depression. This applies equally to measures of severity. However, although biological measures have not yet been incorporated into clinical practice, they are of research interest and may yet yield fruitful applications.

It is never sufficient to consider laboratory tests in isolation, and it is likely that combinations of tests will be more useful in monitoring the progression of disease than in the facilitation of diagnosis.

Greden (1985) notes that there is a variety of types of laboratory tests in psychiatry including neuroendocrine; psychophysiological; biochemical; genetic; brain imaging; and pharmacological challenges. He points out that any of these tests can be used in a variety of ways listed in Table 3.4.

Table 3.4 Uses of biological markers (from Greden, 1985, with permission).

1. Aid to diagnosis
2. Quantify severity
3. Assess prognosis
4. Select specific treatment
5. Serial monitoring
   (a) Monitoring of clinical change
   (b) Prediction of outcome (early or eventual)
   (c) Monitoring remissions
   (d) Early prediction of relapse
6. Assess risk of treatment
7. Screen healthy populations
8. Nosological tool
9. Select research populations or as dependent or independent research variable

Laboratory tests and markers of disease are strongly related to the prevalence of a condition as well as to a variety of technical considerations concerning quality control and the appropriateness of the tests carried out. Greden p—doints out that the objective of having a test which is 100 per cent sensitive and has a specificity of 100 per cent is unrealistic. He notes that sensitivity and specificity figures for the DST (see later) with regard to melancholia are similar to those of ECG criteria for left ventricular enlargement, and in this context the figures for REM latency (see later) as a marker of depression are said to be considerably better.

In the quest for biological markers for depression, excessive emphasis may have been placed on sensitivity and specificity of particular tests. Of more interest to the clinician is the predictor value of a particular test. This may be predictive of either a positive or a negative result and is given by the number/proportion of diseased individuals with a positive test over total number/proportion of persons with a positive test × 100. Vecchio (1966) has elegantly demonstrated that in a population in which the actual disease prevalence is 2 per cent, even with a specificity and a sensitivity of 99 per cent, the predictive value of a positive test is only 66.9 per cent; whereas in the same population the predictive value of a negative test at the modest specificity and sensitivity of 50 per cent each is 98 per cent. The prescreening of patients on whom tests are to be carried out is likely to be a necessary prerequisite in order to make biological tests in psychiatry a useful and rewarding exercise.

One of the first physiological changes associated with depression was hypotonicity and hypomotility of the gastro-intestinal system (Henry, 1931). Decreased secretion of saliva was reported in 1938 and confirmed subsequently by many others (see Bolwig and Rafaelsen, 1972). Uytdenhoef *et al.* (1983) reported hypervascularization in the left cerebral frontal cortex and a hypovascularization in the right posterior cortex in major depressive disorder, compared with various controls. Skin conductance in endogenous depression is less than in controls (Mirkin and Coppen, 1980). The sleep of depressives shows many abnormalities in electro-encephalographic studies (Kupfer and Thase, 1983). At present, the uncertain utility of these measures has meant that they are more confined to research situations. This may be a natural scepticism on the part of clinicians who have often been presented with the gods of biological measures, only to find that they have feet of clay when fully evaluated.

Some biological markers of depression are claimed to be useful in diagnosis, and others to be markers of change or response to treatment. The uptake of serotonin (Stahl *et al.*, 1983), a blunted thyroid stimulating hormone (TSH) response to thyroid releasing hormone (TRH) (Loosen and Prange, 1982) and circadian distribution of GH release (Mendlewicz *et al.*, 1985) have all been considered as potential measures of depression. There is debate regarding the sensitivity, specificity and utility of these markers. Limited optimism for a new 'gold standard' for the measurement of depression often gives way to overly pessimistic conclusions when a range of confounding influences (e.g. age of patients, menstrual status) and studies in other disorders are carried out (see Koslow *et al.*, 1982; Checkley *et al.*, 1987; Lesch *et al.*, 1987, for GH studies in particular).

A range of pharmacological challenge tests, purporting to be either diagnostic or predictive of treatment response, have recently been described and reviewed (Hale *et al.*, 1989; Garcia-Sevilla, 1989; Lopez-Ibor *et al.*, 1988, 1989). These await further validation.

Increasingly, it has been recognized that the use of more than one biological measure is likely to provide a more comprehensive picture of a patient group and may improve sensitivity of measures (Targum *et al.*, 1982) and specificity (Rush *et al.*, 1983). Ansseau *et al.* (1984) state that 92 per cent 'of patients were correctly identified by at least one biological marker' in their study using four tests concurrently. Scepticism is inevitable when considering the sample size (n = 12), but this does not detract from one of their conclusions that 'these four biological markers do not necessarily identify the same population, suggesting that their concurrent use may yield the highest level of diagnostic sensitivity'.

Two of the most widely researched biological markers and measures of depression are those of sleep changes and the dexamethasone suppression test. These will now be considered in more detail.

Sleep

The use of sleep changes in depression have been viewed mostly from the perspective of aids to diagnosis; to a lesser extent for the assessment of whether a specific treatment will be effective; and hardly at all for any of the other reasons indicated in Table 3.4, although it has been noted that the stability of REM latency is greater in those with a family history of depression (Cartwright *et al.*, 1988).

Sleep is a complex process which has long been known to be commonly altered in depressive disorders. Over the last decade a strong case has been made to suggest that the abnormalities of sleep are perhaps the best and possibly the only clear biological marker of depressive illness.

There are a number of cogent reasons for suspecting that an alteration in the REM sleep process is relevant in depression. Besides shortened REM onset latency, it has been clearly demonstrated that most of the treatments which are effective in depression suppress REM sleep. These techniques include tricyclic and monoamine oxidase inhibitor antidepressants; lithium; electroconvulsive therapy; and sleep deprivation. Early results in a study of cognitive therapy show 'no strong relationship between REM latency values and response to cognitive therapy' (Jarrett *et al.*, 1988). In addition, there is the observation that sleep deprivation can trigger mania and that sleep reprovokes depression in those depressed subjects 'treated' by sleep deprivation. There is a regular alteration of sleep time in patients with seasonal affective disorder. The often-reported antidepressant effect of physical activity may be mediated via REM suppression and the increase in slow-wave sleep which follows exercise (Shapiro and Driver, 1989). We have recently demonstrated an association between sleep loss at the time of parturition and increase in incidence of post-natal 'blues'. All these disparate observations point to the possibility of sleep change not simply being an epiphenomenon of depression but in some way causally linked to depression or an integral part of the depressive process. In either of the latter two cases there would be the possibility of sleep changes providing a clear biological marker of depression. Changes in sleep pattern may alter other circadian rhythms with resulting abnormalities of neuroendocrine secretory activity. These changes may precipitate depression.

The supposed characteristic features of sleep changes in patients with depression are:

(1) A disruption of sleep continuity and a prolongation of sleep latency;
(2) A shortening of REM latency (i.e. the time from sleep onset to first appearance of REM sleep);
(3) Decreases in slow-wave sleep (SWS) (stages 3 and 4);
(4) An increase in SWS proportion in the second sleep cycle compared to the first;
(5) Increased REM sleep (particularly in the first third of the night).

It is suggested that these sleep characteristics are most commonly and most extremely found in subgroups of depressed subjects, particularly the psychotic, the elderly and those with other (i.e. non-sleep-related) endogenous features of depression.

Some of the best evidence that there is a fundamental change in REM sleep in depression comes from studies based on the arecholine REM-induction-test (RIT) originally described by Gillin *et al.* (1982). They claimed to have identified a trait marker when they found, in both acutely depressed and recovered depressed patients, that infusion of a muscarinic agonist, arecholine, would provoke a more rapid onset of a subsequent REM period during sleep. This research has been taken further by Berger *et al.* (1988) using a new compound, RS-86. They concluded that their data 'support the assumption that during depression there is a disturbance in the regulation of REM-sleep that seems to be promoted by cholinergic and inhibited by aminergic neurones'. This paper is notable in distinguishing between depressive and non-depressive disorders in addition to healthy controls. In a subsequent publication, Berger *et al.* (1989) give figures indicating that 14 out of 16 depressed patients showed sleep-onset REM after pre-sleep treatment with RS-86 as compared with only one of 20 patients with other diagnoses. They did find REM to be state, rather than trait, dependent.

It is still pertinent to question whether the polysomnographic features of sleep change purported to occur in depressed patients are in fact regularly found. Reynolds and Kupfer in a major review (1987) put the positive case concerning REM latency in depression, and state that the shortened REM latency 'remains a robust and widely replicated finding'. Whether REM latency in depression has a bimodal or normal distribution may be an artifact, with three sources of method variation: (1) age range of the patients studied; (2) the severity of depressive symptoms and (3) subtype of depressive illness. The most extreme picture should therefore occur in delusionally depressed elderly patients. The length of REM sleep in the first REM period is specifically thought to be increased in elderly depressed patients. In a study addressing the question of the best definition of REM latency, Reynolds *et al.* (1983) found that a variety of definitions of REM latency 'correlated about equally well with Hamilton depression ratings ($r = -0.70$)'. Ansseau *et al.* (1985) showed more variability in REM latency in depressed males than in depressed females.

The review a decade ago by Chen (1979) on sleep, depression and antidepressants emphasized that studies have consistently shown that, in comparison to normal controls, depressed people have difficulty in falling asleep, frequent shifts of sleep stages, increased time spent awake, early morning awakening and a considerable reduction of stage 4 sleep, quoting 16 references in support of this statement. Chen goes on to point out that other sleep variables are less consistently described in depressed patients. Interestingly, he notes that REM sleep in depressed patients 'has also been reported to be reduced, normal, or even increased' with reports from Kupfer's laboratory (among others) supporting each of these stances (Kupfer and Foster, 1975; Kupfer and Foster, 1972; Kupfer *et al.*, 1972, respectively).

In reviewing 60 papers in which information about some (if not all) sleep changes of supposed relevance in depression has been documented in depressed and non-depressed groups, one finds that only half show positive results, indicating that a characteristic sleep pattern occurs in depression. It is notable that the preponderance of positive literature is American and consists of studies in which a higher proportion of the participants were female.

Two further important criticisms of the use of sleep measures in the field of biological markers and measures of depression should be cited. First, it is standard procedure in this field to measure sleep in patients who are 'drug-free'. The usual criterion of this has been two weeks post ingestion of psychotropic drugs. The withdrawal of either benzodiazepines or tricyclic antidepressants is likely to have a rebound effect which would include a shortening of REM latency. This effect contaminates the results of many of the studies in this area. Similar reservations relate to the lack of attention to daytime naps in the patterns of sleep.

There is a variety of diagnoses in which a short REM latency has been demonstrated (Table 3.5) and there are groups of depressed patients in whom short REM latency is not documented to occur (Table 3.6). Both these observations will limit the utility of using sleep parameters as a diagnostic tool in depression but do not *a priori* negate many of the other potential uses of this biological marker (see Table 3.4).

Table 3.5 Circumstances in which short REM latency has been documented.

Anxiety disorder	Foster *et al.* (1977)
Alcoholism	Spiker *et al.* (1977)
Alzheimer's disease	Martin *et al.* (1986)
Anorexia nervosa	Neil *et al.* (1980)
Borderline personality	Reynolds *et al.* (1985)
Insomnia in normals	Mullen *et al.* (1986)
Impotence	Schmidt and Shy (1986)
Mania	Gillin *et al.* (1977)
Narcolepsy	Montplaisir (1976)
Korsakov's syndrome	Martin *et al.* (1986)
Panic disorder	Uhde *et al.* (1987)
Obsessive–compulsive disorder	Insel *et al.* (1982)
Schizophrenia	Stern *et al.* (1969)

Table 3.6 Studies in depressed patients not finding short REM latency.

Bipolar patients	Jovanovic (1977)
Young patients	Taub *et al.* (1978)
Recent onset of depression	Thase *et al.* (1986)
Depression in medical disorders	King *et al.* (1981)

In summary, it would appear that changes in sleep may herald therapeutic effects of treatment, and this is a promising development in the measurement of depression. In certain groups, sleep studies may aid diagnosis but such measures are not a universal panacea.

Cortisol and depression

The interaction of the limbic system, hypothalamus, pituitary and adrenal cortex and studies of the activation of this system, particularly in depression (Stokes, 1966), led to the testing of the dexamethasone suppression test (DST) in depressed patients and the claim that dexamethasone non-suppression is more frequent in severe depression than in a variety of other psychiatric disorders (Carroll *et al.*, 1981b; Stokes *et al.*, 1984). The technique and rationale of the dexamethasone suppression test are alluded to in an earlier paper by Carroll *et al.* (1968). In that paper the authors state that 'the midnight dexamethasone suppression test has been extensively used in the assessment of patients with clinical evidence of adrenocortical overactivity'. It is this overactivity that is assessed in depressed patients. Plasma 11-hydroxycorticosteroid levels were shown to be similar at 8.30 a.m. and 4.30 p.m. in a group of 27 depressed patients and 22 non-depressed ones. However, after a midnight dose of 2 mg dexamethasone phosphate, plasma levels of 7,11-hydroxycorticosteroid taken 8½ hours later showed highly significant differences between the depressed group and the non-depressed group, with half of the depressed group having levels above 10 g/100 ml and only three of the non-depressed group evincing this non-suppression. Hundreds of papers have been subsequently published on this subject. Within two years of their original study, Carroll's group (Carroll and Davies, 1970) had already found contradictions with their original study in relation to the effect of severity of illness, and numerous other caveats have been subsequently delineated. Many factors influence the DST, and these are shown in Table 3.7. In a major article over a decade later, Carroll and 11 co-authors (1981b) give a detailed rationale for changing the specific method of carrying out the test and reported on 438 subjects, concluding that with careful selection of the plasma cortisol criterion value, a diagnostic confidence close to 95 per cent can be achieved.

An exemplary review of this subject is provided by Arana *et al.* (1985). These authors outlined many of the technical and theoretical factors which contribute to or limit the usefulness of this test as a measure in depression. They conclude that the sensitivity of the test is greatest in those patients suffering from psychosis (67 per cent) and age groups over 60 years (65 per cent). In contrast, in the less than 18-year-olds sensitivity is only 34 per cent. In this meta-analysis of well over 200 publications, particular attention is paid to the specificity of the DST in major depression as compared with other diagnoses.

A modification of the key table in their publication is shown in Table 3.8. This shows that the specificity depends on the group to which depressed patients are being compared, with figures as high as 93 per cent in comparison to normal controls and percentages only in the fifties if the comparison groups are patients with mania or dementia. The utility of the DST in relation to distinguishing major depressive disorder in selected groups is commented on. In certain situtations (for example, stroke)

Table 3.7. Factors influencing DST

DST	False positive	False negative
Drugs	Barbiturates Carbamazepine Phenytoin Glutethimide Alcoholism and recent withdrawal from alcohol	Synthetic corticosteroids ?Benzodiazepines ?Isoniazid ?Tricylic antidepressants
Endocrine	Cushing's syndrome Pregnancy or high doses of oestrogen Diabetes mellitus Hypercalcaemia Hypothyroidism	Hypopituitarism Addison's disease
Physiological	Rapid metabolism of dexamethasone	Slow metabolism of dexamethasone
Clinical factors	Stress/infections Weight loss Altered sleep and activity	
Age	>60	18
Drug compliance	Failure to take dexamethasone	

relatively high sensitivities and specificities are obtained. The authors go on to describe the predictive power of a positive DST (assuming a prevalence of the index illness among those tested of 50 per cent) and conclude that the 'DST is relatively effective in distinguishing the psychotic affective patients from schizophrenics as well as controls, but less effective in separating the former from patients with other acute psychotic disorders, mania, or even dysthymia'. These observations may lead one to conclude that as a diagnostic test DST has little value.

However, the observation that non-suppression increases the response rate to standard antidepressant treatment by at least 11 per cent and that there is a hierarchical order in the percentage of individuals showing non-suppression from normal controls (7 per cent), acute grief (10 per cent), dysthymic disorders (23 per cent), major depressive disorder (43 per cent), melancholia or endogenous depression (50 per cent), psychotic affective disorders (69 per cent) and depression with suicidal intent (78 per cent) (Arana *et al.*, 1985) indicates that this marker is indexing certain facets of depression and therefore should not be ignored. Subsequent reviews in this area have come to similar conclusions (Stokes and Sikes, 1988; Arana and

Table 3.8 Specificity of the dexamethasone suppression test (DST) in major depression versus other diagnosis (based on Arana *et al.*, 1985, with permission).

Comparison diagnosis	No. of references	No. of patients	Specificity (%)
Normal controls	31 or 34	1130	92.8
Normal subjects with non-psychiatric controls	6	1369	91.3
Acute grief	1	21	90.5
Anxiety/panic/phobia	4	76	88.2
Schizophrenia	25	275	86.9
Alcoholism	10	355	80.0
Dysthymic disorder	14	240	77.1
Acute and atypical psychoses	7	98	65.3
Dementia	11	180	57.2
Mania	14	163	51.5
All psychiatric disorders, not major depressive disorder		1207	76.5

Mossman, 1988) and emphasize the subtlety and complexity of the hypothalamic–pituitary adrenocortical axis in depression. Further tempering of the utility of the DST is offered by the American Psychiatric Association Taskforce (1987). This group does, however, note that 'failure to convert to normal suppression of cortisol with apparent recovery from depression suggests an increased risk for relapse into depression or suicidal behaviour', and gives limited support to the notion of using DST as a clinical aid in decision making.

More clearly negative views of the clinical place of the DST abound (for example, Hirschfeld *et al.*, 1983; Gitlin and Gerner, 1986; Braddock, 1986). Braddock notes that there have been attempts to link results of the DST test with biochemical theories of depression and that 'while intuitively appealing and intensively investigated, have yet to produce any well supported predictions'. She further states 'There is no good reason so far, therefore, to justify the view that the DST is a marker for any underlying pathological process in depressive illness'.

CONCLUSION

The increasing awareness of the multifaceted nature of depression (Gilbert, 1988) suggests that it is best to use a broad span of assessment measures.

Initial attempts in this regard have been recently made (e.g. Ko *et al.*, 1989). Even within areas of measurement, more thoughtful selection of complementary rather than repetitive measures could be achieved. In specific circumstances more clearly defined techniques are likely to be necessary. In the absence of any 'gold standard' it is useful to have common elements in the large number of research studies of depressive disorders, and the use of well-established scales as well as newer measures is to be encouraged. The recognition that one may not be dealing with a unitary condition and that the overlapping measures of different techniques may never focus into a single pattern may help researchers to recognize that the Sisyphean task of looking for a single ideal measure is unlikely to be accomplished. It is possible that there are subgroups of depressed patients who have particular profiles of measures (behavioural and physiological) and who may have different clinical symptoms and/or different treatment responses. For these reasons, a broader approach in the measurement of depression is now highly desirable, if not imperative.

REFERENCES

Adam, K. and Oswald, I. (1989) Can a rapidly-eliminated hypnotic cause daytime anxiety? *Pharmacopsychiatry*, **22**, 115–19.

Aitken, R.C.P. (1969) Measurement of feelings using Visual Analogue Scales. *Proceedings of the Royal Society of Medicine*, **62**, 989–93.

Andreasen, N.J.C. and Pfohl, B. (1976) Linguistic analysis of speech in affective disorders. *Archives of General Psychiatry*, **33**, 1361–7.

Ansseau, M., Schegvaerts, M., Doumont, A., Poirrier, R., Legross, J. and Franck, G. (1984) Concurrent use of REM latency, dexamethasone suppression, clonidine and apomorphine tests as biological markers of endogenous depression: a pilot study. *Psychiatry Research*, **12**, 261–72.

APA Taskforce (1987) The dexamethasone suppression test: overview of its current status in psychiatry. *American Journal of Psychiatry*, **144**, 1253–62.

Arana, G.W. and Mossman, D. (1988) The dexamethasone suppression test and depression: approaches to the use of a laboratory test in psychiatry. *Neurological Clinics*, **6**, 21–39.

Arana, G.W., Baldessarini, R.J. and Ornsteen, M. (1985) The dexamethasone suppression test for diagnosis and prognosis in psychiatry. *Archives of General Psychiatry*, **42**, 1193–204.

Arfwidsson, L., D'Elia, G., Laurell, B., Ottosson, J.-O., Perris, C. and Persson, G. (1974) Can self-rating replace doctors' rating in evaluating anti-depressive treatment? *Acta Psychiatrica Scandinavica*, **50**, 16–22.

Asberg, M., Kragh-Sorensen, P., Mindham, R.H.S. and Tuck, J.R. (1973) Reliability and communicability of a rating scale for depression. *Psychological Medicine*, **3**, 458–65.

Asberg, M., Montgomery, S., Perris, C., Schalling, D. and Sedvall, G. (1978) A Comprehensive Psychopathological Psychiatric Rating Scale (CPRS). *Acta Psychiatrica Scandinavica, Suppl.*, **271**, 5–27.

Association for Methodology and Documentation in Psychiatry (AMDP) (1979) *Das AMDP-System. Manual zur Dokumentation Psychiatrischer Befunde,* 3rd edn, Springer-Verlag, Berlin.

Bailey, J. and Coppen, A. (1976) A comparison between the Hamilton Rating Scale and the Beck Inventory in the measurement of depression. *British Journal of Psychiatry,* **128**, 486–9.

Baumann, U. (1967) Methodische Untersuchungen zur Hamilton-Depression-Skala. *Arch. Psychiat. Nervenkr.,* **222**, 359–75.

Bech, P. and Rafaelsen, O.J. (1980) The use of rating scales exemplified by a comparison of the Hamilton and the Bech–Rafaelsen Melancholia Scale. *Acta Psychiatrica Scandinavica, Suppl.,* **285**, 128–31.

Bech, P., Gram, L.F., Dein, E., Jacobsen, O., Vitger, J. and Bolwig, T.G. (1975) Quantitative rating of depressive states. Correlation between clinical assessment, Beck's self-rating scale and Hamilton's objective rating scale. *Acta Psychiatrica Scandinavica,* **51**, 161–70.

Beck, A.T., Ward, C.H., Mendelson, M., Mock, J.E. and Erbaugh, J. (1961) An inventory for measuring depression. *Archives of General Psychiatry,* **4**, 561–85.

Beck, T.A., Weissman, A., Lester, D. and Trexler, L. (1974) The measurement of pessimism: the hopelessness scale. *Journal of Consulting and Clinical Psychology,* **42**, 861–5.

Berger, M., Riemann, D., Wiegand, M., Joy, D., Hochli, D. and Zulley, J. (1988) Are REM-sleep abnormalities in depression more than an epiphenomenon? In W.P. Koella, F. Obal, H. Schulz and P. Visser (eds), *Sleep,* pp. 218–22, Gustav Fischer Verlag, Stuttgart.

Berger, M., Riemann, C., Hochli, D. and Spiegel, R. (1989) The cholinergic rapid eye movement sleep induction test with RS-86: state or trait marker of depression? *Archives of General Psychiatry,* **46**, 421–8.

Biggs, J.T., Wylie, L.T. and Ziegler, V.E. (1978) Validity of the Zung self-rating depression scale. *British Journal of Psychiatry,* **132**, 381–5.

Blackburn, I.M. (1975) Mental and psychomotor speed in depression and mania. *British Journal of Psychiatry,* **126**, 329–35.

Blackburn, I.M. (1988) Psychological processes in depression. In E. Miller and P.J. Cooper (eds), *Adult Abnormal Psychology,* pp. 128–68, Churchill Livingstone, Edinburgh.

Blackburn, I.M. and Bonham, K.G. (1980) Experimental effects of a cognitive therapy technique in depressed patients. *British Journal of Social and Clinical Psychology,* **19**, 353–63.

Blackburn, I.M., Jones, S. and Lewin, R.J.P. (1986) Cognitive style in depression. *British Journal of Clinical Psychology,* **25**, 241–51.

Blumenthal, M.D. (1975) Measuring depressive symptomatology in a general population. *Archives of General Psychiatry,* **32**, 971–3.

Bolwig, T.G. and Rafaelsen, O.J. (1972) Salivation in affective disorders. *Psychological Medicine,* **2**, 232–8.

Braddock, L. (1986) The dexamethasone suppression test: fact and artefact. *British Journal of Psychiatry,* **148**, 363–74.

Bramley, P.N., Easton, A.M.E., Morley, S. and Snaith, R.P. (1988) The differentiation of anxiety and depression by rating scales. *Acta Psychiatrica Scandinavica* (in press).

Bunney, W.E. and Hamburg, D.A. (1963) Methods for reliable longitudinal observation of behaviour. *Archives of General Psychiatry,* **9**, 280–91.

Carney, M.W.P., Roth, M. and Garside, R.F. (1965) The diagnosis of depressive syndromes and the prediction of ECT response. *British Journal of Psychiatry,***111**, 659–74.

Carr, A.C., Ancill, R.J., Ghosh, A. and Margo, A. (1981) Direct assessment of depression by microcomputer. *Acta Psychiatrica Scandinavica,* **64**, 414–22.

Carroll, B.J. and Davies, B.M. (1970) Clinical associations of 11-hydroxycorticosteroid suppression and non-suppression in severe depressive illnesses. *British Medical Journal,* **1**, 789–91.

Carroll, B.J., Martin, F.I.R. and Davies, B. (1968) Resistance to suppression by dexamethasone of plasma 11-OHCS levels in severe depressive illness. *British Medical Journal,* **3**, 285–7.

Carroll, B.J., Feinberg, M., Smouse, P.E., Rawson, S.G. and Greden, J.P. (1981a) The Carroll Rating Scale for Depression. I. Development, reliability and validation. *British Journal of Psychiatry,* **138**, 194–200.

Carroll, B.J., Feinberg, M., Greden, J.F. *et al.* (1981b) A specific laboratory test for diagnosis of melancholia: standardisation, validation and clinical utility. *Archives of General Psychiatry,* **38**, 15–22.

Cartwright, R.D., Stephenson, K., Kravitz, H. and Eastman, C. (1988) REM latency stability and family history of depression *Sleep Research,* **17**, 119.

Checkley, S.A., Slade, A.P. and Shur, E. (1987) Growth hormone and other responses to clonidine in patients with endogenous depression. *British Journal of Psychiatry,* **138**, 51–5.

Chen, C.-N. (1979) Sleep, depression and antidepressants. *British Journal of Psychiatry,* **135**, 385–402.

Christie, M.J., Little, B.C. and Gordon, A.M. (1980) Peripheral indices of depressive states. In H.M. Von Praag (ed.), *Handbook of Biological Psychiatry Part II,* pp. 145–82, Marcel Dekker, New York.

Cox, J.L., Holden, J.M. and Sagovsky, R. (1987) Detection of postnatal depression—development of the 10-item Edinburgh Postnatal Depression Scale. *British Journal of Psychiatry,* **150**, 782–6.

Coyne, J.C. (1976) Depression and the response of others. *Journal of Abnormal Psychology,* **85**, 189–93.

Cronholm, B. and Ottosson, J.-O. (1960) Experimental studies of the therapeutic action of electroconvulsive therapy in endogénous depression. *Acta Psychiatrica Scandinavica,* **35** (Suppl. 145), 69–101.

Cronholm, B., Schalling, D. and Asberg, M. (1974) Development of a rating scale for depressive illness. In P. Pichot and R. Olivier-Martin (eds), *Psychological Measurements in Psychopharmacology,* pp. 139–50, Karger, Basel.

Derogatis, L.R., Ronald, S., Rickels, K., Uhlenhuth, E.H. and Covi, L. (1974) The Hopkins Symptom Check List (HSCL). A measure of primary symptom dimensions. In P. Pichot and R. Olivier-Martin (eds), *Psychological Measurements in Psychopharmacology,* Karger, Basel.

Derogatis, L.R., Rickels, K. and Rock, A.F. (1976) The SCL-90 and the MMPI: A step in the validation of a new self-report scale. *British Journal of Psychiatry,* **128**, 280–89.

Edwards, B.C., Lambert, M.J., Moran, P.W., McCully, T., Smith, K.C. and Ellingson, A.G. (1984) A meta-analytic comparison of the Beck Depression Inventory and the Hamilton Rating Scale for Depression as measures of treatment outcome. *British Journal of Clinical Psychology,* **23**, 93–9.

Ekman, P. and Friesen, W.V. (1974) Nonverbal behavior in psychopathology. In R.J. Friedman and M.M. Katz (eds), *The Psychology of Depression: Contemporary Theory and Research,* Winston-Wiley, New York.

Endicott, J. and Spitzer, R.L. (1978) A diagnostic interview: The schedule for affective disorders and schizophrenia. *Archives of General Psychiatry*, **38**, 98–103.

Endicott, J., Cohen, J., Nee, J., Fleiss, J. and Sarantakos, S. (1981) Hamilton Depression Rating Scale. Extracted from regular and change versions of the Schedule for Affective Disorders and Schizophrenia. *Archives of General Psychiatry*, **38**, 98–103.

Feighner, J.P., Meredith, C.H., Stern, W.C., Hendrickson, G. and Miller, L.L. (1984) A double-blind study of Buproprion and placebo in depression. *American Journal of Psychiatry*, **141**, 525–29.

Feinberg, M., Carroll, B.J., Smouse, P.E. and Rawson, S.G. (1981) The Carroll rating scale for depression. III. Comparison with other rating instruments. *British Journal of Psychiatry*, **138**, 205–9.

Fennell, M.J.V. and Campbell, E.A. (1984) The cognitions questionnaire: specific thinking errors in depression. *British Journal of Clinical Psychology*, **23**, 81–92.

Ferster, C.G. (1973) A functional analysis of depression. *American Psychologist*, **28**, 857–70.

Fisch, H.U., Frey, S. and Hirsbrunner, H.P. (1983) Analysing non-verbal behavior in depression. *Journal of Abnormal Psychology*, **92**, 307–18.

Folstein, M.F. and Luria, R. (1973) The validity and reliability of the Visual Analogue Mood Scale. *Journal of Psychomatic Research*, **12**, 51–7.

Foster, F.G. and Kupfer, D.J. (1975) Psychomotor activity as a correlate of depression and sleep in acutely disturbed psychiatric inpatients. *American Journal of Psychiatry*, **132**, 928–31.

Foster, F.G., Grau, T., Spiker, D.G. *et al.* (1977) EEG sleep in generalised anxiety disorder. *Sleep Research*, **65**, 145.

Garcia-Sevilla, J.A. (1989) The platelet alpha-2-adrenoceptor as a potential biological marker in depression. *British Journal of Psychiatry*, **154** (Suppl. 14), 67–72.

Gibson, H.B. (1965) *Manual of the Gibson Spiral Maze*, University of London Press.

Gilbert, P. (1988) Psychobiological interaction in depression. In S. Fisher and J. Reason (eds), *Handbook of Life Stress, Cognition and Health*, pp. 559–79, John Wiley, Chichester.

Gillin, J.C., Mazure, C., Post, R.M. *et al.* (1977) An EEG sleep study of a bipolar (manic-depressive) patient with a nocturnal switch process. *Biological Psychiatry*, **12**, 711–18.

Gillin, J.C., Sitaram, N. and Mendelson, W.B. (1982) Acetylcholine, sleep and depression. *Human Neurobiology*, **1**, 211–19.

Gitlin, M. and Gerner, R.H. (1986) The dexamethasone suppression test and response to somatic treatment: a review. *Journal of Clinical Psychiatry*, **47**, 16–21.

Goldberg, D.P. (1972) *The Detection of Psychiatric Illness by Questionnaire*, Oxford University Press, London.

Goldberg, D.P. and Hillier, V.F. (1979) A scaled version of the General Health Questionnaire. *Psychological Medicine*, **9**, 139–45.

Greden, T.F. (1985) Laboratory tests in psychiatry. In H.I. Kaplan and B.J. Sadock (eds), *Comprehensive Textbook of Psychiatry*, 4th edn, Vol. 2, pp. 2028–33, Williams and Wilkins, Baltimore, MD.

Greden, J.F. and Carroll, B.S. (1981) Psychomotor function in affective disorders: an overview of new monitoring techniques. *American Journal of Psychiatry*, **138**, 1441–8.

Guy, W. and Ban, T.A. (eds and translators) (1982) *The AMDP-System*, Springer-Verlag, Berlin/New York.

Hale, A.S., Hannah, P., Sandler, M. and Bridges, P.K. (1989) Tyramine conjugation test for prediction of treatment response in depressed patients. *The Lancet*, **i**, 234–6.

Hamilton, M. (1960) A rating scale for depression. *Journal of Neurological and Neurosurgical Psychiatry*, **23**, 56–62.

Hamilton, M. (1967) Development of a rating scale for primary depressive illness. *British Journal of Social and Clinical Psychology*, **6**, 278–96.

Hamilton, M. (1980) Rating depressive patients. *Journal of Clinical Psychiatry*, **41**, 21–4.

Harris, B., Huckle, P., Thomas, R., Johns, S. and Fung, H. (1989) The use of rating scales to identify postnatal depression. *British Journal of Psychiatry*, **154**, 813–17.

Hathaway, S. and McKinley, C. (1951) *Minnesota Multiphasic Personality Inventory*, The Psychological Corporation, New York.

Hautzinger, M., Linden, M. and Hoffman, N. (1982) Distressed couples with and without a depressed partner: An analysis of their verbal interaction. *Journal of Behaviour Therapy and Experimental Psychiatry*, **13**, 307–14.

Hayes, M.H.S. and Patterson, D.G. (1921) Experimental development of the graphic rating scale. *Psychological Bulletin*, **18**, 98–9.

Hedlund, J.L. and Vieweg, B.W. (1979a) The Hamilton rating scale for depression: A comprehensive review. *Journal of Operational Psychiatry*, **10**, 149–62.

Hedlund, J.L. and Vieweg, B.W. (1979b) The Zung self-rating depression scale. A comprehensive review. *Journal of Operational Psychiatry*, **11**, 48–64.

Hedlund, J.L. and Vieweg, B.W. (1980) The Brief Psychiatric Rating Scale (BPRS): a comprehensive review. *Journal of Operational Psychiatry*, **11**, 48–65.

Heimann, H. and Schmocker, A. (1974) Zur Problematik der Beurteilung des Schweregrades psychiatrischer Zustandbilder. *Arzneim. Forsch.*, **24**, 1004–6.

Heimann, H., Bobon-Schrod, H., Schmocker, A.M. and Bobon, D.P. (1975) Autoévaluation de l'humeur par une liste d'Adjectifs, 1a. Befindlichkeits-Skala (BS) de Zerssen. *L'Encephale*, **1**, 165–83.

Henriques, J.B. and Davidson, R.J. (1989) Affective disorders. In G. Turpin (ed.), *Handbook of Clinical Psychophysiology*, pp. 357–92, John Wiley, Chichester.

Henry, G.W. (1931) Gastro-intestinal motor functions in manic-depressive psychoses. (Recent genological observations). *American Journal of Psychiatry*, **88** (old series), 19–28.

Hersen, M., Eisler, R.M., Alford, G.S. and Agras, W.S. (1973) Effects of token economy on neurotic depression: An experimental analysis. *Behavior Therapy*, **4**, 392–7.

Hinchliffe, M., Lancashire, M. and Roberts, F.J. (1971) Depression: Defense mechanisms in speech. *British Journal of Psychiatry*, **118**, 471–2.

Hirschfeld, R.M.A., Kowlow, S.H. and Kupfer, D.J. (1983) The clinical utility of the dexamethasone suppression test in psychiatry. *Journal of the American Medical Association*, **250**, 2172–5.

Hollon, S.D. and Kendall, P.C. (1980) Cognitive self-statements in depression: development of an automatic thoughts questionnaire. *Cognitive Therapy and Research*, **4**, 383–97.

Iacono, W.G., Peloquin, L.J., Lumry, A.E. *et al.* (1982) Eye-tracking in patients with unipolar and bipolar affective disorders in remission. *Journal of Abnormal Psychology*, **91**, 35–44.

Insel, T.R., Gillin, J.C., Moore, A., Mendelson, W.B., Loewenstein, R.J. and Murphy, D.L. (1982) The sleep of patients with obsessive–compulsive disorder. *Archives of General Psychiatry*, **39**, 1372–7.

Jacobson, N.S. (1981) The assessment of overt behavior in depression. In L.P. Rehm (ed.), *Behavior Therapy for Depression: Present Status and Future Directions*, pp. 279–99, Academic Press, New York.

Jarrett, R.B., Rush, A.J. and Roffwarg, H.P. (1988) The response of depressed outpatients with reduced and nonreduced REM latency to cognitive therapy. *Sleep Research*, **17**, 126.

Johnson, D.A.W. and Heather, B.B. (1974) The sensitivity of the Beck Depression Inventory to change of symptomatology. *British Journal of Psychiatry*, **125**, 184–5.

Jovanovic, U.J. (1977) The sleep profile in manic-depressive patients in the depressive phase. *Waking and Sleeping*, **1**, 199–210.

Kearns, N.P., Cruickshank, C.A., McGuigan, S.A., Siley, S.A., Shaw, S.P. and Snaith, R.P. (1982) A comparison of depression rating scales. *British Journal of Psychiatry*, **125**, 184–5.

Kellner, R. (1986) The Brief Depression Rating Scale. In N. Sartorius and T.A. Ban (eds), *Assessment of Depression*, Springer-Verlag, Berlin.

Kenn, C., Wood, H., Kucyj, M., Wattis, J. and Cunanse, J. (1987) Validation of the hospital anxiety and depression rating scale (HADS) in an elderly psychiatric population. *International Journal of Geriatric Psychiatry*, **2**, 189–93.

King, D., Akiskal, H.S., Lemmi, H., Belluomini, J. and Yerevanian, B.I. (1981) REM density in the differential diagnosis of psychiatric from medical-neurological disorders: a replication. *Psychiatric Research*, **5**, 267–76.

Klein, D.C. and Seligman, M.E.P. (1976) Reversal of performance deficits and perceptual deficits in learned helplessness and depression. *Journal of Abnormal Psychology*, **85**, 11–26.

Knesevitch, J.W., Biggs, J.T., Clayton, P.J. and Ziegler, V.E. (1977) Validity of the Hamilton scale for depression. *British Journal of Psychiatry*, **131**, 49–52.

Ko, H., Lu, R. and Ko, Y. (1989) The comparison of cortisol nonsuppression, cognitive dysfunction and life events among depressive subtypes. *Biological Psychiatry*, **25**, 204A.

Koslow, S.H., Stokes, P.E., Mendels, J., Ramsey, A. and Casper, R. (1982) Insulin tolerance test: human growth hormone response and insulin resistance in primary unipolar depressed, bipolar depressed and control subjects. *Psychological Medicine*, **12**, 45–55.

Krantz, S. and Hammen, C.L. (1979) Assessment of cognitive bias in depression. *Journal of Abnormal Psychology*, **88**, 611–19.

Kupfer, D.J. and Foster, F.G. (1972) Interval between onset of sleep and rapid-eye-movement sleep as an indicator of depression. *The Lancet*, **ii**, 684–6.

Kupfer, D.J. and Foster, F.G. (1975) The sleep of psychotic patients: does it all look alike? In D.X. Freedman (ed.), *The Biology of the Major Psychoses: A Comparative Analysis*, Res. Publ. Assoc. Res. Nerv. Ment. Dis., 54, pp. 143–64. Raven Press, New York.

Kupfer, D. and Thase, M. (1983) The use of the sleep laboratory in the diagnosis of affective disorders. *Psychiatric Clinics of North America*, **6**, 3–25.

Kupfer, D.J., Himmelhoch, J., Swartzburg, M., Anderson, C., Byck, R. and Detre, T.P. (1972) Hypersomnia in manic-depressive disease. *Diseases of the Nervous System*, **33**, 720–24.

Lefebvre, M.F. (1981) Cognitive distortion and cognitive errors in depressed psychiatric and low back pain patients. *Journal of Consulting and Clinical Psychology*, **49**, 517–25.

Lesch, K.-P., Laux, G., Pfuller, H., Erb, A. and Beckmann, H. (1987) Growth hormone (GH) response to GH-releasing hormone in depression. *Journal of Clinical Endocrinology and Metabolism*, **65**, 1278–81.

Lewinsohn, P.M. (1976) Activity schedules in treatment of depression. In J.D. Krumboltz and C.E. Thoresen (eds), *Innovative Treatment Methods of Psychopathology*, Holt, Rinehart and Winston, New York.

Lewinsohn, P.M. and Talkington, J. (1979) Studies on the measurement of unpleasant events and relations with depression. *Applied Psychological Measurement,* **3**, 83–101.

Lipman, R.S., Rickels, K., Covi, L., Derogatis, L.R. and Uhlenhuth, E.H. (1969) Factors of symptom distress. Doctor ratings of anxious neurotic outpatients. *Archives of General Psychiatry,* **21**, 328–38.

Little, J.C. and McPhail, N.I. (1973) Measures of depressive mood at monthly intervals. *British Journal of Psychiatry,* **122**, 447–52.

Lloyd, G.G. and Lishman, W.A. (1975) Effect of depression on the speed of recall of pleasant and unpleasant experiences. *Psychological Medicine,* **5**, 173–80.

Loo, H. (1987) Bilan des recherches biologiques dans la depression chez l'homme. *Psychologie Medicale,* **19**, 2031–55.

Loosen, P.T. and Prange, A.J., Jr (1982) The serum thyrotropin (TSH) response to thyrotropin-releasing hormone (TRH) in depression: a review. *American Journal of Psychiatry,* **139**, 405–16.

Lopez-Ibor, J.J., Saiz-Ruiz, J. and Iglesias, L.M. (1988) The Fenfluramine challenge test in the affective spectrum: a possible marker of endogeneity and severity. *Pharmacopsychiatry,* **21**, 9–14.

Lopez-Ibor, J.J., Saiz-Ruiz, J. and Iglesias, L.M. (1989) Neuroendocrine challenges in the diagnosis of depressive disorders. *British Journal of Psychiatry,* **154**, Suppl. 4, 73–6.

Loudon, J.B. and Tiplady, B. (1981) Assessment of depression and the non-psychiatrist. *Advances in the Biosciences,* **31**, 101–10.

McCormack, H.H., Horne, D.J. de L. and Sheather, S. (1988) Clinical applications of visual analogue scales: a critical review. *Psychological Medicine,* **18**, 1007–19.

MacPhillamy, D.J. and Lewinsohn, P.M. (1971) The pleasant events schedule. Unpublished manuscript, University of Oregon.

Marsella, A.J., Hirschfield, R.M.A. and Katz, M.M. (eds) (1987) *The Measurement of Depression,* John Wiley, Chichester.

Martin, P.R., Loewenstein, R.J., Kaye, W.H., Ebert, M.H., Weingartner, H. and Gillin, J.C. (1986) Sleep EEG in Korsakoff's psychosis and Alzheimer's disease. *Neurology,* **36**, 411–14.

Mendlewicz, J., Linkowski, P., Kerkhofs, M., Desmedt, D., Golstein, J., Copinschi, G. and Van Cauter, E. (1985) Diurnal hypersecretion of growth hormone in depression. *Journal of Clinical and Endocrinological Metabolism,* **60**, 505–12.

Metcalfe, M. and Goldman, E. (1965) Validation of an inventory for measuring depression. *British Journal of Psychiatry,* **111**, 240–42.

Mirkin, A.M. and Coppen, A. (1980) Electrodermal activity in depression: clinical and biochemical correlates. *British Journal of Psychiatry,* **137**, 93–7.

Montgomery, S. and Asberg, M. (1979) A new depression scale designed to be sensitive to change. *British Journal of Psychiatry,* **134**, 382–9.

Montgomery, S.A., Rani, S.J., McAnley, R., Roy, D. and Montgomery, D.B. (1981) The antidepressant activity of zimelidine and maprotiline. *Acta Psychiatrica Scandinavica,* **63**, Suppl. 290, 219–24.

Montplaisir, J. (1976) Disturbed nocturnal sleep. In C. Guilleminault, W. Dement and P. Passouant (eds), *Narcolepsy,* Spectrum, New York.

Morrison, D. and Peck, D.F. (1990) Do self-report measures of affect agree? *British Journal of Clinical Psychology* (in press).

Mullen, P.E., Linsell, C.R. and Parker, D. (1986) Influence of sleep disruption and calorie restriction on biological markers for depression. *Lancet*, **ii**, 1051–5.

Neil, J.F., Merikanges, J.R., Foster, F.G., Merikanges, K.R., Spiker, D.G. and Kupfer, D.J. (1980) Waking and all-night sleep EEG's in anorexia nervosa. *Clinical Electroencephalography*, **11**, 9–15.

Overall, J.E. and Gorham, D.R. (1962) The brief psychiatric rating scale. *Psychopharmacological Bulletin*, **11**, 22–4.

Paykel, E.S. and Norton, K.R.W. (1986) Self-report and clinical interview in the assessment of depression. In N. Sartorius and T.A. Ban (eds), *Assessment of Depression*, pp. 356–66, Springer-Verlag, Berlin.

Paykel, E.S. and Prusoff, B.A. (1973) Response set and observer set in the assessment of depressed patients. *Psychological Medicine*, **3**, 209–16.

Peterson, C., Senimel, A., Von Baeyer, C. Abramson, L.Y., Metalsky, G. and Seligman, M.E.P. (1982) The attributional style questionnaire. *Cognitive Therapy and Research*, **6**, 287–99.

Racagni, G. and Smeraldi, E. (eds) (1987) *Anxious Depression. Assessment and Treatment*, Raven Press, New York.

Radloff, L.S. (1977) The CES-D Scale: A self-report depression scale for research in the general population. *Appied Psychological Measurement*, **1**, 385–401.

Rafaelsen, O.J., Bech, P., Bolwig, T.G., Kramp, P. and Gjerris, A. (1980) The Bech–Rafaelsen combined rating scale for mania and melancholia. *Psychiatria Fennica Suppl.*, 327–31.

Ranelli, C.J. (1978) *Nonverbal Behaviour and Clinical Depression*, Unpublished doctoral dissertation, University of Pittsburg.

Raskin, A., Schulterbrandt, J.G., Reatig, N. and McKeon, J.J. (1970) Differential response to chlorpromazine, imipramine, and a placebo among subgroups of hospitalized depressed patients. *Archives of General Psychiatry*, **23**, 164–73.

Rehm, L.P. (1977) A self-control model of depression. *Behavior Therapy*, **8**, 787–804.

Rehm, L.P. (1987) The measurement of behavioral aspects of depression. In A.J. Marsella, R.M. Hirschfeld and M.M. Katz (eds), *The Measurement of Depression*, pp. 199–239, Guilford Press, New York.

Reynolds, C.F., III and Kupfer, D.J. (1987) State of the Art review: sleep research in affective illness. *Sleep*, **10**, 199–215.

Reynolds, C.F., III, Taska, L.S., Jarrett, D.B., Coble, P.A. and Kupfer, D.J. (1983) REM latency in depression: is there one best definition? *Biological Psychiatry*, **18**, 849–63.

Reynolds, C.F., Soloff, P.H., Kupfer, D.J., Taska, L.S., Restifo, K., Coble, P.A. and McNamara, M.E. (1985) Depression in borderline patients: a prospective EEG sleep study. *Psychiatry Research*, **14**, 1–15.

Rickels, K., Gordon, P.E., Meckelnberg, R., Sablosky, L., Whalen, E.M. and Dion, H. (1968) Iprindole in neurotic depressed general practice patients: A controlled study. *Psychosomatics*, **9**, 208–14.

Robinson, J.C. and Lewinsohn, P.M. (1973) Behavior modification of speech characteristics in a chronically depressed man. *Behavior Therapy*, **4**, 150–2.

Rush, A.J., Schlesser, M.A. and Roffwarg, H.P. (1983) Relationships among the TRH, REM latency and dexamethasone suppression tests: preliminary findings. *Journal of Clinical Psychiatry*, **44**, 23–9.

Sartorius, N. and Ban, T.A. (eds) (1986) *Assessment of Depression*, Published on behalf of the World Health Organization, Springer-Verlag, Berlin.

Schmidt, H.S. and Shy, K. (1986) Short REM latencies and repetitive REM awakenings in impotence without depression. *Sleep Research*, **15**, 203.

Schwab, J.J., Bialow, M.R., Clemmons, R.S. and Holzer, C.E. (1967) Hamilton rating scale for depression with medical in-patients. *British Journal of Psychiatry*, **113**, 83–8.

Schwartz, G.E. (1975) Biofeedback, self-regulation, and the patterning of physiological processes. *American Scientist*, **63**, 314–24.

Schwartz, G.E., Fair, P.L., Salt, P., Mandel, M.R. and Klerman, G.L. (1976) Facial muscle patterning to affective imagery in depressed and non-depressed subjects. *Science*, **192**, 489–91.

Scott, A. (1989) Which depressed patients will respond to electroconvulsive therapy? The search for biological predictors of recovery. *British Journal of Psychiatry*, **154**, 8–17.

Seligman, M.E.P. (1975) *Helplessness: On Depression, Development and Death*, Freeman, San Francisco.

Shapiro, C.M. and Driver, H. (1989) *Sleep and Stress*, NATO Colloquium, Plenum Press, New York.

Simpson, G.M., Lee, H.J., Cuculic, Z. and Kellner, R. (1976) Two dosages of imipramine in hospitalized endogenous and neurotic depressives. *Archives of General Psychiatry*, **33**, 1093–102.

Snaith, R.P., Ahmed, S.N., Mehta, S. and Hamilton, M. (1971) The assessment of primary depressive illness: Wakefield Self-Assessment Inventory. *Psychological Medicine*, **1**, 143–9.

Snaith, R.P., Bridge, G. and Hamilton, M. (1976) The Leeds scales for the self-assessment of anxiety and depression. *British Journal of Psychiatry*, **128**, 156–65.

Spiker, D.G., Foster, F.G., Coble, P.A., Love, D. and Kupfer, D.J. (1977) The sleep disorder in depressed alcoholics. *Sleep Research*, **6**, 161.

Stahl, S.M., Wu, D.J., Mefford, I.N., Berger, P.A. and Ciarenillo, R.D. (1983) Hyperserotonaemia and platelet serotonin uptake and release in schizophrenia and affective disorders. *American Journal of Psychiatry*, **140**, 26–30.

Stern, M., Fram, D., Wyatt, R.J., Grinspoon, L. and Tursky, B. (1969) All night sleep studies of acute schizophrenics. *Archives of General Psychiatry*, **20**, 470–7.

Stokes, P.E. (1966) Pituitary suppression in psychiatric patients. In *Program of the 48th Meeting of the Endocrine Society*, p. 101, Chicago.

Stokes, P.E. and Sikes, C.R. (1988) The hypothalamic–pituitary–adrenocortical axis in major depression. *Endocrinology and Metabolism Clinics of North America*, **17**, 1–19.

Stokes, P.E., Stoll, P.M., Koslow, S.H., Maas, J.W., Davis, J.M., Swann, A.C. and Robins, E. (1984) Pretreatment DST and hypothalamic–pituitary–adrenocortical function in depressed patients and comparison groups. *Archives of General Psychiatry*, **41**, 257–67.

Storrie, M.C., Doerr, H.O. and Johnson, M.H. (1981) Skin conductance characteristics of depressed subjects before and after therapeutic intervention. *Journal of Nervous and Mental Disorders*, **169**, 176–9.

Szabadi, E., Bradshaw, C.M. and Besson, J.A.O. (1976) Elongation of pause-time in speech: a simple objective measure of motor retardation in depression. *British Journal of Psychiatry*, **129**, 592–7.

Targum, S.D., Sullivan, A.C. and Byrnes, S.M. (1982) Neuroendocrine interrelationships in major depressive disorder. *American Journal of Psychiatry*, **139**, 282–6.

Tarnopolsky, A., Hand, D.J., McLean, E.K. and Roberts, H. (1979) Validity and uses of a screening questionnaire (GHQ) in the community. *Neuropharmacology*, **19**, 1211–12.

Taub, J.M., Hawkins, D.R. and Van de Castle, R.L. (1978) Electrographic analysis of the sleep cycle in young depressed patients. *Biological Psychiatry*, **7**, 203–16.

Teasdale, J.D. and Bancroft, J. (1977) Manipulation of thought content as a determinant of mood and corrugator electromyographic activity in depressed patients. *Journal of Abnormal Psychology*, **86**, 235–41.

Teasdale, J.D. and Rezin, V. (1978) Effect of thought-stopping on thoughts, mood and corrugator EMG in depressed patients. *Behaviour Research and Therapy*, **16**, 97–102.

Thase, M.E., Kupfer, D.J. and Ulrich, R.F. (1986) Electroencephalographic sleep in psychotic depression. A valid subtype? *Archives of General Psychiatry*, **43**, 886–92.

Tiplady, B. (1980) A self-rating scale for depression designed to be sensitive to change. *Neuropharmacology*, **19**, 1211–12.

Toedter, L.J., Lasker, J.N. and Alhadeff, J.M. (1988) The perinatal grief scale: development and initial validation. *American Journal of Orthopsychiatry*, **58**, 435–49.

Toone, B.K., Cooke, E. and Lader, M.H. (1981) Electrodermal activity in the affective disorders and schizophrenia. *Psychological Medicine*, **11**, 487–508.

Uhde, T., Mendelson, W.B. and Post, R.M. (1987) Sleep in patients with panic disorder. Submitted for publication.

Uytdenhoef, P., Portelange, P., Jacquar, J., Charles, G., Linkowski, P. and Mendlewicz, J. (1983) Regional cerebral blood flow and lateralized hemispheric dysfunction in depression. *British Journal of Psychiatry*, **143**, 128–32.

Vecchio, T.J. (1966) Predictive value of a single diagnostic test in unselected populations. *New England Journal of Medicine*, **274**, 1171–3.

Watkins, J.T. and Rush, A.J. (1983) Cognitive response test. *Cognitive Therapy and Research*, **7**, 425–35.

Waxer, P. (1974) Nonverbal cues for depression. *Journal of Abnormal Psychology*, **83**, 319–22.

Weingartner, H., Miller, H. and Murphy, D.L. (1977) Mood-state-dependent retrieval of verbal associations. *Journal of Abnormal Psychology*, **86**, 276–84.

Weingartner, H., Cohen, R., Murphy, D.L., Montello, J. and Gerdt, C. (1981) Cognitive processes in depression. *Archives of General Psychiatry*, **38**, 42–7.

Weissman, A. and Beck, A.T. (1978) Development and validation of the Dysfunctional Attitude Scale. Paper presented at the meeting of the Association for Advancement of Behaviour Therapy, Chicago.

Werner, A.E. and Rehm. L.P. (1975) Depressive affect: a test of behavioral hypothesis. *Journal of Abnormal Psychology*, **84**, 221–7.

Widlocher, D. (1983) Salpetriere Retardation Rating Scale. *Psychiatric Clinics of North America*, **6**, No. 1.

Williams, J.B.W. (1988) A structured interview guide for the Hamilton depression rating scale. *Archives of General Psychiatry*, **45**, 742–7.

Wing, J.K. (1983) Use and misuse of PSE. *British Journal of Psychiatry*, **143**, 111–17.

Wing, J.K., Cooper, J.E. and Sartorius, N. (1974) *The Measurement and Classification of Psychiatric Symptoms*, Cambridge University Press, Cambridge.

Wing, J.K., Nixon, J., von Cranach, M. and Strauss, A. (1977) Further developments of the PSE and CATEGO system. *Arch. Psychiat. Nervenkrank.*, **224**, 151–60.

Woggon, B., Baumann, U. and Angst, J. (1978) Inter-rater Reliabilität von AMP-symptomen. *Arch. Psychiatr. Nervenkrank.*, **225**, 73–85.

Zealley, A.K. and Aitken, R.C.P. (1969) Measurement of mood. *Proceedings of the Royal Society of Medicine*, **62**, 993–6.

Zerssen, D. von, Koeller, D.-M. and Rey, E.-R. (1970) Die Befindlichkeits-Skala (BS). *Arztneimittelforsch*, **20**, 915–18.

Zerssen, D. von, Strian, F. and Schwarz, D. (1974) Evaluation of depressive states, especially in longitudinal studies. In P. Pichot and R. Olivier-Martin (eds), *Psychological Measurements in Psychopharmacology*, pp. 189–202, Karger, Basel.

Zigmund, A.S. and Snaith, R.P. (1983) The Hospital Anxiety and Depression Scale. *Acta Psychiatrica Scandinavica*, **67**, 361–70.
Zung, W.W.K. (1965) A self-rating depression scale. *Archives of General Psychiatry*, **12**, 63–70.
Zung, W.W.K. (1967) Factors influencing the self-rating depression scale. *Archives of General Psychiatry*, **16**, 534–47.
Zung, W.W.K. (1972) The Depression Status Inventory: an adjunct to the Self-Rating Depression Scale. *Journal of Clinical Psychology*, **28**, 539–43.

Chapter 4

Clinical Anxiety States

R. PHILIP SNAITH and GRAHAM TURPIN

Techniques for the assessment of anxiety depend upon the setting in which the assessment is to be made (e.g. individual clinical patient, volunteer subject or community survey), resources available (e.g. trained research workers, sophisticated laboratory equipment) and the definition of the construct of 'anxiety' to be used in the study. Attention will first be given to the third of these requirements. Traditionally, in psychological and psychopathological studies constructs such as 'anxiety' and 'depression' are used without further consideration of the complex nature of these concepts or the various mental states to which the terms are applied.

Anxiety is generally considered to be an emotion or state associated with the experience of fear. Fear has a clearly discernible source which may be realistic in terms of the potential for a real threat to well-being or life, or else the focus of the fear may be judged by most people in the person's culture, and indeed by the person himself, to be unrealistic, out of proportion, imaginary or 'neurotic'. In the latter case the psychopathological term *phobia* may be applied.

Anxiety is a more diffuse state than fear; it is more persistent, invading every aspect of the person's life, and its origin may not be obvious although at other times it may be attributed to some event or stress. The pervasive nature of the anxiety state leads to the use of such adjectives as 'free-floating' or 'generalized' to describe it. The latter term will be used here. There is no universally agreed definition of anxiety or of a state of anxiety, although there is a consensus about the features of the state. Lewis (1970) has listed these as follows:

(1) An emotional state with the subjectively experienced quality of fear;
(2) An unpleasant emotion which may be experienced by a feeling of impending death;
(3) Anxiety is directed to the future; implicit is the feeling that there is a threat of some kind;
(4) There may be no recognizable threat, or one which, by reasonable standards, is out of proportion to the emotion it seemingly provokes;

Measuring Human Problems. Edited by D.F. Peck and C.M. Shapiro

(5) There may be subjective bodily discomfort and manifest bodily disturbance.

The anxiety state may be considered to be within the bounds of normality and an understandable reaction to the person's situation, taking into account the background of previous experience and predisposition to be anxious; or it may be recognized to have passed all reasonable bounds and to be a morbid state or psychiatric disorder. The anxiety state is not necessarily a constant state of discomfort but may occur in defined episodic attacks. In fact nosological systems such as DSM III R and ICD 10 recognize the latter to be a separate disorder, and refer to it as Panic Disorder.

There is also a life-long predisposition to be anxious, the trait of anxiety which is chiefly characterized by a proneness to worry needlessly and to be lacking in self-confidence. The person with marked trait anxiety is more prone to develop an anxiety state under adverse circumstances.

There are four major features of the anxiety state: (1) mood, (2) cognitions, (3) physiological symptoms and (4) muscular tension. The mood is that of a sense of dread or of nameless fear. Cognitions are the thoughts and attitudes and these, in the anxiety state, are related to insecurity, disaster or to appearing foolish or incompetent. The physiological symptoms are the wide range of somatic disturbance governed largely, although not entirely, by the sympathetic outflow of the autonomic nervous system. In addition, hyperventilation brings on somatic consequences of paraesthesiae, muscle spasm and faintness. There is also usually tension of the somatic musculature resulting from the state of increased vigilance (hyperarousal). This results in muscular pains and, rarely, muscular spasm, but the popular belief that a persistent muscular tic betrays anxiety is incorrect. There is no exact correspondence between these manifestations. For instance, a person may have markedly anxious thoughts without being physiologically over-aroused; studies of this phenomenon of response system desynchrony are reviewed by Bellack and Lombardo (1984). It has also been pointed out that the term 'anxiety' is no more than a shorthand for the expression of a wider range of psychological states, and that those who purport to 'measure' anxiety must take care to define their particular use of the term. Much confusion has resulted from the disparate usage of this and other psychological states, and the introduction of imprecise instruments has been, and continues to be, a serious impediment to scientific progress (Martin, 1961; Lang, 1968; Bernstein *et al.*, 1986).

Before an instrument is accepted for a particular purpose certain aspects of its validity for that purpose must be carefully considered. This issue is discussed in detail in Chapter 1 of this volume. Following this, some other important information must be sought.

There must be information concerning the score or reading which indicates abnormality or departure from the norm for the general population.

There should also be information as to the scores which indicate various levels of severity of anxiety. Provision of this important information is frequently lacking.

Instructions for use must be clear to the experimenter and to the subject. For instance, a person completing a self-assessment questionnaire must be informed whether his responses are to indicate his state at the time of completion, or in the past week, the past year, his habitual state throughout life, or some other period. Instruments frequently fail to provide such instruction or else couch it in terms easily capable of misinterpretation. For instance, one well-known scale (Zung, 1965), purporting to assess 'trait' anxiety, merely directs the subject to complete the questionnaire to indicate how he 'generally feels'.

Cattell and Scheier (1961) identified over 120 instruments which purported to assess anxiety or some anxiety-related problem. The number has certainly increased. No attempt will be made here to provide a compendium of all anxiety measurement scales and techniques. The present selection is based on three criteria:

(1) The illustration of the procedures and the principles underlying a particular approach;
(2) Techniques and scales which are best known, at least in the English language;
(3) Those recent instruments which have introduced some improvement in the more traditional instruments.

We will shortly outline the procedures necessary to obtain clinical information which is amenable to a behavioural-analytic approach. However, a logical problem which arises from the adoption of this approach should first be highlighted. This concerns the poor intercorrelations which frequently occur between the different response channels employed and also the possible absence of consistency of responding across different situations. For example, in the behavioural treatment of phobias and other anxiety-based disorders the clinician will commonly observe that the rate of improvement (or clinical exacerbation) occurs at different rates across different response channels. A phobic who is rapidly exposed to his or her feared object, as in the case of flooding treatments, may exhibit in a single session pronounced decreases in behavioural avoidance and physiological activation, but may continue to report high and unchanged levels of subjective fear. Although it should be stressed that such a disconcordant pattern of responding is both a prediction and the rational basis of the 'three-systems' approach to anxiety assessment (Lang, 1968), it also raises important questions for the clinician.

Rachman and Hodgson (Rachman and Hodgson, 1974; Hodgson and Rachman, 1974) first drew serious attention to this problem in relation to the clinical practice of behaviour therapy. They termed poor correlations across response channels 'discordance' and dissociations across measures in time 'desynchrony'. Issues which have been identified include the following clinical questions. If a patient is to be considered sufficiently 'treated', should all three response channels demonstrate clinically significant improvements? Do different patterns of desynchrony across individual patients indicate differences in prognosis and/or the size of therapeutic response to different treatments? When attempting to select a particular treatment, which outcome criteria drawn from different response measures should be employed? Not only are these important questions for clinicians to resolve, but if left unresolved, serious problems of interpretation may ensue. For example, Peterson (1984) warns against the arbitrary use of one mode of responding as representative of therapeutic change for such a loosely defined construct as anxiety. Contemporary approaches to this problem emphasize not only the differences between response measures but also their interactions (Cone, 1979; Evans, 1986; Hugdahl, 1989; Kaloupeke and Levis, 1983).

TECHNIQUES OF ANXIETY ASSESSMENT

Two discrete but complementary approaches will be employed to structure the various different methods of anxiety assessment which can be adopted for both clinical practice and research. The first consists of clinical self-report measures which utilize the patients' verbal judgements of their anxiety state or predispositions as obtained using interviews, questionnaires and diaries. This approach is directed to clinical questions concerning diagnosis or classification, and treatment outcome or progress. The second approach, which may be generally construed as a 'behavioural analysis', concerns the general assessment of changes in the construct 'anxiety' within certain specified situations or as a consequence of particular stimuli and therapeutic interventions. Accordingly, anxiety is frequently assessed in terms of three response channels: physiological, cognitive and behavioural (Lang, 1968), and emphasis is placed upon the nature of the relationship between measures derived from these dimensions and anxiety-provoking situations or stimuli. Typically, this approach is adopted in relation to clinical questions concerning the acquisition of anxiety responses, the maintenance of anxiety and accompanying avoidance behaviours, and the processes that may underlie effective treatments which result in anxiety reduction.

It should be emphasized that these two approaches complement each other. Indeed, there is considerable overlap between the two, especially in relation to the measurement of cognitive or subjective aspects of anxiety. They differ, however, in the nature of the clinical questions posed and the level and nature of the analysis, clinical self-report measures being generally applicable to most theoretical frameworks whereas the behavioural measures derive more specifically from a behaviour-analytic perspective (Bernstein *et al.*, 1986).

CLINICAL SELF-REPORT METHODS

At present, self-report methods of anxiety are the most commonly and easily employed techniques for assessment. They have, of course, many drawbacks, including the fact that they cannot be used in situations where the subjects do not have the necessary verbal skill to describe their state. Even in those who are fluent in the language, considerable care must be taken to establish that the subject is using the words in a manner which agrees with the concept required. For instance, the word 'tension' or 'irritability' may be interpreted and used in different senses. The techniques employed are:

(1) Interview by trained interviewer;
(2) Self-assessment methods:
    (a) Questionnaire;
    (b) Completion of a record of events over a period;
    (c) A general estimate of overall severity on a line scale.

Table 4.1 lists the instruments in (1) and (2a) to be considered here.

The Hamilton Anxiety Scale (HAS) (Hamilton, 1959)

The Hamilton Anxiety Scale is composed of 14 items covering the wide range of symptoms generally recognized to be those of an anxiety state. They are: anxious mood; tension; fears; insomnia; difficulty in concentration; depressed mood; muscular tension (tics, aching, trembling); general somatic (tinnitus, blurred vision, faintness, flushing); cardiovascular symptoms; respiratory symptoms; gastro-intestinal symptoms; urogenital symptoms (urological and sexual); other somatic (dryness of mouth, sweating, paraesthesiae); behaviour at interview (appearance of being anxious, restlessness, swallowing frequently, sighing, tremor). Each item is rated on a 5-point scale and the total score represents the severity. There is no information to aid the interpretation of the score. Somatic symptoms account for a large proportion of the total score rendering the Scale unreliable in the setting of physical illness. Some items (e.g. insomnia, depressed mood and some of the somatic symptoms) are as likely to occur in other mood

Table 4.1 Self-report methods of anxiety assessment.

GENERALIZED ANXIETY
(1) *Interview scales*:
The Hamilton Anxiety Scale
The Clinical Anxiety Scale
(2) *Self-assessment scales*:
Taylor Manifest Anxiety Scale
Zung Anxiety Scale
State–Trait Anxiety Inventory (STAI)
Children's STAI
IPAT Anxiety

SITUATIONAL ANXIETY
Self-assessment scales:
Fear Survey Schedule
Fear Questionnaire

ANXIETY WITH OTHER PSYCHOPATHOLOGY
(1) *Interview scales*:
The Brief Psychiatric Rating Scale (BPRS)
The Present State Examination (PSE)
The Comprehensive Psychopathological Rating Scale (CPRS)
(2) *Self-assessment scales*:
The Crown–Crisp Experiential Index
Profile of Mood States (POMS)
The Symptom Distress Check List (SCL-90)
The Irritability Depression and Anxiety Scale (IDA) Scale
The Hospital Anxiety and Depression Scale (HAD Scale)

disorders as in anxiety states, so the Scale will not distinguish between anxiety states and other disorders.

The Clinical Anxiety Scale (CAS) (Snaith *et al.*, 1982)

This instrument was derived from the Hamilton Anxiety Scale by item analysis of the HAS. It is briefer than the parent instrument consisting of just six items each to be assessed on a 0–4 scale of severity. The items cover anxious mood, anxious cognition and motor aspects of anxiety but other somatic symptoms are omitted, thus making the CAS suitable for use in the setting of somatic disorder. A subsequent study (Snaith *et al.*, 1986) provides information on the interpretation of the score in terms of five bands of severity: normal, mild, moderate, severe and very severe. The CAS has been shown to distinguish between the constructs of anxiety and depression (Snaith and Taylor, 1985). The CAS may be reproduced without charge but is subject to copyright law of quotation of its source and title, and is shown in Table 4.2.

Table 4.2

Clinical Anxiety Scale

Instructions for Use

The Scale is an instrument for the assessment of the present state of anxiety: therefore the emphasis on eliciting information for the ratings should be on how the patient feels at the present time. However, the interview itself may raise, or lower, the severity of anxiety and the interviewer should inform the patient that he should describe how he has felt during the period of the past two days.

Psychic tension

(care should be taken to distinguish tension from muscular tension—see next item)

Score 4: Very marked and distressing feeling of being 'on edge', 'keyed up', 'wound up', or 'nervous' which persists with little change throughout the waking hours.

Score 3: As above, but with some fluctuation of severity during the course of the day.

Score 2: A definite experience of being tense which is sufficient to cause some, although not severe, distress.

Score 1: A slight feeling of being tense which does not cause distress.

Score 0: No feeling of being tense apart from the normal degree of tension experienced in response to stress and which is acceptable as normal for the population.

Ability to relax

(muscular tension)

Score 4: The experience of severe tension throughout much of the bodily musculature which may be accompanied by such symptoms as pain, stiffness, spasmodic contractions, and lack of control over movements. The experience is present throughout most of the waking day and there is no ability to produce relaxation at will.

Score 3: As above, but the muscular tension may only be experienced in certain groups of muscles and may fluctuate in severity throughout the day.

Score 2: A definite experience of muscular tension in some part of the musculature sufficient to cause some, but not severe, distress.

Score 1: Slight recurrent muscular tension of which the patient is aware but which does not cause distress. Very mild degrees of tension headache or pain in other groups of muscles should be scored here.

Score 0: No subjective muscular tension or of such degree which, when it occurs, can easily be controlled at will.

Startle response

(hyperarousability)

Score 4: Unexpected noise causes severe distress so that the patient may complain in some such phrase as 'I jump out of my skin'. Distress is experienced in psychic *and* somatic modalities so that, in addition to the experience of fright, there is muscular activity and autonomic symptoms such as sweating or palpitation.

Score 3: Unexpected noise causes severe distress in psychic or somatic, but not in both modalities.

Score 2: Unexpected noise causes definite but not severe distress.

Score 1: The patient agrees that he is slightly 'jumpy' but is not distressed by this.

Score 0: The degree of startle response is entirely acceptable as normal for the population.

Worrying

(the assessment must take into account the degree to which worry is out of proportion to actual stress)

Score 4: The patient experiences almost continuous preoccupation with painful thoughts which cannot be stopped voluntarily and the distress is quite out of proportion to the subject matter of the thoughts.

Score 3: As above, but there is some fluctuation in intensity throughout the waking hours and the distressing thoughts may cease for an hour or two, especially if the patient is distracted by activity requiring his attention.

Score 2: Painful thoughts out of proportion to the patient's situation keep intruding into consciousness but he is able to dispel or dismiss them.

Score 1: The patient agrees that he tends to worry a little more than necessary about minor matters but this does not cause much distress.

Score 0: The tendency to worry is accepted as being normal for the population: for instance even marked worrying over a severe financial crisis or unexpected illness in a relative should be scored as 0 if it is judged to be entirely in keeping with the degree of stress.

Apprehension

Score 4: The experience is that of being on the brink of some disaster which cannot be explained. The experience need not be continuous and may occur in short bursts several times a day.

Score 3: As above, but the experience does not occur more than once a day.

Score 2: A sensation of groundless apprehension of disaster which is not severe although it causes definite distress. The patient may not use strong terms such as 'disaster' or 'catastrophe' but may express his experience in some such phrase as 'I feel as if something bad is about to happen'.

Score 1: A slight degree of apprehensiveness of which the patient is aware but which does not cause distress.

Score 0: No experience of groundless anticipation of disaster.

Restlessness

Score 4: The patient is unable to keep still for more than a few minutes and engages in restless pacing or other purposeless activity.

Score 3: As above, but he is able to keep still for an hour or so at a time.

Score 2: There is a feeling of 'needing to be on the move' which causes some, but not severe, distress.

Score 1: Slight experience of restlessness which causes no distress.

Score 0: Absence of restlessness.

GRADE	RECOVERED	MILD	MODERATE	SEVERE
RANGE	0 – 4	5 – 10	11 – 16	17 – 24

Reproduced from *British Journal of Psychiatry* 1982: **141**: 518 – 23: 1986: **148**: 599 – 601.

The Manifest Anxiety Scale (Taylor, 1953)

This early instrument is derived from the Minnesota Multiphasic Personality Inventory and is presented in two forms: a 50-item and a 28-item version. The presenting study provides normative data for college students (long version) and mixed diagnosis psychiatric patients (short version). The short version has reasonable face validity although the concepts of state and trait are not distinguished.

The Self-Rating Anxiety Scale (Zung, 1971)

This self-assessment scale consists of 20 items, each rated on a 4-point scale. It is heavily dependent upon somatic symptoms which account for 12 of the items. The ability of the anxiety scale and Zung's depression scale to differentiate between the two constructs was reported by Bramley *et al.* (1988).

The State–Trait Anxiety Inventory (STAI) (Spielberger *et al.*, 1987a)

This instrument provides two 20-item questionnaires. The first instructs the respondent to complete the scale 'as you feel right now, that is, at the moment'; the second instructs completion 'as you generally feel'. The face validity of the two questionnaires is reasonable, but it is questionable whether the first rubric of instructions identifies a state independent of the experimental condition and the second rubric a life-long trait of personality. The latest Form Y is said to produce a measure of anxiety more independent of depression.

The Children's State–Trait Inventory (Spielberger *et al.*, 1987b)

This version of the STAI follows the parent instrument and has two separate scales measuring anxiety-proneness and current feelings of anxiety.

The IPAT Anxiety Scale (Cattel and Scheier, 1987)

This 40-item questionnaire covers the concepts of: emotional instability, suspiciousness, guilt-proneness, low integration and tension. These subscales provide a total score, a conscious anxiety score and a covert anxiety score. Norms are provided for American adults and British undergraduate students.

The Fear Survey Schedule (Wolpe and Lange, 1987)

This questionnaire lists 108 items to each of which the responder rates the degree of anxiety on a 0–4 scale. Its main use is as an indication of the major situational anxieties of a subject who may be applying for treatment of a phobic anxiety state.

The Fear Questionnaire (FQ) (Marks and Mathews, 1979)

The instrument provides measures of anxiety focused upon specific situations. The subject records an assessment on 8-point scales of the overall severity of the main phobia in terms of the degree of avoidance of the situation and the severity of emotional distress in that situation. In addition, 15 situations are assessed in terms of the degree of avoidance and these provide measures for agoraphobia, blood-injury and social anxiety. Further work on the FQ, including a suggestion for alternative design of the form, has been given by van Zuuren (1988); she also refers to other studies providing information on norms for the general population and on validation.

The Brief Psychiatric Rating Scale (BPRS) (Overall and Gorham, 1962)

This instrument was introduced in order to assess change resulting from treatment in psychiatric patients. Initially, 14 areas of psychopathology were included but this was later expanded to 18. Ratings for each area are made on 7-point scales and two areas relate to the construct of anxiety:

(2) Anxiety—worry, fear, over-concern for the present or future;
(6) Tension—physical and motor manifestations of nervousness.

The latter therefore admits a wide interpretation. Hedlund and Vieweg (1980) provide a comprehensive survey of studies relating to the use of the BPRS.

The Present State Examination (PSE) (Wing *et al.*, 1974)

This is a comprehensive system for recording the mental state in psychiatric disorder. It has the great advantage of a clear definition of the various symptoms but it may not be used without preliminary training in its administration. A computer program known as CATEGO analyses 140 elements of psychic disturbance (symptoms) into a number of classes or syndromes.

Since scores are allotted to each symptom, overall class scores are derived. The symptoms related to the construct of anxiety comprise: worrying, tension pains, muscular tension, restlessness and fidgeting, nervous tension, free-floating autonomic anxiety, anxious foreboding with autonomic accompaniments, anxiety due to delusions, panic attacks, situational autonomic anxiety, autonomic anxiety on meeting people, specific phobias, avoidance of situations caused by autonomic anxiety, agitation and observed anxiety (anxious appearance). The symptoms are assessed according to their presence and severity over the period of a month before the interview.

The Comprehensive Psychopathological Rating Scale (CPRS) (Åsberg *et al.*, 1978)

This instrument is similar to the Present State Examination but less detailed. Unlike the PSE, supervised training in its use is not mandatory but the following instructions in its use are given in the paper presenting the CPRS:

> The essential requirement for a rater is training and experience in interviewing psychiatric patients. The scale can be used by all trained mental health workers e.g. psychiatrists, psychologists, nurses. It is recommended that all raters should familiarize themselves with the use of the scale in a series of training sessions before it is used for treatment evaluation.

There are explicit descriptions of all the 65 items and each item is rated on a 0 (absence) through 3 (extreme degree) scale. Items relating to the concept of anxiety are:

Item 3 Inner tension: representing feelings of ill-defined discomfort, edginess, inner turmoil, mental tension mounting to panic, dread and anguish. Rate according to intensity, frequency, duration and degree of reassurance called for. Distinguish from sadness, worrying and muscular tension.

Item 9 Worrying over trifles: Representing apprehension, and undue concern over trifles, which is difficult to stop and out of proportion to the circumstances.

Item 11 Phobias: Representing feelings of unreasonable fear in specific situations (such as buses, supermarkets, crowds, feeling enclosed, being alone) which are avoided if possible.

Item 24 Aches and pains: Representing reports of bodily discomfort, aches, and pains. Rate according to intensity, frequency and duration, and also request for relief. Disregard any opinion of organic cause. Distinguish from hypochondriasis, autonomic disturbance and muscular tension.

Item 25 Muscular tension: Representing the description of increased tension in the muscles and a difficulty in relaxing physically. Distinguish from aches and pains.

Item 46 Autonomic disturbances: Representing signs of autonomic dysfunction, hyperventilation or frequent sighing, blushing, sweating, cold hands, enlarged pupils and dry mouth, fainting.

Item 61 Agitation: Representing 'purposeless' motor activity such as hand-wringing, picking at objects and clothes, inability to sit still. Distinguish from overactivity, involuntary movements and mannerisms.

Item 63 Muscular tension: Representing observed muscular tension as shown in facial expression, posture and movements.

The first five items are based upon self-report and the last three upon the interviewer's observation of the subject.

The Crown–Crisp Experiential Index (CCEI) (Crown and Crisp, 1987)

This is a 48-item self-assessment scale which provides measures of severity in the following areas: generalized anxiety, phobic anxiety, obsessionality, somatic symptoms, depression and hysteria. 'Hysteria' is a diffuse concept and the statement in the NFER-Nelson catalogue that the somatic symptoms are related solely to anxiety is doubtful. The ability of the CCEI to distinguish between the constructs of anxiety and depression was examined by Bramley *et al.* (1988).

The Profile of Mood States (POMS) (McNair *et al.*, 1987)

This instrument requires the subject to assess the present state by four degrees of intensity on each of 40 adjectives. It identifies six monopolar dimensions: tension/anxiety, depression/dejection, anger/hostility, vigour/activity, fatigue/inertia and confusion/bewilderment. There is also a bipolar form providing six bipolar scales: composed–anxious, confident–unsure, energetic–tired, elated–depressed, agreeable–hostile and clear-headed–confused.

The POMS provides subscale scores for each of the concepts and also an overall 'total mood disturbance' score. Norms are provided for the general population.

The Hopkins Symptom Check List (SCL-90) (Derogatis *et al.*, 1973)

The 90-item scale provides measures in each of nine areas: somatization; obsessive–compulsive; interpersonal sensitivity; depression; anxiety; hostility; phobic anxiety; paranoid ideation; psychoticism. The SCL-90 is a clinical scale and the ten items of the Anxiety subscale cover anxious mood (pervasive and episodic) muscular tension/restlessness, tachycardia, depersonalization and a feeling of being under pressure to complete tasks. Each item is rated on a 5-point response. The seven-item Phobic subscale is largely confined to the situations usually considered to constitute the agoraphobic complex. The Interpersonal Sensitivity subscale (12 items) provides an indication of social anxiety.

The Irritability, Depression and Anxiety Scale (IDA Scale) (Snaith *et al.*, 1978)

This 18-item self-assessment scale provides four measures: generalized anxiety, depression, and inwardly directed and outwardly directed irritability. Information on interpretation of the subscale scores is provided in terms of normal, borderline and morbid. The ability of the IDA Scale to distinguish between the constructs of anxiety and depression has been examined by Bramley *et al.* (1988). The IDA Scale was devised for the purpose of screening for mood disorder following childbirth and, in this context, the Outward Irritability assessment is useful. The Inward Irritability scale has been shown not to be homogeneous but to consist of two concepts: (1) proneness to suicidal action and (2) self-denigration (Snaith and Taylor, 1985).

The IDA Scale may be reproduced without charge but is subject to copyright quotation of its source and title.

The Hospital Anxiety and Depression Scale (HAD Scale) (Zigmond and Snaith, 1983)

The HAD Scale was designed for use in non-psychiatric hospital departments as a screen for the presence of anxiety and depression. However, it may be used in primary care and in community work. The subscales are each composed of seven items and each item is rated on a 4-point scale. The composition of the items was chosen to diminish the effect of concurrent physical illness on mood and the Anxiety subscale is composed as follows:

Anxiety Scale (1) I feel tense or wound up.

(2) I get a sort of frightened feeling as if something awful is about to happen.
(3) Worrying thoughts go through my mind.
(4) I can sit at ease and feel relaxed.
(5) I get a sort of frightened feeling like butterflies in my stomach.
(6) I feel restless as if I have to be on the move.
(7) I get sudden feelings of panic.

Score ranges are provided for both subscales in the bands: normal, borderline and morbid. The ability of the HAD Scale to distinguish between the concepts of 'depression' and 'anxiety' has been studied by Bramley *et al.* (1988). The HAD Scale has been validated in subsequent studies (*inter alia*: Hicks and Jenkins, 1988).

The HAD Scale may be reproduced from the original article without charge, but is subject to copyright conditions of quotation of the title and source on each copy.

The HAD Scale has been translated into most European and many other languages. These are obtainable free of charge from one of us (RPS).

OTHER METHODS OF ASSESSMENT

The Visual Analogue Scale

This method of self-assessment of subjective states such as pain or anxiety has been explored by Aitken (1969) and Aitken and Zeally (1970). It is based upon the presentation of a horizontal line, usually 10 cm in length (although other lengths may be chosen) with anchoring statements at each end of the line. In the case of the assessment of an anxiety state such statements might be chosen as: 'I feel perfectly calm' and, at the other end, 'I feel as anxious as I have ever felt' or 'I feel as anxious as it is possible to be'. The subject is asked to make a mark on the line at the point to indicate his or her present state and the severity of the state is represented as the distance in millimetres from the end indicating absence of distress. This method is very useful as an indication of change within a single subject but there are frequently problems concerned with the choice of the anchoring statements and in summation of scores for more than one subject. For instance, one person's concept of the statement 'as tense as possible to be' may vary very considerably from another's concept of the meaning of that statement.

'Diary' methods of assessment

The self-recording of distress which occurs episodically may be carried out by the provision of a diary or chart with the days marked out. The subject is then asked to make some agreed mark at any time that the distress is experienced. For instance, the pattern and frequency of panic attacks may be studied by this method over a period or in relation to some other stressful procedures. The method is very useful, but care is required to explain the procedure carefully and to encourage the person to acquire the habit of recording the distress with careful regularity. This is usually best done if the 'diary' is kept at a convenient place where it will be noticed easily (e.g. by the toothbrush or the bedside clock). An example of such a chart in which symptoms may be recorded against the timing of menstrual periods is given in Sims and Snaith (1988).

BEHAVIOURAL APPROACHES

As has already been stated, the concept of anxiety remains a relatively ill-defined and elusive construct. As a consequence, behavioural approaches to the measurement of anxiety over the last 25 years have emphasized the need to measure the overt motoric (behavioural), cognitive (self-report) and physiological (psychophysiological and biochemical) aspects of the behaviour of anxious individuals (Bernstein *et al.*, 1986). In addition, considerable attention is directed towards specifying the nature of the anxiety-provoking situation and the behavioural antecedents and consequences which occur. Accordingly, these measures may be derived *in vivo* when the patient confronts his or her anxiety-provoking stimulus, as a consequence of discussion and directed imagery during the clinical setting, or response to specially contrived situations such as Behavioural Avoidance Tests or Role Play Exercises constructed by the therapist. Measures may be derived from these settings in order to assess either the nature of the acquisition and maintenance of anxiety or the effectiveness of anxiety-reducing interventions at both the level of therapeutic outcome and the processes thought to underlie such changes.

Observed motoric measures

These are frequently referred to as being essentially *behavioural* and consist of observational measures of overt behaviours related to the construct of anxiety. They may be obtained using time-sampling methods (Foster and

Cone, 1986; Foster *et al.*, 1988) to observe directly such behaviours as pacing, trembling, hand tremors, quavering voice, speech blocking, etc. either *in vivo* or from videotape recordings. More commonly, behavioural checklists of anxious behaviours may be completed by a trained observer or therapist and include the Timed Behavioural Checklist (Paul, 1966) for use with adults and the Observer Rating Scale of Anxiety (Melamed and Siegel, 1975) and the Pre-School Observational Scale of Anxiety (Glennon and Weisz, 1978) for use with children and adolescents. In assessing the effectiveness of some anxiety-reducing treatments it might be appropriate not to focus on the reduction of anxiety but to assess the induction of relaxation. Accordingly, Poppen (1988) has developed an observer rating scale of the degree of relaxation which provides both a useful treatment outcome and process measure of relaxation. The major drawbacks with direct observation can be its intrusive nature and the necessity to record large numbers of behavioural categories reliably over time. Other direct measures of anxious behaviours also include speech production and fluency (Bernstein *et al.*, 1986), overall levels of activity as recorded using goniometers, and muscle contraction activity. These latter two measures will be covered in the section on psychophysiological assessment.

Another approach to observational measurement is to indirectly assess anxiety by the degree of behavioural avoidance demonstrated by the patient in a feared situation. Typically, the minimum physical distance tolerated between the patient and the feared object or the period of time spent in the situation is measured either when the patient approaches a feared object or is approached by a therapist with the object. In the case of phobias, this assessment is commonly termed a Behavioural Avoidance Test (cf. Nietzel *et al.*, 1988) and requires the therapist usually to experimentally contrive exposure to the feared object in the therapeutic session.

Although these techniques may be easily incorporated into behavioural exposure treatments such as desensitization, flooding and modelling, it should be pointed out that the assessment technique may also confound the effects of the therapeutic intervention (Rowland and Canavan, 1983). Measures of approach or avoidance may also be obtained in the naturalistic environment. For example, Michelson *et al.* (1985) measured the distance covered by agoraphobics instructed to engage in a standard walk. It should be emphasized that these indirect measures of avoidance are usually accompanied by other behavioural measures of self-report and physiological anxiety. A major issue concerning the use of avoidance and its relationship to other measures of anxiety concerns the demand characteristics imposed by the therapist upon the situation (Kaloupek and Levis, 1983).

Cognitive approaches and subjective reports

The measurement of 'cognition' in behaviour therapy is perhaps one of the most simple but paradoxically equivocal response channels. Traditionally, the cognitive response mode has referred to subjective self-reports of the degree of anxiety level experienced by a patient within a given situation. This may be assessed using fear surveys or questionnaires, as described in the previous section, simple 10- or 100-point fear scales or 'fear thermometers' where the subject rates from 0 (no fear) to 100 (extreme/the most fear I've ever experienced), and visual analogue scales (cf. Bernstein *et al.*, 1986; Neitzel *et al.*, 1988). These scales may be organized into self-monitoring diaries which the patients complete on a daily basis. However, with the advent of cognitive therapy (Beck and Emery, 1986), 'cognition' does not only refer to the act of subjective rating but also to the specific content of thought and language, and to specific attitudes or cognitive styles which may predispose an individual to be anxious or experience anxiety-eliciting thoughts or acts. This is a developing area and requires more extensive discussion than is possible in this chapter. The interested reader should consult Parks and Hollon (1988) for a general review of cognitive assessment methods which include thought listing, thought sampling, diary records of negative or dysfunctional thoughts, cognitive style and attributional questionnaires.

Finally, the role of cognition in anxiety has also been recently approached from the perspective of experimental cognitive psychology. This approach measures performance on information processing tasks such as the Stroop Test (Stroop, 1935) or the Dichotic Listening Paradigm (Kimura, 1967), and sets out to examine patient-related biases in attention to, recognition of and recall of anxiety-related stimuli (Williams *et al.*, 1988). The potential advantage of this innovative approach is that psychopathological differences which might be revealed by these techniques are obtained using tasks whereby patients are *unaware* of any specific biases or deficits in their own performance. Indeed, these techniques are said to reveal biases in encoded material which may not be immediately available to conscious awareness and thus may reflect anxiety-related disruption of so-called 'preconscious' or 'preattentive' processes. However, although these techniques are providing promising results within clinical research settings, they have yet to be properly applied to clinical assessment and treatment (Watts, 1986).

Physiological measures

There are a variety of physiological systems which are said to be affected by anxiety and include the autonomic nervous system (ANS), the central nervous system (CNS) and various endocrine systems. From a behavioural perspective, it is only the first of these that has received much attention. Although anxiety is associated with certain CNS changes as indicated by measurement of the electroencephalogram (EEG) (cf. Zahn, 1986; Turpin, 1989), both the relative non-specific nature of these changes and the technical requirements of the equipment employed have curtailed their clinical use. Similarly, a variety of hormonal responses which are amenable to biochemical assay (e.g. adrenaline, non-adrenaline, adrenocorticotrophic hormone, glucocorticoids, catechol-*o*-methyl transferase) have been cited variously as both antecedents and consequences of anxiety states (Steptoe, 1987; Fredrickson, 1989) but entail considerable practical obstacles to routine clinical assessment. These include the invasive nature of either blood or urine samples, the financial and technical costs of biochemical assays and the limited access to these resources. Nevertheless, from a research perspective, hormonal measures may reveal information concerning the psychophysiological nature of anxiety which is not accessible to study using ANS measures (Fredrickson, 1989).

Behavioural approaches have tended to rely on the measurement of the effects of the autonomic nervous system and, in particular, the cardiovascular and electrodermal systems (cf. Turpin, 1989). Measures of heart rate can be easily obtained using either laboratory polygraphs or commercially available pulsemeters. Similarly, electrical measures of sweating (electrodermal activity) such as skin conductance and resistance (galvanic skin response) can also be obtained using electrodes applied to the fingertips. Other commonly available psychophysiological measures include blood pressure and the electromyogram. For further details of these procedures, a range of technical handbooks are available (Martin and Venables, 1980; Stern *et al.*, 1980; Coles *et al.*, 1986).

As regards the application of psychophysiological methods to the routine assessment of clinical anxiety, there remain several substantive issues to be resolved. These include the reliability of measures, their validity, reactivity to the social setting of the laboratory, individual differences in response reactivity and profiles, and the effects of confounding variables (physical activity, drugs, environmental conditions etc.) (cf. Haynes, *et al.*, 1989; Turpin, 1989). Nevertheless, clinical research has demonstrated the benefits of including measures such as heart rate and skin conductance in the assessment of anxiety and anxiety disorders (cf. Hugdahl, 1989; Ost, 1989; Sartory, 1989). For example, measures of heart rate reactivity have been shown to aid prediction of an individual's response to different treatments and likelihood of subsequent relapse. Indeed, an argument may be made based on these findings to include simple psychophysiological measures routinely in the assessment of some anxiety disorders. In addition, the demonstration of changes in heart rate monitored with a pulsemeter both during and across clinical sessions may provide a very effective means of therapeutic feedback for some patients. Similarly, the monitoring of electrodermal and electromyographic activity can provide additional information for both client and therapist upon the effectiveness of relaxation/anxiety reduction procedures. However, it needs to be strongly emphasized that clinicians wishing to adopt psychophysiological measures routinely should ensure that they are familiar with the technical requirements and interpretative limitations associated with psychophysiological measures (Turpin, in press; Turpin, 1989).

Finally, it should be stated that biological measures are also frequently employed as putative diagnostic markers (cf. Usdin and Hanin, 1982) without specific recourse to behavioural or psychological analysis.

Settings

It is obvious that a behavioural approach describes a wide range of diverse assessment methods. The therapist is therefore confronted by the frequently perplexing question of which particular method is appropriate for any given clinical problem. This choice, however, cannot be prescribed in advance but is dependent upon the therapist's view of the problem and the situations or settings in which the clinical information is to be gathered. Moreover, the essential aim of the assessment ought to be a flexible analysis of the clinical situation (cf. Bernstein *et al.*, 1986). Accordingly, the therapist's hypotheses concerning the aetiology and maintenance of a particular anxiety problem should determine the nature of the measures employed. Ideally, they should also reflect a 'three-systems' approach to the overall description of the problem. In addition, the specific nature of the setting and specific nature of the problem will determine the methods adopted in practice.

Essentially, there is a choice between measures obtained within the clinical setting and those derived in naturalistic settings comprising the client's social environment away from the clinic. It could be argued that the latter approach is a more appropriate and useful source of clinical information. However, obtaining information *in vivo* may present problems relating to the reliability and validity of the data, especially if the therapist is not present, and also may raise practical difficulties. Nevertheless, a range of techniques are amenable to *in vivo* settings and include naturalistic observation, self-monitoring and the use of diary assessments. If the therapist is unavailable, significant others including relatives, care staff or peers may also be a useful source of information and may provide an alternative perspectve to the problem than that reached by either the patient or the therapist. This latter approach is frequently termed social validation (Kazdin, 1977). Occasionally, specific techniques need to be adopted for naturalistic observation.

For example, ambulatory psychophysiological monitoring (Turpin, 1985) has provided an invaluable means of assessing the nature of psychophysiological responding in panic disorder (e.g. Margraf *et al.*, 1987).

Within the clinical setting, the therapist is usually restricted to obtaining clinical information either by self-report from the client or a third party, or perhaps through the use of imagery. Lang's recent emphasis on imagery as an assessment tool (cf. Lang, 1985; Cuthbert and Lang, 1989) provides a means of freeing the assessment from the confines of the clinic setting. Other approaches include the 'artificial' construction of therapeutically relevant situations in which the patient can be engaged. The use of laboratory tasks and Behavioural Avoidance Tests have already been covered. In addition, certain anxiety problems have been approached by the use of role play. In particular, social anxiety and performance of social skills have frequently been assessed using confederates and patients within Social Role Play Tests (cf. Nay, 1986). However, as with all sources of clinic-derived information, the major problem concerns the relationship between clinical/laboratory data and that obtained in real life (cf. Bellack *et al.*, 1978). This issue, known as the 'generalization problem', can frequently be approached using a combination of clinical and naturalistic investigations.

REFERENCES

Aitken, R.C.B. (1969) Measurement of feelings using Visual Analogue Scales. *Proceedings of the Royal Society of Medicine*, **62**, 989–93.

Aitken, R.C.B. and Zeally, A.K. (1970) The measurement of moods. *British Journal of Hospital Medicine*, **4**, 215–24.

Åsberg, M., Montgomery, S.A., Perris, C., Schalling, D. and Sedvall, G. (1978) A comprehensive psychopathological rating scale. *Acta Psychiatrica Scandinavica*, Supplement 271.

Beck, A.T. and Emery, G. (1985) *Anxiety Disorders and Phobias: A Cognitive Perspective*, Basic Books, New York.

Bellack, A.S. and Lombardo, T.W. (1984) Measurement of anxiety. In S.M. Turner (ed.), *Behavioral Theories And Treatment of Anxiety*, pp. 51–89, Plenum Press, New York.

Bellack, A.S., Hersen, M. and Turner, S.M. (1978) Role-play tests for assessing social skills: Are they valid? *Behavior Therapy*, **9**, 448–61.

Bernstein, D.A., Borkovec, T.D. and Coles, M.G.H. (1986) Assessment of anxiety. In A.R. Ciminero, K.S. Calhoun and H.E. Adams (eds), *Handbook of Behavioral Assessment*, John Wiley, New York.

Bramley, P.N., Easton, A.M.E., Morley, S. and Snaith, R.P. (1988) The differentiation of anxiety and depression. *Acta Psychatrica Scandinavica*, **77**, 133–8.

Cattell, R.B. and Scheier, I.H. (1961) *The Meaning And Measurement of Neuroticism And Anxiety*, Ronald Press, New York.

Cattell, R.B. and Scheier, S.H. (1987) *The IPAT Anxiety Scale*, NFER-Nelson, Windsor.

Coles, M.G.H., Donchin, E. and Porges, S.W. (1986) *Psychophysiology: Systems, Processes and Applications*, Guilford Press, New York.

Crown, S. and Crisp, A. (1987) *Crown–Crisp Experiential Index*, NFER-Nelson, Windsor.

Cuthbert, B.N. and Lang, P.J. (1989) Imagery, memory and emotion: A psychophysiological analysis of clinical anxiety. In G. Turpin (ed.), *Handbook of Clinical Psychophysiology*, John Wiley, Chichester.

Derogatis, L.R., Lipman, R.S. and Covi, L. (1973) SCL-90: an outpatient psychiatric rating scale—preliminary report. *Psychopharmacology Bulletin*, **9**, 13–27.

Evans, I.M. (1986) Response strtucture and the triple response mode concept. In R.O. Nelson and S.C. Hayes (eds.), *Conceptual Foundations of Behavioral Assesment*, Guilford, New York.

Foster, S.L., Bell-Dolan, D.J. and Burge, D.A. (1988) Behavioral observation. In A.S. Bellack and M. Hersen (eds), *Behavioral Assessment: A Practical Handbook*, 3rd edn, Pergamon Press, New York.

Foster, S.L. and Cone, J.D. (1986) Design and use of direct observation procedures. In A. Ciminero, K.S. Calhoun and H.E. Adams (eds), *Handbook of Behavioral Assessment*, 2nd edn, John Wiley, New York.

Fredrickson, M. (1989) Psychophysiological and biochemical indices in 'stress' research: Applications to psychopathology and pathophysiology. In G. Turpin (ed.), *Handbook of Clinical Psychophysiology*, John Wiley, Chichester.

Glennon, B. and Weisz, J.R. (1978) An observational approach to the assessment of anxiety in young children. *Journal of Consulting and Clinical Psychology*, **46**, 1246–57.

Hamilton, M. (1959) The assessment of anxiety states by rating. *British Journal of Medical Psychology*, **32**, 50–5.

Haynes, S.N., Falkin, S. and Sexton-Radek, K. (1989) Psychophysiological assessment in behaviour therapy. In G. Turpin (ed.), *Handbook of Clinical Psychophysiology*, John Wiley, Chichester.

Hedlund, J.L. and Vieweg, B.W. (1980) The Brief Psychiatric Rating Scale: A comprehensive review. *Journal of Operational Psychiatry*, **11**, 48–65.

Hicks, J.A. and Jenkins, J.G. (1988) The measurement of preoperative anxiety. *Journal of Royal Society of Medicine*, **81**, 517–19.

Hodgson, R. and Rackman, S.J. (1974) Desynchrony in measures of fear. *Behaviour Research and Therapy*, **12**, 319–326.

Hugdahl, K. (1989) Simple phobias. In G. Turpin (ed.), *Handbook of Clinical Psychophysiology*, John Wiley, Chichester.

Kaloupek, D.G. and Levis, D.J. (1983) Issues in the assessment of fear: response concordance and prediction of avoidance behavior. *Journal of Behavioral Assessment*, **5**, 239–260.

Kazdin, A. (1977) Assessing the clinical or applied importance of behavior change through social validation. *Behavior Modification*, **1**, 427–52.

Kimura, P. (1967) Functional asymmetry of the brain in dichotic listening. *Cortex*, **3**, 163–78.

Lang, P.J. (1968) Fear reduction and fear behavior: problems in treating a construct. In J.M. Schlien (ed.) *Research in Psychotherapy*. American Psychological Association, Washington DC.

Lang, P.J. (1985) The cognitive psychophysiology of emotion: fear and anxiety. In A.H. Tuma and J. Maser (eds), *Anxiety and the Anxiety Disorders*, Lawrence Erlbaum, Hillsdale, NJ.

Lewis, A. (1970) The ambiguous word 'anxiety'. *International Journal of Psychiatry*, **9**, 62–79.

McNair, D., Lorr, M. and Droppleman, L. (1987) *The Profile of Mood States*, NFER-Nelson, Windsor.

Margraf, J., Taylor, B., Ehlers, A., Roth, W.T. and Agras, S.W. (1987) Panic attacks in the natural environment. *The Journal of Nervous and Mental Disease*, **175**, 558–65.

Marks, I.M. and Mathews, A.M. (1979) Brief standard self-rating scale for phobic patients. *Behaviour Research and Therapy*, **17**, 263–7.

Martin, B. (1961) The assessment of anxiety by physiological and behavioral measures. *Psychological Bulletin*, **58**, 234–55.

Martin, I. and Venables, P.H. (1980) *Techniques in Psychophysiology*, John Wiley, Chichester.

Melamed, B.G. and Siegel, L.J. (1975) Reduction of anxiety in children facing hospitalization and surgery by use of filmed modelling. *Journal of Consulting and Clinical Psychology*, **43**, 511–21.

Michelson, L., Mavissakalian, M. and Marchione, K. (1985) Cognitive and behavioral treatments of agoraphobia: clinical, behavioral and psychophysiological outcomes. *Journal of Consulting and Clinical Psychology*, **53**, 913–25.

Nay, W.R. (1986) Analogue measures. In A.R. Ciminero, K.S. Calhoun and H.E. Adams (eds), *Handbook of Behavioral Assessment*, John Wiley, New York.

Neitzel, M.T., Bernstein, D.A. and Russell, R.L. (1988) Assessment of anxiety and fear. In A.S. Bellack and M. Hersen (eds), *Behavioral Assessment: A Practical Handbook*, pp. 280–312, Pergamon Press, New York.

Ost, L. (1989) Panic disorder, agoraphobia, and social phobia. In G. Turpin (ed.), *Handbook of Clinical Psychophysiology*, John Wiley, Chichester.

Overall, J.E. and Gorham, D.R. (1962) The Brief Psychiatric Rating Scale. *Psychological Reports*, **10**, 799–812.

Parks, C.W. and Hollon, S.D. (1988) Cognitive assessment. In A.S. Bellack and M. Hersen (eds), *Behavioral Assessment: A Practical Handbook*, Pergamon Press, New York.

Paul, G.L. (1966) *Insight vs Desensitization in Psychotherapy*, Stanford University Press, Stanford, CA.

Peterson, D.A. and Levis, D.J. (1985) The assessment of bodily injury fears via the behavioral avoidance slide test. *Behavioral Assessment*, **7**, 173–184.

Peterson, L. (1984) A brief methodological comment on possible inaccuracies induced by multimodal measurement analysis and reporting. *Journal of Behavioral Medicine*, **7**, 307–313.

Poppen, R. (1988) *Behavioral Relaxation Training and Assessment*, Pergamon Press, New York.

Rachman, S.J. and Hodgson, R. (1974) Synchrony and desynchrony in fear and avoidance. *Behaviour Research and Therapy*, **12**, 311–318.

Rowland, L.A. and Canavan, A.G.M. (1983) Is a B.A.T. therapeutic? *Behavioural Psychotherapy*, **11**, 139–46.

Sartory, G. (1989) Obsessional–compulsive disorder. In G. Turpin (ed.), *Handbook of Clinical Psychophysiology*, John Wiley, Chichester.

Sims, A.C.P. and Snaith, R.P. (1988) *Anxiety in Clinical Practice*, John Wiley, Chichester.

Snaith, R.P. and Taylor, C.M. (1985) Irritability: definition and associated factors. *British Journal of Psychiatry*, **147**, 127–36.

Snaith, R.P., Constantopoulos, A.A., Jardine, M.Y. and McGuffin, P. (1978) A clinical scale for the self-assessment of irritability, anxiety and depression. *British Journal of Psychiatry*, **132**, 164–71.

Snaith, R.P., Baugh, S.J., Clayden, A.D., Hussain, A. and Sipple, M.A. (1982) The Clinical Anxiety Scale: an instrument derived from the Hamilton Anxiety Scale. *British Journal of Psychiatry*, **141**, 518–23.

Snaith, R.P., Harrop, F.M., Newby, D.A. and Teale, C. (1986) Grade scores of the Montgomery–Asberg Depression and the Clinical Anxiety Scales. *British Journal of Psychiatry*, **148**, 599–601.

Spielberger, C.D., Gorsuch, R. and Lushene, R.E. (1987a) *The State–Trait Anxiety Inventory*, NFER-Nelson, Windsor.

Spielberger, C.D., Edwards, C.D., Mantoun, J. and Lushene, R.E. (1987b) *The Children's State–Trait Anxiety Inventory*, NFER–Nelson, Windsor.

Steptoe, A. (1987) The assessment of sympathetic nervous function in human stress research. *Journal of Psychosomatic Research*, **31**, 141–52.

Stern, R.M., Ray, W.J. and Davis, C.M. (1980) *Psychophysiological Recording*, Oxford University Press, New York.

Stroop, J.R. (1935) Studies of interference in serial verbal reactions. *Journal of Experimental Psychology*, **18**, 643–62.

Taylor, J.A. (1953) A personality scale of manifest anxiety. *Journal of Abnormal and Social Psychology*, **48**, 285–90.

Turpin, G. (1985) Ambulatory psychophysiological monitoring: techniques and applications. In D. Papakostopoulos, F. Butler and I. Martin (eds), *Clinical and Experimental Neuropsychophysiology*, Croom Helm, London.

Turpin, G. (1989) *Handbook of Clinical Psychophysiology*, John Wiley, Chichester.

Turpin, G. (in press). Application of psychophysiology to clinical psychiatry. *British Journal of Hospital Medicine.*

Usdin, E. and Hanin, I. (1982) *Biological Markers in Psychiatry and Neurology*, Pergamon Press, Oxford.

van Zuuren, F.J. (1988) The Fear Questionnaire. Some data on validity, reliability and layout. *British Journal of Psychiatry*, **153**, 659–62.

Watts, F.N. (1986) Cognitive processing in phobias. *Behavioural Psychotherapy*, **14**, 295–301.

Williams, J.M.G., Watts, F.N., McCleod, C. and Mathews, A. (1988) *Cognitive Psychology and Emotional Disorders*, John Wiley, Chichester.

Wing, J.K., Cooper, J.E. and Sartorius, N. (1974) *The Measurement and Classification of Psychiatric Symptoms*, Cambridge University Press, Cambridge.

Wolpe, J. and Lange, P. (1987) *Fear Survey Schedule*, NFER-Nelson, Windsor.

Zahn, T.P. (1986) Psychophysiological approaches to psychopathology. In M.G.H. Coles, E. Donchin and S.W. Porges (eds), *Psychophysiology: Systems, Processes and Applications*, Guilford Press, New York.,

Zigmond, A.S. and Snaith, R.P. (1983) The Hospital Anxiety and Depression Scale. *Acta Psychiatrica Scandinavica*, **67**, 361–70.

Zung, W. (1965) A self-rating depression scale. *Archives of General Psychiatry*, **12**, 63–70.

Zung, W. (1971) A rating instrument for anxiety disorders. *Psychosomatics*, **12**, 271–9.

Chapter 5

Obsessions, Compulsions and Intrusive Cognitions

PAUL M. SALKOVSKIS

CLINICAL AND NON-CLINICAL INTRUSIVE COGNITIONS

Intrusive cognitions are mental events which are perceived as interrupting a person's stream of consciousness by capturing the focus of attention. These cognitive events can take the form of 'verbal' thoughts, images or impulses or some combination of the three. In instances where a previous traumatic event has been prominent there may be an obvious intrinsic emotional element to the intrusion. It may be relevant in conditions like post-traumatic stress disorder to consider this phenomenon as intrusive *affect*. However, negative emotional tone is not an invariant feature of intrusive cognitions, which can be associated with positive affect, negative affect or no affect at all. Furthermore, rather than being the hallmark of psychopathology, intrusive cognitions commonly occur in both clinical and non-clinical populations.

Where problems do arise from these intrusive cognitions, these are a result of the discomfort and impairment associated with frequently occurring negatively evaluated intrusions. The negative impact of intrusions probably results from a combination of factors, including: (1) the way in which the occurrence and content of intrusions are evaluated, (2) because of the context in which they occur and (3) because of associated behavioural reactions (Salkovskis, 1989c). At their most intrusive and distressing, such cognitions are usually identified as clinical obsessional disorders, morbid preoccupations, and worry, and are prominent in generalized anxiety. However, as Rachman and Hodgson (1980) point out, many day-to-day cognitions are intrusive. Salkovskis (1989b) extends this argument by suggesting that the mechanisms governing the occurrence and persistence of clinical intrusive thoughts may be an integral part of normal problem-solving activity. Thus, although intrusiveness of cognitions *can* be a correlate of distress, there is evidence from non-clinical studies that intrusiveness is not sufficient to account for distress associated with such thoughts (England and Dickerson, 1988).

Measuring Human Problems. Edited by D.F. Peck and C.M. Shapiro

In the first part of this chapter a number of issues relevant to the investigation of intrusive cognitions and obsessions will be considered. The bulk of the specific measurement material then emphasizes the assessment of obsessive–compulsive problems. There are three reasons for this emphasis; first, work on measurement of obsessional phenomena is particularly well developed; second, because work on the measurement of obsessional phenomena and many of the measures themselves generalize to related areas and third, because obsessional disorders have a high prevalence in clinic settings and are especially disabling. In the latter part of the chapter some attention will be paid to the assessment of worry and morbid preoccupations, phenomena which have attracted an increasing amount of research attention. Techniques for measuring intrusive cognitions in non-clinical subjects will be considered. Work on non-clinical intrusions is relevant to research into the processes involved in intrusive thoughts experienced by patients with anxiety, depression and obsessional disorders. Finally, techniques from experimental psychology which may be of help in identifying psychological processes involved in the maintenance of intrusive phenomena are briefly considered.

ISSUES AFFECTING THE TYPES OF MEASURES USED

The study of intrusive cognitions is one of the widest and most complex areas of interest in abnormal psychology, impinging on almost all clinical problems and extending into broader non-clinical fields. Most work on intrusive cognitions has been carried out by researchers operating within the framework provided by theories which are behavioural (e.g. Marks, 1987), broadly cognitive (e.g. Reed, 1985) and cognitive–behavioural (e.g. Salkovskis, 1985, 1989c). There has been no recent psychodynamic work of value in this area. This emphasis is reflected by the discussion of measures below and the construction of the measures themselves.

Fuller accounts of the wide range of theoretical issues involved in the conceptualization of obsessive–compulsive disorders can be found in Rachman and Hodgson (1980), Rachman (1981) and Beech (1974; especially Teasdale, Chapter 9). The present discussion is confined to issues most directly relevant to measurement of clinical and non-clinical intrusive cognitions. A useful review of factors affecting the *validity* of measures of cognition has been provided by D.A. Clark (1988). Although Clark's review is not intended to address directly the issue of intrusiveness, a number of measures overlap and the more general conclusions drawn in that review can be applied to the measurement of intrusive thoughts are described here.

Definitions: psychiatric versus psychological

Most studies of intrusive cognitions have concentrated on evaluating clinical problems within a diagnostic framework, within which intrusions are seen as one aspect of a generalized abnormality or clinical syndrome. The clinical definition of intrusive cognitions as an intrinsic part of the obsessional 'syndrome' is based on a problematic set of assumptions concerning the relative invariance of the association between a diverse range of phenomena (such as intrusiveness, discomfort and so on) as relatively imperfect manifestations of 'underlying pathology'; that is, of a specific disease. This type of categorical classification sidesteps key questions concerning the relationship *between* the complex phenomena which are observed in patients suffering from obsessional problems. It is also a major obstacle to the consideration of mechanisms which may be shared with other problems and relevant to normal psychological functioning.

In an attempt to deal with this difficulty, psychological researchers have conceptualized obsessional problems as the outcome of individual differences in psychological processes. For example, Reed (1985) regards the central problem in obsessional disorder as being the experience of compulsion; the disorder, he suggests, is a pathological extension of already exaggerated personality traits. Unfortunately, this work is based on a number of other assumptions which are not supported by the available data (see p. 110). A more promising development is the rapidly expanding body of research derived from the work of Rachman and de Silva (1978), who demonstrated a close similarity between clinical obsessions and normal intrusions. They argued that obsessional disorders could be regarded as an extreme variant of non-clinical intrusive cognitions and hence as the product of normal psychological processes. Obsessional disorders were hypothesized to be acquired as a result of learning experiences which interact with the individual's coping attempts (e.g. avoidance and escape behaviours). This approach arose from and has most in common with recent behavioural and cognitive–behavioural approaches to emotional disorders.

Psychological conceptualizations of obsessional problems and intrusive cognitions are much more demanding in terms of measurement than the psychiatric view of clinical syndromes. Thus, psychological approaches require the accurate description of a wide range of phenomena and their covariation across time. Such measures have to be meaningful across a range of intensities and individuals. Measurement of psychological processes not only allows the assessment of outcome but can also contribute to knowledge of functional relationships (i.e. causal or reciprocal relationships among different variables). On the other hand, psychiatric diagnosis only allows grouping of individuals with a number of symptoms to at least a minimum clinically judged 'threshold'. Diagnostic instruments like the Structured

Clinical Interview for DSM III-R (SCID) are most useful as a relatively reliable way of operationally defining severe clinical populations.

Automaticity and intrusions

When considering psychological aspects of cognition it is important to consider the role of voluntary as opposed to involuntary processing. While intrusive cognitions appear to represent a type of *automatic* processing of current concerns (Anderson, 1985; Salkovskis, 1989b), they are also subject to a surprising degree of cognitive control once they occur. For example, the reader is invited to direct effort towards suppressing any thoughts or images of giraffes. Immediately this is actively attempted, the majority will experience just such an image, as the effort at suppression has an activating effect (Wegner *et al.*, 1987). However, once the image has occurred, voluntary control may be readily exerted. Thus, with a little effort, the imaged giraffe can be made to bend and drink from a clear pool by the shrubs at its feet, straighten, then to turn and walk into the thick jungle behind it.

Although almost nothing is known about this type of interplay between controlled and automatic processing, increasing headway is being made in efforts to measure reliably intrusions and their behavioural correlates. Ultimately this should lead to clarification of this important interaction. The above example illustrates one of the major distinctions which is involved in the measurement and understanding of intrusions. That is, the difference between the involuntary occurrence of an intrusion and the reactions to it (including overt or covert neutralizing and efforts to suppress the cognition) which are under some degree of voluntary control. The paradoxical effect of suppression is an important phenomenon, demonstrating the potential interplay between controlled and automatic processing.

Matching the assessment to the purpose of the investigation

There are two main reasons for the assessment of intrusive cognitions; these correspond to descriptive or clinical measurement and measurements which are intended to investigate psychological processes. For example, as part of research into clinical outcome, researchers may wish to assess the extent of impairment and subsequent improvement in obsessional disorders. To do this, they would take repeated measures of the frequency, duration, extent and severity of obsessional and compulsive phenomena, together with measures of the degree to which obsessional problems are associated with impairment of social and occupational functioning (see p. 102). In order to examine the mechanisms which might be involved in different treatments, measures of habituation rate across a series of standardized exposure sessions might be used (p. 105) together with ratings of the form of intrusive thoughts (e.g. ratings of acceptability, vividness, urge to neutralize and other measures of this type (p. 107)).

The importance of theory

The measurement of intrusive cognitions provides a bewilderingly large array of potential measures, several of which purport to measure almost identical constructs. It is, of course, possible to measure as many variables as possible in the hope of arriving at a useful conclusion. Apart from the practical difficulties (e.g. time spent by the subject completing assessments), this type of 'fishing expedition' seldom produces useful results. For example, finding a difference between two groups on 0–8 ratings of distress but *not* on a questionnaire using a series of True–False options also supposedly measuring distress presents the researcher with considerable difficulties in interpreting the results. It is also relatively easy to arrive at a *post hoc* explanation of a complex pattern of positive and negative results. However, the likelihood of replicating such a pattern is small for both statistical and theoretical reasons. Advances in understanding are more likely to be made if investigators have thought in advance what their hypotheses are, and designed the investigation around these. Studies carried out in this way are more likely to result in refinements (or refutation) of the original hypotheses and generate a series of further studies which clarify key processes. A particularly good example is provided by Roper *et al.* (1973) and Roper and Rachman (1975). Rachman and his colleagues reported data which supported predictions derived from a behavioural hypothesis of obsessional disorder, and demonstrated that Beech's (1974) adverse mood and doubting hypothesis was not consistent with the results of preventing obsessional behaviour. This research also illustrates the way in which research hypotheses have much in common with clinical conceptualizations or formulations used to devise treatment programmes for individual patients.

The ability of a chosen measure to answer the question under investigation also has to be considered. For example, an unreliable measure cannot provide valid results; if a measure of dysfunction does not discriminate between non-clinical and clinical subjects, it is unlikely to discriminate between clinical subgroups. Hypotheses driving a particular investigation do not have to be complex, and can be extremely pragmatic (e.g. 'treatment A produces more generalized improvement of obsessional problems than treatment B'). Often, careful choice of dependent variables can result in a refinement of the hypothesis itself (for example, by the use of subscales measuring different aspects of a construct). Thus, the choice of measures should be based on consideration of the extent to which a particular measure reflects the propositions of the guiding hypothesis. In the immediately preceding example of a clinical hypothesis, the measures required would be of obsessionality and of generalization. However, which measures of obsessionality? What does the treatment actually do? What, therefore, are the specific treatment effects of interest? When generalization is considered, is this to all areas, or just to social and occupational adjustment? Is there any reason to suppose the experimental treatment will have effects on these and other aspects? Why?

Covariation and functional relationships

Rachman and Hodgson (1974) highlighted the fact that there are often systematic differences between different measures in any given individual, and that such *desynchrony* can reflect important functional relationships rather than simply being manifestations of measurement error (cf. Lang's, 1979, description of multiple-response systems). For example, one obsessional patient might report an anxiety rating of 0 on a 0–100 scale during the hour-long period he scrubs his hands, while another may experience intense discomfort (rated at 90) on the same scale while not washing at all. Rachman and Hodgson (1974) describe the importance of evaluating synchrony and desynchrony both as part of the assessment of clinical problems and as a dimension of change, particularly over the course of treatment (see Figure 5.2). Although three dimensions or systems are commonly described (i.e. cognitive/emotional, behaviour and subjective), it is clear that this is an artificially low number reflecting broad aggregations of responses rather than fixed relationships reflecting perfect correlations. In particular, the cognitive/affective dimension can be readily divided into a number of dimensions which are as loosely coupled as the three major divisions initially emphasized. For example, the evaluation of senselessness associated with a particular intrusive thought may vary independently of distress at times and yet be closely correlated at other times. Much recent research has been devoted to attempts to investigate a smaller number of key dimensions. Rachman and Hodgson (1980) summarize this work; particularly promising are investigations of the desynchrony between manifest compulsive behaviour, urge to engage in compulsive behaviour and subjective discomfort. Investigators need to bear in mind the importance of formulating hypotheses in terms of *interactions* between different response systems, and the associated need to measure a range of phenomena. This approach is quite different from the more traditional idea that differences between response systems are facets of some single underlying unitary process, modified only by extraneous error. Instead, the interaction between systems can be regarded as the basis for the maintenance of the problem itself.

OBSESSIONAL DISORDERS

The measurement of obsessions and compulsions has long been an important clinical concern, particularly because of difficulties in defining the boundaries between obsessions and other clinical phenomena such as delusions, morbid preoccupations, worry and depressed and anxious thoughts. The area is further complicated by the observation that obsessional thoughts are commonplace among normal subjects, with up to 90 per cent of non-clinical subjects reporting distressing and unwanted intrusive thoughts, the content of which do not differ from those reported by clinical subjects (Rachman and de Silva, 1978; Salkovskis and Harrison, 1984).

General considerations in the assessment of obsessional disorders

Obsessional patients, almost by definition, tend to regard their thoughts as repugnant and unacceptable. These negative appraisals are often more extreme than those made by patients with other problems. For example, it has, indeed, been demonstrated that people suffering from obsessional problems are unusually sensitive to ideas of criticism and blame (Turner, *et al.*, 1979). The more negative the patient's appraisal of his or her own thinking, the more likely it is that he or she will under-report the extent of symptoms or even fail to report key problems. Obsessional patients often believe that the thoughts reveal that they are unpleasant people, and that others (including their therapist) would criticize or reject them, or believe them to be insane. The obsessional thoughts may concern socially embarrassing topics (e.g. contamination by faeces, urine or semen). Some patients fear that talking about the obsession may make it worse or more real, or even make them act out the thoughts. There may also be specific fears, such as the obsession being a sign of schizophrenia (perhaps implying immediate hospitalization against their will when revealed to the therapist). When the thoughts or impulses concern violence or other illegal or morally repugnant acts, patients may worry that the assessor will have them arrested. Very severe problems (such as extensive compulsive behaviour) can be associated with shame about the extent to which their obsessions are out of control, particularly as most patients regard obsessional thoughts as intrinsically senseless. In chronic cases, the assessment and formulation are made more difficult by the habitual ('over-learned') nature of the behaviours.

These problems mean that great sensitivity is required in assessment, particularly in patients who have not been assessed previously. Ways of overcoming the problems described above in the course of the clinical interview are discussed in detail in Salkovskis and Kirk (1989). Often, patients' beliefs in the acceptability of their problem to the assessor can be modified by the assessor demonstrating an awareness of these problems in a matter-of-fact way. The message which is conveyed is 'OK, yes, I understand your worries about this. These are obsessional thoughts, I've dealt with them before lots of times, and they are not even slightly shocking to me. It's common both to have the thoughts and the worries associated with them.' In chronic cases, compulsive behaviour and avoidance can become so extensive that the patient may have ceased to be aware of the underlying pattern of thinking and voluntary behaviours which pre-empt and mask obsessional thoughts, impulses and images. Behaviour tests (see p. 108) in which avoidance or compulsive behaviour is prevented and/or direct observation in the patient's normal environment will be required to provide a clearer assessment.

However, many of these solutions may not be open to researchers. One obvious way in which accurate reporting can be encouraged in a research setting is to guarantee anonymity. Some of the techniques used in clinical interviews can be extended to questionnaires or to survey studies. For example, in the study by Salkovskis and Harrison (1984), the preamble to the questionnaire identifies the general area of study and attempts to allay possible fears which may affect the way a subject reports their experience (see the top of Figure 5.3).

Diagnostic issues

Clinical obsessional problems have been divided into obsessional or 'anankastic' personality, obsessive–compulsive disorder, and obsessions without overt rituals (often described as ruminations). Although obsessional personality disorder has been described by some authors as a predisposing factor for the development of obsessive–compulsive disorder (Reed, 1985), there is no evidence for this suggestion and some against it (Rachman and Hodgson, 1980; see also below, p. 110). Given this, and the differences between the way in which obsessional symptoms and personality are defined, it seems most sensible to consider these problems separately. The similarities may have more to do with superficial characteristics of behaviour rather than with any similarity in the psychological processes involved. The diagnosis of obsessional disorder is probably most reliably made on the basis of DSM III R criteria assessed using the Structured Clinical Interview for DSM III R (SCID III R). Other diagnostic interviews (such as the Present State Examination (Wing *et al.*, 1974)) include insufficient detail to constitute a useful measure of obsessional problems. The shortcomings of diagnostic interviewing with obsessional problems are vividly highlighted by the great discordance between data from screening and subsequent validatory interviews in the recent large-scale Epidemiologic Catchment Area Study (Karno *et al.*, 1988).

Compared to the obsessional disorder/personality distinction, the case for differentiating between obsessive–compulsive problems and obsessions without overt rituals is less convincing. The presence of motor rituals is probably a superficial difference; patients with 'ruminations' use thought rituals in a way similar to those with overt rituals. Covert ritualizing (referred to here as 'neutralizing') or attempts at deliberate thought suppression probably serve an identical function to overt compulsive behaviour (Salkovskis and Westbrook, 1989).

On clinical and theoretical grounds, a possible distinction between obsessive–compulsive patients whose ritualizing takes the form of excessive washing as opposed to those who repeatedly check has been suggested (Rachman, 1978). Although the functional significance and the clinical utility of this distinction have yet to be fully established, there are enough data to suggest that it reflects an important phenomenon (Steketee *et al.*, 1985). The same type of distinction can also be made in covert neutralizing, where patients can be divided into those who mentally check and those who aim for some kind of cognitive restitution or 'putting right' (i.e. undoing).

Validation of measures

The validation of clinical measures of obsessive–compulsive disorders is problematic because of the low incidence of the clinical condition. Studies validating clinical measures usually have to rely on small sample sizes. The low incidence contrasts with the impact of the disorder on clinical practice. Obsessions tend to be particularly severe and treatment-refractory, and therefore over-represented in the clinic. Furthermore, compared to other disorders an unusually high proportion of patients have already been subjected to several clinical assessments and have undergone unsuccessful treatment programmes, which may have distorted the sample characteristics and the responses themselves. It is therefore not surprising that several measures in common use have not been fully validated.

Obsessional phenomena

Several authors have described the phenomena occurring in obsessional disorders as a sequence (Rachman, 1978; Salkovskis, 1985; de Silva, 1987; Salkovskis and Kirk, 1989). De Silva (1986) identifies key issues with respect to obsessional images; similar specific considerations probably apply to obsessional urges. The components of obsessional experience described by these authors can be summarized as in the sequence below. Some elements may occur simultaneously and not all invariably occur.

Triggers (internal or external)
Avoidance (passive and active)
Intrusion (thought, image, urge)
Appraisal (acceptability, significance/salience, etc.)
Discomfort (anxiety, depression, discomfort)
Physiological arousal (increased heart rate, skin conductance, etc.)
Urges to neutralize, suppress, or distract from the intrusion
Overt neutralizing (compulsive) behaviour (washing, checking)
Covert neutralizing (mental rituals) (restitution, mental checking)
Changes in discomfort (increases or decreases)
Changes in urge to neutralize, etc. (increases or decreases)

No single assessment package includes measures of all of these aspects. As outlined above, the investigator needs to tailor the measures to the issues being examined. The requirements for investigation of outcome, therapy process and the processes involved in the maintenance of a problem usually differ considerably. The formulation of clearly defined and specific hypotheses driving an investigation again provides the key to the choice of measures.

The clinical interview

The clinical interview for obsessional disorders focuses on eliciting a description of the form and content of the obsession itself, and on factors which may be maintaining the obsession and associated discomfort. (See Salkovskis and Kirk, 1989, and Turner and Beidel, 1988, for full accounts of the clinical approach to interview and behavioural assessment for treatment; also Salkovskis, 1989a, for an outline of factors more specific to cognitive therapy.) Clearly, assessment must also take into account the range of information required in a more general behavioural interview; these data are not specific to obsessional disorders, and are not dealt with here (see Kirk, 1989, for a detailed description of behavioural assessment). Specific maintaining factors which are emphasized in the assessment of obsessions include relation to mood state and behaviours which patients use either to prevent them from being exposed to their obsession (avoidant behaviours) and/or behaviours which terminate exposure once it has occurred. The list of phenomena above and on p. 107 provides a guide to the scope of clinical assessment of obsessional problems.

Questionnaire measures

Questionnaire measures are generally designed to provide indices of particular dimensions of obsessional experience, such as frequency of occurrence and degree of distress, and to provide a description of the range of experience. Most of the clinical scales were initially developed to provide measures of outcome. Many questionnaire measures of OCD are symptom checklists or the equivalent, and generally enquire about the relative severity or frequency of obsessive and compulsive behaviours. These may be based on clinical experience of the disorder (e.g. Steketee and Foa, 1985) or on more detailed psychometric studies of obsessional patients (e.g. Hodgson and Rachman, 1978). The most commonly used examples are listed in Table 5.1. One of the most elusive aspects of measurement is content; interview and checklist approaches have been used (e.g. the list of content areas in Table 5.3). A small number of studies have systematically dealt with content of obsessions (Akhtar *et al.*, 1975; Stern and Cobb, 1978).

Clinical rating scales and self-monitoring

Clinical rating scales are widely used with obsessional subjects, either as observer or self-ratings. The best validated are (1) fear-thermometer (0–100) scales as described by Wolpe (1982) and others (e.g. de Silva, 1987; Salkovskis and Kirk, 1989), and (2) 0–8 scales. The scale used at the foot of Figure 5.2 illustrates the way 0–100 scales are commonly represented; note that the anchors are at either end. Such scales are often referred to as *visual analogue scales*. Sometimes no intermediate numbers are displayed, and the position the rater marks on the line (usually of 10 cm total length) is used as the measure. The advantage of intermediate numerical points lies in the possibility of verbal ratings and in general ease of use and scoring. The 0–8 Likert-type scales used by, for example, Rachman *et al.* (1973), Marks (1986) and others have frequently been employed to assess global outcome. An example of this type of scale from our clinic at the Warneford Hospital in Oxford is shown in Figure 5.1.* The rating shown is completed by the patient; similar ratings, with slight changes in the wording, can be completed by the therapist, observers blind to the patients' treatments, or by a lay informant. In the latter instance, it is also helpful to obtain ratings from the relative or friend concerning how well he or she knows the patients' problems, how much day-to-day contact he or she has and in what settings. This information helps in the validation of such ratings.

* The author is grateful to David Westbrook and Joan Kirk who helped in the development of these scales.

Table 5.1. Principal questionnaire measures of obsessional problems.

Leyton Obsessional Inventory (Cooper, 1970)
A 69-item card sort, used to derive scores on (1) symptoms, (2) trait, (3) resistance, (4) interference. It shows good discrimination between obsessives and comparison groups. However, it tends to be time consuming and has an awkward 'postbox' format. It also emphasizes checking rituals and is not a good measure of washing rituals and intrusive thoughts.

Lynfield Obsessional/compulsive Questionnaire (Allen and Tune, 1975)
A short (20-item) self-administered questionnaire version of the Leyton, with added items on ruminations. Its reliability is similar to that of the Leyton.

Compulsive Activity Checklist (Marks *et al.*, 1977; Cottraux *et al.*, 1987)
A 39-item checklist rating impairment arising from ritualizing on daily activities. High scores can be obtained as a result of repetition, slowness or avoidance. The checklist in its present form fails to distinguish among these factors.

Maudsley Obsessive Compulsive Inventory (Hodgson and Rachman, 1978)
A 30-item questionnaire requiring true/false responses yielding a total score, but also subdivided on the basis of factor analysis into checking, slowness/repetition, doubting/conscientiousness and washing subscales. The scale was explicitly designed to measure obsessional ritualizing, and has only two items directly relevant to obsessional thoughts. There are difficulties with some items which involve slightly cumbersome double negatives. This is best dealt with by modifying these items to positives and altering scoring appropriately (Rachman, personal communication). The test–retest reliability of the MOCI is particularly good (r = 0.89). A scoring key is given as an appendix in Rachman and Hodgson (1980).

Cues for Urges to Ritualize Inventory (Steketee and Foa, 1985)
An 18-item true–false questionnaire encompassing cues for urges to ritualize as well as some limited aspects of content of obsessions and feared consequences.

Padua Inventory (Sanavio, 1988)
A 60-item questionnaire using 5-point ratings, designed to evaluate the range of clinical obsessions and compulsions. A factor analysis was used to derive four main factors: impaired control over mental activities; contamination-related items; checking behaviours; and urges and worries of losing control. Reliabilities are good, and good discrimination is found for obsessional and other 'neurotic' disorders.

Rating scales can be used either as assessments of general clinical state or of moment-by-moment changes in discomfort, urges to ritualize and so on. An important application is in the assessment of anxiety changes in the course of behaviour tests and/or prolonged exposure. This type of recording, employing repeated multiple measures over time, is also required if the investigator wishes to assess synchrony and desynchrony. Figure 5.2 shows the way that such measurements were used in the course of treatment of a patient suffering from obsessional ruminations. As part of treatment, the patient listened over headphones to his own voice presenting his ruminative thoughts recorded on a loop tape (as described in Salkovskis and Westbrook, 1989). Discomfort and urge to neutralize were noted on each occurrence of the intrusion (at the same time as implementing response-prevention).

Name . . . . Date . . . .

1: DESCRIPTION

Please write down a brief description of the most troublesome thoughts, images or impulses. Maximum *two* thoughts, from different content areas:

THOUGHT A . . . .

THOUGHT B . . . .

2: THOUGHT RATINGS

Please rate the thoughts on each of the following scales, according to how they have been IN THE PAST WEEK. Each scale should be rated separately for 'Thought A', 'Thought B' and 'All problem thoughts':

(a) Discomfort when this thought occurs is:

0	1	2	3	4	5	6	7	8
Absent		Slight		Definite		Marked		Extreme

A........

B........

All........

(b) How much does this thought interfere with your life?

0	1	2	3	4	5	6	7	8
Not at all		Slight		Definite		Marked		Extreme

A........

B........

All........

(c) Please estimate how long each day you are thinking the thought (i.e. it is in the front of your mind):

A........hours.......minutes

B........hours.......minutes

All........hours........minutes

(d) Please estimate how long each day the thought is 'in the back of your mind':

A........hours.......minutes

B........hours.......minutes

All........hours........minutes

(e) Please estimate about how many times per day you have these thoughts:

A........hours.......minutes

B........hours.......minutes

All........hours........minutes

Figure 5.1

(*continued overleaf*)

Figure 5.1 (*continued*)

3: GENERAL RATINGS

Please use the following scales to rate how far the problem has impaired other areas of your life IN THE PAST WEEK, taking all the problem thoughts into account:

(a) Because of the problem, my ability to WORK is impaired:

0	1	2	3	4	5	6	7	8	All........
Not at all		Slightly		Definitely		Markedly		Very severely I cannot work	

(b) Because of the problem, HOME MANAGEMENT (cleaning, tidying, shopping, cooking, looking after home or children, paying bills, etc.) is impaired:

0	1	2	3	4	5	6	7	8	All........
Not at all		Slightly		Definitely		Markedly		Very severely I cannot do it	

(c) Because of the problem, my SOCIAL LEISURE ACTIVITIES (*with other people*, e.g. parties, pubs, clubs, outings, visits, dating, home entertainment, etc.) are impaired:

0	1	2	3	4	5	6	7	8	All........
Not at all		Slightly		Definitely		Markedly		Very severely I cannot do it	

(d) Because of the problem, my PRIVATE LEISURE ACTIVITIES (*done alone*, e.g. reading, gardening, collecting, sewing, walking alone, etc.) are impaired:

0	1	2	3	4	5	6	7	8	All........
Not at all		Slightly		Definitely		Markedly		Very severely I cannot do it	

(e) Because of the problem, my SEXUAL RELATIONSHIP (enjoyment of sex, frequency of sexual activity, etc.) is impaired:

0	1	2	3	4	5	6	7	8	All........
Not at all		Slightly		Definitely		Markedly		Very severely I cannot enjoy it at all	

(f) Because of the problem, my GENERAL RELATIONSHIP WITH MY PARTNER (e.g. affectionate feelings, number of arguments, enjoying activities together, etc.) is impaired:

0	1	2	3	4	5	6	7	8	All........
Not at all		Slightly		Definitely		Markedly		Very severely I cannot enjoy it at all	

Figure 5.1 Client's ratings.

Two sessions are depicted in Figure 5.2. The chart illustrated could be completed by the patient listening to the tape at home, or drawn up by the assessor from verbal ratings in response to the presentation of a card. Table 5.2 illustrates a number of ways in which the data from Figure 5.2 can be summarized.

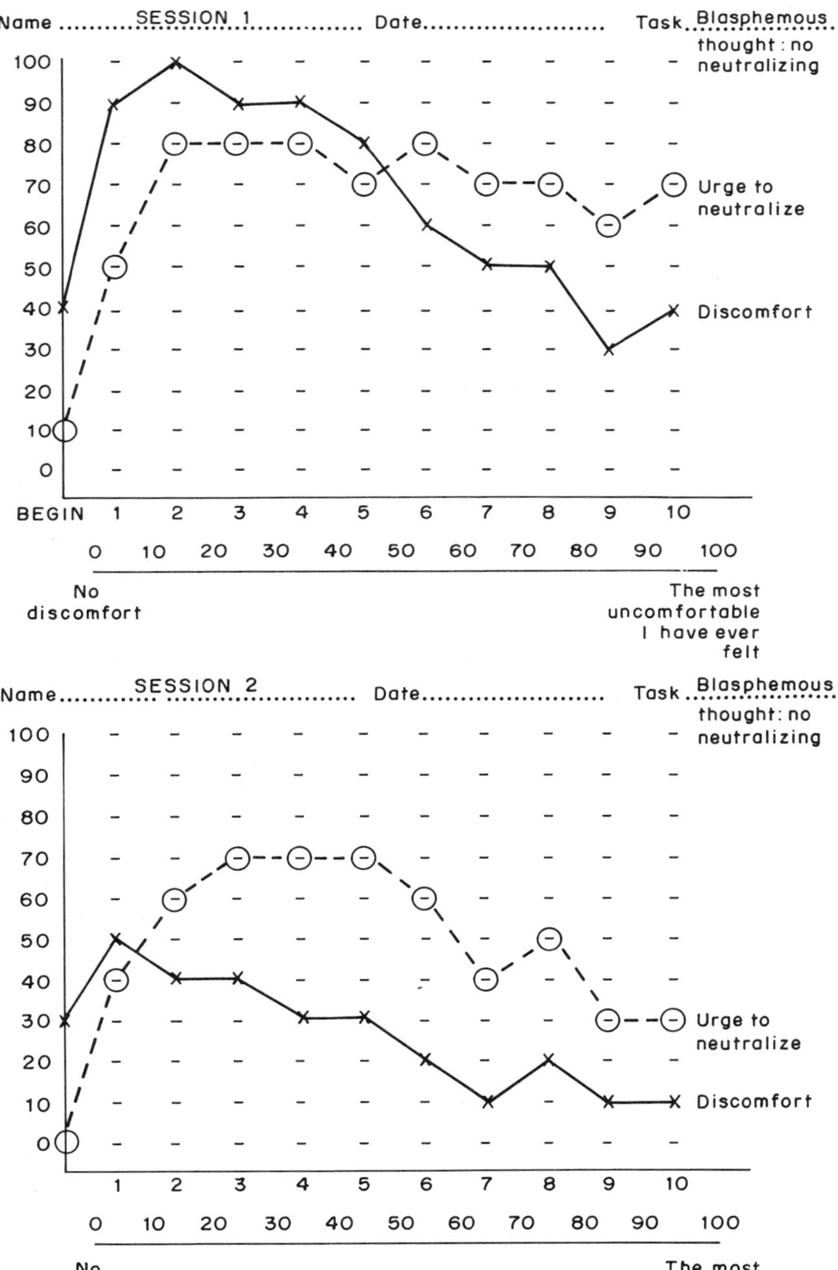
Name SESSION 1 Date
Task Blasphemous thought : no neutralizing
100
90
80
70
60
50
40
30
20
10
0
BEGIN 1 2 3 4 5 6 7 8 9 10
Urge to neutralize
Discomfort
0 10 20 30 40 50 60 70 80 90 100
No discomfort
The most uncomfortable I have ever felt
Name SESSION 2 Date
Task Blasphemous thought: no neutralizing
100
90
80
70
60
50
40
30
20
10
0
1 2 3 4 5 6 7 8 9 10
Urge to neutralize
Discomfort
0 10 20 30 40 50 60 70 80 90 100
No discomfort
The most uncomfortable I have ever felt

Figure 5.2

Table 5.2 Within and between session changes in response to repeated audiotaped exposure to a blasphemous thought (with concurrent response prevention).

	Discomfort rating			Urge to neutralize		
	Session 1		Session 2	Session 1		Session 2
Peak	100		50	80		70
Between session change		–50			–10	
Response	60		20	70		70
Between session change		–40			0	
Presentations to 50% reduction	6		2	no		9
Between session change		–4			–1 minimum	

Note that figures other than those listed in the table can be derived from the same data. Examples might be: initial ratings, number of presentations to peak rating, difference between point 10 in session 1 and point 1 in session 2, and so on. Once again, the choice of measures used would depend on the purpose of the investigation. Discomfort and urge to neutralize are the variables which have been selected here; other measures could equally have been used, such as the vividness or acceptability of the thought, etc. The timing of ratings can be varied (e.g. every third or tenth presentation or at specified time intervals, etc.).

Self-ratings can also include diary measures (see also the example in de Silva, 1987, p. 58). Variables relevant to process and outcome in obsessional problems and which could be measured are listed in Table 5.3.

This list is not exhaustive, again highlighting the need to tailor measures used to the purpose of the investigation being carried out. A number of other scales have been developed and used in one or two clinical studies (see, for example, Pato *et al.*, 1988). These, however, are of little utility as reliability and validity are dubious.

There are a number of adjuncts to self-monitoring which may be helpful; for example, relatively high-frequency events can be monitored by the use of golf counters which the patient carries with them throughout the day. Tick charts can be used in the same way. Timers and stop-watches are helpful where duration is a key variable, and the use of tape recorders (particularly portable dictation machines) can be useful. Mechanical devices such as those which measure approach to particular objects may be helpful, although these almost invariably require considerable technical back-up and can be prone to error.

Table 5.3 Characteristics of obsessional phenomena relevant to process and outcome.

Frequency of cognitions and neutralizing
Duration of cognitions and neutralizing
Repetitiveness of cognitions and neutralizing
Discomfort evoked
Resistance to cognitions and neutralizing (successful and attempted)
Avoidance
Provocation by internal/external stimuli
Intensity and vividness
Ease of dismissal
Intrusiveness (extent to which a cognition interrupts ongoing mental activity)
Acceptability of thoughts and neutralizing to self and to other people
Relationship to anxiety, depression, happiness, anger
Perceived senselessness of cognitions and neutralizing
Ego syntonicity/dystonicity (i.e. alienness)
Actual content:
- Contamination
- Physical violence to self or other, by self or others
- Death
- Accidental harm
- Illness
- Socially unacceptable behaviour
- Sex
- Religion
- Orderliness
- Nonsense
- (See Salkovskis and Kirk, 1989, for examples of content areas)

Consequences of obsessional phenomena:
Associated avoidance
Urges to distract from the obsession
Interference with daily activities
Impairment of: work; home management; social life; leisure; activities; intimate relationships

Observer ratings

Other than 0–8 ratings of the type already described, formal observer ratings are seldom used in obsessional disorders. However, in clinical practice, *ad hoc* ratings or frequency counts by relatives are often used, and therapists sometimes employ direct observation at home or work as part of their assessment (see Salkovskis and Kirk, 1989, for a more comprehensive description of such clinical procedures). Video or audio recording facilities can be helpful and can be combined with the use of independent or blind raters to derive observational scores. This generally means that investigators devise and assess the reliability of operationally defined scoring schemes according to the purposes to which they wish to put the assessment.

Problems with self- and observer ratings

There are a number of problems in self-ratings which are particularly prominent in obsessional problems. Reactivity (see Chapter 7) is probably stronger for self-monitoring of thoughts than almost any other measured variable. This is not surprising, as illustrated in the example on p. 94. Focus on a particular type of thought tends to provoke its occurrence. Sometimes, self-monitoring and self-recording can be (or become) an intrinsic part of obsessional ritualizing, or can themselves provoke ritualizing. Thus, the care with which obsessional patients keep records can become a disadvantage when record keeping becomes a ritual itself (see also Rosenberg and Upper, 1983). Patients can begin to doubt the accuracy of their records, check them, etc. thus biasing the measures. The prospect of keeping records on record keeping is not one to be encouraged!

The presence of an observer can have an impact on obsessional patients' anxiety in two quite different ways. Roper and Rachman (1975) found that less discomfort was induced by provocation of checking rituals when in the presence of a therapist. This is obviously an important consideration, particularly as it is not known whether the impact of an observer on ritualizing changes over time. Another effect can be an increase in anxiety and reduction in ritualizing behaviour, occurring as a result of being under scrutiny (see also p. 97).

Behavioural measures

A range of behavioural measures can be used, often combined with some form of self-rating or self-monitoring. One of the most common behavioural measures is the behavioural avoidance test. As with phobias, there are two ways in which the behaviour test can be carried out:

(1) As a particularly difficult (anxiety-provoking) task which is unlikely to be possible for the patient to complete before treatment, but which might be possible at the end of treatment. The task is subdivided into readily defined and replicable steps (often referred to as a *Behavioural Avoidance Test*); or
(2) As a task which all patients would be able to complete at the beginning of treatment, but which would be expected to provoke considerable anxiety, again divided into steps (often referred to as a *Behaviour Test*).

In the latter instance, it is likely that both the eventual level of exposure involved in the Behavior Test and the intermediate steps will vary considerably from one individual to another, depending on the severity of a particular patient's problem. Both types of behaviour test are repeated on subsequent assessments in the same form as used in the pre-treatment test. In both instances, ratings of anxiety, changes in urges to neutralize, etc. are recorded as required. However, in the first type of test the main measure is the number of steps completed, while the second yields anxiety ratings for each step which can be used to index change.

Some of the anxiety ratings in the first type of test will also allow the measurement of change, but in later steps the number of individuals from whom ratings are available will vary as a function of individual differences in avoidance, thus invalidating any comparison. It can be difficult to standardize behaviour tests across subjects, so individually designed tasks are used. For example, the contaminant or the thing to be left unchecked is not specified, but the level of contact is. An example of the use of such a test is illustrated in Salkovskis and Kirk (1989, pp. 143–5). Unlike phobias, simply asking the patient to approach a feared object or perform a particular activity is not a sufficient definition of the task. It must also be specified whether the patient is to be allowed to engage in neutralizing behaviour (or if this is itself to be a measure, and therefore to be recorded). A detailed protocol for carrying out such a behaviour test can be found in Steketee and Foa (1985). The two styles of behaviour test have different advantages and disadvantages according to the purpose of the investigation being carried out. Behavioural tests can be carried out as contrived tasks in the laboratory or given as homework to be done between sessions.

Behavioural by-products

In some instances, it is possible to collect reliable and easily recorded information from behavioural by-products. Thus, when a patient uses large amounts of soap or toilet paper, it is possible to measure the extent of the problem by evaluating changes in the amounts purchased. With such indirect measures, it is obviously important to be wary of any other influences on the measure itself (e.g. a change in type of soap).

Physiological measures

Physiological measures have been the subject of considerable controversy. Behaviour therapists have tended to be attracted to the use of psychophysiological techniques because of the evident objectivity of the measures themselves. However, this has sometimes led to uncritical use; the objectivity of the measure does not mean that it is impervious to factors other than the independent variable. Furthermore, there has been a tendency to forget that physiological measures primarily reflect biological rather than psychological changes. Where the psychological demands of a task are confounded with the activity level, this can lead to confusion. For example, washing can be an energetic procedure, producing heart rate increases. If the degree of washing is reduced after treatment, this could result in decreased heart rate *even though the degree of anxiety induced by the task may be greater*. That is, the anxiety increase is fully offset by the relatively lower energy demands. Thus, such measures have to be used with considerable caution and with attention to appropriate experimental controls. The magnitude of changes produced by changes in oxygen consumption by exercise can be as much as ten times greater than changes associated with anxiety. The implications of the latter observation *vis-à-vis* using oxygen consumption as a 'physiological' indicator of anxiety are obvious.

Another consideration relates to the pattern of changes. Orientation towards external stimuli is generally accompanied by decreased heart rate, while orientation towards internal stimuli or defensive responding (commonly occurring to anxiety stimuli) is usually followed by heart rate acceleration. A further factor which must be considered is the extent to which patients habituate to the test setting (see Sartory, 1989, for a discussion of the use of psychophysiological measures in obsessions).

Psychophysiological measures can be helpful when stimuli or responses are predominantly covert, or where the verbal description of discomfort ratings would be expected to disrupt the variables under investigation; e.g. habituation to regular tape recorded sequences (see Mills and Salkovskis, 1988, for an example of this type of application in specific phobias). Although many measures can be used, heart rate and skin conductance are most commonly employed, and have generated interesting results (Rachman and Hodgson, 1980, Chapter 16). Recent advances in portable 24-hour monitoring of heart rate and other variables in natural settings are promising, although these techniques have not yet been exploited in the field of obsessional problems. Where a theoretical conceptualization which involves physiological elements is employed, then it is obviously most sensible to use psychophysiological techniques. For example, Kozak *et al.* (1988) have used psychophysiological and self-report measures to index emotional processing within and between exposure sessions.

Obsessional personality

The importance of the concept of obsessional personality has been questioned over the last decade. Reed (1985) is one of the strongest advocates of the utility of obsessional (anankastic) personality. He hypothesizes that, as in obsessive–compulsive disorder, the central, formal phenomenon in obsessional personality is to do with a failure of spontaneous categorization and integration, leading to over-structuring of input (i.e. over-structuring occurring as a compensation for the failure of spontaneous structuring). However, the data used to support this hypothesis are derived almost entirely from patients with obsessional personality, which Reed argues is (1) a unitary phenomenon, and (2) the basis for obsessional symptoms, which are said to be exaggerated extensions of obsessional personality. Rachman and Hodgson (1980, p. 137) have strongly criticized the concept of an obsessional personality. They note the failure to find any meaningful correlations between the wide range of different measures of obsessional or 'anal' personality and obsessional complaints, and found that obsessional patients do not differ from phobics on measures of obsessional personality. They conclude that there is no utility in currently available measures of obsessional personality, and that obsessional personality, however defined, has little to do with the general development of obsessional disorders. They do, however, note a weak association between introversion, neuroticism and obsessional symptoms, and suggest that different types of personality may be involved in determining the type of symptom which appears if an obsessional disorder were developed (e.g. overconscientiousness and checking).

It is reasonable to assume that some individuals can be operationally defined as having relatively enduring characteristics of concern with orderliness, cleanliness or obstinacy, etc. It may be of interest to study such enduring dispositions in terms of a consistent pattern of individual differences in given situations. However, such measures have little to offer the study of obsessional disorders. The labels given to such consistencies by the authors of scales should be treated with great caution and considered in the light of what exactly is being measured at a molar level. In conclusion, the measurement of obsessional personality has not yet been shown to have any validity with respect to obsessional disorder. Instead, the use of the term 'obsessional' in this context is, at best, a misleading hangover from discredited psychoanalytic concepts of obsessional disorder.

WORRY AND PREOCCUPATION

Psychological studies on worry are a recent and exciting development (Borkovec *et al.*, 1983). (Previous work on worry in test anxiety is reviewed by Deffenbacher, 1980.) Borkovec and colleagues defined worry as 'a chain of thoughts and images, negatively affect laden and relatively uncontrollable'. The tendency for anxiety to be disrupted by engagement in ongoing tasks is regarded as important, and provides the foundation for some of the most interesting measures in this area. The measures in the Borkovec *et al.* (1983) study included:

Rating of percentage of a typical day during which worry was experienced.
Mood ratings when worried: 14 adjectives rated on a 5-point scale ('not at all' to 'very much').
Autonomic perception when worried; symptoms rated on a 5-point scale.
Content of worries rated on the same scale; the seven areas were: financial, academic, interpersonal, philosophical, theological, physical harm, personal.
Duration of episodes of worry.
Controllability of worries, on 5-point scale from 'very easy' to 'very difficult'.

A time-sampling procedure was used in one experiment. In this, the subject had to identify the presence or absence of worries in response to a 'beep' signal. In the experiment, the time-sampling procedure was used during a range of experimental tasks requiring varying degrees of concentration. The use of wrist-mounted devices to produce a sampling signal is a possible development (either with pre-programming or telemetry to determine sampling points). Measures of preoccupation can be devised in a way similar to those used to assess worry. For an example of diary-related measures of health preoccupation, see Salkovskis and Warwick (1986). A questionnaire measuring variables relevant to health anxiety, including measures of intrusiveness and preoccupation, has been devised by Warwick and Salkovskis (1989).

NON-CLINICAL INTRUSIVE THOUGHTS

The measurement of non-clinical intrusive thoughts is still in its infancy. Nevertheless, considerable advances have been made in the decade since Rachman and de Silva (1978) reported that intrusions sharing most of the characteristics of clinical obsessions occurred in 80 per cent of the normal population. Rachman and his colleagues went on to clarify the characteristics of normal intrusions (e.g. Parkinson and Rachman, 1981; Rachman, 1981). Much of this work involved the generation of reliable descriptions of the intrusions and their characteristics such as ease of dismissal, duration, etc. Such measurements represent a preliminary stage for studies on the correlates of such cognitions. For example, the illustration in Figure 5.3 was developed from the scale devised by Rachman and de Silva (1978). The version shown here was used to screen subjects for an experimental study (Salkovskis *et al.*, 1989) on the effects of neutralizing.

In this example, subjects were selected for the subsequent experiment if they experienced high levels of discomfort and a high frequency of intrusive thoughts each week, and if they neutralized such intrusions 'often' or 'always'. Previous reliability studies indicated that each of the components used had a test–retest reliability of better than $r = 0.7$.

Age.......... Sex M/F Occupation.........................

Below is a questionnaire regarding the occurrence of unpleasant, unwanted thoughts, impulses and images. Thoughts and impulses of this kind are experienced by many people, and most certainly are not a sign of madness! The information gained from this questionnaire is likely to be of some considerable use in increasing our knowledge of such intrusive thoughts and impulses.

The information collected is fully confidential and anonymous. If, however, you would be prepared to participate in a small, non-stressful experiment (*not* involving drugs) please put your name and where you may be contacted below. *CONFIDENTIALITY WILL BE FULLY PRESERVED IN THESE CIRCUMSTANCES*, and your name will be removed on completion of the experiment.

> Complete this section only if you wish to assist by taking part in the experiment
> Name . . . .
> Contact by . . . .
> . . . . (address or tel. no.)

Do you sometimes experience intrusive, unacceptable and unpleasant thoughts, images/pictures or impulses/urges (e.g. to do with violence, sexual, blasphemous or similar matters)?

IF THE ANSWER ABOVE IS YES, PLEASE COMPLETE THE SECTIONS BELOW WHICH APPLY:

(a) *Thoughts* (images and impulses are on the next page—.

How often have you experienced intrusive, unacceptable and unpleasant thoughts IN THE LAST WEEK?

0 1–5 6–10 11–15 16–20 21–50 51 or more

On average, how easily can you dismiss these thoughts?

1 Yes, usually without effort
2 Yes, but usually with effort
3 Sometimes, usually with considerable effort
4 Not usually

When you have intrusive and unacceptable thoughts, do you want to 'put things right' by

(i) Performing a particular action? Never/Sometimes/Often/Always
(ii) Making yourself think a particular thought? Never/Sometimes/Often/Always

Do you try to avoid situations or things which may trigger such thoughts?
Never/Sometimes/Often/Always

How uncomfortable do the intrusive, unacceptable thoughts make you feel?

0 10 20 30 40 50 60 70 80 90 100

Not at all uncomfortable — The most uncomfortable I have ever been

(continues with urges and images)

Figure 5.3 Screening for intrusive cognitions.

Clark (1988) has demonstrated that, in non-clinical subjects, processes previously demonstrated in clinical subjects are confined to *high-frequency* cognitions (i.e. the same relationships do not operate in low-frequency cognitions). This observation is particularly important, because the modulating effect of frequency was demonstrated on the cognition–affect link (i.e. the association with particular types of thinking and specific affect, such as the link between loss-related thoughts and depression, threat-related thoughts and anxiety). The cognition–affect link is central to cognitive–behavioural models of emotional disorders (e.g. Beck *et al.*, 1987). Studies of this and other such relationships in non-clinical populations must obviously concentrate on high-frequency cognitions.

Using similar techniques, Dickerson and colleagues have attempted to dissect the factors involved in normal intrusions, focusing particularly on the issue of cognitive control. In doing so, they have developed a range of measures which acknowledge the complexity of the phenomena involved without sacrificing relevance and reliability (Edwards, 1988). The scales used in this work are reported in detail by Edwards and Dickerson (1987a). Dickerson and Edwards also describe techniques similar to those employed by Borkovec *et al.* (1983) in the study of worry (see above). Subjects are asked to form and/or replace their worrying thoughts, and the time taken is the main dependent variable. This technique has obvious face validity, and has been widely used as a direct measure of dismissability (see also Wenzlaff *et al.*, 1988; Wegner *et al.*, 1987, for further examples of this type of measurement technique).

Edwards and Dickerson (1987b) also demonstrated that the primary characteristics of positive and negative intrusive thoughts were almost identical, and that the measures which differentiate positive from negative intrusions were the more complex secondary measures such as acceptability. As with the cognitive–behavioural model of obsessional disorders (Salkovskis, 1985, 1989c), this highlights the importance of measures which focus on schema theory (Clark, 1988). The measurement techniques available for such investigations have largely been derived from experimental cognitive psychology, and are methodologically exacting but conceptually crude.

GENERAL ASSESSMENTS

There are a number of assessments which can be useful in the measurement of clinical intrusions, although they are not specific to obsessional problems. The Personal Questionnaire developed by Shapiro (1961) and the rapid-scaling variant devised by Mulhall (1976) are well suited to the assessment and scaling of obsessional and intrusive problems. A more recent development which opens new possibilities for accurate measures is the *Discan* (Discretized analogue) method developed by Singh and Bilsbury (1989).

EXPERIMENTAL METHODS

A number of methods have been adapted from experimental psychology in order to study intrusive thoughts. Foa and McNally (1986) recently reported the use of a dichotic listening task measuring physiological response and detection rates. They were able to demonstrate heightened vigilance for fear-relevant words using a within subjects design in obsessional patients. As with the majority of this type of research, this study did not control for emotionality; a measure of response to emotionally significant material is required in future work. Persons and Foa (1984) used a card-sorting task to evaluate the extent to which obsessional patients were characterized by simple or complex concepts; both number of categories and time taken to sort the cards were used. This task and the tasks employed by Reed (summarized in Reed, 1985) require some clarification with respect to the relationship between the tasks and the processes involved in choosing categories before any useful conclusions can be drawn from studies using these measures. A wide range of other tasks which have not yet been used could prove useful (see Williams *et al.*, 1988). For example, the Stroop paradigm has been extensively used in other anxiety disorders (e.g. Mogg *et al.*, 1989).

CONCLUSION

The measurement of intrusive cognitive phenomena is complicated by a number of factors, including the inherent sensitivity of some individuals to fears of criticism, the importance of non-observable (covert) events, etc. If progress is to be made towards the understanding of intrusive phenomena, empirically testable hypotheses must be employed and refined. Fortunately, recent research into intrusive cognitions in the normal population makes generalizable empirical work a more manageable proposition. An unexpected spin-off has been the way in which work originally developed to foster the understanding of obsessional problems has been applied to the study of anxiety and depression.

ACKNOWLEDGEMENT

The author is grateful for the support of the Medical Research Council of the United Kingdom.

REFERENCES

Akhtar, S., Wig, N.H., Verma, V.K., Pershod, D. and Verma, S.K. (1975) A phenomenological analysis of symptoms in obsessive–compulsive neurosis. *British Journal of Psychiatry*, **127**, 342–8.

Allen, J.J. and Tune, G.S. (1975) The Lynfield Obsessional/Compulsive Questionnaire. *Scottish Medical Journal*, **20** (Supp 1), 21–4.

Anderson, J.R. (1985) *Cognitive Psychology and its Implications*, Freeman, New York.

Beck, A.T., Brown, G., Eidelson, J.I., Steer, R.A. and Riskind, J.H. (1987) Differentiating anxiety and depression: a test of the cognitive content-specificity hypothesis. *Journal of Abnormal Psychology*, **96**, 179–83.

Beech, H.R. (ed.) (1974) *Obsessional States*, Methuen, London.

Borkovec, T.D., Robinson, E., Pruzinsky, T. and DePree, J. (1983) Preliminary exploration of worry: some characteristics and processes. *Behaviour Research and Therapy*, **21**, 9–16.

Clark, D.A. (1988) The validity of measures of cognition: a review of the literature. *Cognitive Therapy and Research*, **12**, 1–20.

Cooper, J. (1970) The Leyton Obsessional Inventory. *Psychological Medicine*, **1**, 48–64.

Cottraux, J., Bouvard, M., Defayolle, M. and Messy, P . (1987) Validity and factorial structure of the compulsive activity checklist. *Behavior Therapy*, **19**, 45–53.

Deffenbacher, J.L. (1980) Worry and emotionality in test anxiety. In I.G. Sarason (ed.), *Test Anxiety: Theory, Research and Application*, Lawrence Erlbaum, Hillsdale, NJ.

de Silva, P. (1986) Obsessional–compulsive imagery. *Behaviour Research and Therapy*, **24**, 333–50.

de Silva, P. (1987) Obsessions and compulsions: investigation. In S. Lindsay and G. Powell (eds), *A Handbook of Clinical Adult Psychology*, Gower, Aldershot.

Edwards, S. and Dickerson, M. (1987a) Intrusive unwanted thoughts: a two stage model of control. *British Journal of Medical Psychology*, **60**, 317–28.

Edwards, S. and Dickerson, M. (1987b) On the similarity of positive and negative intrusions. *Behaviour Research and Therapy*, **25**, 207–11.

England, S.L. and Dickerson, M. (1988) Intrusive thoughts: unpleasantness not the major cause of uncontrollability. *Behaviour Research and Therapy*, **26**, 279–87.

Foa, E.B. and McNally, R.J. (1986) Sensitivity to feared stimuli in Obsessive–compulsives: a dichotic listening analysis. *Cognitive Therapy and Research*, **10**, 477–85.

Hodgson, R.J. and Rachman, S.J. (1978) Obsessional–compulsive complaints. *Behaviour Research and Therapy*, **15**, 389–95.

Karno, M., Golding, J.M., Sorenson, S.B. and Burnham, A. (1988) The epidemiology of obsessive–compulsive disorder in five US communities. *Archives of General Psychiatry*, **45**, 1094–9.

Kirk, J. (1989) Cognitive–behavioural assessment. In K. Hawton, P.M. Salkovskis, J. Kirk and D.M. Clark (eds), *Cognitive–behavioural Treatment for Psychiatric Disorders: a Practical Guide*, Oxford University Press, Oxford.

Kozak, M.J., Foa, E.B. and Steketee, G. (1988) Process and outcome of exposure treatment with obsessive–compulsives: psychophysiological indicators of emotional processing. *Behavior Therapy*, **19**, 157–69.

Lang, P.J. (1979) A bioinformational theory of emotional imagery. *Psychophysiology*, **16**, 495–512.

Marks, I.M. (1986) *Behavioural Psychotherapy: Maudsley Pocket Book of Clinical Management*, Wright, Bristol.

Marks, I.M. (1987) *Fears, Phobias and Rituals*, Oxford University Press, New York.

Marks, I.M., Hallam, R.S., Connelly, J. and Philpott, R. (1977) *Nursing in Behavioural Psychotherapy*, Royal College of Nursing of the United Kingdom, London.

Mills, I.M. and Salkovskis, P.M. (1988) Mood and habituation to phobic stimuli. *Behaviour Research and Therapy*, **26**, 435–9.

Mogg, K., Mathews, A. and Weinman, J. (1989) Selective processing of threat cues in anxiety states: a replication. *Behaviour Research and Therapy*, **27**, 317–23.

Mulhall, D.J. (1976) Systematic self-assessment by PQRST. *Psychological Medicine*, **6**, 591–6.

Parkinson, L. and Rachman, S.J. (1981) The nature of intrusive thoughts. *Advances in Behaviour Research and Therapy*, **3**, 101–10.

Pato, M.T., Zohar-Kadouch, R., Zohar, J. and Murphy, D.L. (1988) Return of symptoms after discontinuation of clomipramine in patients with obsessive–compulsive disorder. *American Journal of Psychiatry*, **145**, 1521–5.

Persons, J.B. and Foa, E.B. (1984) Processing of fearful and neutral information by obsessive–compulsives. *Behaviour Research and Therapy*, **22**, 259–65.

Rachman, S.J. (1978) Anatomy of obsessions. *Behavior Analysis and Modification*. **2**, 253–78.

Rachman, S.J. (1981) Unwanted intrusive cognitions. *Advances in Behaviour Research and Therapy*, **3**, 101–10.

Rachman, S.J. and de Silva, P. (1978) Abnormal and normal obsessions. *Behaviour Research and Therapy*, **16**, 233–8.

Rachman, S.J. and Hodgson, R.J. (1974) Synchrony and desynchrony in fear and avoidance. *Behaviour Research and Therapy*, **12**, 311–18.

Rachman, S.J. and Hodgson, R. (1980) *Obsessions and Compulsions*, Prentice-Hall, Englewood Cliffs, NJ.

Rachman, S.J., Marks, I.M. and Hodgson, R. (1973) The treatment of obsessive–compulsive neurotics by modelling and flooding *in vivo*. *Behaviour Research and Therapy*, **11**, 463–71.

Reed, G.F. (1985) *Obsessional Experience and Compulsive Behaviour: a Cognitive–structural Approach*, Academic Press, London.

Roper, G. and Rachman, S.J. (1975) Obsessional–compulsive checking: replication and development. *Behaviour Research and Therapy*, **13**, 25–32.

Roper, G., Rachman, S.J. and Hodgson, R. (1973) An experiment on obsessional checking. *Behaviour Research and Therapy*, **11**, 271–7.

Rosenberg, H. and Upper, D. (1983) Problems with stimulus response equivalence and reactivity in the assessment and treatment of obsessive–compulsive neurosis. *Behaviour Research and Therapy*, **21**, 177–80.

Salkovskis, P.M. (1985) Obsessional–compulsive problems: a cognitive–behavioural analysis. *Behaviour Research and Therapy*, **25**, 571–83.

Salkovskis, P.M. (1989a) Obsessions and compulsions. In J. Scott, J.M.G. Williams and A.T. Beck (eds), *Cognitive Therapy: a Clinical Casebook*, Routledge, London.

Salkovskis, P.M. (1989b) Obsessive and intrusive thoughts: clinical and non-clinical aspects. In P.M.G. Emmelkamp, W.T.A.M. Everaerd, and M.J.M. van Son (eds), *Fresh Perspectives on Anxiety Disorders*, Swets and Zeitlinger, Amsterdam.

Salkovskis, P.M. (1989c) Cognitive–behavioural factors and the persistence of intrusive thoughts in obsessional problems. *Behaviour Research and Therapy*, **27**, 677–682.

Salkovskis, P.M. and Harrison, J. (1984) Abnormal and normal obsessions: a replication. *Behaviour Research and Therapy*, **22**, 549–52.

Salkovskis, P.M. and Kirk, J. (1989) Obsessional disorders. In K. Hawton, P.M. Salkovskis, J. Kirk and D.M. Clark (eds), *Cognitive-behavioural Treatment for Psychiatric Disorders: a Practical Guide*, Oxford University Press, Oxford.

Salkovskis, P.M. and Warwick, H.M.C. (1986) Morbid preoccupations, health anxiety and reassurance. A cognitive behavioural approach to hypochondriasis. *Behaviour Research and Therapy*, **24**, 597–602.

Salkovskis, P.M. and Westbrook, D. (1989) Behaviour therapy and obsessional ruminations: can failure be turned into success? *Behaviour Research and Therapy*, **27**, 149–60.

Salkovskis, P.M., Westbrook, D., Davis, J., Jeavons, A. and Gledhill, A. (1989) The effects of neutralising on discomfort and persistence of intrusive thoughts: an experiment investigating the aetiology of obsessive–compulsive disorder. Manuscript in preparation.

Sanavio, E. (1988) Obsessions and compulsions: the Padua Inventory. *Behaviour Research and Therapy*, **26**, 169–77.

Sartory, G. (1989) Obsessive–compulsive disorders. In G. Turpin (ed.) *Handbook of Clinical Psychophysiology*, John Wiley, Chichester.

Shapiro, M.B. (1961) A method of measuring psychological changes specific to the individual psychiatric patient. *British Journal of Medical Psychology*, **34**, 151–5.

Singh, A.C. and Bilsbury, C.D. (1989) Measurement of subjective variables: the Discan method. *Acta Psychiatrica Scandinavica*, **79**, Supp. 347, 1–38.

Steketee, G.S. and Foa, E.B. (1985) Obsessive–compulsive disorder. In D.H. Barlow (ed.), *Handbook of Psychological Disorders*, Guilford Press, New York.

Steketee, G.S., Grayson, J.B. and Foa, E.B. (1985) Obsessive–compulsive disorders: differences between washers and checkers. *Behaviour Research and Therapy*, **23**, 197–201.

Stern, R.S. and Cobb, J. (1978) Phenomenology of obsessive–compulsive neurosis. *British Journal of Psychiatry*, **132**, 233–9.

Turner, R.M., Steketee, G.S. and Foa, E.B. (1979) Fear of criticism in washers, checkers and phobics. *Behaviour Research and Therapy*, **17**, 79–81.

Turner, S.M. and Beidel, D.C. (1988) *Treating Obsessive–compulsive Disorder*, Pergamon Press, New York.

Warwick, H.M.C. and Salkovskis, P.M. (1989) A questionnaire study of hypochondriasis. *Scandinavian Journal of Behaviour Therapy*. **18**, 85–92.

Wegner, D.M., Schneider, D.J., Carter, S.R. and White, T.L. (1987) Paradoxical effects of thought suppression. *Journal of Personality and Social Psychology*, **53**, 5–13.

Wenzlaff, R.M., Wegner, D.M. and Roper, D.W. (1988) Depression and mental control: the resurgence of unwanted negative thoughts. *Journal of Personality and Social Psychology*, **55**, 882–92.

Williams, J.M.G., Watts, F.N., MacLeod, C. and Mathews, A. (1988) *Cognitive Psychology and Emotional Disorders*, John Wiley, Chichester.

Wing, J.K., Cooper, J.E. and Sartorius, N. (1974) *The Measurement and Classification of Psychiatric Symptoms*, Cambridge University Press, Cambridge.

Wolpe, J. (1982) *The Practice of Behavior Therapy*, 3rd edn, Pergamon Press, New York.

Chapter 6

Personality Disorder and Social Functioning

PETER TYRER

Traditionally, the measurement of personality and social functioning comes into what is colloquially known as 'soft' data; it is alleged to be unreliable, vague and correspondingly invalid. This particularly applies to personality disorder, which remains a pejorative description that is said to be of limited value and may say as much about the diagnoser as the diagnosed. There are still frequent calls for the diagnosis of personality disorder in its various forms to be abandoned (Blackburn, 1988) because it serves no useful purpose. The author believes this view to be mistaken, and that it is possible to record personality disorder with some degree of accuracy and in a way that has implications for both clinical and research practice.

The measurement of social function is perhaps less contentious but still fraught with difficulties. As with personality, there are problems in defining optimal social function and the criteria by which it can be regarded as impaired. Some of the reasons for the difficulties in measuring personality disorder and social functioning are shown in Table 6.1.

Table 6.1 Some problems of measuring personality disorder and social functioning compared with mental disorder.

	Mental illness	Personality disorder	Social functioning
Clinical state	Can be recorded accurately at interview	Difficult to use positively in diagnosis as very variable	Affected by setting in which assessment is made
Time course	Short	Very long (usually since adolescence)	Short
Source of information	Patient preferable	Informant may be preferable	Uncertain
Contamination by value judgements	Low	High	High

Measuring Human Problems. Edited by D.F. Peck and C.M. Shapiro

Compared with mental illness, the problems in measuring personality disorder and social functioning are more difficult. Clinical examination usually describes the current state of the patient—hence the title of one of the best-known instruments for recording mental illness, the Present State Examination (Wing *et al.*, 1974). In personality disorder the present clinical state may be of little value as it can vary considerably and can also 'contaminate' assessment of underlying personality. Personality *apparently* changes during illness and there is the danger that the change seen during the illness state is misinterpreted as the premorbid personality of the subject. Social functioning also needs to be measured using a different approach from that for assessing mental state. Although it is possible to concentrate on the present social functioning of the individual this can be highly atypical, particularly when the patient is assessed in an alien setting (e.g. a hospital).

The other difficulties in assessment shown in Table 6.1 are also considerable. Personality disorder has a long time-course and traditionally it is formulated during adolescence or shortly afterwards and persists relatively unchanged throughout much of adult life. It is much more difficult to measure a disorder with such a long time span than it is to measure a disorder which is short lived and clearly demarcated. The sort of information necessary to make an adequate diagnosis in mental illness is usually clear. The patient has the illness and direct assessment alone is sufficient in many cases (although in most illnesses it is helpful to have additional information from an informant). In the case of personality disorder, however, there are good theoretical arguments for choosing an informant other than the subject for making assessments. Personality disorder causes suffering in others as well as in the patient, as a consequence of the disorder. As the suffering of others often predates that of the patient it can be argued that the assessment of personality disorder is best carried out with an informant. The same argument could be used with somewhat less force for the assessment of social functioning. When persons feel they are coping well but close relatives with whom they live insist that their functioning is impaired and causing major problems, whom is one to believe? The choice of information can confuse more than illuminate.

Although value judgements can come into the assessment of any mental illness, they are a much greater danger in the assessment of personality disorder and social functioning. It is difficult to describe normal behaviour and personality. The danger is of procrustean conformity being forced on individuals to make them 'normal' because well-meaning people feel that *their* social functioning should be shared by all. This subject will be discussed again later and is particularly important in the field of social functioning.

It is reasonable for personality disorder and social functioning to be discussed together in the same chapter as they have so many common aspects.

Nevertheless, there are obvious differences that need emphasizing even though they will be self-evident to researchers with experience in either of these areas. Personality disorder is often manifest by social dysfunction, but there are many other independent precipitants of such dysfunction, including physical and psychiatric illness, mental handicap, advanced age and social or political considerations that prevent the full potential of the individual from being realized. It would therefore be quite wrong to regard severely impaired social function as necessarily 'due to' personality disorder.

Current attitudes towards personality disorder also do not regard social dysfunction as an essential concomitant. Up to the Ninth Revision of the International Classification of Diseases (ICD-9) personality disorder retained two fixed concepts: the early onset of persistent 'deeply ingrained maladaptive patterns of behaviour' and the Schneiderian aphorism that, as a result of the personality disorder, 'the patient suffers or others have to suffer and there is an adverse effect on the individual and on society' (World Health Organization, 1978). In the latest draft of the Tenth Revision, however, it is acknowledged that some personality disorders can be 'acquired later in life' and that they 'are frequently, *but not always*, associated with various degrees of subjective distress and impaired social functioning' (World Health Organization, 1988). It is therefore possible to envisage a condition presenting after the age of 40 in which there is no social or subjective suffering still being regarded as a personality disorder. For reasons that will become clear later in this chapter, the author regards this description of personality disorder as altogether too catholic for satisfactory classification, but it is likely to be incorporated into the final version of ICD-10 and is already present in published form in the latest American classification, DSM-III-R (American Psychiatric Association, 1987).

The different forms of measurement for both social functioning and personality disorder will therefore be discussed consecutively but individually. As with the other chapters, the use of questionnaires and rating scales are discussed first, followed by physiological, biochemical and behavioural methods where appropriate. For personality disorder and social functioning these are relatively unimportant when compared with the different subjective and informant rating methods.

QUESTIONNAIRES

Social functioning

The measurement of social function includes the assessment of social performance and competence, the degree of social support and networks, and the fulfilment of social roles. These cannot all be covered by a self-rated questionnaire but can roughly be subsumed under two areas; the ability to complete tasks and the amount of distress caused by these tasks. Thus a perfectly competent woman forced to act as a housewife but bored to death by household chores will score well on competence but poorly on stress, whereas her carefree, disorganized neighbour will show the opposite scoring pattern. The available scales measure adjustment at work, at home, in leisure and social situations, with families and spouses, and with money. Those available that are self-explanatory and can be completed by subjects alone are summarized in Table 6.2.

Table 6.2 Self-rating instruments for measuring social adjustment.

Scale	Authors	Main features
Katz Adjustment Scale—Relatives Form	Katz and Lyerly (1963)	205 items rated on 4-point scale by relatives: takes 35 minutes
Social Adjustment Inventory	Berger *et al.* (1964)	33 items rated on 6-point scale by close informant
KDS-15	Frank and Kupfer (1974)	Questionnaire to assess marital relationships (80 items): takes 45 minutes
Self-Assessment guide	Willer and Biggin (1974, 1976)	13-item (brief version); 55-item (full version): takes 20 minutes
Social Adjustment Scale—Self-report (SAS–SR)	Weissman and Bothwell (1976)	42-item scale derived from original observer-rated schedule (see Table 6.4): takes 20 minutes
Social Functioning Questionnaire (SFQ)	Tyrer (1985)	8-item scale (see Appendix 1): takes 5 minutes

The choice of scale depends on the aim of the measurement. The KDS-15 is appropriate for studies of marital satisfaction, the Self-Assessment Guide for general use with psychiatric patients, particularly in studies of treatment outcome, the SAS-SR for community surveys and evaluation of treatment, and the SFQ for screening purposes or for rapid assessment when time is limited. As might be expected with self-ratings, all the scales have a bias towards measurement of perceived social satisfaction; social handicap is not recorded unless it causes distress.

SELF-RATING INSTRUMENTS FOR MEASURING PERSONALITY DISORDERS

Although there are many self-report questionnaires that measure personality attributes, of which the 16PF Questionnaire (Cattell, 1965), the Maudsley Personality Inventory (MPI) (Eysenck, 1959) and the Eysenck Personality Inventory (EPI) (Eysenck and Eysenck, 1964) are perhaps the best known, these do not measure personality disorder. Although it could be argued that personality disorder is at one extreme of a continuum and that such instruments should be perfectly appropriate for recording personality abnormality they are still not directly germane to such measurement. Interest in recording personality disorder using self-report measures has been heightened in recent years because of the great impact of the new personality diagnoses in DSM-III. As these diagnoses are obtained by interviewing the subject, it is hardly surprising that attempts have been made to save time by asking the subject to reveal his or her responses by self-report.

The main instruments used are shown in Table 6.3. The first of these, the Millon Clinical Multiaxial Inventory, preceded DSM-III but as Theodore Millon was an influential member of the task force that prepared DSM-III it is not surprising that they share many common features. Millon derived his instrument from his theory of personality (Millon, 1969) that records personality through the medium of 'social styles', each of which is recorded along a dimension with activity at one extreme and passivity at the other. His four styles are dependent, independent, ambivalent and detached, and by combining these with the activity–passivity dimension eight basic personality types are created. Millon added three further disorders to make up the 11 to correspond closely to the DSM-III groupings. The scores for each personality type are converted to base-rates and a score of greater than 85 suggests personality disorder.

The Minnesota Multiphasic Personality Inventory (MMPI) has long been used to record personality status but is not readily converted into personality disorder diagnoses. However, Morey *et al.* (1985) have derived 11 scales from the MMPI which, they claim, are representative for DSM-III personality disorders. However, the correlations between these derived scales and the MCMI are poor (Streiner and Miller, 1988) and the latter authors conclude that acceptable validity of the modified MMPI scale has not been established.

The Personality Diagnostic Questionnaire (PDQ) is directly matched to the operational criteria of DSM-III and has subsequently been modified (PDQ-R) to comply with the changes made. Although the PDQ shows a certain rough-hewn validity in that patients selected on clinical grounds of having personality disorders have significantly higher scores on the PDQ than those without personality disorder (Hyler *et al.*, 1988), comparison

Table 6.3 Self-rating instruments for measuring DSM-III personality disorders.

Instrument	Authors	Main features
Millon Clinical Multiaxial Inventory (MCMI)	Millon (1983, 1985)	175-item clinical inventory deriving eight basic personality types with three additional personalities corresponding closely to DSM-III personality disorders
Modified Minnesota Multiphasic Personality Inventory (MMPI)	Morey *et al.* (1985)	11 new scales chosen to represent the 11 DSM-III personality disorder diagnoses. 566 items
Personality Diagnostic Questionnaire (PDQ)	Hyler *et al.* (1988)	163-item, true/false questionnaire taking 30 minutes to complete with items specifically chosen to match the operational criteria in DSM-III

between the PDQ and structured clinical interview schedules for assessing personality disorder yield poor agreement (Reich *et al.*, 1987). However, the instrument is probably a good screening tool as a total score of 50 or more on the PDQ suggests that at least one of the DSM-III personality disorders is present.

Although the attractions of self-rating instruments in personality assessment are obvious in view of the length of time it takes to complete a formal interview, there is insufficient evidence that any of the instruments currently available is in itself a satisfactory measure of personality disorder. Of the three available, the MCMI is probably the most satisfactory and is highly recommended. It is not well known in the United Kingdom and at first sight its nomenclature may appear odd. One needs time to become familiar with the scoring system. The PDQ is a possible screening instrument for those wishing to identify DSM-III personality disorders in a population (e.g. in epidemiological studies), but is unsuitable alone as a diagnostic instrument.

INTERVIEW SCHEDULES

Social function

There is an embarrassingly large number of interview schedules available for the assessment of social function in its many aspects. Most of these are subject-completed and take about half an hour. With so many scales available one suspects that none of them is really satisfactory. In most instances investigators have introduced their new scale as an ancillary measure in a study of treatment. As social function is recognized to be separate from psychiatric symptomatology (and has even been given its own axis of classification in DSM-III) it has now become respectable, if not always wise, to include social function among the variables being examined for treatment differences. Examination of existing scales often reveals flaws, and so a new instrument is created primarily for the population being treated. Attempts are made to generalize from this to other populations; these, by and large, fail and so the process is repeated.

Nevertheless, it is important not to be too pessimistic, and it must be acknowledged that the measurement of social functioning in its various forms, however inadequately performed, does convey useful additional information beyond that derived from symptoms, diagnosis and other common psychiatric measures. It often responds to treatment differently from symptoms (Weissman *et al.*, 1974) and shows important differences in severity between psychiatric disorders that might in other respects be regarded as equivalent (Casey *et al.*, 1985).

The main interview scales used for assessing social function are illustrated in Table 6.4. This is not a full list; readers are invited to study the reviews by Weissman (1975); Weissman *et al.* (1981); and, most comprehensively, by McDowell and Newell (1986), in order to obtain a more detailed list. The scales can conveniently be split into three groups; those that measure social adjustment (in the strictest sense of fitting in with the requirements of society), others that attempt to record social function as personal perceptions of adjustment or those of a close informant, and the last measuring social networks to varying degrees of depth. None can be regarded as measuring a global concept of social function and, in any case, it is doubtful whether such a concept is useful.

PERSONALITY DISORDERS

Because the concept of personality disorder is a categorical one based on formal classification it is predictable that most instruments for rating personality disorder are linked to DSM and ICD. The latest versions of these classifications show remarkable congruence (Table 6.5), mainly because of the considerable influence of the third edition, DSM-III, published by the American Psychiatric Association in 1980. The key features of this classification that made it so popular with researchers were the introduction of operational criteria, now also present in somewhat diluted form as 'diagnostic guidelines' in ICD-10 (World Health Organization, 1988). Most interview

Table 6.4 Interview schedules for assessing aspects of social function.

Instrument	Authors	Main features
Normative Social Adjustment Scale (NSAS)	Barrabee *et al*. (1955)	27 items rated on 5-point scales: takes 60 minutes. A prototype for many subsequent scales
Social Role Adjustment Instrument (SRAI)	Cohler *et al*. (1968)	200-item semi-structured interview to assess women's adjustment to roles as friend, wife, mother, daughter, and home maker
Social Dysfunction Rating Scale (SDRS)	Goodman *et al*. (1969)	20 items rated on 6-point scale: takes 40 minutes. Well used in older age groups
Social Adjustment Scale (SAS)	Paykel *et al*. (1971)	Modified from SSIAM, 48 items rated on 5-point scale: takes 50 minutes. A modified form, SAS-II (Glazer *et al*., 1980) is used for schizophrenic patients
Structured and Scaled Interview to Assess Maladjustment (SSIAM)	Gurland *et al*. (1972)	60 items rated on an 11-point scale with defined anchor points: takes 30 minutes. Widely used
Levels of Function Scale	Strauss and Carpenter (1972)	4-item scale using 5 points, and covering adjustment and symptoms over a variable time scale (up to one year): takes 20 minutes. Used mainly with schizophrenic patients
Denver Community Mental Health Questionnaire (DCMHQ)	Ciarlo and Reihman (1975)	Semi-structured interview with 79 items, particularly concerned with psychological distress and satisfaction with mental health services: takes 45 minutes
Psychosocial Adjustment to Illness Scale (PAIS)	Derogatis (1976)	45 questions in seven sections; health care orientation, vocational environment, domestic environment, sexual relationships, extended family relationships, social environment, psychological distress: takes 20–30 minutes
Personal Resources Inventory (PRI)	Clayton and Hirschfeld (1977)	Structured interview of 41 items assessing the period of best social functioning in a defined period of one year

Table 6.4 (*continued*)

Instrument	Authors	Main features
Standardized Interview to Assess Maladjustment	Clare and Cairns (1978)	36 sets of ratings in six areas; housing, occupation/social role, economic situation, leisure/social activities, family and domestic relationships, marital relationship, in which each area is rated with regard to material conditions, management of social affairs and satisfaction. Each rating made on a 4-point scale, higher scores indicating maladjustment: takes 45 minutes
Social Interaction Schedule (SIS)	Henderson *et al.* (1978)	Scale examining an individual's 'primary group interaction' in the week prior to interview with interactions categorized according to three types with duration of content for each
Network Analysis	Cohen and Sokolowsky (1979)	Formal record of size, density, and degree of social contacts: takes about 15 minutes
Social Functioning Schedule (SFS)	Remington and Tyrer (1979)	Semi-structured interview covering areas above (see self-rating section): takes 30 minutes
Social Behaviour Assessment Schedule (SBAS)	Platt *et al.* (1980)	239-item schedule assessing function over 1–3 months, together with patient's behaviour and effects of this behaviour on informants: takes 60–90 minutes
Interview Measure of Social Relationship (IMSR)	Brugha *et al.* (1987)	Modifications of SIS in shortened form for large-scale epidemiological surveys

schedules (Table 6.6) formalize the description of these features and adopt an appropriate scoring system, sometimes with a glossary. Three of the most important schedules (SCID-II, SID-P and the PDE) are intimately linked to DSM-III-R; an example of one of them, the International version of the PDE, is illustrated in Appendix 2 of this chapter.

Although an informant can be interviewed to obtain a DSM-III-R diagnosis, many of the operational criteria involve subjective feelings and attitudes and are difficult to rate independently. As society, and its microcosm, the family, often suffer more than the subject with a personality

Table 6.5 Comparison of current classification of personality disorder.

Code	ICD-10	DSM-III-R	Code
F60.0	Paranoid—excessive sensitivity, suspiciousness, preoccupation with conspiratorial explanation of events, with a persistent tendency to self-reference	Paranoid—interpretation of people's actions as deliberately demeaning or threatening	301.00
F60.1	Schizoid—emotional coldness, detachment, lack of interest in other people, eccentricity and introspective fantasy	Schizoid—indifference to social relationships and restricted range of emotional experience and expression	301.20
	No equivalent	Schizotypal—deficit in interpersonal relatedness with pecularities of ideation, appearance and behaviour	301.22
F60.5	Anankastic—indecisiveness, doubt, excessive caution, pedantry, rigidity and need to plan in immaculate detail	Obsessive–compulsive—pervasive perfectionism and inflexibility	301.40
F60.4	Histrionic—self-dramatization, shallow mood, egocentricity and craving for excitement with persistent manipulative behaviour	Histrionic—excessive emotionality and attention-seeking	301.50
F60.7	Dependent—failure to take responsibility for actions, with subordination of personal needs to those of others, excessive dependence with need for constant reassurance and feelings of helplessness when a close relationship ends	Dependent—persistent dependent and submissive behaviour	301.60
F60.2	Dyssocial—callous unconcern for others, with irresponsibility, irritability and aggression, and incapacity to maintain enduring relationships	Antisocial—evidence of repeated conduct disorder before the age of 15	301.70
	No equivalent	Narcissistic—pervasive grandiosity, lack of empathy, and hypersensitivity to the evaluation of others	301.81
F60.6	Anxious—persistent tension, self-consciousness, exaggeration of risks and dangers, hypersensitivity to rejection, and restricted lifestyle because of insecurity	Avoidant—pervasive social discomfort, fear of negative evaluation and timidity	301.82

Table 6.5 (*continued*)

Code	ICD-10	DSM-III-R	Code
F60.30[a]	Impulsive—inability to control anger, to plan ahead, or to think before acts, with unpredictable mood and quarrelsome behaviour	Borderline—pervasive instability of mood and self-image	301.83
F60.31[a]	Borderline—unclear self-image, involvement in intense and unstable relationships		
	No equivalent	Passive–aggressive—pervasive passive resistance to demands for adequate social and occupational performance	301.84

[a] Included under heading of emotionally unstable personality disorder.

Modified from DSM-III-R and the 1988 draft of ICD-10 and reproduced with permission of the American Psychiatric Association and the World Health Organization, respectively.

disorder, it is often more appropriate to interview an informant as well as (or sometimes instead of) the subject. This is mandatory for one instrument, the Standardized Assessment of Personality (Mann *et al.*, 1981), which was linked to ICD-9 (with two extra categories) but which is now revised to encompass the ICD-10 groupings (unpublished schedule available from Dr Mann at the Institute of Psychiatry, De Crespigny Park, London SE5). The Personality Assessment Schedule (PAS) (Tyrer and Alexander, 1979; Tyrer *et al.*, 1988) derives a computer-coded diagnosis from 24 key personality attributes, each rated on a 9-point scale depending on the degree of social dysfunction caused by the attribute in question. The derived categories, four main (sociopathic, passive-dependent, schizoid and anankastic) and nine subcategories (explosive (impulsive), sensitive–aggressive, histrionic, asthenic, dysthymic, anxious, hypochondriacal, paranoid and avoidant) are similar to ICD-10. A DSM-III-R 'version' (but with no operational criteria) is also available (Tyrer *et al.*, 1988).

The instruments summarized in Table 6.6 are only a few of the many introduced to formalize the assessment of personality disorder. Others are confined to one personality type only, a practice which is not personally recommended (see below) but which may sometimes be considered essential. A full description of other instruments is given by Widiger and Frances (1987).

Table 6.6 Interview schedules for personality disorder.

Structured interview	Author	Features
Structured Clinical Interview for DSM-III-R Personality Disorders (SCID II)	Spitzer *et al.* (1987)	Yields DSM-III-R diagnoses. Has had limited application so far. Normally preceded by Personality Questionnaire. Subject version only
Personality Assessment Schedule (PAS)	Tyrer and Alexander (1979)	Yields five diagnostic categories: sociopathic, schizoid, passive dependent, anankastic and normal. Nine sub-categories in addition to DSM-III-R and ICD-10 equivalent. Also yields dimensional personality trait scores. Subject and informant versions
Standardized Assessment of Personality (SAP)	Mann *et al.* (1981)	Revised version (via author) yields ICD-10 diagnosis plus two other categories (anxious, self-conscious). Informant only interviewed
Personality Disorder Examination (PDE) (International Personality Disorder Examination (IPDE))	Loranger *et al.* (1985)	Present version yields DSM-III-R diagnosis. In early stages of development. Subject version only. Takes up to 4 hours to complete
Structured Interview for DSM-III Personality Disorders (SID-P)	Pfohl *et al.* (1982)	DSM-III and DSM-III-R diagnoses. Utilizes information from subject and informant. Measures personality attributes of past five years where change has occurred

OTHER MEASURES OF PERSONALITY DISORDER

For many years investigators in the biological sciences have attempted to find markers of personality disturbance. No investigator likes the messy business of diagnosis determined only by the subjective responses to questions. The interpretation and presentation of these questions become progressively more rigid and stylized until eventually one has an instrument that can only be administered effectively by a robot.

Unfortunately, the search for such 'independent' measures of personality disorder has been tantalizingly unsuccessful. Despite early evidence that the electroencephalograms (EEGs) of 'aggressive psychopaths' were abnormal in that they contained an excess of slow (theta) waves, particularly in the temporal regions (Hill and Watterson, 1942), we have not progressed much further in the succeeding half century. The brain activity of antisocial personalities is abnormal and can be quantified in a way that allows it to be correlated with behaviour. Thus in one study Mednick *et al.* (1981) found that young multiple offenders, studied both prospectively and retrospectively, had significantly more EEG activity between 8 and 10 Hz than single or non-offenders. They therefore concluded that the EEG could predict recidivism. This is close to being dangerous nonsense; if the claim was true it would make EEG analysis of offenders mandatory and be used to determine sentences in the courts.

Even when more sophisticated cerebral (and peripheral) measurements are used we only find general trends that support the notion of antisocial personality as a state of low arousal in which findings differ to some extent from normal individuals (e.g. Raine and Venables, 1988). Anxious individuals show similar changes in the opposite direction but they are of virtually no diagnostic or therapeutic value.

CHOICE OF SCALE FOR MEASURING SOCIAL FUNCTION

There are currently more than 50 instruments for recording different aspects of social function and it is difficult for the investigator to choose between them. The choice is made more complicated by the fact that there is no common definition of social function or social performance. At a general level good social adjustment suggests harmony between an individual and his or her environment and poor social adjustment suggests disharmony and conflict. It is when one attempts to measure more specific aspects of social function that serious differences of opinion emerge.

This is partly because the boundaries between these different aspects are not drawn clearly. As Weissman *et al.* (1981) point out:

> On the conceptual level, the scales often include overlapping and unspecified concepts. At least five conceptual areas underlying social functioning can be identified and are measured with varying emphasis, depending on the scale. These areas are social supports, social attachments, social competence, social status, and social role performance. Since dysfunctioning in each of these areas may have considerably different implications for intervention, a fruitful task for future development would be the explication and measurement of them.

Unfortunately, many investigators, particularly in the United States, have blurred these boundaries further by introducing external criteria of 'normal' social adjustment against which other individuals can be measured.

Thus the expectations of society rather than the objective measure of performance are measured in most of the instruments emanating from the United States. This is not a coincidence. Conformity to 'role-appropriate behaviour' is considered more important there than in European countries, where apparently inappropriate behaviour for certain roles may often be admired and the person described as 'a real character'.

Platt (1981) has provided a coruscating and comprehensive review of the failure of many adjustment scales to measure what they purport to. He examines the concept of social adjustment in four of the most popular rating scales, the Normative Social Adjustment Scale (NSAS), the Structured and Scaled Interview to Assess Maladjustment (SSIAM), the Social Adjustment Scale (SAS), and the Standardized Interview to Assess Maladjustment (SIAM). Platt points out that all these instruments, to a greater or lesser extent, measure adjustment by comparison with a hypothetical ideal norm and concludes 'that the attempt to establish objective norms of acceptable or reasonable or ideal "social adjustment" is based on a misconception of the sociology of role behavior'. The stage was set in 1955 with the introduction of the NSAS in which social adjustment was defined as 'the degree to which a person fulfils the normative social expectations of behavior that constitute his roles' (Barrabee *et al.*, 1955).

Unfortunately the scale does not live up to this aim because the societal expectations of what constitutes good social adjustment cannot be applied generally and in many instances may be quite inappropriate for a particular role. The insensitive tycoon who rides roughshod over his business rivals by ruthless power play can be regarded as 'well adjusted' in this role, but these qualities would all be handicaps if he was a social worker dealing with problem families. Platt also points out that different subcultures have very different expectations of social function and performance, and to introduce a blanket expectation is quite inappropriate:

> Instead, however, the authors assess behavior against ideal norms, the latter derived from the views of social scientists and their own experience. The ideal norm constitutes a standard for a 'very satisfactory' social adjustment. It is 'what we know we ought to do', as opposed to what we actually do (Platt, 1981).

The same concepts are central to the SSIAM, probably the most widely used of all social adjustment scales. In this scale social maladjustment is defined as 'ineffective performance in the roles and tasks for which an individual has been socialized' (Gurland *et al.*, 1972, p. 259). It is clear from the items in the scale that ineffective performance is based on an ideal notion of roles and tasks that has no external validation. Similarly, the SAS is also scored against general societal norms rather than specific ones from the culture concerned.

In many ways it is understandable why a general norm has been introduced. It is difficult to decide what the norms of each subculture are and there is no doubt that reliability of scales is improved if a single norm is applied for all subjects. Thus an item of behaviour such as the frequency of sexual intercourse is easy to record and comparison with an ideal norm (e.g. frequency of twice weekly) can allow reliable rating to be achieved. This, however, may be an extremely invalid method of measuring social adjustment. Platt provides one good example:

> The male chauvinist wife-beater who comes home drunk every night and forces his wife to make love may very well even reach the top of the scale (the ideal norm) but it is unlikely that his wife perceives his performance in the same way. The researcher is perfectly entitled to measure the subject's frequency of sexual intercourse, but the data he obtains may be irrelevant to an evaluation of role-appropriate behaviour (Platt, 1981, p. 106).

Although the SIAM is more conscious of the different expectations of different subcultures, there is still concern that ideal normative behaviour is in the background when measuring whether performance is adequate in the 'satisfaction' part of the scale.

The best way of overcoming this problem is to use the patient and the important people in his or her life (clumsily termed 'significant others' in the sociological literature) and ask them to decide whether social functioning is adequate or impaired. Thus for each of the major areas of social function the subject or informant is asked for their views irrespective of societal expectations. This approach is formalized in two scales, the Social Behaviour Assessment Schedule (SBAS) (Platt *et al.*, 1978) and the Social Functioning Schedule (SFS) (Remington and Tyrer, 1979).

Of these, the SBAS is by far the more comprehensive and includes (as near as possible) objective assessment of behaviour in all important role areas, but this makes the scale too long for many investigators. The SFS also includes an informant version.

In deciding on a scale for measuring social adjustment the investigator should ask two questions:

(1) Do I want to measure social function or social network?
(2) Does it matter to the investigation whether the assessments are subject-based or norm-based?

The first question is easier to answer. Many investigators in the social sciences are more interested in the supports and social contacts available to subjects and the quality of these relationships rather than their individual social functioning. Although the frequency and content of social contacts are included in all assessments of social adjustment they form only a small part and do not indicate the nature and degree of the social network. A combination of network analysis (e.g. Cohen and Sokolowsky, 1979) and rating scales (e.g. Henderson *et al.*, 1980) is probably the best way to proceed.

Most investigators have tended to ignore the second question, as it is assumed that both subject and society have the same perception of social adjustment. Often they coincide, but when they differ most existing scales fail to detect the changes. For large-scale epidemiological studies it can be argued that it is reasonable to ignore these differences as the large numbers involved come closer to representing a societal view that is an amalgam of several subcultures. This becomes a less tenable proposition when smaller numbers are involved, most commonly in studies of treatment in which social adjustment is just one of several variables measured. If a patient achieves normative criteria for social adjustment, but creates personal suffering or distress to others, this can hardly be described as good social function. Apparently important clinical findings, such as the demonstration that psychotherapy has greater benefit on social adjustment than antidepressant drug therapy (Weissman *et al.*, 1974), may be misleading. This may only indicate better social conformity, not social adjustment in the broadest sense. The issue is bound to remain controversial until more data are available; particularly comparisons of instruments such as the SBAS with the SSIAM. It is likely to assume greater prominence because of the current interest in the measurement of 'quality of life'. This is of particular concern to health planners put in the unenviable position of allocating resources according to agreed priorities. Should more money be given for transplant surgery or more for the community care of the mentally ill? Nobody has yet managed to get half-way to a satisfactory answer, but it is likely that measures of social adjustment may be used for this purpose. If they are going to be determined by societal norms this will set a dangerous precedent.

It is also fair to mention that there is likely to be a higher correlation between social adjustment and clinical symptomatology if a subject-based model of social function is used. The correlation is of the order of +0.7 in patients with definite psychiatric disorder and +0.5 in non-cases (Casey *et al.*, 1985; Casey and Tyrer, 1986). This may go some way to explaining the similar findings in outcome studies for both symptoms and social function (Tyrer and Remington, 1979; Platt *et al.*, 1981; Tyrer *et al.*, 1987). This should not be used as an argument for ignoring the measure of social function. It only acknowledges that both mental state and personality disorder produce marked impairment of function, and that in most instances improvement in disorder leads to improvement in both domains.

CHOICE OF MEASURE FOR ASSESSING PERSONALITY DISORDER

Although the biochemical and physiological 'abnormalities' in some forms of personality disorder are interesting and of theoretical significance they are of little value for diagnostic and assessment purposes (Raine and Venables, 1988). As with the assessment of social function the investigator is left with questionnaires and rating scales as the only measures worth consideration. For reasons already discussed, questionnaires are best used for screening purposes rather than definitive measures of personality disorder, and their use for recording traits in essentially well individuals is likely to remain their main value.

The choice of interview schedule is determined primarily by the type of classification required by the investigator. If DSM-III-R personality disorders are being measured then one of the tailor-made instruments for this purpose (SCID-II, SID-P or PDE) should be used (the exact choice may be determined more by the length of the interview than by any other consideration) and the PDQ may be a less satisfactory alternative or be used for screening.

For assessment of the proposed ICD-10 personality disorders the new International Version of the PDE (IPDE) or the revised SAP can be used, but it is likely that many other instruments will follow once the classification is published. Although the attractions of using instruments that are linked to standard classifications are obvious, they do have the disadvantage of impermanence and other difficulties. These include the problems of classifying two or more personality disorders when the criteria for both are satisfied, the arbitrary divisions between normal personality and disorder, and criteria for diagnosis that increasingly demand that the subject only should be interviewed (Tyrer, 1989).

Instruments that are independent of these classifications (mainly the MCMI and the PAS) allow trait scoring and subcategorization of degrees of personality difficulty, and also have standard procedures for accommodating many simultaneous personality disorders. In many studies there is interest in the effect of personality on outcome. The recording of key traits, present in all subjects, allows additional comparisons to be made independently of the influence of categorically diagnosed personality disorders.

An alternative is to study a defined personality disorder independently of others. Thus borderline personality disorder can be recorded using the Schedule for Interviewing Borderlines (SIB) (Baron, 1981) or the Diagnostic Interview for Borderline Patients (DIP) (Gunderson *et al.*, 1981), antisocial personality disorder measured using the Diagnostic Interview Schedule (DIS) (Robins *et al.*, 1979) (together with mental state assessment), and schizotypal personality disorder using the Schedule for Schizotypal Personalities (SSP) (Baron *et al.*, 1981). The author regards this approach as quite wrong. The overlap between personality disorders is so great that it is artificial to select one group only and ignore all others. Severe personality disorders can cross most of the boundaries in current classifications (Loranger *et al.*, 1987; Mbatia and Tyrer, 1988) and so satisfy the diagnostic criteria for many categories simultaneously. The examination of each singly can only mislead.

The successful measurement of personality disorder and social function is one of the most difficult tasks in mental health assessment. It has to escape the influences of moral values, cultural differences and social engineering in order to achieve validity. Although it has made a start, it has a very long way to go.

ACKNOWLEDGEMENTS

The author would like to acknowledge the help of Stephen Platt, Sheila Hewett, Brian Ferguson and Allen Frances in stimulating the more complicated ideas expressed in this chapter.

APPENDIX 1: SOCIAL FUNCTIONING QUESTIONNAIRE (SFQ)

Name: Date:

Please look at the statements below and tick the reply that comes closest to how you have been over the past two weeks.

		Score
I complete my tasks at work and at home satisfactorily	Most of the time	0
	Quite often	1
	Sometimes	2
	Not at all	3
I find my tasks at work and at home very stressful	Most of the time	3
	Quite often	2
	Sometimes	1
	Not at all	0
I have no money problems.	No problems at all	0
	Slight worries only	1
	Definite difficulties	2
	Very severe problems	3
I have difficulties in getting and keeping close relationships	Severe difficulties	3
	Some problems	2
	Occasional problems	1
	No problems at all	0

I have problems in my sex life.	Severe problems	3
	Moderate problems	2
	Occasional problems	1
	None at all	0
I get on well with my family and other relatives.	Yes, definitely	0
	Yes, usually	1
	No, some problems	2
	No, severe problems	3
I feel lonely and isolated from other people	Almost all the time	3
	Much of the time	2
	Not usually	1
	Not at all	0
I enjoy my spare time.	Very much	0
	Sometimes	1
	Not often	2
	Not at all	3

Total ☐

The Social Functioning Questionnaire (SFQ) (Tyrer, 1985) is unpublished but has been shown to correlate well with interview instruments for recording social functioning in preliminary studies. The scale illustrates the main areas covered by all instruments that attempt to measure social adjustment.

APPENDIX 2: Examples of items from the Personality Disorder Examination (PDE).

This illustrates the use of Interview Schedules to measure the operational criteria of DSM-III and DSM-III-R. The operational criteria are bold type, questions inquiring about their presence or absence are given below and the scoring system is explained by the subsequent glossary. Wherever possible, a 0,1 or 2 score is given and the ? is only used if it is impossible to get a satisfactory reply.

---

67. 0 1 2 ? *0 1 2 ?* **Reads hidden demeaning or threatening meanings into benign remarks or events**
Paranoid: 3

Do you ever find hidden meanings or threats in what people say or do?
If yes: Give me some examples.

68. 0 1 2 ? *0 1 2 ?* **Expects, without sufficient basis, to be exploited or harmed by others**
Paranoid: 1

Has it been your experience that people often try to use you or take advantage of you?
If yes: Give me some examples.

Has anyone ever deliberately tried to harm you, ruin your reputation, or make life difficult for you?
If yes: Give me some examples.

69. 0 1 2 ? *0 1 2 ?* **Ideas of reference (excluding delusions of reference)**
Schizotypal: 1

When you enter a room full of people do you often wonder whether they might be talking about you or even making unflattering remarks about you?
If yes: Give me some examples.

When you're in a public place or walking down the street, do you sometimes worry about whether people might be looking at you, making fun of you, or criticizing you?
If yes: Give me some examples.

Example of Scoring System

Expects, without sufficient basis, to be exploited or harmed by others
Paranoid: 1

Affirmative replies to the questions that assess this criterion require considerable probing and judgment on the part of the examiner, because there must be an assessment of the possible reality basis of the subject's reported experiences. Too much emphasis should not be given to accounts of isolated incidents. The focus should be on identifying a characteristic attitude on the part of the subject suggesting he has an orientation or set toward the expectation of exploitation or harm. His approach to the interview itself may be taken into consideration in the scoring, but should never be the sole basis for a score of 2.

2 Frequently expects, without sufficient basis, to be exploited or harmed by others.

1 Occasionally expects, without sufficient basis, to be exploited or harmed by others.

0 Denied, rare, or not supported by convincing examples.

Extracts with permission from Dr Armand Loranger *et al.*,
The New York Hospital—Cornell Medical Center,
21, Bloomingdale Road,
White Plains,
New York 10605, USA.

REFERENCES

American Psychiatric Association (1987) *Diagnostic and Statistical Manual of Mental Disorders,* 3rd edn revised, American Psychiatric Association, Washington, DC.

Baron, M. (1981) *Schedule for Interviewing Borderlines,* New York State Psychatric Institute, New York.

Barrabee, R., Barrabee, E.L. and Finesinger, J.E.F. (1955) A normative social adjustment scale. *American Journal of Psychiatry,* **112**, 252–9.

Berger, D.G., Rice, C.E., Sewall, L.G. *et al.* (1964) The post-hospital evaluation of psychiatric patients: the social adjustment inventory method. *Psychiatric Study Projects,* **2**, 1–30.

Blackburn, R. (1988) On moral judgements and personality disorders; the myth of psychopathic personality revisited. *British Journal of Psychiatry,* **153**, 505–12.

Brugha, T.S., Sturt, E., McCarthy, B., Potter, J., Wykes, T. and Bebbington, P.E. (1987) The Interview Measure of Social Relationships: the description and evaluation of a survey instrument for assessing personal social resources. *Social Psychiatry,* **22**, 123–8.

Casey, P.R. and Tyrer, P.J. (1986) Personality, functioning and symptomatology. *Journal of Psychiatric Research,* **20**, 363–74.

Casey, P.R., Tyrer, P.J. and Platt, S. (1985) The relationship between social functioning and psychiatric symptomatology in primary care. *Social Psychiatry,* **20**, 5–10.

Cattell, R.B. (1965) *The Scientific Analysis of Personality,* Penguin, Harmondsworth.

Ciarlo, J.A. and Reihman, J. (1975) *The Denver Community Mental Health Questionnaire: Development of a Multi-dimensional Program Evaluation Instrument,* Mental Health Systems Evaluation Project, Northwest Denver Mental Health Center and the University of Denver, Denver.

Clare, A.W. and Cairns, V.E. (1978) Design, development and use of a standardized interview to assess social maladjustment and dysfunction in community studies. *Psychological Medicine,* **8**, 589–604.

Clayton, P. and Hirschfeld, R. (1977) *Personal Resources Inventory (PRI),* Washington University School of Medicine, St Louis.

Cohen, C. and Sokolowsky, J. (1979) Clinical use of network analysis for psychiatric and aged populations. *Community Mental Health Journal,* **15**, 203–13.

Cohler, B., Woolsey, S., Weiss, J. *et al.* (1968) Child rearing attitudes among mothers volunteering and revolunteering for a psychological study. *Psychological Reports*, **23**, 603–12.

Derogatis, L.R. (1976) *Scoring and Procedures Manual for PAIS*, Clinical Psychometric Research, Baltimore.

Derogatis, L.R. (1977) *PAIS: Self Report*, Clinical Psychometric Research, Baltimore.

Eysenck, H.J. (1959) *The Maudsley Personality Inventory (MPI)*, University of London Press, London.

Eysenck, H.J. and Eysenck, S.B.G. (1964) *Manual of the Eysenck Personality Inventory*, University of London Press, London.

Frank, E. and Kupfer, D.J. (1974) *The KDS-15: A Marital Questionnaire*, Western Psychiatric Institute and Clinic, University of Pittsburgh, Pittsburgh.

Glazer, W., Aaronson, H.S., Prusoff, B.A. *et al.* (1980) Assessment of social adjustment in chronic ambulatory schizophrenics. *Journal of Nervous and Mental Disease*, **168**, 493–7.

Goodman, S.P., Schulthorpe, W.B., Evje, M. *et al.* (1969) Social dysfunction among psychiatric and nonpsychiatric outpatients. *Journal of the American Geriatric Society*, **17**, 697–700.

Gunderson, J.G., Kolb, J.E. and Austin, V. (1981) The diagnostic interview for borderline patients. *American Journal of Psychiatry*, **138**, 896–903.

Gurland, B.J., Yorkston, N.J., Stone, A.R., Frank, J.D. and Fleiss, J.L. (1972) The structured and scaled interview to assess maladjustment (SSIAM): I. Description, rationale and development. *Archives of General Psychiatry*, **27**, 259–64.

Henderson, S., Duncan-Jones, P., McAuley, H. and Ritchie, K. (1978) The patient's primary group. *British Journal of Psychiatry*, **132**, 74–86.

Henderson, S., Duncan-Jones, P., Byrne, D.G. *et al.* (1980) Measuring social relationships: The Interview Schedule for Social Interaction. *Psychological Medicine*, **10**, 1–12.

Hill, D. and Watterson, D. (1942) Electroencephalographic studies of psychopathic personalities. *Journal of Neurology and Psychiatry*, **5**, 47–52.

Hyler, S.E., Reider, R.O., Williams, J.B.W. *et al.* (1983) *Personality Diagnostic Questionnaire*, New York State Psychiatric Institute, 722 West 168th Street, New York, NY 10032.

Hyler, S.E., Reider, R.O., Williams, J.B.W., Spitzer, R.L., Hendler, J. and Lyons, M. (1988) The Personality Diagnostic Questionnaire: development and preliminary results. *Journal of Personality Disorders*, **2**, 229–37.

Katz, M.M. and Lyerly, S.B. (1963) Methods of measuring adjustment and social behavior in the community: I. Rationale, description, discriminative validity and scale development. *Psychological Reports*, **13**, 503–35.

Kind, P., Rosser, R. and Williams, A. (1982) Valuation of quality of life: some psychometric evidence. In M.W. Jones-Lee (ed.), *The Value of Life and Safety*, North-Holland, Amsterdam.

Loranger, A.W., Oldham, J.M., Russakoff, L.M. and Susman, V. (1985) Personality Disorder Examination (PDE). A Structured Interview for DSM-III-R and ICD-10 personality disorders. WHO/ADAMHA pilot version, The New York Hospital, Cornell Medical Center, Westchester Division, White Plains, New York.

Loranger, A.W., Oldham, J.M., Russakoff, L.M. and Susman, V. (1987) The Personality Disorder Examination: a preliminary report. *Journal of Personality Disorders*, **1**, 1–13.

McDowell, I. and Newell, C. (1986) *Measuring Health: a Guide to Rating Scales and Questionnaires*, Oxford University Press, New York.

Mann, A.H., Jenkins, R., Cutting, J.C. and Cowen, P.J. (1981) The development and use of a standardized assessment of abnormal personality. *Psychological Medicine*, **11**, 839–47.

Mbatia, J. and Tyrer, P. (1988) Personality status of dangerous patients of a special hospital. In P. Tyrer (ed.), *Personality Disorders: Diagnosis, Management and Course*, pp. 105–11, Wright, London.

Mednick, S.A., Volavka, J., Gabrielli, W.F. and Itil, T.M. (1981) EEG as a predictor of antisocial behavior. *Criminology*, **19**, 219–29.

Millon, T. (1969) *Modern Psychopathology: a Biosocial Approach to Maladaptive Learning and Functioning*, W.B. Saunders, Philadelphia.

Millon, T. (1983) *Millon Clinical Multiaxial Inventory Manual*, 3rd edn, National Computer, Minneapolis.

Millon, T. (1985) The MCMI provides a good assessment of DSM-III disorders: the MCMI-II will prove even better. *Journal of Personality Assessment*, **49**, 379–91.

Morey, L.C., Waugh, P. and Blashfield, R.K. (1985) MMPI scales for DSM-III personality disorders: their derivation and correlates. *Journal of Personality Assessment*, **49**, 245–51.

Morrow, G.R., Chiarello, R.J. and Derogatis, L.R. (1978) A new scale for assessing patients' psychological adjustment to mental illness. *Psychological Medicine*, **8**, 605–10.

Paykel, E.S., Weissman, M.M., Prusoff, B.A. *et al.* (1971) Dimensions of social adjustment. *Journal of Nervous and Mental Disease*, **152**, 158–72.

Pfohl, B., Stangl, D. and Zimmerman, M. (1982) *Structured Interview for DSM-III Personality Disorders (SIDP)*, University of Iowa Hospitals and Clinics, Iowa City.

Platt, S. (1981) Social adjustment as a criterion of success: just what are we measuring? *Psychiatry*, **44**, 95–112.

Platt, S., Weyman, A. and Hirsch, S. (1978) *Social Behaviour Assessment Schedule*, 2nd edn, unpublished schedule, Department of Psychiatry, Charing Cross Hospital, London.

Platt, S., Weyman, A., Hirsch, S. and Hewett, S. (1980) The Social Behaviour Assssment Schedule (SBAS): rationale, contents, scoring and reliability of a new interview schedule. *Social Psychiatry*, **15**, 43–55.

Platt, S.D., Hirsch, S.R. and Knights, A.C. (1981) Effects of brief hospitalization on psychiatric patients' behaviour and social functioning. *Acta Psychiatrica Scandinavica*, **63**, 117–28.

Raine, A. and Venables, P.H. (1988) Enhanced P3 evoked potentials and longer P3 recovery times in psychopaths. *Psychophysiology*, **25**, 30–8.

Reich, J., Noyes, R., Jr and Troughton, E. (1987) Lack of agreement between instruments assessing DSM-III personality disorders. *Proceedings of the First Millon Clinical Multiaxial Inventory Conference* (in press).

Remington, M. and Tyrer, P. (1979) The Social Functioning Schedule—a brief semi-structured interview. *Social Psychiatry*, **14**, 151–7.

Robins, L., Helzer, J., Croughan, J., Williams, J.B.W. and Spitzer, R.L. (1979) *The National Institute of Mental Health Diagnostic Interview Schedule*, NIMH, Rockville, Maryland.

Spitzer, R., Williams, J.B.W. and Gibbon, M. (1987) *Structured Interview for DSM-III-R Personality Disorders*, Biometrics Research Department, New York State Psychiatric Institute, New York.

Strauss, J.S. and Carpenter, W.T. Jr. (1972) The prediction of outcome in schizophrenia: I. Characteristics of outcome. *Archives of General Psychiatry*, **27**, 739–46.

Streiner, D.L. and Miller, H.R. (1988) Validity of MMPI scales for DSM-III personality disorders: what are they measuring? *Journal of Personality Disorders*, **2**, 238–42.
Tyrer, P. (1985) *The Social Functioning Questionnaire*. Unpublished.
Tyrer, P. (1987) Measurement of personality: a review. *Journal of the Royal Society of Medicine*, **80**, 637–9.
Tyrer, P. (1989) What's wrong with DSM-III personality disorders? *Journal of Personality Disorders* (in press).
Tyrer, P. and Alexander, J. (1979) Classification of personality disorder. *British Journal of Psychiatry*, **135**, 163–7.
Tyrer, P.J. and Remington, M. (1979) Controlled comparison of day hospital and outpatient treatment for neurotic disorders. *Lancet*, **i**, 1014–16.
Tyrer, P., Remington, M. and Alexander, J. (1987) The outcome of neurotic disorders after out-patient and day hospital care. *British Journal of Psychiatry*, **151**, 57–62.
Tyrer, P., Alexander, J. and Ferguson, B. (1988) Personality Assessment Schedule (PAS). In P.J. Tyrer (ed.), *Personality Disorders: Diagnosis, Management and Course*, pp. 140–67, Wright, London.
Weissman, M.M. (1975) The assessment of social adjustment: a review of techniques. *Archives of General Psychiatry*, **32**, 357–65.
Weissman, M.M. and Bothwell, S. (1976) The assessment of social adjustment by patient self-report. *Archives of General Psychiatry*, **33**, 1111–15.
Weissman, M.M., Klerman, G.L., Paykel, E.S. *et al.* (1974) Treatment effects on the social adjustment of depressed patients. *Archives of General Psychiatry*, **30**, 771–8.
Weissman, M.M., Sholomskas, D. and John, K. (1981) The assessment of social adjustment: an update. *Archives of General Psychiatry*, **38**, 1250–8.
Widiger, T.A. and Frances, A. (1987) Interviews and inventories for the measurement of personality disorders. *Clinical Psychology Review*, **7**, 49–56.
Willer, B. and Biggin, P. (1974) *Self-assessment Guide: Rationale, Development and Evaluation*, Lakeshore Psychiatric Hospital, Toronto, Canada.
Willer, B. and Biggin, P. (1976) Comparison of rehospitalized and non-hospitalized psychiatric patients on community adjustment: self-assessment guide. *Psychiatry*, **39**, 239–44.
Wing, J.K., Cooper, J.E. and Sartorius, N. (1974) *The Measurement and Classification of Psychiatric Symptoms*, Cambridge University Press, Cambridge.
World Health Organization (1978) Mental disorders: glossary and guide to their classification in accordance with the ninth revision of the International Classification of Diseases, WHO, Geneva.
World Health Organization (1988) International Classification of Diseases, draft for 10th revision, WHO, Geneva.

Chapter 7

Process and Outcome in Psychotherapy

CHRIS P.L. FREEMAN and JENNY K.M. MUNRO

INTRODUCTION

There are literally thousands of psychotherapy rating scales and many large books have been written solely on measuring change in psychotherapy. Unlike other areas in psychiatry such as depression, anxiety and eating disorders, there are virtually no generally agreed outcome measures. The great majority of scales have been used only in one study. The pattern in psychotherapy research until recently appears to have been for the researcher to review the established literature, decide that there was no suitable scale for his particular study available, and then devise his own idiosyncratic measure. We have tried in this review to mention those measures which have been used in several studies and where there is some, usually scant, information available on validity and reliability. As this book is meant to be a practical guide we have not discussed any of the complex issues concerning what is appropriate to be measured in psychotherapy, and for this we would refer the reader to more detailed texts such as Lambert *et al.* (1983), Garfield and Bergin (1986) or Kendall and Butcher (1982).

Most of the chapter refers to rating scales that have been used in dynamically orientated psychotherapies, but there is a relatively comprehensive section on cognitive behavioural therapy. We have dealt only briefly with behaviour therapy. This is because behaviour therapists tend to use relatively straightforward measures, using established ratings scales or constructing simple ways of counting behaviours. Most behaviour therapy research has been on specific groups of patients (e.g. anxious, depressed, etc.) and the appropriate measures are covered in the relevant chapters in this book.

GLOBAL CHANGE MEASURES

Global ratings are useful as summary statements, although they do not supply the detailed information provided by multi-dimensional ratings.

Measuring Human Problems. Edited by D.F. Peck and C.M. Shapiro

They are a means of expressing change as a simple numerical difference between pre- and post-therapy scores. Despite their non-specific nature and emphasis on symptoms as opposed to attitudes and feelings, they have been widely used in psychotherapy studies. In general, global outcome measures tend to produce an outcome more favourable to the therapy being assessed than do measures of specific symptoms (Table 7.1).

Table 7.1 Global rating scales.

Scale	Reference	Comments
The Multiple Affect Checklist (MAACL)	Zuckerman (1960)	Self-report, 132 adjectives describing anxiety, depression and hostility. Anxiety measure most useful for outcome assessment but susceptible to response bias
The Health Sickness Rating Scale (HSRS)	Luborsky (1962)	Observer/therapist rating on 100-point scale up to ideal state of health. Seven subscales and one global rating—vignettes for comparison
Hopkins Symptom Checklist (HSCL)	Main ref.: Derogatis *et al.* (1974)	Recommended as part of the core battery in the NIMH outcome study project.
HSCL 58		58 items—widely used
HSCL 72		72 items include anger and hostility scales
HSCL 90		90 items—allows for more severe psychopathology
General Health Questionnaire (GHQ)	Goldberg (1972)	Self-rating 60 items: takes 10 minutes
GHQ 28	Goldberg and Hillier (1979)	Short version with four subscales, widely used
Symptom Rating Test (SRT)	Kellner and Sheffield (1973)	Checklist of 38 items, optional severity scale. Measures short-term changes in distress. Self-report or interview with cards
Global Adjustment Scale (GAS)	Endicott *et al.* (1976)	100-point scale. Provides more anchor points than HSRS. Simpler to score. Well used in outcome research

The Health Sickness Rating Scale (HSRS) (Luborsky, 1962) is a 100-point scale where the client's level of adjustment is rated from the lowest conceivable to an ideal state of health. There are seven scales linked to a final global rating which is decided on by comparison with 30 brief case vignettes.

Luborsky and Bachrach (1974) have reviewed 18 studies using the HSRS and provide details of reliability and validity.

The Global Adjustment Scale (GAS) was introduced by Endicott *et al.* (1976) as a modification of the HSRS. It provides more anchor points using concrete behavioural examples and excludes the HSRS's seven subscales and case vignettes, and therefore takes considerably less time to use. It has been found sensitive to change and its psychometric properties have been explored more thoroughly than the HSRS. Inter-rater reliability ranges from 0.69 to 0.91 and the GAS reaches acceptable levels of concurrent validity.

The GAS is recommended for use in psychotherapy research by Auerbach (1983) because it provides a brief, simple outcome measure but it is comparable across other studies. It has been modified recently to the unfortunate-sounding GAF, and this version appears in the DSM-III-R handbook (American Psychiatric Association, 1987).

SYMPTOM CHECKLISTS

The Hopkins Symptom Checklist

The HSCL, designed for out-patient groups, is a symptom checklist used frequently in outcome assessment (Lambert *et al.*, 1983; Shapiro and Firth, 1987). The scale was developed as a 58-item self-report measure (Derogatis *et al.*, 1974). Factor analysis revealed five primary dimensions, including interpersonal sensitivity, somatization, anxiety, depression and cognitive performance. The HSCL-72 provides additional information concerning anger and hostility and phobic anxiety. Further adaptation has produced the HSCL-90 with measures of more severe psychiatric problems such as psychotism and paranoid ideation. It is rated on a 5-point scale thus allowing for degrees of severity (Lipman *et al.*, 1979). All three scales are presently in use, therefore the researcher can decide on the most appropriate measure for his or her subject group.

Test–retest reliability for the factors of the HSCL-58 range from 0.75 (for the anxiety scale) to 0.85. The scale has been shown to be sensitive to change in a variety of different outcome studies (for example, Shapiro and Firth, 1987). Derogatis *et al.* (1974) provide normative data.

Measuring psychodynamic change

The process of treating someone with psychodynamic psychotherapy involves a complex and very personal interaction between patient and therapist.

It is perhaps not surprising that dynamic psychotherapists argue that no rating scale, however ingenious, can capture the subtleties of this interaction. Treating someone with psychotherapy is a very different process to that of using a drug or physical method of treatment. In the latter, at least to some extent, the variance due to the treatment can be held reasonably constant. Psychodynamic psychotherapy sees symptoms as only the superficial markers of underlying conflict, and therefore to produce a complete picture of change reliable assessments are needed of these deeper 'neurotic' processes. Change in dynamic psychotheraphy may result in increasing anxiety and depression so that symptom scores may get worse rather than better during treatment. To assess these factors long-term studies are required, and yet remarkably few such investigations have been carried out.

Malan (1959, 1963) has described an individualized method of outcome assessment where a global measure of the optimum change for each client is defined by a panel of judges at the beginning of treatment as a criterion to assess actual change. Agreeing upon 'the basic neurotic conflict' requires a great deal of experienced clinicians' time, but because clinical formulations are integral to the practice of psychodynamic psychotherapy such a method was acceptable to researchers because of its concurrent value in practice and for its high face validity (De Witt *et al.*, 1983).

Measurement of neurotic conflict has been challenged. Mintz (1981) re-examined Malan's data and concluded that, in comparison to symptomatic measures of change, the dynamic component failed to add any further meaning to the understanding of the treatment outcome in the majority of the patients assessed. Mintz suggested that 60 per cent of the variation in the dynamic assessments could be accounted for on the basis of symptomatic change as measured by untrained raters, and that if a patient's initial symptoms did not subside, there was no positive dynamic change. However, dynamic and symptomatic assessments did diverge in cases where initial symptoms improved. This suggests that symptomatic improvement may occur without change at a deeper level but not vice versa. Mintz was not debating the value of assessing dynamic change itself but was questioning the use of a time-consuming method that does have rather low construct and inter-rater reliability, when in most cases a brief measure of symptomatic change provided the same information.

Curtis *et al.* (1988) describe a method for developing a dynamic case formulation and measures of its reliability. They state that from this method it is possible to develop reliable psychodynamic formulations which can be employed in clinically relevant studies of the process and outcome of dynamic psychotherapy.

The problem with case formulations is the difficulty with achieving acceptable levels of reliability. They are usually complex narratives that vary between raters.

Caston (1986) developed a method for dealing with reliability named the 'plan diagnosis' (PD). His procedure involved asking clinical judges to rate how far they agree with the component parts of a formulation developed by a separate team of clinicians rather than developing an entirely independent formulation. The problem of creating complex and dissimilar formulations was resolved by defining uniform components in the formulation. These comprised 'goals', 'obstacles to achieving goals' and 'insights'. Judges were able to weight the importance of the different aspects of a formulation. Therefore interjudge agreement is easily determined, and acceptable reliabilities can be achieved. This procedure has been applied to formulations of brief dynamic psychotherapy with acceptable measures of reliability (Curtis and Silberschatz, 1986; Curtis *et al.*, 1988). However, the authors comment that achieving reliability on a series of discrete items may not be as satisfactory as agreeing on a dynamic formulation as a whole (Caston, 1986).

In an attempt to produce a measure with acceptable reliability Luborsky (1977) developed the Core Conflictual Relationship Theme (CCRT). This involves breaking the clinical formulation into categories of 'wish', 'response from other' and 'response from self'. The CCRT is covered fully in Luborsky's most recent text (Luborsky, 1988).

The 'Change After Psychotherapy' (CHAP) scale is described by Sandell (1987a). This is a method for rating post-therapy information and measures the rate and to what extent the patient has changed during and after psychotherapy in four aspects. These are prevalence and tolerance for symptoms, adaptive capacity, self-insight and resolution of the basic conflict. There are a large number of 'signs' for each of the variables and these are rated first on a rough rating of 0, 0.5 and 1. It is suggested that finer gradations are made after this by comparison with other patients rated on previous occasions. The reliability and validity of the CHAP are discussed by Sandell (1987b).

The Patterns of Individual Change Scale (PICS) (Kaltreider *et al.*, 1981) was designed in an attempt to overcome the psychometric problems of measuring changes occurring 'beyond symptoms' in psychodynamic therapy in a grieving population. The scale is designed for use with video recordings of the therapy sessions and is estimated to take about 2 hours to complete. It is a standardized measure and includes 13 scales such as 'capacity for intimacy', 'self-esteem' and 'work identity'. The scale is designed to provide clear definitions of these areas of self-functioning. The authors suggest the use of a wheel graph to illustrate the clients' patterns of change. The drawback to the PICS is that it is, like clinical formulations, a time-consuming outcome measure requiring trained clinicians. Data from a bereaved population of 28 showed inter-rater reliability of 0.77–0.95 and a factor analysis revealed two main factors, one defined as a measure of social functioning, the other a symptomatic measure of the grief process. The intimacy scale appeared as a separate factor and outcome data suggest that it measures an area of change not detected in measures of symptomatic change (Weiss *et al.*, 1985).

PERSONALITY SCALES AS OUTCOME MEASURES

Wide band measures

It is often assumed that change in psychotherapy involves total personality restructuring and therefore initial personality traits must be assessed and changes measured. In this case, both the stable (source) personality traits and the more flexible (surface) characteristics should be measured in outcome studies. However, it appears from careful inspection of the use of measures of personality in outcome studies that patients generally show a flattening of their profile, i.e. any extreme traits become more 'normal' rather than any real changes in their personality. The use of personality measures in psychotherapy is an area of debate. Gynther and Green (1982) comment in their criticism of personality measures that 'the inability of personality constructs to go beyond the tests of the 1940s and 50s is demonstrated by the continued use of the MMPI and the CPI in the 1980's'. Another drawback to using these instruments as outcome measures is that most of them take at least an hour to complete (see Table 7.2).

The MMPI has been reported to be the most frequently used instrument in psychotherapy research (Lambert *et al.*, 1983). This is a self-report measure of 556 statements divided into ten clinical subscales. It was designed for use as a diagnostic instrument, with strong nosological orientation, not as a measure of change. Cartwright (1975) has suggested that some of the subscales do not show sufficient reliability or sensitivity to change as a result of treatment, although many of them are used independently as outcome measures. However, its use in outcome research, although an area of controversy, has been recommended as one of the core measurements in the NIMH outcome measures project (Waskow and Parloff, 1975). Its benefits include extensive normative data and use across many outcome studies. Restandardization, an update of the language, etc. is in progress by the Minnesota group and Parker *et al.* (1988) provide a thorough update of reliability and stability data.

Another commonly used assessment of change is the Butler–Haig Q sort (Dymond, 1954). This self-report scale comprises 100 statements referring to general aspects of personality, presented independently on cards. The client sorts the cards into piles, on a scale of nine from 'least like me' to 'most like me', producing a normal distribution. Two scores are derived, one being 'The Self and The Ideal Self (QSI), the other the Adjustment Score (QAS).

Table 7.2 Personality change measures.

Scale	Reference	Comments
Butler–Haig Q Sort	Dymond (1954)	Self-report 100 statements on cards sorted on a 9-point scale: takes at least 40 minutes
California Psychological Inventory (CPI)	Gough (1957)	480 true–false items on 18 scales of positive attributes. Lengthy
Personal Orientations Inventory (POI)	Shostrum (1964)	12 scales measuring state of positive mental health
16 Personality Factor Questionnaire (16PF)	Cattell (1966)	187 trichotomous items, value lies in assessment of normal personality variables, takes 1 hour
Minnesota Multi-Phasic Personality Inventory (MMPI)	Dahlstrom *et al.* (1975)	556 self-report statements. Respond true, false, or cannot say. 10 clinical subscales—some commonly used in outcome. Caution required in its use as an outcome measure
Millon Clinical Multi-Axial Inventory (MCMI)	Millon (1982)	175 items. Designed to parallel DSM-III diagnostic criteria. May be promising for use in outcome studies
Interpersonal Style Inventory (ISI)	Lorr and Youniss (1983)	Self-report, 300 true–false items on 15 scales. Measures interpersonal dispositions and impulse control
ISI (Short Form)	Lorr and DeJong (1986)	150 items: takes 20 minutes
Barron Ego Strength	Barron (1953)	68 items from the MMPI, designed to predict response to psychotherapy
Rosenberg Self-Esteem Scale	Rosenberg (1965)	Self-report, 10 items on a 4-point Likert scale. Easy and quick to use
Self-Control Schedule (SCS)	Rosenbaum (1980)	Self-report, 36 items on a 6-point scale. Developed to assess ability to use self-coping strategies
Self-Attitude Inventory (SAI)	Lorr and Wunderlich (1986)	Self-report scale, 32 paired statements. Assesses confidence and perceived social approval
Robson's Self-Esteem Scale	Robson (1989a)	30 items on a 7-point scale. Assesses several aspects of self-esteem

However, the correlation between the two has been reported to be very high before and after treatment, suggesting they both measure the same aspect of change (Lambert *et al.*, 1986). Test–retest reliability is acceptable at 0.76 for the QSI and 0.86 for the QAS (Cartwright, 1975).

Another popular measure is the Personal Orientation Inventory (POI) (Shostrum, 1964), which concerns the client's more positive mental health attributes including self-actualization and capacity for intimacy. The variety of scores and reliability of individual scales make it a potentially valuable instrument for assessing change. Test–retest reliability is reported to be 0.85. An important criticism of this measure is that after therapy, clients' increased awareness of more self-actualized responses may produce false positive results (e.g. as in 'reasons are not needed to justify my feelings'). It has been noted that Shostrum's own outcome group became more homogeneous on every scale (Lambert *et al.*, 1986).

The California Psychological Inventory (CPI) (Gough, 1957) is a source trait scale designed to reflect increasing levels of social and emotional maturity. It consists of 18 subscales of true/false items, and has been criticized because all but four of the subscales are intercorrelated at least 0.5 with another subscale (Gleser, 1975). Dahlstrom (1975) recommends the use of the CPI alongside the MMPI because of its value as a coping measure.

The Millon Clinical Multi-Axial Inventory (MCMI) (Millon, 1982) has produced increasing interest as an outcome measure. It is a 175-item inventory with 20 scales assessing personality styles, pathological personality problems and clinical symptomatology. There is a four-item validity index and a weight-adjustment factor designed to correct for patient inaccuracies. The revised manual (Millon, 1982) provides extensive information about interpretation, reliability and validity. Piersma (1986) has used this scale to assess change in an acute inpatient outcome study. His results indicate that it may hold promise as an outcome measure over a wide range of patients, as predicted by Lambert *et al.* (1983).

Narrow band measures

There are a number of scales specifically measuring self-perception. Their advantage over the above-mentioned measures of personality traits is that they only take about 15 minutes to complete.

The measurement of self-esteem is creating increasing interest in clinical research. This measurement is confused by the looseness of the construct itself, and there are many different questionnaires with differing theoretical bases. Robson (1988) provides a review of the available scales.

Rosenberg (1965) describes self-esteem as a sense of personal worthiness, attractiveness and social aptitude, and the Rosenberg self-esteem scale is a well-known measure of attitudes towards the self, designed specifically for the young individual. Questions are comprehensive (e.g. 'I feel I have a number of things to be proud of') and the scale is brief and simple to score. Although it was designed for use with adolescents it is appropriate in research with adults, as Rosenberg considered self-esteem to be a concept that continues to change through adult experiences.

More recent measures of self-esteem include the Self-Attitude Inventory (SAI) (Lorr and Wunderlich, 1986), which is an interesting 38-item questionnaire with two scales measuring rather different aspects of self-esteem. Both consist of 16 forced-choice items. The Confidence scale consists of statements concerning expectations of success and self-assurance; for example, subjects choose between 'I usually expect to succeed in things I try' or 'Only occasionally do I expect to succeed in things I try'. The Popularity or Social Approval scale measures the individual's perception of how others see him or her (e.g. 'Not many people think well of me' or 'Most people think well of me').

Robson's Self-Esteem Scale (Robson, 1989a) was designed to converge several different components of self-esteem based on Rosenberg's concept and also includes locus of control, competence and self-value. The instructions request a response for 'how you typically feel' on a 7-point scale in an attempt to measure trait rather than state attributes, but some of the questions such as 'I look really awful these days' have a depressive quality to them. However, the questionnaire was designed specifically for use in non-dysphoric problems. Although this scale is fairly new, it is already being used in a wide variety of projects (for example, as a psychotherapy outcome measure for research into eating disorders, sexual abuse and assertiveness training). A factor analysis is available and a shorter version is in development (Robson, 1989b).

Rosenbaum's Self-Control Schedule (1980) is a 36-item measure of use of coping strategies, ability to delay gratification and perceived self-efficacy. Questions are scored by the subject on a 6-point scale from 'very uncharacteristic of me' (–3 to –1) to 'very characteristic of me' (+1 to +3) (for example, 'When I feel depressed I try to keep myself busy with things that I like'). The attaching of positive and negative signs to self-rating scales is a design fault that may result in biased responding. The scale's concurrent validity was assessed against Rotter's I-E scale and also the 'self-control' factor of the 16PF in a non-clinical group. Simons *et al.* (1985) reported that depressed patients with low scores on the S-CS responded poorly to cognitive therapy. We would select this questionnaire only when a measure of self-control is of particular relevance to the research.

Locus of control

The locus of control construct refers to an individual's perceptions and expectancies about his or her power over experiences and events. The most well-known definition of such aspects of self-control and personal effectiveness was developed by Rotter (1966) using concepts of internal and external loci. Internal control refers to the perception of events as being the consequence of one's own behaviour, whereas external control is the attribution of events to be outwith one's control and thus determined by luck or fate (Table 7.3).

Table 7.3 Measures of Locus of Control.

Scale	Reference	Comments
Rotter's Internal–External Scale	Rotter (1966)	29-choice items, takes 10–15 minutes
Internal, Powerful Others and Chance Scale	Levenson (1973)	24 items, three subscales on a 6-point Likert scale
Desired Control and Adjustment Measures	Reid *et al.* (1977)	35-item scale for use with the elderly: takes 20 minutes
Multi-dimensional Multi-attributional Causality Scales	Lefcourt (1981)	Two 24-item Likert scales. Measures attributions of locus of control
Mental Health Locus of Control Scale	Hill (1980)	Measures expectancies of who will be in control during therapy. 28 items: takes 5–10 minutes
Mental Health Locus of Origin of Control Scale	Hill (1980)	Concerns beliefs about the cause of mental illness. 26 items: takes 10 minutes
The Alcoholic Responsibility Scale (ARS)	Worell and Tumilty (1981)	32 forced-choice items. Specific for use in alcohol problems: takes 10–15 minutes
Locus of Control of Behaviour Questionnaire	Craig *et al.* (1984)	17 items on a 6-point scale: takes 5 minutes. Measures client's ability to take control of change in therapy

In a clinical setting it appears that the concept is susceptible to change and a shift towards an internal locus of control appears to correlate with a positive outcome in psychotherapy (Lefcourt, 1982). Research on the prediction of outcome in psychotherapy has revealed that an internal locus of control predicts a more positive outcome than an external measure of control (Foon, 1987).

Another area of possible interest concerning outcome measures is the suggestion that 'internals' tend to deny signs of psychological distress (Rotter, 1975). There are problems in relating locus of control to mental health because of several complexities. First, there is inconsistency about whether locus of control is a stable concept or a process. Holder and Levi (1988) comment that there are gender differences and methodological problems in measuring such a construct, and King (1989) examined locus of control in patients with anorexia nervosa and suggests that locus of control scales act as general measures of psychopathology and add little relevant information over and above this.

Rotter's (1966) locus of control scale is a 29-item forced-choice self-report questionnaire which includes six non-scoring 'filler' items. The subject rates the alternative he or she 'more strongly believes in'. The nature of the forced-choice questions could make this scale rather irritating for the client to use; 'for example, 'No matter how hard you try some people just don't like you' or 'People who can't get others to like them don't understand how to get along with others'. Criticisms of the I-E scale are, *inter alia,* that it assumes that locus of control is a trait and that the questionnaire fails to differentiate between control by fate or by powerful others which may be important in mental health.

Levenson (1973) has provided a multi-dimensional locus of control scale which does distinguish between measures of 'internal', 'powerful others' and 'chance' orientations. This scale has been well used and is the basis for the development of newer measures. These include Hill's (1980) Mental Health Locus of Control Questionnaire, which concerns the responsibility for progress in therapy (for example, 'If psychotherapy is like building a house a good therapist should not only give you the tools but should design the house for you'). Lefcourt (1981) suggests this may be promising for use in explaining behaviour exhibited during therapy.

Craig *et al.* (1984) developed the Locus of Control of Behaviour Questionnaire (LBC), a 17-item scale where subjects choose one out of six responses from 'strongly agree' to 'strongly disagree' for each statement (for example, 'I can control my problem(s) only if I have outside support'). Their argument for the necessity of such a scale is the lack of a scale specifically for use in behaviour therapy where a client's acceptance of responsibility for his or her own continued well-being is essential. They suggest the scale may therefore be an accurate predictor of relapse. Norms are provided for various populations, test–retest reliability was at 0.90 at one week and 0.73 at one month for a non-treatment group. Construct validity was at 0.67 with Rotter's I-E general expectancy scale and it distinguishes between clinical and non-clinical populations. Although the subject number in their follow-up study was small, the scale showed some ability to predict outcome. Further information about the scale's psychometric properties is provided by the authors (Craig *et al.*, 1984).

COGNITIVE MEASURES

Measuring self-statements

An important aspect of cognitive–behavioural therapy involves helping the client to detect and then alter the negative 'automatic thoughts' that are associated with his or her presenting problem. Therefore measurement of the nature and frequency of these thoughts is an important part of therapy and also indicates progress. As part of therapy the client is usually requested to write down his or her automatic thoughts in some kind of record book. Beck *et al.* (1979) provides an example of 'a Daily Record of Dysfunctional Thoughts' form, on which the subject records a detailed account of automatic thoughts, the situation in which they occurred, the degree to which the client believed the thought and the rational alternative thought. These records are of most value as an aid to therapy but are useful as individualized outcome assessments.

An alternative measure of automatic thoughts is the use of standardized questionnaires, and these are widely used as outcome measures. An interesting finding from research in cognitive therapy is that questionnaires differentiate clinical from non-clinical groups more consistently than other individualized techniques. As yet there is no agreed explanation for this observation. Also, an obvious criticism is that automatic thoughts are idiosyncratic and dependent on situations which probably affect the validity of these questionnaires. It is possible that the standardized thoughts are recognized more readily and therefore rated differently than an individual's own thoughts. It is worth noting that the majority of questionnaires concerning cognitive change are constructed by Beck or his associates from the Philadelphia research group.

There is a wide range of such self-statement scales covering anxiety and depression. Clark (1988) provides a thorough critique of their validity and concludes that among those reviewed there is no particularly superior measure of automatic thoughts (Tables 7.4–7.6).

The Distressing Thoughts Questionnaire (DTQ) (Clark, 1986) consists of six anxious thoughts (for example, 'thoughts or images that something is wrong with my health or may be so in the future') and six depressive thoughts based on the ATQ (see below) (for example, 'thoughts or images that my future is bleak'). All 12 thoughts are measured in terms of frequency, sadness, worry, removal (intrusiveness), and disapproval on a 9-point scale. The DTQ reaches acceptable levels of internal reliability and the depressive and anxious thoughts were poorly correlated, thus suggesting that they are useful for measuring different types of cognitions.

The Crandell Cognitions Inventory (Crandell and Chambless, 1986) is a questionnaire concerning depressed cognitions. Forty-five items, 11 of which

Table 7.4 Measures of cognitive change—self-statements.

Scale	Reference	Comments
Automatic Thought Questionnaire (ATQ)	Hollon and Kendall (1980)	These are all brief standardized questionnaires concerning automatic thoughts in depression. As with Table 7.7, we advise that the reader selects whichever scale is most suitable for his or her individual purposes
The Distressing Thought Questionnaire—Depression (DTQ-D)	Clark (1986)	
Crandell Cognitions Inventory (CCI)	Crandell and Chambless (1986)	
The Cognitions Checklist—Depression (CCL-D)	Beck *et al.* (1987)	

Table 7.5 Measures of cognitive change—self-statements.

Scale	Reference	Comments
The Social Interaction Self-Statement Test (SISST)	Glass *et al.* (1982)	These questionnaires are brief standardized measures of anxious automatic thoughts. They all have similar content and psychometric qualities and we advise the reader to choose from the references the scale most appropriate to his or her own requirements
Agoraphobia Cognitions Questionnaire (ACQ)	Chambless *et al.* (1984)	
The Body Sensations Questionnaire	Chambless *et al.* (1984)	
Distressing Thoughts Questionnaire—Anxiety (DTQ-A)	Clark (1986)	
The Cognitions Checklist—Anxiety (CCL-A)	Beck *et al.* (1987)	
The Anxious Self-Statements Questionnaire (ASSQ)	Kendall and Hollon (1989)	

Table 7.6 Other measures of self-statements.

Scale	Reference	Comments
Assertiveness Self-Statement Test (ASST)	Schwartz and Gottman (1976)	Measures positive and negative cognitions during assertiveness tasks
Checklist of Positive and Negative Thoughts	Galassi *et al.* (1981)	Self-statements concerning test-taking situations

are positive statement filler items, are measured on a 5-point frequency scale of 'almost never' to 'almost always'. The statements are divided into four factors: inferiority, detachment, hopelessness and helplessness. An example of a 'hopeless' statement is 'Daytimes are bad but nighttimes are terrible'. Some statements are probably not readily understandable to a non-American subject (for example, 'I just can't cut it'). Internal reliability is reported as 0.95, and scores were found to be significantly correlated with other well-validated questionnaires. The authors have found the scale to be sensitive to change.

The Automatic Thought Questionnaire (ATQ) (Hollon and Kendall, 1980) is the most well-known measure of automatic thoughts in depression. There are 30 items described as 'a variety of thoughts that pop into people's heads' (for example, 'I've let people down'). The subject rates on a 5-point scale how frequently these have occurred in the last week. Many outcome studies in cognitive–behavioural psychotherapy have shown significant reductions in ATQ scores.

The Anxious Self-statements Questionnaire (ASSQ) (Kendall and Hollon, 1989) is a list of 32 brief statements described as in the ATQ (for example, 'I can't stand it'). The score involves the frequency of such thoughts over the preceding week. The scale was found to differentiate anxious and non-anxious subjects as classified by the State–Trait Anxiety Inventory (STAI). The authors suggest that this scale's value lies in its sensitivity to change during therapy.

Other cognitive measures

There has been increasing interest in the nature and stability of dysfunctional thought patterns in depressed patients. This has resulted in the development of rating scales to assess if recovery from a depressive illness results in a restructuring of thinking errors (Table 7.7).

The Attributional Style Questionnaire (ASQ) (Seligman *et al.*, 1979) consists of 12 hypothetical situations which may occur in the individual's life. Six describe a positive outcome to the situation and six are negative. An example of a negative situation is:

'You have been looking for a job unsuccessfully for some time'
Write down one major cause . . . .

This cause is then rated by judges on a 7-point scale referring to the three attributional errors of Seligman's learned helplessness theory, which assumes that an individual internalizes negative events and predicts that these will occur in the future and over a variety of circumstances. These errors are

Table 7.7 Measuring cognitive change.

Scale	Reference	Comments
Symptom Rating Test (SRT)	Kellner and Sheffield (1973)	Designed as outcome measure for drug trials. Either interview with cards or self-report: 38 items measuring 'distress'
Hopelessness Scale	Beck and Weissman (1974)	20 true–false items concerning client's attitude towards the future
Cognitive Response Test	Watkins and Rush (1978)	38 incomplete sentences. The subject completes them and 'Irrational Negative Responses' are counted
Dysfunctional Attitudes Scale (DAS)	Weissman and Beck (1978)	Universally used. Sensitive to change in cognitive therapy. Two parallel forms available, each with 40 items on a 7-point scale
Beck Depression Inventory (BDI)	Beck *et al.* (1961)	Most widely used scale for depressive symptomatology. 30 items with four answer choices
Attributional Style Questionnaire (ASQ)	Seligman *et al.* (1979)	12 life situations. Client answers a series of questions concerning his or her personal beliefs about each one
Cognitions Questionnaire	Fennell and Campbell (1984)	8 complex life situations. Client answers questions about each one
Cognitive Styles Test (CST)	Blackburn *et al.* (1986)	30 life situations. Measures negative thinking errors by client's response choice

named 'internality', 'stability' and 'globality'. There are then a series of questions referring to the attribution errors for each situation. An example of an internality question is as follows:

Is the cause of your unsuccessful job search something about you or other people or circumstances?

Totally due to others					Totally due to me	
1	2	3	4	5	6	7

ASQ scores have been found to correlate with the Beck Depression Inventory (Beck *et al.*, 1961) and the Multiple Affect Adjective Checklist

(Zuckerman, 1960), and significant differences in responses for depressed and non-depressed subjects have been documented (Seligman *et al.*, 1979).

The Cognitions Questionnaire (Fennell and Campbell, 1984) is similar to the ASQ in that eight possible life situations are also used to assess the individual's degree of negative thinking. This questionnaire includes 'neutral outcome situations' and also asks the individual to rate the amount of control he or she may feel over such an event. The eight situations are followed by five fixed-choice questions with four possible options concerning the subject's perception of the event. The situations are quite complex and are somewhat tedious to read. This attempt to design a method of examining the depressed person's thinking style in detail using both Beck's cognitive theory of depression and the learned helplessness model has been found to be lengthy and confusing.

The Cognitive Styles Test (Wilkinson and Blackburn, 1981; Blackburn *et al.*, 1986) was developed as a self-report scale to assess the process of cognitive changes during recovery from a depressive illness again using life situations. It refers to the 'Cognitive Triad' described by Beck (1967) and measures an individual's interpretation of 30 descriptions of everyday events concerning the 'self', the 'world' and the 'future'. There are ten questions for each of these aspects: five are pleasant situations and five unpleasant. Each situation is presented with four possible responses and the client chooses the one that he or she would be most likely to think in the situation. An example of a 'self-pleasant' event is when one meets friends whom one has not seen for a long time, and the client may think:

A. 'I wonder if they still like me.'
B. 'It's good to see old friends.'
C. 'They won't like me any more.'
D. 'They like me a lot.'

There are several possible scores, i.e. self, world and future pleasant and unpleasant scores, total pleasant and unpleasant scores and an overall total can be calculated. This makes the scoring quite complex, and the questionnaire itself takes about 15 minutes to complete, but the situations are presented in a comprehensive, non-invasive style. The CST's concurrent validity with other validated scales is highly significant but its test–retest reliability for a non-clinical group is rather low. CST scores have been found to differ significantly between recovered depressed subjects and in-treatment depressed patients receiving pharmacotherapy. Thus preliminary evidence suggests that it is a sensitive outcome measure. It has high face validity and this may make the scale susceptible to positive changes in an individual's responses while undergoing cognitive therapy. It may not, however, reflect real change in his or her reaction to situations outside the therapeutic environment.

The Hopelessness Scale (Beck and Weissman, 1974) is a brief self-report scale used widely in outcome studies. It consists of 20 statements which are very similar to the ATQ. However, rather than scoring the frequency of the statements it is scored using a true–false format concerning the subject's view of his or her future. An example is 'My future seems dark to me'. Although it was designed as a measure of outcome for depressed patients, the authors suggest that the Hopelessness Scale may be relevant in other areas such as alcohol dependence or physical illness.

The Dysfunctional Attitudes Scale (DAS) (Weissman and Beck, 1978) is a self-report questionnaire with 40 items on a 7-point scale from 'totally agree' to 'totally disagree' (for example, 'If others dislike you, you cannot be happy'). There are two parallel forms available, DAS-A and DAS-B, which have been developed to be highly correlated. It takes about 20 minutes to complete. Some of the questions may seem rather threatening for a depressed patient and, as in the CST, a concern is that development of an awareness of the appropriate response may bias the scores after therapy. This scale is frequently used in outcome studies mainly of depression and has been found in numerous studies to be sensitive to change. It may have value in other patient groups where dysfunctional thoughts are of relevance (for example, in assertiveness training).

Most outcome studies of cognitive therapy have compared this treatment with other active treatments such as drugs. They have tended to use established measures of depressive symptomatology such as the Hamilton Rating Scale (Hamilton, 1967), which incorporates somatic symptoms, or the Beck Depression Inventory (Beck *et al.*, 1961), which is the most widely used measure of depressive cognitions.

MEASURING OUTCOME IN ANXIETY

Probably the most well-known and well-validated measure of anxiety is the State–Trait Anxiety Inventory (STAI) (Spielberger *et al.*, 1970). This is divided into two separate rating scales. The first 20 questions measure the immediate feelings of anxiety (such as 'I feel at ease') and is more frequently used as an indicator of change during therapy (for example, after relaxation). Questions 21 to 40 assess an individual's more stable anxious traits (for example, 'I worry too much over something that really doesn't matter'). Test–retest correlations reflect the different aspects of anxiety that the scales measure with the trait scale being more stable over time.

The Fear Questionnaire (Marks and Mathews, 1979) has three subscales for agoraphobia, social phobia and blood/injury phobia and the intercorrelations between them are reported to be low. Each subscale has five situations all rated on an 8-point severity scale with anchor points of 'would not avoid it', 'slightly avoid it', 'definitely avoid it', 'markedly avoid it' and 'always avoid it'. The clients' main target phobia as described by themselves is also rated. The questionnaire also includes a very brief anxiety depression score and a symptom severity score. It has been found to be sensitive to change. Mavissakalian (1986) provides evidence in her validity study that the agoraphobia subscale is the most sensitive to change. The Fear Questionnaire has been widely used in recent studies (e.g. Michelson *et al.*, 1988). Further details of anxiety measures are provided in Chapter 4.

BEHAVIOURAL MEASURES

There is a very large number of self-report questionnaires measuring different problematic behaviours, ranging from spider anxiety scales to ritualizing inventories. Many of these are designed for specific studies, and care must therefore be taken to consider the reliability and validity of such scales.

A valuable and widely documented measure of behaviour is direct observation. Naturalistic observation is the assessment of a behaviour as it occurs, and it is therefore of superior accuracy to any retrospective measure of an event. Obviously, behaviour cannot be assessed for 24 hours of the day and the timespan allocated must be carefully considered with respect to the frequency of the behaviour and any external conditions (e.g. time of day or day of the week) that may affect the behaviour.

It is recommended that a comprehensive and easily learnt coding system is constructed in order to simplify recording the behaviour and to ensure maximum inter-rater reliability. If a single behaviour such as number of panic attacks in a week is to be recorded, the code can obviously be very simple, but often more complex systems are required such as in social interactions. A useful device for recording what precipitates and maintains behaviour is the 'ABC' chart, where A represents antecedent, B behaviour and C consequences. A comprehensive guide to creating a rater's coding system can be found in Foster *et al.* (1988).

The major drawback to this method is the phenomenon of 'reactivity', which is the extent to which an individual's behaviour changes while under observation. When this occurs, a trend in the change of behaviour is seen, usually over the first few recordings, and this can be assumed to be due to the individual habituating to the observer. Suggestions for reducing reactivity are discussed fully by Foster *et al.* (1988).

Unobtrusive observation where the individual is unaware that a particular behaviour is being observed can be applied in certain conditions (for example, taking speech speed as a measure of dysphoric mood (Teasdale *et al.*, 1980). However, the absence of informed consent and the risk of privacy invasion must be considered in such a method.

Self-recording of behaviours

Self-recording is particularly important in situations where direct observation is not applicable (for instance, in social situations). The design of a self-report diary depends a great deal on the nature of the behaviour in question. Reactivity is again a major methodological consideration, and it should be acknowledged that self-report tends to change behaviour, usually in a clinically desirable direction. This is particularly true in behaviours involving mild self-harm (e.g. hair pulling) or in instances where positive rather than negative behaviours are recorded. A problem with self-report is that people tend to tire of recording their behaviours after a short time period.

Ten-centimetre visual analogue lines are useful in self-recording and can easily be adapted to fit in the specific problem being assessed: for example, 'Because of my problem, my ability to work today has been impaired'

Not at all ———————————————————————— Very severely

Role play

Role play is often used as a therapeutic aid and can be a rough guide to behaviour in social situations. Single- and multiple-response role plays which are artificially created situations are most extensively used in the assessment of social interactions. Another use of role play is the unstructured naturalistic interactions, where the individual is asked to interact with a confederate for a few minutes, and this interaction itself can be assessed by trained raters. Becker and Heimberg (1988) provide examples of role play in behavioural assessment of social skills.

INDIVIDUALIZED MEASURES OF CHANGE

Individual change measures are valuable in psychotherapy outcome studies in that they offer flexibility and idiosyncracity and have good face validity.

They also provide a means of avoiding the problem of evaluating some patients on variables that are irrelevant to their circumstances, as can be the case when using standardized scales. There is no argument that measurement of a therapeutic goal provides much information, and it is considered crucial by Waskow and Parloff (1975) in the NIMH outcome measures project. However, such measures are fraught with methodological problems, mainly because in all goal-setting procedures the correlation between goals tends to be very high. Probably the best application of therapeutic goals is in conjunction with standardized scales.

Target Complaints is a method of assessing change designed as a therapist measure. Battle *et al.* (1966) describe the method as using each patient's spontaneously expressed complaints as criteria for evaluating response to psychotherapy. The targets can be decided upon by the therapist or the client.

It is difficult to divide the complaints into isolated entities and there are as yet no suggestions for a standardized procedure for creating targets. Another drawback is the discrepancy of scoring across different studies. Battle recommends obtaining pre- and post-treatment severity ratings for comparison, but it has been used as a measure of improvement (Hoehn-Saric *et al.*, 1964). Analysis of both approaches reveals problems in reliability, and this is explored fully by Mintz and Keisler (1982).

Goal Attainment Scaling (Kiresuk and Sherman, 1968) is specified for use by a judge who is independent of the therapeutic intervention, and goals are measured on a 5-point scale from 'the most unfavourable outcome' to the 'best anticipated success', the mid-point being 'expected level of outcome'. A formula is provided for overall attainment of all the specific goals where a score of 50 equals outcome reaching the expected level. A comprehensive description of GAS scoring and application is provided by Kiresuk and Lund (1978). They suggest that three to five goals are selected and describe an optional weighting procedure to reflect the importance of each goal. However, weighting can complicate use of the GAS in outcome research. Goals should be defined as concrete behaviours that can be agreed upon and measured by separate independent judges, or they could include standardized rating scales (for example, changes on a Beck Depression Inventory).

Correlations among outcome ratings made by independent raters for the same scales are certainly higher than target complaints at 0.66–0.81 and test–retest scores are reported to be 0.83 (Kiresuk and Lund, 1978). There are, however, several points of concern. First, Goal Attainment Scaling has been reported to take up to 6 hours to construct. Second, the scale is susceptible to the setting of inappropriate goals and interpretation of goals can be misleading (for example, does a rating of below 50, the less than expected outcome, mean that a therapy has failed?). Mintz and Keisler (1982), in their detailed critique of GAS, comment that it offers promise as a psychotherapy outcome measure over a wide range of therapeutic settings. Also it may itself assist clinical practice, as goal setting provides a focus for the therapist, client and any significant others involved as a team. Lewis *et al.* (1987) used the GAS as one of a number of outcome measures in research on family intervention and provide guidelines for its use in controlled research.

PERSONAL QUESTIONNAIRES

Personal questionnaires are designed to measure levels of individual target symptoms over time assessed by the patients themselves. This method was introduced by Shapiro (1961) but, despite the potential value of such an instrument, it was not widely used. Its disadvantages were that it was time consuming to administer and scoring was complex. However, Mulhall (1976) has constructed the Personal Questionnaire Rapid Scaling Technique (PQRST), which overcomes these problems.

The client chooses up to ten symptoms which he or she feels are most important. Once all the symptoms have been drawn up, the patient embarks upon a series of forced-choice descriptions of the severity of each symptom. There are nine of these, ranging from 'absolutely none' to 'very considerable'. Therefore it is important to explain to clients that their 'symptoms' must fit the adjectives. An illustration of this is 'The anxiety I feel in social situations is. . .'. The first severity choice may be 'Little' or 'Moderate', the second may be 'Almost None' or 'Considerable', etc. This presentation therefore removes the bias towards a centre point and also incorporates a measure of internal reliability, making errors readily identifiable.

The only time-consuming aspect of this questionnaire is understanding the rather complicated appearance and procedure (although the manual is very comprehensive) and helping the client to draw up a symptom list. Scoring takes only a few minutes. There are two versions—the PQ10 and the PQ14, differing only in the number of adjective pairs presented. PQ10 takes about 15 minutes and PQ14 takes a little longer. Peck and Dean (1988) state that the PQ is one of the best available measures for assessing change in patients' perceptions of their symptoms, and should have an important role in clinical practice and research.

THE ASSESSMENT OF SOCIAL ADJUSTMENT

Social adjustment scales provide information about an individual's ability to cope within the community, and usually rely on the report of a significant

Table 7.8 Social adjustment, interview scales.

Scale	Reference	Comments
Katz Adjustment Scale—Relatives' Form	Katz and Lyerly (1963)	Used over a wide range of studies: 205 items for significant other
Psychiatric Status Schedule (PSS)	Spitzer *et al*. (1970)	321 descriptions of behaviour concerning work, leisure, role function and alcohol/drug use: takes up to 1 hour. Found sensitive to change. Widely used
Psychiatric Evaluation Form (PEF)	Endicott and Spitzer (1972)	Similar to PSS, but is a shorter, less structured interview. Has been used in psychotherapy outcome studies
Social Dysfunction Rating Scale (SDRS)	Ruesch *et al*. (1972)	20 items on 6-point scale. Semi-structured interview: takes 30–45 minutes. Useful in drug/alcohol studies or with the elderly
Social Adjustment Scale (SAS)	Weissman *et al*. (1971)	48 items, semi-structured interview: takes up to 1 hour. 2-month period assessed
Personal Adjustment and Role Skills (PARS III)	Ellsworth (1975)	For use with significant other. Different forms for men and women: takes under an hour
Social Adjustment Scale II (SASII)	Schooler *et al*. (1979)	52 questions in semi-structured interview with patient or significant other: takes about 1 hour
Social Maladjustment Schedule (SMS)	Clare and Cains (1978)	Measures wide range of relevant information under three main headings. Marital conditions, social management and satisfaction: takes 40 minutes. Requires trained rater
Social Behaviour Assessment Schedule	Platt *et al*. (1980)	Measures the effect of illness on self and family in 1–2 hour interview
Social Functioning Schedule (SFS)	Remington and Tyrer (1979)	12 items on a 10-point scale. Semi-structured with good guidelines: takes up to half an hour. Assess the past four weeks
Personality and Social Network Adjustment Scale	Clark (1968)	17 items on 5-point scale. Quick and simple but role coverage is limited

Table 7.8 (*continued*)

Scale	Reference	Comments
Community Adaptation Schedule	Roen and Burnes (1968)	217 items on 6-point scale. Assess present time: takes up to 45 minutes. Used in psychotherapy outcome but confuses trait and state behaviours
The Self-Assessment Guide	Willer and Biggin (1974); Willer and Miller (1977)	55-item questionnaire designed as an outcome measure with goal attainment—suggest help should be available during completion. 13-item short form
Social Adjustment Scale—Self-Report	Weissman and Bothwell (1976)	42 questions: takes 15–20 minutes. Sensitive to change
People in Your Life Scale (1987)	Marziali (1987)	Assesses patients' perception of quality of supportive relationships. 23 items: takes at least 20 minutes

other (Table 7.8). They are abundant in the literature, and Weissman (1975) and Weissman *et al.* (1981) provide a detailed review of available scales.

The Katz Adjustment Scale—Relatives' Form (KAS-R) (Katz and Lyerly, 1963) consists of 205 items, divided into five forms with each item rated on a 4-point severity scale and 127 items assessing symptoms and social behaviour. Performance in social situations and activities during free time are also measured along with the relatives' own satisfaction concerning these aspects of behaviour.

This scale is recommended on the basis of the extensive literature concerning its use as an outcome measure (Fiske, 1975; Davidson and Davidson, 1983). The timespan to be measured is three weeks, norms are available and reliability values are acceptable (Hogarty and Katz, 1971). The scale takes up to an hour to complete but the questions are written in a straightforward, comprehensive manner. Lambert *et al.* (1986) comment that it may be most applicable for severely disturbed patient groups and lacks built-in validity scales. They suggest that pooled ratings from several significant others would provide the most satisfactory outcome score.

An alternative to the KAS-R is the Personal Adjustment and Role Skills (PARS III) (Ellsworth, 1975). This measures symptoms, alcohol and drug use, adjustment in household management, parenthood and employment over a period of one month. It comprises a 5-point severity scale with 120 items for men and 115 for women. It is less time consuming than the KAS-R and its value lies in its success as a mailed questionnaire (Lambert *et al.*, 1986).

The Social Adjustment Scale (SAS) (Weissman *et al.*, 1971) was designed for a comparative outcome study in a group of depressed women. It is a semi-structured interview with 42 items rated on a 5-point anchored scale measuring two aspects of adjustment, namely work and economic status and social roles. There is also an overall adjustment rating on a 7-point scale and the interview takes around 45 minutes to complete.

A written self-report version (the SAS-SR) has been introduced which does not require a trained rater. It contains 42 questions and each is scored in a 5-point scale. The scale has been reported to correlate well with the interview version, test–retest reliability equals 0.80 and it is sensitive to change (Weissman *et al.*, 1981). It has been used widely in outcome studies (e.g. Shapiro and Firth, 1987). The SAS II has been developed as an interview schedule to measure change specifically in schizophrenic populations. It accommodates the special living requirements often necessary for the chronically mentally ill (Schooler *et al.*, 1979).

Also worth mentioning is the 'People in your Life' (PIYL) scale (Marziali, 1987). This is a self-report scale developed for predicting outcome in psychodynamic therapy but may be of value in other outcome studies (for example, alcohol research). The PIYL provides details on the client's available social support and his or her satisfaction with that support. It was derived from Henderson *et al.*'s interview schedule (1980). Outcome was found to be correlated with the pre-treatment intimacy satisfaction scores. Marziali comments that the PIYL scale picks up a variable that reflects a person's capacity to have satisfying supportive relationships. This may be a contributing factor to the response to the process of psychotherapy, whereas measures of social adjustment provide information about the types of behaviour that result from the therapeutic intervention. Test–retest reliability values for the subscales range from 0.88 to 0.94 and face, concurrent, construct and predictive validity are also reported to be good, although obviously the measure has not been used extensively at present. Further aspects of social adjustment are given in Chapter 6.

THERAPIST RATING SCALES

When measuring outcome in psychotherapy it is important to consider the personal and professional qualities of the therapist, which are required for the formation of the therapeutic relationship with the client (Table 7.9). The Truax scales are the most well-known measure of therapist's empathy, warmth and genuineness, and are direct observation measures for a trained observer to use. The scales have been widely employed in research but their use has been questioned. For example, Mitchell *et al.* (1977) comment that

Table 7.9 Therapist rating scales.

Scale	Reference	Comments
The Relationship Inventory	Barret-Lennard (1962)	85 items on a 6-point scale. Empathy subscale most widely used
The Therapy Session Report	Orlinsky and Howard (1977)	152-item questionnaire for both therapist and client to rate therapy
Accurate Empathy Scale	Truax and Carluff (1967)	9-point scale for observer to rate therapist's empathy
Non-Possessive Warmth Scale		5-point scale for observer rating of therapist's warmth
Genuineness Scale		5-point scale for observer rating of therapist's genuineness
Vanderbilt Psychotherapy Scale	Gomez-Schwartz and Schwartz (1978)	84 items assessing therapist and patient's attitudes and behaviour
Competency Checklist for Cognitive Therapists	Young *et al.* (1979)	Three sections for observer to measure interview technique, cognitive–behavioural skills and empathy
Therapeutic Alliance Scale	Marziali *et al.* (1981)	21 positive and negative items for observer to rate therapist and client's interaction
Helping Alliance Rating (HA-r)	Morgan *et al.* (1982)	Global observer rating of client's perception of how useful therapy is
Helping Alliance Counting Signs (HA-cs)	Luborsky *et al.* (1983)	More standardized rating scale than HA-r. Manual provided
Vanderbilt Negative Indicators	Strupp *et al.* (1981)	42-item scale grouped into five sections. Rates patient and therapist activities thought to be predictive of poor outcome in brief psychotherapy

the scales failed to produce a wide range of scores between individuals, thus making comparison of poor and good therapists difficult. He also questioned the construct validity of the scales.

Marziali *et al.* (1981) developed a therapeutic alliance scale that focuses on interactions beween the therapist and patient. The scale comprises 21 therapist and 21 patient items. There are both positive and negative items measured on a 5-point scale from 'not present' to 'intensely present'. Inter-rater reliability was 0.94 for the therapist ratings and 0.88 for the patient ratings.

The patient's contribution to the therapeutic relationship was found to predict outcome as measured on the HSCL-90 in Marziali's study of brief psychodynamic psychotherapy. She suggests that it is the patient's ability to develop and maintain a positive attitude towards the therapist that achieves greatest benefits in psychotherapy.

Luborsky *et al.* (1983) have designed two Helping Alliance scales for predicting psychotherapy. Helping Alliance is defined as the patient's experience of treatment and how helpful he or she perceives the relationship with the therapist to be. The first scale, Helping Alliance Rating (HAr) (Morgan *et al.*, 1982), is a global method of assessment, relying to a large degree on judges' inferences about the alliance. The second scale is the Helping Alliance Counting Signs (HAcs), which is a scoreable method of assessment and includes a manual which explains two types of helping alliance. The first involves the patient's experience of the therapist providing help, the second is the patient's experience of working with the therapist towards treatment goals which may be of particular interest in cognitive behavioural therapy. These two scales are split into further subtypes which can be scored either positively or negatively on a 5-point scale. Scores on the HAcs were found to be predictive of outcome as measured by Target Complaints.

Luborsky *et al.* (1985) compared supportive psychotherapy, cognitive behavioural psychotherapy and counselling in a group of drug-dependent patients. This study provides further support for the predictive validity of the HA. Luborsky *et al.* also comment on the wide differences they found in therapists' effectiveness. This was discovered to be mainly due to the degree which therapists conformed to the techniques prescribed to them. They suggest from this finding that it is difficult to compare different therapeutic techniques when there are considerable differences across therapists using the same technique. This problem is also illustrated in the Sheffield psychotherapy project (Shapiro *et al.*, 1989). They compared cognitive behavioural therapy and psychodynamic therapy in a crossover design. Cognitive behavioural therapy showed statistically significant superiority over psychodynamic therapy. However, on further analysis it was discovered that one therapist showed significant gains in cognitive behavioural therapy over psychodynamic therapy, thus creating an overall skewness in the results. Although the numbers were small in this study, this finding illustrates the problems that arise when comparing different therapeutic techniques.

The Competency Checklist for Cognitive Therapists was devised by Young *et al.* (1979) for assessing cognitive behavioural therapy. The scale is divided into three sections and consists of a total of 18 items. Part 1 measures general interview procedures and Part 2 is specific to the cognitive behavioural techniques. Part 3 assesses personal and professional characteristics of the therapist. Young *et al.* comment that cognitive behavioural therapy probably requires the same 'subtle therapeutic atmosphere' that has been described in the context of psychodynamic therapy. A full critique of this scale can be found in Blackburn and Davidson (1989).

CONCLUSION

It is difficult to draw together the threads of such a wide area of research endeavour but a number of points are worth emphasizing:

(1) Despite the many hundreds of rating scales available, there is still the need for the development of further good psychotherapy measures of both outcome and process. It would be best if these could be developed jointly by a number of different centres.
(2) One way to solve the current dilemma is for groups of psychotherapy researchers to agree on standard batteries of tests that they will use. These may not be the only dependent variables measured, but if there is a relatively small battery of tests then the usefulness of these tests would be better assessed and patient groups can be more easily compared.
(3) There is a serious problem in psychotherapy research in using rating scales which are treatment-specific, especially when they are self-rating. Psychotherapy is a 'talking' treatment, and the fact that a patient fills in a rating scale differently after many hours of talking to a therapist who speaks a certain way is not in itself evidence of therapeutic change. Therefore it is particularly important in psychotherapy studies that global measures and measures of specific symptomatology are used, and that social, marital and work functioning are assessed. This applies not only to dynamic but to cognitive and behavioural psychotherapies.

REFERENCES

American Psychiatric Association (1987) *Diagnostic and Statistical Manual of Mental Disorders*, 3rd edn revised, Washington, DC.

Auerbach, A.H. (1983) Assessment of psychotherapy outcome from the view of the expert adviser. In M. Lambert, E.R. Christensen and S.S. DeJulio (eds), *The Assessment of Psychotherapy Outcome*, pp. 537–68, Wiley-Interscience, New York.

Barrett-Lennard, G.T. (1962) Dimensions of therapist response as causal factors in therapeutic change. *Psychological Monographs*, **76**, 43–562.

Barron, F. (1953) An ego-strength scale which predicts response to psychotherapy. *Journal of Consulting Psychology*, **17**(5), 327–78.

Battle, C.C., Imber, S.D., Hoehn-Saric, R., Sloane, A.R., Nash, E.R. and Frank, J.D. (1966) Target complaints as criteria for improvement. *American Journal of Psychotherapy*, **20**, 184–92.

Beck, A.T. (1967) *Depression: Clinical Experimental and Theoretical Aspects*, Harper and Row, New York.

Beck, A.T. and Weissman, A. (1974) The measurement of pessimism: the Hopelessness Scale. *Journal of Consulting and Clinical Psychology*, **42**, 861–5.

Beck, A.T., Ward, C.H., Mendelson, M., Mock, J. and Erbaugh, J. (1961) An inventory for measuring depression. *Archives of General Psychiatry*, **4**, 561–71.

Beck, A.T., Rush, A.J., Shaw, B.F. and Emery, G. (1979) *Cognitive Therapy of Depression*, Guilford Press, New York.

Beck, A.T., Brown, G., Steer, R.A., Eidelson, J.I. and Riskind, J.H. (1987) Differentiating anxiety and depression utilizing the Cognition Checklist. *Journal of Abnormal Psychology*, **96**, 179–83.

Becker, R.E. and Heimberg, R.G. (1988) Assessment of social skills. In A.S. Bellack and M. Hersen (eds), *Behavioral Assessment. A Practical Handbook*, 3rd edn, pp. 365–95, Pergamon Press, New York.

Blackburn, I.M. and Davidson, K.M. (1989) *Cognitive Therapy in Depression and Anxiety*, Blackwell Scientific Publications, Oxford.

Blackburn, I.M., Jones, S. and Lewin, R.J.P. (1986) Cognitive style in depression. *British Journal of Clinical Psychology*, **25**, 241–51.

Cartwright, D.F. (1975) Patient self-report measures. In I.E. Waskow and M.B. Parloff (eds), *Psychotherapy Change Measures: Report on Clinical Research Branch Outcome Measures Project*, pp. 48–64, National Institute of Mental Health, Washington.

Caston, J. (1986) The reliability of the diagnosis of the patient's unconscious plan. In J. Weiss, H. Sampson and the Mount Zion Psychotherapy Research Group (eds), *The Psychoanalytic Process: Theory, Clinical Observations and Empirical Research*, pp. 241–55.

Cattell, R.B. and Eber, H.W. (1966) *The Sixteen Personality Factor Personality Questionnaire Test*, revised edition, Institute for Personality and Ability Testing, Champaign, III.

Chambless, D.L., Caputo, G.C., Bright, P. and Gallagher, R. (1984) Assessment of fear in agoraphobics: the Body Sensations Questionnaire and the Agoraphobic Cognitions Questionnaire. *Journal of Consulting and Clinical Psychology*, **52** (6), 1090–7.

Clare, A.W. and Cains, V.E. (1978) Design development and use of a standardised interview to assess social maladjustment and dysfunction in community studies. *Psychological Medicine*, **8**, 589–604.

Clark, A.W. (1968) The personality and social network adjustment scale. *Human Relations*, **21**, 85–96.

Clark, D.A. (1986) Cognitive–affective interaction: a test of the 'Specificity' and 'Generality' hypothesis. *Cognitive Therapy and Research*, **10**, 608–23.

Clark, D.A. (1988) The validity of measures of cognition: a review of the literature. *Cognitive Therapy and Research*, **12**, 1–20.

Craig, A.R., Franklin, J.A. and Andrews, G. (1984) A scale to measure locus of control of behaviour. *British Journal of Medical Psychology*, **57**, 173–80.

Crandell, C.J. and Chambless, D.L. (1986) The validation of an inventory for measuring depressive thoughts: the Crandell Cognitions Inventory. *Behaviour Research and Therapy*, **24**, 403–11.

Curtis, J.T. and Silberschatz, G. (1986) Clinical implications of research on brief psychotherapy. 1. Formulating the patient's problems and goals. *Psychoanalytic Psychology*, **3**, 13–25.

Curtis, J.T., Silberschatz, G., Weiss, J., Sampson, H. and Rosenberg, S.E. (1988) Developing reliable psychodynamic case formulations: an illustration of the Plan Diagnosis Method. *Psychotherapy*, **25** (2), 256–65.

Dahlstrom, W.G. (1975) Recommendations for patient measures in evaluating psychotherapy: test batteries and inventories. In I.E. Waskow and M.B. Parloff (eds), *Psychotherapy Change Measures: Report on Clinical Research Branch Outcome Measures Project*, pp. 14–31, National Institute of Mental Health, Washington, DC.

Dahlstrom, W.G., Welsh, G.S. and Dahlstrom, L.E. (1975) *An MMPI Handbook*, Vol. 2, University of Minnesota Press, Minneapolis.

Davidson, C.V. and Davidson, R.H. (1983) The significant other as data source and data problems in psychotherapy research. In M.J. Lambert, E.R. Christensen and S.S. DeJulio (eds), *The Assessment of Psychotherapy Outcome*, pp. 569–601, Wiley-Interscience, New York.

Derogatis, L.R., Lipman, R.S., Rickels, K., Uhlenhuth, E.H. and Covi, L. (1974) The Hopkins Symptom Checklist (HSCL). A measure of primary symptom dimensions. In P. Pichot (ed.), *Psychological Measurements in Psychopharmacology. Modern Problems of Pharmacopsychiatry*, pp. 79–110, Karger, Basel.

De Witt, K., Kaltreider, N., Weiss, D. and Horowitz, M. (1983) Judging change in psychotherapy: the reliability of clinical formulation. *Archives of General Psychiatry*, **40**, 1121–8.

Dymond, R.F. (1954) Adjustment changes over therapy from self-sorts. In C.R. Rogers and R.F. Dymond (eds), *Psychotherapy and Personality Change*, University of Chicago Press, Chicago.

Ellsworth, R.B. (1975) Consumer feedback in measuring the effectiveness of mental health programs. In E.L. Struening and M. Guttentag (eds), *Handbook of Evaluation Research*, Vol. 2, pp. 239–74, Sage, Beverly Hills.

Endicott, J. and Spitzer, R.L. (1972) What! Another rating scale? The psychiatric evaluation form. *Journal of Nervous and Mental Disease*, **154**, 88–104.

Endicott, J., Spitzer, R.L., Fleiss, J.L. and Cohen, J. (1976) The Global Assessment Scale. A procedure for measuring overall severity of psychiatric disturbance. *Archives of General Psychiatry*, **33**, 767–72.

Fennell, M.J. and Campbell, E.A. (1984) The Cognitions Questionnaire: specific thinking errors in depression. *British Journal of Clinical Psychology*, **23** (2), 81–92.

Fiske, D.W. (1975) The use of significant others in assessing the outcome of psychotherapy. In I.E. Waskow and M.B. Parloff (eds), *Psychotherapy Change Measures: Report on Clinical Research Branch Outcome Measures Project*, pp. 189–201, National Institute of Mental Health, Washington, DC.

Foon, A.E. (1987) Review: locus of control as a predictor of outcome of psychotherapy. *British Journal of Medical Psychology*, **60**, 99–107.

Foster, S.L., Bell-Dolan, D.J. and Burge, D.A. (1988) Behavioral observation. In A.S. Bellack and M. Hersen (eds), *Behavioral Assessment. A Practical Handbook*, 3rd edn, Pergamon Press, New York.

Galissi, J.P., Frierson, H.T. and Sharer, R. (1981) Behavior of high, moderate and low test anxious students during an actual test situation. *Journal of Consulting and Clinical Psychology*, **49**, 51–62.

Garfield, S.L. and Bergin, A.E. (eds) (1986) *Handbook of Psychotherapy and Behavior Change: An Empirical Analysis*, 3rd edn, Wiley-Interscience, New York.

Glass, C.R., Merzulli, T.V., Biever, J.L. and Larsen, K.H. (1982) Cognitive assessment of social anxiety: development and validation of a self-statements questionnaire. *Cognitive Therapy and Research*, **6**, 37–55.

Gleser, G.C. (1975) Evaluation of psychotherapy outcome by psychological tests. In I.E. Waskow and M.B. Parloff (eds), *Psychotherapy Change Measures: Report on Clinical Research Branch Outcome Measures Project*, pp. 32–9, National Institute of Mental Health, Washington, DC.

Goldberg, D. (1972) *The Detection of Psychiatric Illness by Questionnaire*, Maudsley Monograph 21, Oxford University Press, London.

Goldberg, D. and Hillier, V.F. (1979) A scaled version of the General Health Questionnaire. *Psychological Medicine*, **15**, 809.

Gomes-Schwartz, B. and Schwartz, J.M. (1978) Psychotherapy process variables distinguishing the 'inherently helpful' person from the professional therapist. *Journal of Consulting and Clinical Psychology*, **46**, 196–7.

Gough, H.G. (1957) *Manual for the California Personality Inventory*, Consulting Psychologists Press, Palo Alto, California.

Gynther, M.D. and Green, S.D. (1982) Methodological problems in research with self-report inventories. In P.C. Kendall and J.N. Butcher (eds), *Handbook of Research Methods in Clinical Psychology*, pp. 355–86, Wiley-Interscience, New York.

Hamilton, M. (1967) Development of a rating scale for primary depressive illness. *British Journal of Social and Clinical Psychology*, **6**, 278–96.

Henderson, G., Byrne, D.G. and Duncan-Jones, P. (1980) Social relationships, adversity and neurosis: A study of associations in a general population sample. *British Journal of Psychiatry*, **136**, 354–83.

Hill, D.J. (1980) The Development of the Mental Health Locus of Control and Mental Health of Origin Scales. *Journal of Personality Assessment*, **44**(2), 148–56.

Hoehn-Saric, R., Frank, J.D., Imber, S.D., Nash, E.H., Stone, A.R. and Battle, C.C. (1964) Systematic preparation of patients for psychotherapy. 1. Effects on therapy behavior and outcome. *Journal of Psychiatric Research*, **2**, 267–81.

Hogarty, G.E. and Katz, M.M. (1971) Norms of adjustment and social behavior. *Archives of General Psychiatry*, **25**, 470–80.

Holder, E.E. and Levi, D.J. (1988) Mental health and locus of control: SCL-90-R and Levenson's IPC Scales. *Journal of Clinical Psychology*, **44**(5), 753–5.

Hollon, S.D. and Kendall, P.C. (1980) Cognitive self-statements in depression: development of an automatic thoughts questionnaire. *Cognitive Therapy and Research*, **4**(4), 383–95.

Kaltreider, N.B., DeWitt, K.N., Weiss, D.S. and Horowitz, M.J. (1981) Patterns of individual change scales. *Archives of General Psychiatry*, **38**, 1263–9.

Katz, M.M. and Lyerly, S.B. (1963) Methods for measuring adjustment and social behavior in the communty: 1. Rationale, description, discriminative validity and scale development. *Psychological Reports*, **13**, 503–35 (Monograph Supplement 4-V13).

Kellner, R. and Sheffield, B.F. (1973) A self-rating scale of distress. *Psychological Medicine*, **3**, 88.

Kendall, P.C. and Butcher, J.N. (eds) (1982) *Handbook of Research Methods in Clinical Psychology*, Wiley-Interscience, New York.

Kendall, P.C. and Hollon, S.D. (1989) Anxious self talk: development of the Anxious Self-Statements Questionnaire (ASSQ). *Cognitive Therapy and Research*, **13**, 81–95.

King, M. (1989) Locus of control in women with eating pathology. *Psychological Medicine*, **19**, 183–7.

Kiresuk, T.J. and Lund, S.J. (1978) Goal attainment scaling. In C.C. Attkisson, W.A. Hargreaves and M.J. Horowitz (eds), *Evaluation of Human Service Programs*, pp. 341–70, Academic Press, New York.

Kiresuk, T.J. and Sherman, R.E. (1968) Goal attainment scaling: a general method for evaluating comprehensive community mental health programs. *Community Mental Health Journal*, **4**(6), 443–53.

Lambert, M.J., Christensen, E.R. and Dejulio, S.S. (eds) (1983) *The Assessment of Psychotherapy Outcome*, Wiley-Interscience, New York.

Lambert, M.J., Shapiro, D.A. and Bergin, A.E. (1986) The effectiveness of psychotherapy. In S.L. Garfield and A.E. Bergin (eds), *Handbook of Psychotherapy and Behaviour Change*, 3rd edn, pp. 157–212, John Wiley, New York.

Lefcourt, H.M. (1981) *Research with the Locus of Control Construct*, Volume 1, *Assessment Methods*, Academic Press, London.

Lefcourt, H.M. (1982) *Locus of Control: Current Trends in Theory and Research*, 2nd edn, Lawrence Erlbaum, Hillsdale, NJ.

Levenson, H. (1973) Multi-dimensional locus of control in psychiatric patients. *Journal of Consulting and Clinical Psychology*, **41**, 397–404.

Lewis, A.B., Spencer, J.H., Haas, G.L. and DiVittis, A. (1987) Goal attainment scaling: relevance and replicability in follow-up of in-patients. *Journal of Nervous and Mental Disease*, **175**, 408–17.

Lipman, R.S., Covi, L. and Shapiro, A.K. (1979) The Hopkins Symptom Check List (HSCL); factors derived from the HSCL-90. *Journal of Affective Disorders*, **1**, 9–24.

Lorr, M. and DeJong, J. (1986) A short form of the Interpersonal Style Inventory (ISI). *Journal of Clinical Psychology*, **42**(6), 466–9.

Lorr, M. and Wunderlich, R.A. (1986) Two objective measures of self-esteem. *Journal of Personality Assessment*, **50**(1), 18–23.

Lorr, M. and Youniss, J. (1983) *The Interpersonal Style Inventory*, Western Psychological Services, Los Angeles.

Luborsky, L (1962) Clinicians' judgements of mental health. A proposed scale. *Archives of General Psychiatry*, **7**, 407–17.

Luborsky, L. (1977) Measuring a pervasive psychic structure in psychotherapy: the core conflictual relationship theme. In N. Freedman and S. Grand (eds), *Communicative Structures and Psychic Structures*, pp. 367–95, Plenum Press, New York.

Luborsky, L. (1988) *Who will Benefit from Psychotherapy*, Basic Books, New York.

Luborsky, L. and Bachrach, H. (1974) Factors influencing clinicians' judgement of mental health. *Archives of General Psychiatry*, **31**, 292–9.

Luborsky, L., Crits-Christoph, P., Alexander, L., Margolis, M. and Cohen, M. (1983) Two helping alliance methods for predicting outcomes of psychotherapy: a counting signs versus a global method. *Journal of Nervous and Mental Disease*, **171**(8), 480–92.

Luborsky, L., McLellan, T., Woody, G.E., O'Brian, C.P. and Auerbach, A. (1985) Therapist success and its determinants. *Archives of General Psychiatry*, **42**, 602–11.

Malan, D.H. (1959) On assessing the results of psychotherapy. *British Journal of Medical Psychology*, **32**, 86–105.

Malan, D.H. (1963) *A Study of Brief Psychotherapy*, Tavistock, London.

Marks, I.M. and Mathews, A.M. (1979) Brief standard self-rating for phobic patients. *Behaviour Therapy and Research*, **17**, 263–7.

Marziali, E.A. (1987) People in your life: Development of a social support measure for predicting psychotherapy outcome. *Journal of Nervous and Mental Disease*, **175**(6), 327–38.

Marziali, E.A., Marmar, C. and Krupnick, J. (1981) Therapeutic alliance scales: development and relationship to psychotherapy outcome. *American Journal of Psychiatry*, **138**(3), 361–4.

Mavissakalian, M. (1986) The Fear Questionnaire: a validity study. *Behaviour Research and Therapy*, **24**, 83–7.

Michelson, L., Mavissakalian, M. and Marchione, K. (1988) Cognitive, behavioural, and psychophysiological treatment of agoraphobia: a comparative outcome investigation. *Behavior Therapy*, **19**(2), 97–120.

Millon, T. (1982) *Millon Clinical Multiaxial Inventory Manual*, 2nd edn, National Computer Systems, Minneapolis.

Mintz, J. (1981) Measuring outcome in psychodynamic psychotherapy: psychodynamic vs symptomatic assessment. *Archives of General Psychiatry*, **38**, 503–6.

Mintz, J. and Keisler, D. (1982) Individualised measures of psychotherapy outcome. In P.C. Kendall and J.N. Butcher (eds), *Handbook of Research Methods in Clinical Psychology*, pp. 491–534, Wiley-Interscience, New York.

Mitchell, K., Bozarth, J. and Krauft, C. (1977) A reappraisal of the therapeutic effectiveness of accurate empathy, non-possessive warmth and genuineness. In A. Gurman and A. Razin (eds), *Effective Psychotherapy: A Handbook of Research*, pp. 482–502, Pergamon Press, Oxford.

Morgan, R., Luborsky, L., Crits-Christoph, P., Curtis, H. and Solomon, J. (1982) Predicting the outcomes of psychotherapy by the Penn Helping Alliance Rating Method. *Archives of General Psychiatry*, **39**, 397–402.

Mulhall, D.J. (1976) Systematic self-assessment by PQRS (Personal questionnaire rapid scaling technique). *Psychological Medicine*, **6**, 591–7.

Orlinsky, D.E. and Howard, M.I. (1977) The therapist's experience of psychotherapy. In A.S. Gurman and A.M. Razin (eds), *Effective Psychotherapy: A Handbook of Research*, Pergamon Press, Oxford.

Parker, K.C., Hanson, R.K. and Hunsley, J. (1988) MMPI, Rorschach and WAIS, a meta-analytic comparison of reliability, stability and validity. *Psychological Bulletin*, **103**(3), 367–73.

Peck, D.F. and Dean, C. (1988) Measurement in psychiatry. In R.E. Kendell and A.K. Zealley (eds), *Companion to Psychiatric Studies*, 4th edn, Churchill Livingstone, Edinburgh.

Piersma, H.L. (1986) The Millon Clinical Multiaxial Inventory (MCMI) as a treatment outcome measure for psychiatric inpatients. *Journal of Clinical Psychology*, **42**(3), 493–9.

Platt, S., Weyman, A., Hirsh, S. and Hewitt, S. (1980) The social behaviour assessment schedule (SBAS). Rationale, contents, scoring and reliability of a new interview schedule. *Social Psychiatry*, **15**, 43–55.

Reid, D.W., Haas, G. and Hawkings, D. (1977) Locus of desired control and positive self-concept of the elderly. *Journal of Gerontology*, **32**(4), 441–50.

Remington, M. and Tyrer, P. (1979) The social functioning schedule—a brief semi-structured interview. *Social Psychiatry*, **14**, 151–7.

Robson, P. (1988) Self-esteem—a psychiatric point of view. *British Journal of Psychiatry*, **153**, 6–15.

Robson, P. (1989a) Development of a new self-report questionnaire to measure self-esteem. *Psychological Medicine*, **19**, 513–18.

Robson, P. (1989b) Personal communication.

Roen, S.R. and Burnes, A.J. (1968) *Community Adaptation Schedule. Preliminary Manual*, Behavioral Publications, New York.

Rosenbaum, M. (1980) A schedule for assessing self-control behaviors: preliminary findings. *Behavior Therapy*, **11**, 109–21.

Rosenberg, M. (1965) *Society and The Adolescent Self-Image*, Princeton University Press, Princeton, NJ.

Rotter, J.B. (1966) Generalised expectancies for internal versus external control of reinforcement. *Psychological Monographs*, **80**(1), 609.

Rotter, J.B. (1975) Some problems and misconceptions related to the construct of internal versus external control of reinforcement. *Journal of Consulting and Clinical Psychology*, **43**, 56–67.

Ruesch, J., Sabine, J., Peterson, H.W. and Imbeau, S. (1972) The measurement of social disability. *Comprehensive Psychiatry*, **13**, 507–18.

Sandell, R. (1987a) Assessing the effects of psychotherapy, II. A procedure for direct rating of therapeutic change. *Psychotherapy and Psychosomatics*, **47**, 37–43.

Sandell, R. (1987b) Assessing the effects of psychotherapy, III. Reliability and validity of 'Change after psychotherapy'. *Psychotherapy and Psychosomatics*, **47**, 44–52.

Schooler, N., Hogarty, G. and Weissman, M.M. (1979) Social Adjustment Scale II (SASII). In W.A. Hargrieves, C.C. Attkisson and J.E. Sorenson (eds), *Resource Materials for Community Health Program Evaluators*, pp. 290–330, Publication No. (ADM) 79–328, US Dept of Health, Education and Welfare.

Schwartz, R.M. and Gottman, K.M. (1976) Towards a task analysis of assertive behavior. *Journal of Consulting and Clinical Psychology*, **44**, 910–20.

Seligman, M.E.P., Abramson, L.Y., Semmel, A. and von Baeyer, C. (1979). Depressive attributional style. *Journal of Abnormal Psycholgy*, **88**(3), 242–7.

Shapiro, D.A. and Firth, J. (1987) Prescriptive v. exploratory psychotherapy: outcomes of the Sheffield Psychotherapy Project. *British Journal of Psychiatry*, **151**, 790–99.

Shapiro, D.A., Firth-Cozens, J. and Stiles, W.B. (1989) The question of therapists' differential effectiveness: A Sheffield Psychotherapy Project Addendum. *British Journal of Psychiatry*, **154**, 383–5.

Shapiro, M.B. (1961) A method of measuring psychological changes specific to the individual psychiatric patient. *British Journal of Medical Psychology*, **34**, 151.

Shostrum, E.L. (1964) An inventory for the measure of self-actualisation. *Educational and Psychological Measurement*, **24**, 207–18.

Simons, A.D., Lustman, P.J., Wetzel, R.D. and Murphy, G.E. (1985) Predicting response to cognitive therapy of depression: the role of learned resourcefulness. *Cognitive Therapy and Research*, **42**, 79–89.

Speilberger, C.D., Goruch, R.L. and Luchene, R.E. (1970) *Manual for the State–Trait Anxiety Inventory*, Consulting Psychologists Press, Palo Alto, California.

Spitzer, R.L., Endicott, J., Fleiss, J.L. and Cohen, J. (1970) The psychiatric status schedule: a technique for evaluating psychopathology and impairment in role functioning. *Archives of General Psychiatry*, **23**, 41–55.

Strupp, H.M., Moras M. and Sandell, J. (1981) Vanderbilt Negative Indicators Scale: an instrument for the identification of deterrents to process in time limited dynamic psychotherapy. Unpublished manuscript, Vanderbilt University.

Teasdale, J.D., Fogarty, S.D.J. and Williams, J.M. (1980) Speech rate as a measure of short term variation in depression. *British Journal of Social and Clinical Psychology*, **19**(3), 271–8.

Truax, C.B. and Carkhuff, R.R. (1967) *Toward Effective Counselling and Psychotherapy: Training and Practice*, Aldine Publishing Co., Chicago.

Waskow, I.E. and Parloff, M.B. (1975) *Psychotherapy Change Measures: Report on Clinical Research Branch Outcome Measures Project*, National Institute of Mental Health, Washington, DC.

Watkins, J.T. and Rush, A.J. (1978) Measurement of cognitions, beliefs and thought patterns in depressed persons. Paper presented at the Annual Meeting of Association for Advancement of Behaviour Therapy Convention, Chicago, Illinois.

Weiss, D.S., DeWitt, K.N., Kaltreider, N.B. and Horowitz, M.J. (1985) A proposed method for measuring change beyond symptoms. *Archives of General Psychiatry*, **42**, 703–8.
Weissman, M.M. (1975) The assessment of social adjustment: a review of the techniques. *Archives of General Psychiatry*, **32**, 357–65.
Weissman, A.N. and Beck, A.T. (1978) Development and validation of the dysfunctional attitude scale. Paper presented at the Annual Meeting of the Association for Advancement of Behavior Therapy. Chicago, Illinois.
Weissman, M.M. and Bothwell, S. (1976) The assessment of social adjustment by patient self-report. *Archives of General Psychiatry*, **33**, 1111–15.
Weissman, M.M., Paykel, E.S., Siegel, R. and Klerman, G.L. (1971) The social role performance of depressed women: comparisons with a normal group. *American Journal of Orthopsychiatry*, **41**, 390–405.
Weissman, M.M., Sholomskas, D. and John, K. (1981) The assessment of social adjustment: an update. *Archives of General Psychiatry*, **38**, 1250–8.
Wilkinson, I.M. and Blackburn, I.M. (1981) Cognitive style in depressed and recovered depressed patients. *British Journal of Clinical Psychology*, **20**, 283–92.
Willer, B. and Biggin, P. (1974) *Self-Assessment Guide: Rationale, Development, and Evaluation*, Lakeshore Psychiatric Hospital, Toronto.
Willer, B. and Miller, G.A. (1977) A brief scale for predicting rehospitalisation of former psychiatric patients. *Canadian Psychiatric Association Journal*, **22**, 77–81.
Worell, L. and Tumilty, T.N. (1981) The measurement of locus of control among alcoholics. In H.M. Lefcourt (ed.), *Research with the Locus of Control Construct*, Volume 1, pp. 321–31, Academic Press, New York.
Young, J., El Shammaa, K.E. and Beck, A.T. (1979) Competency checklist for cognitive therapists. In A.T. Beck, A.J. Rush, B.F. Shaw and G. Emery (eds), *Cognitive Therapy of Depression*, Guilford Press, New York.
Zuckerman, M. (1960) The development of an affect adjective checklist for the measurement of anxiety. *Journal of Consulting Psychology*, **24**, 457–62.

Chapter 8

Adjustment to Illness

GEOFFREY G. LLOYD

INTRODUCTION

There is convincing evidence that psychiatric and physical illness tend to cluster together. The best evidence of this association comes from primary care and community studies, which have indicated that physically ill people are much more likely to be psychiatrically ill than physically healthy members of the community (Eastwood, 1975; Wells *et al.*, 1988). There are several possible reasons why this association occurs and these are outlined below:

(1) Stressful life events may precipitate episodes of both physical and psychiatric illness as proposed by the cluster theory of Hinkle and Wolff (1957). A retrospective study by Murphy and Brown (1980) showed that the association between the onset of organic illness and stressful events occurring during the previous six months applied only to women aged between 18 and 50, and only when the development of organic disorder was preceded by or coincided with the onset of a psychiatric illness. The authors proposed that the causal link between life events and physical illness had been mediated by a psychiatric illness.

(2) Psychiatric illness may predispose to physical illness either directly or indirectly. The physical morbidity associated with alcoholism and drug abuse is obvious, but there is also evidence that other psychiatric illnesses contribute to physical ill-health. It was apparent from the middle of the nineteenth century that psychiatric patients had an increased mortality rate compared to the rest of the population. Several conditions, especially tuberculosis, contributed to the excess mortality, and there seems little doubt that the effects of chronic institutionalization, with its associated risks of infection and malnutrition, were largely responsible for the high mortality. Recent studies have shown that the excess mortality rate of psychiatrically ill patients has been declining steadily, probably due to improvements in general medical care. Nevertheless, there is still evidence of an increased death rate of patients treated for neurotic illness even when suicide and accidental deaths have been discounted (Rorsman, 1974; Sims and Prior, 1978).

Measuring Human Problems. Edited by D.F. Peck and C.M. Shapiro

(3) Therapeutic drugs contribute significantly to the association. Psychotropic drugs such as antidepressants, lithium and phenothiazines have a wide range of physical side-effects while many drugs used in internal medicine, such as steroids, anticholinergics and anti-hypertensives, can cause affective illnesses or confusional states.
(4) Physical illnesses cause psychiatric disorder because of structural brain disease or disturbance of neurotransmitter function. These are manifest as acute confusional states or organic affective disorders.
(5) Finally, physical illness can cause psychiatric disorder because of its emotional impact and implications for the individual's future well-being. It is this link which will be the predominant concern in this chapter.

PREVALENCE OF PSYCHIATRIC MORBIDITY IN MEDICAL PATIENTS

Most authors who have examined the links between physical and psychiatric illness have studied general hospital populations, either in-patients or out-patients. Two comprehensive reviews have indicated a wide range of reported cases of psychiatric illness (Cavanaugh and Wettstein, 1984; Mayou and Hawton, 1986). Among general hospital in-patients the reported prevalence of psychiatric illness ranged from 13 to 72 per cent while among out-patients the prevalence ranged from 14 to 83 per cent. Higher rates have been reported in studies which have relied on unstandardized clinical interviews. When standardized measures, such as questionnaires and structured interviews, have been used the reported rates are generally lower.

The wide variation in prevalence rates is due to a number of factors, including differences in the age of subjects studied and variations in the hospital setting. However, they do suggest that there are intrinsic difficulties in assessing psychological symptoms in physically ill patients and in agreeing on what constitutes a psychiatric case in this population. One problem immediately apparent in general hospital studies is that prevalence figures include patients with somatic symptoms unexplained by physical illness together with patients with undoubted organic illness. The former group are known to have high rates of psychiatric illness (Lloyd, 1983), and their inclusion will artificially raise the apparent association between physical and psychiatric illness. However, problems remain even if patients without organic illness are excluded from consideration. Cavanaugh and Wettstein (1984) have drawn attention to the fact that little research has been undertaken to define psychiatric illness or to standardize psychiatric measures in medical populations. The concepts of psychiatric illness have been developed from observations on patients in psychiatric hospitals, and these concepts have been applied in a wholesale manner to medical patients.

Only recently has the diagnostic net been cast more widely and detailed consideration been given to the different forms of psychiatric illness seen in primary care and general hospitals. Those studies which have been undertaken show clearly that psychological symptoms in medical populations are distributed continuously. This distribution is similar to that found in community surveys, but in the physically ill the distribution curve is shifted to the right, so that relatively more subjects obtain scores in the higher range (House, 1988). Thus there is no clear separation into two groups, the one being psychiatric cases and the other psychiatrically normal. The point of distinction is often placed in an arbitrary manner because diagnostic criteria are not laid down as clearly as they should be. However, the definition of a case cannot be avoided. The criteria on which a diagnosis is made should include considerations of whether the psychological symptoms are themselves causing the patient distress, whether they are interfering with the patient's adjustment to illness or compliance with treatment and whether the symptoms can be expected to respond to psychiatric intervention. If any of these criteria are satisfied it is reasonable to make a psychiatric diagnosis.

Problems also arise from the nature of the assessments used. With few exceptions, questionnaires and structured interviews have been developed for use in patients with a primary psychiatric illness. They include somatic items such as insomnia, fatigue, anorexia and weight loss, which are crucially important in the assessment of a primary depressive illness but which carry much less significance in patients who are physically ill. Indeed, their presence may be misleading and contribute to a psychiatric diagnosis which is unwarranted.

Several modifications have been introduced to try to overcome this problem. First, questionnaires have been used in shortened form, omitting those items which assess somatic symptoms. Second, higher cut-off points have been used when screening for psychiatric illness in medical patients. In the 30-item version of the General Health Questionnaire a score of 5 or above is usually taken as being the best indicator of probable psychiatric illness. However, in medical patients such a score would lack specificity and yield too many false positives. A higher cut-off point has been shown to have greater validity, studies in neurological patients recommending a score of 12 or above as being the best predictor of psychiatric 'caseness' (Bridges and Goldberg, 1984). Third, a few questionnaires have been designed specifically with medical patients in mind. The best known of these is the Hospital Anxiety and Depression Scale (HAD), introduced by Zigmond and Snaith (1983). This omits somatic items completely, so that anxiety and depression are quantified entirely in terms of their psychological symptoms.

PATTERN OF SYMPTOMS

In most cases the psychological symptoms which arise in association with physical illness take the form of an undifferentiated neurotic reaction with a mixture of anxiety and depression. It is not possible, or even desirable, to separate the two effects although it has been suggested that anxiety predominates in the early stages following the onset of illness while depression is a later development. Several authors have attempted to identify specific characteristics of depression in the medically ill, given that somatic symptoms can be misleading from a diagnostic viewpoint. Moffic and Paykel (1975) compared the symptoms of depressed patients in a medical ward with those treated in a psychiatric setting. The former were not so severely depressed. When the severity of depression was equated the medical depressives more frequently had feelings of pessimism, helplessness, anxiety and self-pity, but they were less inclined to have suicidal thoughts. Clark *et al*. (1983) tried to delineate core symptoms from the Beck Depression Inventory which would discriminate for severity of depression in a medical sample. These symptoms were suicidal ideation, sense of failure, sense of punishment, loss of social interest, indecision and dissatisfaction. Observations such as these have led to the view that anhedonia, the loss of the capacity to experience pleasure, is the best indicator of depression in the physically ill (Snaith, 1987). Klein (1974) had previously suggested that anhedonia is a symptom which may distinguish biogenic from psychogenic states of depression and which may indicate a good response to antidepressant medication.

Mood disturbance following physical illness is often of limited duration, tending to improve within a few weeks, particularly if there is improvement in the patient's physical status. Lloyd and Cawley (1982) carried out a prospective study of men admitted to hospital following a first myocardial infarction. Psychiatric morbidity was common during the first week, 35 per cent being assigned a psychiatric diagnosis after assessment using a standardized interview. In 16 per cent of patients there was evidence of psychiatric morbidity prior to the heart attack. Thus psychological symptoms developed acutely as a result of the cardiac illness (and its implications) in 19 per cent of cases. In the majority of these the psychological symptoms had subsided without specifc treatment when the patients were interviewed again four months later. When their demographic, social and personality characteristics were examined these patients could not be distinguished from those who remained psychologically healthy. In contrast, patients with antecedent psychiatric illness were more likely to be unemployed and unmarried and to have greater levels of social and family maladjustment. Similarly, Mayou *et al*. (1988) observed a marked improvement at follow-up in the mental state of patients diagnosed as having an affective disorder during their hospital admission. This improvement was related to physical recovery; patients with continuing affective symptoms were those who still had serious physical disorder.

Derogatis *et al.* (1983) applied DSM-III criteria in a study of patients with cancer in three centres in the United States. Psychiatric disorder was diagnosed in 47 per cent, and in two-thirds of these the diagnosis assigned was an adjustment disorder with depressed mood, anxiety or a mixture of both. Major affective disorder was diagnosed in only 6 per cent of the total. Dean (1987) studied women undergoing mastectomy for breast cancer and found that psychiatric disorder was highest just before the operation and fell progressively post-operatively. She concluded that psychiatric morbidity was usually of a minor nature and that most women were not ill in the sense that a psychiatrist would have expected them to present for treatment. However, there were serious sexual difficulties following the operation.

By definition, the symptoms of an adjustment disorder improve within a short period, usually a few weeks, as the precipitating illness resolves. If affective symptoms persist longer and are more severe than those seen in adjustment disorder they may satisfy criteria for the diagnosis of a major affective disorder, but it must be stressed that there is no clear-cut distinction between the two categories. In nearly all cases the persistent symptoms are depressive in nature and conform to the category of secondary depression (Lloyd, 1985). The prevalence of secondary depression following physical illness has not been investigated in sufficient detail to allow firm conclusions to be drawn.

Stern *et al.* (1976) studied patients following a heart attack and found that no new cases of affective disorder directly related to the attack developed during the following 12 months. Lloyd and Cawley (1983) observed that 20 per cent of those who had not been psychiatrically ill before their heart attack had developed an affective disorder 4 months later, and 14 per cent still had symptoms of affective disorder 12 months later. In some cases, however, it was evident that psychiatric symptoms had developed as a result of events unrelated to the cardiac illness.

Psychotic symptoms following physical illness are nearly always due to organic brain disease, but occasionally an acute functional psychosis develops, usually in people with a history of previous psychiatric illness or evidence of social or sensory isolation who have been admitted to hospital as emergencies (Cutting, 1980). This takes the form of an acute paranoid reaction, the central feature being a systematized paranoid delusion involving the medical or nursing staff. The psychosis lasts only a few days and responds to neuroleptic medication or particularly to moving the patient to an environment which is perceived as less threatening.

Other psychological reactions are even more difficult to classify. For example, denial of illness refers to a spectrum of attitudes which involve the minimization of evidence of illness or its implications. Denial can be an adaptive response if it protects the patient from distressing levels of anxiety, but it can be an obstacle to recovery if the patient refuses to acknowledge the severity of the illness and the need for treatment. Some patients find it difficult to accept the need to modify their diet, leisure activities and other habits in accordance with medical advice. They may rebel intermittently against this advice, thereby running the risk of aggravating their illness. On the other hand, functional disability may be much greater than would be expected from the degree of physical pathology; it may even persist long after recovery appears complete. The patient continues to complain of pain, fatigue or other somatic symptoms and adopts a pattern of invalidism which is not justified in strictly physical terms. When this pattern is becoming established there is often collusion, albeit unwittingly, on the part of close relatives who take over many of the patient's previous tasks and responsibilities.

STANDARDIZED METHODS OF ASSESSMENT

There are two main methods of measuring the psychological response to illness. These involve the use of either questionnaires or structured interviews. Questionnaires have several advantages in that they are relatively easy to use, are completed quickly and can be administered by people after little training. The items included in a questionnaire are clearly specified and the subject's response to them enables a score to be calculated, thus providing a quantified assessment of psychological symptoms. Some questionnaires provide a single score; others contain a number of different scales derived by grouping items which have similar content. Thus a questionnaire may attempt to quantify several aspects of the patient's mental state. However, questionnaires have a number of shortcomings which limit their value in clinical research. They do not indicate the duration of symptoms nor the relationship between these and the physical illness. The threshold score for case definition needs to be established for each population. Even after this has been accomplished, the questionnaire score does not enable a specific psychiatric diagnosis to be made. It merely indicates the probability of some type of psychiatric disorder being present.

Standardized interviews overcome some of these problems. In addition to providing a quantified assessment they enable the evolution of symptoms to be established and make it possible for the temporal relationship between physical illness and psychological symptoms to be determined. They also allow a specific diagnosis to be assigned. These are often more acceptable to the patient in that they follow the pattern of a routine clinical interview, but they are more time consuming than questionnaires and whoever administers them needs to be appropriately trained before the results can be regarded as reliable.

Most of the assessments available in psychiatry have been used in studies of physically ill subjects, but in this chapter attention will be given only to those measures which have been used frequently and which are most suitable for this type of population. Whenever possible, concurrent measurements should be made of the patient's physical status to assess the severity of the underlying physical illness. These measurements may involve physiological or biochemical parameters or clinical assessment to determine the extent of a disease process, as, for example, is possible in malignant disease. This is not as simple as it sounds, because appropriate assessments are not always available. However, there are measures to quantify the severity or extent of several conditions such as myocardial infarction (Norris *et al.*, 1969) and Hodgkin's disease (Committee on Hodgkin's Disease Classification, 1971). Creatinine clearance is an accepted measure of the severity of renal disease while glycosylated haemoglobin provides a measure of blood glucose control in diabetes. Psychophysiological measures such as heart rate and galvanic skin responses cannot be used as correlates of psychological symptoms because they can be directly affected by the disease process.

General Health Questionnaire (GHQ)

This has been one of the most widely used instruments since its development by Goldberg (1972). It is essentially a screening instrument, a high score on the questionnaire indicating that the patient probably has a psychiatric disorder and that further enquiry, by means of an interview, is necessary (see Chapter 2). Several community studies have indicated its acceptability to subjects who do not regard themselves as psychiatrically ill. It has also been used successfully in many studies of medically ill patients, including gynaecological disorders (Byrne, 1984), hypertension (Mann, 1977), neurological disorders (Depaulo *et al.*, 1980; Bridges and Goldberg, 1984) and breast cancer (Dean, 1987). Other authors have administered the GHQ to unselected medical patients suffering from a wide range of illnesses (Maguire *et al.*, 1974; Cavanaugh, 1983; Feldman *et al.*, 1987).

In its full version the GHQ contains 60 questions, but the abbreviated versions with 30, 28 or 12 items have been preferred for use with medical patients because they contain fewer questions pertaining to somatic symptoms. The 28-item version differs from the others in that, besides providing a global score, it also yields four scale scores which have been derived by factor analysis (Goldberg and Hillier, 1979). These scales are somatic symptoms, anxiety and insomnia, social dysfunction and severe depression.

Goldberg (1985, 1986) has emphasized that the specificity and sensitivity vary according to the patients studied and that the threshold score will be affected by the degree of physical illness. In the case of the 28-item version, 4/5 is the best threshold score for discriminating between cases and non-cases among patients attending general practitioners. However, the threshold needs to be raised to 11/12 when used with patients with neurological disorders (Bridges and Goldberg, 1984).

Some difficulties with this scale are highlighted by Cavanaugh's investigation of 335 medically ill patients in a Chicago hospital (Cavanaugh, 1983). Of the total sample, 61 per cent had a score of 5 or over on the GHQ-30, a much higher percentage than is usually reported for psychiatric disorder in this type of population. However, only 35 per cent had a score of 10 or more while 11 per cent had a score of 20 or more.

Mayou and Hawton (1986) have summarized the GHQ results of several studies of medically ill populations, concluding that both sensitivity and specificity are low, especially in the most severely ill patients. If the GHQ is used as a screening test, as intended, it is necessary to validate it against a standardized interview for each group of patients. For research purposes, when it is necessary to avoid false negatives, it is better to use a low threshold score and then to examine high-scoring subjects in more detail by interviewing them.

Beck Depression Inventory (BDI) (Beck *et al.*, 1961)

This was originally intended to be administered by a trained observer but is now often used in a self-rating form (see Chapter 3). It consists of 21 items each of which has four responses of increasing severity and has been used in several studies. Schwab *et al.* (1967) found that 22 per cent of medical in-patients obtained scores of 14 or more, this usually being taken as indicating a clinically significant degree of depression. Using a similar threshold, Moffic and Paykel (1975) found 24 per cent of medical in-patients to be depressed while Cavanaugh (1983) discovered 36 per cent to have scores of 13 or more. The inclusion of somatic items may give a number of false positive results, and this becomes increasingly evident when lower cut-off points are used. For example, Smith *et al.* (1985) assessed 60 patients with end-stage renal failure and classified 28 (47 per cent) as depressed on the basis of a BDI score of 10 or more. Only six of these were classified as depressed on the Multiple Affect Adjective Check List and only three fulfilled DSM-III criteria for major depression.

Montgomery–Asberg Depression Rating Scale (MADRS) (Montgomery and Asberg, 1979)

This is an observer rating scale derived from a longer instrument. It contains 10 items which are rated on a 4-point scale, each point of which is clearly defined. Kearns *et al.* (1982) compared several depression rating scales in their ability to distinguish different levels of severity of depression. They found the Montgomery–Asberg scale to perform as well as the longer-established Hamilton Depression Scale (Hamilton, 1960) and better than the Beck Depression Inventory and Wakefield Inventory (Snaith *et al.*, 1971). However, they pointed out the different content of the two scales. Whereas in the Hamilton scale there is considerable emphasis on somatic symptoms and observed psychomotor behaviour, the Mongomery–Asberg scale focuses exclusively on the psychological symptoms of depression. The MADRS is therefore more suitable for use with patients who suffer from concurrent physical illness.

Hospital Anxiety and Depression Scale (HAD)

This scale, developed by Zigmond and Snaith (1983), is one of the few instruments to have been introduced specifically for use with physically ill patients. It is brief, contains 14 items, and is completed by the patient. Somatic items likely to result from physical illness have been excluded. Anxiety and depression items have been separated and the concept of depression has been based on the anhedonic state, reflecting loss of pleasure, since it has been considered to be the best clinical marker for biogenic or drug-responsive depression. There are seven items each for anxiety and depression and these are scored on a 4-point scale (0–3). A total score on each scale of 11 or over has been reported to correspond with a clinical diagnosis of anxiety or depression; a score of eight to ten is borderline while one of seven or less is considered normal. The reliability of the scale has been established (Aylard *et al.*, 1987) and it is likely that it will be used frequently in clinical research. A particular asset of this scale is the ease with which it can provide serial measures of affective symptoms.

Similar scales have subsequently been described by Goldberg *et al.* (1988) for use in general medical settings. These consist of nine questions for anxiety and nine for depression. In general practice, patients with an anxiety score of five or depression score of two have a 50 per cent chance of having a clinically important disturbance. The probability rises steeply with scores above these. However, the cut-off scores may need to be revised upwards for use with medically ill patients.

Illness Behaviour Questionnaire (IBQ)

Pilowsky and Spence (1975, 1983) have developed this self-administered questionnaire to assess abnormal illness behaviour as derived from the views of Mechanic (1962). Its chief purpose is to evaluate patients in whom there is a discrepancy between objective organic pathology and their behavioural response. These patients are usually diagnosed as having functional disturbances such as hypochondriasis, conversion reaction or malingering (Pilowsky *et al.*, 1979a). The questionnaire contains 62 items which are answered in a yes/no format. Seven dimensions have been identified using factor analysis; these are general hypochondriasis, disease conviction, psychological or somatic perception of illness, affective inhibition, affective disturbance, denial, and irritability. The IBQ has been used successfully to distinguish patients with chronic pain from those attending a general practitioner (Pilowsky *et al.*, 1979a) and also those with a poor outcome following coronary artery bypass surgery (Pilowsky *et al.*, 1979b). However Wilson-Barnett and Trimble (1985) found that three of the seven scales did not distinguish between patients with hysteria, neurological disorders or primary psychiatric illness. Similarly, Tyrer *et al.* (1989) did not find the IBQ helpful in distinguishing patients with abnormal pain behaviour from the remainder of patients attending a pain clinic.

Visual Analogue Scales (VAS)

These simple scales have been shown to provide a reliable assessment of feelings (Aitken, 1969; Bond and Lader, 1974). They can be constructed to measure a large number of symptoms and are well suited to serial assessments (Lloyd *et al.*, 1984). The scale consists of a 100 mm line at the ends of which are the least severe and the most severe ratings of the symptom. Each patient is asked to indicate the severity of symptoms by marking the scale in the appropriate position. The score is obtained by measuring the distance between this rating and the zero mark. (For further details of VAS see Chapter 3.)

Clinical Interview Schedule (CIS)

This standardized, semi-structured interview is eminently suitable for assessing the range of neurotic problems encountered in medically ill patients (Goldberg *et al.*, 1970). It covers 10 reported symptoms present during the previous week and 12 abnormalities manifest at interview. Psychotic features are included among the manifest abnormalities but the interview is not the best instrument for use with patients in whom psychotic symptoms are likely to be common. A total weighted score is derived by doubling the score for manifest abnormalities and adding this to the score for reported symptoms. No clear instructions are given concerning the threshold for case definition, but the interviewer is encouraged to make a global rating of severity on a 0–4 scale, a score of 2 or more being taken as indicating the presence of psychiatric disorder. The first part of the interview is unstructured and allows the presenting complaints, previous medical and psychiatric history and social background to be recorded. At this time the interview can elucidate the temporal relationship between the onset of physical illness and current psychological symptoms.

The CIS was originally intended for use by experienced psychiatrists but it can also be employed by other professionals involved in mental health provided suitable training is given. Reliability must be established for each interviewer before the quantified assessment can be compared with the results from other studies.

The interview is acceptable to medical patients and has been used in a study of an unselected group of inpatients (Maguire *et al.*, 1974), and also surveys of Parkinson's disease (Mindham *et al.*, 1976), chronic renal disease (Farmer *et al.*, 1979), myocardial infarction (Lloyd and Cawley, 1982) and neurological disorders (Bridges and Goldberg, 1984). The prevalence of psychiatric morbidity in these surveys has been in the range of 20–40 per cent, the majority of cases having affective disorders. In the study of patients following an acute myocardial infarction (Lloyd and Cawley, 1982) follow-up interviews enabled the course of psychological symptoms to be observed. One week after the acute attack 35 per cent were diagnosed as having psychiatric morbidity. In 16 per cent the history suggested that psychological symptoms had antedated the heart attack and these tended to persist throughout the 12-month follow-up period. In the other 19 per cent symptoms had been precipitated by the attack and they tended to subside spontaneously during the following weeks, conforming to the pattern of an adjustment disorder.

Present State Examination (PSE)

The PSE is a semi-structured interview with detailed instructions for the assessment of neurotic and psychotic symptoms (Wing *et al.*, 1974). These are graded into various levels of severity, a level of 5 or over being taken to indicate psychiatric disorder. A computer program, CATEGO, enables a specific diagnosis to be made. The PSE has been used widely in the classification of psychiatric disorders but is not ideally suited for use with medical patients. It has been criticized for not allowing rating of minor degrees of emotional distress and for being awkwardly worded for use with the physically ill (Mayou and Hawton, 1986). Case definition is stringent and therefore the PSE usually records a lower prevalence of psychiatric disorder than other measures. However, its acceptability can be improved if it is modified slightly. Feldman *et al.* (1987) incorporated some modifications into their large survey of general medical in-patients, 14.6 per cent of whom were diagnosed as having an affective disorder based on a PSE Index of Definition of 5 and above. The interview has also been used to examine patients attending a clinic for chronic pain when 32 per cent of patients had sufficient symptoms to be classified as psychiatric cases (Tyrer *et al.*, 1989).

Diagnostic Interview Schedule (DIS)

Robins *et al.* (1981) developed this interview to enable diagnoses to be made according to three systems: DSM-III, Feighner criteria and Research Diagnostic Criteria. It assesses symptoms which may have occurred at any time throughout the subject's life. More detailed enquiry permits the assessment of symptoms during specified periods in the recent past. Its scope is broader than other structured interviews in that it includes assessment of alcoholism, drug abuse and anorexia nervosa. Wells *et al.* (1988) have described its application in a community study which aimed to examine the association between psychiatric disorder and eight chronic medical conditions. This formed part of the National Institute of Mental Health (NIMH) Epidemiologic Catchment Area Program. Among people with one or more medical conditions the sex and age-adjusted prevalence of psychiatric disorder in the preceding 6 months was 24.7 per cent and of lifetime psychiatric disorder 42.5 per cent. The comparable figures for people without a medical condition were 17.5 per cent and 33.0 per cent, respectively. Psychiatric disorders were strongly associated with arthritis, cancer, lung disease, neurological disorder, heart disease and physical handicap but not with hypertension or diabetes.

Psychosocial Adjustment to Illness Scale (PAIS)

The PAIS is a semi-structured interview specifically designed to assess psychosocial adjustment to physical illness (Derogatis, 1986). A self-report version is also available. The interview is composed of 46 items, answers to which are scored on a 0–3 scale. These cover seven areas of adjustment: health care orientation, vocational environment, domestic environment, sexual relationships, extended family relationships, social environments, and psychological distress. The PAIS does not attempt to define psychiatric illness but gives a dimensional score for each of the seven subscales. Internal consistency and inter-rater reliability have been found to be satisfactory and the total score correlates well with other scales of psychological distress with which it has been compared.

This instrument represents a promising development but more studies need to be published before its merits can be established in relation to other questionnaires and interviews.

CONCLUSIONS

There are special problems involved in assessing psychological adjustment to physical illness using quantified measures. Questionnaires and structured interviews may give a misleading estimate of the prevalence of psychiatric morbidity because their scores are influenced by the inclusion of a number of somatic items, responses to which are directly affected by the physical illness. These instruments may need to be modified by omitting certain items and raising the threshold score for case definition. Most research reports have used rating scales or interviews designed for the assessment of primary psychiatric illness and few instruments have been developed specifically for use with a physically ill population. The need to develop such instruments is now being recognized and more research is required to evaluate those which have been introduced in recent years.

Particular attention needs to be given to the evolution of psychological symptoms so that brief emotional reactions can be distinguished from persistent affective syndromes which may require special intervention. Ideally, this requires an assessment of the patient's mental state before becoming ill. Such an assessment is rarely possible, but retrospective enquiries by means of a structured interview enable the clinician to estimate the patient's previous mental state with a high degree of reliability. Adjustment to elective surgery or other major therapeutic procedures can be determined if the patient is examined pre-operatively. Serial assessments after illness or surgery, using the same techniques on each occasion, then enable the severity and duration of psychological symptoms to be determined.

Despite the methodological problems of assessing psychological symptoms associated with physical illness the use of standardized measures has provided a considerable amount of information on the psychological needs of physically ill patients.

REFERENCES

Aitken, R.C.B. (1969) Measurements of feelings using visual analogue scales. *Proceedings of the Royal Society of Medicine*, **62**, 989–93.

Aylard, P.R., Gooding, J.H., McKenna, P.J. and Snaith, R.P. (1987) A validation study of three anxiety and depression self-assessment scales. *Journal of Psychosomatic Research*, **31**, 261–8.

Beck, A.T., Ward, C.H., Mendelson, M., Mock, J. and Erbaugh, J. (1961) An inventory for measuring depression. *Archives of General Psychiatry*, **4**, 561–71.

Bond, A.J. and Lader, M.H. (1974) The use of analogue scales in rating subjective feelings. *British Journal of Medical Psychology*, **47**, 211–18.

Bridges, K. and Goldberg, D. (1984) Psychiatric illness in patients with neurological disorders. *British Medical Journal*, **288**, 268–71.

Byrne, P. (1984) Psychiatric morbidity in a gynaecology clinic: an epidemiological survey. *British Journal of Psychiatry*, **144**, 28–34.

Cavanaugh, S.V. (1983) The prevalence of emotional and cognitive dysfunction in a general medical population: using the MMSE, GHQ and BDI. *General Hospital Psychiatry*, **144**, 28–34.

Cavanaugh, S. and Wettstein, R.M. (1984) Prevalence of psychiatric morbidity in medical populations. In L. Grinspoon (ed.), *Psychiatric Update*, American Psychiatric Press, Washington, DC.

Clark, D.C., Cavanaugh, S.V. and Gibbons, R.D. (1983) The core symptoms of depression in medical and psychiatric patients. *Journal of Nervous and Mental Disease*, **171**, 705–13.

Cutting, J. (1980) Physical illness and psychosis. *British Journal of Psychiatry*, **136**, 109–19.

Dean, C. (1987) Psychiatric morbidity following mastectomy: preoperative predictors and types of illness. *Journal of Psychosomatic Research*, **31**, 385–92.

Depaulo, J.R., Folstein, M.F. and Gordon, B. (1980) Psychiatric screening on a neurological ward. *Psychological Medicine*, **10**, 125–32.

Derogatis, L.R. (1986) The Psychosocial Adjustment to Illness Scale (PAIS). *Journal of Psychosomatic Research*, **30**, 77–91.

Derogatis, L.R., Morrow, G.R., Fetting, J., Penman, D., Piasetsky, S., Schmale, A., Henrichs, M. and Carnicke, C.L.M. (1983) The prevalence of psychiatric disorders among cancer patients. *Journal of the American Medical Association*, **249**, 751–7.

Eastwood, M.R. (1975) *The Relation between Physical and Mental Illness*, University of Toronto Press, Toronto.

Farmer, C.J., Snowden, S.A. and Parsons, V. (1979) The prevalence of psychiatric illness among patients on home dialysis. *Psychological Medcine*, **9**, 509–14.

Feldman, E., Mayou, R., Hawton, K., Ardern, M. and Smith, E.B.O. (1987) Psychiatric disorder in medical inpatients. *Quarterly Journal of Medicine*, **63**, 405–12.

Goldberg, D.P. (1972) *The Detection of Psychiatric Illness by Questionnaire*, Oxford University Press, Oxford.

Goldberg, D.P. (1985) Identifying psychiatric illness among general medical patients. *British Medical Journal*, **291**, 161–2.

Goldberg, D.P. (1986) Use of the general health questionnaire in clinical work. *British Medical Journal*, **293**, 1188–9.

Goldberg, D.P., Cooper, B., Eastwood, M.R., Kedward, H.B. and Shepherd, M. (1970) A standardised psychiatric interview for use in community surveys. *British Journal of Preventive and Social Medicine*, **24**, 18–23.

Goldberg, D.P. and Hillier, V.F. (1979) A scaled version of the General Health Questionnaire. *Psychological Medicine*, **9**, 139–48.

Goldberg, D.P., Bridges, K., Duncan-Jones, P. and Grayson, D. (1988) Detecting anxiety and depression in general medical settings. *British Medical Journal*, **297**, 897–9.

Hamilton, M. (1960) A rating scale for depression. *Journal of Neurology, Neurosurgery and Psychiatry*, **23**, 56–62.

Hinkle, L.E. and Wolff, H.G. (1957) The nature of man's adaptation to his total environment and the relation of this to illness. *Archives of Internal Medicine*, **99**, 442–60.

House, A. (1988) Mood disorders in the physically ill: problems of definition and measurement. *Journal of Psychosomatic Research*, **32**, 345–53.

Kearns, N.P., Cruickshank, C.A., McGuigan, K.J., Riley, S.A., Shaw, S.P. and Snaith, R.P. (1982) A comparison of depression rating scales. *British Journal of Psychiatry*, **141**, 45–9.

Klein, D.F. (1974) Endogenomorphic depression. *Archives of General Psychiatry*, **31**, 447–54.

Lloyd, G.G. (1983) Medicine without signs. *British Medical Journal*, **287**, 539–42.

Lloyd, G.G. (1985) Emotional aspects of physical illness. In K. Granville-Grossman (ed.), *Recent Advances in Clinical Psychiatry*, Volume 5, Churchill Livingstone, Edinburgh.

Lloyd, G.G. and Cawley, R.H. (1982) Psychiatric morbidity after myocardial infarction. *Quarterly Journal of Medicine*, **51**, 33–42.

Lloyd, G.G. and Cawley, R.H. (1983) Distress or illness? A study of psychological symptoms after myocardial infarction. *British Journal of Psychiatry*, **142**, 120–25.

Lloyd, G.G., Parker, A.C., Ludlam, C.A. and McGuire, R.J. (1984) Emotional impact of diagnosis and early treatment of lymphomas. *Journal of Psychosomatic Research*, **28**, 157–62.

Maguire, G.P., Julier, D.L., Hawton, K.E. and Bancroft, J.H.J. (1974) Psychiatric morbidity and referral on two general medical wards. *British Medical Journal*, **i**, 268–70.

Mann, A.H. (1977) The psychological effect of a screening programme and clinical trial for hypertension upon the participants. *Psychological Medicine*, **7**, 431–8.

Mayou, R. and Hawton, K. (1986) Psychiatric disorder in the general hospital. *British Journal of Psychiatry*, **149**, 172–90.

Mayou, R., Hawton, K. and Feldman, E. (1988) What happens to medical patients with psychiatric disorder? *Journal of Psychosomatic Research*, **32**, 541–9.

Mechanic, D., (1962) The concept of illness behaviour. *Journal of Chronic Disease*, **15**, 189–94.

Mindham, R.H.S., Marsden, C.D. and Parkes, J.D. (1976) Psychiatric symptoms during L-dopa therapy for Parkinson's disease and their relationship to physical disability. *Psychological Medicine*, **6**, 23–33.

Moffic, H.S. and Paykel, E.S. (1975) Depression in medical inpatients. *British Journal of Psychiatry*, **126**, 346–53.

Montgomery, S.A. and Asberg, M. (1979) A new depression scale designed to be sensitive to change. *British Journal of Psychiatry*, **134**, 382–9.

Murphy, E. and Brown, G.W. (1980) Life events, psychiatric disturbances and physical illness. *British Journal of Psychiatry*, **136**, 326–38.

Norris, R.M., Brandt, P.W.T., Caughney, D.E., Lee, A.J. and Scott, P.J. (1969) A new coronary prognostic index. *Lancet*, **i**, 274–8.

Pilowsky, I. and Spence, N.D. (1975) Patterns of illness behaviour in patients with intractable pain. *Journal of Psychosomatic Research*, **19**, 279–87.

Pilowsky, I., Murrell, T.G.C. and Gordon, A. (1979a) The development of a screening method for abnormal illness behaviour. *Journal of Psychosomatic Research*, **23**, 203–7.

Pilowsky, I., Spence, N.D. and Waddy, J.L. (1979b) Illness behaviour and coronary artery by-pass surgery. *Journal of Psychosomatic Research*, **23**, 39–44.

Pilowsky, I. and Spence, N.D. (1983) *Manual for the Illness Behaviour Questionnaire (IBQ)*, 2nd edn, University of Adelaide, Adelaide.

Report of the Committee on Hodgkin's Disease Classification (1971) *Cancer Research*, **31**, 1860.

Robins, L.N., Helzer, J.E., Croughan, J. and Ratcliff, K.S. (1981) National Institute of Mental Health diagnostic interview schedule. *Archives of General Psychiatry*, **38**, 381–9.

Rorsman, B. (1974) Mortality among psychiatric patients. *Acta Psychiatrica Scandinavica*, **50**, 354–75.

Schwab, J.J., Bialow, M., Clemmons, R., Martin, P. and Holzer, C.E. (1967) The Beck Depression Inventory with medical inpatients. *Acta Psychiatrica Scandinavica*, **43**, 255–66.

Sims, A.C.P. and Prior, M.P. (1978) The pattern of mortality in severe neuroses. *British Journal of Psychiatry*, **133**, 299–305.

Smith, M.D., Hong, B.A. and Robson, A.M. (1985) Diagnosis of depression in patients with end-stage renal disease. *American Journal of Medicine*, **79**, 160–66.

Snaith, R.P. (1987) The concepts and assessment of depression in oncology. *Journal of Psychosocial Oncology*, **5**, 133–9.

Snaith, R.P., Ahmed, S.N., Mehta, S. and Hamilton, M. (1971) Assessment of the severity of primary depressive illness: the Wakefield self-assessment depression inventory. *Psychological Medicine*, **1**, 143–9.

Stern, M.J., Pascale, L. and McLoone, J.B. (1976) Psychosocial adaptation following an acute myocardial infarction. *Journal of Chronic Diseases*, **29**, 513–26.

Tyrer, S.P., Capon, M., Peterson, D.M., Charlton, J.E. and Thompson, J.W. (1989) The detection of psychiatric illness and psychological handicaps in a British pain clinic population. *Pain*, **36**, 63–74.

Wells, K.B., Golding, J.M. and Burnam, A.M. (1988) Psychiatric disorder in a sample of the general population with and without chronic medical conditions. *American Journal of Psychiatry*, **145**, 976–81.

Wilson-Barnett, J. and Trimble, M.R. (1985) An investigation of hysteria using the Illness Behaviour Questionnaire. *British Journal of Psychiatry*, **146**, 601–8.

Wing, J.K., Cooper, J.E. and Sartorius, N. (1974) *The Measurement and Classification of Psychiatric Symptoms*, Cambridge University Press, Cambridge.

Zigmond, A.S. and Snaith, R.P. (1983) The Hospital Anxiety and Depression Scale. *Acta Psychiatrica Scandinavica*, **67**, 361–70.

Chapter 9

Organic Psychiatry

G. E. Berrios

MEASURING BEHAVIOUR

Measurement is the attribution of numbers to objects, according to rules and objectives (Ellis, 1968). Whether quantification is to be preferred to other descriptive styles will depend upon needs and availability of mathematical models to handle the number arrays. This applies, *mutatis mutandi,* to the measurement of behaviour (Ghiselli *et al.*, 1981). Verbatim accounts may suffice or indeed be more informative when the semantic structure of a mental state needs preserving (Barthes, 1972). Clinical information is lost whenever behaviour is fractionated into symptoms (Berrios, 1984) and when the latter are transformed into the 'items' of a scale. Information relating to structures (e.g. the way in which symptoms hang together) is particularly susceptible to loss.

The quantification of behaviour can be modelled as a variant of analogue-to-digital conversion, i.e. as a process whereby the flow of behaviour is transformed into numbers. In the ideal world it should be possible to reconstruct the 'form' of the flow by plotting the number arrays (Sykes *et al.*, 1981). Successful conversion, however, will depend upon the clinician including sufficient symptoms and choosing the appropriate sampling rate.

Little is known of the sampling patterns required for the optimal quantification of the *organic symptoms*. It is assumed that ascertainment of the symptom *per se* is diagnostically sufficient. Periodic fluctuations in symptom 'saliency', or correlations with other biological events, however, may be equally informative.

Units of analysis

The fractionation of behaviour is controlled by theoretical and empirical rules and the ensuing units of analysis can be considered as information-carrying fragments whose occurrence in real life is almost always enveloped in noise. The information conveyed by symptoms can be assessed qualitatively and quantitatively, but techniques are required to unscramble

Measuring Human Problems. Edited by D.F. Peck and C.M. Shapiro

the signal, increase its 'gain' or reduce the noise. Symptoms of organic mental disease such as memory deficit, emotional lability or orientation failure should be expected to convey more information about the state of the subject's brain than other forms of behaviour (also classed as 'symptoms'), such as 'manipulative behaviour', 'lack of insight' or 'paranoid ideation'. The latter are but theoretical constructs meant to convey information about psychosocial states.

It follows that, to be effective, numerical description in psychopathology must take into consideration the epistemological (informational) value of *each class* of symptom, and that neutral or 'theory-free' descriptions of symptoms, whether verbal (phenomenological) or numerical (i.e. measurements), are not possible (Berrios, 1989a).

The 'existential' space occupied by signs and symptoms lies within the perceptual range of clinical observer and patient. *Macro-symptoms* must be seen, heard or otherwise perceived, i.e. be temporary inhabitants in someone's subjectivity. These symptoms can be identified without technical props and are open to public validation. They are, however, 'noisy' and provide a blurred picture of the neurobiological drama.

Neurobiological events also emit signals lying outside the perceptual range of clinical observer and patient. These *micro-symptoms* can be 'decoded', i.e. brought within 'perceptual' purview by special instrumentation. Some of the so-called neurobiological markers fall within this category. It is likely that micro-symptoms will become particularly important in the area of the organic mental disorders.

Techniques and objectives

Symptoms can be measured on ordinal, interval and ratio scales (Ghiselli *et al.*, 1981). The former two are particularly wasteful of information. The use of a particular type of scale depends on what the measurement is for, and on whether there are adequate statistical techniques to handle the resulting number arrays. Currently available scales are unidimensional and hence cannot convey information on all relevant symptom-dimensions; vectorial structures (e.g. matrices) can do so (Namboodiri, 1984). In this way, important 'structural' information (i.e. how symptoms relate to each other) may be recorded. This type of notation may be also useful for single-case studies.

Measurement techniques can be applied to micro- and macro-symptoms, syndromes, diseases, and to their social consequences. When the output is continuous (e.g. choice reaction time) (Benton, 1986) reference ranges and diagnostic cut-off points can be also determined. When categorical, the objective is to seek meaningful combinations of symptoms and ascertain their relationship to aetiology.

The measurement of the organic mental disorders has general and specific objectives. The former are shared with the quantification of other forms of pathological behaviour. The latter include lesion localization, profiles of functional deficit for the planning of rehabilitation and forensic work. The lesion localization objective is still actively pursued (mainly for theoretical reasons) in the field of neuropsychology. In clinical practice it is being met with by the use of brain-imaging techniques. The organic mental disorders now constitute a hunting ground common to psychiatry, neurology, behavioural neurology and neuropsychology.

THE ORGANIC MENTAL DISORDERS

Concepts and history

The boundaries of this imprecise class of clinical conditions have changed over the years. Textbook definitions are sufficient for teaching and diagnosis but are too vague to identify a *clinical class* to which a common theory of measurement can be applied. Since Kraepelin, 'organic disorders' have been named psychiatric syndromes *causally* related to molar (anatomical) brain pathology. The functional disorders, on the other hand, were *not* defined as the opposite (i.e. as conditions *unaccompanied* by anatomical change) but as resulting from changes *still unknown* (Berrios, 1987).

The debate was on whether *each* aetiology caused its own peculiar symptoms. In other words, could a diagnosis be made of the *physical disease* by examining its psychiatric manifestations? Up to the time of Kraepelin this was the predominant belief. Bonhoeffer (1910), however, suggested that all organic states, regardless of their aetiology, were characterized by the same set of stereotyped symptoms. This view encouraged a narrowing down of the clinical repertoire of the organic disorders, and reinforced the 'cognitive paradigm' of dementia (Berrios, 1989b). The adoption of the latter, in turn, destroyed the nineteenth-century 'gestaltic' pattern of dementia as a form of exogenous psychosis. To compound matters further, 'cognitive' was, at the time, interpreted as 'mnesic', which resulted in an undue emphasis on the measurement of memory. This led to some gains in the diagnostic sensitivity of the concept of dementia but reduced its specificity (Berrios, 1987b).

Early in the twentieth century the 'organic disorders' were redefined as (1) resulting from an identifiable brain lesion, and (2) showing the same stereotyped, *cognitive* symptomatology. This change in perspective occurred against the backdrop of the brain-localization debate. Indeed, the consolidation of the notion of 'organic disorder' coincides with a period of rampant 'brain localizationism', in spite of occasional voices in favour of a hierarchical (e.g. Jackson) or equipotential (e.g. Von Monakow) view (Hecaen and Lanteri-Laura, 1977).

Soon after the First World War, Mourgue, Head, Goldstein, Lashley and others renewed the call for the equipotential view (Bonhoeffer had been influenced by it) and expressed the opinion that the brain responds to insult in a diffuse, stereotyped way, that most of its functions suffer, and also that plastic (adaptational) responses occur during recovery, thus making unreliable any rigid prediction based on localized lesions. The central clinical consequence of this view is that the organic disorders are accompanied by subtle deficits affecting all psychological functioning, which are usually masked by the saliency of cognitive symptoms. Analysis of these deficits might be *more* rewarding, from the point of view of diagnosis and rehabilitation, than, say, the measurement of memory impairment. This sensible view was, however, often packaged in the language of Gestalt, psychodynamic or topological psychology and necessitated for its full expression the development of advanced concepts and instruments.

After the Second World War, signal detection and computational models (Baars, 1986) opened up the possibility of measuring complex forms of cognitive behaviour and even the effect on cognition of all manner of non-cognitive factors (e.g. depression).

Current classifications

ICD-10

The April 1988 draft of ICD-10 defines the organic (including symptomatic) mental disorders (F0) as disorders in which 'aetiology is known by definition' and includes: F00 dementia, Alzheimer type; F01, vascular dementia; F02 dementia in diseases classified elsewhere; F03 dementia not otherwise specified; F04 organic amnesic syndrome (Korsakoff) (other than induced by alcohol or drugs); F05 delirium (other than induced by drugs or alcohol); F06 mental disorders not involving cognitive impairment, due to brain disease, damage or dysfunction, or to physical disease; F07 personality and behaviour disorder due to brain disease, damage or dysfunction; and F09, unspecified or symptomatic mental disorder (Sartorius *et al.*, 1988). It is also suggested in ICD-10 that organic disorders caused by cerebral disease be called *primary*, and by systemic disease *secondary*. Disorders caused by alcohol and drugs are included in another section (F1). The symptomatology of the organic disorders is divided into *cognitive* and *non-cognitive*, and the former favoured on the grounds that it is prominent and invariably present, while the latter, which includes hallucinations, delusions, and affect and personality changes, is also present in non-organic mental disorders. ICD-10 has returned to the original nineteenth-century view that the term 'organic' does not imply that other disorders do not have 'cerebral substrate'.

DSM III-R

DSM III-R (APA, 1987) defines organic mental *syndrome* as a 'constellation of psychological or behavioural signs and symptoms without reference to aetiology' (e.g. organic anxiety symptom and dementia), and organic mental *disorder*, as 'a particular organic mental syndrome in which the aetiology is known or presumed' (e.g. alcohol withdrawal syndrome, multi-infarct dementia). The organic mental syndromes include delirium and dementia, amnestic syndrome and organic hallucinosis, organic delusional, mood, anxiety and personality syndrome, intoxications and withdrawal, and organic mental syndrome not otherwise specified.

Three conclusions can be drawn from the above classifications. First, the organic disorders are believed to consist of 'disturbances in higher cognitive function, such as memory, intellect and learning, or disturbances of sensorium, such as disorders of consciousness and attention' (ICD-10). Second, their assessment requires specific theories and instruments. Third, it is unclear whether the measurement of non-cognitive (but still organic) symptomatology must be earnestly pursued.

THE MEASUREMENT OF THE ORGANIC MENTAL DISORDERS

The first step in the examination of a patient with 'organic' symptoms is to consider the possibility of general medical (e.g. endocrine) causes of psychiatric or psychological presentations. This stage of the procedure only requires measurement when it cannot be qualitatively resolved (e.g. organic symptoms are unclear, or if clear, they are discrepant with other features of the behaviour). In the ordinary clinical process, measurement is only called upon to solve *diagnostic* difficulties. It is, therefore, important to ask how well it can carry out this task. The answer is rather negative. Indeed, measurement is at its most successful after diagnosis has been made. This results from the fact that instruments and cut-off points are validated on groups with clear diagnosis (Grayson, 1988), and their sensitivity is related to disease prevalence (Williams *et al.*, 1982). Therefore the discriminant power of the instrument may be no better than that of clinical diagnosis (Feinstein, 1987; Wasson *et al.*, 1985). Clinical or mathematical adjustments can sometimes make the instrument look better than it is. For example, discrimination may be sharpened in the hands of a clinically experienced psychologist; or cut-off points can be readjusted to improve sensitivity (Galen and Gambino,

1975). Diagnostic cut-off points, however, are not god-given (Veiel, 1988) but are simply mathematical compromises between acceptable levels of sensitivity and specificity (Galen and Gambino, 1975).

Measurement comes into its own when evaluating change (Hadzi-Pavlovic, 1986). Provided that the instrument is reliable (Sanson-Fisher and Martin, 1981), changes in scores usually reflect changes in real life. This is why setting functional baselines is important. This strategy only works when progressive pathology is suspected. In the case of stationary brain lesions, obtaining the same score (or indeed a better one) a year later may lead to the wrong conclusion that there was no organicity in the first place. The evaluation of response to treatment also depends upon the measurement of change.

Measurement is also indicated in the profiling of deficits and assets required for rehabilitation. Organic disorder unevenly affects mental functions. It is important to know which functions have been spared. Rehabilitation programmes can then be based on functional adaptation (Powell, 1981; Miller, 1984). Measurement is also mandatory when the identification of correlations and patterns is needed. Researchers, however, should not feel pressed to force quantification upon all forms of behaviour, particularly when no adequate conceptual models are available to warrant a continuous definition of the symptom.

Factors affecting measurement

The reliability of measurement depends upon the stability of four quasi-independent systems: patient, observer, instrument, and environment. Measurements are designed to register changes in the symptom itself provided that a *ceteris paribus* condition (i.e. other things being equal) is met. In real life, cognitive function changes in response to factors as varied as circadian rhythms, medication (Curran *et al.*, 1988) and mood state (Jorm, 1986). The effect of these factors should be determined. Diagnostic thresholds also vary according to decisional rules often difficult to specify. Observer variability is also affected by changes in diagnostic classifications and operational definitions. On the other hand, the instruments themselves may also become dislocated from their original socio-cultural context. For example, the Wechsler instrument may now be overestimating IQ, as it was validated in groups with means lower than those of the current population (Miller, 1980). Finally, changes in the testing environment can make measuring unstable. For example, the assessment of a subject with obsessive–compulsive disorder may yield lower scores in the clinic than at home.

The measurement of symptoms

The clinician may want to measure *symptoms* (e.g. disorientation, memory deficit, choice reaction time, anxiety, guilt, irritability, etc.) or *disorders* (e.g. severity of delirium, dementia or amnesic syndrome) or level of *psychosocial competence* (e.g. can the patient live in the community?). In each case, different instruments need to be used and different assumptions made.

'Cognitive' symptoms relate either to alterations of awareness (or consciousness) or to dysfunctions of more or less specific brain sites. The former include clouding of consciousness, disorientation, confusion, torpor, stupor, etc.; the latter, memory deficits and the various cortical syndromes ('frontal lobe' dysfunction, aphasia, apraxia, and agnosia). Each of these symptoms belongs to a different level of conceptual organization, and has a different historical origin. Therefore it can only be defined in terms of a given psychological model or measuring technique.

The nosological recognition of new 'organic syndromes' by DSM III-R and ICD-10 has created an interesting problem for the numeric psychopathologist in that 'organic' affective (depression, anxiety), volitional (retardation), neurotic (hypochondriacal, obsessive) and psychotic (hallucinations, delusions) symptoms need measuring now, but it is unclear whether the available instruments (calibrated on the analogous functional disorders) are of any use. Are the instruments in use in the area of the functional disorders adequate for the task? A simple answer to this question is not possible. Preliminary questions must be answered first:

(1) Do the hallucinations and delusions associated with delirium, dementia, brain tumours, epilepsy, anticholinergic syndrome, etc. *belong to the same class of phenomena*? (Berrios, 1985a). Are they *analogous* to similarly named phenomena seen in schizophrenia or delusional depression?
(2) Do the so-called 'depressions' associated with Parkinson's disease, multiple sclerosis, hypothyroidism, carcinoma of pancreas, left frontal lobe injury, beta-blocker drugs, etc. *belong to the same class of disorders of affect* (Berrios and Samuel, 1987)? Are they related to major depression?

Clinicians may answer yes and assume that psychiatric symptoms are stereotyped behavioural forms (the same in all cases regardless of aetiology), and accept that the same instruments apply. Alternatively, they may answer no, and assume that there is no such a thing as a hallucination or depression in abstract; that according to aetiology all symptoms are different, even if they might hold a superficial family resemblance. The consequence of the latter would be to reject the universal applicability of instruments. A solution to this dilemma depends on whether it can be demonstrated that detailed phenomenological differentiation increases the diagnostic and prognostic value of symptoms. In practice, this problem is concealed by the fact that symptoms are rarely dealt with in isolation but judged together with information from the past history of the individual, other symptoms, and even 'intuitive' feelings. Although tautological, this strategy is all that is available at the moment.

The measurement of syndromes

Of the eleven 'Organic mental syndromes' included in DSM III-R (and echoed in ICD-10), Delirium, Dementia, Organic Mood Syndrome, and Amnestic Syndrome are the ones which have received more attention from the psychometric viewpoint. The former three, however, are the commonest in clinical practice. Dementia is covered in Chapter 11. Delirium, the organic mood syndrome and the amnestic syndrome will be dealt with in this chapter. There is little in the way of adequate instruments for the measurement of the other 'organic mental syndromes', and they will not be mentioned further. Nor will anything be said on the ongoing work relating to the psychosocial consequences of having an organic syndrome. The analysis of psychosocial competence is based on different conceptual assumptions, and is dealt with in Chapter 6.

DELIRIUM

Clinical aspects

Occasionally fleeting, frequently incomplete, and always fluctuating, delirium is often missed in clinical practice. The complete picture includes impaired awareness, disorientation, illusions and hallucinations (often visual), paranoid delusional elaboration, mood disorder that can range from severe anxiety to dysphoria, irritability, lability, suicidal ideas, and a defence behavioural syndrome which may include withdrawal, escaping, inopportune demanding and even aggression (Lipowski, 1983, 1987; Berrios, 1981).

Delirium may affect patients' compliance to treatment and occasionally threaten life and limb (Thomas *et al.*, 1988). Advanced age, withdrawal from drugs, neurological and endocrinological disease, history of brain damage, and probably personality traits may increase the risk of developing delirium. Aetiology is multiple and includes any disease above or below the neck which may cause mechanical, vascular, toxic or metabolic cerebral insult

(Lipowski, 1987). It has been suggested that there is a common molecular pathophysiology to delirium, consisting in a fall of cerebral oxidative metabolism which leads to a reduction of acetylcholine synthesis (Blass and Plum, 1983).

Measurement

The attention and communication difficulties of delirium make the assessment of individual mental functions, particularly memory, unreliable. The most common differential diagnoses include dementia, in combination with which it is often found, and depressive pseudodementia (Bulbena and Berrios, 1986). The Sodium Amylobarbitone interview can be of help (Ward *et al.*, 1878; Perry and Jacobs, 1982) but should only be undertaken after a determined medical work-up has ruled out any contra-indication.

Incomplete forms of delirium are often met with. Early delirium, often characterized by changes in mood and social orientation and behaviour, is particularly difficult to diagnose. In these cases the individual is not hallucinated or paranoid and shows little in the way of a disorder of time and space disorientation. Instead he or she exhibits reduced attention and cognitive grasp of the environment, repetitious questioning, over-reactivity, hypersensitivity (what Continental psychiatrists call 'hyperaesthesic state') (Bleuler *et al.*, 1966), irritability, unreasonable complaining, over-familiarity, mild disinhibition, and some sleep disorder.

Often little is known about the pre-morbid state and there is a tendency to assign these psychological changes to personality disorder, anxiety, drug side-effects, or 'regression'. The help of relatives can be invaluable in confirming that the patient's behaviour is out of character. Neuropsychological assessment in these cases is particularly *unhelpful*, as none of the instruments available for the quantification of delirium include the items listed above.

The appearance of disorientation makes the diagnosis clearer. Even in these cases, however, much emphasis is often placed on verbal disorientation, that is, the inability of the individual to reply to standard orientation questions regarding time, place or person. It is likely that by itself this test is insensitive (Klein *et al.*, 1985). Ability to answer orientation questions may also be influenced by factors other than delirium. Assessment of behavioural disorientation, i.e. inability by the patient to find his or her room and other facilities in the ward after a reasonable period (2 days), may be more sensitive and specific (Berrios, 1983).

Measurement of delirious behaviour by dedicated scales can be complemented by seriatim EEG and cerebral imaging. Disorganization of the cerebral rhythms and slowing are a common accompaniment of delirium (Pro and Wells, 1977). Other complementary measurements include deficits in concentration, cognitive flexibility, and visual-motor skills, as detected by Trailmaking and tachistoscopic tests (Reitan, 1958; Trzepacz *et al.*, 1988; Anthony *et al.*, 1985).

Diagnosis of delirium by checklist (such as DSM III-R) must be differentiated from evaluation of severity by special instruments, for which diagnostic cut-off points might be available. One such is the Mini-Mental State Examination (MMSE) (Folstein *et al.*, 1975), which is best described as a measure of diffuse cognitive impairment. It cannot differentiate between delirium and dementia (Anthony *et al.*, 1982), and may be oversensitive to level of education (Bird *et al.*, 1987a) and age. The MMSE is an observer-rated instrument the original description of which included questions testing orientation, registration, attention, calculation, recall and language. Its maximum score is 30 and diagnostic cut-off points of 25, 24 and 20 have been suggested. Teng and Chui (1987) have published a modification of the MMSE that includes four new items and a new scoring system which yields a maximum score of 100. No prospective comparative study has yet been reported for this modified form.

While the MMSE does not purport to be an instrument specific for delirium, the recent Delirium Rating Scale (DRS) does (Trzepacz *et al.*, 1988b). It is a 10-item, observer-rated scale (maximum score = 32), based on DSM III-R diagnostic criteria for delirium, and includes questions recording temporal onset of symptoms, perceptual disturbance, hallucinations, delusions, psychomotor behaviour, cognitive status during formal testing, physical disorder, sleep–wake cycle disturbance, lability of mood and variability of symptoms. However, the name of some of the items is misleading. For example, 'Perceptual disturbances' (include depersonalization and derealization); and 'misperceptions' is illustrated by 'may urinate in wastebasket or mistake bedclothes for something else'. The scale has been validated in 20 delirium subjects (DSM III diagnosed) and three control groups. Another useful instrument to test the 'sensorium' is that reported by Withers and Hinton (1971). It includes items testing orientation, attention and concentration, memory, and general information, and has the advantage of being available in three parallel forms.

A recent article (Nelson *et al.*, 1986) compared the performance of five screening instruments for diffuse cognitive impairment: MMSE, Cognitive capacity screening instrument, Mattis dementia rating scale, Kahn's mental status questionnaire, and the Short portable mental status questionnaire. The authors conclude that all these instruments show a correspondence with clinical descriptions of delirium and dementia, and hence are useful for the quantification of these syndromes. However, they stress that there is no evidence that the tests improve the diagnostic accuracy of the clinical descriptions, particularly in relation to borderline clinical states where the clinician is also in doubt as to the presence of the syndrome.

Discussion

The qualitative diagnosis of delirium remains adequate for most clinical purposes. Instruments available to quantify this syndrome tend to confirm clinical diagnosis and provide scores which are believed to give an idea of severity. Quantification seems unhelpful in doubtful or earlier cases. These cannot be dealt with by simply changing the cut-off points since little is known as to what symptoms actually reflect 'severity' of underlying pathophysiology. Intuitively, it could be assumed that symptoms are hierarchically organized with the disturbances of consciousness, awareness and orientation as the primary changes, followed by release mechanisms (illusions, hallucinations), then by elaborative and defence symptoms such as secondary delusions, and then by congruous mood changes (anxiety, dysphoria, anger, irritability, etc.), and behavioural defence (withdrawal, fleeing, aggression).

If this model is correct, the crucial symptoms to measure would be those of disorders of consciousness (or its clinical concomitant, disorientation). The clinical meaning and value of the other symptoms of delirium remain obscure as they may reflect etiology (drug-induced versus toxic delirium), genetics (tendency to developing psychotic symptoms regardless of underlying condition), personality (e.g. paranoid) or environment (e.g. sensory deprivation). A problem with assessing disorientation alone is that deficits may not show sufficient variance, and often a ceiling effect is found. Two solutions have been considered: first, that time, place and person disorientation constitute states of severity (with person disorientation being the worst). Second, the temporal 'distance' from the public reference system, as expressed by the patient, constitutes a measure of severity (e.g. a subject claiming that it is now 1960 is more ill than one stating that it is 1985) (Levin and Benton, 1975). Little empirical evidence is available to support either of these beliefs (Berrios, 1983).

If it is the case that the symptoms of delirium have different clinical meaning, then it is unlikely that scores including unweighted items will adequately indicate severity, particularly, to establish correlations in neurobiological research (Trzepacz *et al.*, 1988b). Research into the measurement of delirium therefore requires that individual items be analysed independently.

ORGANIC MOOD SYNDROME

Anxiety and depression, whether considered as symptoms or syndromes, often accompany delirium and dementia (Lazarus *et al.*, 1987) or indeed may be the only manifestations of an organic mental syndrome (DSM III-R). It is important, therefore, to ask whether they can be satisfactorily measured by instruments developed in non-organic patients (Montgomery, 1988). Symptoms of physical disease, whether or not neurological, often contaminate depression scales and hence lead to inflated scores and overdiagnosis (Kathol and Petty, 1981; Berrios and Samuel, 1987). This effect may be more marked in the elderly (Gottlieb *et al.*, 1988).

Yesavage *et al.* (1983) have described a Geriatric Depression Screening Scale (GDS), a 30-question, yes/no, self-rating instrument, constructed specially for the elderly. Hyer and Blount (1984) found the GDS to discriminate better between a depressed and non-depressed elderly sample than the Beck Scale. Koenig *et al.* (1988) have used the GDS as a screening instrument in a population of elderly subjects hospitalized with medical illness, and found it to have a sensitivity of 92 per cent and a specificity of 89 per cent when a cut-off point of 11 was used. Doubts have been raised with regard to the screening capabilities of the GDS by Bird *et al.* (1987b), who themselves have reported a self-rating depression questionnaire, Selfcare (D), to be used in conjunction with the larger CARE instrument (Gurland and Wilder, 1984). The Selfcare (D) includes 12 items rated in ordinal points varying from 4 to 8, and suggests weights and corrections for score combinations and for 'don't know' answers. More work is required to ascertain the superiority of this scale in relation to the GDS.

More recently, two more scales for the measurement of mood in the elderly have been reported. The Cornell Scale for Depression in Dementia (Alexopoulus *et al.*, 1988) is a 19-item, observer-rated, 3-point scale, with an internal reliability (Alpha) of +0.84. The Dementia Mood Assessment Scale (Sunderland *et al.*, 1988) is a 24-item, observer-rated instrument, intended to measure intensity of depression in subjects with cognitive impairment. Both scales are at an early stage of development and need to be tried in subjects with a wide degree of impairment.

THE AMNESTIC SYNDROME

Clinical aspects

Korsakov's state

Since its first description, the so-called Korsakov's state (Korsakov, 1889) has become the prime example of the 'amnestic syndrome' (Talland, 1965) and its analysis has influenced the development of most experimental models of memory. Consequently, the Korsakovian defect is difficult to describe *independently* from current theories of memory. As defined by DSM III-R (APA,

1987), the amnestic syndrome includes 'demonstrable evidence of impairment of short- and long-term memory, absence of delirium and dementia and of other cognitive deficits, and evidence of organicity. It may be accompanied by lack of insight or concern, confabulation, personality change, apathy, lack of initiative, and emotional blandness'. Alcoholism is considered as its most common cause. It is also believed that it is a late consequence of a petechial disencephalic haemorrhage (Wernicke's syndrome) (Handler and Perkin, 1983; Harper *et al.*, 1986).

The combination of the acute and chronic syndromes is known as the Wernicke–Korsakov state (WKS) (Victor *et al.*, 1971). Its memory defect, however, must be differentiated from that characterizing the so-called presbyophrenic syndrome (Berrios, 1985b, 1986), Alzheimer's disease, and the amnestic syndrome caused by bilateral temporal lobe impairment. From the aetiological viewpoint three issues remain important:

(1) The role of thiamine deficiency, and perhaps of an inborn error of transketolase activity (Handler and Perkin, 1983) in the development of Wernicke-type lesions;
(2) The role of alcohol in the development of the lesions (i.e. the question of alcoholic dementia) (Cutting, 1978; Thomson and Ron, 1982); and
(3) The fact that similar memory defects can be caused by a variety of brain lesions.

Hence the clinical and pathological boundaries of the amnestic syndrome may prove to be less discrete than once thought (Butters, 1985, Jacobson and Lishman, 1987; Christie *et el.*, 1988).

From the time of Ribot, Richet, Paulhan, Marie and others (Berrios, 1990) clinicians have possessed their own terminology to describe memory disorders. This terminology *differed* from that developed by early experimental psychologists of memory such as Ebbinghaus or Jung, who mainly worked with normal subjects (Berrios, 1990). These two terminological traditions have not yet fully merged. Thus it is not uncommon to hear psychiatrists (e.g. DSM III-R) state that WKS is characterized by a 'short-term memory' defect. Strictly speaking (from the experimental viewpoint), this is incorrect, as STM refers to a conceptual compartment of limited capacity where volatile information is kept by continuous rehearsal. Indeed, there is little evidence that STM is disordered in WKS. Korsakov subjects (like normal individuals) are able successfully to rehearse information in STM. What they cannot do is transfer it to LTM when given a distracting task.

Clinical observation also shows that WKS subjects have difficulty in *retrieving* information already established in LTM. This seems to be time-related, i.e. the more recent the date of storage, the more difficult it is to retrieve it. This has long been known as Ribot's law. Furthermore, within a particular epoch not all information is equally affected. Word meanings and motor skills are less impaired than personalized life episodes. There is also some suggestion that WKS subjects show 'normal forgetting', i.e. that they lose information (and there is evidence that they show some residual learning capacity) at rates not different from normal controls. Nonetheless, it is believed that WKS subjects have difficulties in encoding features of the context in which their experiences occur, i.e. there is a malfunction in the protocols that tag for time, occasion, sensory modality, or accompanying mood state. This would explain why episodic memory is more impaired than semantic memory.

WKS patients may also show other clinical features such as confabulation, which refers to the reactive or spontaneous production of false verbal accounts of past happenings (Mercer *et al.*, 1977; Whitlock, 1981). Confabulatory utterances range from wild and fantastic tales (rare) to jumbled and pedestrian histories (common); in the latter case, fragments from real past happenings may be present. It has been suggested that this type of confabulation results from the distorted recollection of context-free and uncued information. WKS also includes symptoms such as apathy, lethargy, lack of concern and occasionally lack of insight. All these symptoms have been considered to reflect frontal lobe involvement. Indeed, some WKS subjects do badly in the Wisconsin Card Sorting Test or the verbal fluency task, conventionally regarded as measures of frontal lobe function.

Bilateral temporal lobe lesions (TLAS) affecting the hippocampus and amygdala (caused by viral encephalitis or surgical excision of the temporal lobes) may also give rise to amnestic syndromes clinically similar to that of WKS. It has been suggested that the TLAS does not exhibit frontal lobe features or confabulatory behaviour and that it shows less residual learning ability than WKS. There is, however, debate as to whether TLAS and WKS are different on only two points on a severity continuum, with the added fact that WKS has an extra involvement of frontal lobes (Parkin, 1984).

ASSESSMENT OF THE AMNESTIC SYNDROME

With regard to the assessment of subjects suffering from putative memory defect, three points must be kept in mind:

(1) It is unlikely that the amnestic syndrome is a unitary clinical state;
(2) There are important differences in terminology, techniques and objectives between clinicians and experimental psychologists; and
(3) Disorders of perception, attention, cognition and mood may accompany complaints of memory dysfunction and affect their evaluation.

Each point will now be discussed in turn.

Heterogeneity of the amnestic syndrome

Occam's razor would advise that differences between WKS and TLAS be reduced to those resulting from severity of lesion and/or involvement of other structures (such as the frontal lobes). This is not generally accepted, however, and many see these conditions as an expression of neurobiological heterogeneity. It has been suggested, for example, that the amnestic syndromes are clinical composites constituted by elementary lesions of memory each with a separate brain representation (Mayes, 1988). The task of the clinician would then be to tease out each case into elementary units of analysis. To do so, the clinician must make use of *ad hoc* memory tasks.

Terminology, objectives and techniques

Terminology

Different terms are used by clinicians and experimentalists to describe memory complaints; sometimes the same words are given a different meaning. Clinicians should be wary of too hastily borrowing terms from the experimental field before these are shown to have direct clinical usefulness. In practical terms, the clinician wants to describe the following phenomena:

(1) Can the subject acquire new information? Has he been able to do so since he contracted the putative disease?
(2) Can the subject recall information acquired a long time ago ('premorbidly' or before the onset of the disease)?
(3) Is there evidence of *organic* disease?
(4) If not, is there another explanation for the apparent memory defect?

The first three questions require a minimum of terminology. Question (1) refers to *anterograde amnesia*; question (2) to *retrograde amnesia*; question (3) asks whether the amnesia is 'organic', 'functional', 'motivated', 'gain-related', etc. (Whitty and Zangwill, 1977).

Objectives and techniques

Different objectives in testing may also cause confusion. The clinician is interested in ascertaining the presence of a 'DSM III-R amnestic syndrome', in evaluating its severity, and in determining the presence of a brain lesion.

The experimental psychologist is interested in testing hypotheses and identifying new types or variations of the disorder. These objectives demand different testing paradigms. The clinician requires standardized tests and normative data taking into account variables potentially related to memory such as age, sex, intellectual level, education, etc. The experimental psychologist prefers to use *ad hoc* tasks, dictated by theory and which are not in need of normative data. Tests thus born may occasionally graduate as clinical tests, but this is not common. Laboratory tests may correlate adequately with everyday memory tasks (Sunderland *et al.*, 1983).

Amnestic syndrome and clinical context

Perceptual defect, attentional problems, cognitive impairment, severe fatigue, and mood disorder may all inhibit memory mechanisms or hinder their expression. Therefore, before the results of memory tests can be accepted, it is of the essence that clinical tests are used to rule out delirium, dementia, depression, depressive pseudo-dementia, etc. It must be remembered that these differential diagnoses are often harder than the textbooks suggest. In addition to clinical examination, special instruments can be used to carry out this task.

ASSESSMENT TECHNIQUES

General issues

What has been said so far outlines a clinical algorithm for assessment. The first stage is to take a full history, interview carers and/or relatives, and carry out a mental state assessment and physical examination. This will help the clinician to rule out aphasia, eyesight difficulties, deafness, delirium, psychoses, depression, dementia, etc. The second stage is to outline the quality of the memory problem. To do so, the clinician may want to ask the subject and relatives questions concerning the features and circumstances of the memory failure. A number of self-rated or observer-rated questionnaires are now available for both patients and for relatives (Herrmann, 1982).

If the questionnaires confirm the view that there may be a problem with memory then the third step is to make use of some memory tests to gain an idea of severity and type of memory defect. Tests which assess anterograde amnesia are based on a simple principle: the subject is given information and then asked to recall it. If the task is accomplished the clinician may conclude that STM is normal. The clinician may then introduce a distracting task, and after a while ask the subject to recall the information. Typically, the distraction may consist of counting backwards, or any other mental activity that impedes rehearsal. If memory mechanisms are normal the subject will be able to reproduce the information (i.e. he or she has been able successfully to transfer it to long-term store). If the information is lost, the clinician may conclude that there are, prima facie, difficulties in retaining new information, a popular hypothesis being that amnestic subjects suffer from a specific encoding deficit (Butters and Cermak, 1980).

Many variations can be used within these testing parameters. For example, the information may be given in visual (reading words or learning shapes) or auditory *form* (having words read or sounds played); or the information may take the form of word lists, pairs of words, nonsense syllables; or the subject may be asked to *recall* (i.e. to repeat what he or she remembers) or to *recognize* (i.e. to identify from a list the original stimuli); or the distraction may be made to consist of more words or in some task alien to word learning; or the subject can be 'primed' to the task, i.e. given some hint of what the task will be without specifying it completely (Shimamura, 1986). Combinations of these variations give rise to a formidable list of tests, each having a different theoretical interpretation. The clinician, however, does not need to worry about this.

The psychometry of retrograde amnesia has proved to be more difficult than that of anterograde amnesia as the clinician has little control of the material to be recollected. Crude testing, consisting of asking subjects to remember episodes from various epochs of their life, may be sufficient for clinical purposes but is not good enough for quantitative assessment. For this, special tests are required that may be used in groups of patients. Researchers have resorted to constructing tests based on public events, faces or situations whose saliency is sufficient to guarantee their equal exposure to subject cohorts sharing the same cultural characteristics.

The choice of appropriate stimuli, however, has proved difficult. This is due to the fact that most of the great historical events (e.g. President Kennedy's death) are 'publicly rehearsed' (Weiskrantz, 1985). That is, their recognition no longer guarantees a real act of recollection on the part of the subject (i.e. of the actual day on which it took place). Another problem is that, by definition, these tests are culturally bound and cannot be easily exported. One such test has been available in the UK since the early 1970s (Sanders and Warrington, 1971) and others more recently in the USA (Albert *et al.*, 1979; Zola-Morgan *et al.*, 1983).

The Wechsler Memory Scale (WMS)

In spite of its shortcomings the WMS is still widely used (Wechsler, 1945). It includes seven procedures. The first two relate to personal and current information and orientation. The third, called 'mental control', consists of counting backwards in ones from 20, reciting the alphabet, and counting forwards in threes. The fourth, or 'logical memory', consists of the subject hearing a story of approximately 60 words which he or she must immediately recount. The fifth is a digit span task; the sixth a visual reproduction task, and the seventh a paired-associate learning task. It is recommended that the visual reproduction and logical memory tasks be repeated following a 30-minute interval. A memory quotient can be then scored which is measured against a scale of 100 (like the Wechsler IQ). Age must be taken into consideration (Hulicka, 1966).

It has been stated with some reason that the scale is biased in favour of verbal tests, and that its good correlation with IQ scores may reflect an unduly high component of general intelligence. However, factor analysis suggests that at least three components may be tapped by the WMS: short-term memory, verbal memory and figural memory (Russell, 1981). A recent study comparing a number of memory tests on various samples of amnestic patients concludes that, although the WMS is affected by cognitive dysfunctions other than amnesia, it is still useful in the assessment of severity (Squire and Shimamura, 1986). These workers also recommend that the WMS should be accompanied by the WAIS, paired-associate learning tasks, delayed score recall, delayed recall of a complex design, the Rey auditory–verbal learning test, and a dementia rating scale. Similarly, Kopelman (1986) found that the Wechsler logical memory sub-test and the Gresham Questionnaire for memory and orientation had adequate discriminatory power between subjects suffering from WKS and from Alzheimer's disease.

The Benton Visual Retention Test (BVRT)

This simple test taps visual memory and has survived the test of time well. The subject has to identify single lines with various orientations and slopes in a multiple-choice card which includes all eleven stimuli. This test, originally designed to identify subjects with hemisphere lesions (Benton *et al.*, 1975), can be used with profit in subjects with amnestic syndrome and other memory disorders (e.g. depressive pseudodementia).

Rivermead Behavioural Memory Test (RBMT)

Criticism that the WMS included tasks remote from real life led to the development of the RBMT (Wilson *et al.*, 1985), which includes tasks taken directly from real-life situations and has proved of great use in clinical practice, particularly when the effect of memory disorder on psychosocial competence must be ascertained. The RBMT includes tasks such as remembering or interpreting a name, where a hidden belonging is, an appointment, a route in the testing room left to the patient in the form of a message, and two other tasks: face recognition and orientation.

The 'face validity' of this test makes it more acceptable to patients. It has only a low correlation with the WAIS. Its main disadvantage is that it is inadequate for the analysis and comparison of groups and for the testing of memory theories.

The Signal Detection Memory Test (SDMT)

This test, based on signal detection theory (Banks, 1970), seeks to determine the biases used by the subject during the act of recollection. Any information committed to memory seems, upon recollection, to fall into either of three categories: that which one clearly remembers (clear signal), that which is totally forgotten (only noise), and that which is vaguely recollected (faint signal against noise). The SDMT is designed to evaluate biases operating on the third category: what determines that the subject declares information contained therein as 'remembered' or as 'non-remembered'? In this regard, there is some evidence that mood states, personality traits, instructions and other factors may bias response in at least two directions: one of risk or of gambling (with an increase in false positives), the other conservative or of prudence (with an increase in false negatives). A formula allows the clinician to obtain two criteria: *d′*, which relates to the 'real' memory impairment, and *b′*, which indicates the bias (Miller and Lewis, 1977).

The simplest form of the test consists of showing the subject 120 words, out of which 40 are repeated. Repeats will appear at different 'lags' (i.e. distance from the original presentation). Words can be presented on cards or by computer. The advantage of the latter form of presentation is that reaction times can also be recorded and used as an extra variable in the analysis.

SUMMARY AND CONCLUSIONS

This chapter has dealt with some of the theoretical and practical issues relating to the measurement of symptoms and syndromes associated with the 'organic mental disorders', and included a discussion of the main instruments used to evaluate them. It has concentrated on delirium, the organic mood syndrome and the amnestic syndrome, as these are the most common in clinical practice. Dementia is extensively covered in Chapter 11.

Since some of the 'organic symptoms' might be directly related to identifiable brain pathology, it can be safely assumed that their 'signal' is strong and their envelope of psychosocial noise weak. It can be further assumed that their measurement will, on occasions, give an adequate idea of the 'severity' of the damage. The organic disorders, however, are a clinical class in evolution whose boundaries are more historical than empirical. Thus it is not possible to develop a measurement theory common to all. 'Organic disorders' can cause cognitive and non-cognitive symptoms, but the former have received more attention than the latter.

Instruments to evaluate organic symptoms and syndromes may target one or more mental functions; may be simple checklists or structured scales with weighted items; may yield scores reflecting severity; or may offer diagnostic cut-off points, and each will raise its own theoretical and practical problems. The evaluation of delirium is hampered by its transient and fluctuating course and by the frequent involvement of communicational functions. Also, lack of knowledge of its pathophysiology has made difficult the identification of symptoms that might reflect syndrome severity.

REFERENCES

Albert, M.S., Butters, N. and Levin, J. (1979) Temporal gradients in the retrograde amnesia of patients with alcoholic Korsakoff's disease. *Archives of Neurology*, **36**, 211–16.

Alexopoulus, G.S., Adams, R.C., Young, R.C. and Shamoian, C.A. (1988) Cornell Scale for depression in dementia. *Biological Psychiatry*, **23**, 271–84.

Anthony, J.C., LeResche, L., Niaz, U. *et al.* (1982) Limits of the mini-mental state as a screening test for dementia and delirium amongst hospital patients. *Psychological Medicine*, **12**, 397–405.

Anthony, J.C., Le Resche, L., Von Korff *et al.* (1985) Screening for delirium on a general medical ward: the tachistoscope and a global accessibility rating. *General Hospital Psychiatry*, **7**, 36–9.

APA (1987) *Diagnostic and Statistical Manual of Mental Disorders*, 3rd edn, revised, American Psychiatric Association, Washington, DC.

Baars, B.J. (1986) *The Cognitive Revolution in Psychology*, Guilford Press, New York.

Banks, W.P. (1970) Signal detection theory and memory. *Psychological Bulletin*, **74**, 81–99.

Barthes, R. (1972) Sémiologie et Médicine. In R. Bastide (ed.), *Les sciences de la folie*, pp. 37–46, Mouton, Paris.

Benton, A. (1986) Reaction time in brain disease: some reflections. *Cortex*, **22**, 129–40.

Benton, A., Hanay, J. and Varney, N.R. (1975) Visual perception of line direction in patients with unilateral brain disease. *Neurology*, **25**, 907–10.

Berrios, G.E. (1981) Delirium and confusion in the 19th century: a conceptual history. *British Journal of Psychiatry*, **139**, 439–49.

Berrios, G.E. (1983) Orientation failures in medicine and psychiatry: a discussion paper. *Journal of the Royal Society of Medicine*, **76**, 379–85.

Berrios, G.E. (1984) Descriptive psychopathology: conceptual and historical aspects. *Psychological Medicine*, **14**, 303–13.

Berrios, G.E. (1985a) Hallucinosis. In J.A.M. Fredericks (ed.), *Handbook of Clinical Neurology*, Vol. 2 (46), *Neurobehavioral Disorders*, pp. 561–72, Elsevier, New York.

Berrios, G.E. (1985b) Presbyophrenia: clinical aspects. *British Journal of Psychiatry*, **147**, 76–9.

Berrios, G.E. (1986) Presbyophrenia: the rise and fall of a concept. *Psychological Medicine*, **16**, 267–75.

Berrios, G.E. (1987) Historical aspects of the psychoses: 19th century issues. *British Medical Bulletin*, **43**, 484–98.

Berrios, G.E. (1989a) Phenomenology, psychopathology and Jaspers. *American Journal of Psychiatry* (in press).

Berrios, G.E. (1989b) Non-cognitive symptoms and the diagnosis of dementia. Historical and clinical aspects. *British Journal of Psychiatry*, **155** (Suppl. 4), 11–16.

Berrios, G.E. (1990) Memory and its disorders: a conceptual history (submitted for publication).

Berrios, G.E. and Samuel, C. (1987) Affective disorder in the neurological patient. *Journal of Nervous and Mental Disease*, **175**, 173–6.

Bird, H.R., Canino, G., Stipec, M.R. and Shrout, P. (1987a) Use of the mini-mental state examination in a probability sample of a Hispanic population. *Journal of Nervous and Mental Disease*, **175**, 731–7.

Bird, A.S., MacDonald, A.J.D., Mann, A.H. and Philpot, M.P. (1987b) Preliminary experience with the self-care (D): a self rating depression questionnaire for use in elderly, non-institutionalized subjects. *International Journal of Geriatric Psychiatry*, **2**, 31–8.

Blass, J.P. and Plum, F. (1983) Metabolic encephalopathies in older adults. In R. Katzman and R.D. Terry (eds), *The Neurology of Ageing*, pp. 189–220, Davis, Philadelphia.

Bleuler, M., Willi, J. and Bühler, H.R. (1966) *Akute psychische Begleiterscheinungen körperlicher Krankheiten*, Thieme, Stuttgart.

Bonhoeffer, K. (1910) *Die Symptomatischen Psychosen*, Deuticke, Leipzig.

Botwinick, J., Storand, M., Berg, L. and Boland, S. (1988) Senile dementia of the Alzheimer type. Subject attrition and testability in research. *Archives of Neurology*, **45**, 493–6.

Bulbena, A. and Berrios, G.E. (1986) Pseudo-dementia: facts and figures. *British Journal of Psychiatry*, **148**, 87–94.

Butters, N. (1985) Alcoholic Korsakoff's syndrome: some unresolved issues concerning aetiology, neuropathology and cognitive deficits. *Journal of Experimental and Clinical Neuropathology*, **7**, 181–210.

Butters, N. and Cermak, L.S. (1980) *Alcoholic Korsakoff's Syndrome. An Information Processing Approach to Amnesia*, Academic Press, New York.

Christie, J.E., Kean, D.M., Douglas, R.H.B. *et al.* (1988) Magnetic resonance imaging in pre-senile dementia of the Alzheimer-type, multi-infarct dementia and Korsakoff's syndrome. *Psychological Medicine*, **18**, 319–29.

Curran, H.V., Sakulsriprong, M. and Lader, M. (1988) Antidepressants and human memory: an investigation of four drugs with different sedative and anticholinergic profiles. *Psychopharmacology*, **95**, 520–27.

Cutting, J. (1978) The relationship between Korsakov's syndrome and 'alcoholic dementia'. *British Journal of Psychiatry*, **132**, 240–51.

Ellis, B. (1968) *Basic Concepts of Measurement*, Cambridge University Press, Cambridge.

Feinstein, A.R. (1987) *Clinimetrics*, Yale University Press, New Haven, Conn.

Folstein, M.F., Folstein, S.E. and McHugh, P.R. (1975) 'Mini-Mental state'. A practical method for grading the cognitive state of patient for the clinician. *Journal of Psychiatric Research*, **12**, 189–98.

Galen, R.S. and Gambino, S.R. (1975) *Beyond Normality: the Predictive Value and Efficiency of Medical Diagnosis*, John Wiley, New York.

Ghiselli, E.E., Campbell, J.P. and Zedeck, S. (1981) *Measurement Theory for the Behavioral Sciences*, W.H. Freeman, San Francisco.

Gottlieb, G.L., Gur, E. and Gur, R.C. (1988) Reliability of psychiatric scales in patients with dementia of the Alzheimer type. *American Journal of Psychiatry*, **145**, 857–60.

Grayson, D.A. (1988) Limitations on the use of scales in psychiatric research. *Australia and New Zealand Journal of Psychiatry*, **22**, 99–108.

Gurland, B.J. and Wilder, D.E. (1984) The CARE interview revisited: development of an efficient systematic clinical assessment. *Journal of Gerontology*, **39**, 129–37.

Hadzi-Pavolic, D. (1986) Some statistics for analysis of change in psychiatric research. *Australia and New Zealand Journal of Psychiatry*, **20**, 438–51.

Handler, C.E. and Perkin, G.D. (1983) Wernicke's encephalopathy. *Journal of the Royal Society of Medicine*, **76**, 339–42.

Harper, C.G., Giles, M. and Finlay-Jones, R. (1986) Clinical signs in the Wernicke–Korsakoff complex: a retrospective analysis of 131 cases diagnosed at necropsy. *Journal of Neurology, Neurosurgery and Psychiatry*, **49**, 341–5.

Hacaen, H. and Lanteri-Laura, G. (1977) *Evolution des connaisances et des doctrines sur les localisations cérébrales*, Desclée de Brouwer, Paris.

Herrmann, D.J. (1982) Know thy memory: the use of questionnaires to assess and study memory. *Psychological Bulletin*, **82**, 434–52.

Hulika, I.M. (1966) Age differences in Wechsler Memory Scale scores. *Journal of Genetic Psychology*, **109**, 135–45.

Hyer, L. and Blount, J. (1984) Concurrent and discriminant validities of the geriatric depression scale with older psychiatric patients. *Psychological Reports*, **54**, 611–16.

Ineichen, B. (1987) Measuring the rising tide. How many dementia cases will there be by 2002? *British Journal of Psychiatry*, **150**, 193–200.

Israël, L., Kozarević, D. and Sartorius, N. (1984) *Source Book of Geriatric Assessment*, 2 vols, World Health Organization, Geneva.

Jacobson, R.R. and Lishman, W.A. (1987) Selective memory loss and global intellectual deficits in alcoholic Korsakoff's syndrome. *Psychological Medicine*, **17**, 649–55.

Jorm, A.F. (1986) Cognitive deficit in the depressed elderly. A review of some basic unresolved issues. *Australia and New Zealand Journal of Psychiatry*, **20**, 11–22.

Jorm, A.F. and Korten, A.E. (1988) Assessment of cognitive decline in the elderly by informal interview. *British Journal of Psychiatry*, **152**, 209–13.

Kathol, R.G. and Petty, F. (1981) Relationship of depression to medical illness. *Journal of Affective Disorders*, **3**, 111–21.

Klein, L.E., Roca, R.P., McArthur, J. *et al.* (1985) Diagnosing dementia. Univariate and multivariate analysis of the mental status examination. *Journal of the American Geriatric Society*, **33**, 483–8.

Koenig, H.G., Meador, K.G., Cohen, H.J. and Blazer, D.G. (1988) Self-rated depression scales and screening for major depression in the older hospitalized patient with medical illness. *Journal of the American Geriatric Society*, **36**, 699–706.

Kopelman, M.D. (1986) Clinical tests of memory. *British Journal of Psychiatry*, **148**, 517–25.

Korsakov, S.S. (1889) Psychic disorder in conjunction with multiple neuritis (translation by M. Victor and P.I. Yakovlov in *Neurology*, **5**, 394–406, 1955).

Lazarus, L.W., Newton, N., Cohler, B. *et al.* (1987) Frequency and presentation of depressive symptoms in patients with primary degenerative dementia. *American Journal of Psychiatry*, **144**, 41–5.

Levin, H.S. and Benton, A.L. (1975) Temporal orientation in patients with brain disease. *Applied Neuropsychology*, **38**, 56–60.

Lipowski, Z.J. (1983) Transient cognitive disorders (delirium, acute confusional states) in the elderly. *American Journal of Psychiatry*, **140**, 1426–36.

Lipowski, Z.J. (1987) Delirium (acute confusional state). *Journal of the American Medical Association*, **258**, 1789–92.

Mayes, A.R. (1988) *Human Organic Memory Disorders*, Cambridge University Press, Cambridge.

Mercer, B., Wapner, W., Gardner, H. and Benson, F. (1977) A study of confabulation. *Archives of Neurology*, **34**, 429–33.

Miller, E. (1977) *Abnormal Ageing. The Psychology of Senile and Presenile Dementia*, John Wiley, New York.

Miller, E. (1980) Cognitive assessment of the older adult. In J.E. Birren and R.B. Sloane (eds), *Handbook of Mental Health and Ageing*, pp. 520–36, Prentice-Hall, Englewood Cliffs.

Miller, E. (1984) *Recovery and Management of Neuropsychological Impairment*, John Wiley, New York.

Miller, E. and Lewis, P. (1977) Recognition memory in elderly patients with depression and dementia: a signal detection study. *Journal of Abnormal Psychology*, **86**, 84–6.

Montgomery, S. (1988) Measuring mood. In J.P. Wattis and I. Hindmarch (eds), *Psychological Assessment of the Elderly*, pp. 138–50, Churchill Livingstone, Edinburgh.

Nelson, A., Fogel, B.S. and Faust, D. (1986) Bedside cognitive screening instruments. A critical assessment. *Journal of Nervous and Mental Disease*, **174**, 73–83.

Namboodiri, K. (1984) *Matrix Algebra*, Sage Publications, Beverly Hills.

Parkin, A.J. (1984) Amnestic syndrome: a lesion-specific disorder? *Cortex*, **20**, 479–508.

Perry, J.C. and Jacobs, D. (1982) Overview: clinical applications of the Amytal interview in psychiatric emergency settings. *American Journal of Psychiatry*, **139**, 552–9.

Powell, G.E. (1981) *Brain Function Therapy*, Gower, Aldershot.

Pro, J.D. and Wells, C.E. (1977) The use of the electroencephalogram in the diagnosis of delirium. *Diseases of the Nervous System*, **38**, 804–8.

Rattan, G. and Strom, D.A. (1987) The efficacy of a neuropsychological symptom inventory in the differential diagnosis of neurological, depressed and normal patients. *Archives of Clinical Neuropsychology*, **2**, 257–64.

Reitan, R.M. (1958) Trailmaking test as an indicator of organic brain damage. *Perceptual Motor Skills*, **8**, 271–84.

Russell, E.W. (1981) The pathology and clinical examination of memory. In S.B. Filskov and T.J. Boll (eds), *Handbook of Clinical Neuropsychology*, John Wiley, New York.

Sanders, H.I. and Warrington, E.K. (1971) Memory for remote events in amnesia patients. *Brain*, **94**, 661–8.

Sartorius, N., Jablensky, A., Cooper, J.E. and Burke, J.D. (1988) Psychiatric classification in an international perspective. *Appendix 1, British Journal of Psychiatry*, **152** (Suppl.), 44–50.

Sanson-Fisher, R.W. and Martin, C.J. (1981) Standard interviews in psychiatry: issues of reliability. *British Journal of Psychiatry*, **139**, 138–43.

Shimamura, A.P. (1986) Priming effects in amnesia: evidence for a dissociable memory function. *Quarterly Journal of Experimental Psychology*, **38**, 619–44.

Squire, L.R. and Shimamura, A.P. (1986) Characterizing amnesic patients for neurobehavioral study. *Behavioral Neuroscience*, **100**, 866–77.

Sunderland, A., Harris, J.E. and Baddeley, A.D. (1983) Do laboratory tests predict everyday memory? A neuropsychological study. *Journal of Verbal Learning and Verbal Behavior*, **22**, 341–57.

Sunderland, T., Alterman, I.S., Yount, D. *et al.* (1988) A new scale for the assessment of depressed mood in demented patients. *American Journal of Psychiatry*, **145**, 955–9.

Sykes, M.K., Vickers, M.D. and Hull, C.J. (1981) *Principles of Clinical Measurement*, Blackwell, Oxford.

Talland, G.A. (1965) *Deranged Memory. A Psychonomic Study of the Amnesic Syndrome*, Academic Press, New York.

Teng, E.L. and Chui, H.C. (1987) The Modified Mini-Mental State (3MS) Examination. *Journal of Clinical Psychiatry*, **48**, 314–18.

Thomas, R.I., Cameron, D.J. and Fahs, M.C. (1988) A prospective study of delirium and prolonged hospital stay. *Archives of General Psychiatry*, **45**, 937–40.

Thomson, A.D. and Ron, M.A. (1982) Alcohol-related structural brain changes. *British Medical Bulletin*, **38**, 87–94.

Trzepacz, P.T., Brenner, R.P., Coffman, G. and van Thiel, D.H. (1988a) Delirium in liver transplantation candidates: discriminant analysis of multiple tests variables. *Biological Psychiatry*, **24**, 3–14.

Trzepacz, P.T., Baker, R.W. and Greenhouse, J. (1988b) A symptom rating scale for delirium. *Psychiatry Research*, **23**, 89–97.

Veiel. H.O.F. (1988) Base-rates, cut-points and interaction effects; the problem with dichotomized continuous variables. *Psychological Medicine*, **18**, 703–10.

Victor, M., Adams, R.D. and Collins, G.H. (1971) *The Wernicke–Korsakoff Syndrome*, Davis, Philadelphia.

Ward, N.G., Rowlett, D.B. and Burke, P. (1978) Sodium amylobarbitone in the differential diagnosis of confusion. *American Journal of Psychiatry*, **135**, 75–8.

Wasson, J.H., Cox, H.C., Neff, R.K. *et al.* (1985) Clinical prediction rules. *New England Journal of Medicine*, **313**, 793–8.

Wechsler, D. (1945) A standardized memory scale for clinical use. *Journal of Psychology*, **19**, 87–95.

Weiskrantz, L. (1985) Issues and theories in the study of the amnestic syndrome. In N.M. Weinberger, J.L. McGaugh and G. Lynch (eds), *Memory Systems and the Brain*, Guilford Press, New York.

Whitlock, F.A. (1981) Some observations on the meaning of confabulation. *British Journal of Medical Psychology*, **54**, 213–18.

Whitty, C.W.M. and Zangwill, O.L. (eds) (1977) *Amnesia*, Butterworths, London.

Williams, P., Hand, D. and Tarnopolsky, A. (1982) The problem of screening for uncommon disorders. *Psychological Medicine*, **12**, 431–4.

Wilson, B., Cockburn, J. and Baddeley, A. (1985) *The Rivermead Behavioural Memory Test*,Thames Valley Test Company.

Withers, E. and Hinton, J. (1971) Three forms of the clinical tests of the sensorium and their reliability. *British Journal of Psychiatry*, **119**, 1–8.

Yesavage, J.A., Brink, T.L., Rose, T.L. *et al.*, (1983) Development and validation of a geriatric depression screening scale: a preliminary report. *Journal of Psychiatric Research*, **17**, 37–49.

Zola-Morgan, S., Cohen, N.J. and Squire, L.R. (1983) Recall of remote episodic memory in amnesia. *Neuropsychologia*, **21**, 487–500.

Chapter 10

Psychotic Disorders

Erik L. H. M. van de Loo and Elisabeth H. M. Eurelings-Bontekoe

The field of psychosis is wide, complicated and evolving. Although many questions concerning aetiology, diagnosis, classification and treatment are still unanswered, important progress has been made during the last decades. Examples are the growing concensus regarding terminology and classification (see DSM-III-R and ICD-10), the pharmacological treatment of the so-called active psychotic symptoms and the introduction of psychoeducational training for relapse prevention. Because of this complexity and the unanswered questions, there will be a greater emphasis on diagnosis in this chapter.

This chapter presents an overview of factors relevant for the assessment of patients with psychotic symptoms, encompassing assessment of core psychotic symptoms as well as a discussion of those factors that are significant for treatment and rehabilitation. Our approach is integrative; that is, combining the different psychological, biological and social perspectives. This is compatible with the vulnerability–stress model (Zubin *et al.*, 1983). The first part of this chapter deals with psychological assessment and the second with biological and neuropsychological measurement.

PSYCHOTIC SYMPTOMS AND DISORDERS

Psychosis refers to a gross impairment in reality testing and the creation of a new reality. It involves an incorrect evaluation of the accuracy of one's perceptions and thoughts and the making of incorrect inferences about reality (APA, DSM-III-R, p. 404). Psychotic symptoms include delusions, hallucinations, incoherence or marked loosening of associations, catatonic stupor or excitement and grossly disorganized behaviour.

For a description and understanding of psychotic symptomatology it is helpful to distinguish between form and content. The *form* of the psychotic symptomatology refers to type and nature of the observed symptoms (e.g.

Measuring Human Problems. Edited by D.F. Peck and C.M. Shapiro

auditory hallucinations, persecutory delusions). The *content* of the psychotic symptomatology reflects what is actually heard or believed. The form is relevant to biologic, diagnostic and aetiological issues, the content offers a key to the individual's psychological conflicts and may be seen as influenced by personality, individual learning experiences and life history (Arieti, 1974; Maltbie, 1983).

Psychotic symptoms occur in the context of a wide range of mental disorders (see Table 10.1). The differential diagnosis evaluates the possible role of organic factors (organic mental syndrome or disorder), the possible association with mood disorder (mood disorder with psychotic features, schizoaffective disorder), the duration of the psychotic symptoms (schizophrenia, schizophreniform disorder, brief reactive psychosis) and the presence of persistent non-bizarre delusions (delusional or paranoid disorder).

Considering the various possibilities of co-morbidity, Table 10.1 is not complete. For instance, psychotic features can be concomitant with obsessive–compulsive disorder (Insel and Akisal, 1986). In addition, the prognosis of schizophrenia may be codetermined by the presence of obsessive–compulsive symptoms (Fenton and McGlashan, 1986).

Table 10.1 DSM-III-R Axis-1 mental disorders with psychotic symptoms.

I	*Schizophrenia* (types: catatonic, disorganized, paranoid, undifferentiated, residual)
II	*Delusional (paranoid) disorder* (types: erotomanic, grandiose, jealous, persecutory, somatic, unspecified)
III	*Psychotic disorders not elsewhere classified* Brief reactive psychosis Schizophreniform disorder Schizoaffective disorder Induced psychotic disorder Psychotic disorder not otherwise specified (atypical psychosis)
IV	*Mood disorder with mood (in)congruent psychotic features* Manic episode Major depressive episode Bipolar disorder Major depression
V	*Organic mental syndromes and disorders* Delirium Organic delusional syndrome Organic hallucinosis Organic mood syndrome (manic, depressed or mixed) Dementias arising in the senium and presenium Psychoactive substance-induced organic mental disorders Organic mental disorders associated with Axis-III physical disorders or conditions, or whose etiology is unknown

PSYCHOTIC SYMPTOMS AND PERSONALITY DISORDER

According to the descriptive approach of the DSM-III-R, psychotic symptoms are not part of the diagnostic criteria of personality disorders. However, DSM-III-R acknowledges that it is not uncommon to see psychosis as an associated feature or complication of personality disorder. During periods of extreme stress a brief reactive psychosis or transient psychotic symptoms may occur in schizotypal, borderline, histrionic and narcissistic personality disorder (Chopra and Beatson, 1986; APA, 1987). The nature of this association is a matter of discussion. For instance, what is the connection between schizotypal personality disorder and schizophrenic disorders? (Gunderson and Siever, 1985; Frances, 1985). The clinician has a difficult task as the categories of personality disorders themselves still have to be validated and the development of reliable assessment techniques is not as complete as for Axis-I disorders. Nevertheless some instruments are available, such as the Structured Interview for the DSM-III Personality Disorders (SIDP, Stangl *et al.*, 1985) and the Personality Disorder Examination (PDE, Loranger, *et al.*, 1987). A pilot international version of the PDE, the IPDE, is now for use in the WHO/ADAMHA International Study of Personality Disorders. Moreover, many patients show evidence of features of two or more personality disorders (e.g. borderline and histrionic, borderline and schizotypal, or schizotypal and schizoid personality disorder (George and Soloff, 1986).

The paranoid personality disorder should be differentiated from delusional (paranoid) disorder and paranoid schizophrenia, on the basis of criteria shown in Table 10.2. If a patient with paranoid personality disorder suffers from delusions, then it is expected that delusional disorder or paranoid schizophrenic disorder are superimposed upon personality disorder. Hence, presence or absence of delusions is crucial for differentiating between Axis I and Axis II disorders.

In addition to the descriptive diagnostic method there is the structural psychoanalytic approach of Kernberg (1975, 1977). In contrast to the priority that is given to manifest symptoms in the classification according to DSM-III-R, the structural approach intends to assess underlying structural characteristics of personality organization. At its core is the assumption that underlying structural disturbances may or, equally, *may not* lead to manifest symptoms. According to this approach, personality structure is assessed along the following lines: (1) identity integration versus identity diffusion (and the related overall quality of object relations); (2) a constellation of advanced or primitive defence mechanisms, and (3) the quality of reality testing. The structural psychoanalytic approach of Kernberg distinguishes three broad structural organizations of personality: the neurotic, the borderline and the psychotic personality organization. The psychotic person

Table 10.2 Differential criteria on the paranoid spectrum.

	Paranoid personality	Delusional disorder	Paranoid schizophrenia
Delusion system	No delusions	Well systemized	Poorly systemized
Reality testing	Intact	Good except in delusional area	Markedly distorted
Behaviour pattern	Restrained	Rigid	Bizarre
Personality deterioration	None	Mild, if any	Progressive downhill course
Adjustment to society	Reasonable work performance but interpersonal/ marital conflicts common	Struggle to achieve success thwarted by delusional system	Autistic retreat

From Walker and Cavenar (1983b), reproduced by permission of J.B. Lippincott Company, Philadelphia, PA

ality organization, which is important within the scope of this chapter, is characterized by identity diffusion, primitive defences and impaired reality testing. The assessment is made by a so-called *structural interview* (Kernberg, 1977). One of its advantages is that it offers information about structural, hidden aspects of personality that may help to explain the risk of occurrence of psychotic symptomatology.

IDENTIFICATION AND CLASSIFICATION OF PSYCHOTIC SYMPTOMS

The first step in the measurement process is identification and classification of possible psychotic symptoms. The clinician may use the clinical interview as a primary source of information, relying on the clinician's observational skills and the self-report of the patient. Additional sources of information are structured interviews of patients and key relatives, the use of rating scales and psychological tests.

Psychiatric interviews

Frequently used standardized psychiatric interviews are the Present State Examination (PSE, Wing *et al.*, 1974) and the Diagnostic Interview Schedule (DIS, Robins *et al.*, 1981). The PSE interview scores 140 variables, taking 60–90 minutes, and is now available in the 10th version. It is suggested (Slooff *et al.*, 1983) that the PSE is of limited value in the evaluation of patients with a non-affective functional psychosis. The DIS is a highly structured interview that can be administered by lay interviewers. The standard version consists of 264 questions (365 for the complete version). It results in a DSM-III-R diagnosis. Administration time is about 45–75 minutes. Escobar *et al.* (1986) report on a sample of clinically diagnosed DSM-III schizophrenic patients who did not meet DSM-III schizophrenia criteria in the DIS interview. It appeared that some schizophrenic subjects did not report reliable information on the actual or past presence of psychotic symptoms (hallucinations, delusions, thought disorder). This is not automatically a shortcoming of the DIS, as it may be said that psychotic experiences are among the most difficult to assess. Moreover, this may 'have to do with the possible effects of lack of rapport and the difficulties that persons may have in relating psychotic experiences to an interviewer who is a stranger' (Helzer and Robins, 1984).

Other structured interviews are: the Schedule for Affective Disorders and Schizophrenia (SADS) developed by Endicott and Spitzer (1978) (the SADS is also available in a lifetime version (SADS-L) and a version for measuring change (SADS-C)); the Structured Clinical Interview for DSM-III-R (SCID), developed by Spitzer *et al.* (1986); patient and non-patient versions are available, as well as the SCID-II for measuring DSM-III-R personality disorders. For more information see MacKinnon and Yudofsky (1986).

The characteristics shown in Table 10.3, differentiating between several acute psychotic disorders, might be helpful to the clinician for non-standardized interviews.

Psychiatric rating scales

It is suggested that schizophrenia encompasses different subtypes, according to a different symptom distribution. Type I schizophrenia is characterized by positive florid symptoms such as hallucinations, delusions, thought disorder and agitated disorganized behaviour. In Type II schizophrenia negative or defect symptoms are prominent: affective blunting, alogia (poverty of speech, poverty of content of speech), avolition and apathy, anhedonia and asociality and attentional impairment. The Type I and Type II distinction warrants further study and elucidation (Andreasen, 1985). The poor responsivity to psychoactive drugs in the Type II form is discussed below.

For purposes of assessment the following instruments can be used: the Scale for the Assessment of Negative Symptoms (SANS) and the Scale for the Assessment of Positive Symptoms (SAPS) developed by Andreasen (Walker *et al.*, 1988) and the Positive and Negative Syndrome Scale for Schizophrenia (PANSS, Kay *et al.*, 1987).

Table 10.3 Differences among the acute psychoses.

Syndrome	Characteristics
Schizophrenia	Loose associations Flat affect Bizarre delusions Clear sensorium Orientation intact
Mania	Hyperactivity Pressured speech Elevated or irritable mood Orientation usually intact
Organic brain syndrome	Loss of intellectual abilities Poor memory Impaired orientation Possible hallucinations or delusions
Brief reactive psychosis	Sudden onset Dramatic array of hallucinations, derealizations and delusions Visual hallucinations more common than auditory hallucinations Affect tends to be expansive and effervescent Symptoms clear in a day or two
Psychotic depression	Somatic delusions (e.g. spine being eaten by worms) Critical hallucinations Delusions of guilt and self-reproach Paranoid ideation Biological signs—sleep disturbance, change in appetite, altered sex drive

From Walker and Cavenar (1983a), reproduced by permission of J.P. Lippincott Company, Philadelphia, PA

Examples of other relevant psychiatric rating scales are: the Brief Psychiatric Rating Scale (BPRS), the Nurses' Observation Scale For Inpatient Evaluation (NOSIE), the Schizophrenic Subscale of the Comprehensive Psychopathological Rating Scale (CPRS-SS), and the Scales for Rating Psychotic and Psychotic Like Experiences as Continua (SRPPEC). For references see MacKinnon and Yudofsky (1986) and Dingemans (1988).

Psychological tests

If an individual is willing and capable of completing a self-report questionnaire, tests like the MMPI and SCL-90-R may help to identify psychotic symptoms (e.g. hallucinations, delusions, paranoid ideation). We believe that unobtrusive measurement of psychotic symptomatology is possible with the WAIS and projective techniques such as Rorschach, the Thematic Apperception Test (TAT) and projective drawings.

Two basic features of psychosis are inaccurate perception and disordered thinking. The Rorschach, which essentially is not a test of projection but of perception, is capable of identifying these features. The Schizophrenia Index (SCZI) of the Comprehensive System (Exner, 1986) combines both aspects. It consists of five scales rating manifestations of perceptual distortion and thought disorder. Scoring all five scales positively offers a high diagnostic probability of schizophrenia, but it does not exclude false positives. It is an indication of the presence of perceptual distortions and thought disorder. These may also be observed in disorders such as brief reactive psychosis, schizotypal personality disorder, and drug-related or schizoaffective disorders.

In the TAT one is asked to tell a story about a series of pictures. This requires the patient to think, to verbalize and to communicate his thoughts. He is asked to organize or structure his triggered perceptions, fantasies, thoughts, affects and impulses into the plot of a story. Psychotic symptomatology may colour the stories and the storytelling (Rapaport *et al.*, 1968).

Projective drawings may offer an impressive and realistic reflection of the bizarre, disorganized, fragmented or threatened inner world of psychotic individuals. As such, they are often an additional or early source of information about the form and content of psychotic symptomatology. It may be helpful for differentiating between borderline, schizoid and schizophrenic conditions (Hammer, 1978).

Projective responses may reflect higher-order information processing such as cognitive, ideational and affective processes and organizational and structuring activities. For neuropsychological and intelligence tests (e.g. the WAIS) see the last part of this chapter.

ASSESSING THE FEATURES OF PSYCHOSIS

Hallucinations

A hallucination is a sensory perception without external stimulation of the relevant sensory system. Hallucinations may be auditory, visual, gustatory, olfactory, tactile or somatic. Not every hallucination is a sign of psychosis. Crucial is whether the hallucination is associated with a gross impairment of reality testing. Non-psychotic hallucinations may occur as a result of sleep or sensory deprivation. Another example is the hallucinations of widowhood. Olson *et al.* (1985) found that 61 per cent of a group of widows reported hallucinations of the presence of their deceased spouse. In most cases it was a visual experience. As long as they preserve the reality of the death of their spouse, these hallucinations of widowhood are non-psychotic. Hallucinations must be differentiated from *illusions*: the misperceptions or misinterpretations of real external stimuli (e.g. misperceiving a shadow as a man).

The mode of hallucination is not diagnostically specific, but it may be a clinically useful sign (Maltbie, 1983). Auditory hallucinations occur most frequently and are very common in schizophrenia; they may also be found in many other psychiatric conditions. Tactile hallucinations are frequently found in schizophrenia and in delusions of parasitosis (Musaph, 1977), usually accompanied by a delusional explanation. Visual hallucinations without other sensory mode disturbances may be indicative of organic processes. 'Any of the functional or organic psychoses may include simple or complex hallucinations which are identical in form and content and are diagnostically indistinguishable' (Maltbie, 1983).

The clinical assessment should encompass the following aspects of hallucinations (Asaad and Shapiro, 1986): 'Is the patient pretending to hallucinate? What sensory modalities are involved? What is the content of the hallucinatory experience? How real and vivid does it seem? What are the associated thoughts or feelings? When do the experiences occur? Is the experience constant or intermittent? How much is the patient aware of the unreality of the hallucinations? How much do they affect the patient's judgment? Finally, to what extent is the patient likely to act out on the content and in what way?'

Delusions

A delusion is a false personal belief based on incorrect inference about external reality that is not shared by others of the same environment or culture and that is maintained despite clear proof or evidence to the contrary. As a delusion implies impairment in reality testing, it is a psychotic symptom. The most common delusional contents or themes are delusions of being controlled, grandiosity (exaggerated sense of one's importance, power, knowledge, or identity), nihilism (non-existence of the self, part of the self, others, the world), persecution, poverty, reference (events, objects or other people have a particular and unusual significance, usually negative or pejorative), somatic functioning and jealousy (unfaithful sexual partner). For an extended glossary of different delusions see Nash (1983).

The different delusional themes have no diagnostic specificity. Nevertheless, several of them tend to be associated with some of the psychotic disorders (see Table 10.4).

Table 10.4 Characteristics of delusions typical for different psychotic disorders

Disorder	Characteristics
Paranoid disorder	Well-encapsulated persecutory delusions or delusions of jealousy
Schizophrenia	Bizarre, disorganized delusions
Mania	Delusions of grandiloquence
Depression	Somatic delusions or delusions of guilt
Organic mental disorder	Delusions secondary to physical illness

From Walker and Cavenar (1983b), reproduced by permission of J.P. Lippincott Company, Philadelphia, PA

Thought, language and communication

An important manifestation of psychosis may be a severe disturbance of thought process and language production. One may observe incoherence and loosening of associations, flight of ideas, poverty of content of speech, clanging (speech in which sounds, rather than meaningful conceptual relationships, govern word choice), blocking (interruption of speech before a thought or idea has been completed), neologisms, perseveration, pressure of speech and echolalia. When a person, because of a marked disturbance of reality testing, is unaware of these pathological processes, communication can almost become impossible.

Cutting and Murphy (1988) propose four independent components of thought disorder in schizophrenia: (1) disorder of content (delusion, overvalued ideas); (2) disorder of the mechanism of thinking (intrinsic thinking disturbance or dyslogia); (3) formal thought disorder (ability to express and understand conversation); (4) disorder of the way of thinking about events in the real world (deficient real-world knowledge or lack of common sense). Although the last component is considered speculative, the authors report that 75 per cent of the schizophrenic patients displayed markedly higher levels compared to neurotic patients.

DSM-III-R has dropped the term 'formal thought disorder', as distinguished from the content of thought, as the boundaries between the two aspects are not clear. It is far better to speak of disorders of Thought, Language and Communication (TLC).

Andreasen (1986) developed a Scale for the Assessment of TLC. She presents definitions and scoring criteria of 20 TLC disorders:

(1) Poverty of speech;
(2) Poverty of content;
(3) Pressure of speech;
(4) Distractable speech;

(5) Tangentiality;
(6) Derailment;
(7) Incoherence;
(8) Illogicality;
(9) Clanging;
(10) Neologisms;
(11) Word approximations;
(12) Circumstantiality;
(13) Loss of goal;
(14) Perseveration;
(15) Echolalia;
(16) Blocking;
(17) Stilted speech;
(18) Self-reference;
(19) Phonemic paraphasia;
(20) Semantic paraphasia.

According to Andreasen, the first 11 items suggest severe psychopathology.

The Rust Inventory of Schizotypal Cognitions (RISC, Rust, 1988) is a short questionnaire for the assessment of schizotypal cognitions associated with the positive symptoms of acute schizophrenia. The RISC consists of 26 questions, covering the DSM-III-R category A of schizophrenia and several criteria of schizotypal disorder. Reliability and validity are reported as good. The RISC clearly discriminates acute schizophrenics from normal subjects.

The Thought Disorder Index (TDI, Solovay *et al.*, 1986) detects, classifies and measures instances of disordered thinking. The TDI scoring manual contains definitions of 20 TDI categories that are scored at four levels of severity. The material to be investigated may be every transcribed verbatim sample from the subject. Information on reliability and validity is not presented.

Catatonic behaviour

This refers to marked motor anomalies that can be found in the context of a psychotic disorder, that is, not an organic mental syndrome or disorder. This does not exclude the possibility of functional metabolic disturbances in the brain. The DSM-III-R (APA, 1987) specifies several types of catatonic behaviour: catatonic excitement, negativism, posturing, rigidity, stupor and waxy flexibility.

Grossly disorganized behaviour

When the capacity of reality testing is lost, fantasy and external reality become confused and primary process prevails over secondary process thinking; the person may demonstrate bizarre and disorganized behaviour. During acute psychotic episodes some patients act according to their inner felt reality or obey imperative hallucinations. Suicide and homicide may be the most serious consequences. It is often thought that suicidal and homicidal imperative hallucinations should be an indication for emergency hospitalization. It is important to note that violent imperative hallucinations may not be a great risk factor for committing violent acts (Hellerstein, *et al.*, 1987).

Psychosis has been interpreted as a regressive process, a rather primitive defensive strategy that acts to protect the individual against otherwise insuperable problems, conflicts and affects. The depth of the regression correlates with type and stage of the psychotic disorder. The deeper the regression, the more serious the level of behavioural disorganization may be. Arieti (1974), in his longitudinal view of schizophrenia, describes, for example, the 'hoarding habit' that may become manifest in the preterminal stage of schizophrenia. This refers to collecting a large number of objects (e.g. stones, leaves, spoons, faeces, hairs) in pockets, bags or boxes. In an even more regressed stage the patient may deposit the objects in the cavities of his or her own body (nose, ears, mouth, anus, vagina). Although bizarre, it is not without psychological significance. Arieti points out that the hoarding habit may be seen as an attempt to counterbalance the instability of inner reality by trying to get a grip on the outer world by collecting and possessing objects.

RELATED ISSUES ON PSYCHOSIS

Falling into the world of psychosis

Arieti (1974, 1983) describes psychotic symptom formation as a process of falling out of the world of reality into the world of psychosis. Schizophrenic patients may learn to distinguish two stages: the expectation of hearing voices and the actual hallucinated hearing. Arieti mentions the example of a man who comes home after work and expects his neighbours to talk about him. He is in *the listening attitude*: as soon as he expects to hear them, he hears them. Likewise, Arieti describes *the referential attitude* in the emergence of delusions. A man takes a stroll in a park. He believes that the people in the park think that he is a horrible man, a pervert attacking others. In his referential attitude he was searching for references that would corroborate his pre-existing mood. He was almost hoping to find evidence of people thinking badly of him. The delusion can be seen as an attempt to transform a large and vague menace into a concrete threat.

These are examples of how an individual organizes his or her subjective world on the basis of learned information-processing strategies. Only the information is processed for which strategies or cognitive schemata are available. Information that is uncommon for a particular individual tends not to be processed or is distorted (Wexler, 1974).

The detection of a pre-existing mood and acquired attitudes may be a valuable therapeutic tool in the context of teaching patients how to protect themselves against the breakthrough of psychosis (Breier and Strauss, 1983).

Self-protection and coping strategies

In the literature on psychosis emphasis is placed upon pathological aspects. Recently, attention has been given to spontaneous adaptive, self-protective strategies of psychotic patients. The majority of interviewed schizophrenic patients report self-control strategies to counter psychotic experiences. Different coping strategies can be found (Falloon and Talbot, 1981; Van den Bosch, 1988):

(1) Cognitive strategies: for example, self-instruction, positive reinterpretation, attention shifting, thought stopping, learning to differentiate and integrate experiences.
(2) Behavioural strategies: for example, postural change, going out for a walk, seeking social contact, withdrawal from social interaction.
(3) Sensory strategies: seeking of sensory stimulation, most frequently auditory stimulation (loud music), or limiting sensory input (block ears, close eyes).
(4) Physiological strategies: arousal reduction by relaxation, sleep or alcohol consumption; increase of arousal by physical exercise.

Expectations of the effects of these strategies should not be too high. Application is not always possible and not always effective. From a psychodynamic point of view, the usage of these techniques is dependent upon quality and maturity of ego functions (Joos *et al.*, 1986). From a cognitive psychological perspective one may approach these phenomena as aspects of information processing. Within this realm, assessing the degree of healthy ego functioning or information-processing capacity is of crucial importance. That is, to what extent are core psychological (ego) functions like attention, concentration, thinking, memory, perception, language and emotion disturbed by psychosis? The degree of invalidation caused by psychosis is partly determined by the degree of encapsulation of the symptoms. Psychodiagnostic assessment may help to answer this question. For example, is an individual who suffers from a psychotic symptom capable of obtaining adequate results on an intelligence test like the WAIS? If he is, he is able to prevent interference of psychotic symptoms in psychological functions that are decisive for one's level of functioning.

Functional living skills

Psychosis may result in a form of psychiatric invalidity, described as disturbance and deficits of social functioning (Morrison and Bellack, 1987; Giel *et al.*, 1988). A thorough assessment of abilities and disabilities helps to suggest specific training programs. An example is social skills training for schizophrenic individuals at risk for relapse (Liberman *et al.*, 1986).

Wallace (1986) reviews a large series of instruments for the assessment of functional living skills of chronically mentally ill individuals. He concludes that the heterogeneity of the instruments is great, and that none of them is wholly adequate for assessing functional living skills. Some instruments assess performance in major life roles (partner, worker), others are limited to specific behaviours (personal hygiene, food preparation). Sources of information may be patients, significant others or staff members. The instruments range from objective questionnaires to semi-structured interviews and informal observation. The psychometric qualities of the more general instruments are adequate. One may consider usage of one or more of the following: The Katz Adjustment Scale (KAS), Personal Adjustment and Role Skills Scale (PARS), Social Behaviour and Adjustment Scale (SBAS), Psychiatric Status Schedule (PSS), Psychiatric Evaluation Form (PEF), Current and Past Psychopathology Scale (CAPPS). For a thorough review of these and other instruments see Wallace (1986). Some aspects of this are covered in Chapter 6 of this volume. The Morningside Rehabilitation scale (Affleck and McGuire, 1984) has been designed with this population in mind, as has the Rehab scale (Baker and Hall, 1984).

Expressed emotions and burden on the family

Recently much attention has been given to interpersonal and environmental aspects of psychiatric symptomatology. Expressed Emotion (EE) is a measure of relatives' expressed attitudes and feelings about the patient. EE can be measured by the Camberwell Family Interview (Leff and Vaughn, 1985). This semi-structured interview of a key relative of the patient consists of five scales: (1) critical comments about family members; (2) hostility towards the patient; (3) emotional over-involvement (exaggerated emotional response, marked concern and extremely overprotective behaviour towards the patient); (4) warmth; and (5) positive remarks. The newly developed Level of Expressed Emotion Scale (Cole and Kazarian, 1988) is a 60-item self-report measure. It provides an index of the perceived emotional climate in interpersonal relationships. Early reports suggest promising psychometric properties.

It has been repeatedly demonstrated that the family emotional climate, particularly the variables criticism, hostility and emotional over-involvement, relates to the course of schizophrenia. The relapse rate of patients living in low-EE homes is about 15 per cent a year, whereas high-EE homes yield a relapse rate of 40–50 per cent a year (Mintz *et al.*, 1987). Although the exact nature of the relation of EE and relapse rate is still unclear and the concept of EE may be criticized (Hatfield *et al.*, 1987), EE has proved to be an intriguing and useful clinical construct (Koenigsberg and Handley, 1986). In any case, low levels of criticism and emotional over-involvement are protective factors in the course of schizophrenia, as well as of other disorders (such as mood disorders and obesity). Moreover, family intervention and educational programmes are able to lower families' EE levels, with positive effects on course and outcome of the illness (Mintz *et al.*, 1987; Tarrier *et al.*, 1988).

Variability of symptomatology

The course of psychiatric disorder does not follow a straight line. Systematic observation of the course of the disorder reveals a series of longitudinal patterns and individual–environment interactions (Strauss *et al.*, 1985). For example, one may observe moratoria (periods of stability in symptoms and function), change points (considerable shifts in functioning or symptoms over a brief period) and ceilings (highest level of functioning reached in a given period). Such a model underlines the necessity of repeated assessment in order to identify changes in course and variability of symptomatology in the individual case.

Usually, most information about symptomatology is collected by retrospective interviews or questionnaires. The reliability of these methods may be doubted. The interpersonal and intrapersonal variability of symptomatology requires other methods of data collection. DeVries (1987) proposed the method of Experience Sampling (ES), combining diary, behavioural monitoring and spot observation techniques. The patient is asked to fill out a questionnaire ten times a day during one week and scores both the occurrence of psychotic symptoms and other aspects of his or her situation and functioning. This method also provides the opportunity of searching for triggers in the inter- and intrapersonal field. A review of available computer software for behavioural observation and event recording is presented by Noldus *et al.* (1989).

Prognosis

Prognosis depends partly on the type of psychotic disorder. Compared to schizophrenia, the schizophreniform, reactive, atypical and schizoaffective psychoses have a relatively good outcome. Follow-up studies show a poor outcome in schizophrenia in less than 50 per cent of the patients (Möller *et al.*, 1986). Predictors of poor outcome in schizophrenia are: lower age at onset, insidious onset, no precipitating factors, affective blunting, disturbances of premorbid personality or adjustment, and duration of hospitalization before index admission.

Möller *et al.* (1986) present a review of prognostic scales. Most scales are limited to one single predictor: premorbid adjustment (Gittelman–Klein Scale, Philips Scale and Goldstein Scale). Although premorbid adjustment is a strong predictor, better results can be obtained by using the multidimensional Strauss–Carpenter Scale (1974). This is a prognostic scale taking into account various aspects of psychopathology, social functioning and history of illness.

In order to predict outcome in chronic schizophrenic patients, Fenton and McGlashan (1987) developed the Chestnut Lodge Prognostic Scale for Schizophrenia. This scale is easy to administer and is independent of illness duration. It conceptualizes prognosis as a product of the dynamic interplay between the highest level of adaptive occupational and social functioning ever achieved (acquisition of skills and interests), genetic loading (family history of schizophrenia), erosion of reality testing (psychotic assaultiveness), and preservation of affect in psychopathology (depressed mood). Poor outcome was highly correlated with a low scale score (i.e. psychotic assaultiveness, family history of schizophrenia, absence of affect, poor premorbid functioning and skills). It is easier to predict a poor than a good outcome (Fenton and McGlashan, 1987). Familial dysfunctional behaviour is predictive for medium-term (10–19 years) outcome, while genetic vulnerability is prognostic for poor long-term outcome (McGlashan, 1986).

BIOLOGICAL ASPECTS

This section focuses on biological and neuropsychological aspects of major psychoses; in other words, on the biological substratum of ego functioning.

Psychotic disorders as well as prognosis and treatment are strongly determined by the interaction between social, environmental factors and the individual's biological vulnerability, including his or her information-processing capacity. Therefore adequate assessment of biological and neuropsychological aspects is of great clinical importance.

Structural anatomical factors

Structural abnormalities that have been frequently associated with psychotic disorders are enlargement of the third and lateral ventricles and dysfunctions of the frontal and parietal lobes and of the mesolimbic system. Other brain areas are also involved: the basal ganglia, the hypothalamus, the thalamus and the brain stem. Less clear is the role of structural abnormalities of the corpus callosum and the septum pellucidum. Finally, left temporal lobe dysfunction and more general dysfunctions in lateralization are sometimes postulated in schizophrenia.

Recently, many advanced techniques have been developed to assess structural abnormalities of the brain. Examples of these techniques are computerized tomography, magnetic resonance imaging, positron emission tomography, evaluation of cerebral blood flow and computerized evoked potential research. The last-mentioned technique gives insight into higher-order information processing of the brain, and is useful when combined with neuropsychological assessment of higher cognitive functions (Morihisa and McAnulty, 1985). This is compatible with the idea of considering schizophrenia and psychosis as a severe disturbance in the ability to adequately handle both interoceptive and exteroceptive information. The inability to handle information can be considered as the core symptom of the 'deficit syndrome'.

In general, it can be stated that those areas that are involved in higher-order information processing (including the regulation of motor behaviour), especially the (pre)frontal lobes, are of importance. (Pre)frontal lobe dysfunctions will therefore be discussed in more detail.

Neuropsychological deficit syndrome

We believe that the neuropsychological deficit syndrome distinction is far more useful for diagnostic classification in schizophrenia than Crow's (1985) positive and negative symptom dichotomy (Carpenter *et al.*, 1988, Wagman *et al.*, 1987). The deficit syndrome is consistently associated with structural abnormalities in the brain in contrast to the negative symptoms (Kay *et al.*, 1987; Keilp *et al.*, 1988). Moreover, negative symptoms fluctuate over time and also occur as concomitants of other psychiatric disorders such as depression, personality disorders and drug-intoxication (Wagman *et al.*, 1987).

The distinction based on the *presence* of deficit symptoms is probably also more useful than that based on Type I/Type II classification, because Type I schizophrenia is merely *ex negativo* diagnosed by the *absence* of negative symptoms. For purposes of distinguishing subtypes of schizophrenia the presence or absence of stable deficit symptoms are critical. They could even manifest themselves *before* the initial psychotic episode (Carpenter *et al.*, 1988).

Deficit symptoms refer specifically to those negative symptoms that are present as *enduring* traits. They can be found during periods of positive and negative symptom exacerbation as well as periods of clinical remission. The stable presence of the deficit syndrome can be considered as a core manifestation of schizophrenia and as a basic discriminating feature common to the various diagnostic approaches (Carpenter *et al.*, 1988). Because of the uncertainty regarding the neuroleptic responsivity of negative symptoms, clinicians are rather reluctant to give neuroleptics to patients with a predominance of negative symptoms. It is, however, quite possible that only the defect state (those negative symptoms that can be considered as an enduring trait and as primary symptoms) is resistant to neuroleptic treatment. Negative symptoms classified in other ways can be reduced by neuroleptic treatment. Indeed, Breier *et al.* (1987) found that neuroleptics produced improvements in both negative and positive symptoms. This finding leads the authors to advise clinicians to consider a neuroleptic trial in schizophrenic patients who have prominent negative symptoms. In this respect, results of the study carried out by Asarnow *et al.* (1988) may be of interest. They found that the dosage threshold for toxic effects of fluphenazine decanoate seems to be lower in patients with good information-processing capacity. Therefore assessment of information capacity is essential. From this point of view, neuropsychological assessment procedures are, in addition to brain-imaging techniques, of great clinical importance, especially tests that assess the functional integrity of those brain areas that are involved in higher cognitive functioning and attention regulation.

The most comprehensive neuropsychological test batteries are the Halstead–Reitan Neuropsychological Test-Battery and the Luria–Nebraska Neuropsychological Test-Battery. Other commonly used tests are the Wisconsin Card Sorting Test measuring basic abstract thinking and the ability to shift mental sets; the Bender Gestalt Test, a screening device for signs of organic dysfunction; the Meander Test, assessing sustained attention and visual perception, functions mediated by the frontoparietal lobes; the Maze-Tests, assessing eye–hand co-ordination and planning, functions that depend on the integrity of the frontoparietal lobes; and the Stroop Color-Word Test, measuring the ability to cope with interfering information, and to filter out irrelevant information, a frontal lobe function. For a more comprehensive overview of available neuropsychological tests see Lezak (1983) and Eurelings-Bontekoe (1989).

(Pre)frontal lobe dysfunction

The (pre)frontal lobes have an important function in controlled information processing, concentration and selective attention by modulating and regulating the sensory input to the brain, especially by suppressing irrelevant, redundant information. In recent discussions it has been proposed that frontal lobe dysfunction, if not of primary pathogenic importance, may at least explain some of the clinical phenomena associated with schizophrenia. Defect symptoms are similar to the disturbed motivation, flattened affect, thought disorders and other features of frontal lobe disease such as the presence of soft neurological signs. The attentional deficits and cognitive impairment in schizophrenia most consistently involve the frontal lobes.

Recent neuroanatomical and neuropharmacological studies suggest that it is necessary, valid and meaningful to differentiate within the frontal area between the dorsolateral prefrontal cortex and the medio-basal prefrontal areas (Weinberger *et al.*, 1986). The defect symptoms and neuropsychological and cognitive impairments (such as the inability to form abstract concepts, to respond to feedback, to shift mental sets, to use hypothetico-deductive reasoning and to maintain information in working memory over time) and minor neurological signs are mostly associated with dysfunction of the dorsolateral areas of the prefrontal cortex. Dysfunctions of the medio-basal prefrontal areas are rather associated with the 'classical' signs of frontal lobe disease such as disinhibition, impulsivity, 'Witzelsucht' and euphoria (Douma, 1987).

The following tests are especially suitable to assess (pre)frontal dysfunctions. In general, (dorsolateral) prefrontal brain dysfunction leads to a lower total IQ, compared to premorbid level, whereas, in contrast, mediobasal prefrontal dysfunction does not lead to a lowering of total IQ score (Maly and Quatember, 1986). Wechsler subtests that are most sensitive to prefrontal dysfunctions are digit span (especially digits presented in backward order), block design, picture arrangement, picture completion and object assembly. The general opinion that right hemispheric lesions lead to relatively low-performance IQ and left hemispheric lesions to relatively low-verbal IQ does not hold in the case of prefrontal brain dysfunction (Wallesch *et al.*, 1983).

The trail-making test, a subtest of the Halstead Reitan Battery, is also very sensitive in assessing prefrontal brain lesions. In addition, the Stroop Color-Word test (Stroop, 1935), especially the task of naming the colour of words while ignoring the colour they name, is particularly sensitive to the presence of prefrontal brain dysfunction. Also important in this respect is the Wisconsin Card Sorting test, especially the version developed by Nelson (1976). If the number of perseverative incorrect responses is more than 30 per cent of the total of incorrect responses, prefrontal brain dysfunction is to be expected. Also the Complex-Figure Test and the Meander test are sensitive assessors of prefrontal brain pathology. Finally a typical indication of prefrontal brain lesion is the observation that patients are not able to increase the capacity of short-term memory during a 15-word test. When the maximum of words that can be recalled is reached, there is no further increase in the following trials.

Neurotransmission

The dopamine-receptor system, especially the mesolimbic D2-receptor system, has appeared to be of great significance in both the aetiology and the treatment of psychotic disorders. Although noradrenergic and serotonergic systems do play a role, they are of far less clinical significance. Methods to assess mesolimbic DA in the living brain do not exist. However, it is possible to assess the presence of D2 receptors in the living human brain by means of positron emission tomography (Farde *et al.*, 1988). Another indirect method is the measurement of Growth Hormone release (Zemlan *et al.*, 1986).

Very promising are the results of research on the various peptide neurotransmitters, also called neuroactive peptides. Clinical studies using endorphins as agonists have suggested potential clinical applications. It is suggested that neuropeptides interact with dopaminergic systems in the mesolimbic system to decrease its activity. They especially interact with presynaptically located self-inhibiting DA-receptor systems, particularly in the nucleus accumbens. Gamma-type endorphins are thought to be involved in the feedback regulation of DA-receptor systems. Their main role is to potentiate the presynaptic inhibition of DA release. A chronic deficiency of Gamma-type endorphins could eventually lead to a sustained increase of DA release and activity (Verhoeven and Den Boer, 1988). Both positive and negative symptoms can be reduced after administration of Gamma-type endorphins, whereas these substances do not induce extra-pyramidal side-effects, because they influence presynaptic receptors. Further research to assess the effectiveness of Gamma-type endorphins in the treatment of psychosis is needed. Recent results have been intriguing and promising (Bradley and Hirsch, 1986; Verhoeven and Den Boer, 1988).

REFERENCES

Affleck, J.W. and McGuire, R.J. (1984) The Morningside Rehabilitation Status Scale (MRSS). *British Journal of Psychiatry*, **145**, 517–25.

American Psychiatric Association (APA) (1987) *DSM-III-R: Diagnostic and Statistical Manual of Mental Disorders*, American Psychiatric Association, Washington, DC.

Andreasen, N. (1985) Positive vs. negative schizophrenia: A critical evaluation. *Schizophrenia Bulletin*, **11** (3), 380–89.

Andreasen, N. (1986) Scale for the assessment of Thought, Language and Communication (TLC). *Schizophrenia Bulletin*, **12**, 3, 473–96.

Arieti, S. (1974) *Interpretation of Schizophrenia*, 2nd edn, Basic Books, New York.

Arieti, S. (1983) Psychotherapy of schizophrenia: new or revised procedures. In M. Stone, H. Albert, D. Forrest and S. Arieti (eds), *Treating Schizophrenic Patients. A Clinical/Analytical Approach*, pp. 1–19, McGraw-Hill, New York.

Asaad, G. and Shapiro, B. (1986) Hallucinations: theoretical and clinical overview. *American Journal of Pscychiatry*, **143**: 9, 1088–97.

Asarnow, R.F., Marder, S.R., Mintz, J., van Putten, Th. and Zimmerman, K. (1988) Differential effect of low and conventional doses of fluphenazine on schizophrenic outpatients with good or poor information-processing abilities. *Archives of General Psychiatry*, **45**, 822–26.

Baker, R. and Hall, J. (1984) *Rehab: Rehabilitation Evaluation Hall and Baker*, Vine Press, Aberdeen.

Bender, L. (1938) A visual motor gestalt test and its clinical use. *American Orthopsychiatric Association Research Monographs*, No. 3.

Bosch, R.J. van den (1988) Subjectieve belevingen, adaptatie en zelfbeschermingsgedrag. In R. van den Bosch, C. van Meer, P. Dingemans and D. Linszen (eds), *Schizofrenie. Recente ontwikkelingen in onderzoek en behandeling*, pp. 187–202, Van Loghum Slaterus, Deventer.

Bradley, P.B. and Hirsch, S.R. (1986) *The Psychopharmacology and Treatment of Schizophrenia*, Oxford Medical Publications, Oxford.

Breier, A. and Strauss, J. (1983). Self-control in psychotic disorders. *Archives of General Psychiatry*, **40**, 1141–5.

Breier, A., Wolkowitz, O., Doran, A., Roy, A., Boronow, J., Hommer, D. and Pickar, D. (1987) Neuroleptic responsivity of negative and positive symptoms in schizophrenia. *American Journal of Psychiatry*, **144**, 1549–55.

Carpenter, W.T., Heinrichs, D.W. and Wagman, A.M.I. (1988) Deficit and non-deficit forms of schizophrenia: the concept. *American Journal of Psychiatry*, **145**, 578–83.

Chopra, H. and Beatson, J. (1986) Psychotic symptoms in Borderline Personality Disorder. *American Journal of Psychiatry*, **143**, 12, 1605–7.

Cole, J.D. and Kazarian, S.S. (1988) The level of expressed emotion scale: a new measure of expressed emotion. *Journal of Clinical Psychology*, **44** (3), 392–7.

Crow, T.J. (1985) The two-syndrome concept: origins and current status. *Schizophrenia Bulletin*, **11**, 471–86.

Cutting, J. and Murphy, D. (1988) Schizophrenic thought disorder. A psychological and organic interpretation. *British Journal of Psychiatry*, **152**, 310–19.

Devries, M.W. (1987) Investigating mental disorders in their natural settings. *Journal of Nervous and Mental Disease*, **175**, (9), 509–13.

Dingemans, P.M.J.A. (1988) Classificatie en schalen in het onderzoek van schizofrenie. In R. van den Bosch, C. van Meer, P. Dingemans and D. Linszen (eds), *Schizofrenie. Recente ontwikkelingen in onderzoek en behandeling*, pp. 49–71, Van Loghum Slaterus, Deventer.

Douma, M. (1987) De onderkenning van prefrontaal hersenletsel. *Tijdschrift voor Psychiatrie*, **29** (9), 570–84.

Endicott, J. and Spitzer, R.L. (1978) A diagnostic interview: the Schedule for Affective Disorders and Schizophrenia. *Archives of General Psychiatry*, **35**, 837–44.

Escobar, J.I., Randolph, E.T., Asamen, J. and Karno M. (1986) The NIMH-DIS in the assessment of DSM-III Schizophrenic Disorder. *Schizophrenia Bulletin*, **12** (2), 187–94.

Eurelings-Bontekoe, E.H.M. (1989) Biological and neuropsychological aspects of major psychosis. *Leiden Psychological Reports*, CLI 89–01, Leiden University.

Exner, J.E. (1986) *The Rorschach. A Comprehensive System. Vol. 1: Basic Foundations*, 2nd edn, John Wiley, New York.

Falloon, I.R. and Talbot, R.E. (1981) Persistent auditory hallucinations: coping mechanisms and implications for management. *Psychological Medicine*, **11**, 329–39.

Farde, L., Wiesel, F.A. and Sedvall, G. (1988) Central D2-dopamine receptor occupancy in schizophrenic patients treated with antipsychotic drugs. *Archives of General Psychiatry*, **45**, 71–6.

Fenton, W. and McGlashan, Th. (1986) The prognostic significance of obsessive–compulsive symptoms in schizophrenia. *American Journal of Psychiatry*, **143**, 4, 437–41.

Fenton, W. and McGlashan, Th. (1987) Prognostic scale for chronic schizophrenia. *Schizophrenia Bulletin*, **13**, 2, 277–86.

Frances, A. (1985) Validating schizotypal personality disorders: problems with the schizophrenia connection. *Schizophrenia Bulletin*, **11**, 4, 595–7.

George, A. and Soloff, P. (1986) Schizotypal symptoms in patients with borderline personality disorders. *American Journal of Psychiatry*, **143**, 2, 212–15.

Giel, R., De Jong, A. and Wiersma, D. (1988) Sociale aspecten van schizofrenie. In R. van den Bosch, C. van Meer, P. Dingemans and D. Linszen (eds), *Schizofrenie. Recente ontwikkelingen in onderzoek en behandeling*, pp. 284–302, Van Loghum Slaterus, Deventer.

Golden, C.J., Hammeke, T.A. and Purisch, A.D. (1980 *Manual for the Luria–Nebraska Neuropsychological Battery*, Western Psychological Services, Los Angeles.

Grant, D.A. and Berg, E.A. (1948) A behavioural analysis of degree of reinforcement and ease of shifting to new responses in a weight-type card-sorting problem. *Journal of Experimental Psychology*, **38**, 404–11.

Gunderson, J. and Siever, L. (1985) Relatedness of schizotypal to schizophrenic disorders: Editors' introduction. *Schizophrenia Bulletin*, **11**, 4, 532–7.

Halstead, W.C. (1947) *Brain and Intelligence*, University of Chicago Press, Chicago.

Hammer, E.F. (1978) Projective drawings: two areas of differential diagnostic challenge. In B. Wolman (ed.), *Clinical Diagnosis of Mental Disorders*, pp. 281–310, Plenum Press, New York.

Hatfield, A., Spaniol, L. and Zipple, A. (1987) Expressed emotion: a family perspective. *Schizophrenia Bulletin*, **13**, 2, 221–6.

Hellerstein, D., Frosch, W. and Koenigsberg, H. (1987) The clinical significance of command hallucinations. *American Journal of Psychiatry*, **144**, 2, 219–21.

Helzer, J.E. and Robins, L.N. (1984) Lifetime psychotic symptoms assessed with the DIS. *Schizophrenia Bulletin*, **10** (1), 4–7.

Insel, Th. and Akiskal, H. (1986) Obsessive–compulsive disorder with psychotic features: a phenomenological analysis. *American Journal of Psychiatry*, **143**, 12, 1527–33.

Joos, S., Houben, M.E. and Thijs, T. (1986) Psychodiagnostiek bij schizofrenie. De afgrenzingsproblematiek. *Tijdschr. Klin. Psych.*, **16** (4), 209–27.

Kay, S., Fiszbein, A. and Opler, L. (1987) The Positive and Negative Syndrome Scale (PANSS). *Schizophrenia Bulletin*, **13**, 2, 261–73.

Keilp, J.G., Sweeney, J.A., Jacobson, P., Solomon, C., St Louis, L., Deck, M., Frances, A. and John Mann, J. (1988) Cognitive impairment in schizophrenia: specific relations to ventricular size and negative symptomatology. *Biological Psychiatry*, **24**, 47–55.

Kernberg, O. (1975) *Borderline Conditions and Pathological Narcissism*, Jason Aronson. New York.

Kernberg, O. (1977) The structural diagnosis of borderline personality organization. In P. Hartocollis (ed.), *Borderline Personality Disorders*, pp. 87–121, International Universities Press, New York.

Koenigsberg, H. and Handley, R. (1986) Expressed emotion: from predictive index to clinical construct. *American Journal of Psychiatry*, **143**, 11, 1361–73.

Leff, J. and Vaugn, C. (eds) (1985) *Expressed Emotion in Families*, Guilford Press, New York.

Lezak, M.D. (1983) *Neuropsychological Assessment*, 2nd edn, Oxford University Press, New York.

Liberman, R., Mueser, K. and Wallace, Ch. (1986) Social skills training for schizophrenic individuals at risk for relapse. *American Journal of Psychiatry*, **143**, 4, 523–6.

Loranger, A.W., Lehmann Susman, V., Oldham, J.M. and Russakoff, L.M. (1987) The Personality Disorder Examination: A preliminary report. *Journal of Personality Disorders*, **1** (1), 1–13.

MacKinnon, R.A. and Yudofsky, S.C. (1986) *The Psychiatric Evaluation in Clinical Practice*, Lippincott, Philadelphia.

Maltbie, A.A. (1983) Psychosis. In J. Cavenar and H. Brodie (eds), *Signs and Symptoms in Psychiatry*, pp. 413–32, Lippincott, Philadelphia.

Maly, J. and Quatember, R. (1986) Die Neuropsychologische frontobasaler und frontoconvexer Hirnläsionen. *Zeitschrift für Klinische Psychologie und Psychotherapie*, **28**, 267–76.

McGlashan, T. (1986) Predictors of shorter-, medium- and longer-term outcome in schizophrenia. *American Journal of Psychiatry*, **143**, 50–55.

Mintz, L., Liberman, R., Miklowitz, D. and Mintz, J. (1987) Expressed emotion: a call for partnership among relatives, patients and professionals. *Schizophrenia Bulletin*, **13**, 2, 227–35.

Möller, H.J., Schmid-Bode, W. and Zerssen, D. von (1986) Prediction of long-term outcome in schizophrenia by prognostic scales. *Schizophrenia Bulletin*, **12** (2), 225–35.

Morihisa, J.M. and McAnulty, G.B. (1985) Structure and function: brain electrical activity mapping and computed tomography in schizophrenia. *Biological Psychiatry*, **20**, 3–19.

Morrison, R. and Bellack, A. (1987) Social functioning of schizophrenic patients: clinical and research issues. *Schizophrenia Bulletin*, **13**, 4, 715–25.

Musaph, H. (1977) Itching and other dermatoses. In E. Wittkower and H. Warnes (eds), *Psychosomatic Medicine*, pp. 307–15, Harper & Row, Hagerstown.

Nash, J.L. (1983) Delusions. In J. Cavenar and H. Brodie (eds), *Signs and Symptoms in Psychiatry*, pp. 455 –81, Lippincott, Philadelphia.

Nelson, H. (1976) A modified card sorting test sensitive to frontal lobe defects. *Cortex*, **13**, 313–24.

Noldus, L.P.Y.Y., Loo, E.L.H.M. Van de and Timmers, P.H.A. (1989) Computers in behavioural research. *Nature*, **341**, 767–68.

M.Olson, P., Suddeth, J., Peterson, P. and Egelhoff, C. (1985) Hallucinations of widowhood. *Journal of the American Geriatrics Society*, **33**, 8, 543–7.

Osterrieth, P.A. (1944) Le test de copie d'une figure complexe. *Archives de Psychologie*, **30**, 206–356.

Rapaport, D., Gill, M. and Schafer, R. (1968) *Diagnostic Psychological Testing*, revised edition by R. Holt. International Universities Press, New York.

Robins, L.N., Helzer, J.E., Croughan, J. and Ratcliff, K.S. (1981) National Institute of Mental Health Diagnostic Interview Schedule. Its history, characteristics and validity. *Archives of General Psychiatry*, **38**, 381–9.

Rust, J. (1988) The Rust Inventory of Schizotypal Cognitions (RISC). *Schizophrenia Bulletin*, **14**, 2, 317–22.

Sloof, C.J., Mulder-Hajonides van der Meulen, W.R.E.N. and Hoofdakker, R.H. van de (1983) De Nederlandse vertaling van de present state examination 9e editie, I en II. *Tijdschrift voor Psychiatrie*, **25**, 151–63, 280–89.

Solovay, M.R., Shenton, M.E., Gasperetti, C., Coleman, M., Kestnbaum, E., Carpenter, J. and Holzman, Ph. (1986) Scoring Manual for the Thought Disorder Index. *Schizophrenia Bulletin*, **12** (3), 483–96.

Spitzer, R.L., Williams, J.B. and Gibbon, M. (1986). *Structured Clinical Interview for DSM III-R*, Biometrics Research Department, New York State Psychiatric Institute, New York.

Stangl, D., Pfolh, B., Zimmerman, J., Bowers, W. and Corenthal, R. (1985) A structured interview for the DSM–III personality disorders. A preliminary report. *Archives of General Psychiatry*, **42**, 591–6.

Strauss, J.S. and Carpenter, W.T. Jr (1974) Prediction of outcome in schizophrenia. II. Relationships between predictor and outcome variables. *Archives of General Psychiatry*, **31**, 37–42.

Strauss, J., Hafez, H., Lieberman, P. and Harding, C. (1985) The course of psychiatric disorder, III: longitudinal principles. *American Journal of Psychiatry*, **142** (3), 289–96.

Tarrier, N., Barrowclough, C., Vaughn, C., Bamrah, J., Porceddu, K., Watts, S. and Freeman, H. (1988) The community management of schizophrenia: a controlled trial of a behavioural intervention with families to reduce relapse. *British Journal of Psychiatry*, **153**, 532–42.

Verhoeven, W.M.A. and Den Boer, J.A. (1988) Novel atypical antipsychotic compounds: recent developments in the treatment of schizophrenia. In M. Wolf and A. Mosnaim, *Tardive Dyskinesia: Biological Mechanisms and Clinical Aspects*, pp. 245–58, American Psychiatric Press, Washington, DC.

Wagman, A.M.I., Heinrichs, D.W. and Carpenter, W.T. (1987) Deficit and non-deficit forms of schizophrenia. Neuropsychological evaluation. *Psychiatry Research*, **22**, 319–30.

Walker, E.F., Harvey, P. and Perlman, D. (1988) The positive/negative symptom distinction in psychoses. A replication and extension of previous findings. *Journal of Nervous and Mental Disease*, **176** (6), 359–63.

Walker, J.I. and J.O. Cavenar (1983a) Hallucinations. In J. Cavenar and H. Brodie (eds), *Signs and Symptoms in Psychiatry*, pp. 433–54, Lippincott, Philadelphia.

Walker, J.I. and J.O. Cavenar (1983b) Paranoid symptoms and conditions. In J. Cavenar and H. Brodie (eds), *Signs and Symptoms in Psychiatry*, pp. 483–510, Lippincott, Philadelphia.

Wallace, C. (1986) Functional assessment in rehabilitation *Schizophrenia Bulletin*, **12**, 4, 604–30.

Wallesch, C.W., Kornhuber, H.H., Köllner, C., Haas, H.C. and Hufnagl, J.M. (1983) Language and cognitive deficits resulting from medial and dorsalateral frontal lobe lesions. *Archiv für Psychiatrie und Nervenkrankheiten*, **233**, 279–96.

Weinberger, D.R., Faith Berman, K. and Zec, R.F. (1986) Physiologic dysfunction of dorsolateral prefrontal cortex in schizophrenia. *Archives of General Psychiatry*, **43**, 114–24.

Wexler, D.A. (1974) A cognitive theory of experiencing, self-actualization and therapeutic process. In D.A. Wexler and L. North Rice (eds), *Innovations in Client-centered Therapy*, pp. 49–116, John Wiley, New York.

Wing, J.K., Cooper, J.E. and Sartorius, N. (1974) *The Measurement and Classification of Psychiatric Symptoms*, Cambridge University Press, Cambridge.

Zemlan, F.P., Hirschowitz, J. and Garver, D.L. (1986) Relation of clinical symptoms to apomorphine-stimulated growth hormone release in mood-incongruent psychotic patients. *Archives of General Psychiatry*, **43**, 1162–7.

Zubin, J., Magaziner, J. and Steinhauer, S. (1983) The metamorphosis of schizophrenia: from chronicity to vulnerability. *Psychological Medicine*, **13**, 551–71.

Chapter 11

Behavioural and Cognitive Problems in the Elderly

CHRIS J. GILLEARD and JANICE E. CHRISTIE

INTRODUCTION

The elderly are not a problem group in society. They are generally more law abiding and less likely to engage in such deviant activities as drug and alcohol abuse, wife or child beating or tax evasion. The great majority live in their own homes and get on with their own lives as well as history and present circumstances permit. However, what also distinguishes the elderly from other age groups is the rate at which they develop chronic disabling and deteriorative conditions which can make life for them and their families distressing and discouraging. In addition to more long-standing concerns for assessing the mental and behavioural competence of the elderly, there has been an increasing need for measures to assess the disengagement and dysphoria that may accompany the problems of dependency and disability. While the majority of the elderly do not become dysphoric, disengaged or dependent, much of this chapter will be concerned with the measurement of these problem areas, and with the assessment of dementia, especially diagnosis. However, attention will also be paid to areas of assessment such as activity and engagement which are less focused on pathology.

MENTAL COMPETENCE

It is customary to consider intelligence, learning and memory, language and related symbolic functions, and motor executive behaviour as components of what is meant by mental competence. Such a division provides a convenient way to discuss the various performance tests of mental competence and it will be largely adhered to in this section.

Measuring Human Problems. Edited by D.F. Peck and C.M. Shapiro

Intellectual level and intellectual decline

Determining the likelihood that an elderly person is undergoing abnormal intellectual deterioration remains a clinically significant task in the assessment of that person. Current intellectual functioning is typically assessed by the WAIS or WAIS-R (Wechsler, 1981) although the Coloured Progressive Matrices and Mill Hill Vocabulary Scale are sometimes used (Raven, 1965). While these tests are occasionally employed to indicate contrasts between achieved intellectual status and current intellectual efficiency, there is little empirical justification for distinctions between so-called 'hold' and 'don't hold' subtests to indicate the extent of deterioration assumed to have taken place (Bolton *et al.*, 1966). Use of vocabulary tests alone such as the Mill Hill Vocabulary Scale or the WAIS Vocabulary subtest to measure premorbid intellectual level is often recommended, but at present the evidence that such tests are insensitive to the effects of intellectual deterioration is dubious (O'Carroll and Gilleard, 1986: O'Carroll *et al.*, 1987). Indeed, decline in vocabulary scores may be a rather sensitive predictor of dementia in old age (La Rue and Jarvik, 1987).

However, when such tests as the Coloured Progressive Matrices or the WAIS are used as indicators of current intellectual efficiency, there are a number of alternative ways to estimate premorbid intellectual level. Oral reading ability has been found to be closely related to intellectual level in unimpaired adults, and this skill appears to be fairly insensitive to the progressive deterioration associated with mild to moderate dementia (Nelson and McKenna, 1975; O'Carroll *et al.*, 1987). The National Adult Reading Test (NART, Nelson, 1982) employs the number of correct pronunciations from a list of irregularly spelled words such as 'aisle' as a means of providing a reliable estimate of premorbid IQ. NART/WAIS IQ discrepancies have been found useful in discriminating between patients with and without signs of cerebral atrophy derived from neuroradiological investigations (Nelson and O'Connel, 1978: Ruddle and Bradshaw, 1982).

Demographic data have also been used to create regression equations with which to predict premorbid IQ (Wilson *et al.*, 1978; Barona *et al.*, 1984) using data from the standardization of the WAIS or WAIS-R. At present, it is unclear whether contrasts between current IQ and premorbid estimates based upon such formulae possess any incremental validity over the simple use of current WAIS/WAIS-R IQ as an index of deterioration (Eppinger *et al.*, 1987). Nevertheless, as both current and past cognitive skills contribute to present performance levels on cognitive tests ranging from the simplest mental status questionnaire to the most complex of memory tests, it is always useful to have a measure of probable premorbid intellectual achievement by which to judge the nature of any currently observed deficits. Studies of the course and pattern of intellectual decline in dementia may prove misleading without consideration of the role that past cognitive skills have on the way that present intellectual deficits emerge.

Memory and learning

Despite the profusion of experimental models of memory and the dominance of research in this area within psychological gerontology, the clinical tests most widely used in assessing memory and learning in the elderly date from the 1940s and 1950s. While these tests were not devised according to modern experimental paradigms, they retain their value because they have demonstrable validity when set against other clinical criteria of impairment, and they can be administered to moderately disabled elderly people.

A distinction can be made between single tests of memory and memory test batteries. Single tests of non-verbal memory such as Benton's Visual Retention Test (Benton, 1974) have shown characteristically steep declines in level of performance even in normal old age, and hence can have only a limited power to discriminate abnormally impaired memory in the elderly. Effective discrimination for the Benton has been reported between late middle-aged/early old-age patients with either depression or dementia (Crookes and McDonald, 1972), but it seems unlikely that similar discrimination can be anticipated in later old age.

Single verbal learning/memory tests relying upon recall of lists of words or learning pairs of words have often been used to test memory in old-age patients as well as to evaluate the effects of memory-enhancing (or in some cases memory-impairing) drugs. Lezack's handbook on neuropsychological assessment has done much to popularize Rey's Auditory Verbal Learning Test (AVLT, see Lezack, 1978). Since the AVLT incorporates a repeated presentation of a 15-word list, one can assess a patient's rate of learning as well as initial performance level. It is also possible to test for the effects of an interfering word list and to obtain a recognition memory score at the end of the learning trials. As with many serial learning tests that repeatedly expose the patient to their failure, it can prove too wearying for some elderly patients. Although there is promising evidence of the test's discriminative validity (Rosenberg *et al.*, 1984), to date there appear no reports of its comparative efficacy against other simpler tests such as the Inglis Paired Associate Learning Test (IPALT, Inglis, 1959).

The IPALT consists of three versions of a paired-associate learning task each involving the presentation and recall of three pairs of words (the three versions represent difficult, moderate and easy pairs). Developed for use with elderly psychiatric patients, it appears more acceptable than several other verbal learning tests. It has been extensively validated against diagnostic criteria and against outcome among both acute and long-stay elderly patients. It appears to be sensitive to change over time (Whitehead, 1977, 1982) and seems suitable because of its varying difficulty levels for use in treatment studies of memory-disordered patients. The existence of parallel versions of the test would certainly improve its value in this latter respect.

A major problem in the diagnostic use of recall-based tests is that they are sensitive to a number of factors which can depress performance, and as a result they may lack specificity in identifying poor performance due primarily to structural change in the brain. Recognition tests of memory may prove more useful in such cases. Warrington (1984) has recently developed a Recognition Memory Test which contains both a verbal and non-verbal form of the recognition task (words and faces) and age-appropriate norms have been provided. Kapur (1987), while recognizing that the test is 'a significant advance in the assessment of memory', has been critical of the reliability and validity data presented in the test manual. Clearly, further development of the test is needed before it can be uncritically recommended for clinical use, but at present it remains one of the few formal psychometric measures of recognition memory.

Memory test batteries such as the Wechsler Memory Scale continue to be the most widely used form of clinical memory tests (Lubin *et al.*, 1984). While similar batteries have been developed such as the Guild Memory Test (Gilbert and Levee, 1971), they have not introduced any major innovation in format that has not appeared as a modification of the WMS itself (e.g. Russell's version of the WMS employing an additional 30-minute delayed recall for the Logical Memory and Visual Reproduction subtests (Russell, 1975)). While some studies have employed the whole WMS others have used various subtests in diagnostic test batteries, especially in the burgeoning research on Alzheimer's disease (Kaszniak *et al.*, 1978; Weingartner *et al.*, 1981; Storandt *et al.*, 1984). The subtests have proved of value both as discriminators of diagnostic status as well as predictors of outcome and morbidity. Since marked educational effects have been noted in normal elderly subjects' performance (Bak and Greene, 1981) it may be useful to contrast the overall Memory Quotient with estimates of premorbid IQ obtained from the NART or other indices. The existence of parallel forms suggests that the WMS could also be useful as a means of assessing change, but the equivalence of Forms I and II has not yet been established for an older population. As Albert (1981) has noted, there is considerable scope for clinical modification of the WMS subtests and recently there has been a steady output of old-age normative performance data (mainly published in the *Journal of Clinical Psychology*). Until more extensive data on recognition test performance emerge (an area most obviously lacking in the WMS) it seems impossible to identify other tests which can be considered as satisfactory for both clinical and research purposes.

Neuropsychological performance

Assessment of language, praxis and gnosis tend to be assembled under the rubric of neuropsychological tests. This section will first consider neuropsychological test batteries before turning to individual tests. Since most neuropsychological batteries have been developed for younger populations it is not surprising that one has to search outside of the standard manuals and reports to find information on age-related levels of performance. However, since many of the tasks involved in neuropsychological assessments reflect, if not 'automatic' then highly overlearned, cognitive skills which might be expected to be age invariant, such measures should be singularly useful in identifying 'abnormal' features of ageing of the central nervous system.

There are two major neuropsychological batteries which command wide use, particularly in the United States. The first is the Halstead–Reitan Neuropsychological Battery (Reitan, 1977) and the second is the Luria–Nebraska Neuropsychological Battery (Golden *et al.*, 1985). The core tests of the Halstead–Reitan are the Category Test, a Tactual Performance Test, the Seashore Rhythm Test, a Speech Sound Perception Test and a Finger Tapping Test. Often added are measures of bilateral handgrip, the Trail Making Tests and an Aphasia Screening Test. The battery as a whole is lengthy, requiring considerable equipment and cannot be considered suitable for any kind of 'bedside' examination of an elderly patient. Various components of the Halstead–Reitan have been standardized on elderly populations (Bak and Greene, 1980; Bornstein, 1985). Several studies have been reported using parts of this test battery to discriminate early dementia from normal ageing, and to identify different aetiological forms and stages of dementia (Storandt *et al.*, 1984; Filley *et al.*, 1986; Rosen and Mohs, 1982). One may reasonably conclude that the whole test battery is of less value than some of its individual parts. The more recently developed Luria–Nebraska battery has an explicit means of comparing the standardized performance scores against a 'correction factor' of age and education, which the Halstead–Reitan lacks. Unfortunately, the assumption that these background variables exert a constant influence on performance in each area assessed by the Luria–Nebraska (such as motor skills, memory, language expression, tactile recognition) does not appear to hold, Vannieuwkirk and Galbraith (1985) having found correlations with age.

Although there are many promising features, the Luria–Nebraska battery cannot be considered to have a sufficient psychometric base for use as a diagnostic or research tool with elderly patients. Nevertheless, there is an increasing interest in research into the neuropsychological profile in the dementias of old age. In particular, several lines of evidence point to the importance of assessment of language and praxis in the elderly impaired patient. The Minnesota Aphasia Test battery has been applied to a normal elderly population by Walker (1980), who has pointed out evidence of several age-related 'normative' declines in language function. The Sentence Production test from this battery has been found to be associated with poor outcome in dementia (Kaszniak *et al.*, 1978). Receptive language difficulties have been reported to characterize early onset forms of Alzheimer's disease (Filley *et al.*, 1986) and the short version of De Renzi's Token Test (Spellacy and Spreen, 1969) has been found to be as sensitive an index of such difficulties as the longer original version (Taylor, 1986). Word-fluency tests such as producing as many words as possible beginning with F, A and S in one minute also appear useful (Tierney *et al.*, 1987). Valuable normative data on this latter test have been provided by Miller (1984). Tests of praxis have been less extensively examined, but several reports testify to the value of clinical tests of drawing (e.g. a person, a house, a clockface, a cube (Moore and Wyke, 1984)). Kertesz and Hooper's (1980) test of motor praxis has also been found useful as a means of assessing such dysfunctions in elderly impaired patients (Taylor, 1986). As with all neuropsychological measures, it would be useful to establish what may reasonably be called the normal limits of performance on such tasks in old age, in order that a clearer understanding may develop concerning the meaning to be attributed to abnormalities in such areas as language and praxis. At present, many of the 'cut-off' points established for neuropsychological tests overclassify far too many elderly persons as impaired (cf. Bak and Greene, 1980).

Mental state questionnaires

These brief measures of orientation and current personal and general information are probably the most widely used tests of mental competence in the elderly. Despite being virtually identical to each other in general format, no clear consensus has emerged regarding the best set of items to include in such tests. Table 11.1 lists some of the more popular versions.

As Lesher and Whelihan (1986), among others, have observed, these tests tend to be highly correlated with each other, and therefore it is difficult to judge between them. The most extensive normative data in the United States concern the MMS and SPMSQ, while in Britain the CAPE I/O test has been employed in several large-scale community studies (Clarke *et al.*, 1986; Morgan *et al.*, 1987). Unlike the other tests, the MMS does not have a unitary

Table 11.1 Mental status instruments for use with the elderly

Author	Title	Item length	Reliability[a]
Kahn *et al.* (1960)	Mental Status Questionnaire (MSQ)	10	0.80–0.87
Blessed *et al.* (1968)	Information–Concentration–Memory Test (ICMT)	26	0.82–0.88
Hodkinson (1972)	Abbreviated Mental Test (AMT)	10	0.87–0.92
Pfeiffer (1975)	Short Portable Mental Status Questionnaire (SPMSQ)	12	0.82–0.91
Folstein (1975)	Mini-Mental-State (MMS)	19	0.79–0.99
Pattie and Gilleard (1979)	CAPE Information-Orientation Test (CAPE I/0)	12	0.84–0.90
Katzman *et al.* (1983)	Orientation–Memory–Concentration Test (OMCT)	6	0.77–0.80

[a] Split-half and short-term reliability coefficients derived from the original reports and Lesher and Whelihan (1986); Fillenbaum *et al.* (1987); McPherson and Tregaskis (1985); Qureshi and Hodkinson (1974).

factor structure (Fillenbaum *et al.*, 1987) and is influenced by both age and education (Anthony *et al.*, 1982). It is less diagnostically accurate than the CAPE I/O test (Johnston *et al.*, 1987) and adds little to the discrimination achieved by the MSQ (Eastwood *et al.*, 1983). The OMCT has also been found to be as discriminating as the ICMT (Katzma *et al.*, 1983) and to possess advantages over the MMS (Fillenbaum *et al.*, 1987). In short, the brief mental status tests appear preferable to the longer and less homogeneous versions, though the extreme brevity of the OMCT may reduce its stability as a classificatory index (Lesher and Whelihan, 1986).

Apart from their use in classifying and staging broad degrees of mental impairment, mental status tests have frequently been used as dependent measures in studies evaluating therapies to impove memory, orientation and general mental competence. A particular focus upon orientation and personal knowledge and memories has characterized such psychological approaches as Reality Orientation, Reminiscence Therapy and Memory Training. Dissatisfied with the limitations of standard mental status tests to reflect changes in personal orientation and recall, several psychologists have developed 'individualized' mental status/personal orientation questionnaires (Greene *et al.*, 1979; Woods, 1983). These are felt to be more sensitive to change and to represent more faithfully the personal approach of such orienting and training procedures. A good example of the sort of information contained in such personal orientation questionnaires can be found in Greene (1984).

BEHAVIOURAL COMPETENCE

While related to levels of mental competence, it is not possible to predict variations in behavioural competence simply from a knowledge of scores on mental tests (Winograd, 1984). This is no doubt the result of the multiply determined components of behavioural competence. Despite these complexities, it is possible to see two broad areas which in turn relate to the more general issue of what constitutes mental health and adult psychological maturity. One aspect emphasizes autonomy and independence in sustaining an adult life structure; the other stresses the interpersonal engagements that characterize adult identities. The former dimension may be called 'dependency versus autonomy', and relates to such measurement issues as 'self-help' and 'activities of daily living'; the latter may be called 'engagement versus isolation', and relates to such measurement issues as 'apathy' or 'activity level'.

While it may be impossible to remain fully and intimately engaged within an adult social network when one becomes completely dependent upon others, it seems of heuristic value to consider these two areas as separate measurement dimensions, the lower ends of which reflect different aspects of impairment in health and personal well-being. Figure 11.1 represents such a two-dimensional approach to conceptualizing behavioural competence.

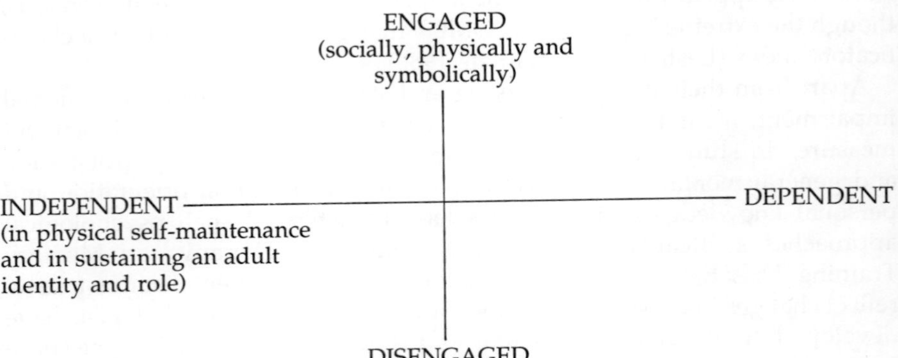

Figure 11.1 Dimensions of behavioural competence in adulthood and ageing

Dependency

Assessment of dependency in old age has usually relied upon observer-completed rating scales, performance ratings or self-report measures to indicate the degree of limitation in activities of daily living. However, cross-method comparability of dependency scores cannot be assumed (cf. Kuriansky *et al.*, 1976; Reifler *et al.*, 1981; Little *et al.*, 1986). Moreover, certain areas of independence in self-care cannot be measured by performance tests (e.g. the ability to retain and void urine appropriately) while other areas are not sensibly measured through self-report (e.g. getting lost and confused). The independent observer completing a rating scale might seem to be the most objective recorder of an old person's dependency, but studies have shown the importance of rater bias in completing such scales (May, 1972). The different measures (self-report, behaviour rating and performance test) have been used in varying settings and for different purposes, while maintaining the semblance of comparability by referring to the measure as one of dependency or disability. As a result, it is difficult to draw comparisons across different sectors of care such as community versus institution. Adapting hospital/nursing home rating scales for use with family informants is often difficult because of the content of the hospital scales (e.g. the Physical and Mental Impairment of Function—Elderly scale (or PAMIE), Gurel *et al.*, 1972; or the Geriatric Rating Scale (or GRS), Plutchik *et al.*, 1970). The CAPE Behaviour Rating Scale (BRS) is a significant exception to many such behaviour rating scales since it provides normative data across a number of different community and institutional settings (Pattie and Gilleard, 1979).

Like other scales such as the GRS or PAMIE, the CAPE BRS employs a much broader concept of dependency than that reflected in Activity of Daily Living (ADL) scales. The latter tend to be unidimensional and restricted to feeding, dressing, bathing and use of the toilet. Performance-based tests of ADL are likewise unidimensional but subject to the unknown influence of the performance setting (e.g. the occupational therapy room). Inevitably, the choice of dependency measure depends upon the goals of the assessment. In Table 11.2 an attempt has been made to include a variety of different approaches to dependency.

Interview-based measures of dependency such as Lawton's Self Care and Instrumental Activities of Daily Living Scale can best be considered for population screening to identify differing levels of need in the community. Performance tests may prove most useful in assessing the progress of rehabilitation and in considering the prognosis for return from hospital to the community. Behaviour ratings of narrow ADL-dependency may also be used to assess rehabilitation needs and outcome, while broader multidimensional ratings can prove of value in determining decisions for appropriate long-term care placement and in evaluating therapy where they may prove

Table 11.2 Measures of dependency for use with elderly people.

Measure	Author	Type of scale
Index of Activities of Daily Living	Katz *et al.* (1963)	Behaviour ratings
Geriatric Rating Scale	Plutchik *et al.* (1970)	Behaviour ratings
Physical and Mental Impairment of Function—Elderly	Gurel *et al.* (1972)	Behaviour ratings
CAPE Behaviour Rating Scale	Pattie and Gilleard (1979)	Behaviour ratings
Barthel Index	Mahoney and Barthel (1965)	Performance ratings
Kenny Self-Care Evaluation Form	Schoening and Iverson (1968)	Performance ratings
Performance Test of Activities of Daily Living	Kuriansky and Gurland (1976)	Performance ratings
Physical Self-Maintenance and Instrumental ADL	Lawton and Brodie (1969)	Self/informant report
Interview Schedule for Disability	Garrard and Bennett (1971)	Self-report/interview
Framingham Disability Index	Pinsky *et al.* (1985)	Self-report/interview

more sensitive to change than cognitive tests. In some clinical situations comparison between performance-based indices of ADL and self-report measures may provide useful information concerning the insight a particular patient may have into his or her own limitations.

Engagement

Like independence, successful engagement may prove difficult to maintain for some people as they grow old. As with independence, engagement is a complex construct that may not easily be measured by a unidimensional instrument. At the lowest end of the dimension degrees of disengagement can be observed, down to the absence of responsivity to one's social and physical surroundings' while at the upper end of the dimension variations in level of engagement will reflect the depth and extent of elderly people's active and symbolic participation in their community. Measures typically concerned with degrees of apathy and disengagement include the structured interview and ratings that make up Farina's Minimal Social Behaviour scale (see Dastoor *et al.*, 1975, for details of the scale and its use with psychogeriatric patients); the 'apathy' subscales of such multidimensional behaviour rating scales as the CAPE BRS and the Multidimensional Observation Scale for Elderly Subjects (MOSES, Helmes *et al.*, 1987); and the numerous direct behaviour observation techniques (Jenkins *et al.*, 1978; McFadyen, 1984).

Direct observation studies have almost entirely been confined to this aspect of functioning in the elderly. Typically, such methods record levels of conversation, participation in tasks and recreation, together with more general aspects of activity such as walking, sitting or dozing. Such techniques are particularly useful as a means of evaluating the nature and quality of life in different institutional settings, where the focus is upon person–environment transactions rather than upon person variables. A particularly valuable illustration of this approach may be found in the work of Godlove and her colleagues, illuminating the nature of institutional life in some of Britain's care settings for the elderly (Godlove *et al.*, 1982). Another valuable illustration of direct behaviour observation of activity and interaction patterns can be found in Hanley (1984), where he examines the reality of '24 hour Reality Orientation' staff practices. When these techniques are used directly to assess more person-related aspects of engagement (as in studies examining engagement levels and depression) the results have proved disappointing (cf. Simpson *et al.*, 1981; Davies and Gledhill, 1983). Because the behaviours studied by such observational techniques reflect the influence of the setting as much as the characteristics of the persons in the setting, they may be less useful in identifying significant individual differences.

Self-report measures of engagement have usually been obtained from individuals who are inherently more independent of their environment (i.e. not institutionalized) and hence more likely to reflect individual differences in the choices of settings where the elderly person is engaged. Surprisingly, such 'higher' levels of engagement have rarely been the topic of psychometric study. The early social gerontological research on disengagement tended to use *ad hoc* indices to classify elderly people into engaged or disengaged categories. Recently, however, Morgan and his colleagues have developed a short questionnaire designed to assess both active (attending clubs) and symbolic (voting, reading a daily paper) levels of engagement (e.g. Morgan *et al.*, 1987). Their scale appears reasonably homogeneous and is significantly related to measures of mood and morale. Extensive normative data have been gathered on samples of young–old and old–old British subjects. Directed at a similar dimension of behaviour, Lawton's Time Use-Effectance scale is another self-report index of the number of ways the elderly person passes his or her time in 'non-instrumental' activity (Lawton *et al.*, 1982). Further research is particularly needed to clarify the interrelationships between engagement, leisure participation and physical activity and how these characteristics in turn influence mood and well-being in the elderly.

MOTOR BEHAVIOUR

The measurement of motor behaviour in the elderly encompasses a number of different phenomena ranging from physical activity and exercise to fine and gross motor control and general response speed. Despite being of considerable relevance to a number of diverse fields in psychology and psychiatry, this is a topic which is often neglected in considering assessment techniques.

Writers such as Welford (1962) and Birren (1974) have considered slowing of response times to be one of the most central features of normal ageing in the central nervous system. While the measurement of reaction times is dependent upon a variety of procedural factors which restrict the utility of such tasks to laboratory-based research, alternative measures of response speed are available which appear to reflect the same general component of psychomotor slowing. Typically, these have involved continuous response measures such as the Digit Copying Test from the Kendrick Battery for the Detection of Dementia (KBDD, Gibson and Kendrick, 1979), the Finger Tapping Test from the Halstead–Reitan test battery (Reitan, 1977), various Letter Cancellation tasks and the Gibson Spiral Maze test (Gibson, 1972). Normative data for most of these measures are available. However, such measures may be less sensitive to changes in CNS functioning than more experimentally based indices, while being of little diagnostic value in identifying 'pathological' aspects of ageing.

In contrast, measures of both fine and gross motor control may bear a much closer relationship to pathological aspects of ageing in the central nervous system. Error rather than slowness may reveal the breakdown of CNS control mechanisms. Thus Morgan (1985) showed that residual sedation effects of hypnotics led to increases in error in a target-tapping task rather than in slowing of tapping speed. Likewise, errors on the Gibson Spiral Maze rather than speed of performance bear the strongest association with mental impairment in the elderly (Pattie and Gilleard, 1979).

Localized deteriorative conditions affecting motor control in old age such as Parkinson's disease and Huntington's chorea have been investigated with instruments designed to assess aspects of motor behaviour. Mortimer *et al.* (1982) describe a form of pursuit rotor test to measure the degree of bradykinesia in Parkinson patients, while Trzepasz and Webb (1987) developed a rod and ring device to record the severity of chorea during voluntary movements. Accelerometers have been applied to study tremor, while electronic motion sensors have been used to assess retardation in elderly depressives. The increasing use of mechanical and electronic equipment to study disorders of motor control in middle-aged and elderly neuropsychiatric populations may lead to more objective and more sensitive evaluations of treatment and disease processes.

At present, such treatment and disease process studies have tended to use rating scales as a means of assessing the severity of movement disorder. Examples include the Colombia University Parkinson's Disease Rating Scale (Lesser *et al.*, 1979) and Simpson's Tardive Dyskinesia Rating Scale (Simpson *et al.* 1978). Increasing awareness of the role of extrapyramidal signs in dementia suggests that such scales may have application outside of the specific disease categories for which they were first developed. At present, studies of impaired motor control in dementia have rarely made use of such assessment procedures.

Measures of physical activity and exercise have begun to be applied to elderly populations, and an extensive review has been published by LaPorte and his colleagues (LaPorte *et al.*, 1985). They identified a variety of approaches to assessing physical activity, ranging from diary keeping to mechanical recording devices like the pedometer and the more recent electronic motion sensors and accelerometers referred to above. Self-report questionnaires and recording devices seem to assess overlapping rather than identical aspects of activity. Both types of measure could usefully be applied to studies examining health activity and morale in the independent elderly, while useful data could be obtained from the impaired elderly using large-scale integrated motor activity monitors which can record aspects of retardation/agitation in psychogeriatric patients. The reliability of such monitors is reportedly high and they are small enough to be used non-intrusively (LaPorte *et al.*, 1985).

SELF-REPORT OF MOOD, MORALE AND TEMPERAMENT

Despite the poor empirical distinction between measures of mood and morale, conceptually these phenomena differ, as the former refers primarily to the affective domain of experience while the latter reflects a superimposed cognitive–evaluative domain of well-being. Self-rated satisfaction with life has been almost as important a dependent measure as intelligence in the field of psychological gerontology. A comprehensive review of concepts and measures of subjective well-being has been given by Diener (1984), where he notes the many different concepts and measures that have tried to pin down this rather elusive construct. Measures of morale or life satisfaction are rather more stable than those restricted to assessing affective experience, and as such they may be rather unhelpful as indicators of short-term changes arising from therapeutic or environmental change interventions. Indeed some authors suggest that morale and life satisfaction may be as much a reflection of stable temperamental characteristics as they are indicators of the objective 'quality of life' of an elderly person. Without further research the clinical applications of such morale scales may be rather limited.

In contrast, several studies have validated the use of standard self-report mood questionnaires such as the Beck Depression Inventory and the Zung Self-rating Depression Scale (Okimoto *et al.*, 1982; Gallagher *et al.*, 1983), although both are rather long and involve response choices which are not always easily accepted by the elderly. Studies by Snowdon (Snowdon, 1986; Hickie and Snowdon, 1986) have validated a simplified version of the Schwab Depression Scale adapted for use with psychogeriatric patients by Gilleard *et al.* (1981). More recently Morgan *et al.* (1987) have provided extensive normative data on both a morale scale (the LSI-Z, Wood *et al.*, 1969) and a brief measure of anxiety and depression (Bedford *et al.*'s (1976) Personal Disturbance Scale). Validation of the latter scale against psychiatric judgements of depression suggested that the depression scale 'over-classified' the number of people with depression and alternative 'cutting' points are recommended. Table 11.3 provides a summary of self-report measures of both mood and morale which have been applied and found useful with elderly people. More detailed reviews can be found in Diener (1984) and Hovaguimian (1986).

Many patients with long-standing 'grumbling' depression appear to have personality traits which have marked them out as being odd, difficult or in some way socially abrasive. In geriatric rehabilitation centres there are

Table 11.3 Self-report measures of mood and morale for use with elderly subjects.

Measure	Author	Item length
Morale/life satisfaction		
Life Satisfaction Index (LSI)	Neugarten *et al.* (1961)	20
Life Satisfaction Index—Z (LSI-Z)	Wood *et al.* (1960)	13
Affect Balance Scale (ABS)	Bradburn (1969)	10
Philadelphia Geriatric Center Morale Scale (PGCMS)	Lawton (1975)	17
Memorial University of Newfoundland Scale of Happiness (MUNSH)	Kozma and Stones (1980)	24
Mood		
Beck Depression Inventory (BDI)	Beck *et al.* (1961)	21
Zung Self-rating Depression Scale (SDS)	Zung (1965)	20
SAD/Personal Disturbance Scale (SAD/PDS)	Bedford *et al.* (1976)	14
Modified Schwab Depression Scale (MSDS)	Gilleard *et al.* (1981)	10
Geriatric Depression Scale (GDS)	Yesavage *et al.* (1983)	30

patients whose lack of progress seems inexplicable in terms of their physical improvement. Both these situations suggest the need to assess aspects of temperament in the elderly when considering their clinical management. Personality questionnaires have usually been developed for younger student-aged populations and only rarely are data presented which permit valid application to the elderly. No formal personality ratings that could be completed by a relative have found wide use, and at present the 'life history' that accompanies the elderly person offers the best insight into those stable and enduring habits that may be said to describe the individual elderly person's character.

OBSERVER-COMPLETED MEASURES OF PSYCHIATRIC STATUS

The increasing use of operational techniques in psychiatric nosology has led to a number of standardized interview and rating schedules such as the Present State Examination and the Schedule for Affective Disorders and Schizophrenia. Parallel developments in geriatric psychiatry have resulted in similar structured interview methods focusing in greater detail upon the more prevalent symptomatology in old age. An added impetus has come from the increasing research on the dementias, and the need for operational methods of staging the severity of dementia and differentiating between dementias of apparently differing aetiology. This section will consider first, semi-structured interview methods and then, standardized ratings as methods of quantifying aspects of psychiatric status in the elderly.

Semi-structured interview methods

Probably the best-known interview technique for use with elderly psychiatric patients is the Geriatric Mental State (GMS, Copeland *et al.*, 1976). Employing a combination of self-report answers to structured questions, indices of performance on mental status type items and behavioural observation, the GMS sought to standardize the routine psychiatric examination of the elderly patient as part of a US/UK cross-national study of mental disorders among the elderly admitted to hospital in New York and London. Since then, a number of revisions have been made, including a shortened version for use in community epidemiological studies and a computerized system of assigning diagnoses on the basis of a hierarchical set of algorithms called AGECAT (Copeland *et al.*, 1987). While there is considerable evidence of the reliability of this procedure, the problem of validating the interview method (in contrast, say, to the AGECAT diagnoses) is difficult to resolve.

Inevitably much of the focus of validation has concerned distinguishing between depression and dementia, and early dementia from 'benign' ageing.

A simpler structured interview schedule that relies entirely upon self-report answers for diagnostic ascertainment is the Survey Psychiatric Assessment Schedule for the elderly (SPAS, Bond *et al.*, 1980). This interview consists of a set of over 50 questions which are grouped into three sections covering 'organic disorders', 'schizophrenic and paranoid disorders' and 'affective and neurotic disorders'. Designed for lay interviewers and resembling an interview-assisted application of a mood questionnaire, mental status test and a very short MMPI, the schedule was found to have moderately high levels of agreement when contrasted with GMS-based diagnoses. In many ways it is a weaker form of the 'Community Version' of the GMS itself.

A more complicated recent instrument, termed the Cambridge Mental Disorders of the Elderly Examination (CAMDEX, Roth *et al.*, 1986), has been described. The CAMDEX consists of structured interview sections, cognitive tests, behavioural observations, plus information from informants. Separate sections record the results of physical and laboratory examinations. The main advantage over the GMS that the CAMDEX seems to offer is the greater differentiation of organic syndromes. These are classified into six different syndrome groups on the CAMDEX, namely delirious states (1) with and (2) without dementia; (3) senile dementia of Alzheimer type; (4) multi-infarct dementia; (5) mixed Alzheimer type/multi-infarct dementia; and (6) dementia due to other causes. Such discriminations are only capable of validation against post-mortem criteria, and hence the value of the CAMDEX awaits the results of the appropriate studies.

Psychopathological rating scales

One of the first rating scales designed specifically to measure the severity of psychopathology in elderly patients was the Sandoz Clinical Assessment—Geriatric scale (SCAG, Shader *et al.*, 1974). This rating scale consisted of 18 symptom areas, each of which is rated on a 7-point scale. The initial report on the scale was not especially encouraging. Several items had low inter-rater reliability and the validity of the scale was based upon only 11 depressed, 15 dementing and 20 healthy elderly subjects. Nevertheless, the SCAG appears to have been used widely in psychopharmacological research and a more detailed manual for users has subsequently been published (Venn, 1983). Although this is likely to improve reliability, it remains to be seen whether the 7-point rating system for each item can be used consistently and discriminatingly in either routine clinical settings or in therapy trials requiring numerous rating occasions.

Psychopharmacological concerns have not been the only motivating force behind attempts to devise rating scales to assess psychopathology in the elderly. Measuring the stage and severity of dementia has been the explicit goal of several recent rating systems. The Global Deterioration Scale (GDS, Reisberg *et al.*, 1982) and the Clinical Dementia Rating Scale (CDR, Hughes *et al.*, 1982) are both designed to grade the severity of dementia on the basis of performance on mental status tests, psychometric tests, behavioural observations and reports from informants. The methods as described are by no means straightforward to apply in practice. The Alzheimer's Disease Assessment Scale (ADAS, Rosen *et al.*, 1984) appears more promising. It covers a wider range of cognitive and non-cognitive behaviours, has high inter-rater reliability and internal reliability, and has shown differential sensitivity to the decline associated with dementia in follow-up studies. It may reflect clinical change more sensitively than either the GDS or CDR and should prove more objective in its scoring than the SCAG. A weakness of the ADAS is that for some items it treats as equivalent the information from the patient or from a relative, an assumption unjustified by research findings addressing this issue (Reifler *et al.*, 1981).

Pre-dating all the above rating systems is the Blessed Dementia Rating Scale (DRS, Blessed *et al.*, 1968). Originally developed as a means of scoring severity of dementia for comparison with post-mortem findings, the successful validation in the original study has not been backed up by data on other psychometric properties of the scale. Recent reports have questioned the diagnostic validity of the ratings (e.g. Eastwood *et al.*, 1983; Roth *et al.*, 1986) but it continues to be widely used.

Another popular yet psychometrically dubious rating measure is the Ischaemia Scale, developed by Hachinski and his colleagues (IS, Hachinski *et al.*, 1975). Based upon 13 items intended to provide a clinical differentiation between dementia due to vascular changes (multi-infarct dementia) and that due to primary atrophy (Alzheimer-type dementia), the scale consists of behavioural observations, neurological examination findings and records of the development of the disease, presumably obtained from an informant. Liston and LaRue (1983a, b) have provided a detailed and critical review of the scale, pointing out that only one independent validation study had been reported, supporting the scale's power to discriminate between these two forms of dementia. In this study (Rosen *et al.*, 1980) only five of the 13 signs proved to be discriminating and these largely referred to the history of past strokes. In the single inter-rater reliability study that they were able to trace, a coefficient of only +0.39 was obtained. Since this review a further validation study has been conducted by Hachinski and his colleagues (Wade *et al.*, 1987). While they found that low scores (4 and below) were consistently related to post-mortem findings of Alzheimer-like pathology, high scores (over 5) were not confined to cases of MID. The IS then is better used to exclude vascular causes in selecting dementia cases for study or therapy trials rather than as a means of positively identifying cases of MID.

In contrast to dementia, relatively little consideration has been given to developing psychiatric rating scales for non-dementing elderly psychiatric patients. The Hamilton Depression Rating Scale (HDRS, Hamilton, 1967) remains the most widely used scale in studies of depression in old age. Hovaguimian (1986), in his review of instruments to measure depression in the elderly, concludes that the HDRS appears sensitive to antidepressant effects in therapy trials. At the same time, it is difficult to find information on the reliability of this scale with elderly patients. One recent study reports an inter-rater reliability of +0.68, which compares unfavourably with reported levels of inter-rater reliability in general adult psychiatry (values of +0.87 to +0.95 are cited by Hamilton, 1986). Griffiths *et al.* (1987) have described a modification of the HDRS for use as a semi-structured interview/questionnaire with elderly subjects in the community, but again reliability data are lacking.

An 8-item Depressive Signs Scale (DSS, Katona and Aldridge, 1985) has also been described as a means of rating affective disturbance in mentally frail elderly patients. The initial report indicates high inter-rater reliability for each item and for the total score, but there appears to have been no further work done on this promising scale.

Finally attention needs to be given to another widely used scale in general adult psychiatry that has also been used with psychogeriatric patients, namely the Brief Psychiatric Rating Scale (BPRS, Overall and Gorham, 1962). Beller and Overall (1983) have described various psychopathological profiles observed from ratings of elderly psychiatric patients, but it seems unlikely that the BPRS encompasses the type of symptomatology that would permit its use as a rating system to discriminate diagnostically or to measure the severity of such conditions as dementia or depression in old age. Table 11.4 briefly summarizes some of the main rating scales for assessing psychopathology in the elderly.

PHYSICAL ASSESSMENTS IN DEMENTIA

Dementia is 'the decline of memory and other cognitive functions in comparison with the patient's previous level of function as determined by a history of decline in performance and by abnormalities noted from clinical examination and neuropsychological tests. A diagnosis of dementia cannot be made when consciousness is impaired by delirium, drowsiness, stupor or coma or when other clinical abnormalities prevent adequate evaluation of mental status' (McKhann *et al.*, 1984).

Table 11.4 Psychopathological rating scales for use with elderly patients.

Measure	Author(s)	Purpose
Dementia Rating Scale (DRS)	Blessed *et al.* (1968)	Rating the severity of dementia
Global Deterioration Scale (GDS)	Reisberg *et al.* (1982)	Staging the course of primary degenerative dementias
Clinical Dementia Rating (CDR)	Hughes *et al.* (1982)	Staging the severity of dementia
Alzheimer's Disease Assessment Scale (ADAS)	Rosen *et al.* (1984)	Evaluating the overall severity of dementia
18-item Brief Psychiatric Rating Scale (BPRS)	Overall and Gorham (1982)	Rating the severity of diffuse psychiatric symptomatology, including depression and dementia
Sandoz Clinical Assessment—Geriatric (SCAG)	Shader *et al.* (1974)	Rating the severity of diffuse psychogeriatric symptomatology, especially depression and dementia
Ischaemia Scale (IS)	Hachinski *et al.* (1975)	Discriminating between primary degenerative dementia and multi-infarct dementia
Hamilton Depression Rating Scale	Hamilton (1967)	Rating the severity of affective symptoms but not specifically designed for elderly
Depressive Signs Scale (DSS)	Katona and Aldridge (1985)	Rating the severity of affective signs and symptoms, especially in the impaired elderly

The emphasis in this section will be on biological measures that may help advance our knowledge about the nature of dementia and they will be considered under the headings of imaging, electrophysiological, biochemical and molecular genetic measures.

Imaging techniques

Computerized tomography (CT)

The advent of CT in 1973 (Hounsfield, 1973; Ambrose, 1973) and its subsequent refinement were major advances in neuroradiology, and CT remains the diagnostic imaging technique most used in routine clinical practice. The CT scan is a computerized reconstruction of the relative radiodensities to

X-rays of a slice of brain. It can differentiate brain tissue, cerebrospinal fluid (CSF), bone and any damage to the brain that alters its radiodensity.

There have been many CT studies in ageing and dementia (Bird, 1982). From the fourth decade onwards, CSF space increases but the major increase only occurs after the age of 60, when there are rapid age-dependent increases in ventricular size and widening of the sulci (Takeda and Matsuzawa, 1984). These changes, which are signs of cerebral atrophy, are substantially greater in patients with dementia compared with age-matched normal subjects. There is, however, considerable overlap with the normal elderly population. Jacoby *et al.* (1980) found that 20 per cent of normal elderly people have ventricles which are larger than expected for their age, whereas 25 per cent of dements have ventricles within the normal range. Thus, evidence of cerebral atrophy on CT can only support a clinical diagnosis of dementia. CT, however, is important in the differential diagnosis of dementia, identifying such pathology as cerebral infarctions, subdural haematomas and brain tumours.

Ventricular enlargement on CT correlates better than enlargement of the sulci with impaired performance in cognitive tests (Jacoby and Levy, 1980; Ford and Winter, 1981; Brinkman *et al.*, 1981). Blind ratings of the degree of cerebral atrophy made by neuroradiologists proved to be a better diagnostic indicator of dementia than various planimetric measures of ventricular size (Jacoby and Levy, 1980).

A CT scan is recommended as a routine measure in the investigation of patients with mild to moderate dementia who would be fit for neurosurgical intervention should a potentially reversible cause be identified (for example, subdural haematoma, cerebral tumour or normotensive hydrocephalus). In a CT investigation of 500 patients with dementia (Bradshaw *et al.*, 1983) four were identified who had a subdural haematoma and six had normotensive hydrocephalus. Cerebral tumours are more frequently found but only a small proportion are operable.

Magnetic resonance imaging

Magnetic resonance imaging (MRI) provides anatomical information on slices through the brain similar to CT (Bydder, 1984) but also provides limited biochemical information since the relaxation parameter T_1 and T_2 (spin–lattice and spin–spin relaxation times, respectively) associated with the magnetic resonance phenomenon broadly correlate with tissue water content and cellular water binding (Mathur de Vre, 1984). MRI uses radiofrequency radiation in the presence of a carefully controlled magnetic field to generate high-quality cross-sectional images of the brain.

The discrimination between grey and white matter and the definition of focal lesions such as infarcts, tumours and demyelination is better with MRI than with CT. A method for the measurement of cerebral atrophy by quantifying ventricular and extra-ventricular CSF volumes using MRI has been described (Condon *et al.*, 1986) but has not been used to relate atrophy to cognitive deficits in dementia.

The utility of quantitative measures of proton density, and of T_1 and T_2, in the investigation of dementia appears to be limited. Besson *et al.* (1985) initially reported that in a population of chronically hospitalized senile dementia patients, proton density and T_1 values were useful in distinguishing between ATD and MID patients and also between dementia patients and control subjects. However, in a recent study of presenile ATD patients, which spanned a wide range of severity of dementia, we found T_1 values to be similar in ATD patients and age-matched control subjects (Christie *et al.*, 1988). Furthermore, there was no relationship between the severity of dementia on neuropsychological testing and T_1 values measured in any of the brain regions of interest, although frontal T_1 values tended to be increased in individual ATD patients when a scan was repeated 18 months after the original scan. In patients with MID and alcoholic Korsakov's syndrome, T_1 values were increased in frontal and parietal grey and white matter, but there was considerable variability and some overlap with the normal population. Therefore, at present MRI is not a particularly useful measure in dementia and its role is similar to that of CT; that is, defining structural lesions in the brain and contributing to the differential diagnosis of dementia.

Cerebral blood flow (CBF)

There have been many advances in the measurement of CBF since the pioneering work of Kety and Schmidt (1948), who developed the nitrous oxide method of measuring hemispheric blood flow. This technique was adapted to allow the external detection of inert gas radiotracers, initially Krypton-85 (Lassen and Ingvar, 1961) and later Xenon-133 (Veall and Mallett, 1966; Risberg *et al.*, 1975). Although there have been advances in detectors and data analysis together with the use of multiple probes, this technique does not allow the measurement of regional CBF (rCBF) in deep brain structures and cannot measure rCBF in transverse sectors of the brain. Recently, tomographic imaging techniques have been developed for the measurement of rCBF, namely single-photon emission tomography (SPET) (Stokely *et al.*, 1980; Devous *et al.*, 1986) and positron emission tomography (PET) (Phelps *et al.*, 1982). These two techniques are not restricted to the measurement of rCBF and PET has been used to measure regional glucose metabolism (rCMR glu) and regional oxygen metabolism (rCMR O_2) and can be used to measure the distribution in the brain of a potentially wide range of radiopharmaceuticals labelled with positron emitters such as oxygen-15, fluorine-18 and carbon-11.

Studies of rCBF in dementia using the xenon-133 inhalation method have in general shown reduced CBF and the greater the reduction, the more severe the dementia. CBF is closely coupled to cerebral metabolism, thus CBF reflects reduced metabolism. Specific patterns of rCBF disturbances are present in different types of dementia (Gustafson and Risberg, 1979). In ATD the major flow reductions are in parietal and parietotemporal regions, whereas in Pick's Disease (in which atrophy affects primarily the frontal cortex) the lowest flow values are seen in premotor, supplementary motor and prefrontal regions.

The highly technical and expensive technique of PET provides unique information on cerebral metabolism and neurotransmission. The resolution of PET, however, is poor compared with CT or MRI because of the distance travelled (± 1 mm) by the emitted positrons before annihilation on collision with an electron. This annihilation reaction results in two high-energy γ-ray photons which travel at 180 degrees to one another and can be registered by a ring of external detectors. A picture of the activity pattern can be built up within a series of contiguous transverse axial brain slides (Phelps *et al.*, 1982). PET is expensive because it requires an on-site cyclotron to generate the radiopharmaceuticals which have an extremely short half-life.

Glucose metabolism, oxygen utilization and blood flow have all been measured in dementia, particularly in ATD, but there have also been studies in patients with Huntington's Disease and in MID. The positron-emitting analogue ^{18}F-fluorodeoxyglucose is used to measure rCMR glu using an adaption of the 2-deoxyglucose method (Sokoloff *et al.*, 1977). Studies in ATD have generally found a significant reduction in cortical CMR glu with the most consistent reductions in parietotemporal regions (Friedland *et al.*, 1983; Foster *et al.*, 1984). In Huntington's Disease there is a characteristic decrease in glucose utilization in the basal ganglia, and this local hypometabolism can be detected early in the disease and may be present in asymptomatic potential carriers of the autosomal dominant gene for Huntington's Disease (Kuhl *et al.*, 1982).

One of the problems of PET is that it provides measurements per unit volume of intracranial contents, and the measurements are affected by the inclusion of metabolically inactive CSF spaces. This leads to artificially low values in the presence of cerebral atrophy, which is a feature of many dementias. Strategies have been developed to correct global PET measurements for the degree of cerebral atrophy using both quantitative CT and PET scans (Herscovitch *et al.*, 1986) or a correction derived from the measurement of CSF volume using MRI (Condon *et al.*, 1986).

Single-photon emission tomography (SPET)

The major advantage of SPET is the use of radionuclides that are widely available for clinical nuclear medicine studies and it is, therefore, much cheaper than PET. There are, however, more difficulties than with PET in reconstructing a three-dimensional brain image because the isotopes produce softer radiation and are subject to greater scatter. Studies in ATD patients with SPET using the 133-xenon inhalation technique have shown, as with PET, reduced CBF in temporoparietal and, to a lesser extent, frontal regions (Bonte *et al.*, 1986). This finding has been confirmed using the radionuclide *N*-isopopyl-*p*-iodoamphetamine labelled within 123-iodine which is distributed in brain proportionally to CBF (Jagust *et al.*, 1987; Johnson *et al.*, 1987). The radionuclide 99-technetium hexamethylpropyleneamine oxime (d, l-HMPAO) has recently been used in studies of demented patients. It is also distributed in proportion to cerebral blood flow and is retained in the brain for a sufficient time to allow tomographic images to be acquired (Neirinckx *et al.*, 1987). Using this radionuclide, Hunter *et al.* (1989) have shown a reduction of rCBF in ATD most strikingly in posterior temporal and parietal areas. The reduced CBF was related to the severity of the dementia as measured by the total score on the section for assessment of cognitive function in the Cambridge Mental Disorders of the Elderly Examination (CAMDEX) (Roth *et al.*, 1986) and the Mini Mental State Examination (Folstein *et al.*, 1975), and comprehension, remote memory, attention and praxis were related to tracer uptake in the left posterior temporal and left parietal regions.

Electroencephalography (EEG) and evoked potentials

In normal ageing there are changes in the EEG with symmetrical slowing of the alpha rhythm and the appearance of theta and delta slow activity (Pedley and Miller, 1983). These changes are accentuated in ATD and there is some relationship between the severity of cognitive impairment and the amount of slow wave activity (Fenton, 1986). Focal changes are likely to be seen on the EEG in MID and where a cerebral tumour is present, but in the frontal dementia of Pick's Disease the EEG is often surprisingly normal (Stigbsy *et al.*, 1981). The spontaneous EEG, however, lacks specificity and there is considerable overlap between demented and normal elderly subjects. Thus, more recent interest has focused on the use of evoked potentials to give more precise information of changes in brain electrical activity in dementia.

Increases in latency of a number of components of evoked responses to auditory, visual and somatosensory stimulation have been reported in ageing and dementia (Pfefferbaum *et al.*, 1984). The most consistent changes are found in event-related potentials which are late components of the auditory evoked response. The P3 wave has been most extensively studied. This is a positive wave which occurs at approximately 300 ms after an unusual or significant stimulus, and is normally recorded using the 'oddball' paradigm in a two-tone discrimination task. The P3 is thought to relate to the speed of cognitive processing (Dochin *et al.*, 1978) and may be generated in the region of the hippocampus and amygdala (Okada *et al.*, 1983). The latency of the P3 increases with age (Goodin *et al.*, 1978) and there is a further increase in latency and a decrease in amplitude in ATD (Pfefferbaum *et al.*, 1984; St Clair *et al.*, 1985).

Unfortunately, there is a lack of specificity with overlap between ATD patients and age-matched control subjects and latency increases occur in other dementias and also in other conditions such as schizophrenia (Blackwood *et al.*, 1987). In individual ATD patients, the P3 latency increases with progression of the dementia and the increase in latency is related to the degree of cognitive decline (St Clair *et al.*, 1988). The amplitude and latency of the P3 did not change during transient memory improvement induced in ATD patients by the cholinomimetic drug physostigmine (Blackwood and Christie, 1986). Thus, event-related potentials are unlikely to be of value for monitoring the effects of putative new therapies in ATD.

Biochemical measures

Over the past decade, post-mortem studies have provided a wealth of data concerning the neurochemical changes that occur in brain in dementia, particularly ATD. The neurotransmitter that is principally involved is acetylcholine, and damage to the cholinergic system is considered, at least in part, to be responsible for the memory impairment in ATD and certain other dementias (Perry, 1986). Other central neurotransmitters which are reduced in ATD, especially in those cases with an early age of onset, are noradrenaline and 5-hydroxytryptamine (5-HT) with 5-HT_1 and 5-HT_2 receptors also reduced (Yates *et al.*, 1983; Roth, 1986; Palmer *et al.*, 1987). The neuropeptides somatostatin and corticotrophine-releasing factor (CRF) are also decreased, as are receptors for somatostatin but not CRF. Other neuropeptide systems do not appear to be significantly involved in ATD (Rossor and Iversen, 1986).

The hallmarks of the neuropathology of ATD remain the senile plaque and the neurofibrillary tangle described by Alzheimer in 1906 (Perry, 1986). Senile plaques are extraneuronal structures 5-200 μm in diameter made up of nerve processes containing paired helical filaments, glial cells and amyloid fibres; some plaques have an amyloid core (Tomlinson and Corsellis, 1985). Tangles are normally intra-neuronal and are aggregates of paired helical filaments. The amyloid core and probably the paired helical filaments contain A4 protein which is possibly part of a membrane-spanning glycoprotein (Glenner and Wong, 1984; Kang *et al.*, 1987). Much recent interest has been focused on A4 protein as it is encoded on chromosome 21, and patients with Down's syndrome (Trisomy 21) who die after the age of 40 invariably have ATD changes in the brain. Plaques and tangles are most widespread in the cerebral cortex and hippocampus, particularly in the temporal and frontal cortex, but are also seen in subcortical nuclei which project diffusely to the cerebral cortex (German *et al.*, 1987).

The diagnosis of definite ATD remains a neuropathological one, but biochemical measures in blood and cerebrospinal fluid (CSF) are being evaluated as potential tools in the differential diagnosis of dementia. Cortical biopsies show impaired synthesis in acetylcholine in early ATD (Sims *et al.*, 1983), but such an invasive procedure can only in rare circumstances be justifiable in ethical terms.

There are a number of routine biochemical measures used in clinical practice to identify possible reversible causes of dementia. Routine haematological and biochemical tests may identify a physical illness which is contributing to the dementia, and hypothyroidism and vitamin B12 deficiency are rare causes of dementia (Mulley, 1986). Neurosyphilis is now a rarity. Other research measures are geared towards identifying alterations in blood or CSF which reflect the neurochemical changes that occur in the brain in dementia.

Acetylcholinesterase, the enzyme that breaks down acetylcholine, is reduced in the brain in ATD. Plasma levels of acetylcholinesterase do not, however, appear to be reduced in ATD, and although some studies have found a reduction in CSF, there is a lack of consistency with other studies reporting normal levels (St Clair *et al.*, 1986; Rasmussin *et al.*, 1988). Reductions in several neurochemical parameters have been found in lumbar CSF; these include 5-HT and its metabolite (5-hydroxyindole acetic acid), the dopamine metabolite homovanillic acid, GABA, CRF and ACTH, but there has been no consistent replication of any of these findings (Volicer *et al.*, 1985; Bareggi *et al.*, 1982; May *et al.*, 1987). The most consistent finding in CSF is a reduction in somatostatin (Wood *et al.*, 1982) but, like many of the other measures, the reduction in somatostatin is not specific to ATD and occurs in other degenerative neurological diseases. Interest is now focused on levels of A4 protein in CSF. None of these measures appear useful at present as diagnostic tests for ATD or other types of dementia.

Neuroendocrine measures

The neuroendocrine approach has been used to determine whether the impaired functioning of central neurotransmitter systems is reflected in plasma concentrations of pituitary hormones whose outputs are controlled by these same neurotransmitter systems. Acetylcholine, noradrenaline, 5-HT, CRF and somatostatin are all reduced in ATD, particularly with early age of onset, and all these neurotransmitter systems are involved in the control of the secretion of pituitary hormones (Reichlin, 1985). The dexamethasone-suppression test was used in several studies to try to discriminate between early dementia and depression in the elderly. These studies suggested that 40–50 per cent of dementia patients had early escape from dexamethasone suppression (Raskind *et al.*, 1982; Balldin *et al.*, 1983; Coppen *et al.*, 1983), an incidence similar to that in endogenous depression (Carroll *et al.*, 1981). More recent studies suggest that only severely demented ATD patients have early escape from dexamethasone suppression and that increased evening cortisol concentrations are correlated with the severity of dementia (Christie *et al.*, 1987).

In a systematic investigation of hormone secretion throughout the day in patients with presenile ATD, patients with other dementias, patients with major depressive disorder and age-matched control subjects, characteristic plasma hormone changes were found to be associated with ATD. Presenile ATD patients, particularly female, have elevated TSH and growth hormone concentrations in the presence of otherwise normal thyroid indices. TSH concentrations above the normal range were found in 47 per cent of female ATD and in none of the other female patients or control subjects (Christie *et al.*, 1988). The high TSH and growth hormone concentrations may reflect the reduced somatostatin concentrations in hypothalamus somatostatin acting to inhibit both TSH and growth hormone secretion. Plasma concentrations of oestrogen-stimulated neurophysin (ESN), the neurophysin associated with oxytocin, were lower throughout the day in ATD compared with all the other groups, and there was a delayed response of ESN secretion after administration of oestrogen in ATD patients. No ATD patient in this study had plasma ESN concentrations greater than 170 pmol, whereas 50 per cent of patients with other presenile dementias had ESN concentrations above this level, and ESN concentrations may provide a test to exclude ATD. In a concurrent post-mortem study, ESN concentrations were shown to be reduced in the pituitary gland in ATD (Christie *et al.*, 1989).

Molecular genetics

A number of dementias have a clear genetic component to their aetiology. Huntington's Disease is inherited as an autosomal gene and there are reports of a small number of ATD families where the pattern of transmission suggests a Mendelian dominant with at least 30 published reports of such families (Goudsmit *et al.*, 1981). Most ATD families, however, have only one affected member with only 15–35 per cent of ATD probands having an affected first-degree relative (Kay, 1986). All the family studies of ATD show there is an increase in cumulative risk in first-degree relatives at successive ages and the cumulative risk is several times higher than in controls. The mode of inheritance of ATD with the exception of the rare subgroup showing an autosomal dominant pattern is unclear. Both a polygenetic mode of transmission (Sjogren *et al.*, 1952) and the age-dependent expression of an autosomal dominant gene (Breitner *et al.*, 1986) have been proposed. Multi-infarct dementia is also increased in families together with other vascular disease.

There is a clear association between ATD and Down's syndrome (trisomy-21), with studies showing that 96–98 per cent of Down's syndrome patients who die over the age of 40 have the characteristic neuropathological and many of the neurochemical changes of ATD (Yates *et al.*, 1983, Wright and Whalley, 1984).

Genetic markers such as specific restriction fragment length polymorphism would be of great value in the differential diagnosis of dementia and in identifying carriers of the defective gene in 'at-risk' relatives. Gusella *et al.* (1983) reported a polymorphic DNA marker on chromosome 4 linked to Huntington's Disease. This G8 probe is not necessarily reliable in identifying who will develop the disease because there is a possibility of heterogeneity on the Huntington's gene locus. Thus, this marker remains restricted in its use to research studies.

Recently there has been great interest in molecular genetic studies of ATD. A complementary DNA clone encoding for the A4 polypeptide has been isolated, sequenced and the gene localized to chromosome 21 (Kang *et al.*, 1987; Goldgaber *et al.*, 1987). The gene is expressed in a number of human tissues in addition to the brain, and, as expected, with the increased gene dosage the messenger RNA for A4 is increased in Down's brain (Tanzi *et al.*, 1987a). In addition, analysis of four families with dominant inheritance of ATD has shown two genetic markers identifying a defective region on the proximal part of the long arm of chromosome 21 which segregates with ATD (St. George-Hyslop *et al.*, 1987). Subsequent to these findings, the hypothesis was proposed that predisposition to ATD was due to an over-expression of A4 protein or an abnormal variant of this protein (Tanzi *et al.*, 1987a; Delabar *et al.*, 1987). This hypothesis has now been rejected because linkage studies show that the A4 gene does not segregate with the familial Alzheimer gene; that is their loci are widely separated on chromosome 21 (van Broeckhoven *et al.*, 1987). The claim by Delabar *et al.* (1987) that 'non-familial' cases of ATD resulted from duplication of the A4 gene has been rejected following two studies which failed to provide confirmation (Tanzi *et al.*, 1987b; van Brockhoven *et al.*, 1987). Although it can now be concluded that the A4 gene is not a marker for ATD, there remains considerable interest in this area, and molecular genetic measures remain a focus for research into the aetiology of and diagnosis of dementias.

REFERENCES

Albert, M.S. (1981) Geriatric neuropsychology. *Journal of Consulting and Clinical Psychology*, **49**, 835–50.

Ambrose, J. (1973) Computerized transverse axial scanning (tomography). Part 2 Clinical application. *British Journal of Radiology*, *46*, 1023–47.

Anthony, J.C., Le Resche, L.A., Niaz, U., Von Korff, M.R. and Folstein, M.F. (1982) Limits of the mini-mental-state as a screening test for dementia and delirium among hospital patients. *Psychological Medicine*, **12**, 397–408.

Bak, J.S. and Greene, R.L. (1980) Changes in neuropsychological functioning in an ageing population. *Journal of Consulting and Clinical Psychology*, **48**, 395–9.

Bak, J.S. and Greene, R.L. (1981) A review of the performance of aged adults on various Wechsler Memory Scale subtests. *Journal of Clinical Psychology*, **37**, 186–8.

Balldin, J., Gottfries, C.G., Karlsson, I., Lindstedt, G., Langstrom, G. and Walinder, J. (1983) Dexamethasone suppression test and serum prolactin in dementia disorders. *British Journal of Psychiatry*, **143**, 277–81.

Bareggi, S.R., Frenceschi, M., Bonini, L., Zecca, L. and Smirne, S. (1982) Decreased CSF concentrations of homovanillic acid and γ-aminobutyric acid in Alzheimer's disease. Age- or disease-related modifications? *Archives of Neurology*, **39**, 709–12.

Barona, A., Reynolds, C.R. and Chastain, R., (1984) A demographically based index of pre-morbid intelligence for the WAIS–R. *Journal of Consulting and Clinical Psychology*, **52**, 885–7.

Beck, A.T., Ward, C.H., Mendelson, M., Mock, J. and Erbaugh, J. (1961) An inventory for measuring depression. *Archives of General Psychiatry*, **4**, 561–71.

Bedford, A., Foulds, G.A. and Sheffield, B.F. (1976) A new personal disturbance scale: DSSI/sAD. *British Journal of Social and Clinical Psychology*, **15**, 387–91.

Beller, A. and Overall, J.E. (1984) The Brief Psychiatric Rating Scale (BPRS) in geropsychiatric practice II. Representative profile patterns. *Journal of Gerontology*, **39**, 194–200.

Benton, A.L. (1974) *The Revised Visual Retention Test*, 4th edn, Psychological Corporation, New York.

Besson, J.A.O., Corrigan, F.M., Iljon Foreman, E., Eastwood, L.M., Smith, F.W. and Ashcroft, G.W. (1985) Nuclear magnetic resonance (NMR): II Imaging in dementia. *British Journal of Psychiatry*, **146**, 31–5.

Bird, J.M. (1982) Computerized tomography, atrophy and dementia: a review. *Progress in Neurobiology*, **19**, 91–115.

Birren, J.E. (1974) Translations in gerontology—from lab to life: psychophysiology and speed of response. *American Psychologist*, **29**, 808–17.

Blackwood, D.H.R. and Christie, J.E. (1986) The effects of physostigmine on memory and auditory P300 in Alzheimer-type dementia. *Biological Psychiatry*, **21**, 557–60.

Blackwood, D.H.R., Whalley, L.J., Christie, J.E., Blackburn, I.M., St Clair, D.M. and McInnes, A. (1987) Changes in auditory P3 event-related potential in schizophrenia and depression. *British Journal of Psychiatry*, **150**, 154–60.

Blessed, G., Tomlinson, B.E. and Roth, M. (1968) The association between quantitative measures of dementia and of senile changes in the cerebral grey matter of elderly subjects. *British Journal of Psychiatry*, **114**, 797–811.

Bolton, N., Britton, P.G. and Savage, R.D. (1966) Some normative data on the WAIS and its indices in an aged population. *Journal of Clinical Psychology*, **22**, 184–8.

Bond, J., Brooks, P., Carstairs, V. and Giles, L. (1980) The reliability of a survey psychiatric assessment schedule for the elderly. *British Journal of Psychiatry*, **137**, 148–62.

Bonte, F.J., Ross, E.D., Chehabi, H.H. and Devous, M.D., Sr (1986) SPECT study of regional cerebral blood flow in Alzheimer disease. *Journal of Computer Assisted Tomography*, **10**, 579–83.

Bornstein, R.A. (1985) Normative data on selected neuropsychological measures from a non-clinical sample. *Journal of Clinical Psychology*, **41**, 651–9.

Bradburn, N.M. (1969) *The Structure of Psychological Well-being*, Aldine, Chicago.

Bradshaw, J.R., Thompson, J.G.L. and Campbell, M.J. (1983) Computed tomography in the investigation of dementia. *British Medical Journal*, **286**, 277–89.

Breitner, J.C.S., Folstein, M.F. and Murphy, E.A. (1986) Familial aggregation in Alzheimer dementia—I. A model for the age-dependent expression of an autosomal dominant gene. *Journal of Psychiatric Research*, **20**, 31–43.

Brinkman, S.D., Sarwar, M., Levin, H.S. and Morris, H.H., III (1981) Quantitative indexes of computed tomography in dementia and normal ageing. *Radiology*, **138**, 89–92.

Bydder, G.M. (1984) Nuclear magnetic resonance imaging of the brain. *British Medical Bulletin*, **40**, 170–74.

Carroll, B.J., Feinberg, M., Greden, J.F., Tarika, J., Albala, A.A., Haskett, R.F., James, N. McI., Kronfol, Z., Lohr, N., Steiner, M., de Vigne, J.P. and Young, E. (1981) A specific laboratory test for the diagnosis of melancholia. *Archives of General Psychiatry*, **38**, 15–22.

Christie, J.E., Kean, D.M., Douglas, R.H.B., Engleman, H.M., St Clair, D. and Blackburn, I.M. (1988) Magnetic resonance imaging in pre-senile dementia of the Alzheimer-type, multi-infarct dementia and Korsakoff's syndrome. *Psychological Medicine*, **18**, 319–29.

Christie, J.E., Whalley, L.J., Bennie, J., Dick, H., Blackburn, I.M. and Fink, G. (1987) Characteristic plasma hormone changes in Alzheimer's disease. *British Journal of Psychiatry*, **150**, 674–81.

Christie, J.E., Whalley, L.J., Bennie, J. and Fink, G. (1988) Characteristic plasma hormone changes in Alzheimer's disease. *British Journal of Psychiatry*, **152**, 434–6.

Christie, J.E., Yates, C.M., Fink, G., Bennie, J., Wilson, H., Carroll, S. and Gordon, A. (1989) Oestrogen stimulated neurophysin in Alzheimer-type dementia. Submitted.

Clarke, M., Lowry, R. and Clarke, S. (1986) Cognitive impairment in the elderly—a community survey. *Age and Ageing*, **15**, 278–84.

Condon, B., Patterson, J., Wyper, D., Hadley, D., Teasdale, G., Grant, R., Jenkins, A., Macpherson, P. and Rowan, J. (1986) A quantitative index of ventricular and extraventricular CSF fluid volumes using MR imaging. *Journal of Computer Assisted Tomography*, **10**, 784–92.

Copeland, J.R.M., Kelleher, M.J., Kellett, J.M., Gourlay, A.J., Gurland, B.J., Fleiss, J.L. and Sharpe, L. (1976) A semi-structured clinical interview for the assessment of diagnosis and mental state in the elderly: the Geriatric Mental State Schedule. *Psychological Medicine*, **6**, 439–49.

Copeland, J.R.M., Dewy, M.E., Wood, N., Searle, R., Davidson, I.A. and McWilliam, C. (1987) Range of mental illness among the elderly in the community: prevalence in Liverpool using the GMS-AGECAT package. *British Journal of Psychiatry*, **150**, 815–23.

Coppen, A., Abou-Saleh, M., Milln, P., Metcalfe, M., Harwood, J. and Bailey, J. (1983) Dexamethasone suppression test in depression and other psychiatric illness. *British Journal of Psychiatry*, **142**, 498–504.

Crookes, T.G. and McDonald, K.G. (1972) Benton's Visual Retention Test in the differentiation of depression and early dementia. *British Journal of Social and Clinical Psychology*, **11**, 66–9.

Dastoor, D.P., Norton, S., Boillat, J., Minty, J., Papadopoulou, F. and Muller, H.F. (1975) A psychogeriatric assessment programme. I Social functioning and ward behaviour. *Journal of the American Geriatrics Society*, **23**, 465–71.

Davies, A.D.M. and Gledhill, K.J. (1983) Engagement and depressive symptoms in a community sample of elderly people. *British Journal of Clinical Psychology*, **22**, 95–106.

Delabar, J.M., Goldgaber, D., Lamour, Y., Nicole, A., Huret, J.L., de Grouchy, J., Brown, P., Gadjusek, D.C. and Sinet, P.M. (1987) Amyloid gene duplication in Alzheimer's disease and karyotypically normal Down syndrome. *Science*, **235**, 1390–92.

Devous, M.D., Stokely, M.E., Chehabi, H.H. and Bonte, F.J. (1986) Normal distribution of regional cerebral blood flow measured by dynamic single-photon emission tomography. *Journal of Cerebral Blood Flow and Metabolism*, **5**, 95–194.

Diener, E. (1984) Subjective well-being. *Psychological Bulletin*, **95**, 542–75.

Donchin, E., Ritter, W. and McCallum, W.C. (1978) Cognitive psychophysiology: the endogenous components of the ERP. In E. Callaway, P. Uteting and S. Koslow (eds), *Event-related Potentials in Man*, pp. 349–411, Academic Press, New York.

Eastwood, M.R., Lautenschlaeger, E. and Corbin, S. (1983) A comparison of clinical methods for assessing dementia. *Journal of the American Geriatrics Society*, **31**, 342–8.

Eppinger, M.G., Craig, P.L., Adams, R.L. and Parsons, O.A. (1987) The WAIS-R index for estimating pre-morbid intelligence: cross-validation and clinical utility. *Journal of Consulting and Clinical Psychology*, **55**, 86–90.

Fenton, G.W. (1986) Electrophysiology of Alzheimer's disease. *British Medical Bulletin*, **42**, 29–33.

Fillenbaum, G.G., Heyman, A., Wilkinson, W.E. and Haynes, C.S. (1987) Comparison of two screening tests in Alzheimer's disease. *Archives of Neurology*, **44**, 924–7.

Filley, C.M., Kelly, J. and Heaton, R.K. (1986) Neuropsychologic findings in early- and late-onset Alzheimer's disease. *Archives of Neurology*, **43**, 574–6.

Folstein, M.F., Folstein, S.E. and McHugh, P.R. (1975) Mini-mental-state: a practical guide for grading the cognitive status of patients for the clinician. *Journal of Psychiatric Research*, **12**, 189–98.

Ford, C.V. and Winter, J. (1981) Computerized axial tomograms and dementia in elderly patients. *Journal of Gerontology*, **36**, 164–9.

Foster, N.L., Chase, T.M., Mansi, L., Brooks, R., Fedio, P., Patronas, N.J. and Di Chirco, G. (1984). Cortical abnormalities in Alzheimer's disease. *Annals of Neurology*, **16**, 649–54.

Friedland, R.P., Budinger, T.F., Yano, Y., Huesman, R.H., Knittel, B., Derenzo, S.E., Koss, B. and Ober, B.A. (1983) Regional cerebral metabolic alterations in Alzheimer-type dementia: kinetic studies with 18-fluorodeoxyglucose. *Journal of Cerebral Blood Flow and Metabolism*, **3**, S510–11.

Gallagher, D., Breckenridge, J., Steinmetz, J. and Thompson, L. (1983) The Beck Depression Inventory and Research Diagnostic Criteria: congruence in an older population. *Journal of Consulting and Clinical Psychology*, **51**, 945–6.

Garrard, J. and Bennett, A.E. (1971) A validated interview schedule for use in population surveys of chronic disease and disability. *British Journal of Preventative and Social Medicine*, **25**, 97–102.

German, D.C., White, C.L., III and Sparkman, D.R. (1987). Alzheimer's disease: neurofibrillary tangles in nuclei that project to the cerebral cortex. *Neuroscience*, **21**, 305–12.

Gibson, A.J. and Kendrick, D.C. (1979) *The Kendrick Battery for the Detection of Dementia in the Elderly*, NFER–Nelson, Windsor.

Gibson, H.B. (1972) *Manual for the Gibson Spiral Maze*, Hodder and Stoughton, London.

Gilbert, J. and Levee, R. (1971) Patterns of declining memory. *Journal of Gerontology*, **26**, 70–75.

Gilleard, C.J., Wilmott, M. and Vaddadi, K.S. (1981) Self-report measures of mood and morale in elderly depressives. *British Journal of Psychiatry*, **138**, 230–35.

Glenner, G.G. and Wong, C.W. (1984) Alzheimer's disease and Down's syndrome: sharing of a unique cerebrovascular amyloid fibril protein. *Biochemical and Biophysical Research Communications*, **122**, 1131–5.

Godlove, C., Richard, L. and Rodwell, G. (1982) Time for Action: an Observation Study of Elderly People in Four Different Care Environments. Joint Unit for Social Services Research. University of Sheffield.

Golden, C.J., Purisch, A. and Hammeke, T.A. (1985) *Luria–Nebraska Neuropsychological Battery: Manual*, Western Psychological Services, Los Angeles.

Goldgaber, D., Lerman, M.I., McBride, O.W., Saffiotti, U. and Gajdusek, D.C. (1987) Characterization and chromosomal localization of a cDNA encoding brain amyloid of Alzheimer's disease. *Science*, **235**, 877–84.

Goodin, D.S., Squires, K.C. and Starr, A. (1978). Long latency event-related components of the auditory evoked potential in dementia. *Brain*, **101**, 635–48.

Goudsmit, J., White, B.J., Weitkamp, L.R., Keats, B.J.B., Morrow, C.H. and Gajdusek, D.C. (1981) Familial Alzheimer's disease in two kindreds of the same geographic and ethnic origin. *Journal of Neurological Sciences*, **49**, 79–89.

Greene, J.G., Nichol, R. and Jamieson, H. (1979) Reality orientation with psychogeriatric patients. *Behaviour Research and Therapy*, **17**, 615–18.

Greene, J.G. (1984) The evaluation of reality orientation. In I. Hanley and J. Hodge (eds), *Psychological Approaches to the Care of the Elderly*, pp. 192–212, Croom Helm, Beckenham.

Griffiths, R.A., Good, W.R., Watson, N.P., O'Donnel, H.F., Fell, P.J. and Shakespere, J.M. (1987) Depression, dementia and disability in the elderly. *British Journal of Psychiatry*, **150**, 482–93.

Gurel, L., Linn, M.W. and Linn, B.S. (1972) Physical and mental impairment of function evaluation in the aged: the PAMIE scale. *Journal of Gerontology*, **27**, 83–90.

Gusella, J.F., Wexler, N.S., Conneally, P.M., Naylor, S.L., Anderson, M.A., Tanzi, R.E., Watkins, P.C., Ottina, K., Wallace, M.R., Sakaguchi, A.Y., Young, A.B., Shoulson, I., Bonilla, E. and Martin, J.B. (1983) A polymorphic DNA marker genetically linked to Huntington's disease. *Nature*, **306**, 234–8.

Gustafson, L. and Risberg, J. (1979) Regional cerebral blood flow measurements by the 133 Xe inhalation technique in differential diagnosis of dementia. *Acta Neurologica Scandinavica*, **60**, 546–7.

Hachinski, V.C., Illiff, L.D., Zilhka, E., Duboulay, C.H., McAllister, V.L., Marshall, J., Russell, R.W.R. and Symon, L. (1975) Cerebral blood flow in dementia. *Archives of Neurology*, **32**, 632–7.

Hamilton, M. (1967) Development of a rating scale for primary depressive illness. *British Journal of Social and Clinical Psychology*, **66**, 278–96.

Hamilton, M. (1986) The Hamilton Rating Scale for Depression. In N. Sartorius and T.A. Ban (eds), *Assessment of Depression*, pp. 143–52, Springer-Verlag, Berlin.

Hanley, I.G. (1984) Theoretical and practical considerations in Reality Orientation therapy with the elderly. In I. Hanley and J. Hodge (eds), *Psychological Approaches to the Care of the Elderly*, Croom Helm, Beckenham.

Helmes, E., Csapo, K.G. and Short, J.A. (1987) Standardisation and validation of the Multidimensional Observation Scale for Elderly Subjects (MOSES). *Journal of Gerontology*, **42**, 395–405.

Herscovitch, P., Auchus, A.P., Gado, M., Chi, D. and Raichle, M.E. (1986) Correction of positron emission tomography data for cerebral atrophy. *Journal of Cerebral Blood Flow and Metabolism*, **6**, 120–24.

Hodkinson, H.M. (1972) Evaluation of a mental test score for assessment of mental impairment in the elderly. *Age and Ageing*, **1**, 233–8.

Hounsfield, G.N. (1973) Computerized transverse axial scanning (tomography): Part I: description of system. *British Journal of Radiology*, **46**, 1016–22.

Hovaguimian, T. (1986) Instruments used in the assessment of depression in psychogeriatric patients. In N. Sartorius and T.A. Ban (eds), *Assessment of Depression*, pp. 343–55, Springer-Verlag, Berlin.

Hughes, C.P., Berg, L., Danziger, W.L., Coben, L.A. and Martin, R.L. (1982) A new clinical scale for the staging of dementia. *British Journal of Psychiatry*, **140**, 566–72.

Hunter, R., McLuskie, R., Wyper, D., Patterson, J., Christie, J.E., Brooks, D.N., McCulloch, J., Fink, G. and Goodwin, G.M. (1989) The pattern of function-related regional cerebral blood flow investigated by single photon emission tomography with ^{99m}Tc-HMPAO in patients with pre-senile Alzheimer's disease and Korsakoff's psychosis. Submitted.

Inglis, J. (1959) A paired associate learning test for use with elderly psychiatric patients. *Journal of Mental Science*, **105**, 440–48.

Jacoby, R.J. and Levy, R. (1980) Computed tomography in the elderly: 2 Senile dementia: diagnosis and functional impairment. *British Journal of Psychiatry*, **136**, 256–69.

Jacoby, R.J., Levy, R. and Dawson, J.M. (1980) Computed tomography in the elderly: 1 The normal population. *British Journal of Psychiatry*, **136**, 249–55.

Jagust, W.J., Budinger, T.F. and Reed, B.R. (1987) The diagnosis of dementia with single photon emission computed tomography. *Archives of Neurology*, **44**, 258–62.

Jenkins, J., Felce, D., Powell, E. and Lunt, B. (1978) *Measuring Client Engagement in Residential Settings for the Elderly*, Research Report No 120, Health Care Evaluation Team, Winchester.

Johnson, K.A., Mueller, S.T., Walshe, T.M., English, R.J. and Holman, B.L. (1987) Cerebral perfusion imaging in Alzheimer's disease. *Archives of Neurology*, **44**, 165–8.

Johnston, M., Wakeling, A., Graham, N. and Stokes, F. (1987) Cognitive impairment, emotional disorder and length of stay of elderly patients in a district general hospital. *British Journal of Medical Psychology*, **60**, 133–9.

Kahn, R.L., Goldfarb, A.I., Pollack, M. and Peck, A. (1960) Brief objective measures for the determination of mental status in the aged. *American Journal of Psychiatry*, **117**, 326–8.

Kang, J., Lemaire, H.G., Unterbeck, A., Salbaum, J.M., Masters, C.L., Grzeschik, K.H., Multhaup, G., Beyreuther, K. and Benno, M.H. (1987) The precursor of Alzheimer's disease amyloid A4 protein resembles a cell-surface receptor. *Nature*, **325**, 733–6.

Kapur, N. (1987) Some comments on the technical acceptability of Warrington's Recognition Memory Test. *British Journal of Clinical Psychology*, **26**, 144–6.

Kaszniak, A.W., Fox, J., Gandell, D.L., Garron, D.C., Huckman, M.S. and Ramsay, R.G. (1978) Predictors of mortality in presenile and senile dementia. *Annals of Neurology*, **3**, 246–52.

Katona, C.L.E. and Aldridge, C.R. (1985) The dexamethasone suppression test and depressive signs in dementia. *Journal of Affective Disorders*, **8**, 83–9.

Katz, S., Ford, A.B., Moskowitch, R.W., Jackson, R.A. and Jaffe, M.W. (1963) Studies of illness in the aged: the index of ADL. *Journal of the American Medical Association*, **185**, 914–19.

Katzman, R., Brown, T., Fuld, P., Peck, A., Schechter, R. and Schimmel, H. (1983) Validation of a short orientation–memory–concentration test of cognitive impairment. *American Journal of Psychiatry*, **140**, 734–9.

Kay, D.W.K. (1986) The genetics of Alzheimer's disease. *British Medical Bulletin*, **42**, 19–23.

Kertesz, A. and Hooper, P. (1982) Praxis and language: the extent and variety of apraxia in aphasia. *Neuropsychologia*, **20**, 275–86.

Kety, S.S. and Schmidt, C.F. (1948) The nitrous oxide method for the quantitative determination of cerebral blood flow in man: theory, procedure and normal values. *Journal of Clinical Investigation*, **27**, 476–83.

Kozma, A. and Stones, M.J. (1980) The measurement of happiness: development of the Memorial University of Newfoundland Scale of Happiness (MUNSH). *Journal of Gerontology*, **35**, 906–12.

Kuhl, D.E., Phelps, M.E., Markham, C.H., Metter, E.J., Riege, W.H. and Winter, J. (1982) Cerebral metabolism and atrophy in Huntington's disease determined by ^{18}FDG and computed tomographic scan. *Annals of Neurology*, **12**, 425–34.

Kuriansky, J.B. and Gurland, B.J. (1976) The performance test of activities of daily living. *International Journal of Ageing and Human Development*, **7**, 343–52.

Kuriansky, J.B., Gurland, B.J. and Fleiss, J.L. (1976) The assessment of self-care capacity in geriatric psychiatry patients by objective and subjective methods. *Journal of Clinical Psychology*, **32**, 95–102.

LaPorte, R.E., Montoye, H.J. and Casperson, C.J. (1985) Assessment of physical activity in epidemiological research: problems and prospects. *Public Health Reports*, **100**, 131–46.

La Rue, A. and Jarvik, L.F. (1987) Cognitive function and prediction of dementia in old age. *International Journal of Ageing and Human Development*, **25**, 79–90.

Lassen, N.A. and Ingvar, D.H. (1961) The blood flow of the cerebral cortex determined by radioactive krypton-85. *Journal of Nuclear Medicine*, **24**, 66–72.

Lawton, M.P. (1975) The Philadelphia Geriatric Centre Morale Scale: a revision. *Journal of Gerontology*, **30**, 85–9.

Lawton, M.P. and Brodie, E.M. (1969) Assessment of older people: self-maintaining and instrumental activities of daily living. *The Gerontologist*, **9**, 179–86.

Lawton, M.P., Moss, M., Fulcomer, M. and Kleban, M.H. (1982) A research and service oriented multilevel assessment instrument. *Journal of Gerontology*, **37**, 91–9.

Lesher, E. and Whelihan, W.M. (1986) Reliability of mental status instruments administered to nursing home residents. *Journal of Consulting and Clinical Psychology*, **54**, 726–7.

Lesser, R.P., Fahn, S., Snider, S.R., Cole, L.J., Isgreen, W.P. and Barrett, R.E. (1979) Analysis of the clinical problems in Parkinsonism and the complications of long-term levadopa therapy. *Neurology (NY)*, **29**, 1253–60.

Lezack, M.D. (1978) *Neuropsychological Assessment*, Oxford University Press, Oxford.

Liston, E.H. and La Rue, A. (1983a) Clinical differentiation of primary degenerative and multi-infarct dementia: a critical review of the evidence. Part I. Clinical studies. *Biological Psychiatry*, **18**, 1451–66.

Liston, E.H. and La Rue, A. (1983b) Clinical differentiation of primary degenerative and multi-infarct dementia: a critical review of the evidence. Part II. Pathological studies. *Biological Psychiatry*, **18**, 1467–84.

Little, A.G., Hemsley, D.R., Volans, P.J. and Bergmann, K. (1986) The relationship between alternative assessments of self-care activity in the elderly. *British Journal of Clinical Psychology*, **25**, 51–9.

Lubin, B.J., Larsen, R.M. and Matarazzo, J.D. (1984) Patterns of psychological test usage in the United States: 1935–1982. *American Psychologist*, **39**, 451–4.

Mahoney, F. and Barthel, D.W. (1965) Functional evaluation: the Barthel Index. *Maryland State Medical Journal*, **14**, 61–5.

McFadyen, M. (1984) The measurement of engagement in the institutionalised elderly. In I. Hanley and J. Hodge (eds), *Psychological Approaches in the Care of the Elderly*, Croom Helm, Beckenham.

McKhann, G., Drachman, D., Fosltein, M., Katzman, R., Price, D. and Stadlan, E.M. (1984) Clinical diagnosis of Alzheimer's disease: report of the NINCDS–ADRDA work group. *Neurology*, **34**, 939–44.

McPherson, F.M. and Tregaskis, D. (1985) The short-term stability of the survey version of the CAPE. *British Journal of Clinical Psychology*, **24**, 205–6.

Mathur-de Vre, R. (1984) Biomedical implications of the relaxation behaviour of water related to NMR imaging. *British Journal of Radiology*, **57**, 955–76.

May, A.E. (1972) The influence of nurses' attitudes on a rating scale for geriatric assessment. *Modern Geriatrics*, **2**, 406–10.

May, C., Rapoport, S.I., Tomai, T.P., Chrousos, G.P. and Gold, P.W. (1987) Cerebrospinal fluid concentrations of corticotropin releasing hormone (CRF) and corticotropin (ACTH) are reduced in patients with Alzheimer's disease. *Neurology*, 37, 535–8.

Miller, E. (1984) Verbal fluency as a function of a measure of verbal intelligence and in relation to different types of cerebral pathology. *British Journal of Clinical Psychology*, **23**, 53–8.

Moore, V. and Wyke, M.A. (1984) Drawing disability in patients with senile dementia. *Psychological Medicine*, **14**, 97–105.

Morgan, K. (1985) Effects of repeated dose Nitrazepam and Lormetazepam on psychomotor performance in the elderly. *Psychopharmacology*, **86**, 209–11.

Morgan, K., Dallasso, H.M., Arie, T., Byrne, E.J., Jones, R. and Waite, J. (1987) Mental health and psychological wellbeing among the old and very old living at home. *British Journal of Psychiatry*, **150**, 801–7.

Mortimer, J.A., Pirozzolo, F.J., Hansch, E.C. and Webster, D.D. (1982) Relationship of motor symptoms to intellectual deficits in Parkinson's disease. *Neurology (NY)*, **32**, 133–7.

Mulley, G.P. (1986) Differential diagnosis of dementia. *British Medical Journal*, **292**, 1416–18.

Nelson, H.E. (1982) *The National Adult Reading Test Manual*, NFER–Nelson, Windsor.

Nelson, H.E. and McKenna, P. (1975) The use of current reading ability in the assessment of dementia. *British Journal of Social and Clinical Psychology*, **14**, 259–67.

Nelson, H.E. and O'Connell, A. (1978) Dementia: the estimation of pre-morbid intelligence levels using the new adult reading test. *Cortex*, **14**, 234–44.

Neirinckx, R.D., Canning, L.R., Piper, I.M., Nowotnik, D.P., Pickett, R.D., Holmes, R.A., Volkert, W.A., Forster, A.M., Weisner, P.S., Marriott, J.A. and Chaplin, S.B. (1987) Technetium-99m d, 1-HM-PAO: a new radiopharmaceutical for SPECT imaging of regional cerebral blood perfusion. *The Journal of Nuclear Medicine*, **28**, 191–202.

Neugarten, B.L., Havighurst, R.J. and Tobin, S.S. (1961) The measurement of life satisfaction. *Journal of Gerontology*, **16**, 134–43.

O'Carroll, R.E. and Gilleard, C.J. (1986) Estimation of pre-morbid intelligence in dementia. *British Journal of Clinical Psychology*, **25**, 157–8.

O'Carroll, R.E., Baikie, E.M. and Whittick, J.E. (1987) Does the National Adult Reading Test hold in dementia? *British Journal of Clinical Psychology*, **26**, 315–16.

Okada, Y.C., Kaufman, L. and Williamson, S.J. (1983) The hippocampal formation as a source of the slow endogenous potentials. *Electroencephalography and Clinical Neurophysiology*, **55**, 417–27.

Okimoto, J.T., Barnes, R.F., Veitch, R.C., Raskind, M.A., Invi, T.S. and Carter, W.B. (1982) Screening for depression in geriatric medical patients. *American Journal of Psychiatry*, **139**, 799–802.

Overall, J.E. and Gorham, D.R. (1962) The brief psychiatric rating scale. *Psychological Reports*, **10**, 799–812.

Palmer, A.M., Francis, P.T., Benton, J.S., Sims, N.R., Mann, D.M.A., Neary, D., Snowden, J.S. and Bowen, D.M. (1987) Presynaptic serotoninergic dysfunction in patients with Alzheimer's disease. *Journal of Neurochemistry*, **48**, 8–15.

Pattie, A.H. and Gilleard, C.J. (1979) *Clifton Assessment Procedures for the Elderly (CAPE): Manual*, Hodder and Stoughton Educational, Sevenoaks.

Pedley, T.A. and Miller, J.A. (1983) Clinical neurophysiology of aging and dementia. In R. Mayeux and W.G. Rosen (eds), *The Dementias*, pp. 31–49, Raven Press, New York.

Perry, E.K. (1986) The cholinergic hypothesis—ten years on. *British Medical Bulletin*, **42**, 63–9.

Perry, R.H. (1986) Recent advances in neuropathology. *British Medical Bulletin*, **42**, 35–41.

Pfefferbaum, A., Wenegrat, B.G., Ford, J.M., Roth, W.T. and Kopell, B.S. (1984) Clinical application of the P3 component of event-related potentials. II Dementia, depression and schizophrenia. *Electroencephalography and Clinical Neurophysiology*, **59**, 104–24.

Pfeiffer, E. (1975) A short portable mental status questionnaire for the assessment of organic brain deficit in elderly patients. *Journal of the American Geriatric Society*, **23**, 433–41.

Phelps, M.E., Mazziotta, J.C. and Huang, S.–C. (1982) Study of cerebral function with positron computed tomography. *Journal of Cerebral Blood Flow and Metabolism*, **2**, 113–62.

Pinsky, J.L., Branch, L.G., Jette, A.M., Haynes, S.G., Feinlab, M., Cornoni-Huntley, J.C. and Bailey, K.R. (1985) Framingham disability study: relationship of disability to cardiovascular risk factors among persons free of diagnosed cardiovascular disease. *American Journal of Epidemiology*, **122**, 644–56.

Plutchik, R., Conte, H., Lieberman, M., Bakur, M., Grossman, J. and Lehrman, N. (1970) Reliability and validity of a scale for assessing the functioning of geriatric patients. *Journal of the American Geriatric Society*, **18**, 491–500.

Qureshi, K.M. and Hodkinson, H.M. (1974) Evaluation of a 10 question mental test in the institutionalised elderly. *Age and Ageing*, **3**, 152–7.

Raskind, M., Peskind, E., Rivard, M.F., Veitch, R. and Barnes, R. (1982) Dexamethasone suppression test and cortisol circadian rhythm in primary degenerative dementia. *American Journal of Psychiatry*, **139**, 1468–71.

Rasmussen, A.G., Adolfsson, R. and Karlsson, T. (1988) New method specific for acetylcholinesterase in cerebrospinal fluid: application to Alzheimer's disease. *Lancet*, **ii**, 571–2.

Raven, J.C. (1965) *Guide to Using the Coloured Progressive Matrices*, H.K. Lewis, London.

Reichlin, S. (1985) Neuroendocrinology, In J.D. Wilson and D.W. Foster (eds), *Williams' Textbook of Endocrinology*, Saunders, London.

Reifler, B.V., Cox, G.B. and Hanley, R.S. (1981) Problems of the mentally ill elderly as perceived by patients, family and clinicians. *The Gerontologist*, **21**, 165–70.

Reisberg, B., Ferris, S.H., DeLeon, M.J. and Crook, T. (1982) The Global Deterioration Scale (GDS): an instrument for the assessment of primary degenerative dementia. *American Journal of Psychiatry*, **139**, 1136–9.

Reitan, R.M. (1977) *Manual for Administration of Neuropsychological Tests for Adults and Children*, Neuropsychology Laboratory, Tucson.

Risberg, J., Ali, Z., Wilson, E.M. *et al.* (1975) Regional cerebral blood flow by 133-xenon inhalation. *Stroke*, **6**, 142–8.

Rosen, W.G. and Mohs, R.C. (1982) Evolution of cognitive decline in dementia. In S. Corkin, K.L. Davis, J.H. Crowdon, E. Usdin and R.J. Wurtman (eds), *Alzheimer's Disease: A Report of Progress in Research*, Raven Press, New York.

Rosen, W.G., Mohs, R.C. and Davis, K.L. (1984) A new rating scale for Alzheimer's disease. *American Journal of Psychiatry*, **141**, 1356–64.

Rosen, W.G., Terry, F.D., Fuld, P.A., Katzman, R. and Peck, A. (1980) Pathological verification of ischaemic score in differentiation of dementias. *Annals of Neurology*, **7**, 486–8.

Rosenberg, S.J., Ryan, J.J. and Prifitera, A. (1984) Rey's Auditory Verbal Learning Test performance of patients with and without memory impairment. *Journal of Clinical Psychology*, **40**, 785–7.

Rossor, M. and Iversen, L.L. (1986) Non-cholinergic neurotransmitter abnormalities in Alzheimer's disease. *British Medical Bulletin*, **42**, 70–4.

Roth, M. (1986) The association of clinical and neurological findings and its bearing on the classification and aetiology of Alzheimer's disease. *British Medical Bulletin*, **42**, 42–50.

Roth, M., Tym, E., Mountjoy, C.Q., Huppert, F.A., Hendrie, H., Verma, S. and Goddard, R. (1986) CAMDEX: A standardised instrument for the diagnosis of mental disorder in the elderly with special reference to the early detection of dementia. *British Journal of Psychiatry*, **149**, 698–709.

Ruddle, H.V. and Bradshaw, C.M. (1982) On the estimation of pre-morbid intellectual functioning: validation of Nelson and McKenna's formulae and some new normative data. *British Journal of Clinical Psychology*, **21**, 159–66.

Russell, E.W. (1975) A multiple scoring method for the assessment of complex memory functions. *Journal of Consulting and Clinical Psychology*, **43**, 800–9.

St Clair, D.M., Blackwood, D.H.R. and Christie, J.E. (1985). P3 and other long latency auditory evoked potentials in presenile dementia Alzheimer type and alcoholic Korsakoff syndrome. *British Journal of Psychiatry*, **147**, 702–6.

St Clair, D.M., Brock, D.J.H. and Barron, L. (1986) A monoclonal antibody assay technique for plasma and red cell acetylcholinesterase activity in Alzheimer's disease. *Journal of the Neurological Sciences*, **73**, 169–76.

St Clair, D., Blackburn, I., Blackwood, D. and Tyrer, G. (1988) Measuring the course of Alzheimer's disease. A longitudinal study of neuropsychological function and changes in P3 event-related potentials. *British Journal of Psychiatry*, **152**, 48–54.

St George-Hyslop, P.H., Tanzi, R.E., Polinsky, R.J., Haines, J.L., Nee, L., Watkins, P.C., Myers, R.H., Feldman, R.G., Pollen, D., Drachman, D., Growdon, J., Bruni, A., Foncin, J.F., Salmon, D., Frommelt, P., Amaducci, L., Sorbi, S., Piacentini, S., Steward, G.D., Hobbs, W.J., Conneally, P.M. and Gusella, J.F. (1987) Genetic defect causing familial Alzheimer's disease maps on chromosome 21. *Science*, **235**, 885–90.

Schoening, H.A. and Iverson, I.A. (1968) Numerical scoring of self-care status. *Archives of Physical Medicine and Rehabilitation*, **49**, 221–9.

Shader, R.I., Harmatz, J.S. and Salzman, C. (1974) A new scale for clinical assessment in geriatric populations: Sandoz Clinical Assessment—Geriatric. *Journal of the American Geriatrics Society*, **22**, 107–13.

Simpson, H., Lee, J.H., Zovbok, B. and Gardos, G. (1979) A rating scale for Tardive Dyskinesia. *Psychopharmacology*, **64**, 171–9.

Simpson, S., Woods, R.T. and Britton, P.G. (1981) Depression and engagement in a residential home for the elderly. *Behaviour Research and Therapy*, **19**, 435–8.

Sims, N.R., Bowen, D.M., Allen, S.J., Smith, C.C.T., Neary, D., Thomas, D.J. and Davison, A.N. (1983) Presynaptic cholinergic dysfunctions in patients with dementia. *Journal of Neurochemistry*, **40**, 503–9.

Sjogren, T., Sjogren, H. and Lindgren, A.G.H. (1952) Morbus Alzheimer and Morbus Pick. *Acta Psychiatrica Neurologica Scandinavica (Suppl.)*, 82, 1–152.

Snowdon, J. (1986) Dementia, depression and life satisfaction in nursing homes. *International Journal of Geriatric Psychiatry*, **1**, 85–92.

Sokoloff, L., Reivich, M., Kennedy, C., Des Rosiers, M.H., Patlak, C.S., Pettigrew, K.D., Sakurada, D. and Shinohara, M. (1977) The (^{14}C) deoxyglucose method for the measurement of local cerebral glucose utilization: theory, procedure and normal values in the conscious and anesthetized albino rat. *Journal of Neurochemistry*, **28**, 897–916.

Spellacy, F.J. and Spreen, O. (1969) A short form of the Token Test. *Cortex*, **5**, 391–7.

Stigsby, B., Johannesson, G. and Ingvar, D.H. (1981) Regional EEG analysis and regional cerebral blood flow in Alzheimer's and Pick's diseases. *Electroencephalography and Clinical Neurophysiology*, **51**, 537–47.

Stokely, E.M., Sveinsdottir, E., Lassen, N.A. and Rommer, P. (1980) A single-photon dynamic computer assisted tomograph (DCAT) for imaging brain function in multiple cross-sections. *Journal of Computer Assisted Tomography*, **4**, 230–40.

Storandt, M.J., Botwinick, J., Danziger, W.L., Berg, L. and Hughes, C.P. (1984) Psychometric differentiation of mild senile dementia of the Alzheimer type. *Archives of Neurology*, **41**, 497–9.

Takeda, S. and Matsuzawa, T. (1984) Brain atrophy during ageing. A quantitative study using computed tomography. *Journal of the American Geriatrics Society*, **32**, 520–24.

Tanzi, R.E., Gusella, J.F., Watkins, P.C., Burns, G.A.P., St George-Hyslop, P., Van Keuren, M.L., Patterson, D., Pagan, S., Kurnit, D.M. and Neve, R.L. (1987) Amyloid β protein gene: cDNA, mRNA distribution, and genetic linkage near the Alzheimer locus. *Science*, **235**, 880–84.

Tanzi, R.E., St George-Hyslop, P.H., Haines, J.L., Polinsky, R.J., Nee, L., Foncin, J.F., Neve, R.L., McClatchey, A.I., Conneally, P.M. and Gusella, J.F. (1987). The genetic defect in familial Alzheimer's disease is not tightly linked to the amyloid β– protein gene. *Nature*, **329**, 156–7.

Taylor, R. (1986) *Patterns of Cognitive Impairment in Dementia*, Unpublished PhD thesis, University of Edinburgh.

Tierney, M.C., Snow, W.G., Reid, D.W., Zorzitto, M.L. and Fisher, R.H. (1987) Psychometric differentiation of dementia. *Archives of Neurology*, **44**, 720–22.

Tomlinson, B.E. and Corsellis, J.A.N. (1985) Ageing and the dementias. In *Greenfield's Neuropathology*, pp. 951–1025, Edward Arnold, London.

Trzepacz, P.T. and Webb, M. (1987) The choreometer: an objective test of chorea during voluntary movements. *Biological Psychiatry*, **22**, 771–6.

Van Broeckhoven, C., Genthe, A.M., Vandenberghe, A., Horsthemke, B., Backhovens, H., Raeymaekers, P., Van Ul, W., Wehnert, A., Gheuens, J., Cras, P., Bruyland, M., Martin, J.J., Salbaum, M., Malthaup, G., Masters, C.L., Beyreuther, K., Gurling, H. D., Mullan, M.J., Holland, A., Barton, A., Irving, N., Williamson, R., Richards, S.J. and Hardy, J.A. (1987) Failure of familial Alzheimer's disease to segregate with the A4-amyloid gene in several European families. *Nature*, **329**, 153–5.

Vanniewkirk, R.R. and Galbraith, G.G. (1985) The relationship to age of performance on the Luria–Nebraska Neuropsychological Battery. *Journal of Clinical Psychology*, **41**, 527–32.

Veall, N. and Mallett, B.L. (1966) Regional cerebral blood flow determination by 133-Xe inhalation and external recording: the effect of arterial recirculation. *Clinical Science*, **30**, 353–69.

Venn, R.D. (1983) The Sandoz Clinical Assessment—Geriatric (SCAG): A general purpose psychogeriatric rating scale. *Gerontology*, **29**, 185–98.

Volicer, L., Langlais, P.J., Matson, W.R., Mark, K.A. and Gamache, P.H. (1985) Serotoninergic system in dementia of the Alzheimer type. *Archives of Neurology*, **42**, 1158–61.

Wade, J.P.H., Mirsen, T.R., Hachinski, V.C., Fisman, M., Lau, C. and Merskey, H. (1987) The clinical diagnosis of Alzheimer's disease. *Archives of Neurology*, **44**, 24–9.

Walker, S.A. (1980) Application of a test for aphasia to normal old people. *Journal of Clinical and Experimental Gerontology*, **2**, 185–98.

Warrington, E.K. (1984) *Recognition Test Manual*, NFER–Nelson, Windsor.

Wechsler, D. (1981) *Manual for the Wechsler Adult Intelligence Scale—Revised*, Psychological Corporation, New York.

Weingartner, H., Kaye, W., Smallberg, S., Evert, M.H., Gillin, J.C. and Sitaram, N. (1981) Memory failures in progressive idiopathic dementia. *Journal of Abnormal Psychology*, **90**, 187–96.

Welford, A.T. (1962) On changes of performance with age. *Lancet*, *ii*, 335–9.

Whitehead, A. (1977) Changes in cognitive functioning in elderly psychiatric patients. *British Journal of Psychiatry*, **130**, 605–8.

Whitehead, A. (1982) Outcome in elderly psychiatric patients: implications of cognitive changes. *British Journal of Clinical Psychology*, **21**, 225–6.

Wilson, R.S., Rosenbaum, G., Brown, G., Rourke, D., Whitman, D. and Grisell, J. (1978) An index of pre-morbid intelligence. *Journal of Consulting and Clinical Psychology*, **46**, 1554–5.

Winograd, C.H. (1984) Mental status tests and the capacity for self-care. *Journal of the American Geriatrics Society*, **32**, 49–55.

Wood, P.L., Etienne, P., Lal, S., Gauthier, S., Cajal, S. and Nair, N.P.V. (1982) Reduced lumbar CSF somatostatin levels in Alzheimer's disease. *Life Sciences*, **31**, 2073–9.

Wood, V., Wylie, M.L. and Sheafer, B. (1969) An analysis of a short self-report measure of life satisfaction: correlation with rater judgements. *Journal of Gerontology*, **24**, 465–9.

Woods, R.T. (1983) Specificity of learning in reality orientation sessions: a single case study. *Behaviour Research and Therapy*, **21**, 173–5.

Wright, A.F. and Whalley, L.J. (1984) Genetics, ageing and dementia. *British Journal of Psychiatry*, **145**, 20–38.

Yates, C.M., Simpson, J., Gordon, A., Maloney, A.F.J., Allison, Y., Ritchie, I.M. and Urquhart, A. (1983) Catecholamines and cholinergic enzymes in pre-senile and senile Alzheimer-type dementia and Down's syndrome. *Brain Research*, **280**, 119–26.

Yesavage, J.A., Brink, T.L. and Rose, T.L. (1983) Development and validation of a geriatric depression screening scale: a preliminary report. *Journal of Psychiatric Research*, **17**, 37–49.

Zung, W.K.K. (1965) A self-rating depression scale. *Archives of General Psychiatry*, **12**, 63–70.

Chapter 12

Drug Problems

SUSAN J. GREY and MICHAEL GOSSOP

INTRODUCTION

In considering the measurement of drug use there are a number of ways of categorizing assessment approaches. For example, there are at least three major settings in which drug use may be assessed. First, the information may be required for clinical use, either as a way of monitoring and evaluating the progress of an individual drug user in a treatment programme or as part of a systematic study of treatment methods in a clinical trial. Second, it may be necessary to assess drug use in the context of a theoretical study to elucidate the pharmacological mechanisms and psychological processes involved. Third, epidemiological or other survey methods might be used to establish incidence and prevalence rates for sociological studies or for strategic planning of services.

Traditionally, distinctions have also been made on the basis of the type of substance used, and there are a number of substance-specific checklists and questionnaires. However, although there are differences between classes of drugs in terms of their route of administration, patterns of use and physiological, cognitive and emotional effects, there is increasing interest in the common features of addictive substances. These include the ability to induce tolerance, physical dependence and withdrawal distress if used regularly and in sufficient quantities. Sobell and Sobell (1976) were among the first to develop this line of research by grouping alcohol, opiates and barbiturates together on the basis of their common addictive properties. The notion of a broad-based model of addictive processes has been developed further by various authors (Miller, 1980; Cummings *et al.*, 1980; Orford, 1985) to include other behaviours such as gambling and eating.

The increased interest in the process of addiction as opposed to the properties of the individual substances has stimulated research into the factors involved in the development and maintenance of addiction and the relapse process, and a greater acknowledgement of the interrelationships between physiological, psychological, cognitive and social factors. Donovan (1989) has described in detail the implications of the biopsychosocial model of

Measuring Human Problems. Edited by D.F. Peck and C.M. Shapiro

addiction for assessment and the need for a broad-spectrum approach. In this chapter we will focus on measurement of behavioural, psychological and physiological indices of drug use, following the multiple systems approach to the analysis of behavioural disorders pioneered by Lang (1968) and developed by others (Kratochwill and Mace, 1983; Donovan and Marlatt, 1989). This approach has been chosen in preference to analysis in terms of drug type or purpose of assessment in order to emphasize the multifactorial nature of the process involved in drug use. Reference will be made within each section to the applicability of particular methods to different contexts.

The Advisory Council on the Misuse of Drugs (1982) has defined a problem drug taker as 'Any person who experiences social, psychological, physical or legal problems related to the intoxication and/or regular excessive consumption and/or dependence as a consequence of his or her use of drugs or other chemical substances (excluding alcohol or tobacco)'. The range of drugs implicit in this definition will be considered in this chapter.

ASSESSMENT OF DRUG-TAKING BEHAVIOUR

In discussion of specific scales and monitoring systems it is worth considering data collection for epidemiological purposes separately from data collection in a clinical context since the information required for this is, on the whole, less detailed and more substance-oriented than that needed for assessment in a clinical or theoretical study.

Epidemiological data

In Britain the pattern of illicit drug taking has undergone several remarkable transformations since the early 1960s. The Home Office Index (1985) shows an increase in notified drug addicts from 1349 in 1966 to 12 489 in 1984. Police and Customs and Excise information suggests a massive increase in the size of the illegal market for heroin from the early 1970s to the present day. In addition, there is growing evidence of illicit intravenous use of amphetamines and non-notifiable drugs such as Temgesic. Unfortunately, however, there is still no adequate research base from which to monitor such trends nationally.

The Home Office Index has deficiencies which have been well documented (Strang and Shah, 1985), some of which remain even after its recent revisions. It consists of information sent to a central register by medical practitioners only. Notification is required for certain controlled drugs only, together with full personal details of the drug taker. Information is also requested on intravenous use of either the notified drug or any others. However, there is no formal requirement to notify users of other drugs, such as amphetamines, whether injected or not; indeed this section of the form is worded somewhat ambiguously. The lack of anonymity is a disincentive to notify and the restricted range of notifiable drugs makes the Index insensitive to recent trends. A requirement for non-medical agencies to submit notifications to the Index could greatly increase the notification rate and would be consistent with the change in central policy for treatment services towards a greater role for the voluntary sector and for generalist workers.

The core items used by the WHO (Hughes *et al.*, 1980) in their cross-cultural study require detailed and lengthy interviewing by trained staff. Information is collected on the agency, demographic details, drug type, pattern of use, drug-use history and treatment and referral details. However, the system depends upon the use of relatively skilled interviewers and is more suitable for individual in-depth studies than as a national monitoring system.

Local monitoring systems, which are easier to manage and tailor to local conditions, have been more successful in gathering data from a variety of sources. The anonymous case register system introduced by the Manchester Drugs Project gathers information from GPs, Community Drugs Teams, voluntary sector agencies, social services and others. Data are collected on types, frequency and quantity of drug used, route of administration, prescribing and other action taken and other demographic information. The register operates in all health districts in north-west England and has the advantage of allowing multi-agency enumeration by the use of unique subject identification codes, consisting of initials, date of birth and sex. This system preserves the client's anonymity and has been found acceptable by many agencies.

A modest core data set, for use by non-specialist staff with minimal commitment to research, might consist of age, sex, date seen, agency, source of referral, plus details of up to three drugs used, together with route of administration and age of first use. Information on whether the drug user shares injecting equipment is also useful and it may be worth making a distinction between sharing with one person only and sharing with several people. Details of quantity and frequency of drug use are of interest, but many staff find this difficult to record, particularly in cases of multiple or chaotic drug use. To ask for such detail can lead to diminishing returns in the form of decreased validity and reduced staff compliance with data collection.

The data obtained from local research projects allow the researcher to gather information about the demographic characteristics of the drug users presenting for treatment as well as their patterns of drug use. They also form the basis for a continuous monitoring system which can show changing trends in drug taking over time, and can provide the basis for evaluation of the effectiveness of services reaching target populations (Grey, 1989). A major disadvantage is that the data sets used by monitoring systems in different areas are not standardized, and there is no real agreement between agencies on the definition of problem drug use. The Department of Health has recently instructed all regional health authorities to provide six-monthly statistical returns on drug users attending helping agencies. This should lead to greater consistency between monitoring systems.

Most monitoring systems give information about drug users coming to the attention of participating agencies, and in most cases this is where the drug use is part of the reason for presenting. The data obtained, therefore, give estimates of treatment prevalence and treatment incidence, as opposed to true incidence and prevalence in the population. Other methods are needed to piece together information about drug takers not making contact with official agencies. This would include Customs and Excise data on seizures of illegal drugs, police data on arrests, information on accidental deaths and other data from a variety of sources. A useful resource book which gives guidelines on methods of estimating the extent of drug use on a local basis is that by Hartnoll *et al.* (1985).

Assessment of drug taking in a clinical setting

Reliability and validity of self-report

In assessing drug-taking behaviour the investigator is almost always dependent on self-report by the drug user. It is rarely possible to set up the conditions required to allow objective observer measurement of behaviour, although Hartnoll *et al.*, (1985) provide some guidance on how field workers can study drug users' activities by spending time in the drug-using environment.

The more common method is to use self-report, either through structured interviews or questionnaires. Retrospective self-reporting of any behaviour is always prone to error simply because of the limitations of human memory. Accuracy will be influenced by many factors, such as period covered, presence or absence of observable clues, individual differences in memory skills, motivational factors, state-dependent learning effects and the salience of the material, to mention but a few.

In the field of drug addiction these difficulties are further compounded by other factors which may lead to distortions in reporting. For example, although a heroin user may know quite precisely the weight and cost of the drug he has bought on a particular day, he cannot be sure of its purity. If he has shared it with friends, supplemented it with other drugs and varied the route of administration he may be quite unsure of exactly how much he has used altogether. In addition, his report will be less accurate, the longer the period of recall. There are, however, additional factors operating at the time of reporting, which influence the drug user's motivation and make accuracy even less likely. A drug user who is being assessed for treatment with methadone may tend to overestimate his heroin consumption in order to ensure a generous level of medication; a drug user under threat of legal sanctions may underestimate or deny his drug use.

Several studies have shown acceptable levels of reliability for self-report of drug use. These involve assessment of internal consistency within an interview, comparisons with responses at re-interview, and consistency between interviewers. Amsel *et al.* (1976) found inconsistencies in only 13 per cent or less of questionnaires for each of eight content areas relating to drug use and illegal activity. Cottrell and O'Donnell (1967) discovered over 90 per cent agreement across repeated interviews with heroin users seeking help. Stephens (1972) reported over 84 per cent agreement between clients and their counsellors.

Validity studies have shown mixed results. Amsel *et al.* (1976) found good agreement between interview data and urinanalysis in former committed addicts, as did Page *et al.* (1977) in male arrestees and Bale *et al.* (1981) in veteran heroin addicts. Validity of self-report among clients in methadone maintenance programmes, however, is more variable. Cox and Langwell (1974) reported 86 per cent agreement between interview data and urinanalysis, whereas Chambers and Taylor (1973) reported only 34 per cent agreement. In a study of reliability and validity of self-report of 34 chronic heroin users, Maddux and Desmond (1975) found mixed results and particularly low validity on items relating to past drug use and treatment history, when using hospital records as a comparison. Gossop *et al.* (1989), however, found that self-reports of opiate use in heroin addicts after treatment were consistent with urine screening.

It seems likely that this variability reflects not only the differences in measures used and validation criteria but also the context in which assessment is being carried out. In several studies it is suggested that where disclosure of drug use may lead to legal sanctions or to termination of treatment there may be a greater chance of deception (Maddux and Desmond, 1975; Bale, 1979; Callahan and Rawson, 1980). Clearly, in assessing drug use by means of self-report it is important to pay due regard to the legal and social pressures experienced by the client and the possible consequences for treatment.

Apart from the usual precautions, such as the use of structured interviews, trained interviewers and guaranteed confidentiality, it is likely that the factor most likely to enhance validity is for the client to be aware that a biochemical measure is also to be used. The importance of these measures justifies their discussion in some detail in a separate section of this chapter.

Content of interview schedules and questionnaires

Assessment of drug-taking behaviour is an essential first step in developing a treatment plan. However, information on drug-taking behaviour alone is insufficient to provide a basis for a comprehensive treatment programme geared to maximizing the client's personal resources for maintaining abstinence following treatment. Furthermore, because many clients are ambivalent about their drug use, treatment centres have increasingly used intermediate as well as long-term goals, with a broader focus on several aspects of behaviour change (Strang *et al.*, 1987).

This broad focus is particularly relevant to the treatment of intravenous opiate users, where the prevention of spread of HIV infection is being perceived as a more urgent goal than abstinence. The use of prescribed methadone as a substitute for opiates was introduced in the 1960s and the practice of prescribing on a long-term basis has been popular for many years in the USA. Although there has been some disillusionment with methadone maintenance as a treatment option, it has undergone something of a revival in the form of 'flexible prescribing'. Thus, methadone maintenance might be used to stabilize the client's opiate intake while short-term treatment could focus on reduction of needle sharing, use of sterile needles, changing from intravenous to oral drug use or changing from use of street drugs to prescribed drugs. Each treatment objective can be seen as a goal in itself and an acceptable step towards long-term abstinence in the case of those drug users who would not otherwise participate in treatment.

Structured interviews and questionnaires

In clinical practice most investigators modify interview schedules and questionnaires to meet their current needs, with the result that there is no single well-tested measurement instrument to provide quantified data on drug use. The Addiction Severity Index (McLellan *et al.*, 1980) is designed to provide a reliable, valid and standardized diagnostic and evaluative instrument in the field of alcohol and drug abuse. Information is collected in the form of client self-report of problems requiring treatment in the following areas: (1) chemical abuse, (2) medical, (3) psychological, (4) legal, (5) family/social and (6) employment/support. Ratings are also made by the assessor on the basis of interview and other verifiable data, such as test results, laboratory reports, etc. Although the basic interview is relatively brief, taking only about 30 minutes, the procedures for administering and collating other information to form the objective section of the report appear more cumbersome. However, in common with many such assessment schedules it is comprehensive for clinical use and, if further refined, may prove useful in research.

A series of standardized questions have been suggested by Roffman and George (1988) for measuring present and past consumption of marijuana in behavioural interviewing. The items include information on age of first use of marijuana, number of times ever used, time since most recent use, frequency of use in the last twelve months, frequency of use in the last 30 days, quantity smoked in the last 30 days. For those subjects who have ever used marijuana almost daily for a period of one month, there are additional questions about how often and for how long such daily use took place. These questions are supplemented with a guide to enquiring about current use to provide information about other issues such as how the client learned about marijuana, what were the circumstances of first marijuana use, subjective response to drug unavailability, first concern about marijuana use, attempts at abstinence and use of other drugs. A questionnaire is used for postal follow-up after treatment. No reliability or validity data are given, the emphasis being placed on the use of the questionnaires for formulating treatment goals, maintaining motivation and teaching clients to think about their behaviour in more objective terms.

An extensive assessment questionnaire has been developed by Washton *et al.* (1988) to facilitate accurate reporting of drug use by patients attending for treatment of cocaine abuse. The Cocaine Abuse Assessment Profile (CAAP) is a self-report form completed by patients at intake. The CAAP elicits information on previous and current use of cocaine, alcohol and other drugs, the nature and extent of drug-related consequences, history of psychiatric or psychological problems, history of previous treatment for drug or alcohol problems and family history of drug, alcohol or psychiatric problems.

In common with other assessment schedules designed primarily for clinical purposes, the information covers psychological aspects of drug use such as anxiety about withdrawal, concern about the social and legal consequences of drug use, subjective sense of dependency, loss of control and changes in personality or attitudes due to cocaine use. These items are contained in the Addiction/Dependency Self-Test section of the CAAP and for clinical purposes give an indication of the severity of cocaine abuse.

The Drug Abuse Screening Test (DAST; Skinner, 1982) is a self-report measure designed for clinical screening and treatment evaluation. The items are concerned with the consequences of drug abuse, such as inability to stop drug use, problems getting through the week without drugs and signs of withdrawal on cessation of drug use. It has good internal consistency, and appears to be a unidimensional scale which is independent of other indices of psychopathology and other variables related to drug use.

Several questionnaires have been developed to collect information about injecting practices and sexual habits of drug users (Robertson *et al.*, 1986; Strang *et al.*, 1988; Morrison, 1989) in order to assess the extent of 'high-risk' behaviour of drug addicts. In a review of methods of assessment of drug use for treatment studies, Wells *et al.* (1988) point out that single-substance questionnaires are insensitive to multiple drug use, and those dealing separately with every drug used can lead to misleading estimates of overall drug use in the sample or in the individual, depending on how the results are reported. These authors categorize drug-use measures in terms of five types, namely, measures of consumption (including measures of abstinence), classification by drug-use history, indices combining 'seriousness' of drug use with frequency, composite indices of severity (including impact of substance use and functioning in other life areas) and measures of patterns of use over time. They suggest that the large choice of measurement methods may be responsible for the variability in treatment outcome results. They recommend that further research should focus on examining the properties of existing measures and particularly on those measures which deal with the timing and sequence of the relapse process.

Self-monitoring

Ongoing self-monitoring has also been used as an adjunct to structured interviews and self-report questionnaires and may be particularly valuable for the continuous assessment of progress during treatment and follow-up where relapse prevention is a major focus of treatment. Self-monitoring is often central to psychological treatment, since it helps to teach clients skills in observing their own behaviour and its consequences. During treatment, objective data are not always available to corroborate self-report, so validity must be ensured in other ways. For monitoring illegal drug use, where the goal is abstinence, it is important to ensure that the consequences of reporting of relapses are not so severe as to encourage deception. Important work has been done in this area (Boudin, 1972; Boudin *et al.*, 1980). These researchers taught addicts to monitor events leading to increased probability of drug use. Self-monitoring methods have also been used by Callahan and Rawson (1980) in the behavioural treatment of drug abuse.

Roffman and George (1988) also used self-monitoring for the measurement of marijuana use during treatment. The procedure involves the recording of information about quantity and frequency of use, circumstances of use, urges to smoke, use of other substances, level of intoxication and mood. Clients are encouraged to produce graphs or other summaries of the data in order to reveal patterns of use and drug-use precipitants.

ASSESSMENT OF SUBJECTIVE ASPECTS OF DRUG USE

In the assessment of subjective aspects of drug use, such as attitudes, cognitions and emotions, the primary method of assessment is self-report, sometimes supported by assessor ratings. The use of self-report with drug users has already been discussed in the context of assessment of behaviour, with the conclusion that reliability and validity are dependent to a great extent on the circumstances in which measurement takes place.

For the assessment of internal and subjective states and events, self-report is the most direct method, and when the purpose of investigation is primarily theoretical the researcher can be more confident about the reliability and validity of the results. Although our understanding of the internal processes involved in drug use and addiction is relatively unsophisticated, several areas of research have shown promising results.

Craving

Subjective measurement of craving has been found to be related to heroin self-administration. Meyer and Mirin (1979) asked subjects to report levels of 'craving' before and after heroin administration. Craving was measured by having subjects cross a 100 mm line at the point that would indicate levels of craving from most to least. This simple measure was regarded as adequate for experimental purposes, and even more basic methods may be used (for example, with 5- or 7-point scales of intensity). Such scales are widely used in behavioural work with anxiety and have been useful in determining hierarchies of anxiety-provoking situations and in ensuring that the pace of exposure treatment and the duration of treatment sessions are appropriate to the needs and responses of the patient. There are no standardized or routine procedures or forms for the assessment of craving.

There have been problems associated with the definition of terms such as craving. A 1955 World Health Organization report condemned the term and recommended that it be avoided in the scientific literature. More recently, Kozlowski and Wilkinson (1987) have criticized the term on the grounds that it carries excess meaning. Instead it has been suggested that the simpler phrase 'strong desires' be used. However, other workers have tried to rehabilitate the term 'craving' by explicitly removing it from earlier and simplistic formulations which equated it with 'physical craving' and using it to refer to a multidimensional construct with subjective, behavioural and physiological components (Hodgson *et al.*, 1978). Recent research has studied the similarities and differences between different types of addictive behaviour, and Gossop *et al.* (1990) found that when opiate addicts and cigarette smokers were asked to rate their experiences of craving on an adjective checklist both groups described craving primarily in terms of dysphoric mood states (e.g. anxious, desperate, frustrated). The experience differed between the groups in that it was more intense for the opiate addicts than for the smokers.

One study which has had some impact upon this question is that of Shiffman and Jarvik (1976), who devised a 7-item scale for the measurement of craving among cigarette smokers. Although devised for smokers, many of these questions may be adapted relatively easily for use with other forms of addictive behaviour. The questions within the Shiffman–Jarvik questionnaire were:

(1) If you could smoke freely, would you like a cigarette this minute?
(2) If you had just eaten would you want a cigarette?
(3) Are you thinking of cigarettes more than usual?
(4) If you were permitted to smoke, would you refuse a cigarette right now? (negative loading).
(5) Do you miss a cigarette?
(6) Do you have an urge to smoke right now?
(7) Would you find a cigarette unpleasant right now? (negative loading).

Withdrawal

The opiate withdrawal syndrome has often mistakenly been regarded as a purely physical response to abstinence. Recent research has indicated that psychological factors such as anxiety may have a powerful effect upon the severity of withdrawal symptoms and may influence withdrawal more strongly than such 'physical' factors as drug dosage (Phillips *et al.*, 1986).

Fear of detoxification has been examined by Milby *et al.* (1987) by means of the Detoxification Fear Survey Schedule (DFSS). This is designed to measure negative emotional reactions to detoxification, and the authors report that a pathological fear of detoxification exists among some addicts and may contribute to the poor success rate of many detoxification programmes. It has been found that the provision of simple, reassuring information about withdrawal may help to alleviate withdrawal severity (Green and Gossop, 1988).

Withdrawal distress has been measured by means of versions of the Opiate Withdrawal Scale (OWS) (Bradley *et al.*, 1987). The OWS was originally a 32-item scale consisting of various signs and symptoms associated with the heroin withdrawal syndrome. Subjects responded to these on a 4-point scale by rating each symptom nil (0), mild (1), moderate (2) and severe (3). This simple and straightforward instrument was found to produce a total score with a strong single factor loading which had good discriminative efficiency in differentiating between withdrawal and post-withdrawal phases of treatment of heroin addicts. It also discriminated well between addicts and controls. In view of the high intercorrelation of the original 32 items, the OWS contained a certain redundancy, and subsequent research has refined the scale from 32 to 20 to 12 and finally to a 10-item scale (Gossop, in press). The 10-item Short Opiate Withdrawal Scale (SOWS) performs the same task as the original scale but with less redundancy of items. The final 10 items and the format of the SOWS are shown in Figure 12.1. Because of its ease of administration (most addicts can complete the form in less than one minute), the SOWS has been regarded as a useful instrument in both research and clinical practice.

Name: Date:

Please put a tick in the appropriate box if you have suffered from any of the following conditions in the last 24 hours

	Nil	Mild	Moderate	Severe
Feeling sick				
Stomach cramps				
Muscle spasms/twitching				
Feelings of coldness				
Heart pounding				
Muscular tension				
Aches and pains				
Yawning				
Runny eyes				
Insomnia/problem sleeping				

Figure 12.1 The Short Opiate Withdrawal Scale.

Dependence

The notion of dependence as a dimension for describing and explaining addictive behaviours has become increasingly important (Edwards, 1986). The idea that *dependence* constitutes a separate dimension from *problems* was originally put forward by a WHO Scientific Group and has been developed by Edwards *et al.* (1981). In the study of alcohol problems, the Severity of Alcohol Dependence Questionnaire (SADQ) has been found to be a useful instrument (Stockwell *et al.*, 1979). As originally described, the SADQ comprised 35 questions dealing with physical withdrawal symptoms, affective symptoms of withdrawal, relief drinking, level of alcohol consumption and rapidity of reinstatement after withdrawal.

A similar attempt has been made to develop a Severity of Opiate Dependence Questionnaire (SODQ) (Sutherland *et al.*, 1986, 1988; Phillips *et al.*, 1987). Since the SODQ was designed to be similar to the SADQ there are marked structural similarities between the two questionnaires. The original version of the SODQ consisted of five main sections corresponding to (1) Quantity and pattern of opiate use, (2) Physical symptoms of withdrawal, (3) Affective symptoms of withdrawal including craving, (4) Withdrawal-relief drug taking, and (5) Rapidity of reinstatement of withdrawal symptoms after a period of abstinence.

The study of Sutherland *et al.* (1986) also included an interesting set of further questions which are referred to as the Opiate Subjective Dependence Questionnaire (OSDQ). This consisted of just five questions relating to 'a typical recent period of drug taking':

(1) Did you think that your opiate use was out of control?
(2) Did the prospect of missing a fix (or dose) make you very anxious or worried?
(3) Did you worry about your opiate use?
(4) Did you wish you could stop?
(5) How difficult would you find it to stop or go without drugs?

There were significant correlations between the SODQ scores and the five OSDQ items, and well as between SODQ scores and important drug-related behaviours (for instance, number of fixes per day).

Motivation and stages of change

A number of workers have commented on the apparent changes in motivational states at different stages of the natural history of addiction. O'Brien *et al.* (1986), describing the cycle of addiction for heroin addicts, distinguish between an initial phase where incentive motivation is predominant; an addictive phase where frequency of use increases, voluntary periods of abstinence decrease, tolerance increases and incentive motivation becomes less important; and a further phase where the addict uses methadone regularly, is less preoccupied with withdrawal and may be able to learn new, adaptive, non-drug behaviour. The initial recognition of the problem and readiness to consider change does not occur until late in the addictive phase, when tolerance has increased and the pursuit of euphoria is no longer a motivating factor.

Prochaska and DiClemente (1986) have described a model comprising four stages of change in the treatment of dependence:

(1) Precontemplation, when the addict does not regard drug taking as a problem;
(2) Contemplation, where the problem is recognized and educational and conscious-raising techniques may be helpful.
(3) Action, where the decision is taken to modify or cease drug taking and action-oriented interventions are appropriate; and
(4) Maintenance, where continued abstinence or control is achieved.

If relapses occur, the drug user returns to the precontemplation or contemplation stage of the cycle and may move towards taking action again.

This model has proved extremely influential, particularly in the field of alcohol problems, and provides a helpful conceptual framework for assessment by allowing treatment approaches to be tailored to fit the motivational state of the client.

PHYSIOLOGICAL MEASURES

Physical signs of drug use

Physical signs alone cannot be regarded as conclusive evidence of drug use, since they vary greatly between individuals, drugs and methods of administration. However, as part of a clinical assessment it can be useful to record signs of intoxication or symptoms such as venepuncture marks and dilated or pinpoint pupils, since they may indicate recent drug use. These data provide an additional source of information to self-report and can contribute to assessment prior to and during treatment.

Biochemical tests for drug use

Urinanalysis

Urine testing has many advantages over other methods in that it is non-invasive, easily carried out and can be used for a wide variety of substances. For these reasons it is the most widely used technique and provides an essential component of most assessment and treatment programmes. The method is useful not only because it provides an objective biological measure of drug use but also because if the patient is aware that the test is being carried out he or she can be held more accountable for drug taking and is more likely to give reliable self-reports. However, it is a sensible precaution to ensure that urine collection is supervised in order to avoid substitution of another sample.

Urine analysis cannot be employed to plot a dose–response curve, so its main use is as a qualitative measure to detect and identify drug use in the period up to 72 hours after last use. As a qualitative test it is not a satisfactory measure of compliance in methadone maintenance programmes, since it cannot show whether the client is taking all or only part of his or her supplied methadone. If there is a suspicion that the client is selling part of his or her methadone, blood serum checks must be carried out to provide quantitative data.

The most commonly used procedure is the enzyme multiple-immunoassay technique (EMIT), which can be used for detection of a variety of drugs (Green 1982). These drugs include amphetamines, morphine, heroin, methadone, antihistamines, barbiturates, cannabis, ephedrine, flurazepam, methaqualone, phenothiazines, codeine, meperidine, propoxyphene, benzodiazepines, ethanol, phencyclidene, phenytoin and salicylates.

The accuracy of EMIT testing is reduced when dosage levels are low, when length of time since drug taking is greater and, for some drugs, when the drug has been chronically abused. It is thought that chronic drug use may lead to increased metabolic efficiency in clearing the drug from the system (Stewart, 1982). Experienced heroin users frequently know and may take advantage of the fact that by drinking large quantities of beer or water they can flush out their systems and produce a drug-free specimen within 24 hours. A test of the specific gravity of the urine may be helpful to give an indication of whether or not flushing has taken place.

Chromatography can also be used to analyse urine samples. This method identifies the substances in the urine sample by comparing the distance between the mobile and stationary phases of the substance with that of known standards. There are three procedures which can be used to determine this distance: thin-layer chromatography (TLC), gas–liquid chromatography (GLC), and high-pressure liquid chromatography (HPLC)

(Gough and Baker, 1983). TLC is a relatively straightforward and inexpensive procedure. However, the results are only qualitative and it is less accurate than other techniques. GLC can provide quantitative and qualitative results, but can only be used for certain substances, and can be expensive for some substances. HPLC uses a spectrophotometer or fluorometer to detect and identify multiple substances, but it is a more costly and complex procedure, and therefore less useful for routine screening.

When urine testing is used to enhance treatment compliance it is important to take urine samples on a regular basis throughout. Many in-patient treatment programmes insist on daily samples. Some treatment centres take daily samples but only analyse a small proportion of them in order to reduce costs. In deciding to adopt this course of action it is important to be aware that most addicts may realize that not all their samples are tested. Any non-random system of selecting the samples to be tested or any system whereby the patient is in contact with the person who decides which samples to test may weaken the credibility of the procedure as a validity check on verbal self-reports. Some treatment centres ask for urine samples on a random basis, and others leave it to the discretion of the primary worker or the doctor. The latter arrangement has the disadvantage that it may introduce an unnecessarily challenging element into an already sensitive therapeutic relationship. For a therapist to decide to ask for a urine sample on one day rather than another may be interpreted as an accusation that the patient has aroused suspicions. On the other hand, the therapist may be deceived by the appearance of compliance and may fail to ask for sufficient urine tests to find out otherwise. For these reasons, it is preferable to ask for samples routinely either at a regular frequency or on a truly random basis.

Blood serum analysis

Analysis of blood serum can provide quantitative measures of drug use, unlike urine analysis. However, the procedures involved are more lengthy and expensive than those used for urinanalysis. There are a number of factors which may affect the accuracy of serum analysis, including age, sex, degree of adiposity, presence of concomitant disease, drug tolerance and inherited metabolic differences (Pribor *et al.*, 1981). Longer histories of drug use tend to be associated with lower serum levels, possibly as a result of increased efficiency of metabolizing the substance. Other factors, such as route of administration, dose size and route of elimination, can also influence serum levels. It must also be recognized that obtaining blood from many intravenous drug abusers is complicated by the poor state of their superficial veins and may be a difficult and sometimes painful process. Obtaining blood from the femoral vein should be done with great circumspection, since it may encourage addicts to inject drugs by this hazardous route on future occasions. For these reasons, blood serum analysis is not usually the most appropriate routine screening method for therapeutic purposes.

Symptoms of withdrawal

There are physical and subjective indicators of withdrawal, and assessment frequently includes both. Drug users' own experiences and reports of withdrawal and craving have been discussed in the section on subjective assessment. Other methods of measuring withdrawal have been developed for medical purposes when assessing the severity of dependence or determining appropriate medication.

Naloxone can be used to assess opiate dependence because its properties as a narcotic antagonist cause it to produce measurable withdrawal symptoms (Wang *et al.*, 1982). A 0.8 mg intramuscular injection of naloxone is given and subsequent withdrawal symptoms are observed and recorded. A withdrawal score is calculated for each of three successive 10-minute intervals following the injection based on presence or absence, severity and time of onset of the following symptoms: gooseflesh, vomiting, tremor, profuse sweating, restlessness, lacrimation, nasal congestion and yawning. The severity of opiate dependence is estimated from the changes in withdrawal over time.

Methadone may be used in the treatment of opiate addiction to enable the client to attain emotional and physical stability before withdrawing completely. In these cases it is necessary to determine the appropriate amount of methadone to prevent unpleasant withdrawal symptoms without overmedicating. It is also important to confirm that the client actually is opiate dependent.

Aylett (1982) assessed methadone dosage by measuring objective signs of withdrawal and titrating the dose until these were abolished. The procedure was caried out on an out-patient basis, with clients required to undergo a 12–24-hour drug fast prior to assessment. Urine was tested for drug content and blood pressure and pulse rate were measured. Observer ratings were recorded for pallor, cold skin, sweating, 'edginess', sniffing and cramps. Clients were also questioned about withdrawal sensations. Methadone mixture was given in 10 mg steps orally. BP and pulse were measured 1 minute after each dose. Doses were delayed 5 or 10 minutes if signs warranted and BP and pulse measurement was repeated at 5-minute intervals following the final dose for up to 1 hour.

Out of 49 subjects, four were identified as 'not currently using addicts', on the basis of sedation, flushing and/or tachycardia following a 10 mg oral dose of methadone. The results for the other clients showed that they were able to tolerate doses in excess of that required to achieve pathophysiological stability. It was concluded that the addict's common viewpoint that he or she must have a particular exact dose of methadone to achieve emotional and physical control of the habit was not confirmed, and that drug addicts can be accommodated on 35 mg if they are non-hypertensive and 87 mg if they are hypertensive in this withdrawal test.

Psychophysiological assessment

Psychophysiological assessment has been used in the investigation of classical conditioning in opiate addicts, pioneered by Wikler (1965) and developed by Siegel (1976), Wikler (1980) and O'Brien *et al.* (1986). In a study of conditioned craving and conditioned withdrawal Childress *et al.* found that when opiate users who had completed 30 days' abstinence in a therapeutic setting were exposed to drug-related stimuli many experienced intense subjective craving and some showed symptoms of conditioned withdrawal. They also showed increased arousal, as indicated by electrodermal responding and decreased peripheral skin temperature to drug-related activities as opposed to neutral activities. There was no significant effect on heart rate. During extinction sessions to drug-related stimuli and activities, effects on psychophysiological indices were not clear cut and the authors suggest that subjective and physiological measures are only loosely related (see Chapter 1).

CONCLUSIONS

The assessment procedures discussed in this chapter have been mainly concerned with data collection in a clinical setting, although some reference has been made to epidemiological methods and theoretical issues. Our understanding of the psychological mechanisms involved in the misuse of drugs is still somewhat primitive, and this is reflected in the multiplicity of comprehensive assessment procedures each designed to meet the needs of a particular drug-treatment programme. Some of these have been described, where there has been an attempt to provide standardized procedures which can be replicated and refined for use elsewhere.

The extensive past literature on personality assessment in drug addicts has not been included on the grounds that it is of limited relevance to current models of addiction, and has not led to the development of effective strategies for treatment (Cohen *et al.*, 1982). A behavioural–analytic approach is seen as more valuable in assisting clients to recognize the behavioural, cognitive and physiological consequences of drug use and to identify aspects of patterns of and attitude to drug use, and personal circumstances which can be used as a focus for treatment.

The organization of the chapter in terms of behavioural, subjective and physiological aspects of drug use is an attempt to accommodate the increasingly psychological interpretation of drug use and drug addiction. It seems likely that there will be continuing interest in the theoretical basis of addiction and that this will lead to less redundancy and greater validity in assessment.

REFERENCES

Advisory Council on the Misuse of Drugs (1982) *Report of the Working Party on Treatment and Rehabilitation*, HMSO, London.

Amsel, Z., Mandell, W., Matthias, L., Mason, G., and Hocherman, I. (1976) Reliability and validity of self-reported illegal activities and drug use collected from narcotics addicts. *International Journal of the Addictions*, **11**, 325–36.

Aylett, P. (1982) Methadone dose assessment in heroin addiction. *International Journal of the Addictions*, **17**, 1329–36.

Bale, R.N. (1979) The validity and reliability of self-reported data from heroin addicts: Mailed questionnaires compared with face-to-face interviews. *International Journal of the Addictions*, **14**, 993–1000.

Bale, R.N., Van Stone, W.W., Engelsing, T.M.J., Zarcone, V.P. and Kuldau, J.M. (1981) The validity of self-reported heroin use. *The International Journal of the Addictions*, **16**, 1387–98.

Boudin, H.M. (1972) Contingency contracting as a therapeutic tool in the deceleration of amphetamine use. *Behavior Therapy*, **3**, 604–5.

Boudin, H.M., Valentine, V.E., Ruiz, M.R. and Regan, E.J. (1980) Contingency contracting for drug addiction: An outcome evaluation. In L. Sobell, M.C. Sobell and E. Ward (eds), *Evaluating Alcohol and Drug Abuse Treatment Effectiveness: Recent Advances*, pp. 109–29, Pergamon Press, New York.

Bradley, B.P., Gossop, M., Phillips, G.T. and Legarda, J.J. (1987) The development of an Opiate Withdrawal Scale (OWS). *British Journal of Addiction*, **82**, 1139–42.

Callahan, E.J. and Rawson, R.A. (1980) Behavioral assessment and treatment evaluation of narcotic addiction. In L.S. Sobell, M.C. Sobell and E. Ward (eds), *Evaluating Alcohol and Drug Abuse Treatment Effectiveness: Recent Advances*, Pergamon Press, New York.

Chambers, C.D. and Taylor, W.J.R. (1973) The incidence and patterns of drug abuse during maintenance therapy. In C.D. Chambers and L. Brill (eds), *Methadone: Experiences and Issues*, Behavioral Publications, New York.

Childress, A.R., McLellen, A.T. and O'Brien, C. (1986) Abstinent opiate abusers exhibit conditioned craving, conditioned withdrawal and reductions in both through extinction. *British Journal of Addiction*, **81**, 655–60.

Cohen, G.H., Griffin, P.T. and Wiltz, G.M. (1982) Stereotyping as a negative factor in substance abuse treatment. *International Journal of the Addictions*, **17**, 371–6.

Cottrell, E.S. and O'Donnell, J.A. (1967) *Reliability of Admission Data*, Unpublished report, National Institute of Mental Health Clinical Research Centre, Lexington, Kentucky.

Cox, T. and Langwell, B. (1974) Reliability of interview data concerning heroin use from heroin addicts on methadone. *International Journal of the Addictions*, **9**, 162–5.

Cummings, C., Gordon, J.R. and Marlatt, G.A. (1980) Relapse: Strategies of prevention and prediction. In W.R. Miller (ed.), *The Addictive Behaviours: Treatment of Alcoholism, Drug Abuse, Smoking and Obesity*, pp. 291–321. Pergamon Press, Oxford.

Donovan, D.M. (1989) Assessment of addictive behaviours: implications of an emerging biopsychosocial model. In D.M. Donovan and G.A. Marlatt (eds), *Assessment of Addictive Behaviours*, pp. 3–48, Hutchinson, London.

Donovan, D.M. and Marlatt, G.A. (1989) *Assessment of Addictive Behaviours*, Hutchinson, London.

Edwards, G. (1986) The alcohol dependence syndrome: a concept as stimulus to enquiry. *British Journal of Addiction*, **81**, 171–83.

Edwards, G., Arif, A. and Hodgson, R. (1981) Nomenclature and classification of drug- and alcohol-related problems. *Bulletin of the World Health Organization*, **59**, 225–42.

Gossop, M. (in press) The development of a Short Opiate Withdrawal Scale (SOWS). *Addictive Behaviors*.

Gossop, M., Green, L., Phillips, G. and Bradley, B. (1989) Lapse, relapse and survival after treatment: a prospective follow-up study. *British Journal of Psychiatry*, **154**, 348–53.

Gossop, M., Powell, J., Grey, S. and Hajek, P. (in press) What do opiate addicts and cigarette smokers mean by 'craving'? A preliminary investigation. Drug and Alcohol Dependence.

Gough, T.A. and Baker, P.B. (1983) Identification of major drugs of abuse using chromatography: An update. *Chromatography*, **21**, 145–53.

Green, L. and Gossop, M. (1988) Effects of information on the Opiate Withdrawal Syndrome. *British Journal of Addiction*, **83**, 305–9.

Green, S. (1982) Use of the toxicology laboratory. *Critical Care Quarterly*, **2**, 19–23.

Grey, S.J. (1989) Statistical report on the Community Drug Team 1988–89. South Glamorgan Clinical Psychology Dept, unpublished report.

Hartnoll, R., Lewis, R., Daviaud, E. and Mitcheson, M. (1985) *Drug Problems: Assessing Local Needs*, Drug Indicators Project, London.

Hodgson, R., Rankin, H. and Stockwell, T. (1978) Craving and loss of control. In P. Nathan, G.A. Marlatt and T. Loberg (eds), *Alcoholism: New Directions in Behavioral Research and Treatment*, Plenum Press, New York.

Home Office (1985) *Statistics for the Misuse of Drugs in the United Kingdom: 1984 (and Supplementary Tables)*, Head Office, Statistical Bulletin, Statistical Department, Surbiton, Surrey.

Hughes, P.H., Venulet, J., Khant, U., Medina Mora, M.E., Navaratnam, V., Poschyachinda, V., Rootman, I., Salan, R. and Wadud, K.A. (1980) *Core Data for Epidemiological Studies of Non-medical Drug Use*, Offset Publication No. 56, World Health Organization, Geneva.

Kozlowski, L.T. and Wilkinson, D.A. (1987) Use and misuse of the concept of 'craving' by alcohol, tobacco and drug researchers. *British Journal of Addiction*, **82**, 31–6.

Kratcochwill, T.R. and Mace, F.C. (1983) Experimental research in clinical psychology. In M. Hersen, A.E. Kazdin and A.S. Bellack (eds), *The Clinical Psychology Handbook*, pp. 197–221, Pergamon Press, New York.

Lang, P.J. (1968) Fear reduction and fear behavior: Problems in treating a construct. In J.M. Shlien (ed.), *Research in Psychotherapy*, **3**, 90–103, American Psychological Association, Washington, DC.

Maddux, J.F. and Desmond, D.P. (1975) Reliability and validity of information from chronic heroin users. *Journal of Psychiatric Research*, **12**, 87–95.

McLennan, A.T., Luborsky, L., O'Brien, C.P. and Woody, G.E. (1980) An improved evaluation instrument for substance abuse patients: the Addiction Severity Index. *Journal of Nervous and Mental Disease*, **168**, 26–33.

Meyer, R. and Mirin, S. (1979) *The Heroin Stimulus*, Plenum Press, New York.

Milby, J., Gurwitch, R.H., Hohmann, A. and Wiebe, D. (1987) Assessing pathological detoxification fear among methadone maintenance patients: the DFSS. *Journal of Clinical Psychology*, **43**, 528–38.

Miller, P.M. (1980) Theoretical and practical issues in substance abuse assessment and treatment. In W.R. Miller (ed.), *The Addictive Behaviours: Treatment of Alcoholism, Drug Abuse, Smoking and Obesity*, pp. 265–90, Pergamon Press, Oxford.

Morrison, V. (1989) Psychoactive substance use-related behaviours of 135 regular illicit drug users in Scotland. *Drug and Alcohol Dependence* (in press).

O'Brien, C.P., Ehrman, R.N. and Ternes, J.W. (1986) Classical conditioning in human opioid dependence. In S. Goldberg and I.P. Stolerman (eds), *Behavioral Analysis of Drug Dependence*, pp. 329–56, Academic Press, New York.

Orford, J. (1985) *Excessive Appetites: A Psychological View of Addictions*, John Wiley, New York.

Page, W.F., Davies, J.E., Ladner, R.A., Afassal, J., and Tennis, H. (1977) Urinanalysis screened vs verbally reported drug use: The identification of discrepant groups. *International Journal of the Addictions*, **12**, 439–50.

Phillips, G., Gossop, M. and Bradley, B. (1986) The influence of psychological factors on the Opiate Withdrawal Syndrome. *British Journal of Psychiatry*, **149**, 235–8.

Phillips, G., Gossop, M., Edwards, G., Sutherland, G., Taylor, C. and Strang, J. (1987) The application of the SODQ to the measurement of the severity of opiate dependence in a British sample. *British Journal of Addiction*, **82**, 691–9.

Pribor, H., Morrel, G. and Schen, G. (1981) *Drug Monitoring and Pharmacokinetic Data*, Pathotox, Park Forest, IL.

Prochaska, J.O. and DiClemente, C.C. (1986) Toward a comprehensive model of change. In W.R. Miller and N. Heather (eds), *Treating Addictive Behaviors: Processing of Change*, pp. 3–27, Plenum Press, New York.

Robertson, J.R., Bucknall, A.B.V. and Wiggins, P. (1986) Regional variations in HIV antibody seropositivity in British drug users. *Lancet*, **i**, 1435.

Roffman, R.A. and George, W.H. (1988) Cannabis abuse. In D. Donovan and G.A. Marlatt (eds), *Assessment of Addictive Behaviours*, Hutchinson, London.

Shiffman, S. and Jarvik, M. (1976) Smoking withdrawal symptoms in two weeks of abstinence. *Psychopharmacology*, **50**, 35–9.

Siegel, S. (1976) Morphine analgesic tolerance: its situation-specificity supports a Pavlovian conditioning model. *Science*, **193**, 323–5.

Skinner, M.A. (1982) The Drug Abuse Screening Test. *Addictive Behaviors*, **7**, 363–71.

Sobell, L. and Sobell, M.C. (1976) Assessment of addictive behavior. In M. Hersen and A.S. Bellack (eds), *Behavioral Assessment: A Practical Handbook*, pp. 305–36, Pergamon Press, New York.

Stephens, R. (1972) The truthfulness of addict respondents in research projects. *International Journal of the Addictions*, **7**, 549.

Stewart, D.C. (1982) The use of the clinical laboratory in the diagnosis and treatment of substance abuse. *Paediatric Annals*, **11**, 669–82.

Stockwell, T., Hodgson, R., Edwards, G., Taylor, C. and Rankin, H. (1979) The development of a questionnaire to measure severity of alcohol dependence. *British Journal of Addiction*, **74**, 79–87.

Strang, J., Ghodse, H. and Johns, A. (1987) Responding flexibly but not gullibly to drug addiction. *British Medical Journal*, **295**, 1364.

Strang, J., Johns, A. and Hunt, S. (1988) Syringe exchange schemes. *British Medical Journal*, **297**, 200.

Strang, J. and Shah, A. (1985) Notification of addicts and the medical practitioner. *British Journal of Psychiatry*, **147**, 195–7.

Sutherland, G., Edwards, G., Taylor, C., Phillips, G., Gossop, M. and Bradley, R. (1986) The measurement of opiate dependence. *British Journal of Addiction*, **81**, 485–94.

Sutherland, G., Edwards, G., Taylor, C., Phillips, G. and Gossop, M. (1988) The Opiate Dependence Syndrome: replication study using the SODQ in a New York clinic. *British Journal of Addiction*, **83**, 755–60.

Wang, R.I., Kochar, C., Hasegawa, A.T. and Roth, B.L. (1982) Initial methadone dose in treating opiate addiction. *International Journal of the Addictions*, **17**, 357–63.

Washton, A.M., Stone, N.S. and Hendrickson, E.C. (1988) Cocaine abuse. In D.M. Donovan and G.A. Marlatt (eds), *Assessment of Addictive Behaviours*, pp. 364–89, Hutchinson, London.

Wells, E.A., Hawkins, J.D. and Catalano, R.F. (1988) Choosing drug use measures for treatment outcome studies. I. The influence of measurement approach on treatment results. *International Journal of the Addictions*, **23**, 851–73.

WHO Expert Committees on Mental Health and on Alcohol (1955) The 'craving' for alcohol. *Quarterly Journal of Studies on Alcohol*, **16**, 33–66.

Wikler, A. (1965) Conditioning factors in opiate addiction and relapse. In D.I. Wiher and G.G. Kassebaum (eds), *Narcotics*, McGraw-Hill, New York.

Wikler, A. (1980) *Opioid Dependence: Mechanisms and Treatment*, Plenum Press, New York.

Chapter 13

People with Mental Handicaps

CHRIS CULLEN and PAUL DICKENS

INTRODUCTION

First, a note on terminology. We are aware that different people prefer to use different terms when describing the group we will refer to as *mentally handicapped people* or *people with mental handicaps*. This sometimes reflects national or cultural differences or, for some, ideology. Nevertheless, we wish to assert at the outset that our client group are first and foremost *people*, and the issues important in assessment are as relevant for them as for other groups.

In particular, we wish to draw attention to an issue which we will return to later and which is mentioned by other authors in this volume. *Assessment cannot stand alone as an activity or process in its own right, nor can people be 'assessed', independently of the context in which they exist*, as when their height or weight is being measured. Assessment has a *purpose*, and it is important to be clear about the purpose before the process is started. Knowledge of the purpose will largely determine the type of assessment process to be undertaken.

THE PROCESS

Hawkins (1979) has identified five separable functions of assessment:

(1) Screening and identifying aspects of general disposition;
(2) Definition and general quantification of problems or achievement;
(3) Pinpointing and design of interventions;
(4) Monitoring of progress;
(5) Follow-up.

These form an 'assessment funnel', and in this chapter we will touch upon aspects of the assessment process relevant to each function.

The last ten years has seen the rapid development of assessment techniques for use with people with a mental handicap. This has been brought about by a number of factors:

Measuring Human Problems. Edited by D.F. Peck and C.M. Shapiro

(1) The passing of legislation requiring professionals to assess the needs of this client group;
(2) The extensive use of Individual Programme Planning and Goal Planning techniques for intervention;
(3) The trend towards de-institutionalization of people with a mental handicap;
(4) The increasing de-professionalization of services, with a resulting emphasis on the development of appropriate assessment techniques for those without specific professional training.

At the same time, there has been the recognition referred to above that assessment is influenced by environmental variables, particularly those associated with the provision of opportunities to gain and practise skills. Dickens (1984) has suggested that assessment can be considered on three levels:

Primary—at a client-centred level, using face-to-face methods of individual evaluation;
Secondary—at an immediate environment level;
Tertiary—where the social and environmental system of a person or group of people is evaluated.

The history of assessment of people with a mental handicap has seen first, the development of detection instruments such as the early Binet and Simon tests (Anastasi, 1961), and then the rise of measures of social functioning and skills such as the Vineland Social Maturity Scale (Doll, 1947), which led to the modern scales of adaptive behaviour brought about by the adoption of the dual criteria of intellectual and social handicap by the American Association on Mental Deficiency (now Retardation) (1965). More recently there has been the development of criterion-referenced tests as opposed to norm-referenced tests, and the use of total teaching packages where a dedicated assessment tool is linked directly to the provision of goal plans or treatment programmes. Dickens and Stallard (1987), in providing a comprehensive listing of specific assessment devices available for use with mentally handicapped people, have pointed out that they are often expected to serve sometimes disparate functions, such as:

(1) Supplying information to aid the setting up of training programmes for individuals;
(2) Supplying information to aid placement in residential, work or educational settings;
(3) The evaluation of programme success;

(4) Large-scale surveys of need providing vital information for the planning and provision of services;
(5) For comparative and research purposes.

Whatever use is planned, it is important that the purpose of the assessment, and the appropriate level, are clear at the outset, so that a correct choice of method can be made.

TYPES OF ASSESSMENT

The background literature on assessment with this client group has been reviewed elsewhere (Mittler, 1970; Clark, 1975; Matson and Breuning, 1983; Hogg and Raynes, 1987). Each of these sources identifies a wide range of available assessment devices summarized under general headings, including intellectual and vocational inventories, personality and psychopathological measures, and specific ability tests. This is not exhaustive, and there are many instances where tests and measures are not readily classifiable under one category or another, or overlap across many. This is particularly true of many adaptive behaviour measures.

It is also noticeable that the categories of measures mentioned above tend to lend themselves to particular types of assessment method. Those in the intellectual and cognitive category tend to be psychometric, with standardized administration. Those in the adaptive behaviour category tend to be either observational checklists or rating scales completed on the information of third-party informants. Given the three-level model of assessment described above, we might mention measures designed to assess at secondary and tertiary levels. Many of these are not specific to the mental handicap field (e.g. the Program Analysis of Service Systems (PASS); Wolfensberger and Glenn, 1975), but are used widely in human services.

Intellectual and cognitive tests

The development of measures of intellectual functioning closely paralleled the early psychological study of mental handicap. Binet and Simon's first attempt (1905) at such a measure was in response to the need to discriminate between non-handicapped (or educable) and handicapped (or ineducable) children. Not surprisingly, therefore, the Stanford–Binet Intelligence Scale is still in use today, although in its present standardization it is not recommended. The Wechsler Scales (Wechsler Preschool and Primary Scale (WPPSI) (1967), Wechsler Intelligence Scale for Children (WISC) (1949) and

Wechsler Adult Intelligence Scale (WAIS) (1955)) have widespread acceptance, although they are not really standardized on a handicapped population. Furthermore, they have a high-ability baseline, so that their use with moderately or severely handicapped people is limited. Similarly, the British Ability Scale (Elliott *et al.*, 1983) has not proved as useful in clinical practice with mentally handicapped people as it might have been, although the subtests are a good source of individual cognitive tests.

All these tests require the subject to possess language, which is often not the case with people with a mental handicap. There are, therefore, a number of tests that rely on non-verbal input. Chief among these is the Coloured Progressive Matrices (Raven, 1962), which has the additional advantages of British and handicapped norms. The British Picture Vocabulary Scale (Dunn *et al.*, 1982) is often used as an intellectual measure, because of its ease of administration and non-verbal input. It is also useful with people with motor problems that prohibit or discourage the use of other tests requiring motor input. Similarly, the Columbia Mental Maturity Scale (Burgemeister *et al.*, 1959) relies on non-verbal and non-motor input. The Leiter International Performance Scale (Leiter, 1969) is a pure non-verbal measure, consisting of mental-age grouped subtests presented without speech, and requiring non-linguistic skills.

Because of the restricted input modalities, such measures described above often sample a restricted set of cognitive abilities, with the emphasis on logical deductive reasoning. It is precisely these skills that are usually lacking in people with learning difficulties, so the test situation is biased against obtaining a valid assessment of the person's capabilities.

Psychologists working with this group of people often employ more specific measures of discrete individual cognitive skills. The Wechsler Memory Scale (Wechsler, 1945) or the more recent Rivermead Test (Wilson *et al.*, 1985) are used where a clinical examination of memory is required, although the use of the standard test norms is not possible. Information gained has to be interpreted with care, therefore, and the results should be reported tentatively. Many psychologists also have their own 'clinical instruments' which they use for judging the extent of cognitive skills, usually on a criterion-referenced basis. A good published example is Form C of the Paton's Assessment Schedules (cf. Dickens and Stallard, 1987), which is a comprehensive set of subtests for examining what might be termed functional intelligence, in ways that are relevant to people with a mental handicap, who often have a history of poor educational exposure and institutionalization.

Scales for assessing adaptive behaviour

The concept of adaptive behaviour is of vital importance in considering the assessment of people with a mental handicap. It owes its origin to the adoption of a dual-criteria approach to the diagnosis of mental handicap by the American Association on Mental Deficiency (now Retardation) in 1961. A standard definition is 'the degree to which a person meets the standards of personal independence and social responsibility expected of their age and cultural group' (AAMD, 1965).

Adaptive behaviour is a collection of skills and attributes, with significant dimensions of age and culture. The concepts of personal independence (the skills that are needed for everyday living) and social responsibility (the adherence to norms, standards and rules of behaviour) form the basic structure of a number of assessment measures. The use of this concept has given rise to many scales, although the parallel idea of 'social competence' employed by Gunzburg (1968) has also been used as a starting point. Indeed, the scales quoted below represent many different views of essentially the same concept, with consequent differences in terminology.

The earliest work in this area was reported by Doll (1925), with his Vineland Social Maturity Scale. Although still available, it is not recommended for current use, having been superseded by a major revision, the Vineland Adaptive Behavior Scale (Sparrow *et al.*, 1985). This new scale represents a major step forward in the psychometrics of adaptive behaviour, having by far the best normative and standardization sample of any of these scales, besides being 'user-friendly' with the option of computer-generated scoring and data display. In keeping with the definition of adaptive behaviour given above, the new Vineland covers behaviour domains of Communication (Receptive, Expressive and Written), Daily Living Skills (Personal Skills, Domestic Living Skills and Community Skills), Socialization (Interpersonal Relationships, Play and Leisure Time and Coping Skills), Motor Skills and Maladaptive Behaviour. The last two domains are optional. Norms are available for institutional and non-institutional groups of people with a mental handicap, ambulant and non-ambulant people, and blind, deaf and emotionally disturbed non-handicapped children. Data are in the form of ratings made on the basis of information gathered from a structured interview with the parent or carer of the client. The scale exists in two forms, the Survey Form, which is intended for shorter diagnostic use, and the Extended Form, which is primarily for programme planning. Each has separate scoring systems reflecting this difference in emphasis, and there are also more items in the longer Extended Form.

The Vineland Scale is a significant advance on the widely used AAMD Adaptive Behavior Scale (Nihira *et al.*, 1974). This scale was originally developed to measure the adaptive behaviour component of the dual diagnostic criteria adopted by the AAMD, and was based on existing scales, including the Vineland Social Maturity Scale already mentioned and the Gunzburg scales (see below). The resulting scale is in two parts, Adaptive Behaviour and Maladaptive Behaviour, each of which is subdivided into a number of domains which are, in turn, divided into subdomains. These are collections of items reflecting discrete skills, and information to compile them (most being in the form of rating scales) is gathered by direct testing of the client or from an interview with a carer or parent. There is a considerable body of literature on the ABS, and it has wide acceptance and usage in research and clinical practice, since it yields reliable results that are of direct use in diagnosis. It is less useful in programme planning, however, a fact which has led to the development of other scales that use the ABS as a source of items and validation. Significant problems with the ABS include difficulties in the scoring and interpretation of the second part that measures maladaptive or problem behaviour. This part is not only value-laden but also does not equate for severity of problem. There are a number of papers that have attempted to tackle this issue (e.g. McDevitt *et al.*, 1977).

Besides being a useful diagnostic concept, adaptive behaviour has great utility in the planning and execution of treatment and training. This has led to the recent development of 'dedicated' assessment tools that are linked directly to a set of pre-prepared teaching plans or to a system for devising individual programme plans. One of the earliest of these was the Portage Guide to Early Education (Bluma *et al.*, 1976), which consists of a developmental checklist in which each item on that list is cross-referenced to a teaching card in a similar skill area that gives teaching suggestions or goals. A similar system has been devised in the United Kingdom, for adults, the Bereweeke Skill Teaching System, which is mentioned in more detail later in the chapter. Another aspect of the usefulness of adaptive behaviour measures in treatment has been the development of maladaptive behaviour scales that can provide global baseline information on behaviour disorder prior to fine-grain behavioural analysis and intervention. A good example is the Aberrant Behavior Checklist (Aman *et al.*, 1985).

CONCEPTUAL ISSUES

Having outlined just a few of the many instruments which are commonly used in assessing people with mental handicaps we want now to discuss some conceptual issues which are currently of particular concern in the field. We have already emphasized the importance of choosing an assessment process only after it is clear what are the purposes of the assessment (cf. Hawkins, 1979), and although we will not cover this any further, its pervading influence will be seen below. Nor will we dwell on crucial matters such as reliability and its assessment, or the relation between reliability, validity and accuracy, issues which are of the utmost importance (cf. Suen, 1988) and which are often overlooked when assessing in mental handicap services. These have been dealt with elsewhere in this volume.

We have chosen to concentrate on three issues which have particular relevance in the field of mental handicap: (1) age-appropriateness, (2) direct observation, and (3) assessment of the causes of behaviour.

AGE-APPROPRIATENESS

It is clear that, in the eyes of many, including some professionals, people with mental handicaps are 'eternal children'. Adults are thought to be operating at developmentally early stages and the public often seems to be content to ask, of a person with a mental handicap, 'at what age would a (normal) child behave thus'. Nowhere is this more apparent than in the legal system, where it is quite common to find courts requesting the mental age of a mentally handicapped person. It is as if judges feel that they have a better understanding if they are told that the 23-year-old in front of them has a mental age of 7 years. Put crudely, they can judge the behaviour of the person with a mental handicap as if it were the behaviour of a 7-year-old child.

This has damaging social repercussions which have been outlined many times by Wolfensberger and his colleagues (cf. Wolfensberger, 1972). Unfortunately, many of the assessment procedures in common usage perpetuate the situation. Instruments are used which are standardized on populations of children or materials are employed which are more appropriate for use with young people rather than adults. There is an urgent need to introduce and maintain awareness of age-appropriateness in assessment for people with mental handicaps.

This applies to all the functions of assessment. It is particularly relevant when a person's adaptive behaviour is being surveyed. Felce *et al.* (1984) has compared, for example, child-orientated and adult-orientated items which might be included in a typical checklist designed to assess a person's grasping and releasing skills (Table 13.1). Felce and his colleagues have also adapted the already successful Bereweeke Skill Teaching System (Mansell *et al.*, 1984) to provide items which are more relevant to adults (Felce *et al.*, 1986). For example, in order to assess matching abilities, labels from tins and jars are used. Sorting by shape is assessed by using knives, forks and spoons, while sorting by colour is measured by using piles of different coloured clothes or towels.

Table 13.1 Comparison of child-orientated checklist and adult-orientated checklist (adapted from Felce *et al.*, 1984).

Ability	Child-orientated procedure	Adult-orientated procedure
Pincer-grip	Assessed using crayon	Assessed using toothbrush
Pushes object	Assessed using toy car	Assessed using cloth to wipe surface
Removes object	Assessed using four buttons in a box	Assessed using coins in purse

DIRECT OBSERVATION

Assessing a person's abilities by asking them, or others, how they *would* perform is time efficient, practical and has a long history. It is the basis of many assessment procedures and clearly has its place. However, it is often an exceedingly fallible way of obtaining information. An anecdote will serve to illustrate the point.

One of us (CC) was using a standard checklist to assess the level of self-care skills of a group of mentally handicapped men who lived in an institution. Many of them were severely or profoundly handicapped. Questions such as 'can he pour hot liquids?' were invariably answered in the negative. After having been asked such questions of the residents in her ward, one enterprising nurse obtained a domestic-style teapot and gave it to one of the elderly residents of the ward, a man with reasonable physical abilities. To her surprise, he lifted the teapot, poured tea into a cup, added milk and one spoonful of sugar, and drank the tea. For the previous ten years he had been having his tea prepared according to the prevailing institutional practice, whereby one large jug of tea was made for the whole ward containing milk and the equivalent of two or three spoonfuls of sugar per cup for each resident. This was a situation where a person's abilities are *assumed* to be different (usually less) than they actually are because the environment does not present opportunities to behave appropriately (cf. Cullen, 1987). This is not uncommon and assessment instruments should take this into account.

The past decade has seen a marked increase in the number of reports of direct observations of behaviour and this has become a field in its own right. We do not have the space to review much of the methodology. The interested reader is advised to consult recent texts such as Bellack and Hersen (1988) or Nelson and Hayes (1986). The foundations of the methodology of direct observation, which come mainly from the field of ethology, are described clearly in Martin and Bateson (1986, reprinted 1988), and the journal

Behavioral Assessment, which is in its twelfth volume in 1990, publishes state-of-the-art papers covering different populations and methodologies.

It is undoubtedly true that improvements in instrumentation often lead to new discoveries, indeed whole new fields of science, and this is also the case in the direct observation of behaviour. Not long ago, if direct observation was to be undertaken it was necessary to use paper-and-pencil methodology, with tick-charts and stop-watches. The complexity of the behavioural stream together with the need to write down what was happening, or find the appropriate box to tick, often made it necessary to use various sampling methods. While these have continuing utility, it is important to note that they have limitations in terms of their accuracy and how much of the behaviour stream can be dealt with at one time (cf. Springer *et al.*, 1981). The advent of portable computing devices has made the direct observation of behaviour, and the subsequent analysis of data, much more comprehensive. An early example will serve to illustrate.

Using a portable keyboard, Cullen *et al.* (1983) observed the behaviour of ten mentally handicapped men in a British institution. Each key corresponded to a particular category of behaviour, and each key depression resulted in a recording in real time of the depression. Thus, it was possible to compute the duration of behaviours as well as their relative frequency, without the need for time sampling. Each person was observed continuously for 10 minutes at a time, and their behaviour categorized as *appropriate, inappropriate* or *neutral*. The behaviour of staff members (reacting to the behaviour of the mentally handicapped person) was recorded using additional keys as *positive* or *negative*, and the reactions of other mentally handicapped people to the person being observed were also categorized as *positive* or *negative*. An eighth key was depressed when there was *no attention* being given to the person under observation. A full description of the methodology can be found in Cullen *et al.* (1983). Table 13.2 shows the type of information obtained using this methodology. From this it emerges that the ten mentally handicapped people who were observed in this setting spent the large majority of their time engaged in neutral or inappropriate behaviour, and that 92 per cent of their behaviour received no attention of any kind from other people!

There is clearly a value in having these kinds of data, either for individuals or for groups. The picture obtained corroborates the more impressionistic or qualitative descriptions to be found in critical texts such as Ryan and Thomas (1988) and provides data against which change may be assessed. For example, one of us (CC) is currently engaged in research using such direct observations as one of the dependent variables with which to judge the efficacy of a staff training programme. Using a portable computer (a Psion Organizer) the size of a pocket calculator, which is considerably more powerful and flexible than that used in Cullen *et al.* (1983), data on the

Table 13.2 Percentage of time spent in each category.

Residents' behaviour	Reaction: From other residents: Positive	Reaction: From other residents: Negative	Reaction: From staff: Positive	Reaction: From staff: Negative	None	Total
Appropriate	1	0	1	0	5	7
Neutral	1	0	1	0	55	57
Inappropriate	1	0	3	0	32	36
Total	3	0	5	0	92	100

interactions between staff and residents are being collected before and after staff are taught how to interact with residents. Using two observers, each with their own Psion (which are now relatively inexpensive), reliability of the observations can be assessed.

Repp *et al.* (1989) describe the ways in which another portable computer—the Epson HX-20—has been used to record up to 43 behaviours in real-time, providing durations and frequencies of behaviours as well as a ready means of performing sequential analyses to find out if any of the behaviours act as antecedents for other behaviours, an issue to which we turn in the next section. They outline how the instrument has been used to examine the effects of moving a group of adults from institutions to group homes; the effects of various staff : client ratios; and the effects of task-demand on stereotyped behaviour.

It is clear that the considerable savings in time and effort, and the ability to analyse complex behaviour–environment relations, are reasons for the continued interest in, and development of, direct observation methodology. It is perhaps not too fanciful to hope that direct observations by care staff, using portable computers, may one day become a common practice and will replace some of the more indirect (and less accurate) assessment procedures in general usage.

ASSESSMENT OF THE CAUSES OF BEHAVIOUR

It is rarely the case that assessment of an individual in order to describe that individual is sufficient. This will only be so when we are interested in screening and describing general disposition (cf. Hawkins, 1979), although even in this case it would be helpful to know what factors influence, or are responsible for, a person's behaviour. That is, if a person scores such-and-such on an instrument, why this level and not better? Behaviour occurs in a context, and it is one of the hallmarks of modern approaches in mental handicap that, in order to understand behaviour, it is not sufficient to describe the behaviour alone; we must also have some understanding of the environment and context in which the behaviour occurs. Contextual events may be proximal or distal, external or internal (Dumas, 1989).

We have emphasized that assessment in mental handicap services should be undertaken to serve a function, and since most of the services for people with mental handicaps exist to help the person to *change* in some way it follows that assessment should be a part of that process. First Iwata *et al.* (1982) and subsequently others (e.g. Parrish *et al.*, 1985; Repp *et al.*, 1988; Sturmey *et al.*, 1988) have devised methodologies for basing interventions on an assessment of the causes of, or functions served by, behaviour. This type of approach fully integrates assessment into the process of behaviour analysis which comprises the four stages of assessment, interpretation, intervention and re-assessment (cf. Cullen *et al.*, 1977; Tennant *et al.*, 1981), and takes us away from seeing assessment as a process on its own which can be meaningful independent of the context of intervention. It also illustrates the point that assessment does not have to be a formal and rigorous procedure in order to be useful.

The Iwata *et al.* (1982) methodology is based on the hypothesis that self-injurious and stereotyped behaviours are difficult to treat because individuals engage in them for different reasons. A successful intervention therefore depends on an assessment of the likely causes for a particular person. Three possibilities have become obvious as a result of various studies over the years; positive reinforcement, negative reinforcement and self-stimulation. Positive reinforcement would be the situation where self-injury or stereotyped behaviour resulted in otherwise scarce consequences such as staff attention. Negative reinforcement would be the situation where self-injury or self-stimulation leads to the removal of some event such as a demand on the person to engage in some task. Self-stimulation may be assumed to be an important factor if the behaviour occurs following a period of no stimulation or when the person is alone.

Iwata *et al.* (1982) took eight children who each engaged in self-injury and put them into four different experimental conditions. *Social disapproval* was when self-injury resulted in the child being mildly reprimanded by an adult who otherwise was not engaged with the child. This took the form of a statement of concern (e.g. 'Don't do that, you're going to hurt yourself') paired with brief contact such as a hand on the child's shoulder. The adult's attention was thus contingent only on the child's self-injury and might act as a reinforcer.

Academic demand was in effect when the adult was trying to get the child to engage in an educational task, such as stacking rings on a peg, and self-injury resulted in the adult terminating the trial and turning away for 30 seconds. This was meant to assess whether the negative reinforcement (removing demand) served to maintain self-injury on an avoidance schedule.

Unstructured play was essentially a control condition where no particular demands were put on the child, self-injury was ignored as far as possible, and the child was in an enriched environment with plenty of attention for appropriate behaviour. In a fourth condition the child was *alone*, with no toys, to see whether the absence of external stimulation led to self-injury, perhaps to bring about self-stimulation.

Iwata *et al.* found that different children exhibited different effects dependent on the condition. Some children's self-injurious behaviour was maintained by reinforcement; some on avoidance schedules; and some by self-stimulation. These findings have been replicated by others (e.g. Sturmey *et al.*, 1988) for other stereotyped behaviours. This kind of procedure is an attempt—albeit still in its early stages—to assess the effects of environmental variables so that more adequate treatment procedures may be devised. It is moving us in a direction away from making 'decisions based on a "best guess" as to what might constitute the most effective means of intervention' (Iwata *et al.*, 1982).

CONCLUSION

In this chapter we have deliberately moved towards assessment which is directly linked to intervention. We asserted at the outset that the *purpose* of assessment has to be considered before embarking on the exercise. Intervention, rather than classification or description, seems to be a useful aim for the helping professions, and assessment must play its part in that process.

REFERENCES

Anastasi, A. (1961) *Psychological Testing*, 2nd edn, Macmillan, New York.

Aman, N.G., Singh, N.N., Stewart, E.W. and Field, C.J. (1985) The Aberrant Behavior Checklist. A behavior rating scale for the assessment of treatment effects. *American Journal of Mental Deficiency*, **89**, 485–91.

American Association on Mental Deficiency (1965) *Manual on Terminology and Classification in Mental Retardation*, 2nd edn, AAMD, Washington, DC.

Bellack, A.S. and Hersen, M. (eds) (1988) *Behavioral Assessment: a Practical Handbook*, 3rd edn, Pergamon Press, New York.

Binet, A. and Simon, T.H. (1905) Méthodes nouvelles pour le diagnostic du niveau intellectuel des anormaux. *Année Psychologie*, **11**, 191–244.

Bluma, S., Shearer, M., Frohmann, A. and Hilliard, J. (1976) *The Portage Guide to Early Education*, Portage Project.

Burgemeister, B., Blum, L.H. and Lorge, I. (1959) *Columbia Mental Maturity Scale*, revised edition, Harcourt Brace and World, New York.

Clark, D. (1975) Psychological Assessment. In A.D.B. Clarke and A.M. Clarke (eds), *Mental Deficiency—the Changing Outlook*, 3rd edn., Methuen, London.

Cullen, C. (1987) Nurse training and institutional constraints. In J. Hogg and P. Mittler (eds), *Staff Training in Mental Handicap*, Croom Helm, Beckenham.

Cullen, C., Burton, M., Watts, S. and Thomas, M. (1983) A preliminary report on the nature of interactions in a mental handicap institution. *Behaviour Research and Therapy*, **21**, 579–83.

Cullen, C., Hattersley, J. and Tennant, L. (1977) Behaviour modification: some implications of a radical behaviourist view. *Bulletin of the British Psychological Society*, **30**, 65–9.

Dickens, P. (1984) The evaluation of services for people with a mental handicap using PASS. *Mental Handicap*, **12**, 102–3.

Dickens, P. and Stallard, A. (1987) *Assessing Mentally Handicapped People—A Guide for Care Staff*, NFER-Nelson, Windsor.

Doll, E. (1925) *The Measurement of Social Competence*, American Guidance Service Inc., Circle Pines.

Doll, E.A. (1947) *Vineland Social Maturity Scale*, Educational Test Bureau, Minneapolis.

Dumas, J.E. (1989) Let's not forget the context in behavioral assessment. *Behavioral Assessment*, **11**, 231–47.

Dunn, L., Dunn, L., Whetton, C. and Pintilie, D. (1982) *British Picture Vocabulary Scale*, NFER–Nelson, Windsor.

Elliott, C.D., Murray, D.J. and Pearson, L.S. (1983) *British Ability Scale*, NFER–Nelson, Windsor.

Felce, D., Jenkins, J., de Kock, U. and Mansell, J. (1986) *The Bereweeke Skill-teaching System: Goal Setting Checklist for Adults*, NFER–Nelson, Windsor.

Felce, D., de Kock, U., Mansell, J. and Jenkins, J. (1984) *Assessing Mentally Handicapped Adults*, Unpublished manuscript.

Gunzberg, H.C. (1968) *Social Competence and Mental Handicap*, Baillière Tindall and Cassell, London.

Hawkins, R.P. (1979) The functions of assessment: implications for selection and development of devices for assessing repertoires in clinical, educational, and other settings. *Journal of Applied Behavior Analysis*, **12**, 501–16.

Hogg, J. and Raynes, N.V. (1987) *Assessment in Mental Handicap*, Chapman and Hall, London.

Iwata, B.A., Dorsey, M.F., Slifer, K.J., Bauman, K.E. and Richman, G.S. (1982) Toward a functional analysis of self-injury. *Analysis and Intervention in Developmental Disabilities*, **2**, 3–20.

Leiter, R.G. (1969) *Examiner's Manual for the Leiter International Performance Scale*, Stoelting Co., Chicago.

Mansell, J., Felce, D., Jenkins, J. and Flight, C. (1984) *Bereweeke Skill Teaching System*, NFER–Nelson, Windsor.

Martin, P. and Bateson, P. (1988) *Measuring Behaviour: an Introductory Guide*, Cambridge University Press, Cambridge.

Matson, J.L. and Breuning, S.E. (1983) *Assessing the Mentally Retarded*, Grune & Stratton, London.

McDevitt, S.C., McDevitt, S.C. and Rosen, M. (1977) Adaptive Behavior Scale, Part II; a cautionary note and suggestions for revisions. *American Journal of Mental Deficiency*, **82**, 210–12.

Mittler, P. (ed.) (1970) *The Psychological Assessment of Mental and Physical Handicaps*, Methuen, London.

Nelson, R.O. and Hayes, S.C. (eds) (1986) *Conceptual Foundations of Behavioral Assessment*, Guilford Press, New York.

Nihira, K., Foster, R., Shellhaas, M. and Leland, H. (1974) *AAMD Adaptive Behavior Scale (1975 Revision)*, AAMD, Washington, DC.

Parrish, J.M., Iwata, B.A., Dawsey, M.F., Bunck, T.J. and Slifer, K.J. (1985) Behavior analysis, program development and transfer of control in self-injury. *Journal of Behavior Therapy and Experimental Psychiatry*, **16**, 159–68.

Raven, J.C. (1962) *Coloured Progressive Matrices (Revised Order, 1956)*, H.K. Lewis, London.

Repp, A.C., Felce, D. and Barton, L.E. (1988) Basing the treatment of stereotypic and self-injurious behaviors on hypotheses of their causes. *Journal of Applied Behavior Analysis*, **21**, 281–9.

Repp, A.C., Harman, M.L., Felce, D., Van Acker, R. and Karsh, K.G. (1989) Conducting behavioral assessments on computer collected data. *Behavioral Assessment*, **11**, 249–68.

Ryan, J. and Thomas, F. (1988) *The Politics of Mental Handicap*, Penguin Books, London.

Sparrow, S.S., Balla, D.A. and Cicchetti, D.V. (1985) *The Vineland Adaptive Behavior Scale*, American Guidance Service Inc., Circle Pines.

Springer, B., Brown, T. and Duncan, P.K. (1981) Current measurement in applied behavior analysis. *The Behavior Analyst*, **4**, 19–31.

Sturmey, P., Carlsen, A., Crisp, A.G. and Newton, J.T. (1988) A functional analysis of multiple aberrant responses: a refinement and extension of Iwata *et al.*'s (1982) methodology. *Journal of Mental Deficiency Research*, **32**, 31–46.

Suen, H.K. (1988) Agreement, reliability, accuracy, and validity: toward a clarification. *Behavioral Assessment*, **10**, 343–66.

Tennant, L., Cullen, C. and Hattersley, J. (1981) Applied behaviour analysis: intervention with retarded people. In G. Davey (ed.), *Applications of Conditioning Theory*, Methuen, London.

Wechsler, D. (1945) A standardized memory scale for clinical use. *Journal of Psychology*, **19**, 87–95.

Wechsler, D. (1949) *Wechsler Intelligence Scale for Children: Manual*, Psychological Corporation, New York.

Wechsler, D. (1955) *Wechsler Adult Intelligence Scale: Manual*, Psychological Corporation, New York.

Wechsler, D. (1967) *Wechsler Preschool and Primary Scale of Intelligence*, Psychological Corporation, New York.

Wilson, B., Cockburn, J. and Baddeley, A. (1985) *The Rivermead Behavioural Memory Test*, Thames Valley Test Company.

Wolfensberger, W. (1972) *Normalisation: the Principle of Normalisation in Human Services*, National Institute on Mental Retardation, Toronto.

Wolfensberger, W. and Glenn, L. (1975) *Program Analysis of Service Systems*, National Institute on Mental Retardation, Toronto.

Chapter 14

Eating Disorders

CHRIS P.L. FREEMAN and FIONA BARRY

INTRODUCTION

Systematic research in eating disorders has a relatively short history, and until a few years ago there were no rating scales available for the measurement of these disorders. The emergence over the past ten years of the syndromes of bulimia, bulimia nervosa and compulsive eating have provided a stimulus to enquiry in this area, and the clinician and researcher now have a reasonably comprehensive battery of measures available.

Development of measures which incorporate specific diagnostic cut-offs has been hampered by the lack of agreement about what the diagnostic criteria of each disorder should be. There are several competing operational definitions for bulimia nervosa. Anorexia nervosa has recently been redefined in the DSM-IIIR in a much broader way, so the weight criteria are now minus 15 per cent rather than minus 25 per cent of mean matched population weight for height (MMPW). Despite this, the field has moved through the characteristic stages of measurement, namely global clinical ratings, followed by self-rating scales to observer rating scales administered using structured clinical interviews, in just a few years.

OPERATIONAL DEFINITIONS

The criteria which have been developed for eating disorders are important both as diagnostic tools and outcome measures. Several studies have used 'failure to meet' a given set of diagnostic criteria as a measure of outcome during a treatment study.

DSM-IIIR diagnostic criteria for anorexia nervosa (1987)

(A) Intense fear of becoming obese, even when underweight;

Measuring Human Problems. Edited by D.F. Peck and C.M. Shapiro

(B) Disturbance of the way in which one's body weight, size or shape is experienced, e.g. claiming to 'feel fat' even when emaciated; belief that one area of the body is 'too fat' even when obviously underweight;
(C) Refusal to maintain body weight over a minimal normal weight for age and height, e.g. weight loss leading to maintenance of body weight 15 per cent below expected: failure to make expected weight gain during period of growth, leading to body weight 15 per cent below expected;
(D) In females, absence of at least three consecutive menstrual cycles when otherwise expected to occur (primary or secondary amenorrhoea).

The concept of anorexia nervosa described above is a much wider one than previously adopted because of the changes in the weight loss required for age, sex and height. However, amenorrhoea is included, the subject being required to have missed at least three consecutive menstrual cycles for a diagnosis of anorexia nervosa to be made.

Russell's (1983) diagnostic criteria for post-pubertal anorexia nervosa have been the most widely used in Britain. He states that there are three necessary sets of clinical disturbances:

(1) Marked loss of weight that is self-induced usually through a systematic avoidance of 'fattening' foods (e.g. high-carbohydrate foods) and excessive exercise. Self-induced vomiting and purging are less frequent (cf. bulimia nervosa);
(2) A specific psychopathology; an overvalued idea that fatness is a dreadful state to be avoided at all costs;
(3) A specific endocrine disorder. In the female amenorrhoea is an early symptom. In the male there is loss of sexual interest and potency.

This set of criteria is more vague than those of the DSM-IIIR, giving no levels of severity either with regard to amount of weight lost or number of periods missed, and does not include distorted body image as a necessary condition for a diagnosis of anorexia nervosa to be made.

There has been a great deal of discussion and controversy over the diagnostic criteria of bulimia nervosa which has reflected the confusion surrounding its aetiology and clinical features. The picture was further confused by the fact that different researchers gave different names to what was essentially the same disorder. However, it was clearly vital that diagnostic criteria be agreed upon so that people could be identified and meaningful research carried out.

The DSM-III criteria for bulimia nervosa were published in 1980. They were found to be over-inclusive; in particular, it was fairly common for a person with a primary diagnosis of depressive illness to meet the criteria for bulimia. The revised criteria for bulimic disorder published in DSM-IIIR are less vague. They specify the frequency of bingeing required for a diagnosis of bulimic disorder to be made, as well as making behaviour specifically engaged in to counteract the effects of eating (severely restrictive diets, self-induced vomiting, or use of laxative and/or diuretics) another necessary condition for a diagnosis.

DSM-IIIR diagnostic criteria for bulimia (1987)

(A) Recurrent episodes of binge-eating (rapid consumption of a large amount of food in a discrete period of time, usually less than 2 hours);
(B) During the eating binges there is a feeling of lack of control over the eating behaviour.
(C) The individual regularly engages in either self-induced vomiting, use of laxatives, or rigorous dieting or fasting in order to counteract the effects of the binge-eating;
(D) A minimum average of two binge-eating episodes per week for at least 3 months.

Although the American DSM-III criteria are widely used, Russell's revised criteria for bulimia nervosa have remained popular, particularly in Britain.

Bulimia nervosa—revised criteria (Russell, 1983)

(1) Preoccupations with food, irresistible cravings for food and repeated episodes of overeating;
(2) Devices aimed at counteracting the 'fattening' effects of food;
(3) A psychopathology resembling that of classical anorexia nervosa;
(4) A previous overt or cryptic episode of anorexia nervosa.

Russell enlarges the diagnostic category by allowing that some bulimics counteract the 'fattening' effects of food by severely restricting their food intake, rather than by self-induced vomiting or purgative abuse. He also addresses the relationship between anorexia nervosa and bulimia nervosa, albeit in a vague way. Russell accounts for the bulimics who do not have a history of anorexia nervosa by saying that they have had a 'cryptic' episode of anorexia nervosa in the past. By this he seems to mean a period of weight loss which would not have been enough to warrant a diagnosis of anorexia nervosa.

GLOBAL MEASURES

The Morgan–Russell assessment schedule (1975)

This set of measures was originally devised as a way of comparing outcomes from different follow-up studies (Morgan, 1973; Morgan and Russell, 1975). Essentially, 14 scaled ratings are made on items such as menstrual pattern, attitude towards sexual matters, relationship with the family, etc. Each of these items is scored on a 0–12 scale with 0 indicating that the behaviour is carried out all the time and 12 that it is not carried out at all; the higher the score, the more normal the behaviour. The authors recommend that information for scoring be collected by means of a guided interview and that the final score should be the average of scale data obtained from the patient, a key informant and information gathered over the previous 6 months. This method of rating differs from the original Morgan–Russell scales (1975), when outcome for eat scales were simply categorized as good, intermediate or poor. The advantages of these schedules are that they are sufficiently simple and quick for routine use in everyday clinical practice.

SELF-MONITORING

Diaries

The most basic self-report measure used to assess a subject's eating pattern is an eating diary (Figure 14.1). These vary in the amount of detail they contain, but usually the subject is required to record everything which he or she eats and drinks, the time, and whether alone or in company. Any counteractive measures taken, such as self-induced vomiting, laxative or diuretic abuse or exercise, are also recorded. Binges are identified in some way, e.g. by bracketing the food which makes up the binge. There is usually also some record of mood and as much as a page may be devoted to the subject's record of 'comments' on the day, which usually describes the subject's feelings and emotions. Sometimes 10 cm lines are used to record mood as they are easy to 'read' and take up little space.

SELF-RATING SCALES

Most eating questionnaires are self-report measures which are vulnerable to response style bias and to inaccurate reporting by the subject. Using a self-

NAME ....

Your next appointment is on:

at:

Please call extension
if you cannot keep your appointment

Please record daily everything that you eat and drink, the number of binges that you have, and the number of times that you vomit and the number of laxatives you take.

______ st ______ lb
______ kg

PLEASE BRACKET ALL BINGES

NUMBER OF BINGES ________

Date Day

		Vomit	Lax.	Other
Breakfast				
Lunch				
Evening meal				
Totals				

Comments:

The desire to starve myself today has been:

Not at all |———————| As strong as it possibly could be

Today's urge to overeat has been:

Not there at all |———————| As strong as it possibly could be

Today in general I have felt:

Not emotionally upset at all |———————| Extremely emotionally upset

Figure 14.1 An eating diary.

report measure may also mean that the clinician or researcher misses relevant information which might have been elicited by probe questions on issues which he or she senses are particularly relevant to the individual. A number of questionnaires taking the form of semi-structured interviews have been developed to overcome these problems.

Global eating disorders rating scales such as EAT26 and 40, EDI and DSEDR are used as screening instruments to identify subjects who have a particular eating disorder and sometimes to measure response to therapy.

The Eating Attitudes Test (EAT)

The Eating Attitudes Test was developed by Garner and Garfinkel (1979) to measure the symptoms of anorexia nervosa, because they felt that there was no rating scale which covered the whole range of behaviours and attitudes which are found in the disorder. It has been used in most studies of eating disorders, in particular anorexia nervosa, since then.

There are two forms of the questionnaire: the first has 40 items and the second is a shorter 26-item version of the original. The questionnaires have cut-off scores of 30 and 20, respectively. Scores above these cut-off points indicate the presence of the symptoms of anorexia nervosa. However, subjects who have abnormal eating patterns, but who would not be diagnosed as having anorexia nervosa, may also score highly on the EAT, so it would be inappropriate to use the EAT as a diagnostic tool for the detection of anorexia nervosa in non-clinical populations.

Both versions of the EAT are presented in the form of 6-point, forced-choice Likert scales. The subject has to rate whether each item applies 'always', 'usually', 'often', 'sometimes', 'rarely' or 'never'. Subjects find it easy to complete, and most do so in under 5 minutes. It is slightly complicated to score: 3 is scored for the most 'anorexic' response, 2 for the adjacent response, 1 for the response adjacent to that, and 0 for the other three responses, on each item. This instrument is not specific to any particular eating disorder.

The Eating Disorder Inventory (EDI)

The Eating Disorder Inventory (EDI) was developed by Garner *et al.* (1983) to measure some of the psychological and behavioural traits relevant to anorexia nervosa and bulimia. It is a 64-item self-report questionnaire which has the same format as the EAT: 6-point, forced-choice Likert scales. It has eight subscales: Drive for Thinness, Bulimia, Body Dissatisfaction, Ineffectiveness, Perfectionism, Interpersonal Distrust, Interoceptive Awareness

Example of question used in the EAT

I am terrified about being overweight	3	2	1	0	0	0

3 Always

2 Very often

1 Often

0 Sometimes

0 Rarely

0 Never

and Maturity Fears. The first three subscales assess attitudes and behaviours related to eating and body shape which are central features of anorexia nervosa, but which can also be found in dieters in general. The other five subscales measure traits which Garner *et al.* saw as having been identified as features central to the psychopathology of anorexia nervosa.

Subjects with anorexia nervosa of the restrictive and bulimic types and normal-weight bulimic subjects were found to score significantly higher than normal control subjects on the EDI subscales Drive for Thinness, Bulimia and Body Dissatisfaction. The EDI was also found to discriminate between subjects with anorexia nervosa, obese and formerly obese subjects, so it does not simply seem to be measuring concern about weight or dieting. When anorexic bulimic subjects and normal-weight bulimic subjects were compared, their EDI scores were similar, except that the anorexic bulimic subjects scored higher on the Maturity Fears subscale.

Unfortunately, Garner *et al.* did not examine whether the five more general subscales are specific to subjects with eating disorders. Cooper *et al.* (1985) administered the EDI to a sample of psychiatric outpatients who did not have an eating disorder. They found that although their scores on the three subscales related to eating and attitudes to weight and shape were significantly lower than Garner *et al.*'s anorexic subjects, there were few differences between the anorexic group and the psychiatric out-patients who had high scores on the General Health Questionnaire (GHQ). The authors felt that this suggests that these subscales may reflect a general level of psychological disturbance rather than features specific to patients with eating disorders.

The EDI is slightly longer than the EAT but it is scored in exactly the same way. It does not have a cut-off score like the EAT as the subscale scores are considered separately rather than being added together to produce one total EDI score. Like the EAT, it is easily and rapidly filled in by most subjects. It is vulnerable to the problems of any self-report measure.

BULIMIA

Several questionnaires have been developed specifically to assess bulimia and its symptoms. Most of them were compiled by researchers using their clinical experience and based on DSM-III criteria for bulimia, usually developed for specific purposes and seldom used in research carried out elsewhere.

The Binge-Eating Questionnaire

The Binge-Eating Questionnaire was developed by Halmi *et al.* (1981) in order to estimate the prevalence of bulimia in a college population. It is a 23-item questionnaire which elicits demographic information, weight history, use of diet aids and medication, and the behavioural symptoms of bulimia as described in the DSM-III diagnostic criteria for bulimia. As the diagnostic criteria have been revised since then, the questionnaire would not be of use as it stands. However, it could be easily updated by simply incorporating the changes made to the criteria into the relevant questions. When Halmi *et al.* surveyed a college population using the Binge-Eating Questionnaire they found a higher prevalence rate of bulimia (13 per cent) than other surveys of college populations in different locations. This is probably a reflection of the fact that the DSM-III criteria for bulimia were over-inclusive, as they contained no necessary level of frequency of binge eating and did not require that a person use the drastic measures of either strict dieting or fasting, self-induced vomiting or use of laxatives in order to counteract binge eating and to try to control weight. The Binge-Eating Questionnaire has not been widely used and does not seem to have been updated. However, this basic short questionnaire is useful for large surveys of normal populations, provided that it is recognized that the diagnostic criteria upon which it is based have been revised.

The Bulimia Test (BULIT)

The Bulimia Test (BULIT) was developed by Smith and Thelen (1984). It is a 32-item, self-report, multiple-choice scale. The authors compiled it with the following aims in mind: that it would discriminate (1) between individuals with bulimia and those with no eating problem; (2) between individuals with bulimia and those with other eating disorders; (3) between the different subgroups of bulimia; and (4) that the scale would achieve these objectives both for those who had and those who had not sought treatment.

The items which discriminated most strongly between a group of bulimic subjects and a group of normal control subjects were chosen to make up the scale and every criterion area described in DSM-III was included. The BULIT is a self-report, multiple-choice scale with each item having five possible answers, the most symptomatic response scoring 5. There is a cut-off score of 102 above which a subject is likely to meet the diagnostic criteria for bulimia. The authors suggest that if the BULIT is being used as a screening instrument to pick out subclinical cases of bulimia in subjects who have not yet sought treatment, the cut-off point can be reduced to 88 and special attention paid to item 15, which covers self-induced vomiting, so that subjects who respond with any response other than 'less than once a month or never' can be picked out. The Bulimia Test is straightforward and is fairly quickly completed by most subjects. Although it was based on the DSM-III criteria for bulimia which have now been revised, it would not need to be revised as it includes items which cover the changes in the criteria. It has not been widely used in research in Britain.

The Bulimic Investigatory Test, Edinburgh (BITE)

The BITE was developed by Henderson and Freeman (1987) specifically to identify subjects with symptoms of bulimia nervosa. When it is used as a screening instrument subjects answer on the basis of their feelings and behaviour over the previous 3 months. It can also be used to measure severity and response to treatment. When it is utilized to monitor progress in treatment, subjects answer on the basis of their feelings and behaviour over the previous month.

The BITE is a 33-item, self-report measure which is easily completed by most subjects in under 10 minutes. It consists of two subscales. The Symptom subscale is made up of 30 items to which the subject is required to answer 'yes' or 'no'. The Scale is scored by giving one point for each 'bulimic' answer circled. Scores can be divided into three groups: a symptom score of 20 or more indicates a very disordered eating pattern and it is highly likely that a subject whose score is in this range will meet DSM-IIIR criteria for bulimic disorder. A medium-range symptom score (10–19) indicates a disordered eating pattern but would be unlikely to warrant a diagnosis of bulimic disorder. A symptom score of 0–10 indicates that the subject has a normal eating pattern. The Severity Scale consists of three questions and measures the severity of bingeing and purging behaviour as defined by its frequency. It is scored by adding the circled scores together. A severity score of 5 or more is considered to be clinically significant and one of 10 or more indicates a high degree of severity.

The BITE is a useful measure as it can be used as a screening instrument and as an assessment of severity and response to treatment. It also identifies both subjects with bulimic disorder and those who, although they do not meet DSM-IIIR criteria for bulimic disorder, have certain symptoms of that disorder (for example, psychogenic vomiting, laxative abuse or compulsive eating).

OBSERVER RATING SCALES

The Eating Disorders Examination (EDE) (1987)

The Eating Disorders Examination was developed by Cooper and Fairburn (1987) as a semi-structured interview for the assessment of the specific psychopathology of eating disorders. It was felt that although a number of eating questionnaires existed, none of them were detailed, sensitive or flexible enough for use in studies of the psychopathology of eating disorders or of the effects of treatment. The usual format is the self-report questionnaire which has inherent limitations, particularly in this field, as the specific psychopathology of eating disorders is complex and often difficult to define and to interpret.

The EDE is a 62-item semi-structured clinical interview. It is concerned with the patient's current state and all questions refer to the previous four weeks. For each item there is a mandatory probe question as well as a number of optional subsidiary questions which are designed to help the interviewer to give the client as accurate a rating as possible. The interviewer can ask any additional questions which he or she feels are necessary. Most of the ratings are made on 7-point scales which have at least four clearly defined anchor points. Other items concerning the frequency of certain behaviours are marked in terms of severity or frequency of occurrence at a certain level of severity. The EDE takes between 30 minutes and 1 hour to administer and brief training in its administration is required.

A recent paper evaluating the EDE by Wilson and Smith (1988) compared it with the EDI, which was also designed to assess the specific psychopathology of eating disorders and the Restraint Scale, which assesses concern about dieting, one of the main clinical features in bulimia nervosa. The three measures were compared with regard to how well they were able to discriminate between patients with bulimia nervosa and severely restrained, non-bulimic controls. The groups' scores were significantly different only on the total score and the bulimia scale with the EDI. However, their scores were significantly different on four out of five subscales of the EDE, the exception being the 'restraint' subscale. The authors felt that this demonstrated that the EDE was the best available measure of the specific psychopathology of bulimia nervosa.

The Clinical Eating Disorder Rating Instrument (CEDRI) (1987)

The Clinical Eating Disorder Rating Instrument (CEDRI) was developed by Palmer *et al.* (1987) to provide a systematic way of documenting clinical observation of patients with anorexia nervosa and bulimia. It can also be used to assess progress. Palmer *et al.* felt that this was necessary, as most of the measures of the specific psychopathology and clinical features of eating disorders take the form of self-report questionnaires. It is made up of 31 items covering the range of features which the authors consider to be important in the diagnosis and description of clinical eating disorders. There is also a standardized information sheet for recording other relevant details about the patient.

Each item takes the form of a standard question followed by a list of probe questions. In addition, interviewers may add their own questions to clarify the response to each item. Anchor points are defined for the individual ratings for each question. One of the purposes of the interview is to measure change over time, and so the patient is asked to respond to each item only referring to the previous four weeks. The authors advise that the CEDRI should be administered by an experienced clinical interviewer who is able to ask appropriate additional probe questions when necessary, and to adequately clarify questions to ensure that the subject fully understands each question.

OTHER MEASURES

The Diagnostic Survey for Eating Disorders (DSED)

The DSED is a standardized multi-item interview for obtaining detailed intake information which was developed by Johnson (1985). It can be used in both a purely clinical and in a research setting and as a self-report measure or as a semi-structured interview guide. It is divided into twelve sections which focus on various aspects of anorexia nervosa and bulimia nervosa: demographic factors, weight history and body image, dieting behaviour, binge-eating behaviour, purging behaviour, exercise, related behaviours, sexual functioning, menstruation, medical and psychiatric history, life adjustment and family history. It was not intended as a scaled instrument, but as a standardized format for collecting relevant information which makes communication between different treatment centres easier. As such, it is an extremely useful measure to use in the initial assessment of a patient with an eating disorder. Patients can be asked to fill in the DSED as fully as possible on their own and interviewers can then review the self-reported information with the patients, eliciting more detailed information where necessary and assessing the affective responses of patients to the topics covered in the survey.

Body-image measures

It is well established that body-image distortion is a feature of both anorexia nervosa and bulimia nervosa, and a number of different methods have been employed to measure that distortion. These can be divided into distorting-image techniques and size-estimation techniques.

Distorting-image techniques

The *Distorting Mirror* was developed by Traub and Orbach (1964). It is a metal mirror which can be bent horizontally and vertically in order to distort the image. The subject is required to reset the mirror to produce what is believed to be the correct image. A more sophisticated distorting mirror has recently been developed by Slade (eg. Slade, 1985).

A *Distorting Photograph Technique* was developed by Glucksman and Hirsch (1969). A slide is taken of the subject with an anamorphic lens which can be distorted by up to 20 per cent in the underestimation direction. The subject is required to decide which image most closely resembles a correct image of his or her body.

The *Distorting Television Technique* was developed by Allbeck *et al.* (1976). It consists of the subject being photographed by a video camera and his or her image being reproduced on a television screen. That image can be distorted in both the overestimation and underestimation direction, and the subject is required to alter the image so that it corresponds with his or her view of correct body size.

Size-estimation techniques

Slade and Russell (1973) modified a *visual size estimation task* which was developed by Reitman and Cleveland (1964). It involves subjects estimating the physical widths of certain parts of their bodies using two light sources. From this a measure of body perception accuracy (BPI) could be calculated:

$$\text{BPI} = \frac{\text{Perceived size}}{\text{Real size}} \times 100$$

Image-marking technique

The image-marking technique was developed by Askevold (1975). It involves subjects standing facing a blank expanse of paper attached to a wall or screen. They are required to mark on the paper in front of them the widths between certain parts of their bodies as they were touched (for example, shoulders, waist and hips).

The different methods have produced different results (Slade, 1985), and so it is important that one of the techniques from each of the two categories, Distorting-image Techniques and Size-estimation Techniques, be used in studies of body-size estimation. Size-estimation techniques seem to be more sensitive to both external and internal influences and are therefore most useful in monitoring aspects of ongoing treatment, whereas image-marking techniques produce more stable responses and are therefore most useful in monitoring more long-term responses to treatment. The former seems to measure the extent of body-size sensitivity and the latter a more fixed irrational belief about body size.

Body shape questionnaires

It is well established that extreme concern about body shape is a central feature of both anorexia nervosa and bulimia nervosa. Although there are a number of measures which assess dissatisfaction with different parts of the body (e.g. the Body-image Satisfaction Scale (Marsella *et al.*, 1981) and the Body Dissatisfaction subscale of the Eating Disorder Inventory (Garner *et al.*, 1983), none has provided a specific assessment of concerns about body shape including details of antecedents and consequences. The Eating Disorder Examination (Cooper and Fairbairn, 1987) does include questions about concern about body shape, but it was designed as a research interview which covers all the specific psychopathology of anorexia nervosa and bulimia nervosa, rather than only concern about body shape.

The Body Shape Questionnaire was developed by Cooper *et al.* in 1987 specifically to assess concern about body shape and the experience of 'feeling fat'. It is a self-report measure which consists of 34 questions each of which have six possible answers ranging from 'never' = 1 to 'always' = 6. The items were chosen after interviews with both patients with eating disorders and 'normal' women. The BSQ scores of the patient groups were significantly higher than those of the 'normal' group, and within 'the non-patient' group those who admitted to being concerned about weight and shape had significantly higher BSQ scores than those who were not concerned about weight and shape.

Cooper *et al.* recommend that the BSQ should not be used for case detection but as a measure of the extent of psychopathology. The BSQ is easily completed by most subjects in under 10 minutes and is the only measure which has been developed specifically to assess concern about body shape.

THE ASSESSMENT OF OBESITY

Obesity and overweight are not the same thing. Obesity exists when fat makes up a greater than 'normal' fraction of total body weight. In adult males fat tends to comprise 15–18 per cent of total body weight and an adult male might be described as obese if his body fat content is over 25 per cent. In adult females the figures are slightly higher: fat tends to make up 20–25 per cent of total body weight and an adult female might be described as obese if her body fat content is over 30 per cent. Several laboratory procedures can provide very accurate measures of body fat (for example, measurement of body density, body potassium, underwater weighing and gas uptake). However, these measures are not widely available, they can be very time consuming and they can also involve some physical discomfort and embarrassment. Simple skinfold calipers used at various sites on the body provide a good measure of subcutaneous fat.

Overweight is more easily assessed than obesity, and it is usually defined in relation to tables of desirable weight which are usually derived from information from insurance companies (for example, Geigy, 1962). Degree of 'overweight' can be expressed in two ways:

(1) Relative weight, which is the ratio of percentage of actual to desirable weight, desirable weight being associated with minimum mortality. Using tables such as the Metropolitan Life Insurance weight for height tables, overweight can be defined as body weight above the upper weight for each height.
(2) Body Mass Index (BMI). Various ratios of height and weight are used, BMI being the most popular. It is calculated as follows:

$$\text{BMI} = \frac{\text{Weight (kg)}}{\text{Height (m)}^2}$$

and gives the following categories:

<15	emaciated	
15 – 19.9	underweight	
20 – 24.9	normal weight	
25 – 30.9	mildly obese	Grade I
30 – 39.9	moderately obese	Grade II
40 +	severely obese	Grade III

The BMI classification is the same as Quetelet's Index, which was proposed by the Belgian astromer Quetelet in 1871. There are objections to the classification. First, as it is derived from body weight and height it does not necessarily follow that overweight indicates fatness or adiposity; it might be an indication of heavy musculature. Second, although the normal weight range 20–25 was chosen specifically because it is associated with minimum mortality and corresponds to the 'desirable weight' range in the Metropolitan Life Insurance weight-for-height tables, the choice of 25, 30 and 40 as the cut-off points between Grades I, II and III is purely arbitrary.

However, it is a widely used classification which enables professionals who are involved with obese people to communicate meaningfully about obesity (Figure 14.2).

The *Master Questionnaire (MQ)* was developed by Straw *et al.* (1984) specifically for use in obesity research. It was designed to be used as an outcome measure and as a predictor of change in obesity status. The authors felt that a questionnaire was required which covered areas other than eating and exercise habits, which have come to be thought of as important in the treatment of obesity. The current version includes measures of Hopelessness, Physical Attribution, Motivation, Stimulus Control and Energy Balance Knowledge.

The MQ is a useful measure of response to treatment and prediction of outcome and is the only questionnaire specifically for use with the obese. It is fairly short and is easily completed by most subjects in under 15 minutes. However, it requires further refinement and validation.

'Eating style' questionnaires

'Restraint' is an aspect of eating behaviour described by Hermann and Mack

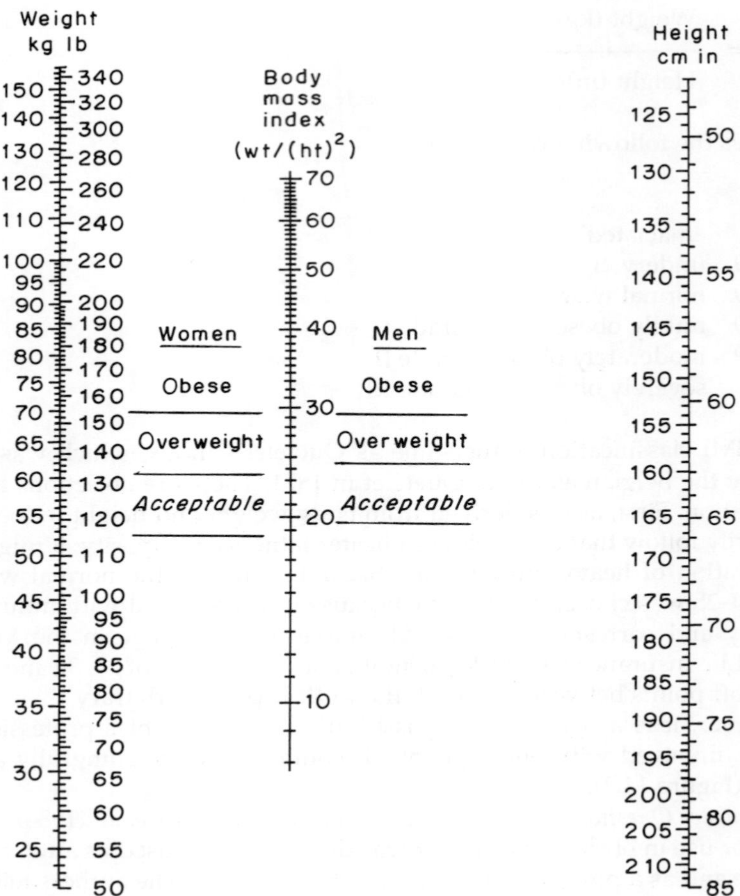

Figure 14.2 A nomogram for body mass index. To use this nomogram, place a ruler or straight edge between the body weight in kilograms or pounds (without clothes) and the height in centimetres or inches (without shoes). The body mass index is read from the middle of the scale and is in metric units.

(1975). Until recently it was the only 'eating style' variable to have been psychometrically assessed. Hermann proposed the concept of restraint to explain individual differences in eating behaviour and external responsibility. It was based on Nisbett's (1972) set-point theory. Nisbett suggested that individuals who were dieting, or exhibiting restraint, might be trying to maintain a lower weight than their biologically predetermined set-point. He suggested that the resulting state of hunger might lead to increased responsivity to external food cues and a tendency to overeat. The Restraint Scale was developed to assess how far normal individuals exhibit behavioural and attitudinal concern about dieting and keeping their weight down. The original version had only five items and this has been expanded and revised a number of times.

The Restraint Scale now consists of 10 items and has a simple scoring system. The scale has been found to contain two robust subscales: 'weight fluctuation' (WF) and 'concern for dieting' (CD). Although there is no agreement about the relative importance of these two subscales as yet, it is now generally accepted that a total RS score can no longer be seen as a simple measure of 'dietary restraint'. One of the other problems that the discovery of the two subscales has uncovered is that while most subjects can easily answer all the CD items, low-restraint subjects who are more likely to be unconcerned about their weight frequently cannot answer the WF questions, which require specific information about weight variation. This is a problem if the questionnaire is used in research, because complete usable questionnaires are more likely to be obtained from subjects who are relatively more concerned about their weight.

Two questionnaires have been developed more recently which contain 'eating style' variables in addition to 'restraint', The Three-Factor Eating Questionnaire was developed by Stunkard and Messick (1985) to measure three dimensions of eating behaviour: 'dietary restraint', 'disinhibition' and 'hunger'. The items were derived from the Restraint Scale, the Latent Obesity Questionnaire and 17 items from the clinical experience of the authors. The original questionnaire was administered to several groups who were selected to cover the whole range from extreme dietary restraint to extreme lack of restraint. The responses were factor analysed and the resulting factor structure was used to revise the questionnaire. This process was repeated and the three stable factors mentioned above emerged. The final questionnaire consists of 51 items. The 36 items in Part I are simply answered 'true' or 'false' and the remaining 15 items in Part II have four choices of response, apart from item 50, which has five possible responses. The Three-Factor eating Questionnaire has uncovered three dimensions within the global concepts of restrained eating and latent obesity and is a useful measure for the study of eating behaviours.

The Dutch Eating Behaviour Questionnaire (DEBQ) was developed by Van Strien *et al.* (1986). It was designed to assess the eating style characteristics which the authors considered to contribute to the development of eating disorders; namely, restraint, emotional eating and external eating. The current version consists of 33 items, all of which have the response format: 'never' (1); 'seldom'; (2); 'sometimes' (3); 'often' (4); and 'very often' (5). The DEBQ is easily completed by most subjects in less than 10 minutes and is a useful measure for studying eating style characteristics, and seems to be able to identify those styles associated with obesity, anorexia nervosa and bulimia nervosa.

Meyer and Pudel (1977) developed the 40-item Latent Obesity Questionnaire. They discovered that the rate of consumption during a 20-minute test meal differentiated obese from non-obese people, the rate of eating of non-obese people slowing down during the meal while the rate of eating of the obese people did not. They felt that this suggested an impairment of satiety. Meyer and Pudel discovered a subgroup of non-obese people whose rate of eating also did not slow down during a 20-minute test meal and came up with the concept of 'latent obesity' to explain this. The latent obese were seen as people who were biologically predetermined to be obese but who were able to maintain a normal body weight by restricting their food intake. The Latent Obesity Questionnaire identified as latent obese normal-weight people whose eating rate did not slow down during the 20-minute test meal. However, the questionnaire has only been applied in this particular laboratory experiment.

CONCLUSIONS

We have described the main assessment methods currently available for eating disorders. While there is a wide range none are ideal. The recent introduction of standardized semi-structured clinical interviews such as the EDE and, to a lesser extent, the CEDRI represent an advance. Many studies in the past have relied solely on self-report questionnaires. In our view, the following developments are required:

(1) A short semi-structured interview which takes less time than the EDE or the CEDRI, perhaps incorporating cut-off points or optional sections so it can be tailored to the specific pathology being examined.
(2) An observer-rated measure of change in eating disorders. This may need to incorporate a separate measure for bulimia nervosa and anorexia. An equivalent of the Hamilton Depression Scale but with better validity and reliability would be desirable in assessing eating disorders.
(3) Self-rating scales which attempt to measure the core pathology of eating disorders, namely disturbed eating habits, extreme methods of weight control and excessive concerns about weight and shape.
(4) Measures which are comprehensive enough to allow for the likely changes in diagnostic criteria which will occur with DSM-IV and thereafter. It is important that any measures currently being developed are flexible enough to allow investigators to determine whether their subjects fit such criteria.
(5) The development of a core set of criteria which are reported in all

> scientific studies. There is an urgent need to proceed beyond outcome measures such as percentage of matched mean population weight for height. All patients should be reported in terms of current height, current weight, height and weight at the onset of the disorder, menstrual status, and an assessment of eating pattern and habits, methods of weight control, anorexic/bulimic attitudes. The recently modified Morgan and Russell Scales for anorexia nervosa mentioned earlier in the chapter go some way towards meeting this need, but they are not based on a standardized interview schedule, nor do they include satisfactory measures of anorexic attitudes or beliefs.

The development of other more objective measures of assessment should be actively pursued. For anorexia nervosa these could include body composition studies, measure of ovarian size, measure of bone density and cognitive measures. There has been recent interest in the Stroop Colour Naming Task. This test appears to be able to demonstrate which words an individual finds emotive, alarming or of high personal significance. The test has so far been used in spider phobics (Watts *et al.*, 1986), generalized anxiety disorder patients (Mathews and McLeod, 1985) and those who have attempted suicide (Williams and Broadbent, 1986). It may be that such a measure could provide a simple and relatively bias-free indication of disordered beliefs in eating disorders.

For the present, the best that we can do is to use a range of different outcome measures and at least attempt to address the list of essential items mentioned above.

REFERENCES

Allbeck, P., Hallberg, D. and Espmark, S. (1976) Body Image—an apparatus for measuring disturbances in estimation of size and shape. *Journal of Psychosomatic Research*, **20**, 583–9.

American Psychiatric Association (1980) *DSM-III: Diagnostic and Statistical Manual of Mental Disorders*, 3rd edn, American Psychiatric Association, Washington, DC.

American Psychiatric Association (1987) *DSM-IIIR: Diagnostic and Statistical Manual of Mental Disorders*, 4th edn, American Psychiatric Association, Washington, DC.

Askevold, F. (1975) Measuring body image. *Psychotherapy and Psychosomatics*, **26**, 71–7.

Cooper, Z., Cooper, P.J. and Fairburn, C.G. (1985) The specificity of the Eating Disorder Inventory. *British Journal of Clinical Psychology*, **24**, 129–30.

Cooper, Z. and Fairburn, C. (1987) The eating disorder examination: a semi-structured interview for the assessment of the specific psychopathology of eating disorders. *International Journal of Eating Disorders*, **6**, 1–8.

Cooper, P.J., Tawor, M.J., Cooper, Z. and Fairburn, C.G. (1987) The Development and Evaluation of the Body Shape Questionnaire. *International Journal of Eating Disorders*, **6**, 485–494.

Garner, D.M. and Garfinkel, P.E. (1979) The Eating Attitudes Test: an index of symptoms of anorexia nervosa. *Psychological Medicine*, **9**, 273–9.

Garner, D.M., Olmstead, M.P. and Polivy, J. (1983) Development and validation of a multi-dimensional eating disorder inventory for anorexia nervosa and bulimia. *International Journal of Eating Disorders*, **2**, 15–34.

Geigy (1962) *Average Weights of Adults*, Society of Actuaries: Build and Blood Pressure Study, Chicago, 1959, 623, Documenta Geigy, Scientific Tables, Geigy Pharmaceuticals, Manchester.

Glucksman, M.L. and Hirsch, J. (1969) The response of obese patients to weight reduction. 3. The perception of body size. *Psychosomatic Medicine*, **31**, 1–7.

Gormally, J., Black, S., Daston, S. and Rardin, D. (1982) The assessment of binge-eating severity among obese persons. *Addictive Behaviors*, **7**, 47–55.

Halmi, K.A., Falk, J.R. and Schwartz, E. (1981) Binge-eating and vomiting: a survey of a college population. *Psychological Medicine*, **11**, 697–706.

Hawkins, R.C. and Clement, P.F. (1980) Development and validation of a self-report measure of binge eating tendencies. *Addictive Behaviors*, **5**, 219–26.

Herman, C.P. and Mack, D. (1975) Restrained and unrestrained eating. *Journal of Personality*, **43**, 647–660.

Henderson, M. and Freeman, C.P.L. (1987) A self-rating scale for bulimia: the 'BITE'. *British Journal of Psychiatry*, **150**, 18–24.

Johnson, C. (1985) Initial consultation for patients with bulimia and anorexia nervosa. In D. Garner and P. Garfinkel (eds), *Handbook of Psychotherapy for Anorexia Nervosa and Bulimia*, Guilford Press, New York.

Marsella, A.J., Shizuru, L., Brennan, J. and Kameoka, V. (1981) Depression and body image satisfaction. *Journal of Cross-cultural Psychology*, **12**, 360–71.

Mathews, A. and McLeod, C. (1985) Selective processing of threat cues in anxiety states. *Behaviour Research and Therapy*, **23**, 563–9.

Meyer, J.E. and Pudel, V. (1977) Experimental feeding in man: a behavioural approach to obesity. *Psychosomatic Medicine*, **39**, 153–7.

Morgan, H.G. (1973) *Anorexia Nervosa: a Prognostic Study*. MD thesis, University of Cambridge.

Morgan, H.G. and Russell, G.F.M. (1975) Value of family background and clinical features as predictors of long term outcome in anorexia nervosa. *Psychological Medicine*, **5**, 355–71.

Nisbett, R.E. (1972) Hunger, obesity, and the ventromedial hypothalamus. *Psychological Review*, **79**, 433–53.

Palmer, R., Christie, M., Cordle, C., Davies, D. and Kerrick, J. (1987) The Clinical Eating Disorder Rating Instrument (CEDRI): a preliminary description. *International Journal of Eating Disorders*, **6**, 9–16.

Reitman, E.E. and Cleveland, S.E. (1964) Changes in body image following sensory deprivation in schizophrenia and control groups. *Journal of Abnormal and Social Psychology*, **68**, 168–76.

Russell, G.F.M. (1979) Bulimia nervosa: an ominous variant of anorexia nervosa. *Psychological Medicine*, **9**, 429–48.

Russell, G.F.M. (1983) Anorexia nervosa and bulimia nervosa. In G.F.M. Russell and L. Hersov (eds), *Handbook of Psychiatry*, Vol. 4, *The Neuroses and Personality Disorders*, pp. 285–98, Cambridge University Press, Cambridge.

Slade, P.D. and Russell, G.F.M. (1973) Awareness of body dimensions in anorexia nervosa: cross-sectional and longitudinal studies. *Psychological Medicine*, **3**, 188–99.
Slade, P. (1985) A review of body image studies in anorexia nervosa and bulimia nervosa. *Journal of Psychiatric Research*, **19**, 255–65.
Smith, M.C. and Thelen, M.H. (1984) Development and validation of a test for bulimia. *Journal of Consulting and Clinical Psychology*, **52**, 863–72.
Straw, M.K., Straw, R.B., Mahoney, M.J., Rogers, T., Mahoney, B.K. *et al.* (1984) The Master Questionnaire: preliminary report on an obesity assessment device. *Addictive Behaviors*, **9**, 1–10.
Stunkard, A.J. and Messick, S. (1985) The Three-Factor Eating Questionnaire to measure restraint, disinhibition and hunger. *Journal of Psychosomatic Research*, **29**, 71–83.
Traub, A.C. and Orbach, J. (1964) Psychological studies of body image. 1. The adjustable body-distorting mirror. *Archives General Psychiatry*, **11**, 33–66.
Van Strien, T. Frijters, J.E.R., Bergers, A. and Defares, P.B. (1986) The Dutch Eating Behaviour Questionnaire (DEBQ) for assessment of restrained emotional and external behaviour. *International Journal of Eating Disorders*, **5**, 295–315.
Watts, F.N., McKenna, F.P., Sharrock, R. and Trezise, L. (1986) Colour naming of phobia-related words. *British Journal of Psychology*, **77**, 97–108.
Williams, J.M.G. and Broadbent, K. (1986) Distraction by emotional stimuli: use of a Stroop task with suicide attempters. *British Journal of Clinical Psychology*, **25**, 101–10.
Wilson, G.T. and Smith, D. (1988) Assessment of bulimia nervosa: an evaluation of the Eating Disorders Examination. *International Journal of Eating Disorders*, **8**, 173–9.

Chapter 15

Sexual Behaviour

John Bancroft

The measurement of human sexual experience presents us with problems of unique complexity. The occurrence of particular categories of behaviour (e.g. coitus, masturbation) is relatively easily recorded; the psychophysiological responses which accompany them, such as penile erection, vaginal lubrication and orgasm, are less easily quantified. A fundamental dimension of the sexual experience, sexual desire, is particularly resistant to measurement. Whereas such desire may be manifested as thoughts about sex, it is also expressed in terms of arousal and excitement. There are problematic interrelationships between such phenomena. Are sexual thoughts or fantasies stimuli or responses or both? The unique essence of the sexual experience is perhaps its potential for escalation; thoughts about sex may lead to arousal and perceived physiological change, which in turn stimulate further thoughts and incentive for action. The closest parallel to sexuality in this respect is the behaviour related to food intake, where the experience of appetite for food has the same complex substrate of cognitive and physiological phenomena, and where the consequences of the consummatory behaviour, and hence its reinforcers, extend beyond the mere reduction of hunger.

Elsewhere, the author has described the sexual experience as a complex which can be observed through various windows, e.g. the 'cognitive', the 'affective' and the 'psychophysiological' windows. But as with the blind men examining the elephant, it is always important to remember that any one window produces only a partial view (Bancroft, 1988). Given the inherent complexity of this subject, it is first necessary to choose the 'window' through which to make our measurements. This process of conceptual analysis is essential, not only for measurement but also for deriving scientifically useful models of sexuality which lend themselves to empirical investigation. In the author's particular field of research, the relationship between reproductive hormones and sexual behaviour, an important first step is to make a clear distinction between sexual desire and genital response. Surprisingly, this seemingly obvious distinction had been noticeably lacking in most of the early literature. Studies of 'impotence' made no distinction between loss of sexual desire and erectile failure. Once this

Measuring Human Problems. Edited by D.F. Peck and C.M. Shapiro

distinction was made, it soon became apparent that in men hormones played a fundamental role in maintaining sexual desire, but their role in erectile responsiveness was more complex and depended on the context, or on the types of erotic stimuli involved (Bancroft, 1988).

Of the early attempts to provide a conceptual analysis of human sexual experience (e.g. Winoker, 1963; Hardy, 1964), the most influential has been that of Whalen (1966), who described the following components:

(1) Gender identity—the gender role;
(2) Object choice (i.e. sexual orientation or preference);
(3) Sexual gratification—the 'reinforcers' or 'pleasure' associated with or caused by sexual activity;
(4) Sexual arousal—the momentary 'state' level of sexual excitation;
(5) Sexual arousability—'an individual's characteristic rate of approach to orgasm as a result of sexual stimulation' (i.e. a 'rate' characteristic indicating the capacity for sexual arousal);
(6) Sexual activity—exemplified by fantasy as well as overt behaviour.

According to Whalen, sexual motivation is a function of the current state of arousal and the individual's arousability. Arousal is modulated by the presence or absence of relevant stimuli; arousability is determined by physiological factors such as hormonal mechanisms, as well as effects of previous experience and learning.

In this chapter we will restrict our attention to the last four of Whalen's components. More particularly, we will focus on the measurement of sexual attitudes, overt sexual behaviour, the assessment of sexual dysfunction and the measurement of change in sexuality that might follow treatment or illness. We will concentrate on psychometric and psychophysiological methods. The rapidly growing field of diagnosis of erectile dysfunction in men, using vascular, neurological and pharmacological procedures, is not dealt with in this chapter (for a review, see Bancroft, 1989). We will not deal with gender-related issues (e.g. masculinity or femininity), sexual orientation or preference, the assessment of sexual knowledge or education, of criminal sexual behaviour or of the varieties of sexual behaviour which only affect a tiny minority of individuals.

We will use three 'windows': (1) self-description of sexual behaviour, (2) measurement of sexual attitudes and (3) psychophysiological measurement of sexual arousability.

MEASURING SEXUAL BEHAVIOUR

Purposes

The principal purposes for 'measuring' sexual behaviour are:

(1) To establish norms of behaviour by means of social surveys. While always of interest, this issue has become of particular importance in recent years with the growing concern about 'safe sex' and the risks of sexually transmitted diseases such as AIDS. Social problems such as teenage pregnancy have generated the need for information about teenage sexuality and use of contraception;
(2) The diagnosis of sexual problems, i.e. sexual dysfunction, sexual relationship problems and how they interact;
(3) Measuring change of sexual behaviour over time, not only to establish social trends but also to identify the natural history of sexual problems and assess response to treatment.

Methods

Direct observation of sexual behaviour, the cornerstone of studies of animal sexuality, is, with a few special exceptions, not appropriate for human research. Masters and Johnson (1966) made observations in their laboratory of various aspects of sexual physiology in large numbers of men and women engaging in various forms of sexual activity. Their published reports of these studies are, however, curiously devoid of any attempt to measure or quantify the changes they observed and reported. Some studies have systematically measured changes during sexual arousal induced by masturbation or the use of vibrators (e.g. Fox and Fox, 1969; Levin and Wagner, 1985; Riley and Riley, 1986), but in general we must rely on self-report. The most basic issue concerning information obtained by self-report is its validity. It would not be surprising if, with information as sensitive and confidential as this, people gave false accounts or strove for social desirability in their answers. However, most experienced researchers are of the opinion that provided there is a good reason for obtaining the information, and that it is seen to be treated with respect and confidentiality, most people are prepared to be frank and honest.

Such reporting can be retrospective, covering various periods of time in the past, from a week to a lifetime, or 'prospective', with daily recording of behaviours over a limited time period of weeks or months. The prospective approach, while possibly essential for certain types of research, is demanding of the subject and very time consuming for the researcher. For most purposes, particularly where large numbers are required, as in population surveys, retrospective reporting is the only feasible method.

Retrospective reports

The main methodological question is whether to use a face-to-face interview or a self-rated questionnaire. There is now a third approach to consider—the use of computerized interviews. A recent report by Binik *et al.* (1989) is encouraging in this respect, though it is too early to assess the place of such methods in human sex research. This issue is central to much of social and psychological research, and there is a substantial literature on this general topic. But sexual surveys and enquiries do pose special problems, and there are particular advantages and disadvantages of both interview and questionnaire methods.

The interview

The obvious *advantages* of the face-to-face interview are as follows:

(1) It is possible to ensure that the questions are comprehended—questions can be phrased in more than one way, the subject's interpretation can be checked and inconsistencies cross-checked. A wide range of information can therefore be obtained by this method, and as the interviewer can respond appropriately, subjects with relatively low intelligence can be involved.
(2) It is possible to establish a good rapport and engender trust so that the subject will feel that the information will be treated with respect. Obviously this can work both ways—a poor relationship between interviewer and subject may seriously impair the information obtained. A good relationship often means that the subject gains from having someone to confide in. The fact that, not infrequently, subjects gain emotionally from being able to discuss sensitive issues increases the likelihood that they will give honest answers while at the same time increasing the ethical justification for the research.

The main *disadvantages* of the interview method are:

(1) It is extremely time consuming for the researcher, particularly if time is allowed to listen to what the subject wants to say rather than just concentrating on the research items, an allowance that is usually necessary to ensure the good relationship needed.

(2) The interviewer is obviously susceptible to bias in the ways questions are asked or answers interpreted.
(3) Anonymity is not possible, hence confidentiality of records becomes a major concern.

The questionnaire

The main *advantages* are that:

(1) Questions can be standardized, hence avoiding interviewer bias;
(2) Information can be collected relatively cheaply;
(3) Anonymity is possible, rendering safeguards for confidentiality less problematic.

The *disadvantages* are:

(1) The impossibility of checking whether the proper meaning of a question had been grasped. Even with careful design and piloting, there are serious limits to the questions that can be asked about sex without ambiguity or misinterpretation. Some aspects of sexual response and behaviour are difficult to define in simple terms. Orgasm, for example, may require some explanation. Whereas a sensitive interviewer can use appropriate vernacular to aid comprehension, such use in a questionnaire is likely to be offensive to some respondents. The avoidance of ambiguity may also lead to stark or absurd wording on such sensitive issues (e.g. a question in Sorensen's, 1973, questionnaire for adolescents asked the 'number of different boys whose sex organs I have felt in the past month').
(2) The method of answering often requires a level of sophistication in form-filling that is beyond large sections of the population. Questionnaires tend to be more successful with the better educated.

To some extent the two methods can be combined. The Sexual Experience Scale (Frenken and Vennix, 1981) was designed to be completed by the subject in the presence of a researcher who could clarify any uncertain meanings that arose. This, of course, jeopardizes many of the advantages of the questionnaire method. Also, it is possible, and often appropriate, to incorporate sections of 'questionnaire' enquiry during the course of an interview.

Kinsey and his colleagues had no doubts about the need for a lengthy face-to-face interview. The same conclusion was reached by Schofield (1965), Gorer (1971) and Farrell (1978). Zelnik and Kantner (1977) used a self-administered questionnaire to deal with the more sensitive questions during the interview of their first 1971 sample. For their later 1976 sample they used face-to-face interviews throughout and concluded that their previously used questionnaire method had no advantage.

Wyatt *et al.* (1988), reporting on their recent study of sexual behaviour in Californian women, compared their interview method with that used by Kinsey and his associates (Kinsey *et al.*, 1948). The Kinsey interview lasted from 45 minutes to 'several hours'; the Wyatt interview from 3 to 8 hours. The former covered 300 items, the latter 478. Both interviews were organized chronologically. Whereas Kinsey asked subjects *when* particular behaviours occurred, 'placing the burden of denial on the respondent', Wyatt asked *whether* specific behaviours occurred. Both methods used general questions leading to more specific ones. Wyatt used visual aids when long lists of alternative responses were offered. Wyatt and Peters (1986), in reviewing studies of the prevalence of child sexual abuse, concluded that the face-to-face interview method is associated with much higher prevalence rates than self-administered questionnaires. Also, the use of multiple questions to ask about specific behaviours leads to higher rates of reporting. More research is required to establish what information can effectively be obtained by questionnaire, and which aspects need a sensitive, trained interviewer. In many studies, questionnaires appear to have been used for simple expediency with little effort made to establish the appropriateness of such methods.

At present, most interview methods have been designed on an *ad hoc* basis to suit specific studies. Interviews such as those reported by Wyatt *et al.* (1988), that cover longer time periods, are of such a length as to make detailed reporting in the literature impractical. Hence we do not have an established interview schedule which is widely used. Meyer-Bahlburg and Ehrhardt (1983) have published a detailed and comprehensive interview outline as the Sexual Behaviour Assessment Schedule. This is, however, highly structured and does not lend itself easily to sensitive interviewing technique, and its usefulness and applicability have yet to be demonstrated. A comprehensive but shorter 'checklist' of questions that can be used to guide an interview has been published as the Sex History Form (Schover *et al.*, 1982); this is designed principally for assessment of sexual dysfunction. Reading and Wiest (1984) reported data from a 54-item semi-structured interview that was designed to cover only the preceding 4 weeks. This had been developed and reported by a WHO task force and has been published (WHO, 1980).

Prospective assessment—daily ratings

The use of daily ratings of various aspects of sexuality has increased over the past 10 years. Once again there is no single method that has gained general acceptance or has demonstrable superiority over others. As with semi-structured interviews, most have evolved on an *ad hoc* basis to meet the requirements of particular studies. The author has used such measures in a number of studies and there is now enough experience of their use to justify some general conclusions, and some examples of daily rating forms in use will be given.

Such ratings are demanding of both the subject and the researcher. They require reasonably high motivation and co-operation on the subjects' part if such ratings are to be completed conscientiously over a number of weeks. Although each rating form can be completed in 2 or 3 minutes once the subject is used to it, this needs to be done daily, preferably at the same time of day, and some systematic thought about the previous day's experiences is obviously necessary (see Appendix to this chapter). For the researcher it generates a fair amount of work in scoring and data processing (although computerized methods of reading and analysis should be available for adaptation). Reading and Wiest (1984) concluded that their 4-week retrospective interview yielded 'high quality data very close to the far more expensive and time consuming procedure of having respondents complete a daily checklist via a diary card'. This may well be the case when studies, such as theirs, are simply establishing 'base line' levels of behaviour. In the author's experience, however, daily ratings have provided the most robust and valuable measures of *change* in sexual behaviour, sexual interest and aspects of sexual function. For treatment studies, where considerable time and effort is expended on a relatively small number of subjects, the author regards them as the outcome measures of first choice, particularly when a cross-over design is used. Retrospective assessments are particularly susceptible to 'halo effects' in treatment studies when the subject reaches conclusions about whether a treatment method has been successful or not. Prospective methods are also essential for investigating temporal relationships between changing levels of sexual behaviour or interest and other variables such as hormone levels (e.g. Bancroft *et al.*, 1983). They can also be usefully combined with other methods of assessment. For example, after looking through the daily diaries for a time period, questions can be asked about specific occurrences, physiological responses, etc.

A variety of behaviours, responses and related subjective states can be rated on a daily basis, e.g. specific sexual acts, with or without partner, accompanying physiological responses (orgasm/ejaculation, erection), the presence of erections on waking, more subjective experiences such as sexual fantasies. Sexual desire presents the most difficult task. For a stable sexual pair, sexual desire may be readily manifested as sexual activity, and as a consequence there will be little prevailing sexual desire after the activity has occurred. In the absence of sexual activity, feelings of sexual desire may be much more prominent. (Similarly, if one eats food on a regular basis, there may be little awareness of hunger, in spite of a perfectly normal appetite.) There is therefore a complex interaction between sexual desire and sexual activity. In addition to daily recording of sexual activity we have used two ratings: (1) frequency of sexual thoughts during the day and (2) sexual excitement accompanying such thoughts. These have proved to be useful measures in assessing treatment effects (e.g. Skaakebaek *et al.*, 1981; O'Carroll and Bancroft, 1984; O'Carroll *et al.*, 1985). But subjects often confuse *spontaneous* desire, which is likely to lead to the initiation of sexual activity, with a sexually interested response to their partner's sexual approach. The frequency of sexual thoughts often increases on days when sexual activity occurs, but this increase can be as much a consequence as a cause of the sexual activity, reflecting pleasant musing over the recent experience. Questions about who initiated particular acts can be asked but are often difficult to answer, particularly when sexual behaviour results from a subtle interaction of the two partners (e.g. Bancroft *et al.*, 1983). We have not as yet found a better way to deal with this issue.

Other methodological considerations

Daily rating forms should not be too complex and the questions should be restricted to those of particular importance to the study. They should be easily scored, and the layout of the form is important in that respect. They should be discreet; if a subject is to complete such a form daily for several weeks or months the forms are likely to be around the house and may be seen by children, or other family members. The wording on the daily forms should not therefore be too explicit. We normally use abbreviations, letters or codes together with an instruction sheet explaining each item and how to answer it.

The occurrence of a specific act can be recorded on a yes/no basis, although some allowance for more than one occurrence per day may be needed. This then allows a simple frequency count for a specific time period. The frequency of sexual thoughts is difficult to count, and we provide a rating scale which allows the subject to assess, on his or her personal range, where the day's frequency fell (Figure 15.1). Similarly, with subjective ratings such as enjoyment, or satisfaction, rating scales are required.

Debate continues about the relative merits of different types of rating scales for such purposes, in particular whether to use a visual analogue scale or a 'defined point' scale. We have used both. If the 'defined points' are of degree (e.g. slight, moderate, marked, extreme) then there seems little to choose between them and visual analogue scales. They share the same psychometric limitations, and many people use the VAS as a 5- or 10-point scale.

For many purposes it is helpful to incorporate some daily rating of well-being or mood. In our menstrual cycle studies we have shown an important association between well-being and sexuality, particularly in women who experience marked variations in well-being through the cycle (e.g. Sanders *et al.*, 1983; Warner and Bancroft, 1988; Walker and Bancroft, 1989). The relationship between well-being and sexuality in men has not been so clearly demonstrated but should not be ignored.

It is important to have a 'trial run' with daily ratings. In a treatment study it is desirable to have a baseline period of ratings which provides an opportunity for the subject to adapt to this method. The subject's ratings should be checked to ensure that instructions are being followed correctly *before* ratings are made which will be used in the analysis. It is helpful, when giving a subject the rating form for the first time, to ask him or her at the time to complete it for the previous day, and then check it in his presence. Subjects should be asked to leave any day's form if they forget to complete it, rather than fill it in retrospectively. Daily ratings should be returned on a regular basis at least once every two weeks. If subjects are returning for interview less frequently we provide them with stamped addressed envelopes in which to return their rating forms. Failure of these to arrive on time should be quickly followed up by an enquiring phone call or letter.

Questionnaire methods

Conte (1983) provides a useful review, whereas Davis *et al.* (1988) have recently published a compendium of sexuality-related measures which, while not complete, is helpful and includes measures related to fertility control, sex education, homosexuality and 'love'. An earlier review by Schiavi *et al.* (1979) provided a motley selection of scales many of which have not been psychometrically established or have failed to stand the test of time.

Unidimensional (Guttman-type) scales of sexual behaviour

A unidimensional questionnaire is used to assess the extent of occurrence of specific behaviours. It is based on the assumption that the behaviours included in the scale are 'scalable', i.e. if an infrequent behaviour is said to have been experienced by an individual, then all the more frequent behaviours in that scale will also have been experienced. Podell and Perkins (1957) and Brady and Levitt (1965) pioneered such scales for sexual behaviour. The most substantially developed version was produced by Bentler (1968a, b), with one scale for men and one for women. Each consists of 21 classes of behaviour forming a cumulative ordinal scale. A high degree of scalability and internal consistency was demonstrated.

The main limitations of the Bentler scales are that they (1) are restricted

CODE ____________ DAY ____________ DATE ____________

I. Morning? F. ☐ P. ☐ N. ☐

II. How did you feel today?

Cheerful	0 ______________________	10
Fatigued	0 ______________________	10
Energetic	0 ______________________	10
Anxious	0 ______________________	10
Irritable	0 ______________________	10
Unhappy	0 ______________________	10
________	0 ______________________	10

(Please specify and mark any other feeling you had today on this line)

III. Activity?

No activity ☐

M? ☐ Enjoyment 0 ______________________ 10
Fullness 0 ______________________ 10

E(m) ☐

S? ☐ Enjoyment 0 ______________________ 10
Fullness 0 ______________________ 10

You ☐ Partner ☐ Both ☐

E(s) ☐

IV. Thoughts

Frequency	0 ______________________	10
Excitement	0 ______________________	10

(Leave blank if no thoughts)

Figure 15.1 An example of a daily rating form for men. Instructions for use are given in the appendix

to heterosexual behaviour; (2) only include a relatively narrow range of behaviours; (3) do not assess the relative frequency of different behaviours and (4) have been established only in relatively young college-educated populations. Anderson and Brofitt (1988) found rather different hierarchical ordering of behaviours in a group of older women in stable relationships, indicating that such scaling of sexual behaviour may be very sensitive to age, social class and other cultural influences.

Zuckerman (1973) has developed a further Guttman-type scale, including a limited amount of homosexual behaviour as well as heterosexual, and combined with various attitudinal measures (Zuckerman, 1988). However, there has been less psychometric development of this scale.

Such scales do, with appropriate adaptation, lend themselves to establishing the occurrence of specific behaviours in defined populations, but as yet they have been little used for such purposes.

Multidimensional questionnaires

The most widely used questionnaires vary in the ranges and complexity of behaviours covered, in the extent to which they have been psychometrically established, and in the amount of normative data.

The Sexual Experience Scales (SES) (Frenken and Vennix, 1981)

This Dutch questionnaire has normative data from a general population 'broad middle class' random sample of 250 couples. Its reliability and validity have been well established (Frenken and Vennix, 1981). There are four scales covered by this questionnaire:

SES1 (Sexual morality): covers attitudes, norms and values concerning marital sexual behaviour, premarital sex, and sexual socialization of children and young people. At one pole there is 'restrictive sexual morality', the prevention, avoidance or control of such aspects of sexuality. At the other pole is 'permissive sexual morality' or acceptance. There are three subscales measuring 'sexual morality within marriage', 'premarital sexual experience' and for men, 'premarital sexual attitude', for women 'morality of sexual socialization'.

SES2 (Psychosexual stimulation): refers to the extent that one seeks or accepts (rather than avoids or rejects) sexual stimuli of an auditory-visual or imaginary kind. Questionnaire items refer to experiences in non-interactional, socio-sexual situations. There are three subscales, 'interpersonal sexual attraction', 'evaluation of exposure to erotic imagery' and 'arousal by erotic imagery'.

SES3 (Sexual motivation): refers to sexual interaction with one's normal partner. It covers (a) the degree of sexual response, problems with arousal, orgasm or ejaculation, actual and preferred coital frequency, length of foreplay; (b) the pleasantness of various kinds of activity, e.g. touching partner's genitals, tongue kissing, being naked, variations in positions; (c) the occurrence and frequency of certain emotional reactions during lovemaking, such as fear, aversion, apathy, tension. One pole of the scale is described as 'sexual aversion', the other as 'sexual appetite'. There are five subscales: 'enjoyment potential', 'orgasm adequacy during intercourse', 'sexual inhibition', 'frequency of sexual intercourse' and 'length of foreplay'.

SES4 (attraction to marriage): refers to three particular reasons a person may have to continue or to end a marriage; (a) the social and emotional attraction to the partner; (b) the acceptability or unacceptability of ending the relationship; (c) sexual attraction to the partner. There are three subscales: 'marital satisfaction', 'attitude to extramarital involvement' and 'evaluation of partner as a sexual partner'.

These scales have now been used in a variety of studies and have proved themselves acceptable to a wide variety of research subjects. SES3 has been used as an outcome measure in treatment studies (e.g. Everaerd, 1977; Everaerd and Dekker, 1982) and as a measure of change in relation to other events such as hysterectomy or pregnancy, breastfeeding, etc. (e.g. Alder and Bancroft, 1988).

There is a male and a female version. Each is designed to be administered in the presence of a researcher so that any uncertain meanings can be clarified. It usually takes 20 to 30 minutes to complete.

The Derogatis Sexual Functioning Inventory (DSFI; Derogatis, 1978)

This American questionnaire has a total of 258 items that cover sexual function and sexuality under eight headings; information, sexual experience, drive, attitudes, gender role, fantasy, body image and satisfaction. These can be combined to provide an overall score, the Sexual Functioning Index. There is also a Global Sexual Satisfaction Index (GSSI) that judges the quality of the subject's sexual activity on a 9-point scale from 'couldn't be better' to 'couldn't be worse'.

The total DSFI is long, taking 30 to 40 minutes to complete, and includes two scales ('affect' and 'psychological symptoms') which are not directly related to sexuality and cover areas for which there are probably better psychometric measures.

There are data for a group of 200 or so 'normals' and a similar number of sexually dysfunctional patients. Psychometrically it is only partially established. Derogatis has reported reasonable reliability, but less evidence of validity. Derogatis and Meyer (1979) compared 47 dysfunctional and 57 'normal' men, and 40 dysfunctional and 143 'normal' women. The Sexual Experience and Drive subscales differentiated between the male groups but not the females. The GSSI differentiated between groups for both sexes. Anderson and Brofitt (1988) applied the Sexual Experience subscale (covering 24 individual hererosexual behaviours) in two groups of women, one recently diagnosed with gynaecological malignancy, the other 'healthy' controls attending for routine gynaecological checks. The scale was re-administered on three further occasions with intervals of 4 months. These authors reported some dissatisfaction with this scale. Reliability and stability were questionable, the changing level of sexual activity in the patient group was not well reflected, and the occurrence of sexual dysfunction was missed in the majority of cases.

As yet, there is little other published research based on the DSFI (e.g. Schreiner-Engel *et al.*, 1985) and its general usefulness for sex research is not well established. Some of its scales require fairly high reading ability.

The Sexual Interaction Inventory (LoPiccolo and Steger, 1974)

The most notable features of this inventory are that it is designed for couples and it assesses both real and ideal frequencies of specific sexual behaviours. Each partner answers 6 questions about 17 items of sexual behaviour, including such items as 'the male seeing the female when she is nude', 'the female caressing the male's genitals with her hands', 'the female caressing the male's genitals with her mouth until he ejaculates', 'the male and female having intercourse'. The 6 questions per item cover real and ideal frequency, and pleasantness and unpleasantness for each partner. Reliability and validity were shown to be satisfactory but on a small sample. McCoy and D'Agnostino (1977) published a psychometric critique based on an even smaller sample. The scores from both partners are used to derive an 11-scale profile which is sensitive to change and can be used as a treatment outcome measure (e.g. McGovern *et al.*, 1975).

This inventory has some disadvantages. It is relatively lengthy, taking 30 to 40 minutes to complete; it can only be used if both partners complete it—hence is of no use for individual patients; it is fairly explicit, made more so by the accompanying line drawings of each of the 17 behaviours. Schover and Jensen (1988) consider it likely to cause offence in some patient groups. Also its reported use has been very limited considering the length of time since it was introduced.

The Sexual Arousability Inventory (SAI; Hoon et al., 1976)

This was devised to provide a measure of dysfunctional sexual arousal in women. There are 28 erotic situations listed, included 'when a loved one fondles your breast with his/her hands', 'when you read a pornographic or "dirty" story', 'when you dance with a loved one', 'when a loved one kisses you with an exploring tongue', 'when you masturbate'. Each item is rated on a bipolar 7-point scale of sexual arousal. Reliability and validity have been shown to be satisfactory, though based on a somewhat unrepresentative sample of women, predominantly graduates, undergraduates or members of women's groups. It discriminated between normal women and women seeking sex therapy (Hoon *et al.*, 1976).

The SAI is relatively short, easy to administer and suitable for homosexual as well as heterosexual women. It does appear to have diagnostic value and to reflect changes in response to treatment (e.g. Murphy *et al.*, 1980). However, it does not assess current sexual functioning and its directly explicit questions, established with a highly educated sample, may be unacceptable for many women.

An expanded version, the Sexual Arousal Inventory—Expanded (SAI-E), has been published, in which similar questions covering anxiety responses as well as sexual arousal are added (Chambless and Lifshitz, 1984: Hoon and Chambless, 1988). Once again there is as yet little published evidence of its usefulness.

The Golombok–Rust Inventory of Sexual Satisfaction (GRISS; Golombok and Rust, 1985)

This short measure of sexual dysfunction has separate forms for men and women. Each form has 28 questions, such as 'Do you have intercourse as often as you would like?', 'Do you lose your erection during intercourse?' 'Does your vagina become moist during lovemaking?', 'Do you ejaculate by accident just before your penis is about to enter your partner's vagina?' Each question has five possible answers, varying from 'always' to 'never'.

This inventory has been established in several small groups of couples with and without sexual dysfunction. Factor analysis has led to subscales for anorgasmia and vaginismus for women, impotence and premature ejaculation for men, plus 'avoidance', 'dissatisfaction', 'non-sensuality', 'infrequency' and 'non-communication' for both sexes. There is also a global score for each sex. Reliability has been shown to be satisfactory. Validity was established by comparing scale scores and change scores following treatment with ratings made by therapists. This showed the inventory to be appropriate for both diagnosis and the measurement of therapeutic change (Golombok and Rust, 1988).

The main virtues of this scale are its brevity (it takes 4 to 5 minutes to complete) and its straightforward non-offensive language. It is promising but its value has yet to be demonstrated with results from substantial studies.

Assessment of sexual fantasy

Systematic assessment of sexual fantasy has received relatively little attention. The most extensively used measure has been the Sexual Daydreaming Scale of the Imaginal Processes Inventory of Singer and Antrobus (1972). There are 12 specifically sexual items, including 'my daydreams about love are so vivid, I actually feel they are occurring', 'while working intently at a job, my mind wanders to thoughts about sex', 'whenever I'm bored I daydream about the opposite sex', 'my daydreams tend to arouse me physically'. Based on factor analysis, frequency ratings of these items provide scores for 'sexual daydreaming in general', 'the intensity' and 'the visual quality' of such daydreaming. Giambra has reported several studies using this scale (e.g. Giambra and Martin, 1977; Giambra, 1983). The author has used it recently in a study of young women (Bancroft *et al.*, 1990).

Crepault *et al.* (1977), in a study of women, used a list of 31 fantasies covering a variety of 'normal' and deviant sexual activities. Each subject was asked to indicate how often each fantasy was used (1) during intercourse and (2) during masturbation. A modification, involving 38 items, was used in a study of men (Crepault and Couture, 1980), and this data set was more closely analysed with factor analysis.

A comparable approach has been described by Wilson (1988). He uses a list of 40 erotic situations and each is rated for its frequency as (1) a daytime fantasy, (2) a fantasy during intercourse or masturbation, (3) a dream while asleep, (4) an overt behaviour, (5) a desired overt behaviour. Principal components analysis resulted in four principal components; 'Exploratory' (e.g. group sex, promiscuity), 'Intimate' (e.g. kissing passionately, oral sex), 'Impersonal' (e.g. sex with a stranger) and 'Sadomasochistic'.

Sexual attitudes

The Eysenck Inventory of Attitudes to Sex (Eysenck, 1971)

This questionnaire, and details of its psychometric qualities, are most fully reported in Eysenck (1976). It has a long form of 158 items and a 96-item short form. The items are questions requiring yes/no, agree/disagree or true/false answers. Although many of the questions deal with explicit sexual activity, it is easily understood and the long version takes from 20 to 60 minutes to complete.

Oblique factor analysis generated 12 factors: (1) permissiveness, (2) satisfaction, (3) neurotic sex, (4) impersonal sex, (5) pornography, (6) sexual shyness, (7) prudishness, (8) dominance/submission, (9) sexual disgust, (10) sexual excitement, (11) physical sex and (12) aggressive sex. The first six factors were virtually identical for men and women. The intercorrelations between these oblique factors generated two 'super-factors' called 'sexual libido' and 'sexual satisfaction', similar for the two sexes.

Eysenck's main interest in developing this scale was to relate the attitudes measured to his other measures of personality, extraversion (E), neuroticism (N) and psychoticism (P). He found that extraverts were high on 'libido' and tended to the positive end of the 'satisfaction' factor. Introverts were at the low end of the 'libido' factor, although they showed greater satisfaction at older age levels. 'Extraversion is more appropriate to youth.'

High N scorers complained more of sexual dysfunction of various kinds and reported high anxiety about sex (i.e. low satisfaction) while being high on the 'libido' dimension. According to Eysenck, high N scorers showed a conflict between their strong desires and equally strong inhibitions. High P scorers emerged as advocates of impersonal permissive sex practices. They are high on 'libido' but low on 'satisfaction'.

Others have questioned Eysenck's conclusions. Farley *et al.* (1977), using different but comparable measures, concluded that there was a 'general lack of contribution of personality variables to sexuality'. Shenk *et al.* (1981) found that in a study of married couples the quality of the marriage was more important than personality variables in determining the sexual relationship. In a study of single men, Shenk and Pfrang (1986) found some support for a link between sexuality and extraversion but not neuroticism.

The Sexual Experience Scales (Frenken and Vennix, 1981)

The SES1 scale of the SES, measuring sexual morality, has already been described. They concluded that the predictive power of personality characteristics was weak; gender, age and the frequency of church attendance were the best predictors of sexual behaviour.

The Sexual Opinion Survey (Fisher et al., 1988)

This questionnaire involves 21 items, each requiring a response on a 7-point bipolar scale from 'strongly agree' to 'strongly disagree'. Examples of items are 'I think it would be very entertaining to look at hardcore pornography', 'I do not enjoy daydreaming about sexual matters', 'masturbation can be an exciting experience'. The selection of 21 items was from an original pool of

53 and based on significant correlations with effective response to viewing erotic slides. The scale is regarded as measuring a dimension of *erotophobia-erotophilia*—i.e. responding to sexual cues along a negative–positive dimension of affect and evaluation. The authors of this scale report satisfactory internal consistency and convergent and discriminant validity. The total scale scores correlate with 'authoritarianism' and adherence to traditional sex roles. In general, erotophilia is scored higher by men than women, by the younger than the older (though it is not clear whether this is an age or a cohort effect), by higher than lower socio-economic groups and by the non-religious than the religious.

Factor analysis has produced three factors; 'open sexual display', accounting for 34 per cent of the variance; 'sexual variety' (11 per cent of the variance); and 'homoeroticism' (7 per cent of variance). A short 5-item version has been produced which predicts well the total scale score. The use of this short version is recommended when there are time constraints or a need to avoid sexually sensitive items (e.g. with young teenagers).

A number of studies using this scale have been published (e.g. Becker and Byrne, 1985; Fisher, 1984; Fisher *et al.*, 1979; Kelley, 1979), although they have predominantly involved undergraduate or graduate subjects.

PSYCHOPHYSIOLOGICAL ASSESSMENT OF SEXUAL RESPONSE

The use of psychophysiological techniques to measure sexual responses in a variety of situations has increased substantially in the past 15 years. Rosen and Beck (1988) provide an excellent, detailed and comprehensive review of this field.

Reflecting the cautious approach of sex researchers at the time, early psychophysiological studies predominantly measured non-genital parameters such as electrodermal activity (i.e. skin conductance) and cardiovascular changes in heart rate and blood pressure. Such measures have proved to be of limited value, mainly because of their non-specificity. It is difficult to distinguish between autonomic arousal associated with emotional states, such as anxiety or anger, and sexual excitement (Zuckerman, 1971). Also, the patterns of non-genital autonomic responses to erotic stimulation are highly variable across individuals and occasions, reflecting individual and situational types of response specificity (Bancroft and Mathews, 1971).

Pupillometry initially offered interesting possibilities. Hess and his colleagues (Hess and Poll, 1960; Hess *et al.*, 1965) postulated that pupillary dilatation may be a more specifically sexual response to erotic or other sexually relevant stimuli than electrodermal and cardiovascular responses, with the added possibility that pupillary dilatation reflected a positive and constriction a negative response. Since then, disappointing attempts to replicate these early findings, combined with the considerable technological complexity and expense of the method, has resulted in a loss of interest in this approach.

Of the cardiovascular responses, blood pressure remains potentially the most interesting, particularly at relatively low levels of sexual arousal. Zuckerman (1971) concluded that changes in both systolic and diastolic blood pressure were unusual among non-genital responses in their tendency to vary proportionally with the strength of the sexual stimulus employed (e.g. Wenger *et al.*, 1968; Wincze *et al.*, 1976). Although Kockott *et al.* (1980) found that blood pressure measurement did not discriminate between functional and dysfunctional men, Bancroft *et al.* (1985), in a study of diabetic men with erectile dysfunction, found that blood pressure response was less in those dysfunctional men who had evidence of psychogenesis in addition to their diabetes, compared with those whose erectile dysfunction was probably simply organic. This raised the possibility that the blood pressure response reflected central arousal, which was likely to be more inhibited in predominantly psychogenic cases. This possibility deserves further study.

The measurement of central arousal during sexual response remains the most formidable problem in this field. Earlier studies of evoked cortical potentials (Lifshitz, 1966), and the 'expectancy wave' or 'contingent negative variation' in the EEG (Costell *et al.*, 1972) in response to visual erotic stimuli, probably measured indices of attention to the stimuli rather than the arousal in response to those stimuli. More recently interhemispheric EEG differences with non-dominant hemisphere 'lateralization' have been found to be related to central sexual arousal (Tucker and Dawson, 1984; Cohen *et al.*, 1985). Two further studies have also indicated that non-dominant hemisphere EEG activity is associated with spontaneous erections during sleep (Hirshkowitz *et al.*, 1979; Rosen *et al.*, 1986). While these findings are of considerable theoretical interest, it is probably premature to regard such EEG indices as measures of central sexual response appropriate for other than research purposes.

Measures of genital response

Vascular changes in the genitalia provide the most specific sexual responses to erotic stimuli. Measurement of penile erection in the male is, by comparison with genital measures in the female, straightforward and more readily interpreted, and much more research has been carried out with such measures in male subjects.

Male genital responses

The simplest method for measuring penile erection involves strain gauge measurement of penile circumference, usually at the base of the penile shaft. Strain gauges of either mercury-in-rubber (e.g. Fisher *et al.*, 1965; Bancroft *et al.*, 1966) or 'solid state' (i.e. a semiconductor strain gauge attached to a spring metal ring; Barlow *et al.*, 1970) have been widely used. Rosen and Keefe (1978) compared the performance of these two types and found them similar in most respects. The solid-state type may be more susceptible to movement artefact. The main deficiency of these otherwise reliable methods is that they do not reflect changes in the length of the penis, which often occur to a substantial extent during the early stages of an erection, sometimes to the extent that circumference is transiently reduced. Volumetric penile plethysmography, which involves the whole shaft of the penis, has been used, principally by Freund and his colleagues (e.g. Freund *et al.*, 1965) and McConaghy (1967). These devices are cumbersome, obtrusive and prone to a variety of artefactual problems, particularly with movement. Wheeler and Rubin (1987) concluded that they had no advantage over the circumferential methods.

Neither circumferential nor volumetric measures indicate the degree of rigidity of the erection. Maximum circumference can be attained with less than maximum rigidity, and after a certain amount of tumescence, circumference change ceases to have a linear relationship with intracavernosal pressure (Metz and Wagner, 1981). This is clearly important in diagnosing erectile dysfunction, as evidence of full tumescence, in terms of circumference increase, may conceal the fact that there is inadequate rigidity for vaginal entry. In spite of this, circumference measurement is useful in its own right for a variety of research and clinical purposes, e.g. discriminating between the erotic significance of different stimuli, or different types of erectile dysfunction where erectile response is clearly impaired. However, a recent study (Carani *et al.*, 1989) of the effects of exogenous testosterone on the nocturnal penile tumescence (NPT) of normal young men showed that the testosterone had no effect on the frequency or circumference but did enhance the rigidity of NPT. In other words, this effect of hormones would not have been identified if only circumference measures had been used. The addition of a rigidity measure in this study extended the scope for measurable change. Earlier comparable studies of erectile response, which did not measure rigidity (e.g. Bancroft and Wu, 1983), may have to be reappraised in the light of these results.

Unfortunately, measurement of ridigity is technically difficult. Various attempts to produce devices for continuous monitoring of rigidity have been made. One such device, the Rigiscan (Dacomed Inc), used in the study cited above (Carani *et al.*, 1990), is commercially available but expensive. There have been some favourable reports of its validity (e.g. Bradley *et al.*, 1985) and others expressing reservations, suggesting that it underestimates the rigidity (e.g. Wooten and Fields, 1987). It is likely that other devices of this kind will soon become commercially available, which should at least result in a reduction in cost.

Measurement of erectile response is carried out in two types of situation (1) during sleep, i.e. spontaneous erections during sleep or nocturnal penile tumescence (NPT), and (2) in a psychophysiological laboratory, usually in response to erotic stimuli.

Nocturnal penile tumescence (NPT)

It has been known for some time that men normally have erections at intervals during sleep. Erections on waking, noticed by most men, are the last of these nocturnal responses which precede and continue beyond the point of waking (they are not, as is often supposed, the result of a full bladder).

There are now substantial normative data on these responses, showing them to vary in important ways throughout the life cycle. Their frequency, duration and degree increase during childhood to reach a peak in adolescence and thereafter to gradually decline. There is a close association between sleep erections and Rapid Eye Movement (REM) sleep, though they are to some extent independent and show different patterns of change through the life cycle (Karacan *et al.*, 1976). At age 13, NPT occupies 32 per cent of total sleep time. This declines to 20 per cent in the 60 to 69 age group. In teenagers and young adults, more than 90 per cent of all NPT episodes occur at least in part during a REM period; 90 per cent of REM periods are associated with NPT, but by age 60 this has fallen to 66 per cent. In the 13–15 age group an average maximum of four erections occur per night, three in the 30 to 39 age group, 2+ in the 40–67 year group and 1.7 for the 70+ age group (Schiavi and Fisher, 1982).

Karacan (1970) was the first to suggest that measurement of NPT might be useful in distinguishing between organic and psychogenic causes of erectile failure. If organic factors, impairing the basic mechanisms of erection, are involved then sleep erections should also be impaired. On the other hand, psychogenic factors should have little influence during sleep, and hence in psychogenic erectile dysfunction NPT should be relatively normal. Since Fisher *et al.*, (1975) and Karacan *et al.* (1978) started publishing results of NPT as a diagnostic procedure, there have been numerous other similar reports. There has been a noticeable lack of validation, however, and the recent realization that rigidity is also important diagnostically has increased the uncertainty about many of these results. While it is true thạt in a proportion of cases the results of NPT testing are relatively clear cut, in the majority of clinical cases the results are somethat equivocal. We cannot *exclude* psychogenesis on the basis of an abnormal NPT, whereas the presence of a *normal* NPT does increase the likelihood of psychogenesis. It is also becoming clear that changes in NPT may precede erectile dysfunction. As already mentioned, NPT decreases with advancing age. Recently Schiavi (personal communication) found NPT to be impaired, to an extent often regarded as indicative of organic failure, in a group of older men who had no problems during their lovemaking. Presumably, in some way the capacity for spontaneous erections declines while the capacity to respond to tactile stimulation continues.

There is other evidence indicating that impairment of NPT is not necessarily a result of organic pathology directly affecting the erectile mechanisms. NPT is impaired in men with androgen deficiency and improves with androgen replacement (Kwan *et al.*, 1983; O'Carroll *et al.*, 1985). NPT is often impaired in men with loss of sexual desire (Schiavi *et al.*, 1988) and with depressive illness (Roose *et al.*, 1982; Thase *et al.*, 1987). We thus find NPT providing a link between sexual desire (which is androgen dependent in men), androgen status and depressive illness. This raises the important possibility that measurement of NPT, rather than simply testing the integrity of the peripheral erectile mechanisms, its traditional role, also provides a 'window' into this aspect of central nervous system function (Bancroft, 1988). Looked at this way, NPT offers some exciting possibilities for assessing the neurophysiological substrate of sexual desire. As yet, the usefulness of such an approach awaits demonstration, but deserves serious consideration.

There are a number of methodological issues to consider. NPT does not appear to be affected by previous sexual activity (Brissette *et al.*, 1985) or exposure to visual erotic stimuli shortly before sleep (Carani *et al.*, 1990). For diagnostic purposes, most authorities recommend a minimum of two consecutive nights, preferably three, the first being regarded as an 'adaptation night'. Quite often sleep is impaired on the first night, although it is not unusual to get a normal NPT response on the first night. With repeated testing at intervals (e.g. during a controlled experiment) it is probably unnecessary to have an adaptation night before each test night providing that no more than one week lapses between tests.

Some workers recommend the use of two strain gauges, one at the base, the other near the tip. Apart from occasionally identifying some abnormality of erection (e.g. Peyronie's Disease), we doubt that this adds much of value. An important methodological issue is the concurrent measurement of sleep. This involves a much more substantial procedure, can only really be carried out in a sleep laboratory and is consequently much more expensive. On the other hand, for research purposes it is undoubtedly important to establish the normality of the sleep pattern before interpreting the NPT. For diagnostic purposes this advantage has to be set against cost. Providing the NPT is one of a number of methods of assessment then it is probably better to measure NPT without sleep measurement than to have no NPT measurement at all. The use of portable home monitoring does have potential (Procci *et al.*, 1983), but other relatively cheap devices such as the 'snap gauge' or erectiometer are of very doubtful value.

The most contentious methodological issue concerns the definition of a normal or adequate response. As discussed above, it is now increasingly recognized that rigidity as well as circumference needs to be measured. Apart from rigidity, the usual parameters measured are latency to first NPT, duration of NPT above a criterion level, number of separate NPTs above a criterion, the maximum response and the mean maximum response.

Measurement of erections to erotic stimuli

The laboratory-based measurement of erectile responses to erotic stimuli has been used for a variety of purposes, including the assessment and treatment of sexual deviance (Bancroft, 1974), assessment of response to erotica (Reifler *et al.*, 1971), effects of drugs (Tennent *et al.*, 1974; Rosen *et al.*, 1988) and alcohol (Wilson and Lawson, 1976) on sexual response, the role of hormones in sexual response (Bancroft *et al.*, 1974; Bancroft and Wu, 1983) and more recently the investigation of erectile dysfunction (Kockott *et al.*, 1980; Bancroft *et al.*, 1985; Zuckerman *et al.*, 1985).

In comparison with spontaneous response occurring during sleep (i.e. NPT), the elicitation of erections in the laboratory is obviously open to influence by situational factors. One of the main problems with this approach to measurement is to standardize the procedure and conditions sufficiently to allow comparability across individuals and across studies.

The types of stimuli to be used is a prime consideration. Visual stimuli (in the form of films or slides), auditory stimuli, literature read by the subject and self-generated fantasies have all been used. In general, erotic films have proved to be the most effective in eliciting an erectile response. Fantasy is usually the least effective, but there is considerable intersubject variability in this respect. Some individuals find their favourite fantasy more powerful than any external stimulus. In two apparently similar studies of dysfunctional men, involving diabetic and non-diabetic dysfunctional subjects and controls, there were substantial differences in the mean levels of erectile response reported. For the controls, Bancroft *et al.* (1985) reported a mean circumference increase of 31 mm, whereas Zuckerman *et al.* (1985) reported 21.3 mm. Similar discrepancies were apparent for the dysfunctional men. Although, with the relatively small numbers of subjects involved in such studies, variability of responsiveness is to be expected, it is possible that the erotic stimuli used in the first study were more effective than in the second. More basic work is required on the characteristics of erotic stimuli to allow selection of appropriate material for such studies. Unfortunately, in terms of visual material, the researcher is usually limited to that produced for the 'hard' or 'soft' pornography market. This raises ethical issues about its use. The author has always been careful to select material which portrays reasonably 'normal' sexual activity. Although it is not unusual for a subject to say that he does not like the stimuli shown to him, we have encountered very little adverse reaction to being exposed to erotica in this way. It is sometimes striking the extent to which individuals show genital responses which are in apparent conflict with their subjective assessment of the stimulus. It is therefore important to emphasize that a genital response to a stimulus in no way implies that the subject finds that stimulus acceptable. It is helpful to explain that at a physiological level most people will show some response to visual presentation of sexually explicit activity, whether they like it or not.

Habituation to erotic stimuli is another factor which complicates this type of assessment. Several studies for the US Commission on Obscenity and Pornography set out to evaluate the effect of repeated exposure, with somewhat inconclusive results (Bancroft, 1978). The key question, which from a methodological point of view has not been adequately answered, is how the interval between repeated exposure to a stimulus relates to habituation to that stimulus. It is usually assumed that changing the stimulus will avoid, or at least reduce, such habituation, but to do that in a predictable way requires knowledge of the comparable 'strength' of different erotic stimuli. Given the individual variability in this respect, such information is not readily available. At the very least, experiments involving repeated exposure to erotic stimuli require a design which adequately controls for order effect, and until we have more information to guide us, it would seem prudent to reduce the number of testing occasions to the minimum compatible with the aims of the study.

The experimental (i.e. laboratory) setting and the attitude and behaviour of the experimenter are two other potentially important sources of variance. Privacy is desirable and should be consistent. Too great an exposure to experimenter observation will inhibit many subjects, while some may even find this situation sexually arousing. The experimenter needs to combine a reasonably open and friendly attitude to avoid reinforcing the otherwise 'clinical', impersonal atmosphere of the laboratory test, while at the same time avoiding any suggestion of prurient interest or vicarious pleasure. Although we know of no systematic study of relevance, it is desirable, in conforming to the above requirements, to use experimenters of the same sex as the subjects, a view shared by Rosen and Beck (1988).

Measurement of penile circumference poses some 'baseline' problems; there is no clear physiological baseline for penile circumference. This leaves two alternatives; measuring the increase in circumference above the lowest point preceding the stimulus (Bancroft, 1974), or measuring the percentage of full erection obtained. The latter method is only appropriate if a full erection is elicited at some point, which is unlikely for many dysfunctional subjects. Most studies have used the first method, expressing response as millimetre increase in circumference or diameter. Earls *et al.* (1987) have suggested that a z transformation of circumference change scores best explains the variance within a data set. Obviously, the appropriateness of this or other methods depends on the precise questions being asked. Other parameters which can be measured are latency to reach a defined criterion (e.g. 15 mm or 30 mm increase in circumference). Latency to maximum response is sometimes used, but is difficult to interpret as the maximum response is likely to vary from test to test.

Most studies have attempted to measure subjective sexual arousal in parallel with psychophysiological assessment. This has either involved a Likert-type scaling procedure at the end of each stimulus presentation or a form of continuous monitoring involving a subject-controlled variable-resistance potentiometer and dial, or 'cognitive lever'. The first, retrospective type of rating tends to produce high correlations, particularly when higher degrees of erectile response occur (probably reflecting the tendency for men to judge their degree of sexual arousal according to their degree of genital response, a characteristic which may distinguish men from women). The second, continuous type of assessment tends to produce lower correlations, raising the question whether the first 'global' rating produces spuriously high correlations, or whether the continuous method sufficiently distracts the subject to reduce his awareness of his response.

The measurement of circumference change and rigidity may only be reflecting part of the erectile process. Recently, Bancroft and Bell (1985) and Bancroft *et al.* (1985) reported on the use of a photometer which, attached to the dorsum of the penis, measures pulsatile flow in the dorsal penile arteries (see below). The variable relationship between circumference change and pulse amplitude change raises the possibility that these two parameters are reflecting different components of the erectile response, which has both theoretical and diagnostic implications. However, this approach should still be seen as experimental, and further work is needed before its place as a method of measuring genital response is established.

Female genital responses

The genital response of the female is anatomically more complex than that of the male. Rather than being neatly confined to one exposed and measurable structure like the penis, changes occur in the vaginal wall, the clitoris, the vulva and the uterus. A variety of measurement techniques have been applied to these different anatomical sites, including the clitoris (Karacan *et al.* 1970), the uterus (with measures of contraction (Bardwick and Behrman, 1967) or intra-uterine pressure (Fox *et al.*, 1970)), and temperature changes in the labia (Henson *et al.*, 1977). The physiological response that is probably most directly comparable to penile erection is vasocongestion of the vaginal wall. Of the various techniques applied to this site, the most interpretable physiological signal has been obtained by the oxygenation-temperature measure introduced by Levin and Wagner (1977). This device, which is attached to the vaginal wall by a small suction cup, measures blood flow in two ways: first, by measuring the power necessary to maintain a constant temperature, and second, by measuring the pO_2 of the blood in the underlying tissues. This method is, however, relatively invasive (the cup has to be attached by the experimenter) and requires expensive equipment. So far, its main function has been to validate physiologically other measures. The most widely used measure is the vaginal photometer and this will be described in more detail.

This device incorporates a reflectance photometer and a light-emitting diode into a plastic probe, shaped like a tampon and insertable into the vagina. This method was first described by Sintchak and Geer (1975) and has been extensively used since.

Two types of signal are produced; an AC-coupled signal of pulse amplitude and a DC-coupled signal. The physiological interpretation of both these signals is far from clear. Changes in the DC signal are believed to reflect changes in the amount of blood pooled in the vaginal wall (i.e. VBV) and the AC signal changes in pulsatile flow in the arterioles (VPA) (Hatch, 1979). However, there has been no validation of either of these assumptions (Cook, 1974; Jennings *et al.*, 1980). The relative merits of these two signals has become a continuing *cause célébre* among sexual psychophysiologists, with some such as Geer *et al.* (1974), Heiman (1977) and Beck *et al.* (1983) favouring the VPA, while Hoon *et al.* (1976) prefer the VBV. The proponents of VPA point to its greater ability to discriminate between erotic and neutral stimuli, whereas the VBV is seen to be less distorted by variations in heart rate and cardiac stroke volume. It is probably fair to say, at this point in time, that neither measure is physiologically interpretable but both provide empirical evidence of some form of vascular response to erotic stimulation.

There are various methodological problems. Neither signal can be meaningfully calibrated. Both, particularly VPA, are susceptible to movement artefact. There is some evidence that position in the vagina is important (Gillan and Brindley, 1979), requiring carefully standardized placement if results are to be reproducible. A variety of methods of summarizing or sampling and analysing the VPA response have been described, but none has been shown to be clearly superior (Hatch, 1979). The main advantage of this technique is that it is easy to use and relatively unobtrusive (the subject can insert the probe herself, and with appropriate additions to the probe, can do so with consistency of placement, and be tested more or less normally clothed).

A continuing concern with most methods of measuring female genital response is the low correspondence between the physiological response and subjective reporting of arousal. In general, correlations have been higher with VPA, but the lack of significant correlations reported by Geer *et al.* (1974) has persisted in most other studies (Rosen and Beck, 1988). This raises an important and interesting issue. As mentioned earlier, the relatively high correlations between penile erection and subjective arousal in men may simply reflect the male's greater tendency to judge his stage of arousal by his perceived degree of erection. Women may not only have less easily quantifiable signals of genital response but also be more influenced by other non-genital cues of arousal or excitement. In an earlier study, Levi (1969) used urinary catecholamine excretion as the physiological index of arousal. He reported no correlation with subjective ratings of arousal in men after watching erotic films, but a significant correlation in women. We have suggested previously that this could result from women basing their assessment of arousal on cues of excitement more predictably related to catecholamine excretion than genital response would be (Bancroft, 1978). The common tendency in the literature to equate genital response with sexual arousal is a source of theoretical confusion (Bancroft and Mathews, 1971). The commonly expressed concern about these low correlations in women could be telling us more about our inappropriate expectations than about the validity of the physiological measures. This issue is of crucial importance when applying these psychophysiological techniques to treatment studies, either as a component of treatment (e.g. 'feedback') or as outcome measures. Although several interesting reports relating to treatment have appeared (e.g. Wincze *et al.*, 1978; Heiman, 1980), Rosen and Beck (1988) recently concluded that more research is needed before we can use sexual psychophysiology as an index of treatment efficacy.

In most respects, including the use of appropriate stimuli and the experimental setting, the comments made in relation to men apply also to women. There is also some evidence of spontaneous episodes of vaginal vasocongestion occurring periodically during sleep in women, comparable to the NPT of the male although with a less predictable relationship to REM sleep. The vascular changes occurring in such responses were as great as those during orgasm in the waking state (Fisher *et al.*, 1983). As yet, very little attention has been paid to the possible research or diagnostic implications of this sleep response in women.

CONCLUSIONS

A consistent finding, in the psychometric literature reviewed in this chapter, is for methods of assessment to be devised and used by the originators and only a handful of other researchers. In comparison with measures of, say, personality, there has been a lack of wide acceptance of any one method in the field. To some extent this reflects the special needs of many research studies, but also the sensitive nature of this type of enquiry and hence a greater reluctance to use methods which have evolved in a different culture or research setting. This has held back progress in this field, and it is to be hoped that a suitable selection of the measures reviewed here, or others yet to be devised, will gain wider acceptance.

In the psychophysiological field, the main obstacle to standardization of practice lies in the use of erotic stimuli. These simply do not lend themselves to standardization. There may be no simple solution to that particular problem.

APPENDIX: HELP SHEET FOR ANSWERING DAILY REPORT QUESTIONS

This daily report lets us know how you feel from day to day. It is important that you fill it in accurately at about the same time each day, and should only take a few minutes of your time after a little practice.

I Morning

Did you wake this morning with an erection? Please tick the appropriate box: Yes, a *full* erection (F); Yes, a *partial* erection (P); or no erection (N).

II How did you feel today?

Your physical and emotional state can affect how sexy you feel, so we want to know a little about your moods each day. Each feeling is marked on a 0 to 10 scale, 0 always means 'not at all' and 10 means 'more than I can remember'. So, for instance, if a line was marked like this:

Cheerful 0 ________________________________x______ 10

we would say that the person was very cheerful, but not the happiest he could ever remember. If it was like this:

Cheerful 0 ______x________________________________ 10

we would say that the person was not very cheerful. Please mark *each* scale *each* day. The blank line is for any feeling which is important for you which we have missed.

III Sexual activity

If there was no sexual activity today, please tick the box marked 'no activity' and pass on to section IV.

If you *masturbated* today, please tick box M, then use the lines beside it to say how enjoyable it felt (0 = unpleasurable—10 = wonderful), and how full the erection was (0 = no erection—10 = full, rigid, sustained erection). If this led to ejaculation, tick box E(m).

If you had *sexual activity with a partner* today, please tick box S, then use the lines as above to say how pleasurable it was and to describe the fullness of the erection. Please tick the appropriate box to say whether *you*, your *partner*, or *both* of you started the sexual activity, and if you ejaculated tick box E(s).

IV Sexual thoughts

Please tell us how often you found yourself thinking sexy thoughts today on the line called 'frequency' (0 = no sexual thoughts—10 = very frequent sexual thoughts).

Please tell us on the next line, how many of your sexy thoughts were accompanied by feelings of sexual excitement. (0 = none of the thoughts were accompanied by feelings of excitement—10 = all of the thoughts were accompanied by feelings of excitement). If you *did not have* any sexy thoughts today please leave this line blank.

REFERENCES

Alder, E. and Bancroft, J. (1988) The relationship between breastfeeding persistence, sexuality and mood in postpartum women. *Psychological Medicine*, **18**, 389–96.

Anderson, B.L. and Broffitt, B. (1988) Is there a reliable self-report measure of sexual behavior? *Archives Sexual Behavior*, **17**, 509–26.

Bancroft, J. (1974) *Deviant Sexual Behaviour*, Clarendon Press, Oxford.

Bancroft, J. (1978) Psychological and physiological responses to sexual stimuli in men and women. In L. Levi (ed.), *Society, Stress and Disease*, Vol. 3. *The Productive and Reproductive Age*, pp. 154–63, Oxford University Press, Oxford.

Bancroft, J. (1988) Sexual desire and the brain. *Sexual and Marital Therapy*, **3**, 11–28.

Bancroft, J. (1989) *Human Sexuality and its Problems*, 2nd edn, Churchill Livingstone, Edinburgh.

Bancroft, J. and Bell, C. (1985) Simultaneous recording of penile diameter and penile arterial pulse during laboratory based erotic stimulation in normal subjects. *Journal of Psychosomatic Research*, **29**, 303–13.

Bancroft, J., Bell, C., Ewing, D.J., McCulloch, D.K., Warner, P. and Clarke, B.F. (1985) Assessment of erectile function in diabetic and non-diabetic impotence by simultaneous recording of penile diameter and penile arterial pulse. *Journal of Psychosomatic Research*, **29**, 315–24.

Bancroft, J., Gwynne Jones, H.E. and Pullan, B.P. (1966) A simple transducer for measuring penile erection with comments on its use in the treatment of sexual disorder. *Behaviour Research and Therapy*, **4**, 239–41.

Bancroft J. and Mathews, A. (1971) Autonomic correlates of penile erection. *Journal of Psychosomatic Research*, **15**, 159–67.

Bancroft, J., Sanders, D., Davidson, D.W. and Warner, P. (1983) Mood, sexuality, hormones and the menstrual cycle. III Sexuality and the role of androgens. *Psychosomatic Medicine*, **45**, 509–16.

Bancroft, J., Sherwin, B., Alexander, G.M., Davidson, D.W. and Walker, A. (1990) Oral contraceptives, androgens and the sexuality of young women. I A comparison of sexual experience, sexual attitudes and gender role in oral contraceptive users and non-users. *Archives of Sexual Behavior* (in press).

Bancroft, J., Tennent, T.G., Loucas, K. and Cass, J. (1974) Control of deviant sexual behaviour by drugs: behavioural effects of oestrogens and anti-androgens. *British Journal of Psychiatry*, **125**, 310–15.

Bancroft, J. and Wu, F.C.W. (1983) Changes in erectile responsiveness during androgen replacement therapy. *Archives Sexual Behaviour*, **12**, 59–66.

Bardwick, J.M. and Behrman, S.J. (1967) Investigation into the effects of anxiety, sexual arousal and menstrual cycle phase on uterine contractions. *Psychosomatic Medicine*, **29**, 468–82.

Barlow, D.H., Becker, R., Leitenberg, H. and Agras, S. (1970) A mechanical strain gauge for recording penile circumference change. *Journal of Applied Behavior Analysis*, **3**, 73–6.

Beck, J.G., Sakheim, D.K. and Barlow, D.H. (1983) Operating characteristics of the vaginal photoplethsymograph; some implications for its use. *Archives of Sexual Behavior*, **12**, 43–58.

Becker, M.A. and Byrne, D. (1985) Self-regulated exposure to erotica, recall errors, and subjective reactions as a function of erotophobia and type A coronary prone behavior. *Journal of Personality Social Psychology*, **48**, 135–51.

Bentler, P. (1968a) Heterosexual behavior assessment. I Male. *Behaviour Research and Therapy*, **6**, 21–5.

Bentler, P. (1968b) Heterosexual behavior assessment. II Female *Behavior Research and Therapy*, **6**, 27–30.

Binik, Y.M., Servan-Schreiber, D., Freiwald, S. and Hall, K.S.K. (1989) Intelligent computer-based assessment and psychotherapy; an expert system for sexual dysfunction. *Journal of Nervous and Mental Disease* (in press).

Bradley, W.E., Timm, G.W., Gallagher, J.M. and Johnson, B.K. (1985) New method for continuous measurement of nocturnal penile tumescence rigidity. *Urology*, **26**, 4–9.

Brady, J.R. and Levitt, E.E. (1965) The scalability of sexual experience. *Psychological Record*, **15**, 275–9.

Brissette, S., Montplaisir, J., Godbout, R. and Lavoisier, P. (1985) Sexual activity and sleep in humans. *Biological Psychiatry*, **20**, 758–63.

Caram, C., Bancroft, J. *et al.* (1989) The effects of testosterone administration on nocturnal penile tumescence in normal men. *Hormones and Behavior* (in press).

Chambless, D.L. and Lifshitz, J.L. (1984) Self-reported sexual anxiety and arousal; the Expanded Sexual Arousal Inventory. *J. Sex Research*, **20**, 241–54.

Cohen, H.D., Rosen, R.C. and Goldstein, L. (1985) EEG hemispheric asymmetry during sexual arousal: psychophysiological patterns in responding, unresponsive and dysfunctional males. *Journal of Abnormal Psychology*, **94**, 580–90.

Conte, H.R. (1983) Development and use of self-report techniques for assessing sexual functioning: a review and critique. *Archives of Sexual Behavior*, **12**, 555–76.

Cook, M.R. (1974) Psychophysiology of peripheral vascular changes. In P.A. Obrist, A. Black, J. Brener and L.V. DiCara (eds), *Cardiovascular Physiology; Current Issues in Response Mechanisms, Biofeedback and Methodology*, pp. 60–84, Aldine, Chicago.

Costell, R.M., Lunde, D.J., Kopell, B.S. and Wittner, W.K. (1972) Contingent negative variation as an indicator of sexual object preference. *Science*, **177**, 718–20.

Crepault, C., Abraham, G., Porto, R. and Couture, M. (1977) Erotic imagery in women. In R. Gemme and C.C. Wheeler (eds), *Progress in Sexology*, Plenum Press, New York.

Crepault, C. and Couture, M. (1980) Men's erotic fantasies. *Archives of Sexual Behavior*, **9**, 565–82.

Davis, C.M., Yarber, W.L. and Davis, S.L. (1988) Sexuality-related measures; a compendium. Obtained from W.L. Yarber, Department of Psychology, Indiana University.

Derogatis, L.R. (1978) *Derogatis Sexual Functioning Inventory*, revised edition, Clinical Psychometric Research, Baltimore.

Derogatis, L.R. and Meyer, J.R. (1979) A psychological profile of the sexual dysfunctions. *Archives of Sexual Behavior*, **8**, 201–23.

Earls, C.M., Quinsey, V.L. and Castonguay, L.G. (1987) A comparison of three methods of scoring penile circumference change. *Archives Sexual Behavior*, **16**, 493–500.

Everaerd, W. (1977) Comparative studies of short-term treatment methods for sexual inadequacy. In R. Gemme and C.C. Wheeler (eds), *Progress in Sexology*, pp. 153–65, Plenum Press, New York.

Everaerd, W. and Dekker, J. (1982) Treatment of secondary orgasmic dysfunction. A comparison of systemic desensitisation and sex therapy. *Behaviour Research and Therapy*, **20**, 269–74.

Eysenck, H.J. (1971) Personality and sexual adjustment. *British Journal of Psychiatry*, **118**, 593–608.

Eysenck, H.J. (1976) *Sex and Personality*, Open Books, London.

Farley, F., Nelson, J.G., Knight, W.C. and Garcia-Colberg, E. (1977) Sex, politics and personality: a multidimensional study of college students. *Archives of Sexual Behavior*, **6**, 105–20.

Farrell, C. (1978) *My Mother Said . . . the way young people learn about sex and birth control*, Routledge & Kegan Paul, London.

Fisher, C., Cohen, H.D., Schiavi, R.C., Davis, D., Furman, B., Ward, K., Edwards, A. and Cunningham, J. (1983) Patterns of female sexual arousal during sleep and waking; vaginal thermo-conductance studies. *Archives of Sexual Behavior*, **12**, 97–122.

Fisher, C., Gross, J. and Zuch, J. (1965) Cycle of penile erection synchronous with dreaming (REM) sleep: preliminary report. *Archives of General Psychiatry*, **12**, 29–45.

Fisher, C., Schiavi, R.C., Lear, H., Edwards, A., Davis, D.M. and Witkin, A.P. (1975) The assessment of nocturnal REM erection in the differential diagnosis of sexual impotence. *Journal of Sex and Marital Therapy*, **1**, 277–89.

Fisher, W.A. (1984) Predicting contraceptive behavior among university men: the roles of emotions and behavioral intentions. *Journal of Applied Social Psychology*, **14**, 104–23.

Fisher, W.A., Byrne, D., Edmunds, M., Miller, C.T., Kelley, K. and White, L.A. (1979) Psychological and situation-specific correlates of contraceptive behavior among university women. *Journal of Sex Research*, **15**, 38–55.

Fisher, W.A., Byrne, D., White, L.A. and Kelley, K. (1988) Erotophobia–erotophilia as a dimension of personality. *Journal of Sex Research* (in press).

Fox, C.A. and Fox, B. (1969) Blood pressure and respiratory patterns during human coitus. *Journal of Reproduction and Fertility*, **19**, 405–15.

Fox, C.A., Wolff, H.S. and Baker, J.A. (1970) Measurement of intravaginal and intrauterine pressures during human coitus by radio-telemetry. *Journal of Reproduction and Fertility*, **22**, 243–51.

Frenken, J. and Vennix, P. (1981) *Sexuality Experience Scales Manual*, Swets & Zeitlinger BV, Lisse.

Freund, K., Sedlacek, F. and Knob, K. (1965) A simple transducer for mechanical plethysmography of the male genital. *Journal of Experimental Analysis of Behavior*, **8**, 169–70.

Geer, J.H., Morokoff, P. and Greenwood, P. (1974) Sexual arousal in women: the development of a measurement device for vaginal blood volume. *Archives of Sexual Behavior*, **3**, 559–64.

Giambra, L.M. (1983) Daydreaming in 40 to 60 year old women; menopause, health values and sexuality. *Journal of Clinical Psychology*, **39**, 11–21.

Giambra, L.M. and Martin, C.E. (1977) Sexual daydreams and quantitative aspects of sexual activity; some relations for males across adulthood. *Archives of Sexual Behavior*, **6**, 497–505.

Gillan, P. and Brindley, G.S. (1979) Vaginal and pelvic floor responses to sexual stimulation. *Psychophysiology*, **16**, 471–81.

Golombok, S. and Rust, J. (1985) The Golombok-Rust Inventory of Sexual Satisfaction (GRISS). *British Journal of Clinical Psychology*, **24**, 63–4.

Golombok, S. and Rust, J. (1988) The GRISS: a psychometric scale and profile of sexual dysfunction. In C.M. Davis, W.L. Yarber and S.L. Davis (eds), *Sexuality-related Measures: a Compendium*, pp. 241–3.

Gorer, G. (1971) *Sex and Marriage in England Today*, Nelson, London.

Hardy, K.R. (1964) An appetitional theory of sexual motivation. *Psychological Review*, **71**, 1–18.

Hatch, J.P. (1979) Vaginal photoplethysmography: methodological considerations. *Archives of Sexual Behavior*, **8**, 357–74.

Heiman, J.R. (1977) A psychophysiological exploration of sexual arousal patterns in females and males. *Psychophysiology*, **14**, 266–73.

Heiman, J.R. (1980) Female sexual response patterns; interactions of physiological, affective and contextual cues. *Archives of General Psychiatry*, **37**, 1311–16.

Henson, D.E., Rubin, H.B., Henson, C. and Williams, J. (1977) Temperature changes of the labia minora as an objective measure of human female eroticism. *Journal of Behavior Therapy and Experimental Psychiatry*, **8**, 401–10.

Hess, E.H. and Polt, J.M. (1960) Pupil size as related to interest value of visual stimuli. *Science*, **132**, 349–50.

Hess. E.H., Seltzer, A.L. and Shlien, J.M. (1965) Pupil response of hetero- and homosexual males to pictures of men and women: a pilot study. *Journal of Abnormal Psychology*, **70**, 165–8.

Hirshkowitz, M., Ware, J.C., Turner, D. and Karacan, I. (1979) EEG amplitude asymmetry during sleep. *Sleep Research*, **8**, 25.

Hoon, E.F. and Chambless, D. (1988) Sexual Arousability Inventory (SAI) and Sexual Arousability Inventory-Expanded (SAI-E). In C.M. Davis, W.L. Yarber and S.L. Davis (eds), *Sexuality-related Measures: a Compendium*, pp. 21–4.

Hoon, E.F., Hoon, P.W. and Wincze, J.P. (1976) The SAI: an inventory for the measurement of female sexual arousability. *Archives of Sexual Behavior*, **5**, 291–300.

Hoon, P.W., Wincze, J.P. and Hoon, E.F. (1976) Physiological assessment of sexual arousal in women. *Psychophysiology*, **13**, 196–204.

Jennings, J.R., Tahmoush, A.J. and Redmond, D.P. (1980) Non-invasive measurement of peripheral vascular activity. In I. Martin and P.H. Venables (eds), *Techniques in Psychophysiology*, pp. 86–116, John Wiley, Chichester.

Karacan, I. (1970) Clinical value of nocturnal erection in the prognosis and diagnosis of impotence. *Medical Aspects of Human Sexuality*, **4**, 27–34.

Karacan, I., Rosenbloom, A. and Williams, R.L. (1970) The clitoral erection cycle during sleep. *Psychophysiology*, **7**, 338 (abstract).

Karacan, I., Salis, P.J., Thornby, J.I. and Williams, R.L. (1976) The ontogeny of nocturnal penile tumescence. *Waking and Sleeping*, **1**, 27–44.

Karacan, I., Salis, P.J. and Williams, R.L. (1978) The role of the sleep laboratory in diagnosis and treatment of impotence. In R.L. Williams and I. Karacan (eds), *Sleep Disorders: Diagnosis and Treatment*, pp. 353–82, John Wiley, New York.

Kelley, K. (1979) Socialisation factors in contraceptive attitudes: roles of affective responses, parental attitudes and sexual experience. *Journal of Sex Research*, **15**, 6–20.

Kinsey, A.C., Pomeroy, W.B. and Martin, C.F. (1948) *Sexual Behavior in the Human Male*, Saunders, Philadelphia.

Kockott, G., Feil, W., Ferstl, R., Aldenhoff, J. and Besinger, V. (1980) Psychophysiological aspects of male sexual inadequacy; results of an experimental study. *Archives of Sexual Behavior*, **9**, 477–93.

Kwan, M., Greenleaf, W.J., Mann, J., Crapo, L. and Davidson, J.M. (1983) The nature of androgen action on male sexuality; a combined laboratory-self-report study on hypogonadal men. *Journal of Clinical Endocrinology and Metabolism*, **57**, 557–62.

Levi, L. (1969) Sympatho-adreno-medullary activity, diuresis and emotional reactions during visual sexual stimulation in human males and females. *Psychosomatic Medicine*, **31**, 251–68.

Levin, R.J. and Wagner, G. (1985) Orgasm in women in the laboratory—quantitive studies on duration, intensity, latency and vaginal blood flow. *Archives of Sexual Behavior*, **14**, 439–50.

Lifshitz, K. (1966) The average evoked cortical response to complex visual stimuli. *Psychophysiology*, **3**, 55–68.

LoPiccolo, J. and Steger, J.C. (1974) The sexual interaction inventory; a new instrument for the assessment of sexual dysfunction. *Archives of Sexual Behavior*, **3**, 585–96.

McConaghy, N. (1967) Penile volume change to moving pictures of male and female nudes in heterosexual and homosexual males. *Behavior Therapy*, **5**, 43–8.

McCoy, N.N. and D'Agostino, P.A. (1977) Factor analysis of the sexual interaction inventory. *Archives of Sexual Behavior*, **6**, 25–35.

McGovern, K.B., Stewart, R.C. and LoPiccolo, J. (1975) Secondary orgasmic dysfunction. I. Analysis and strategies for treatment. *Archives of Sexual Behavior*, **4**, 205.

Masters, W. and Johnson, V.E. (1966) *Human Sexual Response*, Churchill Livingstone, Edinburgh.

Metz, P. and Wagner, G. (1981) Penile circumference and erection. *Urology*, **18**, 268–70.

Meyer-Bahlberg, H.F.L. and Ehrhard, A.A. (1983) *Sexual Behavior Assessment Schedule—Adult SEBAS-A.* Published by the authors, Dept Psychiatry, College of Physicians and Surgeons of Columbia University, 722 West 168th Street, New York, NY 10032, USA.

Murphy, W., Coleman, E., Hoon, E.F. and Scott, C. (1980) Sexual dysfunction and treatment in alcoholic women. *Sexuality and Disability*, **3**, 240–55.

O'Carroll R. and Bancroft, J. (1984) Testosterone therapy for low sexual interest and erectile dysfunction in men: a controlled study. *British Journal of Psychiatry*, **145**, 146–51.

O'Carroll, R., Shapiro, C. and Bancroft, J. (1985) Androgens, behaviour and nocturnal erections in hypogonadal men; the effects of varying the replacement dose. *Clinical Endocrinology*, **23**, 527–38.

Podell, L. and Perkins, J.C. (1957) A Guttman scale for sexual experience—a methodological note. *Journal of Abnornal and Social Psychology*, **54**, 420–22.

Procci, W.R., Moss, H.B., Boyd, J.L. and Baron, D.A.S. (1983) Consecutive night reliability of portable penile tumescence monitor. *Archives of Sexual Behavior*, **12**, 307–16.

Reading, A.E. and Wiest, W.M. (1984) An analysis of self-reported behavior in a sample of normal males. *Archives of Sexual Behavior*, **13**, 69–84.

Reifler, C.B., Howard, J., Lipton, M.A., Liptzin, M.B. and Widmann, D.E. (1971) Pornography: an experimental study of effects. *American Journal of Psychiatry*, **128**, 575–82.

Riley, A.J. and Riley, E.J. (1986) The effects of single dose diazepam on female sexual response induced by masturbation. *Sexual and Marital Therapy*, **1**, 49–54.

Roose, S.P., Glassman, A.H., Walsh, B.T. and Cullen, K. (1982) Reversible loss of nocturnal penile tumescence during depression; a preliminary report. *Neuropsychobiology*, **8**, 284–8.

Rosen, R.C. and Beck, J.G. (1988) *Patterns of Sexual Arousal. Psychophysiological Processes and Clinical Applications*, Guilford Press, New York.

Rosen, R.C., Goldstein, L., Scoles, V. and Lazarus, C. (1986) Psychophysiological correlates of nocturnal penile tumescence in normal males. *Psychosomatic Medicine*, **48**, 423–9.

Rosen, R.C. and Keefe, F.J. (1978) The measurement of human penile tumescence. *Psychophysiology*, **15**, 366–76.

Rosen, R.C., Kostis, J.B. and Jekelis, A.W. (1988) Beta blocker effects on sexual function in normal males. *Archives of Sexual Behavior*, **17**, 241–56.

Sanders, D., Warner, P., Backstrom, T. and Bancroft, J. (1983) Mood, sexuality, hormones and the menstrual cycle I. Changes in mood and physical state: description of subjects and methods. *Psychosomatic Medicine*, **45**, 487–501.

Schiavi, R.C., Derogatis, L.R., Kurianski, J., O'Connor, D.and Sharpe, L. (1979) The assessment of sexual function and marital interaction. *Journal of Sex and Marital Therapy*, **5**, 169–222.

Schiavi, R.C. and Fisher, C. (1982) Assessment of diabetic impotence: measurement of nocturnal erections. *Clinics in Endocrinology and Metabolism*, **11**(3), 769–84.

Schiavi, R.C., Schreiner-Engel, P., White, D. and Mandell, J. (1988) Pituitary-gonadal function during sleep in men with hypoactive sexual desire and in normal controls. *Psychosomatic Medicine*, **50**, 304–18.

Schofield, M. (1965) *The Sexual Behaviour of Young People*, Longman, London.

Schover, L.R., Friedman, J.M., Weiler, S.J., Heiman, J.R. and LoPiccolo, J. (1982) Multiaxial problem-oriented system for sexual dysfunction *Archives of General Psychiatry*, **39**, 614–19.

Schover, L.R. and Jensen, S.B. (1988) *Sexuality and Chronic Illness. A Comprehensive Approach*, Guilford Press, New York.

Schreiner-Engel, P., Schiavi, R.C., Vietorisz, D., Eichel, J. de S. and Smith, H. (1985) Diabetes and female sexuality; a comparative study of women in relationships. *Journal of Sex Marital Therapy*, **11**, 165–75.

Shenk, J. and Pfrang, H. (1986) Extraversion, neuroticism and sexual behavior: interrelationships in a sample of young men. *Archives of Sexual Behavior*, **12**, 31–42.

Shenk, J., Pfrang, H. and Rausche, A. (1981) Personality traits versus the quality of the marital relationship as the determinants of marital sexuality. *Archives of Sexual Behavior*, **15**, 449–56.

Singer, J.L. and Antrobus, J.S. (1972) Daydreaming, imaginal processes, and personality; a normative study. In P. Sheehan (ed.), *The Function and Nature of Imagery*, pp. 175–202, Academic Press, New York.

Sintchak, G. and Geer, J.H. (1975) A vaginal plethysmograph system. *Psychophysiology*, **12**, 113–15.

Skaakeback, N.E., Bancroft, J., Davidson, D.W. and Warner, P. (1981) Androgen replacement with oral testosterone undecanoate in hypogonadal men: a double-blind cross-over study. *Clinical Endocrinology*, **14**, 49–67.

Sorensen, R.C. (1973) *Adolescent Sexuality in Contemporary America*, World Publishing, New York.

Tennent, G., Bancroft, J. and Cass, J. (1974) The control of deviant sexual behaviour by drugs: a double blind controlled study of benperidol, chlorpromazine and placebo. *Archives of Sexual Behavior*, **3**, 261–71.

Thase, M.E., Reynolds, C.F., Glanz, L.M. *et al.* (1987) Nocturnal penile tumescence in depressed men. *American Journal of Psychiatry*, **144**, 89–92.

Tucker, D.M. and Dawson, S.L. (1984) Asymmetric EEG changes as Method actors generated emotions. *Biological Psychology*, **19**, 63–75.

Walker, A. and Bancroft, J. (1989) The relationship between oral contraceptive use and premenstrual symptoms; a controlled study. *Psychosomatic Medicine*, **52**, 86–96.

Warner, P. and Bancroft, L. (1988) Mood, sexuality, oral contraceptives and the menstrual cycle. *Journal of Psychosomatic Research*, **32**, 417–27.

Wenger, M.A., Averill, J.R. and Smith, D.D. (1968) Autonomic activity during sexual arousal. *Psychophysiology*, **4**, 468–78.

Whalen, R.E. (1966) Sexual motivation. *Psychological Review*, **73**, 151–63.

Wheeler, D. and Rubin, H.B. (1987) A comparison of volumetric and circumferential measures of penile erection. *Archives of Sexual Behavior*, **16**, 289–300.

Wilson, G.D. (1988) Measurement of sexual fantasy. *Sexual and Marital Therapy*, **3**, 45–55.

Wilson, G.T. and Lawson, D.M. (1976) Expectancies, alcohol and sexual arousal in male social drinkers. *Journal of Abnormal Psychology*, **85**, 587–94.

Winoker, G. (1963) Aspects of sexual behavior; a classification. In G. Winoker (ed.), *Determinants of Human Sexual Behavior*, pp. vii–viii, Charles C. Thomas, Springfield, Ill.

Wincze, J.P., Hoon, E.F. and Hoon, P.W. (1976) Physiological responsivity of normal and sexually dysfunctional women during erotic stimulus exposure. *Journal of Psychosomatic Research*, **20**, 445–51.

Wincze, J.P., Hoon, E.F. and Hoon, P.W. (1978) Multiple measure analysis of women experiencing low sexual arousal. *Behaviour Research and Therapy*, **16**, 43–9.

Wooten, V. and Fields, T.J. (1987) Evaluation of the Dacomed Rigiscan device. Paper presented at International Sleep Conference.

World Health Organization Task Force on Psychosocial Research in Family Planning (1980) Acceptability of drugs for male fertility regulation; a prospective study and some preliminary data. *Contraception*, **21**, 121–34.

Wyatt, G.E. and Peters, S.D. (1986) Methodological considerations in research on the prevalence of child sexual abuse. *Child Abuse and Neglect*, **10**, 241–51.

Wyatt, G.E., Peters, S.D. and Guttrie, D. (1988) Kinsey revisited. Part 1 Comparison of the sexual socialisation and sexual behavior of white women over 33 years. *Archives of Sexual Behavior*, **17**, 201-40.

Zelnick, M. and Kantner, J.F. (1977) Sexual and contraceptive experience of young unmarried women in the United States 1970 & 1971. *Family Planning Perspectives*, **9**, 55–71.

Zuckerman, M. (1971) Physiological measures of sexual arousal in the human. *Psychological Bulletin*, **75**, 297–329.

Zuckerman, M. (1973) Scales for sexual experience for males and females. *Journal of Consulting and Clinical Psychology*, **41**, 27–9.

Zuckerman, M. (1988) Human sexuality questionnaire. In C.M. Davis, W.L. Yarber and S.L. Davis, *Sexuality-related Measures: a Compendium*, pp. 92–8.

Zuckerman, M., Neeb, M., Fiches, M. *et al.*, (1985) Nocturnal penile tumescence and penile response in the resting state in diabetic and non-diabetic sexual dysfunctionals. *Archives of Sexual Behavior*, **15**, 366–76.

Zuckerman, M., Tushup, R. and Finner, S. (1976) Sexual attitudes and experience: attitude and personality correlates and changes produced by a course in sexuality, Journal of Consulting and Clinical Psychology, 44, 7–19.

Chapter 16

Sleep Disorders

COLIN M. SHAPIRO and KATHERINE RATHOUSE

MEASUREMENTS OF SLEEP

Introduction

Information about sleep has grown considerably over the last three decades, and has followed the EEG description of sleep stages and states. There has been a great deal of 'have technique, will study' research with limited attention to methodology in the wider context. In many respects this honeymoon is over, and the careful selection of techniques and particularly the combination of techniques for studies aimed at answering questions rather than at being descriptive will be increasingly important. In this context, it is surprising that there is no single review of the measurement of different facets of sleep and sleepiness. This may be a consequence of the breadth of the subject, or that sleep research is particularly multidisciplinary and that no group can cover the spectrum of measures that have been applied. This review omits measures related to dreams, biochemical measures of sleep factors and details in specific areas (for example, the techniques used in ear oximetry and breathing analysis) that have been developed specifically with sleep studies in mind. It will be surprising to some that ear oximetry has a sensitivity for classifying non-REM sleep of 0.85 (Farney *et al.*, 1986). This indicates the potential of a range of techniques which can be applied to sleep assessment and measurement.

The most extensive description of detailed techniques to date is the book edited by Guilleminault (1982).0 The purpose of this review is to make accessible the basic techniques of sleep recordings and to provide an integrated synthesis of the range of measures which might be used. Recent well-conducted studies (e.g. Adam *et al.*, 1986) have shown the value of the combination of subjective measures (both idiographic and nomothetic) and objective sleep stage analysis. It is intended that this review emphasizes the use of multiple measure1s but the description of the techniques is, of necessity, sequential and separate.

Certain measures during sleep (for example, of metabolic rate during

Measuring Human Problems. Edited by D.F. Peck and C.M. Shapiro

sleep) are likely to alter that which is being measured (Shapiro, 1985). The search for specific solutions for specific measurement problems remains.

Electroencephalographic measures of sleep

Electroencephalography (EEG) was first described by Berger in 1929 and is the study of the small, constantly changing electrical potentials from the brain which can be recorded from the scalp. A sleep polysomnograph also involves recording eye movements (electro-occulograph (EOG)) and movement from muscle tone (electromyograph (EMG)).

The descriptions of sleep-recording techniques and sleep staging which follow are based on the scheme outlined by Dement and Kleitman (1957). This was refined by the Association for the Psychophysiological Study of Sleep, who published a manual for recording and scoring human sleep stages (Rechtshaffen and Kales, 1968).

It should be mentioned here that the electrode placement for polysomnograph recordings differs slightly between sleep centres in the USA and the majority of the sleep laboratories in Europe, although sleep-staging criteria are standard. Sleep pattern is a particularly stable biological parameter. A first-night effect has been often reported (e.g. Agnew *et al.*, 1966) in which the first night of recording is different from subsequent nights, but this is not invariably detected (Clausen *et al.*, 1974).

EEG measures are important for exploring the neuropsychological and neurophysiological basis of sleep, correlating them with other physiological measures (e.g. hormone levels, body temperature, ECG, respiration, etc.) to obtain measures of normal sleep in attempts to elucidate the functions of sleep. Further, they can be used to test the effects of drugs and compare their actions by determining the speed of onset and the 'depth' of sleep. Certain abnormalities (e.g. some focal epileptic discharges) are enhanced by the change in the patient from the alert to the sleeping state. A sleep EEG combined with respiratory monitoring and a daytime multiple sleep latency test (MSLT) is used for diagnosing sleep disorders (for example, sleep apnea and narcolepsy; Guilleminault, 1982). Sleep disturbances as indicated by sleep recordings are considered by some to be a useful diagnostic aid in patients suffering from endogenous depression (see Chapter 3).

In the decade since Smith (1978) reviewed the role of computers in sleep research, there have been considerable developments, and interactive programs or computer-aided analyses of sleep are becoming increasingly available. This area is beyond the scope of this review.

Equipment

The most standard method of recording the polysomnograph is using an ink-on-paper electroencephalograph machine. A number of EEG systems which produce compressed tape recorded tracings are available, some having an added facility of automatically analysing sleep stages according to the criteria of Rechtshaffen and Kales (1968). At present, however, visual scoring by properly trained personnel for sleep stage analysis is still the most popular. Details concerning the practical aspects of carrying out sleep recordings and the attachment of electrodes, etc. are available from the authors.

Sleep staging (scoring)

The quality and characteristics of the polysomnograph tracings depend on the technique used, and this should be standardized in a laboratory. The sleep stage designations are standardized and are defined as stage 1, 2, 3 and 4 of non-REM sleep (NREM) and rapid eye movement REM sleep. Stages 3 and 4 in combination are sometimes referred to as slow-wave sleep (SWS) or delta sleep.

The major scoring criteria are based on the criteria of Rechtshaffen and Kales (1968). Stage W, which corresponds to the waking state, is characterized by alpha activity and/or a low-voltage mixed-frequency EEG, eye blinks are present in the EOG and there is a relatively high tonic EMG.

Stage 1: Greater than 50 per cent abundance of low-voltage 2–7 Hz activity in the epoch 'low-voltage, mixed-frequency EEG'. Vertex sharp waves may occur and K complexes and sleep spindles (these two terms are described below) are absent. This stage, especially following wakefulness, is characterized by the presence of slow rolling eye movements (SEMs) lasting several seconds. Rapid eye movements are absent. Tonic EMG levels are usually below those of relaxed wakefulness. For a more detailed description of the transition from wakefulness to sleep see Roth (1961).

K complexes are defined as EEG waves having a well-delineated negative sharp wave followed immediately by a positive component. These may or may not be combined with a sleep spindle. K complexes can occur in response to sudden stimuli. The sleep spindle describes activity of 12–14 cps (cycles per second) and one should be able to count six or seven distinct waves within a half-second period.

Stage 2: Sleep spindles and/or K complexes occur with a duration of greater than 0.5 second. Eye movements do not occur and tonic EMG levels are usually the same or lower than during stage 1. Sleep spindles and K complexes are transient, however, and if less than 3 minutes of intervening epochs occur between recognizable sleep spindles and/or K complexes this time is classed as stage 2 unless it is clearly recognizable as stage 1.

Stage 3: An EEG record in which between 20 per cent and 50 per cent of the epoch consists of delta activity or slow waves of 2 cps or slower, with amplitudes greater than 50 μV (European) at 75 μV (peak to trough). In practice, it is necessary to bear in mind that the amplitude of the slow waves (delta waves) is lower in older patients or if the patient is on CNS depressants. The amplitude also decreases across the night's recording. Apart from cerebral activity, the amplitude is also influenced by other factors (e.g. inter-electrode distance, electrode placement, time constants). Sleep spindles are usually present.

Stage 4: More than 50 per cent of an epoch consists of delta activity of waves of 2 cps or lower and 50 μV amplitude. Sleep spindles may or may not be present.

Stage REM: There is a concomitant appearance of relatively low-voltage, mixed-frequency EEG activity and episodic rapid eye movements (REMs) with a marked reduced tonic EMG and phasic bursts of muscle activity (EMG tone is always lowest during REM sleep). The EEG pattern resembles the one described for stage 1, except that vertex sharp waves are not prominent and distinctive 'sawtooth' waves may occur (Berger *et al.*, 1962). Alpha activity may be present but there is an absence of sleep spindles and K complexes. In unusual circumstances (e.g. recovery sleep following sleep deprivation) sleep spindles may occur during REM. Sleep staging is then based on striking a balance in favour of the dominant features of either REM or stage 2, particularly at the beginning and end of REM sleep.

Table 16.1 Sleep stages.

Wakefulness: stage W, O or stage A.
Stage 1: drowsy sleep, transitional sleep, low voltage fast, descending stage 1, sleep onset 1, stage B.
Stage 2: spindle sleep, light sleep, stage C.
Stage 3 and/or Stage 4: deep sleep, quiet sleep, delta sleep, slow wave sleep, transitional sleep, orthosleep, telencephalic sleep, synchronous sleep, stage D and E.
Stage REM: paradoxical sleep, rhombencephalic sleep, stage 1-REM, activated sleep, fast sleep, low voltage-fast sleep, desynchronized sleep, D-sleep, stage 5.

Movement: When the EMG and EOG show increased muscle tone, which also tends to obscure the EEG for approximately half an epoch (depending on paper speed), then movement time is noted for that epoch. This movement, when not resulting in awakening, may lead to a slight arousal, as indicated by a couple of epochs of stage 1. It is left to the scorer to decide on setting his or her limit for scoring movement time.

A sleep hypnogram can be mapped out showing sleep stage change over the night. Other graphic techniques (for example, using colour coding or, more recently, the direct linkage of fast Fourier transformation and colour graphics with colour density spectral array; Salinsky *et al.*, 1988) have been used and were found to have approximately 90 per cent agreement with traditional polygraphic techniques. Automated techniques for scoring sleep records have increasingly been employed. A study in which the same sleep records were scored by nine separate groups as well as by automated techniques has recently been reported (Ferri *et al.*, 1989), and it cautions against assessing reliability of scoring by automated techniques when these are contrasted with the results of one or two scorers using standard visual techniques.

Movement and position during sleep

One facet of sleep is 'rest'. This can be assessed by a variety of criteria (for example, energy change and metabolic rate). For theoretical reasons and for practical reasons (for example, in conditions such as certain parasomnias and nocturnal myoclonus) it is often desirable to measure movement during sleep. A variety of techniques have been applied, some being very innovative.

Photography/video

The advantage of such a system is that the subject is completely unaffected by being filmed. Low light (Aaronson *et al.*, 1980) or infrared (Bardsley and Bell, 1975) systems can be used so as not to disturb the subject. The camera can be set up in the subject's normal surroundings. For these reasons, this technique is particularly favoured for studying infants (Anders and Sostek, 1976). Further advantages include the relative cheapness of such a system and the fact that a technician or attendant is not required to be present during the recordings.

Unfortunately, with photography the recording is intermittent, either occurring at fixed intervals (Aaronson *et al.*, 1980) or following movement which triggers the camera by a sensitive bed mechanism (Bardsley and Bell, 1975), and the covers may obscure some movements, particularly small ones. Despite these difficulties, the correlation between photography and polysomnographic (PSG) measures of sleep in young babies is quite high, although varying between REM and non-REM and waking states (Anders and Sostek, 1976). Inter-rater reliability is very high (Aaronson *et al.*, 1980).

Recently, Stradling *et al.* (1988) described a technique using photodiodes attached to the video screen, which is a simple and relatively cheap technique of detecting movement in bed.

Observation

Although superficially this may appear to be a method with the same advantages and disadvantages as photography, it seems to be less reliable, perhaps partially as a result of the inability to attend to all parts of the body at once. EEG and simultaneous nursing observations of psychiatric patients show that the main drawback is mistaking wakefulness for sleep. Reliability is influenced by the disorder of the patient being studied and tends to be worse for depressed patients as compared with manic or schizo-affective patients (Kupfer *et al.*, 1970; Weiss *et al.*, 1973). Methods for checking inter-observer reliability have recently been described (Carroll *et al.*, 1989) with encouraging results.

Sensitive bed

Sensitive bed techniques are entirely non-invasive. Mechanical sensitive beds have been used in a variety of studies (see Oswald *et al.*, 1963; Crisp *et al.*, 1970; Bardsley and Bell, 1975), but they cannot record small movements (e.g. finger movements).

The static charge sensitive bed, SCSB (Alihanka and Vaahtoranta,1979), is sensitive to small movements as well as to larger ones and it is reliable. A similar number of movements were recorded by the SCSB as in the study by Gardner and Grossman (1975), using a number of techniques including EEG, photography and direct observation. Polo *et al.* (1988) have shown that the SCSB has a sensitivity of 0.95 in detecting obstructive apnea in a group of sleep apnea patients. Specificity in detecting apneic events in 2-minute epochs was 0.64 in sleep apneics but approached unity in normal controls. Recently a technique using sixteen temperature sensors arranged on the surface of the bed has been used to detect body movement (Tamura *et al.*, 1988). Schmidt-Nowara and Scantlen (1983) report the use of two mercury switches in the bed to monitor movement and position.

Photoelectric beams

A simple burglar alarm technique can be used to detect the presence or absence of movement. This approach has found application in both theoretical research studies (for example, for detecting movement in a study of oxygen consumption during sleep; Shapiro *et al.*, 1984) and in clinical studies of behavioural conditioning during sleep in which body movements at night were successfully suppressed using a scanning device that, when interrupted, triggered a flashing light (unreported case study).

Transducers attached to the body

As with polysomnographic techniques, the apparatus is attached to the subject's body for the whole night. It is claimed that the transducers are small, comfortable, easy to apply and relatively cheap as compared with polysomnographic techniques. These systems also permit recording of sleep variables in the subject's own home.

Recently, piezoelectric transducers have been used (for example, the wrist actograph weighing only ±90 g and not much bigger than a large wrist watch). Mullaney *et al.* (1979, 1980) found that it gave a slightly longer measure of total sleep time than the EEG but Levine *et al.* (1986) stated that it underestimated sleep at night and overestimated sleep during the day. Wrist actography is an accurate and reliable technique for identifying sleep onset, prolonged arousals and awakening but not for short arousals or entry to REM sleep. A large number of studies have used actography in the detection of sleep in specific circumstances—for example, monitoring change in patients with sleep apnea during treatment and periodic body movements during sleep, especially in the elderly (Kripke *et al.*, 1978; Mullaney *et al.*, 1980; Webster *et al.*, 1982; Redmond and Hegge, 1985; Dzvonik *et al.*, 1986).

The use of this technique in the screening of sleep disorders has been considered by Urbach *et al.* (1988). Aubert-Tulkens *et al.* (1987), on discussing the wrist actograph, conclude that 'with respect to polysomnographic diagnosis of sleep apnea syndromes, the sensitivity of activity recordings was 89 per cent, whereas the specificity was 95 per cent'.

Messin *et al.* (1974) applied a similar transducer to the eyelid which senses globe movements through the closed lid. This type of sensor has both advantages and disadvantages as compared with standard EEG recordings.

Physiological measures characterizing sleep

Spontaneous electrodermal response

Several attempts have been made to obtain a measure of certain facets of sleep. There were claims by Niimi *et al.* (1968) that skin potential fluctuations were related to sleep stage. A distinction between wake and sleep was achieved (Koumans *et al.*, 1968) but not the sleep stage differentiation. Subsequent studies have made claims regarding the utility of this approach in psychological and physiological conditions (Wyatt *et al.*, 1970; McDonald *et al.*, 1976).

Responses to intermittent stimulation

The duration of sleep can be measured by recording responses to intermittent stimulation. This technique has been used recently in the treatment of insomnia (Espie *et al.*, 1989). It is assumed that the subjects are still awake if they respond and are asleep if they do not.

These assumptions may be incorrect. If a subject is sleepy or unmotivated, but not asleep, he may not respond. It may also be possible that the subject can respond while asleep. The experiments by Oswald *et al.* (1960) and MacDonald *et al.* (1975) show that information processing may take place during sleep.

Johnson and Kitching (1972) used a light which came on intermittently and required the subject to press a button in response. Unfortunately they did not compare this estimate of total sleep time with any other measure. Lichstein *et al.* (1982) used a different stimulus (a soft tone), and the subject was required to make a verbal rather than mechanical response.

Arousal threshold

One of the key features of sleep is that it is state reversible, unlike coma, and yet there is no simple way of measuring this facet of sleep. A number of factors influence arousal threshold during sleep, including: sleep stage; form of stimulus (e.g. auditory sound and hypoxaemia may have different effects); relevance of stimulus (e.g. baby's cry for a mother is attended to whereas other, louder, stimuli are ignored); and response criteria (e.g. perception of wakefulness, change in EEG or change in heart rate may be valid criteria but all produce different results). Other factors which have been shown to be pertinent include stimulus intensity, time of night and time lag between stimulus and response.

Evoked potentials

There have been a number of attempts to relate average evoked response (ER) to depth of sleep. These have been equivocal at best. Several authors describe a clear change with sleeping (Broughton *et al.*, 1987). Shapiro *et al.* (1980) could detect no post-sleep differences on ER in controls subjected to extremely fatiguing procedures, nor any effect of different fatiguing procedures. Evoked potentials have been used as an index of sleepiness (Broughton *et al.*, 1988) in narcoleptics and are claimed to be a useful adjunct to other measures of sleepiness (see below).

Middle ear muscle activity

Compliance of the tympanic membrane is known to change during normal sleep in humans. This is believed to be due to spontaneous contraction of the middle ear muscles. When awake, middle ear muscle activity (MEMA) is governed by either noise or tactile stimulation. However, during sleep MEMA occurs predominantly during REM sleep with approximately 80 per cent of all night-time MEMA occurring at this time (Pessah and Roffwarg, 1972). The remaining 20 per cent is mostly concentrated in NREM sleep prior to the REM period (Benson and Zarcone, 1979). Temporal distribution of middle ear muscle activity is not uniform but is more dense during the early part of the night. The discrimination of these events between REM and NREM sleep is not good enough for use as a solitary criterion of sleep classification. The same would apply to the other REM-related phasic events, including PGO waves, integrated activity of the extraocular muscles, apnea and K complexes.

Nocturnal penile tumescence

Shortly after the description of REM sleep, the association between REM sleep and nocturnal penile tumescence was postulated and confirmed (Oswald, 1962; Karacan *et al.*, 1966). This observation has been used extensively in the investigation of erectile dysfunction (see Schiavi, 1988, for review). The use of this procedure has been made in other disorders. Despite the observation that most patients with endogenous depression show diminished erectile function (Janovic, 1972) this has not been applied to differential diagnosis in psychiatric disorders. The technique is well established for the distinction between organic and psychogenic impotence with an efficiency of 80–90 per cent and specificity and sensitivity depending on the criteria used (Shapiro *et al.*, 1990).

Reliability of sleep parameters

Until recently, overnight polysomnographic recordings were necessarily carried out in sleep laboratories, but ambulatory monitoring systems have now been introduced. Some record variables similar to those recorded in the sleep laboratory. Others (for example, the use of wrist actography; Webster *et al.*, 1982) detect sleep and sleep state by virtue of a motility parameter. Both are useful alternatives and can be used in the subject's own home.

Other factors related to the laboratory recordings may influence sleep patterns: overall estimates may be biased. Frankel *et al.* (1976) have reported that some normal subjects feel that their sleep is worse in the laboratory than at home. Subjects used to sleeping with a partner tend to have less REM and more stage 4 sleep when they sleep alone (Monroe, 1969).

Most studies that have compared home and laboratory recordings have shown little or no differences in reliability or validity between the two (Nino-Murcia *et al.*, 1985; Sewitch and Kupfer, 1985; Sharpley *et al.*, 1988). However, Coates *et al.* (1979) did find that laboratory recordings produced more precise estimates of minutes awake after sleep onset and other variables. Rosekind *et al.* (1978) also claim that home recordings eliminate first-night effects.

Subjective measures

There are many advantages in recording subjective measures of sleep compared with objective techniques, and they are quick, simple and cheap to use, in contrast to the measures described above. They provide easy access to large samples of subjects, and questionnaires can address a greater variety of details concerning sleep at one time as compared with other methods of assessment. There is a dearth of scales and questionnaires regarding sleep (Jenkins *et al.*, 1988). Douglass *et al.* (1989) provide a clear, brief introduction to sleep-assessment questionnaires. There are also a number of features about sleep which cannot be measured in any other way (e.g. habitual sleep length, which can only be investigated on a particular night using polysomnography). Similarly, sleep satisfaction can only be rated in a subjective way.

The subject's judgement of sleep quality is an essential dimension because of the implications for treatment. The prescription of hypnotics depends on subjective sleep quality. Monroe (1967) states that this judgement is based on subjective estimations of sleep latency, depth of sleep and restedness on awakening. This last criterion was found to be the most important in a study by Kamens *et al.* (1982). Other criteria judged to be subjectively important were sleep onset latency, number of awakenings, depth and length of sleep and how the subject felt late in the day. In contrast, the number of movements during the night, ease of awakening and number of dreams were not believed to affect the quality of sleep.

Monroe (1967) also found that these parameters objectively measured do differ in self-rated good and poor sleepers, although not as markedly as in questionnaires. They have been modified by Adam *et al.* (1984), who demonstrated more profound differences in relation to temperature in good and poor sleepers. This emphasizes the importance of considering alternative forms of measurement in assessing behaviour in general and sleep in particular. The distinction between poor sleepers and insomniacs should be noted.

Insomniacs suffer from a difficulty in falling asleep and staying asleep.

They differ significantly from normal controls in sleep onset latency, total sleep time and number of arousals (Frankel *et al.*, 1973).

Subjective estimates of absolute values of sleep parameters and changes following experimentally induced alterations in sleep have been compared to objective measures in several studies. These studies have shown that although changes are in the expected direction, absolute estimates are rather unreliable, particularly in insomniacs. Surprisingly, the number of arousals is consistently underestimated by insomniacs as well as by normal controls. Carskadon *et al.* (1976) suggest four reasons why this may be so; sleep may interfere with memory, several short arousals may be perceived as one long arousal, the subject may not perceive having fallen asleep nor having woken up.

Estimates following questions about a specific night's sleep were found to correspond more closely to objective measures than questions about the subject's sleep habits (Carskadon *et al.*, 1976; Tepas *et al.*, 1980). This may be because such estimates are less reliable. Alternatively, it may show that a few nights' sleep recording is not representative of the subject's normal sleep pattern.

The following is a list of questionnaires that have been used in assessing sleep quality and other facets of sleep:

(1) Stanford Sleepiness Scale (Hoddes *et al.*, 1973);
(2) Leeds Sleep Evaluation Questionnaire (Parrott and Hindmarch, 1978);
(3) Post-Sleep Inventory (Webb *et al.*, 1976);
(4) ASDC Sleep Disorders Questionnaire (Douglass *et al.*, 1986);
(5) St Mary's Hospital Sleep Questionnaire (Ellis *et al.*, 1981).

There are a variety of other questionnaires which are used to assess different facets of sleep. Many of these are created by individual sleep clinics, are not validated and have never been published. Recently, a group of Scandinavian laboratories have developed the Basic Nordic Sleep Questionnaire. Other examples of questionnaires are those developed at the Toronto Western Hospital (Sleep–Wake Questionnaire; Morningness–Eveningness, Questionnaire and Sleep Diary). The Stanford Sleepiness Scale (SSS) and sleep diaries have been widely used.

Most recently, a Dutch group has produced the 'Sleep–Wake Experience List' (SWEL) (Die Slaap–Waak Ervaring Lijst in its original form) (van Diest and Markusse, in press) and have used this scale to show that deviant sleep patterns represent a risk factor for coronary heart disease (van Diest, in press). This questionnaire consists of 15 items covering six areas: sleep onset; sleep maintenance; early morning awakening; difficulty in waking up; tired on waking up; daytime sleepiness. For each of these consideration of severity, duration and frequency is attempted.

MEASUREMENT OF SLEEPINESS

Introduction

Sleepiness is the tendency to fall asleep and the desire for sleep, which are accompanied by other behavioural changes. The three main methods of measuring sleepiness correspond to these three major aspects of daytime functioning. They are physiological measurements; introspective assessment; and tests of performance.

These methods may not all assess the same qualities. Dement and Carskadon (1982) suggest that objective measures are concerned with the relatively stable physiological sleepiness, whereas the facets measured by subjective tests vary as a result of a wide range of short-term psychological factors, including motivation in carrying out the tests, muscular activity and sensory stimulation. They suggest that behavioural measures are closely related to subjective measures. Evidence exists for the imperfect correspondence of these three measures. Monk (1987) points out that diurnal variation of each is different. Freeman *et al.* (1988) found a high correlation among the subjective measures and among the objective measures used to assess sleepiness, but little correlation between them at most times of the day.

Physiological measures

The Multiple Sleep Latency Test (MSLT)

The time taken to fall asleep is a measure of sleepiness with high face validity. This is believed to be a measure of the underlying physiological tendency to fall asleep in the absence of arousing factors. There are, however, many factors which affect sleep onset, and accordingly a standard procedure has been developed (Carskadon/ASDC Task Force, 1986). It has been found that the retest reliability of the MSLT is high, even with long intervals between testing sessions, and irrespective of level of sleeplessness (e.g. Roehrs *et al.*, 1988). The MSLT is sensitive to a number of effects due to time of day and disruptions in the normal sleep/wake cycle (for example, total sleep deprivation, partial deprivation, sleep fragmentation and sleep extension; Carskadon and Dement, 1981). It is sensitive to the effects of hypnotics, and has been used to detect disorders of excessive daytime sleepiness (e.g. Roth *et al.*, 1980). However, its value in the diagnosis of narcolepsy is not clear (Rendells *et al.*, 1982).

Similarly, the ability of the MSLT to detect treatment effects has not been clearly established. Carskadon and Dement (1982) suggest that this may be due to a floor affect in the pre-treatment measurement. Mitler *et al.* (1982)

and Erman *et al.* (1987) have suggested a number of measures to improve the sensitivity to treatment effects of the MSLT. Broughton *et al.* (1988) provide a useful discussion of the MSLT, and introduce the use of evoked potentials as a discriminating factor in the sleepiness of narcoleptics. They produced clear evidence of changes in brain processing of new information during wakefulness in narcolepsy, but such measures may not be as reliable as the MSLT.

Waking EEG

It has recently been discovered that certain characteristics of waking PSG correlate with other sleepiness scores. Torsvall and Akerstedt (1987) monitored train drivers with EEG and EOG throughout both night and day. They also recorded self-rated sleepiness (unfortunately not describing the technique they used). Not surprisingly, subjectively rated sleepiness increased during the night. This was accompanied by an increase in alpha spectral power density, slow eye movements and, to a lesser extent, slower features on the EEG. In contrast, values for all these measures were lower during the day and there was no trend in their variation. Akerstedt (1988) and Torsvall and Akerstedt (1988) report further studies with similar findings, but Seidel *et al.* (1988), who measured EEG and EOG in subjects undergoing MSLT, surprisingly found that high levels of alpha and delta power before sleep onset were correlated significantly, but not strongly, with long sleep latencies.

Pupillography

Pupil size, instability and response to changes in light intensity have been investigated for use as indices of sleepiness. Alert subjects have large stable pupils (e.g. Yoss *et al.*, 1970). Smaller pupils and an increased number of oscillations accompany higher levels of sleepiness in patients with disorders of excessive somnolence (Korczyn, 1987). Similar observations occur in normal subjects following sleep deprivation and during the course of the day (Lavie and Schulz, 1978). Pupil diameter was found to vary during a 90-minute period in narcoleptics following the same pattern as variations in sleepiness measured by the Stanford Sleepiness Scale (SSS, Pressman *et al.*, 1980). Pupillary response to high light intensity stimuli is affected by sleepiness (Schmidt and Fortin, 1982). Schmidt *et al.* (1981) have considered the abnormal response to low light intensity as a means of diagnosing narcolepsy and distinguishing narcolepsy from other sleep disorders. Those advocating this technique consider it quick and easy to use and to be a method which has not had its potential fully realized.

Subjective measures

There are four different methods of quantifying subjective sleepiness (Monk, 1987). The subject may be provided with (1) a numerical scale; (2) a visual analogue scale representing sleepiness (e.g. Weitzman *et al.*, 1982; Folkard *et al.*, 1978) and asked to state or mark how sleepy he or she is on the scale; (3) a list of adjectives which the subject rates according to appropriateness (e.g. Pearson and Byars, 1956; Thayer *et al.*, 1978); or (4) a list of sentences from which the subject chooses one which best describes his or her condition (e.g. the Stanford Sleepiness Scale (SSS) (Hoddes *et al.*, 1972, 1973)). Subjective measures are quick to explain and easy to carry out and score, particularly the numerical and visual analogue scale, but are subject to several difficulties (Aitken, 1969; Bond and Lader, 1974). Social desirability may influence a subject's response; different frames of reference and idiosyncratic interpretation of terms make inter-subject comparisons difficult; and the magnitude of a change cannot be determined, even on numerical and visual analogue scales.

Jenkins *et al.* (1988) take a pragmatic view in the development of a scale for the estimation of sleep problems and provide one of the few validated measures available using different samples and reporting test–retest reliability.

Reliability and validity of visual analogue scales

This technique is sensitive to complete sleep loss (Hoddes *et al.*, 1973), partial sleep loss (Herscovitch and Broughton, 1981) and recovery (Hoddes *et al.*, 1973) and it differentiates between REM and SWS deprivation (Carskadon and Dement, 1977). SSS cross-validates with performance (Hoddes *et al.*, 1972, 1973). Its reliability in chronically sleepy patients, however, is questionable (Dement *et al.*, 1978). The technique of standardizing VAS measurements (Morgan *et al.*, 1984) is an important methodological advance. The VAS is most valuable in a series of recorded nights and should not be used on a one-off basis.

Subjective measures of other dimensions that are related to sleep have also been developed. The Pre-Sleep Arousal scale (Nicassio *et al.*, 1985) has proved useful in discriminating insomniacs from normal sleepers. In terms of validity it correlates with anxiety, depression and, to a smaller extent, sleeping difficulties. Monk's (1988) measure for Global Vigour and Affect is sensitive to jet lag and to diurnal variation in sleepiness.

Performance measures of sleepiness

Anecdotal evidence suggests that when people are tired they perform more slowly and make more mistakes. Many tasks have been used in an attempt to use changes in performance to detect alterations in the sleep–wake cycle. A distinction between poor sleepers and restless sleepers on the basis of physiological recordings, subjective reports and performance measures has been made (Williams and Williams, 1966). Morgan *et al.* (1984) have emphasized the value of idiographic subjective reports in the documentation of pharmacological manipulations.

Cognitive tasks

A number of cognitive skills have been tested. Addition has been popular since Wilkinson (1966) found it to be sensitive to large sleep reductions. Bonnet (1986) found that sleep disruption produced a significant detriment but many other studies have shown no change following various manipulations of the sleep–wake cycle (Friedmann *et al.*, 1977; Webb and Agnew, 1974). Significant effects have been found on the performance of other skills. For example, the ability to solve logic tasks is impaired after total sleep deprivation (Smith and Whittaker, 1987) and divergent thinking is reduced following selective REM deprivation (Glaubman *et al.*, 1978).

Tests of short-term memory have also been fairly widely used. As in the case with addition, they have shown no significant decrease in many studies (for example, Friedmann *et al.*, 1977; Glenville *et al.*, 1978). In fact, sleep deprivation enhances performance under some circumstances. Spence and Wilkinson (1973) gave subjects digit span tests for 30 minutes. During the first half of the testing session sleep-deprived subjects had an advantage over non-sleep-deprived subjects, but in the second half of testing the advantage was reversed. They attributed the original effect to above-optimal arousal following a normal night's sleep.

The cognitive tasks probably most sensitive to manipulations of the sleep–wake cycle are attention tests. The Wilkinson Auditory Vigilance Test (Wilkinson *et al.*, 1966) is the best known, but variants, for example, the x-test (another auditory vigilance test) and the Pentagon Test (visual vigilance) (Webb and Agnew, 1965) have also been developed. Declining performance on the Wilkinson Auditory Vigilance Task following sleep deprivation has been replicated several times (e.g. Webb and Agnew, 1974; Glenville *et al.*, 1978), but Friedmann *et al.* (1977) found no significant effects of gradual sleep reduction.

Signal detection theory has been applied to vigilance tasks (Horne *et al.*, 1983) in order to distinguish between a drop in performance due to a change in motivation or in intrinsic capacity for sensory discrimination. Naitoh

(1983) has, however, criticized the use of signal detection theory in this context.

Wilkinson has emphasized that the repetitive nature and the duration of the task are key factors (Wilkinson, 1964) in the sensitivity of performance measures to detect sleepiness. It has been found that the most sensitive tests are long and monotonous (e.g. card sorting, threading beads through a narrow-bore tube, listening to a continuous auditory task when the interruptions are unpredictable). The tests are also more sensitive when experimenter rather than subject paced.

Motor tasks

A wide variety of motor tasks has been tried, from grip strength (Webb and Agnew, 1974—no significant effect) and rapid alteration (Friedmann *et al.*, 1977—significant increase in variability) to pinball (Taub *et al.*, 1971—significant decrement) and handwriting (Glenville *et al.*, 1978—no significant change in size) with varying success. Simple and complex reaction time tests (e.g. Glenville *et al.*, 1978; Bonnet, 1986) are fairly sensitive.

It has become common practice to use a battery of tests, including some with increased face validity, e.g. driving motor skills tasks, inspection time, reaction time, critical flicker fusion tests, among others.

Properties of good tests for sleepiness

Wilkinson (1968) has summarized these as follows:

(1) They should be long;
(2) The subjects should be given no feedback;
(3) The tests should be repeated (but, as Bonnet, 1986, points out, care must be taken to control for the effects of learning);
(4) The sleep manipulation should be repeated;
(5) The test should be difficult, without making it interesting.

Other factors that may affect performance under sleep deprivation include (Johnson, 1982): (1) Task pacing; (2) Proficiency level; (3) Task complexity; (4) Memory requirements.

Finally, there are several non-task, situational factors that can affect performance under sleep deprivation (Johnson, 1982): (1) Exercise; (2) Noise; (3) Temperature; (4) Drugs; (5) Breathing atmosphere.

There are few studies which consider the relationship between performance measures and other measures of sleepiness. The limited information that does exist includes studies by Taub and Berger (1969) and Charles *et al.* (1987). Taub and Berger (1969) were able to demonstrate, using simple vigilance and calculation tasks, that extend sleep (11 hours versus 8 hours) produced decrements in function similar to those produced by sleep loss. Charles *et al.* (1987) have shown the value of both subjective and objective measures in the assessment of performance (for example, after taking hypnotic drugs).

CONCLUSION

There is a wide variety of techniques used in the measurement of sleep. This is one area of measurement of human problems in which the objective measures have exceeded, in usage and quality, the subjective measures. Currently, there is considerable emphasis on the automation and computer analysis of sleep scoring. Techniques such as the use of power density analysis of EEGs are increasingly being used. It would seem that the range of choices with regard to measures of sleep will increase and with this development further attention will have to be paid to the choice of the specifics of change. Psychometric instruments clearly need further development. The integration of sleep measures with measures of circadian changes requires and is receiving considerable attention.

ACKNOWLEDGEMENTS

We thank H. Driver and E. Fossey for assistance. K. Rathouse was supported by the Edinburgh Sleep Research Trust when working on this review.

REFERENCES

Aaronson, S.T., Biper, M.P., Rashed, S. and Hobson, J.A. (1980) Use of time lapse video tape recording in sleep research: method of study and sleep latency determination. *Sleep Research*, **9**, 118.

Adam, K., Tomeny, M. and Oswald, I. (1984) Do poor sleepers have less restorative sleep than good sleepers. In W.P. Koella, E. Ruther and H. Schultz (eds), *Sleep '84*, pp. 48–9, Gustav Fischer Verlag, Stuttgart.

Adam, K., Tomeny, M. and Oswald, I. (1986) Physiological and psychological differences between good and poor sleepers. *Journal of Psychiatric Research*, **20**(4), 301–16.

Agnew, H.W., Webb, W.B. and Williams, R.I. (1966) The first night effect: an EEG study of sleep. *Psychophysiology*, **2**, 263–6.

Aitken, R.C.B. (1969) Measurement of feelings using visual analogue scales. *Proceedings of the Royal Society of Medicine*, **62**, 989–93.

Akerstedt, T. (1988) Sleepiness as a consequence of shift work. *Sleep*, **11**(1), 17–34.

Alihanka, J. and Vaahtoranta, K. (1979) A static charge sensitive bed; a new method for recording body movements during sleep. *Electroencephalography and Clinical Neurophysiology*, **46**, 731–4.

Anders, T.F. and Sostek, A.M. (1976) The use of time lapse video recording of sleep–wake behaviour in human infants. *Psychophysiology*, **13**, 155–8.

Aubert-Tulkens, G., Culee, C., Harmant-van Rijckevorsel, K. and Rodenstein, D.O. (1987) Ambulatory evaluation of sleep disturbance and therapeutic effects in sleep apnea syndrome by wrist activity monitoring. *American Review of Respiratory Disease*, **136**, 851–6.

Bardsley, G.I. and Bell, F. (1975) A technique using load cells and infra-red photography for monitoring movements during sleep. *Sleep Research*, **4**, 249.

Benson, K. and Zarcone, V.P., Jr (1979) Phasic events of REM sleep: Phenomenology of middle ear muscle activity and periorbital integrated potentials in the same normal population. *Sleep*, **2**, 199–213.

Berger, R.J., Olley, P. and Oswald, I. (1962) The EEG, eye movements and dreams of the blind. *Quarterly Journal of Experimental Psychology*, **14**, 183–6.

Bond, A. and Lader, M. (1974) The use of analogue scales in rating subjective feeling. *British Journal of Medical Psychology*, **47**, 211–18.

Bonnet, M.H. (1986) Performance and sleepiness as a function of frequency and placement of sleep. *Psychophysiology*, **23**, 263–71.

Broughton, R.J. and Aguirre, M. (1987) Differences between REM and NREM sleepiness measured by event-related potentials (P300, CNV) MSLT and subjective estimate in narcolepsy–cataplexy. *Electroencephalography and Clinical Neurophysiology*, **67**(4), 317–26.

Broughton, R., Aguirre, M. and Dunham, W. (1988) A comparison of multiple and single sleep latency and cerebral evoked potential (P300) measures in the assessment of excessive daytime sleepiness in narcolepsy–cataplexy. *Sleep*, **11**, 537–45.

Carroll, J.S., Bliwise, D.L. and Dement, W.C. (1989) A method for checking interobserver reliability in observational sleep studies. *Sleep*, **12**(4), 363–7.

Carskadon, M.A. (1986) ASDC Task Force on Excessive Sleepiness Guidelines for Multiple Sleep Latency Test (MSLT): a standard measure of sleepiness. *Sleep*, **9**, 519–24.

Carskadon, M.A. and Dement, W.C. (1977) Sleepiness and sleep state on a 90-min schedule. *Psychophysiology*, **14**, 127–33.

Carskadon, M.A. and Dement, W.C. (1981) Cumulative effects of sleep restriction on daytime sleepiness. *Psychophysiology*, **18**(2), 107–13.

Carskadon, M.A. and Dement, W.C. (1982) The multiple sleep latency test: what does it measure? *Sleep*, **5** (Suppl. 2), 567–73.

Carskadon, M.A., Dement, W.C., Mitler, M.M., Guilleminault, C., Zarcone, V.P. and Spiegel, R. (1976) Self-reports vs sleep laboratory findings in 122 drug-free subjects with complaints of insomnia. *American Journal of Psychiatry*, **133**, 1382–8.

Charles, R.B., Kirkham, A.J.T., Guyatt, A.R. and Parker, S.P. (1987) Psychomotor, pulmonary and exercise responses to sleep medication. *British Journal of Clinical Pharmacology*, **24**, 191–7.

Clausen, J., Sersen, E.A. and Lidsky, A. (1974) Variability of sleep measures in normal subjects. *Psychophysiology*, **11**, 509–16.

Coates, T.J., Rosekind, M.R., Strossen, R.J., Thoresen, C.E. and Kirmil-Gray, K. (1979) Sleep recordings in the laboratory and at home: A comparative analysis. *Psychophysiology*, **16**, 339–46.

Crisp, A.H., Stonehill, E. and Eversden, I.D. (1970) The design of a motility bed including its calibration for the subject's weight. *Medical Biology and Engineering*, **8**, 455–63.

Dement, W.C. and Carskadon, M.A. (1982) Current perspectives on daytime sleepiness: the issues. *Sleep*, **5** (Suppl. 2), S56–67.

Dement, W.C., Carskadon, M.A. and Richardson, G. (1978) Excessive daytime sleepiness in the sleep apnea syndrome. In C. Guilleminault and W.C. Dement (eds), *Sleep Apnea Syndromes*, pp. 23–46, Alan R. Liss, New York.

Dement, W.C. and Kleitman, N. (1957) Cyclic variations of EEG during sleep and their relation to eye movements, body motility and dreaming. *Electroencephalography and Clinical Neurophysiology*, **9**, 673–90.

Douglass, A.B., Bornstein, R.A., Nino-Murcia, G., Keenan, S., Miles, L., Zarcone, V.P., Guilleminault, C. and Dement, W.C. (1986) Creation of the ASDC sleep disorders questionnaire. *Sleep Research*, **15**, 117.

Douglass, A.B., Carskadon, M. and Houser, R. (1989) Historical data base, questionnaires, sleep and life cycle diaries. In L. Miles (ed.), *Clinical Evaluation and Physiological Monitoring in the Home and Work Environment*, Raven Press, New York.

Dumont, M., Montplaisir, J. and Infante-Rivard, C. (1988) Insomnia index among nursing personnel with past experience of night work. Results of a survey. *Sleep Research*, **17**, 371.

Dzvonik, M.L., Kripke, D.F., Klauber, M. and Ancoli-Israel, S. (1986) Body position changes and periodic movements in sleep. *Sleep*, **9**, 484–91.

Ellis, B.W., Johns, M.W., Lancaster, R., Raptopoulos, P., Angelopoulos, N. and Priest, R.G. (1981) The St Mary's Hospital Sleep Questionnaire: a study of reliability. *Sleep*, **4**, 93–7.

Erman, M.K., Beckham, B., Gardner, D.A. and Roffwarg, H.P. (1987) Modified Assessment of Sleepiness Test (MAST). *Sleep Research*, **16**, 550.

Espie, C.A., Lindsay, W.R. and Espie, L.C. (1989) Use of the Sleep Assessment Device (Kelley and Lichstein, 1980) to validate insomniacs' self-report of sleep pattern. *Journal of Psychopathology and Behavioral Assessment*, **11** (in press).

Farney, R.J., Walker, L.E., Jensen, R.L. and Walker, J.M. (1986) Ear oximetry to detect apnea and differentiate rapid eye movement (REM and non-REM (NREM) sleep. *Chest*, **4**, 533–9.

Ferri, R., Ferri, P., Colognola, R.M., Petrella, M.A., Musumeci, S.A. and Bergonzi, P. (1989) Comparison between the results of an automatic and a visual scoring of sleep EEG recordings. *Sleep*, **12**(4), 354–62.

Folkard, S., Monk, T.A. and Lobban, M.C. (1978) Short and long-term adjustment of circadian rhythms in 'permanent night nurses'. *Ergonomics*, **21**, 785–99.

Folstein, M.F. and Luria, R. (1973) Reliability, validity and clinical application of the Visual Analogue Mood Scale. *Psychological Medicine*, 3, 479–86.

Frankel, B.L., Buchbinder, R., Coursey, R. and Snyder, F. (1973) Sleep patterns and psychological test characteristics of chronic primary insomniacs. *Sleep Research*, **2**, 149.

Frankel, B.L., Coursey, R.D., Buchbinder, R. and Snyder, F. (1976) Recorded and reported sleep in primary insomnia. *Archives of General Psychiatry*, **33**, 615–23.

Freeman, C.R., Johnson, L.C., Spinweber, C.L. and Gomex, S.A. (1988) Relationship among four measures of sleepiness. *Sleep Research*, **17**, 334.

Friedmann, J., Globus, G., Huntley, A., Mullaney, D., Naitoh, P. and Johnson, L. (1977) Performance and mood during and after gradual sleep reduction. *Psychophysiology*, **14**, 245–50.

Gardner, R. and Grossman, W.L. (1975) Normal motor pattern, patterns in sleep in man. In E.D. Weitzman (ed.), *Advances in Sleep Research*, Vol. 2, pp. 67–107, Spectrum Publications, New York.

Glaubman, H., Orbach, I., Aviram, O., Frieder, I., Frieman, M., Pelled, O. and Glaubman, R. (1978) REM deprivation and divergent thinking. *Psychophysiology*, **15**, 75–9.

Glenville, M., Broughton, R.J., Wing, A.M. and Wilkinson, R.T. (1978) Effects of sleep deprivation on short duration performance measures compared to the Wilkinson Auditory Vigilance Task. *Sleep*, **1**, 169–76.

Guilleminault, C. (ed.) (1982) *Sleeping and Waking Disorders: Indications and Techniques*, Addison-Wesley, Menlo Park, California.

Helfand, R., Lavie, P. and Hobson, J.A. (1986) REM/NREM discrimination via ocular and limb movement monitoring: correlation with polygraphic data and development of a REM state algorithm. *Psychophysiology*, **23**, 334–9.

Hersovitch, J. and Broughton, R. (1981) Sensitivity of the Stanford Sleepiness Scale to the effects of cumulative partial sleep deprivation and recovery oversleeping. *Sleep*, **4**, 83–92.

Hoddes, E., Dement, W.C. and Zarcone, V. (1972) The development and use of the Stanford Sleepiness Scale. *Psychophysiology*, **9**, 150.

Hoddes, E., Zarcone, V. and Dement, W.C. (1972) Cross-validation of the Stanford Sleepiness Scale. *Sleep Research*, **1**, 91.

Hoddes, E., Zarcone, V., Smythe, M., Phillips, R. and Dement, W.C. (1973) Quantification of sleepiness: a new approach. *Psychophysiology*, **10**, 431–6.

Horne, J.A., Anderson, N.R. and Wilkinson, R.T. (1983) Effects of sleep deprivation on signal detection measures of vigilance: implications for sleep function. *Sleep*, **6**, 347–58.

Jenkins, C.D., Stanton, B-A., Niemcryk, S.J. and Rose, R.M. (1988) A scale for the estimation of sleep problems in clinical research. *Journal of Clinical Epidemiology*, **41**, 313–21.

Johnson, J. and Kitching, R. (1972) A simple sleep recorder for clinical situations. *British Journal of Psychiatry*, **120**, 569–71.

Johnson, L.C. (1982) Sleep deprivation and performance. In W.B. Webb (ed.), *Biological Rhythms, Sleep, and Performance*, p. 120, John Wiley, New York.

Jovanovic, U.J. (1969) Der Effect der ersten Untersuchungsnacht auf die Erektionen im Schlaf. *Psychotherapy Psychosomatics*, **7**, 295–308.

Jovanovic, V.J. (1972) Sexuelle Reaktizer und Schlafperiodik bei Menschen. Ergebnisse experimenteller Untersuchungen. *Beitrage für Sexualforschung*, **51**, 1–292.

Kamens, L., Carlson, M.L., Falkin, S., Laman, M.S., O'Donnell, R.R. and Tepas, D.I. (1982) Relative importance of subjective criteria for judging sleep quality. *Sleep Research*, **11**, 201.

Karacan, I., Goodenough, D.R., Shapiro, A. and Starker, S. (1966) Erection cycle during sleep in relation to dream anxiety. *Archives of General Psychiatry*, **15**, 183–9.

Kelley, J.E. and Lichstein, K.L. (1980) A sleep assessment device. *Behavioral Assessment*, **2**, 135–46.

Korczyn, A.D. (1987) The pupil and vigilance. *Functional Neurology*, **11**, 539–44.

Koumans, A.J.R., Tursky, B. and Solomon, P. (1968) Electrodermal levels and fluctuations during normal sleep. *Psychophysiology*, **5**, 300–6.

Kripke, D.F., Mullaney, D.J., Messin, S. and Wyborney, V.G. (1978) Wrist actographic measures of sleep and rhythms. *Electroencephalography and Clinical Neurophysiology*, **44**(5), 674–6.

Kupfer, D.J., Wyatt, R.J. and Snyder, F. (1970) Comparison between EEG and systematic nursing observations on sleep in psychiatric patients. *Journal of Nervous Mental Disorders*, **151**, 361–8.

Lavie, P. and Schulz, H. (1978) Ultradian rhythms in the pupil. *Sleep Research*, **7**, 307.

Levine, B., Moyles, T., Roehrs, T., Fortier, T. and Roth, T. (1986) Actigraphic monitoring and polygraphic recording in determination of sleep and wake. *Sleep Research*, **15**, 247.

Lichstein, K.L., Nickel, R., Hoelschoer, T.J. and Kelley, J.E. (1982) Clinical validation of a sleep assessment device. *Behavior Research and Therapy*, **20**, 292–7.

McDonald, D.G., Schmidt, W.W., Trazier, R.E., Shallen-Berger, H.D. and Edwards, D.J. (1975) Studies of information processing in sleep. *Psychophysiology*, **12**, 624–9.

McDonald, D.G., Shallen-Berger, H.D., Koresko, R.L. and Kinzy, B.G. (1976) Studies of spontaneous electrodermal responses in sleep. *Psychophysiology*, **13**, 128–34.

McPartland, R.J., Foster, F.G., Matthews, G., Coble, P. and Kupfer, D.J. (1975) The LSI Movement Activated Recording Monitor—an instrument to study motor rhythms. *Sleep Research*, **4**, 261.

Messin, S., Kripke, D.F. and Atkinson, M. (1974) A miniature eye movement transducer. *Sleep Research*, **3**, 162.

Mitler, M.M., van den Hoed, J., Carskadon, M.A., Richardson, G., Park, R., Guilleminault, C. and Dement, W.C. (1979) REM sleep episodes during multiple sleep test in narcoleptic patients. *Electroencephalography and Clinical Neurophysiology*, **46**, 479–81.

Mitler, M.M., Gujavarty, S. and Browman, C.P. (1982) Maintenance of Wakefulness test: a polysomnographic technique for evaluating treatment efficacy in patients with excessive somnolence. *Electroencephalography and Clinical Neurophysiology*, **53**, 658–61.

Monk, T.H. (1987) Subjective ratings of sleepiness—the underlying circadian mechanisms. *Sleep*, **10**(4), 343–53.

Monk, T.H. (1988) A technique to measure Global Vigor and Affect (GVA) *Sleep Research*, **17**, 341.

Monroe, L.J. (1967) Psychological and physiological differences between good and poor sleepers. *Journal of Abnormal Psychology*, **72**, 255.

Monroe, L.J. (1969) Transient changes in EEG sleep patterns of married good sleepers: The effects of altering sleeping arrangements. *Psychophysiology*, **6**, 330–37.

Morgan, K., Adam, K. and Oswald, I. (1984) Effects of loprazolam and of triazolam on psychological functions. *Psychopharmacology*, **82**, 386–8.

Mullaney, D.J., Kripke, D.F. and Messin, S. (1979) Wrist actograph measures sleep duration. *Science Research*, **8**, 266.

Mullaney, D.J., Kripke, D.F. and Messin, S. (1980) Wrist actographic estimation of sleep time. *Sleep*, **3**, 83–92.

Muzet, A., Becht, J., Jacquot, P. and Koenig, P. (1972) A technique for recording human body posture during sleep. *Psychophysiology*, **9**(6), 660–62.

Naitoh, P. (1983) Signal detection theory as applied to vigilance performance of sleep-deprived subjects. *Sleep*, **6**, 359–61.

Nicassio, P.M., Mendlowitz, D.R., Fussell, J.J. and Petras, L. (1985) The phenomenology of the presleep state: the development of the Presleep Arousal Scale (PSAS). *Behaviour Research and Therapy*, **23**(3), 263–71.

Niimi, Y., Watanabe, T. and Hori, T. (1968) Skin potential activities as a function of stages of sleep. *Journal of the Physiological Society of Japan*, **30**, 231–44.

Nino-Murcia, G., Bliwise, D., Keenan, S., MacGregor, P., Foster, R., Butkov, N., Huthison, D., Kramer, H., Sink, V., Dement, W. and Miles, L. (1985) Respiration monitoring in sleep: Comparison of judgements based on conventional polysomnography (PSG) and an ambulatory microprocessor-derived recording (AMC). *Sleep Research*, **14**, 274.

Oswald, I. (1962) *Sleeping and Waking*: Physiology and Psychology, Elsevier, Amsterdam.

Oswald, I., Taylor, A.M. and Treisman, M. (1960) Responses to stimulation during human sleep. *Brain*, **83**, 440–53.

Oswald, I., Berger, R.J., Jaramillo, R.A., Keddie, K.M.G., Olley, P.C. and Plunkett, G.B. (1963) Melancholia and barbiturates: a controlled EEG, body and eye movement study of sleep. *British Journal of Psychiatry*, **109**, 66–78.

Parrott, A.C. and Hindmarch, I. (1978) Factor analysis of a sleep evaluation questionnaire. *Psychological Medicine*, **8**, 325–9.

Pearson, R.G. and Byars, G.E. Jr (1956) The development and validation of a checklist for measuring subjective fatigue. *Rep. 56–115*, School of Aviation Medicine, USAF, Texas.

Pessah, M.A. and Roffwarg, H.P. (1972) Spontaneous middle ear muscle activity in man: A rapid eye movement sleep phenomenon. *Science*, **178**, 773–6.

Polo, O., Brissaud, L., Sales, B., Besset, A. and Billiard, M. (1988) The validity of the static charge sensitive bed in detecting obstructive sleep apnoeas. *European Respiratory Journal*, **1**, 330–36.

Pressman, M.R., Spielman, A.J. and Korczyn, A. (1980) Pupillometry in normals and narcoleptics throughout the course of a day. *Sleep Research*, **9**, 218.

Rechtshaffen, A. and Kales, A. (1968) *A Manual of Standardized Terminology, Techniques and Scoring System for Sleep stages of Human Subjects*, US Public Health Service, US Government Printing Office, Washington, DC.

Redmond, D.P. and Hegge, F.W. (1985) Observations on the design and specification of a wrist worn human activity monitoring system. *Behavior Research Methods, Instruments and Computers*, **17**, 659–69.

Reynolds, C.F., Coble, P.A., Kupfer, D.J. and Holzer, B.C. (1982) Application of the Multiple Sleep Latency Test in disorders of excessive sleepiness. *Electroencephalography and Clinical Neurophysiology*, **53**, 443–52.

Roehrs, T., Zwyghuizen-Doorenbos, A., Schaefer, M., Sicklesteel, J., Wittig, R. and Roth, T. (1988) Test–retest reliability of the MSLT. *Sleep Research*, **17**, 348.

Rosekind, M.R., Coates, T.J. and Thoresen, C.E. (1978) Telephone transmission of polysomnographic data from subjects' homes. *Journal of Nervous and Mental Disease*, **166**, 438–41.

Roth, B. (1961) The clinical and theoretical importance of EEG rhythms corresponding to states of lowered vigilance. *Electroencephalography and Clinical Neurophysiology*, **13**, 395–9.

Roth, T., Hartse, K., Zorick, F. and Conway, W. (1980) Multiple naps and the evaluation of daytime sleepiness in patients with upper airway sleep apnea. *Sleep*, **3**, 425–39.

Salinsky, M., Goins, S., Sutula, T., Roscoe, D. and Weber, S. (1988) Comparison of sleep staging by polygraph and color density spectral array. *Sleep*, **11**, 131–8.

Schiavi, R.C. (1988) Nocturnal penile tumescence in the evaluation of erectile disorders: a critical review. *Journal of Sexual and Marital Therapy*, **14**, 84–96.

Schmidt, H.S. and Fortin, L.D. (1982) Electronic pupillography in disorders of arousal. In C. Guilleminault (ed.), *Sleeping and Waking Disorders: Indications and Techniques*, pp. 127–43, Addison-Wesley, Menlo Park, California.

Schmidt, H.S., Kackson, E.I. and Knopp, W. (1981) Electronic Pupillography (EPG): objective assessment of sleepiness and differentiation of disorders of excessive somnolence. *Sleep Research*, **10**, 48.

Schmidt-Nowara, W.W. and Scantlen, G.E. (1983) A head position monitor for polysomnography. *Sleep*, **6**, 384–5.

Seidel, W.F., Edgar, D.M., Wheatland, R., Cohen, S.A., Eder, D. and Dement, W.C. (1988) Spectral correlates of MSLT during relaxed wakefulness. *Sleep Research*, **17**, 352.

Sewitch, D.E. and Kupfer, D.J. (1985) Polysomnographic telemetry using telediagnostic and Oxford Medilog 9000 systems. *Sleep*, **8**, 288–93.

Shapiro, C.M. (1985) *Human Metabolism and Sleep*, Unpublished PhD thesis, University of Edinburgh.

Shapiro, C.M., Bartel, P.R. and Griesel, R.D. (1980) Effect of fatigue on electrocerebral excitability. *Neurological Psychology*, **11**, 282.

Shapiro, C.M., Goll, C.C., Cohen, G. and Oswald, I. (1984) Heat production during sleep. *Journal of Applied Physiology*, **56**, 671–7.

Shapiro, C.M., Bancroft, J. and Montgomery, I. (1990) Nocturnal erections: a diagnostic tool in impotent patients. In press.

Sharpley, L., Solomon, R.A. and Cowen, P.J. (1988) Evaluation of first night effect using ambulatory monitoring and automatic sleep stage analysis. *Sleep*, **11**, 273–6.

Smith, C. and Whittaker, M. (1987) Effects of total sleep deprivation in humans on the ability to solve a logic task. *Sleep Research*, **16**, 536.

Smith, J.R. (1978) Computers in sleep research. *CRC Critical Reviews in Bioengineering*, **3**, 93–148.

Spence, M.T. and Wilkinson, R.T. (1973) Total sleep deprivation and short term memory. *Sleep Research*, **2**, 172.

Stradling, J.R., Thomas, G. and Belcher, R. (1988) Analysis of overnight sleep patterns by automatic detection of movement on video recordings. *Journal of Ambulatory Monitoring*, **1**, 217–22.

Tamura, T., Togawa, T. and Murata, M. (1988) A bed temperature monitoring system for assessing body movement during sleep. *Clinical Physical and Physiological Measures*, **9**, 139–45.

Taub, J.M. and Berger, R.J. (1969) Extended sleep and performance: the Rip Van Winkle effect. *Psychonomic Science*, **16**, 204–5.

Taub, J.M., Globus, G.G., Phoebus, E. and Drury, R. (1971) Extended sleep and performance. *Nature*, **233**, 142–3.

Tepas, D.I., Canning, P.M., Moss, P.D., Armstrong, D. and Walsh, J.K. (1980) How should one measure human sleep length in surveys? *Sleep Research*, **9**, 266.

Thayer, R.E. (1978) Toward a psychological theory of multidimensional activation (arousal). *Motivation and Emotion*, **2**, 1–34.

Torsvall, L. and Akerstedt, T. (1987) Sleepiness on the job: continuously measured EEG changes in train drivers. *Electroencephalography Clinical Neurophysiology*, **66**(6), 502–11.

Torsvall, L. and Akerstedt, T. (1988) Extreme sleepiness: quantification of EOG and spectral EEG parameters. *International Journal of Neuroscience*, **38**, 435–41.

Urbach, D., Lavie, P. and Alster, J. (1988) Screening for sleep disorders by actographic recordings. *Sleep Research*, **17**, 357.

van Diest, R. Subjective sleep characteristics as coronary risk factors. Their association with Type A behaviour and vital exhaustion. In press.

van Diest, R. and Markusse, R. De Slaap–Waak Ervaring Lijst. In press.

Webb, W.B. and Agnew, H.W., Jr (1965) Sleep: effects of a restricted regime. *Science*, **150**, 1745–7.

Webb, W.B. and Agnew, H.R., Jr (1974) The effects of chronic limitation of sleep length. *Psychophysiology*, **11**, 265–74.

Webb, W.B., Bonnet, M. and Blume, G. (1976) A post-sleep inventory. *Perceptual and Motor Skills*, **43**, 987–93.

Webster, J.B., Kripke, D.F., Messin, S., Mullaney, D.J. and Wyborney, G. (1982) An activity-based sleep monitor system for ambulatory use. *Sleep*, **5**(4), 389–99.

Weiss, B.L., McPartland, R.J. and Kupfer, D.J. (1973) Once more: the inaccuracy of non-EEG estimations of sleep. *American Journal of Psychiatry*, **130**, 1282–5.

Weitzman, E.D., Czeisler, C.A., Zimmerman, J.C., Ronda, R.M. and Knaver, R.S. (1982) Chronobiological disorders: analytic and therapeutic techniques. In C. Guilleminault (ed.), *Disorders of Sleeping and Waking: Indications and Techniques*, pp. 297–329, Addison-Wesley, Menlo Park, California.

Wilde-Frenz, J. and Schulz, H. (1983) Rate and distribution of body movements during sleep in humans. *Perceptual and Motor Skills*, **56**, 275–83.

Wilkinson, R.T. (1964) Effects of up to 60 hours of sleep deprivation on different types of work. *Ergonomics*, **7**, 175–86.

Wilkinson, R.T. (1968) Sleep deprivation: performance tests for partial and selective sleep deprivation. In L.E. Abt and B.F. Reiss (eds), *Progress in Clinical Psychology*, Vol. 8, pp. 28–43. Grune and Stratton, New York.

Wilkinson, R.T., Edwards, R.S. and Haines, E. (1966) Performance following a night of reduced sleep. *Psychonomic Science*, **5**, 471–2.

Williams, H.L. and Williams, C.L. (1966) Nocturnal EEG profiles and performance. *Psychophysiology*, **2**, 164–75.

Wyatt, R.J., Stern, M., Fram, D.H., Tursky, B. and Grinspoon, L. (1970) Abnormalities in skin potential fluctuations during the sleep of acute schizophrenic patients. *Psychosomatic Medicine*, **32**, 301–8.

Yoss, R.E., Mayer, N.J. and Hollenhurst, R.W. (1970) Pupillary size and activity—well established indicator of alertness and sleepiness. *Neurology*, **20**, 545–54.

Index